DRINK- AND DRUG-DRIVE CASE NOTES

FOURTH EDITION

DRINK- AND DRUG-DRIVE CASE NOTES

FOURTH EDITION

Compiled and edited by
P. M. Callow, LL.M, Ph.D

WS
&H

Wildy, Simmonds & Hill Publishing

ISBN: 9780854903092

British Library Cataloguing in Publication Data

A catalogue record for this book is available from the British Library

First edition 2002
Second edition 2007
Third edition 2015

This edition published in 2025 by

Wildy, Simmonds & Hill Publishing
Wildy & Sons Ltd
Lincoln's Inn Archway
Carey Street
London WC2A 2JD
www.wildy.com

Printed in Great Britain by CPI Group (UK) Ltd, Croydon CR0 4YY.

FSC www.fsc.org MIX Paper | Supporting responsible forestry FSC® C013604

Preface

Drink- and Drug-Drive Case Notes comprises summaries of the many cases on the drink- and drug-driving offences which have come before the higher courts. The cases go back, broadly, to 1984, although some earlier, leading, decisions are also included. Judgments available up to the end of January 2025 are covered. Over 600 judgments are summarised. Each note is presented as a short statement of the facts of the case, the issue(s) in the appeal and an extract from the judgment. The notes are intended to provide a broad outline of the trends in the case law and as starting points for readers seeking guidance on particular points.

As far as possible, the material is arranged according to the subject matter of the cases, but overlaps are inevitable. Each case note has a headnote, giving an attempt at a single-sentence (sometimes longer) summary of the ratio of the case. Headnotes to the various sections include cross-references to other cases touching on like subjects.

This fourth edition includes notes of some 50 or more cases added since the third edition was published in 2015. Themes running through the new cases include the availability of judicial review as a means of challenge, case management, the appropriateness of adjournments and preparedness for trial. Longer-standing issues have also been revisited – the disclosure of records, consulting the forms completed during the investigation to refresh memory at trial, the discretion to admit or exclude evidence and burdens of proof.

At the time of writing, the drug-driving offences in ss 3A(1)(ba) and 5A, Road Traffic Act 1988 have been in place for 10 years, and now account for almost as many convictions as the alcohol offences. The drug offences are framed in broadly the same terms as the equivalent alcohol offences, although testing for drugs is by the analysis of blood or urine only. Much of the case law concerning the alcohol offences is relevant. Definitive sentencing guidelines for the drug offences were not introduced until 2023, but now clarify certain issues which had given rise to sentencing appeals.

The option in s 8(2), Road Traffic Act 1988, under which suspects could, in so-called borderline cases, choose to have their breath specimens replaced by specimens of blood or urine was finally removed in 2015. Cases dealing solely with the exercise of the option no longer appear in this edition of *Drink- and Drug-Drive Case Notes*. Others, notably those relating to the procedure once the option has been exercised in favour of providing alternative specimens, are likely to continue to be relevant, and remain in the text.

I am indebted to the late Dr Paul Williams, who first sparked my interest in this vast area of law, which became the subject of my Ph.D thesis.

P. M. Callow
January 2025

Contents

Table of Cases

*References are to page numbers. Page numbers in **bold** indicate a case note.*

Table of Legislation

References are to page numbers.

Table of Attorney General's Guidelines and Practice Directions

References are to page numbers.

Chapter 1

The Requirement to Provide Specimens

For the powers of the police to administer preliminary tests and to require specimens for analysis, see ss 6–7A, Road Traffic Act 1988.

1. THE ARREST

See also the cases in Chapter 8 under the heading "Bad Faith", page 394; and DPP v Godwin, page 347, where the justices' decision to exclude evidence following an unlawful arrest was upheld; and Harper v DPP, page 358, where the unlawfulness of the arrest was a matter of form rather than substance.

R v Fox, Fox v Chief Constable of Gwent

[1986] AC 281, [1985] 1 WLR 1126, [1985] 3 All ER 392, [1985] RTR 337, [1986] Crim LR 59, 17 October 1985, HL

Lawful arrest is not a prerequisite for requiring a breath specimen.

A motorist had been convicted of, *inter alia*, driving with excess alcohol, contrary to s 6(1), Road Traffic Act 1972 as substituted by s 25 and Sch 8, Transport Act 1981. He appealed to the Divisional Court, which upheld the conviction on the ground that the fact that the motorist had been at the police station because of a wrongful arrest did not bear on the question of whether the breath specimen, the basis for the conviction, had been unfairly obtained. The motorist further appealed.

CERTIFIED QUESTION: "Were the justices correct in convicting the appellant … on the basis of the proportion of alcohol in a specimen of breath which he had been required to provide at a police station when the appellant was present at that police station because he had been wrongly arrested?"

HELD: "… the statutory provisions have been amended [by the Transport Act 1981] in two respects which are important for present purposes … the substituted section 6(1) … is not now dependent upon the accused having been validly arrested. Secondly, and more important for present purposes, the substituted section 8(1) … does not contain the words 'A person who has been arrested under section 5(5) or 8 …'. Accordingly a lawful arrest is not now specified as an essential prerequisite of a breath test … there is nothing in *Morris v Beardmore* [page 18] which supports a general principle that conviction for an offence under section 6(1) will be invalid if the evidence by which it is proved has been obtained unlawfully … any evidence which is relevant is admissible even if it has been obtained illegally … Accordingly the Divisional Court … was … right in treating the fact that the appellant was in the police station because he had been unlawfully arrested merely as a historical fact, with which the court was not concerned … Of course, if the appellant had been lured to the police station by some trick or deception, or if the police officers had behaved oppressively towards the appellant, the justices' jurisdiction to exclude otherwise admissible evidence recognised in *R v Sang* [[1980] AC 402, [1979] 3 WLR 263, [1979] 2 All ER 1222, [1979] Crim LR 655 (HL)] might have come into play. But there is nothing of that sort suggested here."

Appeal dismissed.

Gull v Scarborough

[1987] RTR 261, 12 November 1985, QBD (DC)

Lawful arrest is not a prerequisite for requiring a blood or urine specimen.

A motorist had been charged with failing without reasonable excuse to provide a specimen for a breath test, contrary to s 7(4), Road Traffic Act 1972 as substituted by s 25 and Sch 8, Transport Act 1981; and with failing without reasonable excuse to provide a specimen of blood for a laboratory test, contrary to s 8(7), Road Traffic Act 1972 as likewise substituted. He refused to take a roadside screening test; at the police station, the evidential breath machine was not operating and the police officer therefore required a specimen of blood; the defendant refused. The magistrate found that the police officer had had no reasonable cause to suspect that the motorist had been driving the car in question with an excess of alcohol; the arrest had therefore been unlawful and there had been no proper request for a specimen of blood. The magistrate dismissed both informations.

The prosecutor appealed against the dismissal of the information under s 8(7).

QUESTION(S) FOR THE COURT: Having dismissed the information under s 7(4) because the magistrate was not satisfied that the constable requiring the specimen of breath had reasonable cause to suspect that the defendant had alcohol in his body when driving, whether the magistrate was correct in law in deciding that the prosecutor had no power to require the defendant to provide a specimen of blood for a laboratory test and to find there was no case for the defendant to answer under s 8(7).

HELD: "… The defendant in the present case was never asked to provide a specimen of breath and therefore did not refuse to provide such a specimen. … Nor did he give a specimen of breath so the case is different on the facts from *Fox v Chief Constable of Gwent* [above] … Nevertheless, it appears to me quite plain that the reasoning … applies just as much to the present facts … The essence of the decision [in *Fox*] is that 'a lawful arrest is not now specified as an essential prerequisite of a breath test'. That being so, in circumstances where the machine for testing the breath is not available it must follow that the requirement under section 8(1)(b) [to provide a blood or urine specimen] read with section 8(3)(b) [reliable device not available] and section 8(4) [constable to decide whether specimen to be of blood or urine] is also not qualified by any requirement of a previous valid arrest. Accordingly … the defendant was in breach of section 8(7) … ."

Appeal allowed.

Hartland v Alden

[1987] RTR 253, 30 April 1986, QBD (DC)

Not only does an unlawful arrest not invalidate the requirement to provide specimens, but neither is it a reasonable excuse for failing to provide a specimen.

A motorist had been charged with, *inter alia,* failing without reasonable excuse to provide a specimen of breath for analysis, contrary to s 8(7), Road Traffic Act 1972 as substituted by s 25 and Sch 8, Transport Act 1981. He had been driving erratically and police officers followed him home. They went into his home, and asked for a breath sample for a test. The defendant made clear that he did not consent to their being there, saying, either before they made the request or at the time they made it, "No, in my house you can't do me, so there". They arrested him and took him to the police station where he was required, under s 8(1), Road Traffic Act 1972 as likewise substituted (power to require specimens), to provide breath specimens for analysis. He refused.

At the hearing the defendant argued that, although the police had acted in good faith, the arrest was wrongful, therefore all subsequent proceedings had been vitiated and could not be used in evidence; or that the unlawful arrest constituted a reasonable excuse.

The justices convicted him. He appealed.

QUESTION(S) FOR THE COURT: (1) The defendant having been unlawfully arrested and being unlawfully held at a police station, whether he could be lawfully required to provide a specimen under s 8(1), Road Traffic Act 1972 as substituted; (2) if so, whether the justices were right in law in holding that he did not have a reasonable excuse for refusal.

HELD: "… It is the law, unpalatable though it may appear, that Parliament has provided that what has brought a motorist to a police station is of no account. All that matters is that the proceedings at the police station are conducted by a police officer strictly in accordance with the provisions of section 8. What happened beforehand is in effect merely a matter of history. Consequently, … there was unquestionably a right in the officer conducting the proceedings under section 8 to put the question he did to the defendant and an obligation on the defendant to reply affirmatively to that question, otherwise be prosecuted for the offence of which he was convicted …

"… We are invited to say that an unlawful arrest on which the defendant is, on the one hand, not entitled to rely under section 8 can, on the other, be used as a reasonable excuse for not complying with a request properly made of him under that section. That seems to me to be wholly illogical and the submission to that effect cannot … be sustained."

The answers to both questions were "yes". Appeal dismissed.

DPP v Kay (John)

[1999] RTR 109, 4 March 1998, QBD (DC)

The officer at the roadside is under no duty to ask when the motorist last drank or smoked. On the facts of this case (the motorist's appearance, his slurred speech, his breath smelling of alcohol), the officer had ample reason to suspect the motorist had alcohol in his body. The magistrates were in error to exclude the officer's evidence under s 78, Police and Criminal Evidence Act 1984. See also Grant v DPP, page 16, where the court was entitled to find that the motorist had not had a drink within the 20 minutes preceding the requirement; and DPP v Carey, page 72, where the officer's failure to follow the manufacturer's instructions for a roadside breath testing device did not vitiate the procedure.

A motorist had been charged with failing without reasonable excuse to provide two specimens of breath for analysis, contrary to s 7(6), Road Traffic Act 1988. A roadside breath test had been administered, but the constable did not ask the motorist when he had last taken alcoholic drink; he was unaware of the manufacturer's instruction that there should be an interval of at least 20 minutes between the defendant's last drink and the administration of the test; in fact the interval was only 5 minutes. The test was positive; the motorist was arrested and, at the police station, failed to provide specimens of breath for analysis.

The magistrates found that the constable's failure to comply with the manufacturer's instructions rendered the result of the breath test so unreliable that it would not have been fair to allow the Crown Prosecution Service to rely on it; the constable had acted negligently and, at worst, in bad faith. They exercised their discretion under s 78, Police and Criminal Evidence Act 1984 (discretion to exclude evidence which would have such an adverse effect on the fairness of the proceedings that the court ought not to admit it) to exclude the constable's evidence and any further evidence obtained as a consequence of the constable's involvement in the case. They dismissed the information. The prosecutor appealed.

QUESTION(S) FOR THE COURT: (1) Whether there was any requirement that the arresting officer should enquire when the respondent had taken his last drink. (2) Whether there was any evidence upon which the justices could properly have found bad faith on the part of the arresting officer. (3) Even if there was no evidence of bad faith, whether there was any basis upon which the justices could properly have exercised a discretion to exclude the evidence of the Intoximeter procedure under s 78, Police and Criminal Evidence Act 1984.

HELD: "[On (1)] … *DPP v Carey* [see page 72] … is still good law. Consequently there is no duty on a police officer to ask when the respondent had taken his last drink or smoked his last cigarette … Failure to ask either or both of those questions does not invalidate the roadside breath test nor the subsequent arrest …

"[On (2)] There was no evidence … which could have justified [a finding of bad faith]. The magistrates found that the reason why [the arresting officer] had not complied with the manufacturer's instruction was that he was unaware of the requirement that there should be a time interval of not less than twenty minutes … [the arresting officer's] account of the respondent's appearance, of his speech being slurred and his breath smelling of alcohol and of what the respondent had said to him at the road side was not challenged in any way in cross-examination. The officer had ample cause to suspect the respondent of having alcohol in his body, and that that alcohol exceeded the prescribed limit …

"[On (3)] … the magistrates' exercise of their discretion under s 78 was in error … Parliament altered the form of the original 1972 Act deliberately to remove as a pre-condition for the valid taking of a specimen at a police station or hospital the taking of a road side breath test correct in every detail … It is only if the admission of the second officer's evidence in the light of what had gone wrong at the road side would have such an adverse effect on the fairness of proceedings that the court ought not to admit it that the second officer's evidence may be excluded. …"

Appeal allowed.

DPP v Porter (Paul Nicholas)

Unreported, CO/3434/1999, 15 February 2000, QBD (DC)

There is no material distinction between arrest and detention; neither is a prerequisite of a lawful requirement for a specimen.

A motorist had been required to provide specimens of breath for analysis. He replied that he had a medical condition, asthma, which prevented him from doing so. He was then required to provide a specimen of blood or urine. He replied "Nobody's sticking a needle in me. I'll give urine". The officer decided this was not a medical reason. The police surgeon was called and, in his presence, a specimen of blood was requested. The defendant refused.

It was argued before the magistrates that there was no case to answer in that the defendant had not been lawfully detained and that the breath analysis procedure, including the respondent's failure to provide a blood sample, was therefore invalid. The magistrates accepted that argument and dismissed the charge. The prosecutor appealed.

QUESTION(S) FOR THE COURT: (a) Whether proof of lawful detention authorised by the custody officer is relevant in a charge of failing to provide a specimen for analysis under s 7(6), Road Traffic Act 1988. (b) Whether the Intoximeter procedure is a separate issue from the issue of respondent's lawful detention.

HELD: "… 8. The central argument advanced here by the appellant/prosecutor is that it is entirely unnecessary to prove a defendant's lawful detention in order to establish a case of this nature against him. That that is so is perfectly plain from a whole succession of authorities. One of them, *Anderton v Royle*, [[1985] RTR 91 (DC)] was considered by the Justices and, somewhat surprisingly … they were advised by their clerk that it could be distinguished on the footing that, whereas that case was concerned with valid arrest, the argument advanced on the submission of no case to answer here related to lawful detention. There is no material distinction between the two for present purposes.

"9. Other cases which are fatal to the Justices' conclusion are *Fox v Chief Constable of Gwent* [see page 1] … and *Hawes v DPP* [see page 22] … ."

The answers to the questions were: (a) "no"; and (b) "yes". Appeal allowed.

DPP v Robertson (Steven Gary)

[2002] EWHC 542 (Admin), [2002] RTR 383, 4 March 2002, QBD (Admin)

The fact that a motorist provided a negative roadside breath test did not preclude the police from arresting on suspicion of driving while impaired.

A motorist was stopped by police officers as part of a routine stop check. One of the officers smelt alcohol on his breath and asked him to accompany him to the police car. He was asked whether he had been drinking. He said he had, and that his last drink was about 10–15 minutes before. He provided a negative roadside breath specimen.

There was further conversation in the police car, during which the police officers concluded that the motorist slurred his speech. They arrested him under s 4, Road Traffic Act 1988 on suspicion of driving whilst impaired through alcohol. At the police station the motorist provided breath specimens and the lower reading was 41 µg alcohol in 100 ml breath.

The magistrates found that the motorist had been arrested unlawfully; in the police car, there was no evidence upon which the police could have arrested him because the result of the test had been negative. They found that the procedures at the police station were so tainted by the conduct of the police at the roadside that they excluded the evidence obtained at the police station under s 78, Police and Criminal Evidence Act 1984 (discretion to exclude evidence which would have such an adverse effect on the fairness of the proceedings that the court ought not to admit it). The prosecutor appealed.

QUESTION(S) FOR THE COURT: Whether police officers have power to arrest a motorist on the grounds that they suspect he is unfit to drive through drink, when a roadside breath test under s 6, Road Traffic Act 1988 has proved negative.

HELD: "16. … the prosecutor submits that there are two parallel and quite distinct areas in which a constable has a power to arrest when dealing with motorists. Under section 4 the critical question … is that the constable must have reasonable cause to suspect that the person is, or has been … driving when impaired. The provisions in connection with breath tests are directed towards cases of a person driving, or being in charge of a motor vehicle, with an alcohol concentration above a prescribed limit. Section 6 provides for the tests, and the equivalent power under section 6(5) [see now s 6D(1)] is that the officer may arrest without warrant if, as a result of a breath test, he has reasonable cause to suspect that the portion of alcohol in that person's breath or blood exceeds the prescribed limit.

"17. [The prosecutor further] submits the police officers were faced with a driver who from his breath and from his admission to them had been drinking. He … provided a test and as a result of the test the constables did not have reasonable cause to suspect that the portion of alcohol in his breath or blood exceeded the prescribed limit. … But [it is argued] that does not mean, having operated their powers under section 6, assuming they have reasonable cause to suspect that he is impaired, they have no power to arrest …

"18. … that submission is entirely correct. Plainly the police have powers which subsist under section 4 which do not fall away simply because they have embarked upon a procedure under section 6 by the way of administration of a breath test. But obviously the result of a test, if it is negative, would fall to be considered as a factor in any case where, notwithstanding that result, the police went on to arrest on the ground that they had a reasonable suspicion under section 4(6) … ."

The magistrates were wrong to conclude that the respondent had been unlawfully arrested and wrong to exclude the evidence. Appeal allowed.

DPP v Wilson

[2009] EWHC 1988 (Admin), [2009] RTR 29, 21 July 2009, QBD (DC)

The fact that a person was arrested while at hospital as a patient (which is prohibited by s 6D(3), Road Traffic Act 1988) did not invalidate the subsequent procedures.

A motorist had been charged with driving with excess alcohol in blood, contrary to s 5(1)(a), Road Traffic Act 1988. He had been involved in a road traffic accident and was taken to hospital. With the consent of the doctor in charge, a breath specimen was taken and was positive. An officer then arrested and cautioned the motorist. The officer was unaware that s 6D(3), Road Traffic Act 1988 prohibits the arrest of a person being treated at hospital. Again with the consent of the doctor in charge, a blood specimen was taken. The motorist was later discharged from hospital and the officer took him to the police station. Analysis of the blood specimen revealed 133 mg alcohol in 100 ml blood. The justices found the specimen had been taken unlawfully and dismissed the charge.

QUESTION(S) FOR THE COURT: Whether the justices were wrong to decide the blood specimen had been taken unlawfully because the defendant had been arrested while at hospital, even though he remained there until his treatment was concluded.

HELD: "7. … the only issue relates to the consequence of the statutory provision, which states that a person may not be arrested whilst a patient in hospital. The issue in this case is what the effect is in relation to subsequent blood tests. …

"10. [It is argued for the motorist] that the fact that the arrest was prohibited means that all procedures subsequent to the arrest are not valid. In my view this is not correct. There is nothing in the statutory provisions which requires there to be a valid arrest for subsequent procedures to be so valid. Furthermore, there is no logical reason or any principled reason as to why evidence obtained after an unfair or an unlawful arrest should be admissible, but not that obtained after a prohibited arrest. The fact that an arrest is prohibited does not have the effect of invalidating subsequent procedures provided they are carried out in accordance with the other statutory requirements. …"

The answer to the question was "yes". Case remitted to the magistrates' court with a direction to convict.

R (CPS) v Wolverhampton Magistrates' Court

[2009] EWHC 3467 (Admin), 27 November 2009, QBD (DC)

On the facts (arrest without any preliminary test), the evidence of breath analysis should not have been excluded under s 78, Police and Criminal Evidence Act 1984. In any event, it was still open to police to arrest on suspicion of having been in charge with excess alcohol.

The defendant had been charged with driving with excess alcohol, contrary to s 5(1)(a), Road Traffic Act 1988. Police officers saw a motor car. The driver spotted them and quickly reversed away. The officers went after the car on foot. It collided with a bank and a hedge and came to a stop. One of the officers saw that the driver's eyes were glazed and could smell intoxicants on his breath. The officer did not conduct a preliminary breath test because he did not have the equipment with him. Nor did he carry out a preliminary impairment test because he had not been trained to do so. The driver was arrested for driving while unfit through drink. Breath analysis gave a lower reading of 44 µg in 100 ml of breath, and a replacement blood specimen given under s 8(2), Road Traffic Act 1988 (lower breath reading no more than 50 – now repealed; see page v) also showed excess alcohol.

The defendant submitted there was no case to answer. The district judge severely criticised the police for not having trained sufficient officers to conduct preliminary impairment testing. He found that since none of the conditions in s 6B, Road Traffic Act 1988 (preliminary impairment testing) had been met, the arrest was unlawful. He went on to exclude the evidence of the blood analysis under the discretion in s 78, Police and Criminal Evidence Act 1984 (to exclude evidence which would have such an adverse effect on the fairness of the proceedings that the court ought not to admit it) and allowed the defendant's submission of no case to answer.

The prosecutor sought judicial review of the finding of no case to answer.

HELD: "11. … The real issue here is the District Judge's application of s 78 of PACE. The District Judge has used this power … as a rod with which to beat the police for failure to put in place sufficient training in the new procedures enacted in sections 6A to 6D. … The District Judge has not considered the critical section 78 question, namely, whether admission of the evidence in issue would have such an adverse effect on the fairness of the proceedings that it should not be admitted. … I am unable to see how the unlawfulness of the arrest, constituted by the want of any preliminary road side test, occasioned the least unfairness to the defendant. Given the readings at the police station it is surely inconceivable that a breath test at the scene would have been favourable to the defendant. And whatever the result of a road side test, the officer would still have been entitled to arrest the defendant if he had reasonable cause to suspect that he had committed a section 4 offence."

The court granted the prosecutor's application for judicial review and quashed the acquittal.

Kohler v DPP

[2010] EWHC 2886 (Admin), 9 July 2010, QBD (Admin)

Breath analysis following a breach of s 6D(3), Road Traffic Act 1988 is admissible in evidence. The results of breath analysis are admissible even if there has been no preliminary breath test.

A motorist had been charged with driving with excess alcohol, contrary to s 5(1), Road Traffic Act 1988. She was a patient at a hospital but there was no doctor on duty and she was not under the charge of a medical practitioner. A nurse had made arrangements for her to be transferred to another hospital and she was awaiting an ambulance. A police officer arrived at the hospital and the patient admitted that she had been driving. Without first establishing whether a medical practitioner had any objection to the requirement for, or the provision of, a specimen (as required by s 9(1), Road Traffic Act 1988), the officer required a preliminary breath test. It was positive and the officer arrested the motorist, in breach of s 6D(3), Road Traffic Act 1988 (a person may not be arrested under s 6D while at a hospital as a patient). He took her to the police station, where breath analysis showed excess alcohol. The motorist was convicted and appealed.

QUESTION(S) FOR THE COURT (AS REFORMULATED IN THE JUDGMENT): Whether the result of the evidential breath testing was admissible in evidence.

HELD: "[On the argument that the breath analysis should not be admitted, as the officer had not, before requiring the preliminary breath test, sought to see if the medical practitioner in immediate charge of her case objected] 23. … Section 9 by definition relates to a person only while they are at hospital as a patient. Therefore section 7, where it deals with a suspect at a police station, cannot sensibly be made subject to the additional requirements of section 9. …

"24. I am fortified in this conclusion by the acceptance by [counsel for the appellant] that if no preliminary breath test at all had been administered, nonetheless it would have been open to the police officer to arrest Mrs Kohler and to have the subsequent samples provided at the police station admitted in evidence. It is not a necessary prerequisite of an admissible section 7 sample that there be a preliminary breath test. …

"[On the argument that the evidence of the breath analysis should be excluded on the ground that the protection of the physical body or mental state of a patient was, as a matter of public policy, of such importance as to render inadmissible that which would otherwise (though obtained unlawfully) be admissible] 26. …evidence which is said to be illegally obtained, as, for instance, by breach of a mandatory statutory procedure, is nonetheless admissible. That has been the common law position in this jurisdiction for many years, if not longer. …

"31. In this case … there was a prohibited arrest at a hospital. It was contrary to statute. … If, on the authorities, it is plain that a prohibited or unlawful arrest does not invalidate a specimen of breath or urine thereafter obtained in accordance with section 7, it seems to me impossible to see any good reason why public policy should provide that the antecedent failure to comply with section 9 should have that effect."

The answer to the question was "yes". Appeal dismissed.

2. RANDOM STOPPING OF VEHICLES

Chief Constable of Gwent v Dash

[1986] RTR 41, [1985] Crim LR 674, 13 June 1985, QBD

Officers may randomly stop vehicles but may not randomly require breath tests. See also the Scottish case of Stewart v Crowe 1999 SLT 899, to the same effect.

Magistrates had convicted a motorist, under s 6(1), Road Traffic Act 1972 as substituted by s 25 and Sch 8, Transport Act 1981, of driving with excess alcohol. The police had been randomly stopping cars to find whether the drivers had been drinking, and stopped the motorist; they smelt alcohol on his breath, which led to the breath testing procedure, prosecution and conviction.

The motorist appealed to the Crown Court, which overturned the conviction on the ground that randomly stopping cars to ascertain if the drivers had been drinking was malpractice and unlawful. The prosecutor appealed.

QUESTION(S) FOR THE COURT: Whether on the facts found the Crown Court was entitled to conclude that there was such malpractice as to render unlawful the requirement of a specimen of breath and the subsequent procedure.

HELD: "… there is no express requirement of reasonable cause for suspicion that alcohol has been consumed set out in section 8 or anywhere else in the Act before a car can be stopped … That requirement of s 8(1)(a) [authorising a constable to require a specimen of breath if he has reasonable cause to suspect a driver has alcohol in his body] governs the administration of the first breath test and not the stopping of the car … provided there is no malpractice or oppression or caprice or opprobrious conduct … there is no restriction upon the stopping of motorists by a policeman in the execution of his duty and the subsequent requirement for a breath test should the policeman then and there genuinely suspect the ingestion of alcohol … the police are … not prohibited from the random stopping of cars within the limits already referred to; but are, of course, prohibited from requiring breath tests at random, which is a very different thing … The officers' conduct did not, on the proved facts, amount to malpractice as such."

Appeal allowed.

DPP v Minton

[2002] EWHC 805 (Admin), 15 March 2002, QBD (Admin)

Officers may randomly stop vehicles but may not randomly require breath tests.

A motorist had been charged with driving with excess alcohol, contrary to s 5(1)(a), Road Traffic Act 1988. He had been stopped as part of a routine check. At the time he was stopped, the officer in question had no cause to suspect that he had an excess of alcohol; the officer shouted across the road, asking him whether he had had anything to drink; the motorist replied that he had had two pints of lager. A roadside breath test was positive. The motorist was arrested and taken to the police station. Analysis of a blood specimen revealed 92 mg alcohol in 100 ml blood.

The justices accepted an argument that since the motorist had been stopped as part of a routine check, the officer had no reasonable cause to suspect excess alcohol; they exercised their discretion to exclude the subsequent procedures at the police station and the analysis of the blood. The motorist was acquitted; the prosecutor appealed.

QUESTION(S) FOR THE COURT: (1) On the facts found, was the court entitled to conclude that the [officer], in requiring the respondent to provide a roadside specimen of breath, and in arresting the defendant, acted in such a way as to: (a) render inadmissible the evidence of the subsequent procedures at the police station and the analysis of blood? (b) justify the exclusion of such evidence? (2) On the facts found, was the court entitled to acquit the respondent?

HELD: "6. … The justices appeared to have confused the power of a PC in the execution of his duty randomly to stop motorists with the question of when, for the purposes of section 6(1), reasonable cause to suspect has to arise. Reasonable cause to suspect must not be confused with the power to stop a vehicle at random. The law prohibits police officers from requiring breath tests at random, but does not prohibit the random stopping of cars provided that that stopping is in the execution of a police officer's duty and is not as a result of some oppression, caprice or malpractice. No finding was made of oppression, caprice and malpractice. The police officer had acted perfectly properly in routinely stopping the driver. The error of the justices was in thinking that in some way the procedures under the Road Traffic Act were vitiated because the suspicion did not arise until the driver had made an admission that he had been drinking."

The answer to questions (1)(a) and (b) and (2) was "no". Appeal allowed.

3. REASONABLE SUSPICION AND REASONABLE BELIEF

See s 6(2)–(5), Road Traffic Act 1988 – power to administer preliminary tests. See also R v South Norfolk JJ ex p Keymer, page 23 – reasonable cause to suspect not required in relation to a requirement for an evidential specimen; the tests under s 6 and s 7 are different; and DPP v Godwin, page 347, where the officer did not have reasonable cause to suspect.

Johnson v Whitehouse

[1984] RTR 38, 22 March 1983, QBD (DC)

In the circumstances of this case, the officer had ample grounds to believe the subject had been driving; the fact that he used the word "suspect" rather than "believe" was no more than an inaccurate use of language.

A person had been charged with failing without reasonable excuse to provide a specimen of breath for a breath test, contrary to s 8(2) (accident; power to require breath specimen from person whom a constable has reasonable cause to believe was driving) and (3), Road Traffic Act 1972; and with failing without reasonable excuse to provide a specimen for analysis, contrary to s 9(3), Road Traffic Act 1972. An accident had occurred and a witness had seen a single person alight from a car, lock it and walk away. A police officer arrived 10 minutes later; he found blood on the front seats of the car, and documents bearing the defendant's name in the car. He went to the address and saw the defendant enter the garden and fall over in a drunken state. He was bleeding and had in his possession keys which fitted the car. The officer required a breath specimen on the basis that he had reasonable cause to suspect him of having driven the car when it was involved in an accident.

At the hearing, it was submitted that there was no case to answer on the ground that s 8(2) requires the constable to have a reasonable belief, not merely to suspect, that the person has been driving, and that there was insufficient evidence to ground such a belief. The justices rejected that submission and convicted the defendant, who appealed.

QUESTION(S) FOR THE COURT: Whether, if an accident occurred owing to the presence of a motor vehicle on a road, a constable in uniform was entitled to require the person whom he had reasonable cause to believe was driving the motor vehicle to provide a specimen of breath for the breath test if he "suspects" as distinct from "believes" him of having been the driver of the motor vehicle, in accordance with s 8(2), Road Traffic Act 1972.

HELD: "… there can be no doubt at all that there was ample ground on which the constable … could reasonably believe that the defendant was the driver of the car … the constable found in the crashed car documents bearing the defendant's name and address, the time lapse between the accident and the defendant arriving at his home being consistent with the progress made by an injured person to cover that distance, and the defendant's recent injuries being consistent with those received in a car crash … it was found also that the defendant was bleeding from the face and that there was blood on the steering wheel as well as on both the front seats of the car.

"... the greater force of the word 'believe' is an essential part of the law and ... the police constable in the present case, having said 'suspect' rather than 'believe' was guilty of no more than an inaccurate use of language ... when accuracy of language was not essential."

Appeal dismissed.

Blake v Pope

[1986] 1 WLR 1152, [1986] 3 All ER 185, [1987] RTR 77, [1986] Crim LR 749, 14 May 1986, QBD (DC)

The suspicion that a person has been driving need not arise while the person is actually driving; nor need there be any nexus between the driving and the police arriving and the suspicion arising.

A motorist had been charged, *inter alia*, with driving with excess alcohol, contrary to s 6(1)(a), Road Traffic Act 1972 as substituted by s 25 and Sch 8, Transport Act 1981. Another motorist had caused the defendant to stop his car, leaving his car so that the defendant's car was blocked in, and a third motorist removed the defendant's keys before calling the police. When the police arrived some 10 or 15 minutes later, an officer smelt alcohol on the defendant's breath and saw that he was unsteady on his feet. He required a breath sample for a roadside breath test under s 7(1)(b), Road Traffic Act 1972 as likewise substituted; the defendant refused and was arrested. At the police station, breath analysis revealed 108 μg alcohol in 100 ml breath.

At the trial, the motorist contended that since he had ceased driving some 10 minutes before the police arrived, and had effectively been prevented from driving by others, the nexus between his driving and the intervention of the police had been severed; the police officer's suspicion about his condition could not have arisen while he was driving. The justices accepted this argument and dismissed the information. The prosecutor appealed.

QUESTION(S) FOR THE COURT: Whether the justices were right in law in accepting the defendant's defence and dismissing the charge of driving with excess alcohol.

HELD: "Section 7(1)(b) does not require that the suspicion of the officers can only justify the exercise of the power to require a breath test if the suspicion that the driver has excess alcohol arises whilst the driver is still driving or if there is a nexus between such driving and the arrival and suspicion of the police ... section 7(1)(b) is expressly to the contrary effect.

"... the justices misdirected themselves with regard to the proper construction of section 6(1) and 7 of the Road Traffic Act 1972."

Appeal allowed.

DPP v Redling

Unreported, CO/331/88, 10 October 1988, QBD (DC)

In the circumstances of this case, there was nothing in the justices' findings to contradict the fact that the officer had reasonably come to the conclusion that the defendant had been driving.

A person had been charged, *inter alia*, with failing without reasonable excuse to provide a specimen for a breath test, contrary to s 7(4), Road Traffic Act 1972 as substituted by s 25 and Sch 8, Transport Act 1981; and with failing without reasonable excuse to provide a specimen of breath for analysis, contrary to s 8(7), Road Traffic Act 1972 as likewise substituted.

The justices heard evidence from a witness to an accident who could not identify the defendant as the driver; one police officer said the defendant had admitted driving; another said he had not. There was other evidence suggesting that the defendant had not been driving.

The justices found that the defendant had not driven the car at all on the evening in question, and dismissed the charges. The prosecutor appealed.

QUESTION(S) FOR THE COURT: Whether the question of the defendant's driving or otherwise was relevant to the reasonableness of the officer's suspicion, and whether the fact that the defendant was not driving could amount to a reasonable excuse for not providing specimens under either section.

HELD: "… There is ample authority … to show that when a police officer reasonably suspects a person has been or may have been driving a car and has alcohol on his breath, he is entitled to request that person to provide a sample of breath, both at the roadside and later, if he is taken there, at a police station … there is nothing in [the justices'] findings to contradict [that the officer] had reasonably come to the conclusion upon facts known to him at the material time that the Respondent had been driving the car. Therefore he was entitled to make the request that he made and the Respondent disentitled by law to refuse it. The like consideration applies to what happened at the police station."

The answer to the question was "no". Appeal allowed.

DPP v McGladrigan

[1991] RTR 297, [1991] Crim LR 851, 22 April 1991, QBD (DC)

An officer's reasonable cause to suspect that a driver has alcohol in his body is sufficient if it arises after the driver has been stopped.

A motorist had been charged with driving with excess alcohol, contrary to s 5(1)(a), Road Traffic Act 1988. He had been seen manoeuvring his vehicle out of a car parking space; the engine stalled and he restarted it. He then drove a short way until he was stopped by police; the motorist admitted he had consumed alcohol; a roadside breath test was positive and the motorist was arrested and taken to the police station, where breath analysis proved positive.

The justices found that the constable had had no reasonable grounds to suspect that the defendant had alcohol in his body when he was seen driving, and that the arrest was unlawful, which vitiated the subsequent procedure and rendered inadmissible evidence of those procedures. They dismissed the charge. The prosecutor appealed.

QUESTION(S) FOR THE COURT: Whether the justices were correct in holding that their doubts as to the circumstances in which the defendant had been stopped whilst driving or their finding that there had been an unlawful arrest, without more, vitiated the subsequent procedures under s 7, Road Traffic Act 1988 thereby entitling them to dismiss the charge.

HELD: "… the time when the constable had reasonable cause to suspect was after the car had been stopped and after the defendant had himself confirmed that he had consumed alcohol. That was a firm, and indeed complete, basis for the constable to have the necessary reasonable cause and to require the defendant to provide a specimen, and thereafter to arrest him if the test was a positive one … the justices were wrong on their own findings of fact in restricting their consideration to the reasonable cause the constable had whilst the car was being driven, and on the finding of fact the defendant had himself confirmed that he had consumed alcohol."

Appeal allowed.

Whelehan v DPP

[1995] RTR 177, 16 November 1994, QBD (DC)

Where an officer did not caution a motorist until after he had admitted driving and had given a positive roadside breath test, there was no procedural flaw. Compare CPS v O'Shea, page 458, where questioning did amount to an interview such that a caution should have been administered.

A person had been charged with driving with excess alcohol, contrary to s 5(1), Road Traffic Act 1988. He had been found by police in the driving seat of his stationary car; the keys were in the ignition; it was apparent that he had been drinking. In answer to a question from the officer, he admitted he had driven there. The officer then administered a roadside breath test, which was positive. The officer arrested and cautioned him, and at the police station, breath analysis revealed excess alcohol.

At the hearing, it was argued that there was no case to answer on the ground that the defendant's admission that he had driven was inadmissible, in that it had been obtained in breach of PACE Code C, paragraph 10.1 of the PACE Codes of Practice under s 66, Police and Criminal Evidence Act 1984, the officer having failed to caution the motorist before asking the question. The justices found that the constable's suspicion that an offence had been committed arose only after the roadside breath test had been taken and therefore the caution had been administered at the correct time. They found a case to answer and went on to convict the motorist, who appealed.

QUESTION(S) FOR THE COURT: (1) Whether PACE Code C, paragraph 10.1 applied so that the officer should have cautioned the defendant before asking him whether he had driven to the place where he was found; (2) if so, whether the justices were right to reject a submission of no case to answer when the only evidence that the defendant had driven at all had been his answer "yes"; (3) in particular, whether the justices were right to reject the submission that the answer should not be admitted in evidence when it had been obtained in breach of paragraph 10.1; and (4) whether the answer was sufficient evidence that the defendant had driven at the material time.

HELD: "... It seems ... that the justices were led into the belief ... that the answer 'Yes' to the question posed by the constable was the only evidence that the defendant had driven to the place of arrest on the road. I ... do not think that that is so. The time of 1.20 a.m., the place and the circumstances, ... afforded sufficient evidence at that stage of the proceedings on which it could be inferred, by necessary and proper deduction by the court, that he had driven the motor car ...

"... even if the submission is well founded that the constable should have cautioned the defendant at an earlier stage, any court properly directing itself would not rule this answer out, either under section 76(2) or in its discretion under section 78 ... or, for that matter, under the residual powers of the court at common law ...

"... the need to caution did not apply until the screening test ... the constable did not need to caution him until after the question 'Did you drive here?' and receiving the answer 'Yes'."

The answer to question (1) was "no"; question (2) did not apply. The answer to questions (3) and (4) was "yes". Appeal dismissed.

Grant v DPP

[2003] EWHC 130 (Admin), (2003) 167 JP 459, 22 January 2003, QBD (DC)

In the circumstances of this case, the court was entitled to find that the motorist had not had a drink within the 20 minutes preceding the requirement for a breath specimen, and the requirement was lawful. The motorist's challenge to the approval of the breath analysis device failed. See also DPP v Kay (John), page 4 – officer under no duty to ask when the motorist last drank or smoked; and DPP v Carey, page 72 – officer's failure to follow manufacturer's instructions for roadside breath testing device did not vitiate the procedure.

A motorist had been charged with failing without reasonable excuse to provide a specimen for a breath test, contrary to s 6(4), Road Traffic Act 1988, and with driving with excess alcohol, contrary to s 5(1)(a), Road Traffic Act 1988. He had been followed by the police for about 4 miles. When they stopped him, he said he had had a drink within the preceding 5 minutes, that he knew his rights and that the officer had to wait 20 minutes. He refused to give a roadside breath test. At the police station, breath analysis revealed excess alcohol.

At the trial, the defendant argued that the requirement for a roadside breath test was unlawful because, contrary to the manufacturer's instructions, there had not been an interval of least 20 minutes since his last drink; and challenged the type approval of the breath analysis device used.

The motorist was convicted and his appeal to the Crown Court was dismissed. He appealed further.

QUESTION(S) FOR THE COURT: (1) Whether there was evidence upon which the court could conclude that the defendant was lawfully required to provide a specimen of breath; (2) whether the court was correct to follow *DPP v Brown* and *DPP v Teixeira* (see page 297) that evidence should not be put before the court as to whether the EC/IR instrument should have been approved by the Secretary of State and/or that approval should have been revoked and/or that it had been modified.

HELD: "[On (1)] 6. … The court expressly held that the police officers were wholly reliable and honest witnesses … whereas the appellant was not a witness whose evidence they could accept save when corroborated by the testimony of others …

"15. … there is no doubt that [the officer] had reasonable cause to suspect both that the appellant was driving with alcohol in his body and he had committed a moving traffic offence, namely speeding.

"16. It follows that on the plain words of the section the officer was entitled to require the appellant to provide him with a specimen of breath for a breath test. …

"19. The question … is whether [the officer] acted *bona fide* in requiring the appellant to take the breath test when he did. In particular did he have reasonable cause to suspect that the appellant had been drinking in the 20 minutes before he was required to take the test? …

"22. … the court were entitled to conclude that the appellant was clearly lying when he said that he had had a drink within the previous five minutes …

"23. I would reject [the] submission that there was no evidence on which the officer could have reasonable grounds for disbelieving the appellant. …

"[On (2)] 25. [Counsel for the appellant] challenged the approval of the intoximeter device known as EC/IR for three reasons: (1), it was *Wednesbury* unreasonable for the Secretary of State to approve it in the first place; (2), it was *Wednesbury* unreasonable for the Secretary of State not to have revoked its approval; and, (3), the alterations to it had caused it to lose its seal of approval. …

"27. [In *DPP v Brown* and *DPP v Teixiera*, the court] underlined the general principle that it is not open to defendants to assert that the intoximeter EC/IR should not have received the approval of the Secretary of State … [Following *DPP v Brown, DPP v Teixiera* and *DPP v Memery* [2002] EWHC 1720 (Admin), [2003] RTR 18 arguments (1) and (2) were rejected.]

"[On (3)] 44. … I … assume for present purposes, one, that alterations to a device can be so fundamental that they cause the device to be such that it is no longer the device approved and, two, that once the issue is sufficiently raised the burden is on the Crown to prove beyond reasonable doubt that the device is an approved device. However, I would not accept … that the court did not consider the relevant evidence …

"45. … [the court] permitted [counsel] to ask appropriate questions of [the appellant's expert witness] designed to show that the devices had been modified, but they plainly rejected [the] evidence that there had been such a modification."

The answer to question (1) was "yes"; the answer to question (2), omitting the words "and/or it had been modified" was "yes". Appeal dismissed.

4. TRESPASS

See also Matto v Wolverhampton Crown Court, page 394, where officers acted in bad faith.

Morris v Beardmore

[1981] AC 446, [1980] 3 WLR 283, [1980] 2 All ER 753, [1980] RTR 321, 17 July 1980, HL

A requirement to provide a breath specimen is not lawful where the officer making the requirement is trespassing in the defendant's home.

The defendant had been charged with failing to supply a specimen of breath, contrary to s 8(3), Road Traffic Act 1972 and with failing to supply a specimen for a laboratory test contrary to s 9(3) of that Act. He had collided with another vehicle; he went home. Later, police went to his home where the motorist's son let them in. The motorist did not wish to speak to the officers and sent them a message, via his son, that they were trespassers and that he wished them to leave. The officers went upstairs into a bedroom, where they asked the defendant to supply a specimen of breath. He refused and was arrested. At the police station he refused to supply a specimen for a laboratory test. The magistrates dismissed both charges on the ground that in the circumstances the requirement was unlawful. The Divisional Court allowed the prosecutor's appeal. The motorist appealed further.

QUESTION(S) FOR THE COURT: Whether a constable in uniform who has been invited into a private house by someone other than the occupier, and whose permission to remain therein is subsequently withdrawn by the occupier, continues to be a constable in uniform empowered under s 8, Road Traffic Act 1972 to require a person in that house, whom he has reasonable cause to believe was driving or attempting to drive a motor vehicle which had been involved in an accident on a public road, to provide a specimen of breath for a breath test, and in the event of a refusal to provide such a specimen to effect a lawful arrest of that person.

HELD: "… The presumption is that in the absence of express provision to the contrary, Parliament did not intend to authorise tortious conduct … to constitute a valid requirement the constable who makes it must be acting lawfully towards the person whom he requires to undergo a breath test at the moment that he makes the requirement. He is not acting lawfully if he is then committing the tort of trespass on that person's property, for section 8(2) gives him no authority to do so."

Appeal allowed.

Clarke v DPP

Unreported, CO/3993/95, 30 April 1996, QBD (DC)

In the circumstances of this case the police were not trespassers in the defendant's home; the requirement for a breath test was lawful.

The appellant had been charged with failing without reasonable excuse to provide a specimen for a breath test, contrary to s 6(4), Road Traffic Act 1988; and with failing without reasonable excuse to provide two specimens of breath for analysis, contrary to s 7(6), Road Traffic Act 1988.

Police had received a report of erratic driving. They went to the appellant's home, where they saw the car in question on the drive. They were admitted to the house by a Mrs Dawson, who was providing medical attention to the appellant's wife. She introduced Mrs Clarke, the appellant's wife, as "the lady of the house". Mrs Clarke did not object to the presence of the officers, co-operated with them, and told them that the appellant had been the last driver of the car. The appellant then appeared, but would not give his name; the police smelt alcohol on him; he remonstrated with the police and asked them to leave. They explained why they were there and that they had been invited in; one of the officers asked for a specimen of breath, which was refused. The officer arrested the driver.

In his defence, the appellant contended that, although the officers had been invited into his home, he had asked them to leave before they asked for a sample of breath; they were therefore trespassers; the arrest which followed was unlawful; and the refusals to provide should have been excluded as evidence.

The justices rejected that contention and convicted the appellant. He appealed.

QUESTION(S) FOR THE COURT: Whether the justices should have excluded the evidence of the appellant's failure to provide a specimen of breath for a breath test and the subsequent police station procedure where it was contended by the appellant that the police officers were trespassers at the time the first request for a specimen of breath was made.

HELD: "… One cannot determine upon the available material whether Mrs Dawson, when she opened the door and invited [the officers] in specifically acted under instructions from Mrs Clarke. One does not know for what reason she took them into the living room. [Counsel for the appellant] is unable to overcome the effect of the evidence that when they were taken into the living room Mrs Clarke, who was the lady of the house, received them and had a conversation with them. She was capable of granting a licence to them to be there …

"… There was evidence upon which … the magistrates were entitled to conclude that a licence had been granted by the way in which Mrs Dawson and Mrs Clarke conducted themselves, and there was no basis … for a submission that in law Mr Clarke had the authority to determine any licence which had been granted by Mrs Clarke."

Appeal dismissed.

5. IN THE COURSE OF AN INVESTIGATION

See s 7(1) and (1A), Road Traffic Act 1988 – power to require specimens in the course of an investigation into whether an offence has been committed under s 3A, s 4, s 5 or s 5A. See also Butterworth v DPP, page 614 – the investigation may be into any offence under s 4 or s 5.

Graham v Albert
[1985] RTR 352, 28 January 1985, QBD (DC)

A requirement for a breath test following an accident was lawful; the officer was inquiring into whether the driver had committed an offence under s 6; he was not investigating the accident.

A motorist had been charged with failing without reasonable excuse to provide a specimen of breath for analysis, contrary to s 8(7), Road Traffic Act 1972 as substituted by s 25 and Sch 8, Transport Act 1981. An accident had occurred; the defendant had been the driver of one of the vehicles involved. She got out of her car, became agitated, and was escorted back to her car by a police officer, who smelt alcohol on her breath. He requested a breath specimen for a roadside breath test. The defendant refused and was arrested. At the police station, the station sergeant told her she had been arrested for failing to take a breath test and was suspected of driving having had too much to drink. He requested breath specimens for analysis under s 8(1), Road Traffic Act 1972. She refused.

At the trial, the motorist submitted there was no case to answer on the ground, *inter alia*, that the request for specimens at the police station was unlawful as the station officer was investigating an accident, not a possible offence under s 5 or s 6, Road Traffic Act 1972.

The justices dismissed the information. The prosecutor appealed.

QUESTION(S) FOR THE COURT: Whether the justices were correct in law in concluding that the prosecutor was not investigating a possible offence under s 5 or s 6, Road Traffic Act 1972 when he asked the defendant to provide two specimens of breath for analysis.

HELD: "… The prosecutor is the station officer. He was not investigating the road traffic accident. He was investigating an allegation … by the arresting officer …

of a potential offence under either section 5 or, in this particular case … under section 6 of the Road Traffic Act 1972 … When the prosecutor required the defendant to give a breath specimen pursuant to section 8, he was … inquiring into the possibility that the defendant had committed an offence under section 6 of the Act … his requirement of her to take a test was wholly lawful, her refusal constituted an offence under section 8(7) which was properly charged and the justices reached a wrong conclusion … ."

Appeal allowed.

Pearson v Commissioner of Police of the Metropolis

[1988] RTR 276, 24 June 1987, QBD (DC)

Where an officer suspects a number of people have been drinking, and that one was the driver, he is in the course of an investigation and it is lawful to require them all to provide specimens.

Three persons had been charged with failing without reasonable excuse to provide specimens of breath for analysis, contrary to s 8(7), Road Traffic Act 1972 as substituted by s 25 and Sch 8, Transport Act 1981. They had been arrested on suspicion of theft and interference with a motor vehicle. At the police station, suspecting that all three had been drinking, and that one had been the driver, but not knowing which, the police asked all three to provide breath specimens. All refused and were convicted by justices.

Their appeals to the Crown Court were unsuccessful, that court finding that in each case the officer had been genuinely investigating whether an offence under s 5 or s 6 of the Act (driving or in charge while unfit or with excess alcohol) had been committed, and that the breath specimens had been properly required under s 8(1) (in the course of an investigation whether a person had committed an offence under s 5 or s 6, a constable may require specimens of breath, etc). One of the three appealed further.

QUESTION(S) FOR THE COURT: (i) Whether, under s 8, Road Traffic Act 1972, a constable was entitled to require specimens of breath from more than one person where more than one person was suspected of having been the driver or having been in charge of a motor vehicle; (ii) whether the suspicion of an offence under s 5 or s 6 of the Act must relate to one particular person before the requirement was made; (iii) whether requirements for tests could be made to all members of a group, of which one unidentified member was suspected of having committed an offence under s 5 or s 6; and (iv) whether the Crown Court's determination was correct in point of law.

HELD: "[Dismissing the argument that breath specimens can be required only when the driver has already been identified] … in the context of section 8(1) of the Road Traffic Act 1972 when, as occurred in this case, a police officer had good reason to believe that one of three persons and no one else, was the driver of a vehicle, and that each of those three persons had consumed alcohol to such an extent that it was appropriate for the officer to require that person to provide a sample, then, what he was doing in making his request … was 'in the course of an investigation whether (the person to whom the request was addressed) has committed an offence'."

Appeal dismissed.

Hawes v DPP

[1993] RTR 116, 28 April 1992, QBD (DC)

As long as the officer is bona fide investigating whether or not an offence has been committed, a requirement for specimens is lawful even if it later transpires that no offence was in fact committed.

A motorist had been charged with driving in a public place while unfit, contrary to s 4(1), Road Traffic Act 1988; and with failing without reasonable excuse to provide two specimens of breath for analysis, contrary to s 7(6), Road Traffic Act 1988. Police had seen him driving on the car park of a public house. They believed he was drunk and arrested him. At the police station, he refused to provide breath specimens.

At the hearing, it was found that the car park was not a public place, and the s 4(1) charge was dismissed. The motorist submitted that since he had been driving on private land, there could be no offence under s 4 (driving while unfit) or s 5 (driving with excess alcohol), and that therefore he could not be convicted of an offence under s 7. The justices found that s 7 (in the course of an investigation into whether a person may have committed an offence under s 4 or s 5) stood alone and that all that was necessary was that a *bona fide* investigation was being carried out. They therefore convicted on the s 7(6) charge. The motorist appealed.

QUESTION(S) FOR THE COURT: Whether the justices were correct in law in finding: (a) that it was not a prerequisite to a s 7 offence that there was in fact an offence committed under s 4 or s 5 even though the investigation might in time have revealed that the place of the offence was in fact not a public place; and (b) that it was not necessary for there to be evidence at trial regarding the police officer's investigation into the alleged offences, provided the court was satisfied that the investigation was *bona fide*.

HELD: "There being no challenge to the good faith of the police officers, it is clear that what they were concerned with was to discover whether indeed the defendant had, in driving on the car park that night, been guilty of an offence under section 4 or section 5. They were not concerned with anything else. No doubt they assumed that the car park of the public house was a public place … It seems … difficult to suppose … that … the officer was doing anything other than investigating … whether a section 4 or 5 offence had been committed …

"Where a question arises, whether a constable has lawfully required a person to provide a specimen under [s 7(1)], the court trying the matter is simply concerned to know whether there was or was not a *bona fide* investigation of the question of whether the suspect had committed an offence under section 4 or 5 …

"On the facts here, … the requirement of a breath test was lawfully administered by the police officer under section 7. It follows that the defendant, who failed without reasonable excuse to provide it, was guilty of the offence under section 7(6)."

The answer to the question was "yes". Appeal dismissed.

R v South Norfolk JJ ex p Keymer

Unreported, CO 2813/93, 12 October 1994, QBD (DC)

A requirement to provide specimens is lawful where an officer is, in good faith, investigating whether a person has committed an offence under s 4 or s 5, Road Traffic Act 1988; the officer does not have to have reasonable cause to suspect that such an offence has been committed. The tests under ss 6 and 7, Road Traffic Act 1988 are different.

A motorist had been charged with failing without reasonable excuse to provide a specimen for a breath test, contrary to s 6(4), Road Traffic Act 1988; and with failing without reasonable excuse to provide two specimens of breath for analysis, contrary to s 7(6), Road Traffic Act 1988.

The magistrates dismissed the first matter on a submission of no case to answer, because they were not satisfied that the police officer had had reasonable cause to suspect that an offence under s 4 or s 5, Road Traffic Act 1988 had been committed. They found the second matter proved because, although not satisfied that the arresting officer had had reasonable cause to suspect that an offence under s 4 or s 5 had been committed, they were satisfied that, in continuing the investigation, he did so in good faith and without *mala fides*. The motorist sought to have a case stated in respect of that matter but the magistrates refused to do so. The motorist appealed further, seeking an order that the magistrates state a case.

HELD: "… Section 6 deals with a situation where, under section 6(1), a constable … has reasonable cause to suspect various matters, including that a person driving a vehicle or in charge of a vehicle has alcohol in his body or has committed a road traffic offence. That reasonable cause is the precondition to the application of section 6. Section 7 is in notably different terms. Section 7(1) applies when in the course of an investigation into whether a person has committed an offence under section 4 or 5 of this Act a constable requires him to do various things including providing a breath specimen. Section 6, therefore, imports a precondition of reasonable cause to suspect. Section 7 does not in its terms have any requirement as to reasonable cause, but simply that, as a matter of fact, the request should be made in the course of an investigation.

"… all that the tribunal of fact has to be satisfied about in respect of section 7(1) is that there was in progress an investigation that can properly be described as an investigation. That is how the Magistrates interpreted this section in this case and that is what they found … the Magistrates were right in declining to state a case."

Application dismissed.

DPP v Earnshaw (Neil Graham)

Unreported, CO/1425/98, 11 June 1998, QBD (DC)

On the facts of this case (another person was in the driving seat, but the defendant was standing by the car; he admitted he was the owner; he said, "we're putting the car round the back"; he tried to make off), the officer was in the course of an investigation.

A person had been charged with, in the course of an investigation into whether he had committed an offence under s 4(1) or s 5(1)(a) or (b), Road Traffic Act 1988, failing without reasonable excuse to provide two specimens of breath for analysis, contrary to s 7(6), Road Traffic Act 1988. A police officer observed a car at the entrance of an industrial estate; one man was sitting in the driver's seat and another, the defendant, was standing next to the car. The latter was unsteady on his feet, and the car was parked in an "unconventional position". The officer asked the man standing what they were doing; he replied that they were "putting the car round the back". The officer asked the man in the driver's seat if it was his car, had he been drinking and had he just driven there. He answered no to all questions. The defendant said he was the owner. The other man was uncooperative and confrontational and made off. The defendant attempted to do the same but was arrested for being drunk in charge of a vehicle.

At the police station, the arresting officer told the custody sergeant that he suspected both men had been drinking, and suspected drink driving. The defendant was asked to provide specimens of breath for analysis, but said he had not driven the car and made no attempt to blow into the breath analysis device.

The justices concluded that the arresting officer could not reasonably infer from the defendant's actions that he was in charge of the vehicle; the officer was more concerned with the other man; there was no *bona fide* investigation into the defendant's actions, but merely a "speculative inquiry"; he was not obliged to provide specimens of breath. They dismissed the case. The prosecutor appealed.

HELD: "… the test for determining whether the officer is 'in the course of an investigation into whether a person has committed' one of the specified offences is: (i) Was the officer investigating the offence? (ii) If so, did the officer believe that the person, to whom the requirement to provide a specimen was being made, had or may have committed the offence. The offence must, of course, be one of the offences identified in section 7(1) and the burden of proof is on the prosecution. The use of the words '*bona fide*' may cause difficulties. In deciding whether or not the officer had that belief, the court is entitled to inquire whether he had good reason for the belief, but the question remains …: 'Did he believe that the person had committed the offence or did he believe that he may have committed the offence?' If that be the state of his belief, then the officer is entitled under the section to require a specimen.

"[In the present case, there] are four relevant facts …: (i) the Respondent was standing by the car; (ii) he said he was the owner; (iii) he said 'We're putting the car round the back'; and (iv) he ran away …

"Having regard to those four facts against the background of what happened that evening, it was irrational to reach any conclusion other than that the officer was in the course of an investigation within the meaning of section 7…".

Appeal allowed.

6. MEDICAL REASONS WHY BREATH SPECIMENS CANNOT BE PROVIDED OR SHOULD NOT BE REQUIRED

See s 7(3)(a), Road Traffic Act 1988 – where the constable has reasonable cause to believe that for medical reasons a specimen of breath cannot be provided or should not be required, a blood or urine specimen may be required instead. See also May v DPP, page 189, where it was unclear whether or not the officer had formed the view that there were medical reasons why breath could not be provided or should not be required; Piggott v DPP, page 214 – there is no requirement in the legislation that a suspect communicate a reasonable excuse for failing to provide a breath specimen; McMahon v CPS, page 231 – where the medical examiner found no reason not to provide, there were no medical reasons why breath could not be provided or should not be required. Compare Medical Reasons Why a Blood Specimen Cannot or Should Not Be Taken (page 91); and medical reasons in the context of failing without reasonable excuse to provide specimens (page 220).

Horrocks v Binns

[1986] RTR 202, 26 July 1984, QBD (DC)

It is unlawful to require a specimen of blood or urine where there are no medical reasons why breath cannot be provided or should not be required, a reliable breath analysis device is available, and it is practicable to use it.

A motorist had been charged with failing without reasonable excuse to provide a specimen of blood for a laboratory test, contrary to s 8(7), Road Traffic Act 1972 as substituted by s 25 and Sch 8, Transport Act 1981. He had failed to provide breath specimens for analysis, saying he had difficulty because of a cut on his head. A doctor found insufficient evidence that the motorist's driving ability was impaired due to alcohol but was not asked whether the injuries would affect his ability to provide a specimen of breath. The police did not believe the cut affected the motorist's ability to provide breath specimens, but concluded that it was not practicable to require them; they asked instead for a specimen of blood. The motorist refused.

The magistrate found no good reason for requesting blood; there was no reasonable cause to believe that medical reasons prevented a sample of breath being taken; a reliable device was available and it was practicable to use it; the doctor's advice on the motorist's ability to provide a breath specimen had not been sought. The magistrate dismissed the charge. The prosecutor appealed.

QUESTION(S) FOR THE COURT: Whether, in the circumstances, the prosecutor made a valid requirement of the defendant to provide a specimen of blood.

HELD: "A blood or urine sample is only to be requested in the circumstances set out in section 8(3) paragraphs (a) [medical reasons], (b) [device or reliable device not available or not practicable to use it] or (c), although paragraph (c) does not apply to this case. …

"… the magistrate … was justified in finding as a fact that the provisions of paragraph (a) were not made out because the prosecutor himself said that he did not think that the defendant had any medical reason which prevented him from providing a specimen of breath. The magistrate then went on to consider paragraph (b) and he found, on the evidence, that not only was the device available, but there was no reason why it was not practicable to use it."

Appeal dismissed.

White & Gaskell v Proudlock

[1988] RTR 163, 23 November 1984, QBD (DC)

Having reasonable cause to believe that for medical reasons breath specimens cannot be provided or should not be required does not mean that the officer must in fact believe that.

A motorist had been charged, under s 8(7), Road Traffic Act 1972 as substituted by s 25 and Sch 8, Transport Act 1981, with failing without reasonable excuse to provide two specimens of breath; and, under s 8(1)(b) of the Act as likewise substituted, of failing without reasonable excuse to provide a specimen of blood. The motorist had not given breath specimens because he suffered from an asthmatic condition; the police had formed the view that he might have a medical condition and, under s 8(3)(a), required a specimen of blood, which the motorist refused to give.

The magistrates dismissed the first charge on the ground that the motorist suffered an asthmatic condition; and the second on the ground that at the time of requiring a blood specimen the police had not met the statutory requirement in s 8(3)(a) of "having reasonable cause to believe" that a specimen of breath could not be provided for medical reasons; the justices interpreted "reasonable cause to believe" as meaning "has reasonable cause to believe and does believe". The prosecutor appealed.

QUESTION(S) FOR THE COURT: Whether the justices were correct: (i) in concluding that because the officer had not formed the view that the failure to provide the two specimens of breath was due to a medical condition he was not entitled to require a specimen of blood; and (ii) in law in dismissing both charges.

HELD: It was not necessary to put an extended interpretation on the words "reasonable cause to believe"; the officer must have only reasonable cause to believe; he need not in fact believe; there may be cases where the officer does not know whether or not to believe a suspect has a medical condition: "I cannot see why the fact that he could not know whether or not to believe him should undermine the existence of a power to make the requirement".

"The justices were incorrect in their conclusion and wrong in dismissing the second charge. The answer to question (i) was "no"; the answer to question (ii) was that the justices erred in law in dismissing the charge relating to the provision of a specimen of blood".

Appeal allowed.

Dempsey v Catton

[1986] RTR 194, 21 November 1985, QBD (DC)

When deciding whether there are medical reasons why breath cannot be provided or should not be required it is sufficient to determine only whether the matter raised is capable of being a medical reason; the officer need not take medical advice.

A motorist had been charged with failing without reasonable excuse to provide a specimen of blood for a laboratory test, contrary to s 8(7), Road Traffic Act 1972 as substituted by s 25 and Sch 8, Transport Act 1981. In response to requests for breath specimens, the motorist said, *inter alia*, that he suffered from agoraphobia and had a "phobia about machines". On the basis of the latter only, the officer required a blood specimen instead, under s 8(3)(a), Road Traffic Act 1972 as likewise substituted. The defendant refused to provide a blood specimen.

The justices found that the officer had had reasonable cause to believe that for medical reasons the motorist could not provide breath specimens and that the blood specimen was correctly required. They convicted the motorist and he appealed.

QUESTION(S) FOR THE COURT: Whether the requirement to provide a specimen of blood pursuant to s 8(3), Road Traffic Act 1972 as substituted was valid.

HELD: "The constable is not required under the sections material to this appeal to determine whether a phobia asserted by a person whose condition is being investigated is or is not a phobia recognised by medical science; all that he can do as a layman is to determine whether or not that which is raised is capable of being such a condition. If on sufficient material, he concludes that it is, that amounts to medical reasons upon which he then has to consider whether or not he has reasonable cause to believe that a specimen of breath cannot be provided or should not be required … the decision is the constable's alone. There is no provision in or requirement of the statute at that stage for a doctor to be summoned or to give an opinion."

Appeal dismissed.

Davis (Paul) v DPP

[1988] RTR 156, [1988] Crim LR 249, 14 October 1987, QBD (DC)

Whether or not an officer had reasonable cause to believe that for medical reasons breath could not be provided or should not be required is to be determined objectively; it is immaterial whether the officer actually believed, or was dubious, sceptical or disbelieving.

A motorist had been charged with driving with excess alcohol in blood, contrary to s 6(1), Road Traffic Act 1972 as substituted by s 25 and Sch 8, Transport Act 1981. He had been asked to provide breath specimens, but failed, saying he was suffering from asthma and had a heavy cold. The police officer administering the procedure took the view that for medical reasons a breath specimen could not or should not be provided, although his personal opinion was that the motorist could have provided breath but had not made a determined effort. The officer proceeded to require a blood specimen under s 8(3)(a), Road Traffic Act 1972 as likewise substituted (constable having reasonable cause to believe that for medical reasons a breath specimen cannot be provided or should not be required).

The magistrate rejected the motorist's argument that the police had not been empowered to require a blood specimen, and convicted. The motorist appealed.

QUESTION(S) FOR THE COURT: Whether the prosecutor made a valid requirement of the defendant to provide a specimen of blood pursuant to s 8(3)(a), Road Traffic Act 1972.

HELD: "… what is or is not a reasonable cause to believe is a question of fact to be objectively determined … if there is objectively determined as a matter of fact a reasonable cause to believe, put into the possession of the police constable, it is … immaterial whether the police constable actually believes, is dubious, sceptical, or, as here, disbelieving … ."

The answer to the question was "yes". Appeal dismissed.

Davies (Gordon Edward) v DPP

[1989] RTR 391, [1990] Crim LR 60, 29 June 1989, QBD (DC)

In the circumstances of this case (medication; haemophiliac tendencies; vitamins), the officer had reasonable cause to believe that for medical reasons breath specimens could not be provided or should not be required; it was lawful then to require first a blood, then a urine, specimen.

A motorist had been charged with failing without reasonable excuse to provide a specimen of urine for a laboratory test, contrary to s 8(7), Road Traffic Act 1972 as substituted by s 25 and Sch 8, Transport Act 1981. He had been asked to provide breath specimens, but refused, saying he was taking a drug, which a psychiatrist had told him would influence the alcoholic content of his blood stream. The police officer conducting the procedure accepted this as a medical reason for not supplying breath and asked for a specimen of blood under s 8(3)(a); the motorist declined, saying he had haemophiliac tendencies; again the police officer accepted this, and went on to ask for a specimen of urine; the motorist replied that there was no medical reason why he could not do so but that he was taking various vitamins which would influence the result, and refused to supply specimens.

The magistrates accepted that the sergeant had had a reasonable belief that, for medical reasons, specimens of breath and blood could not be provided, and that he had been entitled to ask for the alternative specimens. They convicted the motorist. He appealed.

QUESTION(S) FOR THE COURT: (a) Whether a reasonable bench, properly directed, could have found that a reasonable cause to believe that for medical reasons a specimen of breath could not be provided, or should not be required, existed where the defendant claimed to be taking medication which would affect either the analysis of his breath or the alcohol content of his blood; (b) whether a reasonable bench, properly directed, could have found that there was reasonable cause to believe that for medical reasons a specimen of blood could not be provided or should not be required; (c) whether the police sergeant made a valid requirement for the defendant to supply a specimen of urine pursuant to s 8(3)(a).

HELD: "I see great force in the argument that the [appellant's] reason was incapable of leading to the reasonable belief that a specimen of breath could not be provided. But even if it be right that the words 'cannot be provided' in section 8(3)(a) relate exclusively to physical or mental capacity to provide a specimen no similar restriction can be placed on the words 'should not be required'...

"The sergeant's task was to obtain reliable and admissible evidence. The defendant gave the sergeant a medical reason why he should not persist in asking for specimens of breath. On the information before him, as provided by the defendant himself, the sergeant had reasonable cause to believe that for medical reasons a specimen of breath should not be required ... [he] was therefore entitled to proceed to ask for a specimen of blood and then a specimen of urine."

The answer to questions (a) and (b) was "yes"; question (c) should be directed to s 8(4), Road Traffic Act 1972. Appeal dismissed.

Webb v DPP

[1992] RTR 299, 6 March 1992, QBD (DC)

Trying one's best, but being distressed, shaken, upset, of slight build and having taken alcohol, are capable of constituting a medical reason why breath cannot be provided or should not be required.

A motorist had been charged with driving with excess alcohol in blood, contrary to s 5(1)(a), Road Traffic Act 1988. She had made three attempts to blow into the breath analysis device, and each time the machine had aborted. She said she did not suffer from any medical condition and was blowing as hard as she could. The officer conducting the procedure saw that she was shaken, upset, apparently distressed, and of slight build; he concluded that for medical reasons a specimen of breath could not be provided under s 7(3)(a), Road Traffic Act 1988. He therefore required an alternative specimen; a blood specimen was provided and on analysis it proved positive.

At the hearing, the motorist argued that the officer had not had reasonable cause to believe she could not give breath specimens for medical reasons and that the blood analysis was not therefore admissible. The justices rejected this argument and convicted. The motorist appealed.

QUESTION(S) FOR THE COURT: (i) Whether incapacity due to the defendant's physical state, namely, being upset and shaken, shocked, distressed, intoxicated and of slight build, could amount to "medical reasons" within the meaning of s 7(3)(a), Road Traffic Act 1988; (ii) if so, whether any bench properly directed could conclude on the evidence that the police officer had reasonable grounds to believe that for medical reasons a specimen of breath could not be provided by the defendant.

HELD: "… The sergeant was entitled to require a specimen of urine or blood but only if he had reasonable cause to believe for medical reasons a specimen of breath could not be provided or should not be required [which is, quoting] 'a question of fact to be objectively determined by justices' …

"… it is difficult to envisage a situation in which a failure will not be due either to a medical condition or wilful refusal. In the instant case it seems to me that the material upon which the justices came to their conclusion was material from which they were entitled to find that there was a medical condition. The defendant was apparently doing her best; there was therefore no other reason why she should not comply. She was in a distressed condition, she was shaken and upset, she had obviously taken alcohol and she was of slight build. Those matters seem to me to be capable of amounting to a medical condition within the meaning of section 7(3)(a)."

Appeal dismissed.

Young (Paula) v DPP

[1992] RTR 328, [1992] Crim LR 893, 24 March 1992, QBD (DC)

Intoxication can amount to a medical reason under s 7, Road Traffic Act 1988 why breath cannot be provided or should not be required.

A motorist had been charged with failing without reasonable excuse to provide two specimens of breath for analysis, contrary to s 7(6), Road Traffic Act 1988. She had been arrested and, at the police station, was required to provide specimens of breath for analysis, but failed to do so. The police officer administering the procedure observed that she was heavily intoxicated but considered she was otherwise fit and well, and recorded that she was "unable to provide [breath] due to state of intoxication (numerous attempts)". He therefore required a specimen of blood; she refused.

At the hearing, it was argued on behalf of the motorist that there was no case to answer because the requirement to provide a specimen of blood pursuant to s 7(3)(a), Road Traffic Act 1988 (constable having reasonable cause to believe that for medical reasons a specimen of breath cannot be provided or should not be required) had been invalid. The justices rejected that submission and convicted the motorist. She appealed.

QUESTION(S) FOR THE COURT: (a) Whether intoxication by alcohol was capable of amounting to a medical reason within s 7(3)(a), Road Traffic Act 1988; (b) whether there was sufficient material to found a reasonable belief that there were medical reasons why a specimen of breath could not be provided or should not be required; and, accordingly, (c) whether the justices were correct to hold that the request for a specimen of blood was lawful.

HELD: "... I can see no reason why intoxication should not constitute a medical reason for the purposes of section 7(3) of the Act of 1988 because it is a medical condition recognised by doctors. I have not been persuaded that there is any practical or other reason why 'medical reasons' in this statutory provision should not be given its full ordinary meaning."

Appeal dismissed.

Francis v DPP

[1997] RTR 113, 29 April 1996, QBD (DC)

Where the defendant understood the request for breath specimens and the penal consequences, it made no difference that he had been detained under the Mental Health Act 1983. The requirements of the Police and Criminal Evidence Act 1984 in respect of such persons did not apply to the breath analysis procedure. See also DPP v Billington, page 216, on the non-applicability of the Police and Criminal Evidence Act 1984 to the procedure.

A motorist had been charged with, *inter alia*, failing without reasonable excuse to provide two specimens of breath for analysis, contrary to s 7(6), Road Traffic Act 1988. He had been drinking and had had a row with his girlfriend; he took LSD and another hallucinogenic drug. He then drove; he got out of his vehicle and was approached by a member of the public. His behaviour was bizarre. The police arrived, formed the view that he was suffering a mental disorder, and detained him under s 136, Mental Health Act 1983 (power to remove to a place of safety a person in a public place who appears to be suffering mental disorder and to be in immediate need of care and control). The motorist struggled and was violent.

At the police station, the officer administering the breath testing procedure concluded that the motorist had calmed down and appeared to understand the request for breath specimens. No appropriate person under PACE Code C, Annex E of the Codes of Practice under s 66, Police and Criminal Evidence Act 1984 was present. No medical practitioner was present when the officer asked for breath specimens and the motorist refused.

The motorist was convicted by justices and his appeal to the Crown Court was dismissed. He appealed further.

QUESTION(S) FOR THE COURT: (a) Whether a person detained under s 136, Mental Health Act 1983 could become fit to be requested to provide a breath specimen without being examined by a medical practitioner; (b) whether such a person could be interviewed otherwise than in the presence of an appropriate adult under the PACE Codes of Practice; (c) whether such a person could be requested to give a breath specimen otherwise than in the presence of an appropriate adult.

HELD: "… the sergeant who requested the specimen was of the view that the defendant understood the position … the opinion of a police constable … that someone should be detained under section 136 of the Mental Health Act 1983 … is not a diagnosis; it is an opinion, the foundation for which … can be undermined or put in question by later events. The position, as found by the Crown Court, stands and stands unqualified, namely, that at the time that the defendant was requested to give a specimen of breath he did understand what was being asked of him and … that what he was being asked to do, … could carry penal consequences …

"… there was … sufficient evidence before the court … that the taking of the drug was a voluntary intoxication which disentitled the defendant from relying upon that state as a defence to the charges which he faced.

"… the fact of detention under the Mental Health Act 1983 … is not determinative of the issue in this case. It does give rise [to] obligations on the police … [PACE Code C, Annex E] is something which is strictly related only to interviews proper and not to a breath test procedure. There is good authority … that the breath test procedure is not an interview … I can see no reason for excluding the consequences of [the police] inquiry and their test simply because they had parallel obligations in relation to [the defendant's] detention under the Mental Health Act 1983 …".

Appeal dismissed.

Steadman v DPP

[2002] EWHC 810 (Admin), [2003] RTR 2, 15 April 2002, QBD (DC)

Section 7(4), Road Traffic Act 1988 (medical reasons why a specimen of blood cannot or should not be taken) has no bearing on a requirement for breath specimens under s 7(3)(a). The fact that a motorist took sleeping pills and had with him a tablet he was not asked about, could not give the officer reasonable cause to believe that the motorist should not be required to provide specimens of breath.

A motorist had been charged with driving with excess alcohol, contrary to s 5(1)(a), Road Traffic Act 1988. At the police station, a tablet was found on him; he was not asked what the tablet was or what it was for, but he was asked whether he suffered from any illness or injury, and whether he had any medical problems. He said he took sleeping tablets. He was asked whether he was suffering from mental illness, or whether he was dependent on drugs. He said that he was not, and that he had not taken any drugs that evening. Breath analysis revealed 70 μg alcohol in 100 ml breath.

At the hearing, it was argued that if the officer who had administered the procedure at the police station had considered whether there was reasonable cause to believe that for medical reasons the motorist could not or should not provide specimens of breath, he may have concluded that there was such reasonable cause; and that the breath analysis should not therefore be allowed in evidence.

The magistrates rejected that argument and convicted the motorist. He appealed.

QUESTION(S) FOR THE COURT: (1) Whether the decision in *Wade v DPP* (see page 92) relating to the definition of medical reasons and the duty of officers to consider them under s 7(4), Road Traffic Act 1988 equally apply to s 7(3)(a), Road Traffic Act 1988. (2) Whether the justices' finding that the constable had no reasonable cause to believe that there were any medical reasons why a specimen of breath could not or should not be provided was one which a reasonable bench of magistrates could reach on the evidence.

HELD: "16. … the regime laid down by section 7(3)(a) is … so different from that laid down by section 7(4) that the decision in [*Wade*] has no application to the question whether there was reasonable cause to believe that for medical reasons a defendant could not provide, or should not be required to provide, specimens of breath.

"19. … the defendant said that he had not taken any drugs that evening. Nor did he say that the sleeping pills which he took, or the tablet which was found on him (if it was not one of the sleeping pills) might have an adverse impact on the reliability of any reading produced by the device into which he had to blow … the mere fact that the defendant was taking sleeping pills, and had a tablet on him which he was not asked about, could not have given the police sergeant reasonable cause to believe that the appellant should not be required to provide specimens of breath."

The answer to question (1) was "no"; the answer to question (2) was "yes". Appeal dismissed.

Bodhaniya v CPS

[2013] EWHC 1743 (Admin), (2014) 178 JP 1, 14 May 2013, QBD (Admin)

In the circumstances of this case (suspect having been involved in a major motorway accident and unable to provide a second breath specimen despite five attempts; inference that officer attributed this to the trauma of the incident), the officer had reasonable cause to believe that for medical reasons breath specimens could not be provided or should not be required.

A motorist had been charged with driving with excess alcohol in blood, contrary to s 5(1), Road Traffic Act 1988. He had been involved in a major motorway accident. At the police station, he provided one specimen of breath but, despite five attempts, did not provide a second specimen. The investigating officer decided instead to require a blood specimen, which was taken and in due course revealed excess alcohol.

The district judge found it was reasonable to infer that the officer had decided that the appellant had not been able to provide the specimen because of the shock of the road traffic accident, that in law this could amount to a medical reason to require a blood specimen under s 7(3), and that the constable had reasonable cause for that belief. The motorist was convicted and appealed.

QUESTION(S) FOR THE COURT: Not recited in the judgment.

HELD: "[On the argument that the requirement for a blood specimen was unlawful] 16. … the inference drawn by the district judge in this case was … open to him. … The constable gave positive evidence that he was satisfied that the appellant had tried his best on five occasions to provide a second specimen of breath. The district judge accepted that evidence. So what then was the inevitable conclusion? It was that the appellant was incapable of providing a second sample. For whatever reason, he simply did not have the necessary lung-function to do so on that occasion. That was a medical reason. The district judge saw it likely to be explained by the nature of the trauma in which the appellant had earlier been involved.

"[On whether or not the evidence might have been excluded if the requirement had been unlawful] 17. … Section 7 of the Road Traffic 1988 does not in terms provide that a failure to comply with section 7(3) has the consequence that the results of the analysis of a blood sample cannot be given in evidence. … The general position in English law is that evidence obtained illegally remains admissible, even in criminal cases. … In the overwhelming majority of cases it may be that a failure to comply with section 7(3) of the Road Traffic Act 1988, before requiring an accused to provide a specimen of blood, will have the result that all evidence of that specimen will be excluded. But it is not necessarily so. The facts of this case, where on any view the constable concerned bent over backwards to try to assist the appellant in difficult circumstances, provides an example where exclusion … would not have been appropriate."

Appeal dismissed.

7. BREATH ANALYSIS DEVICE UNRELIABLE, UNAVAILABLE, OR NOT PRACTICABLE TO USE

See s 7(3)(b), Road Traffic Act 1988 – where a device or a reliable device is not available, or it is not practicable to use such a device, a blood or urine specimen may be required instead. See also Horrocks v Binns, page 25 – it is unlawful to require a specimen of blood or urine where there are no medical reasons why breath cannot be provided or should not be required, a reliable breath analysis device is available, and it is practicable to use it;

Clayton v DPP, page 83 – it is sufficient for the officer to say that breath specimens cannot be taken because a breath analysis device is not available; there is no need to elaborate further; and Rawal (Sushil) v DPP, page 179, where the suspect was sufficiently informed of the reasons why breath specimens could not be taken. See also Chapter 5, Challenging the Breath Testing and Analysis Devices.

Cotter v Kamil

[1984] RTR 371, 3 May 1984, QBD (DC)

The time at which the breath analysis device is to be found unreliable is the time at which the blood/urine specimen (not the breath specimen) is required. See also Oxford v Baxendale, page 40, and Chief Constable of Avon & Somerset v Kelliher, page 41, both on the same point.

A motorist had been charged, under s 8(7) and Sch 4, Road Traffic Act 1972 as substituted by s 25 and Sch 8, Transport Act 1981, with failing without reasonable excuse to provide a specimen of blood for a laboratory test. The breath analysis procedure had been started, but the machine indicated that it had reached a temperature at which analysis became unsatisfactory. The officer asked for a specimen of blood, which the motorist refused to supply. The magistrate found that because the device appeared reliable when the request for breath specimens was made, and was only later found to be defective, it was unsafe to proceed with the case, and therefore dismissed it. The prosecutor appealed.

QUESTION(S) FOR THE COURT: Whether, when the device available showed itself to be defective after two specimens of breath had been provided by the defendant, it was then proper for the prosecutor to take the view that the equipment was unreliable, or that it was impracticable to use it and he was therefore entitled to require a specimen of blood pursuant to section 8(3), Road Traffic Act 1972 as substituted.

HELD: The case concerned the construction of s 8(3)(b), providing that a specimen of blood or urine can be requested only if "at the time the requirement is made a device or a reliable device … is not available at the police station or it is then for any other reason not practicable to use such a device there". The words "at the time …" refer to the time of requesting blood or urine, not breath. The breath analysis device, before it had completed its function of analysis, had signalled that it was not operating properly. "So it followed that a reliable device was not available at the police station to carry out its function of analysis of the specimen of breath. That was so at the time when the requirement was made for the provision of a specimen of blood."

Appeal allowed.

Slender v Boothby

[1986] RTR 385, 27 November 1984, QBD (DC)

Where the breath analysis device did not take account of leap years and showed the date as 1 March instead of 29 February, the officer was entitled to find it unreliable and to require a specimen of blood. Compare the cases in Chapter 5 under the heading "The Date and Time", page 292.

A motorist had been convicted, under s 8(7), Road Traffic Act 1972 as substituted by s 25(3) and Sch 8, Transport Act 1981, of failing without reasonable excuse to provide a specimen of blood for a laboratory test. He had provided two specimens of breath for analysis by a Lion Intoximeter 3000. The machine timed the first at 23:59 GMT on 28 February 1984, the second at 00:01 GMT on 1 March 1984; it was a leap year and the Intoximeter had not taken account of the extra day. The police took the view that the device was not reliable and therefore required a specimen of blood under s 8(3)(b) (reliable device not available). The motorist refused.

The justices found that the police had been entitled to require the alternative sample. The motorist appealed.

QUESTION(S) FOR THE COURT: Whether a specimen of blood may be required on the grounds that the printout shows the date to be 1 March 1984 rather than 29 February 1984 (the true date) because the said instrument cannot take account of leap years and was therefore not reliable.

HELD: "We have ... simply to ask ourselves whether or not, at the time the requirement was made, a reliable device of the type mentioned was available at the police station ... if the machine in question is not at the relevant time capable of producing an accurate date on the printout, it cannot be said to be a reliable machine ... the pre-requisite of the constable's power to make the requirement [for blood] under s 8 is fulfilled."

The answer to the question was "yes". Appeal dismissed.

Morgan v Lee

[1985] RTR 409, 3 April 1985, QBD (DC)

Failure of the breath analysis device to produce a printout did not render it unreliable. Compare Haghigat-Khou v Chambers, page 43 – officer entitled to require a blood specimen where he knew the printer was malfunctioning before commencing the procedure.

A motorist had been charged, under s 8(7), Road Traffic Act 1972 as substituted by s 25 and Sch 8, Transport Act 1981, with failing without reasonable excuse to provide a specimen of blood for a laboratory test. The breath analysis device had operated correctly but failed to produce a printout because the paper was tangled. The police sergeant recorded the result from the display panel on the machine, but concluded that the device was inoperative and required a specimen of blood under s 8(3)(b) (device or reliable device not available, etc) and (4) of the Act. The motorist refused.

The justices found that there was nothing to exclude the sergeant from giving evidence of the result of the breath analyses from what he had seen on the display panel; the device had been capable and available; the sergeant had not therefore been entitled to request a blood specimen. They dismissed the charge. The prosecutor appealed.

QUESTION(S) FOR THE COURT: Whether a police officer was lawfully entitled to require the driver, in all the circumstances, to provide a specimen of blood under s 8(3)(b).

HELD: "That a police officer may give evidence of the results of breath tests which he has seen on the display panel ... there is no doubt ... If what was observed on the display panel of the calibration checks showed that the device was working satisfactorily, then the fact that a printout is not expelled from the device is no more than an indication that a part of the mechanism ... was not ... functioning properly. But that ... would not render the whole of the device unreliable ... the sergeant ... was in a position to inform the justices of satisfactory results of the calibration check and of the analyses of the specimens of breath [and] cannot be said to have tested the defendant on other than a reliable device ... he was not entitled to ask the defendant to provide a specimen of blood and the defendant was not acting unlawfully when he declined to comply with that request."

The answer to the case stated was "no". Appeal dismissed.

Waite v Smith

[1986] Crim LR 405, 4 December 1985, QBD (DC)

Where a calibration check is outside the manufacturer's specified range, the breath analysis device is unreliable.

A motorist had been charged with driving with excess alcohol, contrary to s 6(1)(a), Road Traffic Act 1972 as substituted by s 25 and Sch 8, Transport Act 1981. He had provided two breath specimens, and the lower reading was 96 µg alcohol in 100 ml breath. The final calibration check was "38° C High"; the maximum permissible temperature, according to the manufacturer's handbook, was 37.9° C. The officer therefore considered the device unreliable and required a specimen of blood under s 8(3), Road Traffic Act 1972 as likewise substituted. Analysis revealed 230 mg alcohol in 100 ml blood.

The justices found that the device had in fact been reliable and that the police had not therefore been entitled to require a specimen of blood. They acquitted the motorist. The prosecutor appealed.

QUESTION(S) FOR THE COURT: Whether the appellant was entitled pursuant to ss 8(1)(b) and 8(3)(b), Road Traffic Act 1972 as substituted to require the respondent to provide a specimen of blood for a laboratory test when the respondent had provided two specimens of breath for analysis using the Lion

Intoximeter 3000 and the second calibration check read "38° C High", which is outside the specified check calibration range prescribed by the Lion Intoximeter 3000 Operator Handbook.

HELD: It was "impermissible for justices themselves to regard such a device as reliable when they have … evidence to the effect – which was not controverted – that the device was operating outside the area of tolerance and, therefore, in the clear view of the manufacturers, unreliably … They were certainly wrong, therefore, in coming to the conclusion … that the officer … was not empowered within the terms of section 8 to ask the respondent to give a specimen of blood. In my judgment he was clearly so empowered properly to ask the question and the evidence of the analysis of the blood was properly admissible by the court and should have been so admitted."

Appeal allowed.

Dye v Manns

[1987] RTR 90, [1986] Crim LR 337, 14 January 1986, QBD (DC)

It must be proved that a breath analysis device was not available at the time a blood specimen was requested; in the circumstances of this case, that was not done.

A motorist had been charged with failing without reasonable excuse to provide a specimen of blood for a laboratory test, contrary to s 8(7), Road Traffic Act 1972 as substituted by s 25 and Sch 8, Transport Act 1981. At the police station, the officer told the motorist that no approved breath testing device was available and that he therefore required a blood specimen. The motorist refused. At the trial, although the police had not adduced evidence that no device had been available, the magistrate found that there had been a valid request for a blood specimen and convicted the motorist. The motorist appealed.

QUESTION(S) FOR THE COURT: Where a constable made the requirement and purported to exercise his power under s 8(3)(b) to require a specimen of blood, whether it was necessary for the prosecutor to adduce evidence that, at the time the requirement was made, a device or a reliable device was not available at the police station or it was then for any other reason not practicable to use such a device there; and, if so, whether evidence that the defendant was informed by the constable that such a device was not available was capable of providing such proof without any further evidence.

HELD: "Two questions arise. The first is whether the prosecutor must prove that a device was not available … they must do that. It is inherent in that that they must do it according to the laws of evidence.

"The second question … is whether the evidence in fact given was sufficient to prove the offence … In my judgment, there was no evidence to support the finding made by the magistrate. The fact that the statement was made by [the arresting officer] in the presence of the [station sergeant] by itself proves nothing. It is totally neutral. It could only prove something if there had been some response from the defendant which indicated that he accepted that … or was not prepared to contradict it. In my judgment, there is no evidence at all here to prove the facts required by section 8(3)(b) in order to justify a requirement to provide a specimen of blood. In those circumstances, there was not a valid requirement for the specimen of blood."

Appeal allowed.

Thompson v Thynne

[1986] RTR 293, [1986] Crim LR 629, 18 March 1986, QBD (DC)

A reliable device is one which the officer "reasonably believes to be reliable" (see also Dixon v Yardley, page 48, on the reasonableness of the officer's decision that a device is unreliable). Where the readings were so different that the officer believed the device to be unreliable, he was entitled to require a specimen of blood or urine.

A motorist had been charged with driving with excess alcohol in blood, contrary to s 6(1), Road Traffic Act 1972 as substituted by s 25 and Sch 8, Transport Act 1981. He had provided two samples of breath which, on analysis, produced readings of 145 and 117 μg alcohol in 100 ml breath. In view of the wide discrepancy, the police officer conducting the test took the view that the machine was not reliable and therefore requested a blood specimen under s 8(3)(b), Road Traffic Act 1972, as likewise substituted. On analysis, the blood specimen showed 309 mg alcohol in 100 ml blood. The motorist was convicted by the justices on the basis of the blood specimen.

He appealed to the Crown Court, arguing that the breath analysis machine had in fact been reliable and that the police had not been entitled to require a specimen of blood. That appeal was dismissed. The motorist further appealed.

QUESTION(S) FOR THE COURT: Whether the Crown Court was correct in holding that: (1) the operator had to make up his mind whether the machine was reliable or not, and was entitled on the basis of the varying readings to find that the machine was unreliable; (2) in view of the operator's belief that no reliable device was available, no reliable device was available within the meaning of s 8(3)(b); (3) the operator was therefore entitled to require the provision of a sample of blood.

HELD: "... the natural answer to the question [whether the words 'a reliable device' are to be construed objectively or subjectively] would seem to be that the words are to be construed subjectively; for the whole scheme of section 8 provides for, or involves, the making by the constable concerned of a series of decisions, of which the decision whether the device is reliable is one ... the words 'a reliable device' are to be given the meaning 'a device which he reasonably believes to be reliable'; and in consequence ... the defendant's appeal to the Crown Court was rightly dismissed ... As ... it has not been suggested ... that the justices were not entitled on the evidence ... to find that [the sergeant's] belief, namely, that the machine was not reliable, was reasonable, the answer to each question is 'yes'."

Appeal dismissed.

Oxford v Baxendale

[1987] RTR 247, [1986] Crim LR 631, 21 April 1986, QBD (DC)

In the absence of evidence to the contrary, it is open to a court to find that a breath analysis device which was unreliable when it analysed breath specimens, remained unreliable 1 hour and 45 minutes later when a blood specimen was required. See also Cotter v Kamil, page 35 and Chief Constable of Avon & Somerset v Kelliher, page 41 – the time at which the device is to be found unreliable (Cotter v Kamil) or impracticable to use (Chief Constable of Avon & Somerset v Kellliher) is the time at which the blood/urine specimen is required.

A motorist had been charged with failing without reasonable excuse to provide a specimen of blood for a laboratory test, contrary to s 8(7), Road Traffic Act 1972 as substituted by s 25 and Sch 8, Transport Act 1981. He had provided breath specimens which, on analysis, proved positive. Some 1½ hours later, the police realised that the instrument's final calibration check had shown an irregularity which had not been noticed earlier; they then, some 100 minutes after the breath analysis, required a specimen of blood instead. The motorist refused. The justices found that, although there was evidence of malfunction at the time of the breath analysis, there was no evidence of the unreliability of the machine at the time the police requested the blood specimen. They therefore found no case to answer. The prosecutor appealed.

QUESTION(S) FOR THE COURT: Where a defendant provided the statutory specimens of breath and at a substantially later time it became apparent to the operator that the approved device was unreliable at the time of the breath analysis, and evidence of that unreliability had been adduced to the court, whether it was incumbent upon the prosecution to adduce further evidence to show that a device or a reliable device was not then available when the requirement for blood or urine was made under section 8(3)(b).

HELD: "It seems to me that the justices had proceeded on the assumption that they could not be satisfied purely on consideration of the evidence that there was not [a reliable device available] an hour and three-quarters earlier. In my judgment, that is a mistake on their part and they could have been so satisfied. Whether they should have been we do not need to consider. In my judgment, it was open to them to draw the conclusion that, if the machine did not work at 14.01 GMT and was unreliable then, as they state, in the absence of further evidence it was open to them to come to the conclusion that the machine was not reliable an hour and three-quarters later."

The answer to the question was "no". Appeal allowed.

Chief Constable of Avon & Somerset v Kelliher
[1987] RTR 305, [1986] Crim LR 635, 13 May 1986, QBD (DC)

The time at which it must be shown that it was not practicable to use the breath analysis device is the time the requirement for blood is made (see also Cotter v Kamil, page 35 and Oxford v Baxendale, page 41, on this point); where a trained operator was not at the police station at that time, it was impracticable to use the device.

A person in charge of a motor vehicle was charged with failing without reasonable excuse to provide a specimen of breath for analysis, contrary to s 8(7), Road Traffic Act 1972 as substituted by s 25 and Sch 8, Transport Act 1981. He had been left in charge of the car while the driver went for petrol. The police found him there and, at the police station, asked for blood specimens; a breath analysis machine was available but no officer trained to use it was on duty. The request for blood specimens was refused. The justices dismissed the information, finding that it would have been practicable to bring an officer trained in the use of the approved device from a neighbouring police station. The prosecutor appealed.

QUESTION(S) FOR THE COURT: Whether the justices were correct in law to decide that the absence of a trained operator at the police station where a laboratory specimen was requested does not make it impracticable to use the device provided that a trained operator could be summoned from a neighbouring police station.

HELD: "… The argument before us has proceeded on the final sentence of subsection (b) [of s 8(3), Road Traffic Act 1972 as substituted]: 'or it is then for any other reason not practicable to use such a device there' … the only construction which can properly be put upon that subsection, having regard to the use of the word 'then', is that at the time the requirement is made, it is for any other reason not practicable to use such a device. One has therefore to pose the question: was it practicable to use the device at the time the requirement to provide a specimen of blood was made? … the Crown have established that it was not, having regard to the fact that there was no one there to operate it … an officer … is not and cannot in practice be required at the time the request for blood is made to telephone around to other local police stations to see if there is somebody available to come and work the machine.

"… the magistrates were in error and came to the wrong conclusion in dismissing the information."

Appeal allowed.

Chief Constable of Kent v Berry

[1986] RTR 321, [1986] Crim LR 748, 3 July 1986, QBD (DC)

Where a breath analysis device is unreliable and the motorist is required to provide a blood specimen, and is taken to another police station where there is a doctor, and there is a breath analysis device at that station, it is not necessary to show that that second device was unreliable or that it was impracticable to use it.

A motorist had been charged with driving with excess alcohol in his blood, contrary to s 6(1)(a), Road Traffic Act 1972 as substituted by s 25 and Sch 8, Transport Act 1981. At Faversham police station he had been required to provide breath specimens for analysis; the first specimen proved positive, but the machine failed correctly to purge itself and recorded no second sample. The officer administering the test, concluding that the device was not reliable, required the motorist to provide a blood specimen, under s 8(3)(b), Road Traffic Act 1972 as likewise substituted (reliable device not available or impracticable to use). For this purpose the motorist was taken to another police station (Canterbury) where a doctor was available; the requirement for a blood specimen was repeated there, and the specimen taken; analysis proved positive. A breath analysis device was present at Canterbury but the officer did not inquire into the possibility of using it.

The justices accepted the motorist's argument that there had been a device at the second police station, that the prosecutor had not adduced evidence that it had been unreliable or that it had been otherwise impracticable to use it, and that the blood specimen had therefore been unlawfully required; the justices dismissed the information. The prosecutor appealed.

QUESTION(S) FOR THE COURT: (1) Where a constable makes a requirement for the provision of a blood specimen at a police station and it then becomes necessary to transfer the defendant to another police station for the purpose of taking a blood specimen, and that second police station is equipped with a Lion Intoximeter device, but the constable does not purport to require the provision of two specimens of breath for analysis by that device pursuant to s 9(1)(a), Road Traffic Act 1972, whether the court is required to hear evidence that the second device was unreliable or that it was impracticable to use it before admitting evidence of a blood specimen. (2) If not, whether the court is required to hear the said evidence before admitting evidence of a blood specimen if upon arrival at the second police station the constable purports to repeat the requirement for the provision of a blood specimen? (3) If the answer to (1) or (2) is "yes", whether the court is required to hear the said evidence before admitting evidence of a blood specimen if the Lion Intoximeter at the first police station showed itself to be defective after a specimen of breath had been provided and analysed.

HELD: "... the requirement which was effective and operative was that which had been made at Faversham ... what was said at Canterbury could not affect the validity of the requirement which had already been made. The mere repeating of the words of the requirement was, from the legal point of view, surplusage, and did not in any shape or form operate to begin the whole process again."

The answer to questions (1) and (2) was "no"; question (3) did not arise. Appeal allowed.

Haghigat-Khou v Chambers

[1988] RTR 95, [1987] Crim LR 340, 7 November 1986, QBD (DC)

Where the officer knows the printer is malfunctioning before commencing a breath analysis, he is entitled to find the device unreliable and request a blood specimen instead; Morgan v Lee (page 36) distinguished.

A motorist had been charged with driving with excess alcohol, contrary to s 6(1), Road Traffic Act 1972 as substituted by s 25 and Sch 8, Transport Act 1981. The police officer conducting the testing considered the Intoximeter defective in that the printout apparatus was not functioning correctly; he therefore required a specimen of blood under s 8(3)(b), Road Traffic Act 1972 as likewise substituted (reliable device not available, etc). Blood analysis proved positive. It was argued on behalf of the motorist that, under *Morgan v Lee* (see page 36), a reliable device had been available; the blood specimen had therefore been unlawfully required and was inadmissible in evidence.

The magistrate distinguished *Morgan v Lee*, where the malfunction became known only after the provision of breath specimens, the results had been noted and the officer could have given oral evidence of them; in the present case, the malfunction had been known before testing. He found that the officer had been reasonable in believing that the machine was unreliable, that the requirement to provide a blood specimen had been lawful, and that the blood analysis was therefore admissible. The magistrate convicted the motorist, who appealed.

QUESTION(S) FOR THE COURT: Whether the analysis of the defendant's blood was admissible in evidence in view of the decision in *Morgan v Lee*.

HELD: "*Morgan v Lee* establishes that an analysis carried out by a device, which has functioned satisfactorily … but failed to produce a printout, is available as evidence; … the device cannot be held to be not 'reliable' … when it has already performed its function … at the time when the officer purports to make a requirement … for a specimen of blood. … Before an investigation has commenced, the position is different.

"[Applying *Thompson v Thynne*, see page 39] … it was permissible for the officer to have regard to the malfunction of the printout in forming his conclusion that the device was not a reliable device. Although … the printout is not an indispensable mode of proof of the analysis … the ordinary working of the device contemplated by the statutory provisions … included the production by the machine and independently of the officer conducting the investigation of the printout. … The inability of the machine to produce this printout meant that the machine was not able to function, in one important respect, in the way in which it was intended to function for the purposes of the investigation … the requirement for a specimen was therefore lawfully made."

Appeal dismissed.

Stokes v Sayers

[1988] RTR 89, 20 February 1987, QBD (DC)

To justify requiring a blood specimen, it must be shown that the officer believed the breath analysis device was unreliable and that there was evidence upon which he could have formed that view.

A motorist had been charged, *inter alia*, with driving with excess alcohol, contrary to s 6(1)(a), Road Traffic Act 1972 as substituted by s 25 and Sch 8, Transport Act 1981. At the police station, before the breath testing procedure began, the operating officer saw on the visual display the words "34 Low Abort". He concluded that the machine was unreliable and therefore requested a blood specimen under s 8(3)(b) Road Traffic Act 1972 as likewise substituted (reliable device not available). The blood specimen was taken and was positive. At the trial, no evidence was adduced about the visual display message or about the officer's belief that the machine had been unreliable.

The justices upheld a defence submission that, in the absence of any evidence to explain the reading on the visual display, it had not been proved that the device had been unreliable; the blood specimen had therefore been wrongly required and the analysis inadmissible; they dismissed the charge. The prosecutor appealed.

QUESTION(S) FOR THE COURT: Whether the justices were correct in concluding that the prosecution had failed to establish that the device was not a reliable device thereby enabling the police officer to require a blood sample.

HELD: Applying cases decided since the justices' decision in the present case, "What the prosecution had to show by evidence is, first, that the relevant officer did believe that the Intoximeter was unreliable and, secondly, that there was some material or evidence upon which at the time he could reasonably form that view.

"… [I could not conclude] that no reasonable bench of justices … could properly come to the conclusion to which they did come … [they] were … giving their minds to the question whether there was evidence before them that there was material on which the officer could have reached the conclusion he did reasonably and properly, they were entitled to decide that there was not."

Appeal dismissed.

Tobi v Nicholas

[1988] RTR 343, 1 July 1987, QBD (DC)

Oral evidence that a breath analysis device was not available is evidence of that fact. A doctor's certificate of taking a blood specimen is not admissible unless it has been served as required by the Act. In the circumstances of this case, evidence of the identity of the driver was inadmissible.

A defendant had been convicted of, *inter alia*, driving with excess alcohol, contrary to s 6(1), Road Traffic Act 1972 as substituted by s 25 and Sch 8, Transport Act 1981. There had been an accident, causing damage to a coach; the car which caused the damage did not stop. The coach driver and a police officer went to the defendant's nearby house; his damaged car was in the driveway. The coach driver said the defendant had been driving the car and had collided with his coach some 20 minutes before; he pointed to the defendant and said, "That is the guy". The defendant denied having driven the car. The police officer detected alcohol on his breath and arrested him for driving while unfit. After caution and while being escorted to the police car, the defendant said his wife had been driving; she said, "No I wasn't; don't make it worse than it is". The defendant was taken to the police station; the officer told him that no breath testing device was available and required a blood specimen. It proved positive.

The coach driver was not present at the hearing; the prosecution unsuccessfully sought an adjournment to secure his attendance. The doctor's certificate that he had taken the blood from the defendant had not been served at least 7 days before the hearing. The magistrate was minded to allow an adjournment for service of the certificate, but the defendant agreed that the matter proceed on the basis of the certificate being put in evidence.

The defendant was convicted, and appealed.

QUESTION(S) FOR THE COURT: (1) Whether there was any and if so sufficient evidence that the defendant was the driver of the car at the material time; (2)(a) whether there was any evidence that any of the exceptions which justified the request for a sample of blood applied; (b) whether defence counsel at the trial should have been or was forced to accept the admission into evidence of the doctor's certificate when: (i) it had not been served on the defendant at least 7 days before the hearing as required by s 10(5), and (ii) if not accepted as admissible at that point, proceedings would have been adjourned for the doctor to give oral evidence.

HELD: "[On question (2)(a) and the argument that the police evidence was of what the officer had said (that no device was available), rather than of the fact of the availability of the device] That the sergeant says no device is available and then comes along and gives evidence that he said no device was available inherently includes evidence that no device was available."

The answer to this question was "yes".

"[On question (2)(b)] The phrase 'admissible in evidence only if' [in s 10(5), Road Traffic Act 1972 as substituted] means what it says. If the requirements of the subsection have not been complied with, the document as such is not admissible evidence, and if it is not admissible then no purported waiver of objection by counsel for the defendant can make it admissible."

The answer to question 2(b) was "no".

"[On question (1), and the defence submission that the police officer's evidence of the coach driver's words 'That is the guy' was hearsay, and the prosecutor's submission that those words were admissible as part of the *res gestae*, and after an examination of authorities] I am not satisfied that the necessary conditions for the admission of hearsay evidence as to the identification of the appellant by [the coach driver] are present here and accordingly … the appeal must be allowed on this ground also."

The answer to the question was "no".

Appeal allowed.

Badkin v DPP

[1988] RTR 401, 10 July 1987, QBD (DC)

Where the breath analysis device has been found unreliable and a blood specimen provided, it is not open to the prosecution then to seek to show that the device was in fact reliable and adduce the breath analysis in evidence; in any event, the motorist's appeal succeeded because there was no evidence to show that the device was reliable, and because the prosecution did not notify the motorist of the blood analysis results. See also the cases in Chapter 5 under the heading "The Date and Time", page 292.

A motorist had been charged with driving with excess alcohol in breath, contrary to s 6(1)(a), Road Traffic Act 1972 as substituted by s 25 and Sch 8, Transport Act 1981. Breath specimens were analysed and the visual display showed a lower reading of 56 µg alcohol in 100 ml breath, but the breath analysis device failed to produce a printout. The officer conducting the testing procedure therefore decided the device could be unreliable and required a blood specimen. It later transpired that the clock mechanism in the device had been inaccurate by some 5 minutes. The blood specimen was analysed, but the results were not served on the motorist and were not adduced in evidence at the trial. Two police officers gave evidence of the breath analysis as shown on the visual display, on the basis of which the motorist was convicted. The motorist appealed.

QUESTION(S) FOR THE COURT: (1) Where a police officer has reason to believe that the breath testing device is malfunctioning because its printer had failed to produce a printout, is the officer entitled to require a specimen of blood under s 8(3)(b), Road Traffic Act 1972 as likewise substituted (reliable device not available)? (2) Would the fact that evidence came to light during the court hearing that the clock mechanism in the device was inaccurate, make any difference? (3) If a requirement to provide a specimen of blood is complied with, in the circumstances in (1), and the blood specimen is thereafter forensically analysed, can the court admit evidence relating to specimens of breath initially provided for analysis when trying an information under s 6(1)(a)?

HELD: "Since the officer's decision that the breath analysis device was unreliable was the basis for the requirement for a blood specimen ... it seems to me to be inconsistent with the scheme of the Act for the prosecuting authority thereafter to seek to prove that the breath analysis device was reliable and thus that the requirement for a blood specimen was not justified.

"... even if the principle ... outlined above is not correct [the appeal would still be allowed]. First, the facts found not merely include the failure by the device to produce a printout, but also that it was apparently indicating an incorrect time. To counter these two pieces of evidence that the machine was unreliable, there was no evidence to prove its reliability ... Secondly ... the failure by the prosecution to give notice to the defendant of the results of the blood analysis and to call evidence of the results of that analysis, is a breach of the requirement in section 10(2) of the Act that 'Evidence of the proportion of alcohol ... in a specimen of ... blood ... provided by the accused shall in all cases be taken into account ...'... The failure to do so ... vitiated the prosecution case."

The answer to question (1) was "yes"; the answer to question (2) was "No, it reinforces the answer to question (1)"; the answer to question (3) was "No, and particularly not when no evidence of the results of the blood analysis is tendered". Appeal allowed.

Denny v DPP

[1990] RTR 417, 9 March 1989, QBD (DC)

Where a motorist provides two specimens of breath and the breath analysis device then proves unreliable, it is lawful to require two further specimens of breath for analysis by another device.

A motorist had been charged with driving with excess alcohol, contrary to s 6(1), Road Traffic Act 1972 as substituted by s 25 and Sch 8, Transport Act 1981. The breath analysis device had stopped functioning properly after the second breath specimen had been given, so the motorist was taken to another police station where a reliable device was available. Two specimens of breath were provided there, and the lower reading was 53 µg alcohol in 100 ml breath.

At the hearing, the motorist contended that, once the first device had become unreliable, the police officer could only request a specimen of blood or urine under s 8(3)(b); since the motorist had already complied with a request for breath, the second request for two specimens was unlawful.

The magistrates rejected this argument and convicted. The motorist appealed.

QUESTION(S) FOR THE COURT: Whether a defendant who has apparently provided two specimens of breath for analysis by means of an approved device under section 8(1)(a), Road Traffic Act 1972 and the device having then been found to be faulty, may be lawfully required to provide two further specimens of breath for analysis by another device of the same type instead of being called upon to provide a specimen of blood or urine in accordance with s 8(3)(b), Road Traffic Act 1972.

HELD: "It is of course true that … section 8 [lays] down an alternative procedure which a police officer may adopt upon the provision by a motorist of specimens of breath into an approved device which is at the time unreliable …

"… in section 8(1)(a) the material words used are 'to provide two specimens of breath for analysis'… there is no such provision of specimens unless the result of a motorist blowing into a device is the provision of two valid specimens of breath, by which I mean that the motorist has, for his part, blown properly into the device and the device is working properly so as to receive and properly analyse those specimens and, further, to record truly the result …

"I can see nothing in the terms of section 8(1), (2) or (3) which confines a police officer to asking a motorist for a specimen of either his blood or his urine when a device into which a motorist is breathing becomes defective and accordingly cannot correctly analyse breath so as to provide two valid specimens … the provisions of section 8 do not operate in that way."

The answer to the question was "yes". Appeal dismissed.

Dixon v Yardley

[1993] RTR 22, 21 May 1992, QBD (DC)

To justify a requirement for a blood or urine specimen, there must be a finding that the officer's decision (that the breath analysis device was unreliable) was, in the circumstances, reasonable. See also Thompson v Thynne, page 39 – a reliable device is one which the officer "reasonably believes to be reliable".

A motorist had been charged with driving with excess alcohol in blood, contrary to s 5(1)(a), Road Traffic Act 1988. He had provided breath specimens, which had been analysed and produced readings of 189 and 191 μg alcohol in 100 ml breath. The officer administering the procedure signed the printout. He then took the view that the high readings and the apparent absence of symptoms of intoxication in the motorist meant that the breath analysis device might not be reliable. He therefore asked for a blood specimen, which was given, and, upon analysis, revealed 391 mg alcohol in 100 ml blood, which broadly equated with the breath analysis results.

At the hearing, it was argued, *inter alia*, that there was no evidence upon which the officer could have formed an opinion as to the unreliability of the device; s 7(3)(b), Road Traffic Act 1988 (reliable device not available, etc) did not therefore apply and the blood specimen had been obtained unlawfully and was inadmissible.

The justices found that the officer had properly required a blood sample, having decided that the device was unreliable, which he could do even after breath samples had been given. They convicted the motorist, who appealed.

QUESTION(S) FOR THE COURT: (2) Whether, in the circumstances, the police officer could lawfully require the appellant to provide a sample of blood for analysis; (3) whether evidence was properly admitted regarding the proportion of alcohol in the breath of the defendant.

HELD: "The test ... is a subjective one ... what has to be regarded was not whether that was so or not but whether or not the officer concerned reasonably believed that the device was not reliable ... in their findings of fact the justices nowhere expressed a conclusion as to whether the opinion formed by [the officer] was in the circumstances a reasonable one ... there is an unresolved and unresolvable conflict between the facts as found, or not found, and the conclusions reached by these justices ... the justices can rightly be said to have made a perverse conclusion, which cannot possibly be upheld ... ."

The answer to question (2) was "... yes if it be found that the officer in charge of the procedure holds the belief not that the device might be unreliable but the reasonable belief that it actually was at the material time unreliable." The answer to question (3) was "yes". Appeal allowed.

Wootton v DPP

Unreported, CO/2347/90, 16 June 1992, QBD (DC)

The court would not go outside the magistrates' finding that the officer reasonably believed the breath analysis device to be unreliable, the words "trace acetone" appearing on the display but not on the printout.

A motorist had been charged with driving with excess alcohol in blood, contrary to s 5(1)(a), Road Traffic Act 1988. He had provided breath specimens; the first showed on the visual display 44 μg alcohol in 100 ml breath, and the word "trace" (acetone); the second specimen showed on the visual display 41 μg alcohol in 100 ml breath but no indication of acetone. The printout did not, however, include the word "trace". The officer administering the procedure therefore believed the device was unreliable; she asked the motorist to provide a specimen of blood or urine; a specimen of blood was taken, which, upon analysis, proved positive.

The magistrates found that the officer reasonably believed that a reliable device had not been available and that she was therefore legally entitled to request a blood or urine sample pursuant to s 7(3)(b), Road Traffic Act 1988 (reliable device not available). They convicted the motorist, who appealed.

QUESTION(S) FOR THE COURT: Whether a police officer was legally entitled to require the driver of a motor vehicle, who had just provided a positive specimen at the roadside and two specimens of breath for analysis at the police station, to provide an additional specimen of blood under s 7(3)(b), Road Traffic Act 1988 when the breath analysis device used to analyse the specimen registered on the display a trace of acetone in the first specimen of breath provided which was not recorded on the printed certificate of analysis.

HELD: "[On the argument that there was at least reasonable doubt whether the officer did indeed reasonably believe the device to be defective, there having been no evidence of malfunction or explanation of why the printout had not referred to trace acetone] … while it could perhaps be sensibly argued, as [the appellant] did argue, that this, that or the other piece of evidence could have been obtained and advanced before the justices, the fact is that that course was not taken. This case stated … must be taken as it stands. This court cannot go outside the stated facts or the findings of the justices based upon those stated facts."

The answer to the question was "yes". Appeal dismissed.

Rathbone v DPP

Unreported, CO 2878/93, 20 January 1995, QBD (DC)

In the circumstances of this case, the officer had formed the view that the breath analysis device was unreliable. In the absence of a doctor's certificate, the officer's oral evidence of the taking of the blood specimen was sufficient.

A motorist had been charged with driving with excess alcohol, contrary to s 5(1)(a), Road Traffic Act 1988. He had been stopped by police and a breath test was positive. At the police station, the breath analysis procedure was commenced. On the first specimen, the display showed 58 µg alcohol in 100 ml breath, but the machine produced no printout. Three further attempts produced no reading and no printout. The sergeant was unsure whether the suspect had failed to provide sufficient air, or the machine was malfunctioning; he decided that since it appeared not to be working properly it was not available, and accordingly required a specimen of blood. Blood was taken and later revealed 120 mg alcohol in 100 ml blood. No certificate of taking the blood was served in advance of the hearing, and the doctor who took the specimen was not called to give evidence.

At the hearing, the motorist contended that the requirement to provide a blood specimen was unlawful in that the officer had been wrong to conclude that the breath analysis device was not available; and that in the absence of the certificate under s 16(2), Road Traffic Offenders Act 1988 (documentary evidence as to specimens) there was no satisfactory evidence of the status of the doctor who took the blood. The justices rejected both arguments and convicted the motorist. He appealed.

QUESTION(S) FOR THE COURT: Whether the justices were right in law to conclude that: (i) it was unnecessary for the officer at the time or the justices in court to be absolutely certain that the machine had malfunctioned and whether the officer's belief (which they found to have been reasonable) that it had malfunctioned was sufficient to enable him to require a specimen of blood; and (ii) s 16(2), Road Traffic Offenders Act 1988 was simply an enabling provision rather than a mandatory requirement and that therefore the justices were entitled to accept the police officer's evidence as to the correct procedure and nexus.

HELD: "[On (i)] What has to be considered is whether or not a constable reasonably believes that the device … is unreliable … [counsel for the appellant submits that the sergeant] … did not … form the necessary reasonable belief and the Magistrates were not entitled to conclude that he did … [In the case stated] the Magistrates are making it quite clear that they were finding as a fact that the Police Sergeant did draw that inference [that the device was malfunctioning]; although he was not certain about it, he formed that conclusion and that was a conclusion which was reasonable … [The failure to produce a printout] was not the only factor which was disturbing the officer … but it was one of them, and that factor alone would have been sufficient to enable the officer to come to the conclusion that the device was unreliable …

"[On (ii), counsel for the appellant] submits that in the absence of a certificate pursuant to section 16(2) there was no proper evidence to support the admissibility of the specimen which was taken by [the doctor] … the prosecution … had to prove … that the specimen of blood was taken with the consent of the Appellant and … that it was taken by a medical practitioner. They did so by relying upon the evidence of [the police sergeant] who was present throughout when [the doctor] took the sample … Section 16(2) is … simply permissive; it is not mandatory. It indicates how the necessary evidence may be given. In this particular case it was given in a different way, but it is nonetheless evidence for that … ."

Appeal dismissed.

Jarvis v DPP

[1996] RTR 192, 8 February 1995, QBD (DC)

Magistrates may not use personal knowledge that only one breath analysis device is available at a particular police station, although in this case there was other evidence of that fact.

A motorist had been charged with failing without reasonable excuse to provide specimens for analysis, contrary to s 7(6), Road Traffic Act 1988. At the police station, the breath analysis device would not start when the start button was pressed and the police officer conducting the procedure therefore required an alternative specimen under s 7(3)(b), Road Traffic Act 1988 (reliable device not available). The motorist agreed to provide a specimen of blood, but, after the arrival of the doctor to take the specimen, refused.

At the hearing, the motorist submitted there no case to answer in that there was no evidence that only one approved device was installed at the particular police station and that the provisions of s 7(3)(b), Road Traffic Act 1988 had not therefore been satisfied. The magistrate used his personal knowledge, from similar cases in the same court, that only one machine was installed at the police station. He convicted the motorist, who appealed.

QUESTION(S) FOR THE COURT: (1) Whether the magistrate was entitled to use his personal knowledge and take judicial notice that only one Lion Intoximeter 3000 was installed at the police station on the date in question; (2) whether the evidence was sufficient to support his findings of fact; (3) whether, on notice taken and/or the facts found, the magistrate was correct in holding that there was no approved device available at the police station when the defendant was required to provide a specimen of blood or urine; (4) whether the magistrate came to a correct decision in law in convicting the defendant.

HELD: "… it was wrong in principle for the stipendiary magistrate to use evidence that he had heard in other cases in order to supplement the evidence in the case he was now trying … this was not a case where judicial notice was appropriate to fill a gap in the evidence, if there was one.

"… The record of evidence … is as follows: 'The [sergeant] … pressed the start button on the Lion Intoximeter 3000 on numerous occasions, it failed to operate. He informed the defendant … that it was not therefore possible to take specimens of breath and that he would … require the provision of a specimen of blood or of urine'… his evidence can only mean that there was only one in the police station and that that was not working. There was no cross-examination on that evidence and no issue was raised on it until the close of the prosecution case.

"… the magistrate was … not only entitled but bound to draw the inference that no approved device was available at [the] police station."

The answer to question (1) was "no"; the answer to questions (2) to (4) was "yes". Appeal dismissed.

Hague v DPP

[1997] RTR 146, 6 November 1995, QBD (DC)

Where the officer mistakenly believed the breath analysis device was not reliable and required a blood specimen, which the motorist refused to provide, the breath analysis was admissible, it having been realised that the device had in fact been reliable.

A motorist had been charged with driving with excess alcohol in breath, contrary to s 5(1)(a), Road Traffic Act 1988. At the police station, breath specimens were provided and analysed, showing excess alcohol. The officer administering the procedure mistakenly but honestly believed that the device had not been properly calibrated and therefore required a blood specimen under s 7(3)(b), Road Traffic Act 1988 (reliable device not available). The motorist refused to supply a blood specimen. It later became clear that the breath analysis device was correctly calibrated and was reliable.

The magistrate found that the breath specimen had not been replaced by an alternative sample and was therefore admissible. He convicted the motorist, who appealed.

QUESTION(S) FOR THE COURT: Whether it was right as a point of law that, after the operator of an approved breath testing device in a police station had a reasonable belief that such device was not reliable and therefore requested a specimen for laboratory analysis and the requirement was for blood and no such specimen was provided, the prosecutor could at a later date on discovery that the device was reliable revert to the breath testing procedure and successfully prosecute for driving with excess alcohol.

HELD: "… the breath sample remains admissible in evidence unless and until it is replaced by an appropriately admissible sample of blood or urine … the breath specimens provided under section 7(1) were obtained lawfully and in accordance with the statutory procedure by what was accepted and found at the trial to be a properly calibrated device".

Appeal dismissed.

Evans (Cyril) v DPP

The Times 30 May 1996, 9 May 1996, QBD (DC)

Where the officer concluded that the motorist was not blowing satisfactorily and that the breath analysis results were therefore unreliable, and went on (unlawfully) to require a urine specimen, the breath analysis was not admissible in evidence, the motorist having been charged with driving with excess alcohol in urine.

A motorist had been charged, *inter alia*, with driving with excess alcohol in urine, contrary to s 5(1)(a), Road Traffic Act 1988. At the police station, the breath analysis device was in good working order and calibrating properly. Breath specimens produced "disparate readings". The officer administering the procedure concluded that the motorist was not blowing satisfactorily and that the results were unreliable. He therefore required an alternative specimen. The motorist provided a specimen of urine, which, on analysis, revealed excess alcohol. He was convicted by the justices and appealed to the Crown Court.

At the Crown Court, the motorist argued that the urine specimen had been taken unlawfully, the machine being in proper order, and was therefore inadmissible. The Crown Court accepted that, but went on to dismiss the appeal on the basis that they were entitled to look at the breath analysis results. The motorist appealed further.

HELD: "… since the Appellant was charged with driving with a proportion of alcohol in his urine which exceeded the prescribed limit, it was necessary for the prosecution to have available evidence which was probative and relevant to enable the court to so conclude … once the court had concluded that the only direct evidence which was available in that regard was that which had been unlawfully obtained, they were left … with simply the evidence provided by the breath samples. The evidence provided by the breath sample was not sufficient, it was not relevant to the issue or sufficiently cogent to enable the court to come to the conclusion it did."

Appeal allowed.

Slasor v DPP

[1999] RTR 432, 9 November 1998, QBD (DC)

If there is some relevant and clearly identified purpose, and subject to the court's discretion, evidence of breath analysis may be admissible where the prosecution is based on blood analysis.

A motorist had provided a positive roadside breath test and was arrested. At the police station, he provided breath specimens, the lower reading being 102 µg alcohol in 100 ml breath, but the breath analysis device then failed its final calibration test. The motorist was therefore required, pursuant to s 7(3), Road Traffic Act 1988 (reliable device not available), to provide a specimen of blood, which was duly taken. While transferring the blood from the syringe to the two bottles, it was seen that one of the bottles was cracked. This was noticed almost immediately, and, using a different syringe, the doctor transferred the blood from the damaged bottle to another. Analysis later revealed 246 mg alcohol in 100 ml blood. The motorist was charged with driving with excess alcohol in blood, contrary to s 5(1)(a), Road Traffic Act 1988.

At the trial, the motorist contended that the blood specimen may have been contaminated. The prosecutor argued that evidence of the breath test should be admitted to show its compatibility with the blood analysis; and that it was "far more probative than prejudicial". The justices accepted that argument, finding also that the blood specimen was of a quality and quantity capable of analysis and had not been contaminated. The results of the blood analysis were reliable, even without the evidence of breath analysis. They convicted the motorist, who appealed.

QUESTION(S) FOR THE COURT: Whether the evidence of the breath specimens should have been excluded as a result of the decision in the case of *Badkin v DPP* (page 46).

HELD: "… Subject to there being some relevant and clearly identified purpose for which it is to be adduced and subject to the exercise of the court's discretion, evidence of breath test results may properly be admissible in cases where the prosecution is based on the result of a blood alcohol analysis.

"… If the breath test result was compatible with, in the sense of being broadly equivalent to, the blood analysis result, then, notwithstanding the reason for requiring the appellant to provide blood, such evidence was at least capable of tending to support the reliability of the blood analysis result.

"… it seems to me to have been perfectly legitimate for [the justices] to have come to the conclusion that the blood analysis result was a completely reliable one, even without having regard to the evidence relating to the breath test."

The answer to the question was "no". Appeal dismissed.

Bobin v DPP

[1999] RTR 375, 6 July 1999, QBD (DC)

The reason specimens of breath cannot be taken can be given by an officer other than the officer requiring the blood or urine specimen. Information given by an officer (that failure to provide would not mean "definite disqualification") which affected his decision not to provide a specimen, can amount to a special reason for not disqualifying (see Chapter 10).

A motorist had provided a positive roadside breath test. He was arrested and taken to the police station where the arresting officer, in the presence of the custody officer, required him to provide two specimens of breath for analysis. The motorist agreed, but calibration checks on the breath analysis device demonstrated that it was not reliable. The custody officer, in the presence and hearing of the arresting officer, told the appellant that the device could not be used because it was not working properly and any breath test could not be relied on. The arresting officer then required the motorist to provide a specimen of blood or urine. The motorist asked the arresting officer whether a failure to provide a specimen "was a definite disqualification". The officer said it was not. The motorist then refused to provide a specimen of blood. He was charged with failing to provide a specimen, contrary to s 7(6), Road Traffic Act 1988.

He was convicted, fined and disqualified for 18 months. He appealed to the Crown Court, which rejected his appeal against conviction, and found no special reasons for not disqualifying under s 34(1), Road Traffic Offenders Act 1988, but reduced the period of disqualification to the minimum obligatory period of 12 months. He further appealed against conviction and sentence.

QUESTION(S) FOR THE COURT: (1) Whether the mandatory requirement that the constable, in requiring a specimen of blood or urine under s 7(4), Road Traffic Act 1988, tell the driver the reason why specimens of breath cannot be taken or used was satisfied when another constable made the appellant aware of the factual ground upon which the requirement of blood or urine was based, and the constable making the requirement of blood or urine failed to tell the appellant the reason. (2) Whether a requirement for a specimen can be conducted by more than one constable.

HELD: "… It obviously is essential from the terms of section 7(3) that the officer who is making the request for the sample must have cause to believe that there is no reliable device available to analyse the driver's breath at the police station. The driver must be made aware of that fact … But … there is no reason to impose a requirement that the driver must be informed of that fact by the officer making the request for the sample of blood or urine. One asks the rhetorical question, what conceivable prejudice can result if the information is supplied by some other officer? … this appeal against conviction should be dismissed.

"[On the sentence] … the inaccurate information given to the appellant, which affected his decision not to provide a sample, is capable of amounting to a special reason. To that extent, therefore, the Crown Court … was wrong when it found as a fact that the refusal was not, as a matter of law, capable of amounting to a special reason."

Kneale v DPP

Unreported, CO/1986/1999, 15 May 2000, QBD (DC)

Relying on an inspector's written note (that if the clock on the breath analysis device was more than one minute wrong) was reasonable cause to believe that the device was unreliable.

A motorist had been arrested on suspicion of driving with excess alcohol. At the police station, the clock on the breath analysis device was found to be 1½ minutes wrong. Attached to the machine was a memorandum from an inspector saying that if the clock was more than a minute in error, alternative means of testing a suspect's alcohol level should be adopted. The sergeant in question knew that the manufacturer's handbook suggested a tolerance of 4 minutes, but relied on the memorandum and her knowledge that defendants were being acquitted if their breath was analysed in machines whose clocks were more than one minute wrong. A blood specimen was therefore required and the motorist was charged with driving with excess alcohol.

He argued that the sergeant was not entitled to require the blood specimen because she had simply followed the inspector's advice rather than forming her own view as to the machine's reliability. The sergeant gave evidence that she reasonably believed the device was not reliable.

The magistrates convicted the defendant. He appealed.

QUESTION(S) FOR THE COURT: Whether (1) the justices were entitled to find on those facts that the sergeant reasonably believed that there was no reliable breath test machine available; (2) the sergeant was lawfully entitled, on those facts, to request a specimen of blood; (3) the justices were right to convict.

HELD: "17. … on what basis must the officer's judgment be made and tested in court? On the one hand, a whimsical judgment would not do. On the other, the judgment does not have to be right. It seems … quite clear from the context of the statute and the decided cases that the officer making the judgment must have a belief based upon reasonable cause or grounds that the machine is unreliable. … It is possible reasonably to hold the belief that something is so when it is not. …

"18. … The sergeant's judgment or belief was that because the clock on the machine was sufficiently wrong, it was not a reliable indicator of the applicant's alcohol level, having regard to the terms of the advice contained in the memorandum. … She was obviously entitled to heed that advice, whether it was right or wrong. It was for the magistrates to say whether, having regard to her evidence, she did believe that the machine was unreliable, and secondly, whether or not she had reasonable grounds for her belief … The magistrates expressly found as a fact that the sergeant reasonably believed that the only available intoximeter was not a reliable device at that time."

The answers to all three questions were "yes". Appeal dismissed.

Kelsey v DPP

[2008] EWHC 127 (Admin), 17 January 2008, QBD (Admin)

The test under section 7(3)(b), Road Traffic Act 1988 (reliable device not available or not practicable to use it) remains a subjective test and, where the officer was told by the custody sergeant that the device was not available because of a technical fault, the test was met.

A motorist had been charged with driving with excess alcohol, contrary to s 5(1)(a), Road Traffic Act 1988. The officer conducting the procedure was told by the custody sergeant that the breath analysis device was not available because of a technical fault. The officer therefore required a urine sample, which was provided, and revealed excess alcohol. The motorist was convicted, and appealed.

QUESTION(S) FOR THE COURT: Whether the requirement for a urine sample was lawful.

HELD: "10. … [It was contended for the appellant] that … section 7(3)(b), in the light of amendments … made … by the Criminal Procedure and Investigations Act 1996 [the insertion of subss 7(3)(bb) and (bc)], should now be construed as meaning that the question of whether a reliable intoximeter device was available had to be answered by reference to objective fact; that is to say, the prosecution had to demonstrate that the machine at the police station was not reliable or not available. …

"[After reviewing the authorities, which establish a subjective test] 20. … the interpretation of section 7(3)(b) as consistently maintained … and which has never been doubted remains the way in which section 7(3)(b) should be interpreted.… [Parliament] … saw no need to make an amendment, content with the way in which that provision consistently and authoritatively had been interpreted. …

"30. [It is submitted that] the forming of a reasonable belief can only be done by someone who has some personal knowledge of what the fault is thought by him to be. As an alternative, [it is argued] that even if the officer can rely upon what he is told by another, what he is told by that other person has to include what the nature of the fault is believed to be. …

"31. … A reasonable belief can be formed as a result of information provided by another. I regard that as self-evident. It is also evident that giving evidence as to the basis for one's belief does not involve giving inadmissible hearsay evidence. …

"32. … I can see neither principle nor statutory provision which precludes reliance, in forming a reasonable belief, upon what an officer is told. …

"33. As to [the argument] that a specific cause had to be assigned, … there is nothing as a matter of principle, which is the basis upon which this case has been argued, to show that some such cause must actually be adduced, whether the fault referred to is truly the fault or not.

"34. The court in deciding whether the belief is reasonably held is also entitled to consider the position of the person who provides the information, which is the basis of the constable's belief, and to consider whether it was reasonable for the officer to rely upon what was said in reaching that belief."

The answer to the question was "yes". Appeal dismissed.

8. DEVICE HAVING PRODUCED UNRELIABLE INDICATION

See s 7(3)(bb), Road Traffic Act 1988 – where the officer has reasonable cause to believe that the breath analysis device has not produced a reliable indication, a blood or urine specimen may be required instead. See also Jubb v DPP, page 341 – s 16(1), Road Traffic Offenders Act, on production of printouts from the breath analysis device, does not apply where the printout is in evidence only to show that the officer had reason to believe that the device had produced an unreliable indication; and Stewart (John Kimball) v DPP, page 114 – where the device generated the message "breath difference", the officer was not obliged to go on to require a blood specimen; he could instead offer to take, or require, further breath specimens.

DPP v Smith (Robert James)

[1999] EWHC 836 (Admin), [2000] RTR 341, 25 November 1999, QBD (DC)

Relying on the table of breath difference ranges in Forms MG DD/A and B provides reasonable cause to believe that a breath analysis device has not produced a reliable indication; the pro formas are a plain man's guide to the procedures.

A motorist had been charged with driving with excess alcohol, contrary to s 5(1)(a), Road Traffic Act 1988. A roadside breath test was positive. At the police station a calibration check showed the breath analysis device to be in working order. Two specimens were analysed, showing 43 and 33 µg alcohol in 100 ml breath. Referring to a *pro forma* (MG DD/A and B), the officer conducting the procedure consulted a table of breath difference ranges appended to the *pro forma*, from which he concluded that the indication obtained from the breath analysis was unreliable. He therefore required a blood specimen; analysis revealed 80 mg alcohol per 100 ml.

At the hearing, the motorist argued that the legality of Form MG DD/A was in issue; if the reason the officer had required a specimen of blood was his reliance on the form and the court concluded that the form was unlawful then the evidence relating to the specimen of blood should be excluded; in any event, a belief based on reliance on the instructions in the *pro forma* was not capable of constituting a reasonable cause for belief for the purposes of s 7(3)(b) and (bb), Road Traffic Act 1988.

The justices dismissed the charges; the prosecutor appealed.

QUESTION(S) FOR THE COURT: Whether the justices were right to hold that the officer's decision to request a sample of blood was not founded upon a reasonable cause for belief that a reliable device was not available, and/or was not founded on a reasonable cause for belief that the device had not produced a reliable indication, based as it was on automatic adherence to a form in which he had received no formal training, and the genesis and scientific basis of which there was no evidence before the court.

HELD: "… forms MG DD/A and B … are, in essence, no more than what I would describe as the 'plain man's guide' to a simple understanding of the procedures provided by the 1988 Act to ensure, in a practical way, that those called upon to operate the procedures do not omit a relevant step; that at stages where there is a choice of steps, they appreciate that such a choice exists, and it also offers quite clearly common sense guidance as to the way in which choices should be exercised when they fall to be made.

"… going back to the facts of this case: as the result of the pre and post breath procedure calibrations on this particular device show, … the device itself was not unreliable. The calibration checks showed that to be the position. If then, two breath specimens are taken within the space of a minute or so, which showed a disparity in reading (the higher being some 30.3 per cent higher than the lower) any reasonable person would be minded to conclude that the indication given by the device was unreliable … there was no obligation on the prosecution to call evidence as to the provenance of the form …

"[On whether or not the officer had reasonable cause to believe that the machine had not produced a reliable indication] given the simple facts of this case … he did. The form suggested that he understood it and applied it correctly … ."

The answer to the question was "no". Appeal allowed.

Hussain v DPP

[2008] EWHC 901 (Admin), [2008] RTR 30, 19 March 2008, QBD (DC)

Where valid breath specimens had not been provided, the device registering "ambient fail" after a single specimen in each of two cycles, the device had not produced a reliable indication and an officer was entitled to require two further breath specimens, at a different police station.

A motorist had been charged with failing without reasonable excuse to provide two specimens of breath for analysis, contrary to s 7(6), Road Traffic Act 1988. At the police station, he provided a first specimen of breath, but the breath analysis device would not allow a second specimen to be provided, the words "ambient fail" appearing on the screen. A second cycle was commenced but the result was the same. The officer conducting the procedure believed the device had not produced a reliable indication, and took the suspect to another police station, where another officer asked the motorist to provide specimens into the machine there. The motorist refused.

The district judge found that the first officer had reasonable cause to believe that the device had not produced a reliable indication of the proportion of alcohol in the breath; that the specimens had not been provided so as to enable the objective of the analysis to be carried out, as required by s 11(3), Road Traffic Act 1988 (a person does not provide a specimen of breath for analysis unless the specimen is sufficient to enable the analysis to be carried out, etc); and that the second officer was entitled to require further specimens of breath. He convicted the motorist, who appealed.

QUESTION(S) FOR THE COURT: (1) Whether the specimens provided at the first police station constituted valid specimens for the purposes of s 11(3); (2) where the officer had reasonable cause to believe that the breath testing device had not produced a reliable indication of the proportion of alcohol in the breath, whether another officer could require that person to provide further specimens of breath.

HELD: "18. … the machine indicated during the course of each of the cycles that there was an ambient fail. That seems to me to provide a clear indication that the readings provided during the course of the cycle could not be relied upon for the purposes of section 11(3)(b). They were not reliable readings. Moreover, it is a striking feature of this case that the ambient fail was indicated by the machine not on one occasion but on two occasions. Those two occasions were only minutes apart. The fact that on each occasion the machine indicated 'ambient fail' before the second reading could be taken demonstrates … that there was something wrong with this machine which rendered the readings unreliable.

"20. … in the circumstances of this case, where no valid specimens of breath have been provided, the officer was entitled to require the appellant to provide two further specimens of breath. His refusal to do so constituted the offence of which he was convicted."

The answer to question (1) was "no"; it was not appropriate to answer the second question. Appeal dismissed.

McNeil v DPP

[2008] EWHC 1254 (Admin), [2008] RTR 27, 28 April 2008, QBD (DC)

The fact that a breath specimen might have been affected by eructation did not give the investigating officer reasonable cause to believe that the device had not produced a reliable indication.

A motorist had been charged with driving with excess alcohol, contrary to s 5(1)(a), Road Traffic Act 1988. At the police station, before providing specimens of breath, the investigating officer asked a standard question, from the contemporaneous record Form MG DD/A, about whether or not the suspect had brought up anything from his stomach; the reply was "no". After providing the specimens, on being asked a further question from the standard form – whether he had burped since the earlier question had been asked – he replied that he had. The officer therefore required a specimen of blood under s 7(3)(bb), Road Traffic

Act 1988, as advised in the notes to Form MG DD/A. The motorist was convicted on the basis of the blood analysis. He appealed.

QUESTION(S) FOR THE COURT: Whether the justices were right to hold that the blood specimen had been lawfully taken on the basis that the officer had reasonable cause to believe that the breath analysis reading was unreliable.

HELD: "9. It is the appellant's case that the taking of the blood sample was unlawful because [the officer] had not had reasonable cause to believe that the Intoximeter had not produced a reliable indication. … First, [it is submitted] that the officer did not believe that the Intoximeter had produced an unreliable indication. Secondly, [it is submitted] that even if he did so believe, or if his subjective belief is immaterial, there was in fact no reasonable cause for any such belief.

"10. It is convenient to take the second question first. It may at first sight be attractive to say that there was plainly reasonable cause for [the officer's] belief because it was based on what he was told on an official form. However, it is not as straightforward as that. [The appellant] submits that the note in the form … incorporates a view of the law which has been shown to be wrong by the decision of this court in *Zafar v Director of Public Prosecutions* [see page 439], since endorsed in other cases, in particular *Woolfe v Director of Public Prosecutions* [see page 440]. On the basis of those authorities it is now settled that a specimen of breath affected, or potentially affected, by reflux or regurgitation from the stomach is not to be treated in any way differently: it is simply 'breath' within the meaning of the statute. [It is argued] that it follows that a sample cannot be treated for the purpose of Section 7(3)(bb) as an unreliable indication of the proportion of alcohol in the appellant's breath simply because it may have been so affected. The same must apply to the case of specimens potentially affected by burping or, to give it a more dignified name, eructation. *Zafar* had not been decided at the time [the form used in this case] was drafted …

"11. I can see no answer to that submission. No blame attaches to the officer personally for following the procedure specified by the form. But the fact remains that the cause which he thought that he had to believe that the breath samples tested on the Intoximeter did not give a reliable indication of the proportion of alcohol in the appellant's breath namely having been told that the appellant had recently burped was not in law capable of rendering that indication unreliable. In those circumstances the subsequent request for a blood sample was not one which the officer was entitled to make. The conviction based on that sample cannot be sustained."

Appeal allowed.

Taylor v DPP

[2009] EWHC 2824 (Admin), 20 October 2009, QBD (DC)

Where the breath analysis readings were 63 and 52, and the device recorded "breath difference", the officer was entitled to require a blood specimen. On the facts (matching names, matching police station, but a minor discrepancy in transcribing the serial number), the justices were right to find that the blood specimen analysed was that taken from the defendant.

A motorist had been charged with driving with excess alcohol in blood, contrary to s 5(1)(a), Road Traffic Act 1988. At Leamington Spa police station, evidential breath specimens showed 63 and 52 µg alcohol in 100 ml of breath, and the device registered "breath difference". The officer administering the procedure thought this was because the motorist had blown too hard and too fast when giving the second specimen. Following the guidance on the MG DD/A form, he decided that, although the device appeared reliable, it may not have produced a reliable indication of the proportion of alcohol. He therefore required a specimen of blood under s 7(3)(bb), Road Traffic Act 1988 (officer having reasonable cause to believe that the device has not produced a reliable indication). A specimen was taken, the vial was marked with the motorist's name (Martin Taylor) and a serial number, and placed in the fridge. The person who took the specimen from the fridge later the same day and sent it for analysis recorded the serial number, but made an error in one of the digits. The blood specimen showed excess alcohol and the motorist was convicted. He appealed.

QUESTION(S) FOR THE COURT: (1) Whether the officer was entitled to ask for a blood specimen on the basis that: (a) although the machine appeared to be working properly, it may not have given a reliable indication of the alcohol concentration because the printout said "breath difference"; and (b) he thought the reason for the "breath difference" was that the appellant had blown too hard on the second analysis. (2) Whether there was admissible evidence that the blood analysed was that of the motorist.

HELD: "[On (1)] 13. … the officer's evidence as to why a wide breath difference may have occurred, namely that the appellant had been blowing too hard or too fast, would not of itself constitute reasonable grounds for doubting the veracity of the test results. …

"14. … The discrepancy [between the two breath readings] is …in the region of 20 per cent in a period of some three or four minutes … that fully entitled the Justices to conclude that this factor, coupled … with the fact that the printout … referred to breath difference, constituted reasonable cause for the officer to determine that the blood test should be taken. …

"[On (2)] 18. … The question here is whether on the information available to them the Justices could properly be satisfied to the criminal standard of proof that the blood provided was the sample that ultimately was tested. …

"19. … There were three factors … which seem to me to support that conclusion. First, … the sample bore the appellant's name. There was not just the name of

Taylor but it was identified with the name Mark [*sic*] Taylor. Second, it was taken from the Leamington Spa Police Station. Third, the sample that was sent was taken from the fridge only some eight hours – probably less than that in fact – after a sample had been taken from the defendant, and both bore the name Martin Taylor. Plainly in such a short period it is highly unlikely that there would be a confusion resulting from there being two samples with exactly the same name.

"23. … although the serial number was not identical, it was very similar. The Justices did not specifically rely on this but … the discrepancy of the kind demonstrated here is the kind of every day error of transcription that will arise when individuals are putting down strings of numbers. Had the serial number been markedly different, then that might have raised greater doubts and it would have been a different case."

The answers to both questions were "yes". Appeal dismissed.

DPP v Vince; Kang v DPP

[2016] EWHC 3014 (Admin), 25 November 2016, QBD (Admin)

Where the breath analysis device registered "ambient fail" and the procedure was recommenced and completed without any error message, the resulting reading was reliable; there was no requirement to require a blood or urine specimen instead. See also Richardson v DPP, page 263 – no breach of art 6, European Convention on Human Rights where, following a positive breath test, officers refused to allow the motorist to give a blood specimen; and DPP v Camp, page 257 – once the offence of failing without reasonable excuse to provide a breath specimen is complete, there is no duty on the investigating officer to require an alternative specimen. A roadside breath reading may be taken into account as confirming the procedure at the police station.

For the decision in *DPP v Vince*, see page 602. In *Kang*, a motorist had been charged with being in charge of a motor vehicle with excess alcohol, contrary to s 5(1)(b), Road Traffic Act 1988. A roadside test showed 157 µg of alcohol in 100 ml of breath. At the police station, the breath analysis procedure was begun. The calibration check was satisfactory, but, before the first breath specimen was provided, the device produced the message 'ambient fail' and aborted the procedure. The procedure was begun again, the error message did not recur, and the lower reading was 143. The officer did not require blood or urine instead of breath. The district judge found that the error message had occurred because the suspect held the breath tube too close to his mouth before providing the first specimen, and that the reading of 143 was reliable. The defendant was convicted. He appealed.

QUESTION(S) FOR THE COURT: (1) Whether the court was entitled to conclude that the reading of 143 was reliable and admissible, notwithstanding the 'ambient fail' message and the decision of the officer to re-start the Intoxilyser rather than offer the choice to provide a sample of blood or urine; (2) whether the court was entitled to regard the evidence of the reading of 157 provided in the roadside test as evidence which supported the reliability of the station procedure.

HELD: "9. … it was submitted that [the officer conducting the procedure] failed to follow the prescribed statutory procedure in three respects … 1. continuing with the breath test procedure despite the 'Ambient Fail' message instead of offering … the option to provide a blood or urine sample; 2. failing to complete paragraph A18 of the MG DD/A form which requires reasons for an incomplete procedure to be set out; and 3. failing to complete paragraph A19 of the form which provides that where a breath testing device stops working or is working unreliably, details should be given.

11. "The District Judge (Magistrates Court) found as facts (1) that the cause of the 'Ambient Fail' message was that [the appellant] had held the breathing tube of the machine in the vicinity of his mouth before providing the first specimen of breath for analysis, (2) that the machine was working perfectly, and (3) that its readings were reliable. These are findings of fact. … Accordingly, the only issues arising so far as the first question is concerned is whether in any of the three respects set out above [the officer] failed to follow the correct statutory procedure and, if he did, whether the consequence is that the results obtained are invalid and inadmissible as a matter of law. That question must be determined on the facts found by the District Judge including the three findings referred to above. …

"17. I can see nothing in the legislation which required [the officer] to insist on a blood or urine sample instead of completing the breath test procedure as he did. …

"18. [The appellant's] argument is based, not on the legislation, but on the terms of form MG DD/A…

"21. It was because the machine would not allow the test to continue that it had to be aborted and started all over again. Although the form indicates that in such circumstances 'it will be usual' to proceed by way of blood or urine sample, that is not stated to be mandatory but only to represent usual practice. … Even applying the terms of the form, therefore, there was no breach of any procedure. In any event, … the provisions of the form have no statutory force.

"22. I would therefore reject [the appellant's] first ground for saying that the statutory procedure was not correctly followed.

"23. The second and third grounds can be taken together shortly. Paragraphs A18 and A19 of the MG DD/A form deal respectively with what should happen when the breath analysis procedure is not completed satisfactorily and when no reliable indication can be obtained of the proportion of alcohol in a person's breath. … However, these paragraphs have no application in the present case. At the second attempt the procedure was completed satisfactorily and a reliable indication was obtained. …

"24. … the decision of the officer to re-start the Intoxilyzer and to continue with analysis of a specimen of breath despite the 'Ambient Fail' message; and/or the failure of the officer to complete paragraphs A18 and A19 of form MG DD/A did not render the results thereby obtained invalid or inadmissible.

"[On the second question] 27. … the District Judge relied on a number of factors in reaching his conclusion as to the reliability of the machine. These included not only the roadside test itself, but also (1) the consistency between the roadside test reading and the station test result, (2) the absence of any explanation why this should be so if the machine was defective, (3) [the appellant's] demeanour both at the roadside (smelling of alcohol, eyes glazed, unsteady on his feet and leaning on PC Smith) and in the police station (unsteady on his feet, speech slurred, eyes heavily glazed), (4) rejection of [the appellant's] evidence as to what he had drunk on the day in question, (5) the 'entirely plausible' explanation for the 'Ambient Fail' message being displayed, and (6) the evidence of PC Smith, a highly experienced officer, as to the checks carried out to ensure that the machine was working properly. …

"29. I can see no reason why the District Judge was not entitled to rely on the roadside test reading as one piece of evidence among others supporting the reliability of the station procedure. It is important to understand that the District Judge did not treat the roadside test as the basis for [the appellant's] conviction. [He] was convicted because of the reading obtained by a test carried out at the police station in accordance with the requirements of section 7. …"

Appeal dismissed.

9. DRIVER'S CONDITION DUE TO SOME DRUG

See s 7(3)(c), Road Traffic Act 1988 – specimen of blood or urine not to be required unless the suspected offence is under s 3A, s 4 or s 5A and the constable has been advised by a medical practitioner that the suspect's condition may be due to some drug.

Cole v DPP

[1988] RTR 224, 17 June 1987, QBD (DC)

A requirement for a blood specimen under s 8(3)(c), Road Traffic Act 1972 was unlawful unless a doctor had given the officer a clear statement that the driver's condition might be due to some drug.

A motorist had been charged, *inter alia*, with failing without reasonable excuse to provide a specimen of blood for a laboratory test, contrary to s 8(7), Road Traffic Act 1972 as substituted by s 25 and Sch 8, Transport Act 1981. He had provided breath specimens which produced zero readings; the police officer administering the test thought, because of the motorist's appearance and behaviour, that he might be under the influence of drugs; he called a doctor with a view to ascertaining whether a blood specimen could be required under s 8(3)(c) (requirement for blood specimen not to be made unless the constable has been advised by a medical practitioner that the condition of the person might be due to some drug). Although the doctor formed the view that the motorist's condition could have been due to drugs or epilepsy, he did not communicate this to the officer, first saying that the motorist was incapable of understanding a request for a blood specimen, and later, that the motorist was then capable of understanding the request. The constable requested a blood specimen, and the motorist refused.

The justices rejected the motorist's contention that, in the absence of a direct communication from the doctor to the constable that the motorist's condition might be due to drugs, the request for blood had been unlawful under s 8(3)(c), and convicted. The motorist appealed.

QUESTION(S) FOR THE COURT: (1) Whether the justices were correct in law in finding that the requirement for a blood specimen complied with s 8(3)(c), Road Traffic Act 1972 as substituted; (2) whether the evidence justified the finding of fact that the constable making the requirement for a specimen of blood had been advised by a medical practitioner that the condition of the person required to provide the specimen might be due to some drug.

HELD: "When section 8(3)(c) was enacted … Parliament intended that there should be a clear indication from a doctor to a police officer at a police station in circumstances such as this of the doctor's view as to the possible cause of a defendant's condition as found by him at the police station – by a clear indication I mean a clear oral statement by the doctor to the police officer of his opinion. Here, obviously, there was none. The justices were disentitled … from drawing the inference which they appear to have drawn."

The answers to both questions were "no". Appeal allowed.

Bell v DPP

Unreported, CO 2950-95, 30 July 1997, QBD (DC)

In the circumstances of this case, the justices were entitled to find that the doctor had clearly told the officer that the defendant's condition might be due to some drug. See also DPP v Gibbons, page 94, where such an opinion was also given.

A motorist had been charged with driving when unfit through drink or drugs, contrary to s 4(1), Road Traffic Act 1988. His driving was erratic; police officers stopped him and suspected he was under the influence of drugs. They found white powder on him; he admitted it was amphetamine; that he had used it the night before; and that he used it most days. At the police station, the custody sergeant was of the opinion that his condition might be due to drugs; he called a Dr Gold, who examined the motorist. The form (Form 300) recording the drink/drugs procedure showed, in paragraph G, certain observations of the doctor, signed by the doctor. The sergeant had completed paragraph E of the form (reasons for requiring a blood specimen) by selecting the option "impairment through drugs after medical advice". The officer then sought a blood specimen, which was duly taken, and, on analysis, revealed a level of amphetamine incompatible with the safe control of a motor vehicle.

The doctor was not called to give evidence before the justices nor was any statement by him served by the prosecution on the defence. At the hearing, the motorist argued that s 7(3)(c), Road Traffic Act 1988 (requirement that the officer be advised by a medical practitioner that the condition of the person required to provide the specimen might be due to some drug) had not been complied with, in that the doctor had not advised the sergeant that the motorist's condition might be due to some drug; the specimen was not therefore legally taken and the analysis inadmissible. The justices, however, accepted that it was a proper inference from the manner in which the record of the procedure had been completed that the requirement had been complied with. They convicted the motorist. He appealed.

QUESTION(S) FOR THE COURT: (1) Whether the justices were correct in law in finding that the requirement for the specimen of blood complied with s 7(3)(c); (2) whether the justices were justified in concluding that the sergeant had been advised by a medical practitioner that the condition of the appellant might be due to some drug; (3) whether, in the absence of any evidence from Dr Gold, the way in which the officer had completed Form 300 and/or the endorsement apparently signed by Dr Gold as part of that record could provide a proper foundation for a finding of fact that the doctor had advised the sergeant that the condition of the appellant might be due to some drug.

HELD: "… it was manifestly Parliament's intention that a clear indication should be given from a doctor to a police officer at a police station as to the possible cause of the defendant's condition. [That] can be proved, plainly, by the doctor being called to say what he said [or] by the police officer saying what the doctor said to him. But how it is to be proved must depend on the circumstances of the particular case. In my judgment, the only question which arises on this appeal is whether there was evidence before the Justices entitling them to draw the inference that the sergeant had been clearly told by the doctor that the condition of the defendant might be due to drugs.

"… on the material before them, namely the unchallenged evidence of the custody sergeant as to what he said and did and as to the filling in by him of Form 300, paragraph E, and in the light of the contents of paragraph G, the Justices were entitled to find as they did."

The answer to questions (1) and (2) was "yes". On question (3), "… the fact that the doctor had signed the endorsement and that the endorsement was then followed by the words … which led the officer to complete paragraph E in the manner to which I have referred, was something to which the Justices were entitled to have regard.

"I would therefore answer question [3] in the affirmative subject to those comments and subject to deleting from it the words 'and/or the endorsement apparently signed by Dr Gold at Section G of Form 300', so that the answer to the question is affirmatively given by reference to the way in which the Custody Sergeant had completed Form 300."

Appeal dismissed.

Angel v Chief Constable of South Yorkshire

[2010] EWHC 883 (Admin), 23 March 2010, QB (Admin)

The issue to be addressed by the medical practitioner is the suspect's condition at the time of the alleged offence rather than at the time of the medical examination.

A motorist had been charged with failing without reasonable excuse to provide a specimen of blood for a laboratory test, contrary to s 7(6), Road Traffic Act 1988. He was stopped because he was driving very slowly. The officer smelled cannabis and asked the driver how much cannabis he had had that night. The motorist replied, "only a bit, not much". The officer conducted a preliminary impairment test and concluded that the motorist was unfit to drive. At the police station, breath analysis was carried out and a police surgeon was then called. The officer recounted what had happened at the roadside and the police surgeon said that she could find no medical reason for the driver's impairment at the roadside 2 hours earlier, and that his condition might be due to drugs. He was convicted of failing to provide a blood specimen and appealed.

QUESTION(S) FOR THE COURT: Whether the medical practitioner's advice should address only the condition of the person as it appears at the police station, or whether he or she can also address his condition at the time of the offence under investigation as related to the doctor by the police officers.

HELD: "11. ... The purpose of the medical advice is to provide a protection against the invasive requirement of a blood test when there is a clear medical explanation of the person's condition which excludes the influence of drugs. ...

"12. [It is] plainly correct that the condition referred to in section 7(3)(c) of the 1988 Act (requirement that the officer be advised by a medical practitioner that the condition of the person required to provide the specimen might be due to some drug) is the person's condition at the time he was driving. It is that for which he has been arrested and is under investigation and it is to that condition that the specimen of blood will be relevant. Insofar as it might be different, his condition later at the police station is not that to which the investigation is directed. ...

"13. It is common sense, therefore, that the doctor is entitled to take into account all relevant information relating to the person's earlier condition. In some cases, of course, the person's condition at the police station may alone be sufficient to enable the doctor to give the necessary advice, but the doctor is not limited to the finding of his or her own police station examination. In my judgment, the requiring of the blood specimen in this case was lawful."

The answer to the question was that "the issue to be addressed by the medical practitioner ... is the suspect's condition at the time of the alleged offence".

Appeal dismissed.

Watling v Chief Constable of Suffolk Constabulary and G4S Health Service (UK) Ltd
[2019] EWHC 2342 (QB), 2 August 2019, QBD

Where there were no grounds for police officers reasonably to have known that a driver was someone other than a suspected drug-driver (in fact he had had a stroke), a claim for damages for violation of arts 3 and 8, European Convention on Human Rights failed; meaning of "public authority".

Police stopped a vehicle which was being driven erratically. The driver was unable to speak or answer questions; there was phlegm around his mouth; his body and arm were shaking; there was no smell of alcohol; the officer had to help him switch off the car engine. A roadside breath test was negative. The officer suspected that the erratic driving was a result of being under the influence of drugs, and arrested the driver for driving while under the influence of drugs.

The custody record was opened 2.47 am; at 3.04 am an officer contacted G4S (the company contracted to the Suffolk Constabulary to provide forensic and medical services to detainees), requesting a forensic medical examiner to assess the detainee and test him for drugs. The doctor arrived at the police station at 5.19 am and saw the detainee at about 5.40 am. The doctor was of the opinion that the detainee had had a stroke or transient ischaemic accident (TIA) and referred him to hospital for investigation. The claimant arrived at hospital between 6.15 am and 6.30 am

The claimant sought declarations and damages under the Human Rights Act 1998, alleging that the police and G4S, as public authorities, had violated art 3 (prohibition on torture, inhuman or degrading treatment or punishment) and/or art 8 (the right to respect for private and family life) of the European Convention on Human Rights, in that, had he been dealt with more quickly, the medical outcome would have been better.

HELD: "52. At no stage at the roadside or at the PIC [Police Investigation Centre] did any of the police officers know the claimant was presenting as a stroke victim or as any sort of medical emergency, nor were there grounds on which they reasonably ought to have known or foreseen that he might potentially become an emergency case. In all the circumstances there were no grounds on which any of the police officers ought to have known or foreseen that the claimant presented as one at risk of Article 3 ill treatment or at any stage as someone other than a suspected drug-driver. Signs of stroke were subtle even by the time [the forensic medical examiner] examined the claimant. The signs were so subtle that even a health care professional other than a doctor would not be expected to notice them, much less, I conclude, a police officer or other layman. …

"62. Article 3 and 8 duties apply to public authorities as defined by section 6 and 6(3)(b) and (5) of the Human Rights Act 1998 …

"[On whether G4S is a public authority for the purposes of this action] 66. … G4S is a 'hybrid' authority and falls within the scope of section 6(3)(b) of the HRA; it is an authority that exercises both private and public functions … .

"70. … none of the relevant acts at issue in the present case were private acts… . G4S is, therefore, a public authority for the purposes of Articles 3 and 8 in the present case … .

"72. The claimant's case is that the system as out-sourced to and designed by G4S was demonstrably inadequate … the geographical area covered … was too large to allow for appropriate response times; it was not robust enough to deal with occasions where staff were off sick; the triage process was not manned by or overseen by a clinician and the information available to assist unqualified call-handlers … was too limited …

"81. … failure to provide appropriate medical care to a detainee may, in principle, constitute a violation of the operational duty imposed by Article 3 … .

"82. To engage Article 3 at all the behaviour alleged to constitute the inhuman or degrading treatment must attain a minimum level of severity and must go beyond that which is considered reasonably coincidental to the fact of detention.

"84. … I am not satisfied that the threshold minimum level of severity has been established in the present case … the police officers had neither actual nor constructive knowledge that the claimant had had a stroke or was showing discernible signs of being at risk of medical deterioration or was otherwise in need of immediate medical attention … all that can be said is that the police officers' inaction between about 3.04 am and 5.19 am has been shown with the benefit of hindsight to have been a non- negligent mistake … .

"95. The system devised by G4S clinical staff and implemented in the present case was adequate.

"96. … The claimant was not exhibiting extensive signs of stroke at the roadside or at the police station. His was an unusual presentation. There was no justification for the police to exclude drug ingestion as a result of any profiling. The police officers conscientiously kept the claimant under review throughout his time in custody in a properly open-minded fashion but on the basis of all the information available to them about the claimant reasonably concluded he was a section 4 case and was not presenting as a medical emergency. Neither Defendant knew or ought to have known otherwise … ."

Claims dismissed.

Twigg v R

[2019] EWCA Crim 1553, 13 September 2019, CA (Crim)

Where a suspect lied to the healthcare professional by saying he had not taken drugs, and she did not tell the investigating officer that his condition might be due to some drug, the analysis of the blood specimen then taken was nevertheless admissible in evidence and the trial judge was correct not to exclude it under s 78, Police and Criminal Evidence Act 1984.

A motorist was charged with causing death by careless driving while over the limit for a specified drug, contrary to s 3A(1)(ba), Road Traffic Act 1988. He had left the scene of an accident. He was arrested at home. The arresting officer smelt cannabis and asked the driver if he had smoked anything; he replied, "not recently". He told the healthcare professional who was to take a blood specimen that he had not taken any drugs. The healthcare professional reported that there were no alcohol or drug issues and took the specimen, which showed an excess of delta-9-tetrahydrocannabinol (cannabis). In interview, he again lied to police, saying that he had not smoked cannabis for months. At trial, the motorist admitted he was a cannabis user at the relevant time. The healthcare professional said she took the specimen because the police had asked for it, but that if the appellant had answered honestly about his drug use, she would have reviewed her opinion about whether he was affected by cannabis. The trial judge concluded that, although there had been a breach of procedure in taking the sample, in all the circumstances, admission of that evidence would not have such an adverse impact on the fairness of the trial that it would be unfair to allow the prosecution to adduce it. The driver was convicted and appealed against conviction.

GROUNDS OF APPEAL: The judge should have exercised her discretion under s 78, Police and Criminal Evidence Act 1984 (to exclude evidence which would have such an adverse effect on the fairness of the proceedings that the court ought not to admit it) to exclude the blood sample evidence; the healthcare professional had not advised the police that the appellant's condition might be due to some drug, as required by s 7(3)(c), Road Traffic Act 1988; without that opinion, the police were not lawfully allowed to make the request.

HELD: "29. … [S]ubsection (3)(c) [Road Traffic Act 1988] … was not complied with in the present case, since the healthcare professional did not advise the police that the Appellant's condition might be due to some drug. …

"[After reviewing authorities] 44. … the general approach of English law is to regard the manner in which evidence was obtained (including where it was obtained unlawfully) as not leading to its automatic exclusion. The manner in which it was obtained will be a relevant factor to be taken into account when performing the exercise required by section 78 of PACE and Article 6 of the ECHR [right to a fair trial] but ultimately the question for the court is whether there will be a fair trial. However, in the present case, it is submitted on behalf of the Appellant that, even before one gets to that issue, the blood sample in question was inadmissible as a matter of law, so there could be no question of admitting it at all. …

"72. … We … reject [that] submission …

"73. … the trial judge was entitled to exercise the judgement which she did under section 78 of PACE and to refuse to exclude the evidence of the blood sample. This is essentially for the reason that she gave, namely that the Appellant lied to the health care professional about whether he had been taking drugs. If he had not lied it was likely that the healthcare professional would have altered the opinion which she formed as to whether his condition might have been due to drugs."

Appeal dismissed.

10. THE PROCEDURE

See ss 6 and 7, Road Traffic Act 1988 – preliminary tests and provision of specimens for analysis. On the procedure for taking and dividing specimens, see Chapter 3. For cases concerning hospital patients, see page 98.

DPP v Carey

[1970] AC 1072, [1969] 3 WLR 1169, [1969] 3 All ER 1662, [1970] RTR 14, 10 and 11 November 1969 and 3 December 1969, HL

The officer's failure to follow the manufacturer's instructions for using a roadside breath testing device did not vitiate the procedure, but an officer should seek to use the device correctly.

See also Blake v Bickmore, page 108, where there was no evidence that the officer had not complied with the manufacturer's instructions for a roadside breath test; Grant v DPP, page 16, where the court was entitled to find that the motorist had not had a drink within the 20 minutes preceding the requirement; DPP v Kay (John), page 4 – the officer at the roadside is under no duty to ask when the motorist last drank or smoked; and DPP v Kennedy, page 366, where the mouthpiece on the roadside device was not changed between attempts to blow.

A motorist had been charged with driving with excess alcohol in blood, contrary to s 1(1), Road Safety Act 1967. He was stopped and a roadside breath test administered. The officer did not ask the driver when he had last drunk alcohol or smoked; the manufacturer's instructions for the use of the device said that a test should not be administered within 20 minutes of either. Nor did the officer give the instructions recommended by the manufacturer for inflating the bag. The test was positive; the driver was arrested and at the police station another test was administered. The motorist was told only that he should take a deep breath and inflate the bag fully. A blood specimen was taken which showed excess alcohol.

The magistrates acquitted the motorist. The prosecutor appealed to the Divisional Court, which found that the breath test must be conducted in strict compliance with the manufacturer's instructions; failure to do so vitiated the breath test and the subsequent procedure. The prosecutor appealed further.

HELD: "I do not agree … that the instructions 'are printed as an integral part of the device'. I think that the wording of the Schedule to the [approval] order shows that they form no part of the device approved by the Home Secretary … While the Act requires a device of a type approved by the Home Secretary to be used it does not require his approval of the instructions, and whether or not he had approved them is … immaterial. … in the absence of knowledge of and in the absence of reasonable cause to suspect the consumption of alcohol within the preceding 20 minutes, a police officer is not to be regarded as failing to carry out the instructions if he does not delay carrying out the test. I do not think it is incumbent on him to establish the negative, that no alcohol has been consumed with the 20 minutes.

"… there is not … any absolute requirement, express or implied, that a test in order to be a 'breath test' within the meaning of the Act must be carried out in perfect compliance with the manufacturer's instructions. There is an express requirement that the test must be carried out for the purpose of obtaining an indication of the proportion of alcohol in the blood, and it follows that the police officer must be trying to use the device correctly in order to obtain a true indication. I think also that there probably is an implied requirement … that the test must be carried out with such accuracy as is reasonably attainable in the circumstances. I do not think on the facts of this case there was any failure to comply with those requirements."

Appeal allowed.

Chief Constable of Avon & Somerset v Singh

[1988] RTR 107, 12 March 1987, QBD (DC)

Where the defendant did not understand the warning of the consequences of failure to provide breath specimens for analysis, because of his inability to understand English, acquittal would follow.

A motorist had been charged with, *inter alia*, failing without reasonable excuse to provide a specimen of breath for analysis, contrary to s 8(7), Road Traffic Act 1972 as substituted by s 25 and Sch 8, Transport Act 1981. His first language was Punjabi. The police officer administering the breath analysis procedure considered there was no language barrier and read the statutory warning to the motorist.

The justices found that, because of his limited understanding of English, the motorist had not been able to understand the consequences of failure to provide, and acquitted him. The prosecutor appealed.

QUESTION(S) FOR THE COURT: (1) Whether the justices were correct in holding that the defendant had to understand the penal consequences of a refusal or failure to provide two specimens of breath for analysis if he knew why he had been asked to blow into the machine and attempted on three occasions to do so.

HELD: "... when a person is charged with an offence under section 8, but the necessary warning is not given, there must be an acquittal … Thus, even though a warning may be given … if that warning is not understood by the person to whom it is given, perhaps because of his inability to understand English … there must be an acquittal."

Appeal dismissed.

Murray v DPP

[1993] RTR 209, [1993] Crim LR 968, 4 February 1993, QBD (DC)

In this old "driver's option" case, where the driver declined the option and was prosecuted on the basis of the breath analysis, the driver was acquitted because he had not been warned of the consequences of failing to provide a specimen. See also Worsley v DPP, page 352 – the statutory warning is not required in relation to preliminary testing.

A motorist had been charged with driving with excess alcohol, contrary to s 5(1)(a), Road Traffic Act 1988. He had been arrested and, at the police station, provided breath specimens for analysis. The lower reading was 47 µg alcohol in 100 ml breath. The officer administering the procedure therefore told the motorist of his right, under s 8(2), Road Traffic Act 1988 (lower breath reading no more than 50 µg alcohol in 100 ml breath – now repealed; see page v), to have the breath specimens replaced by an alternative specimen. He declined.

At the hearing, the officer gave evidence that she had completed the "standard procedure" form, but could not recall the exact words she had used to the motorist. She was not cross-examined on this point. It was submitted on behalf of the motorist that the breath analysis was not admissible, since there was no evidence that the motorist had been warned, as required by s 7(7), Road Traffic Act 1988, that failure to provide specimens could render him liable to prosecution. The justices accepted that no warning had been given, but found that this had not prejudiced him and that the breath analysis result was admissible. They convicted him. He appealed.

QUESTION(S) FOR THE COURT: (1) Whether the justices were right to admit the evidence of the breath analysis when the defendant had not been warned that failure to provide would result in prosecution; (5) whether there was sufficient evidence on which to convict.

HELD: "... The justices admitted the results of the breath tests in evidence, although the defendant ... had not been warned before he provided the specimens of his liability to prosecution if he declined to do so. On the face of it, therefore, the specimens had been obtained without compliance with part of the statutory procedure, and the tests ... should not have been admitted since the specimens had not been provided 'pursuant to the provisions of the Act'.

"... There remains the question whether this court should hold as a matter of principle that where no prejudice to a defendant is occasioned by failure to warn because he has in any event given the specimen required of him, ... the results of the consequent test can be admitted despite the breach of procedure. We are unable to arrive at such a conclusion. Once it is accepted ... that the admission in evidence of the results of tests is ... dependent upon the statutory procedure having been carried out ... it is impossible to carve out an exception to cater for the cases where the breach of procedure causes no prejudice ... ."

Appeal allowed.

DPP v Warren

[1993] AC 319, [1992] 3 WLR 814, [1992] 4 All ER 865, [1993] RTR 585, 5 November 1992, HL

The House of Lords endorsed the form of words used in this case to require a specimen of blood or urine under s 7(3), Road Traffic Act 1988, and set out what is to be said when offering the driver the option under s 8(2) (alternative specimen where lower breath reading no more than 50 – repealed, with effect from 10 April 2015, by s 52 and Sch 11, Deregulation Act 2015). In neither situation is there any need to invite the driver to express a preference for giving blood or urine. See also DPP v Jackson, Stanley v DPP, page 79.

A motorist had been charged with driving with excess alcohol, contrary to s 5(1)(a), Road Traffic Act 1988. At the police station, the breath analysis device was not working properly and the officer administering the procedure therefore required a specimen of blood or urine under s 7(3)(b), Road Traffic Act 1988 (reliable device not available). He used the following words: "The approved evidential breath testing device cannot be used on this occasion because the calibration check has proved unsatisfactory. Accordingly, I require you to provide an alternative specimen, which will be submitted for laboratory analysis. The specimen may be of blood or urine but it is for me to decide which. If you provide a specimen you will be offered part of it in a suitable container. If you fail to provide a specimen you may be liable to prosecution. Are there any reasons why a specimen of blood cannot or should not be taken by a doctor? … Will you provide a specimen of blood?". A blood specimen was taken and showed excess alcohol.

The magistrate found no case to answer because the wording used did not allow the motorist an opportunity of making representations as to which type of specimen he would prefer to supply, as required under *DPP v Byrne (Paul)* [1991] RTR 119 (DC). The Divisional Court upheld the magistrate's decision. The prosecutor appealed further.

CERTIFIED QUESTION(S): (1) If a requirement is made, pursuant to s 7(3), Road Traffic Act 1988 for a specimen of blood or urine, is the constable making that requirement under a duty, by virtue of s 7(4) (constable to decide whether specimen to be of blood or urine), Road Traffic Act 1988 to: (a) convey to the suspect that the specimen to be provided may be of blood or urine; and/or (b) give to that suspect an opportunity to consider which type of specimen he would prefer to supply, if the choice was his; and/or (c) give, expressly or otherwise, to that suspect an opportunity to give any reasons (including non-medical reasons) in support of any expression of choice?

(2) Can a constable, when authorised by s 7(3), Road Traffic Act 1988 to require a specimen of blood or urine (and absent any medical opinion that for medical reasons a blood specimen cannot or should not be taken), lawfully require the provision of blood (or urine) alone without, in speaking to the suspect, making reference to the alternative?

(3) Do the words used by the officer in the instant case, sufficiently comply with the requirements of s 7, Road Traffic Act 1988?

HELD: "… where the necessity to require a specimen of blood or urine under section 7(4) arises for one of the reasons specified in section 7(3), what is required is no more and no less than the formula used in the instant case or words to the like effect. … In neither [a s 7(3) case nor a s 8(2) case] is there any need to invite the driver to express his preference for giving blood or urine."

The answer to question (3) was "yes". Appeal allowed.

For cases in which the principles established in *DPP v Warren* were applied, see *Edge v DPP* [1993] RTR 146; *Meade v DPP* [1993] RTR 151; *Ogburn v DPP; Williams v DPP; DPP v Duffy; R v Cheshire JJ ex p Cunningham and Other Cases* [1995] RTR 287; *R v Cheshire JJ ex p Sinnott and Other Cases* [1995] RTR 281; *Beaufont v DPP* [1998] RTR 175.

DPP v Garrett

[1995] RTR 302, 31 January 1995, QBD (DC)

Where the procedure for requiring a blood specimen was not correctly followed, but it was not then possible to obtain a blood specimen and a urine specimen was required instead, the analysis of the urine specimen was admissible. See also Barnes v Chief Constable of Durham, page 118, where an unproductive request for one specimen did not prevent a subsequent request for another specimen; and Wyllie v CPS, page 117, and DPP v Taylor, page 119, both to the effect that there is nothing to prevent an officer requiring a urine specimen following failure to provide a blood specimen.

A motorist had been charged with driving with excess alcohol in urine, contrary to s 5(1)(a), Road Traffic Act 1988. A roadside breath test was positive and the driver was arrested and taken to the police station. The breath analysis device was not working, and the officer administering the procedure therefore required an alternative specimen under s 7(3)(b), Road Traffic Act 1988 (reliable device not available, etc). The record of the procedure did not contain the question whether there was any reason why a specimen of blood could not be given. A doctor was called, but when he tried to take a blood specimen, the motorist's vein collapsed. The officer therefore required a specimen of urine, saying that the doctor was of the opinion that, for medical reasons, a specimen of blood could not or should not be taken. A urine specimen was provided and revealed excess alcohol.

At the hearing, the motorist submitted that there was a procedural defect in that the officer had not asked whether there was any reason why a blood specimen could not or should not be taken, and that invalidated the subsequent procedure. The justices accepted that contention and dismissed the charge. The prosecutor appealed.

QUESTION(S) FOR THE COURT: Whether, on a trial in respect of an allegation contrary to s 5(1)(a), Road Traffic Act 1988, an invalid but unproductive request for a specimen of blood rendered inadmissible evidence of the analysis of a subsequent correctly taken specimen of urine.

HELD: "… the sergeant is entitled to change his mind as to the type of specimen to be required … That right … continues up to the time at which the blood sample, if it be a sample of blood, is actually taken. The procedure is … a continuing process and it crystallises only when a sample is actually obtained … what section 7 requires is that the person who is at the police station and whose conduct is being investigated shall provide a sample. He is required by section 7(1) to provide it, and if no blood is actually given he has not done that which section 7(1) requires.

"Once blood is given then, of course, the right of the officer to change his mind about the nature of the sample to be given has come to an end, because the suspect has complied with section 7(1) and … there is no obligation on him to provide a specimen of urine."

The answer to the question was "no". Appeal allowed.

See also *Hayes v DPP* [1994] RTR 163, [1993] Crim LR 966, 12 March 1993, QBD (DC) – a "statutory option" case under s 8(2), Road Traffic Act 1988 (now repealed; see page v), where it was held that the investigating officer, having decided that the specimen would be of blood, was free to change his mind and choose a specimen of urine instead. The fact that the officer did not, when indicating that the replacement specimen would be of blood, say that the specimen would be taken by a doctor unless the doctor considered there were medical reasons for not taking blood, did not invalidate the procedure.

DPP v Palmer (Carlton Lloyd)

Unreported, CO 4566/96, 21 March 1997, QBD (DC)

It is a matter of fact and degree whether a warning of the consequences of failure to provide should be repeated if there is a delay; in the circumstances of this case, the warning should have been repeated. See also Edmond v DPP, page 115, where, on the facts, there was no need to repeat the warning.

Police required a motorist to provide a specimen of breath for a roadside breath test; it was positive. The motorist was arrested and taken to the police station. The statutory warning in s 7(7), Road Traffic Act 1988 (that failure to provide may render the subject liable to prosecution) was given. He was required to provide specimens of breath for analysis. He did so, but the breath analysis device then broke down. The officer conducting the procedure therefore took the motorist some 6 miles to another police station to use the breath analysis device there. At the second police station, the statutory warning was not repeated; two further specimens of breath were given.

The motorist submitted to the magistrates that the failure to give the warning at the second police station invalidated the procedure and rendered inadmissible the analysis of the specimens given there. The magistrates found that the chain of events had been broken by the transfer to the second police station and that the procedure should have been started *de novo*. They dismissed the information. The prosecutor appealed.

QUESTION(S) FOR THE COURT: Whether it is right as a point of law in deciding that after the operator of an approved breath testing device in a police station had a reasonable belief that such device was not reliable, that operator should repeat the statutory warning required by s 7(7), Road Traffic Act 1988 before requiring further specimens of breath for analysis when using another approved breath testing device in a different police station and that such failure to repeat the statutory warning rendered the specimens of breath subsequently obtained inadmissible in evidence.

HELD: "… Here we have a time lapse of 39 minutes and a topographical distance of six miles between two police stations. This is not a case where no warning was given; … a warning was given. The question is whether it was sufficient in all the circumstances. This is … a matter of fact and degree …

"… [T]he Justices considered the right point. They decided, as a question of fact and degree, on the particular facts of the case as they found, having heard the evidence, that the warning in this case was insufficient and did not operate on the mind of the then defendant at the time when he was requested to give further samples at [the second police station].

"For my part, I am not prepared to say that that decision was perverse."

Appeal dismissed.

DPP v Ward (Andrew Stuart)

Unreported, CO/3281/97, 12 February 1998, QBD (DC)

In deciding whether the warning (of the consequences of failure to provide) was given before breath specimens were provided, the sequence of events is more important than the accuracy of the timing.

A motorist had been charged with driving with excess alcohol in breath, contrary to s 5(1)(a), Road Traffic Act 1988.

At the hearing, a statement of the officer who administered the breath testing procedure was admitted in evidence. It recited that the warning required by s 7(7), Road Traffic Act 1988 (of the consequences of failure to provide specimens) had been given at 01.55 hours, but the test record from the breath analysis device showed that the first specimen of breath was given at 01.54 hours. The magistrates concluded that the specimen had been taken before the warning was given, and found the results of the breath test inadmissible. They dismissed the charge. The prosecutor appealed.

QUESTION(S) FOR THE COURT: Whether the justices were entitled to acquit on the basis that there was admissible evidence that the warning which must be given pursuant to s 7(7), Road Traffic Act 1988 may have been given after the respondent provided specimens of breath.

HELD: "… if one reads [the officer's] statement apart from the test record one sees that the sequence of events that she describes is that the warning was given (allegedly at 01:55) and that the encoding of the accused's details and the commencement of the test procedure took place thereafter (allegedly at 01:56) … it is the sequence of events which matters for the purpose of any submissions about the warning, not the accuracy of the timing.

"… So far as sequence is concerned, it seems to me manifest from the totality of the evidence … that [the officer] intended to convey that the test was started after the warning had been given. I do not think that any other reading of the written evidence was open to the magistrates … I do not think it was open to the magistrates to regard the small discrepancy in the timings shown on the printout and those shown in handwriting [in the statement] as providing material from which the magistrates could conclude that the warning might not [have] been given until after the first specimen had been provided. Much the most likely explanation for the differences in precise timing is that [the officer's] watch had not been synchronised with the machine, or because she misread her watch or because she misread the machine."

Appeal allowed.

DPP v Jackson; Stanley v DPP

[1999] 1 AC 406, [1998] 3 WLR 514, [1998] 3 All ER 769, [1998] RTR 397, 29 July 1998, HL

With certain exceptions, the requirements in DPP v Warren (page 75) are not mandatory in the sense that non-compliance should lead to acquittal. The exceptions are: (1) in a s 7(3) case (mandatory requirement for specimen of blood or urine), the warning of the risk of prosecution for failure to provide; (2) in a s 7(3) case, the statement of reason why breath specimens cannot be taken or used; ((3) concerned s 8(2), Road Traffic Act 1988 (lower breath reading no more than 50 μg alcohol in 100 ml breath giving rise to the "driver's option" – repealed, with effect from 10 April 2015, by s 52 and Sch 11, Deregulation Act 2015) and is not considered here.) The driver must understand the role of the doctor and should be asked whether there are any medical reasons why a specimen could not or should not be taken.

In *Jackson*, a motorist had been charged with failing without reasonable excuse to provide a specimen of blood for analysis, contrary to s 7(6), Road Traffic Act 1988. He had been stopped by police who saw that his eyes were red and glazed and noticed his speech was slurred. They arrested him on suspicion of having driven while unfit through drink or drugs. At the police station, he was examined by a doctor, whose opinion was that his symptoms were consistent with having taken drugs. The sergeant conducting the procedure then requested a sample of blood or urine, warning of the consequences of refusal; the motorist refused. He was warned for a second time and asked if he had any representations whether the sample should be of blood or urine, and again refused. The sergeant asked if there was any reason why a specimen could not be taken, adding that his only right to object to giving blood and to give urine instead would be for a medical reason to be determined by a doctor. The motorist replied, "I don't like needles but I'm not giving anything anyway". He was convicted by justices and appealed to the Divisional Court, which allowed the appeal. The prosecutor appealed further.

The case of *Stanley* concerned s 8(2), Road Traffic Act 1988 (lower breath reading no more than 50 µg alcohol in 100 ml breath giving rise to the "driver's option" – repealed, with effect from 10 April 2015, by s 52 and Sch 11, Deregulation Act 2015) and is not considered here.

CERTIFIED QUESTION: *Jackson*: To what extent if at all should the guidance in *DPP v Warren* as to the procedure to be followed when a request is made for a sample of blood under s 7(4), Road Traffic Act 1988 be applied beyond the issue arising in that case of whether the driver should be invited to express a preference for giving blood or urine? If that guidance does not apply other than in respect of that issue, what on the true construction of the Road Traffic Act 1988 is the procedure to be followed when a request is made under ss 7(3), (4) (and 8(2)), Road Traffic Act 1988?

HELD: "… The principal difficulty which has arisen following … *Warren's* case is that different approaches have been taken in two lines of cases to the question whether the requirements stated [in *Warren*] are mandatory, so that a failure to observe a requirement must lead to an acquittal, or whether a breach of a requirement is not necessarily a bar to a conviction …

"… Section 7(4) provides that if a specimen other than a specimen of breath may be required under that section it is for the police officer to decide whether the specimen will be blood or urine. But section 11(4) provides that the specimen of blood is to be taken by a doctor. In addition the right of the police officer to choose whether the specimen will be of blood or urine is subject to the qualification that if a medical reason is raised why a specimen of blood cannot or should not be taken, the issue is to be decided by a doctor and not by the police officer …

"… the guidance given in *Warren's* case should be regarded as having the following effect. The requirements stated by Lord Bridge, with three exceptions, are not to be treated as mandatory but as indicating the matters of which a driver should be aware so that … he may know the role of a doctor in the taking of a specimen of blood and in determining any medical objections which he may raise to the giving of such a specimen. The requirements, constituting the three exceptions, which should be regarded as mandatory so that non-compliance should lead to an acquittal are:

(1) in a section 7(3) case the warning as to the risk of prosecution required by section 7(7);

(2) in a section 7(3) case the statement of the reason under that subsection why breath specimens cannot be taken or used; and

(3) [concerned s 8(2), now repealed; see above].

"… what is necessary is that the driver should be aware (whether or not he is told by the police officer) of the role of the doctor so that he does not suffer prejudice.

Therefore if the driver appreciates that a specimen of blood will be taken by a doctor and not by a police officer, the charge should not be dismissed by the justices because the police officer failed to tell the driver that the specimen would be taken by a doctor.

"Accordingly in relation to the *Warren* requirements there will be two issues for the justices to decide. The first issue is whether the matters set out in the *Warren* formula … have been brought to the attention of the driver by the police officer. The second issue [concerned s 8(2) cases only].

"… there are two respects in which I would word the requirements stated by Lord Bridge in a different way. (1) I consider that there is nothing in the wording of the relevant subsections and there are no considerations of fairness which require a police officer to ask the driver if there are any non-medical reasons why a specimen of blood cannot or should not be taken … Therefore I am of opinion that in Lord Bridge's speech … in relation to a section 7(3) case the words 'ask the driver if there are any reasons why a specimen cannot or should not be taken from him by a doctor' should read 'ask the driver if there are any medical reasons why a specimen cannot or should not be taken from him by a doctor.' (2) [concerned s 8(2) cases only].

"In *Jackson* … the Divisional Court was right to reject the defendant's argument that the statement … 'I don't like needles' raised a potential medical reason for not providing a specimen of blood. It was a question of fact … and the Divisional Court was entitled to find on the facts … that the police officer was not under an obligation to investigate further … there is no need for a police officer to ask whether there are non-medical reasons for a blood specimen not being given. Moreover the defendant made it entirely clear to the police officer that he was not going to give a specimen of blood or urine, and therefore the defendant suffered no prejudice … ."

Appeal in *Jackson* allowed.

On the importance attached to the suspect's understanding that any blood specimen would be taken by a medical practitioner, see also the following cases, all based on the "statutory option" under s 8(2), Road Traffic Act 1988 (now repealed; see above):

- *Hayes v DPP* [1994] RTR 163, [1993] Crim LR 966, 12 March 1993, QBD (DC): The fact that the officer did not, when indicating that the replacement specimen would be of blood, say that the specimen would be taken by a doctor unless the doctor considered there were medical reasons for not taking blood, did not invalidate the procedure under s 8(2).
- *Robinson (Dena) v DPP* [1997] RTR 403, 23 April 1996, QBD (DC): Where the officer put the option without explaining that any blood specimen would be taken by a doctor and that the only right to object would be for medical reasons to be determined by the doctor, in the circumstances of the case, the motorist was not prejudiced and there was no flaw in the procedure.

- *Chatelard v DPP* [1997] RTR 362, 11 October 1996, QBD (DC): Where the driver was not told that any blood specimen would be taken by a doctor, and there was no finding whether or not that prejudiced him, his appeal against conviction succeeded.
- *DPP v Orchard* unreported, CO/2706/2000, 17 October 2000, QBD (Admin): There was nothing in the circumstances of this case to suggest that the driver was prejudiced by not being asked whether there were any reasons why a blood specimen could not or should not be taken by a doctor.

Maudling v DPP

Unreported, CO 2565/96, 4 December 1996, QBD (DC)

On the facts of this case (suspect violent and drunk, requirement for a specimen incomplete), the requirement for a breath test had not been made and it was unlawful to arrest him for failing to provide.

A motorist had been charged with assaulting a police constable in the execution of his duty. He had parked his car at an unusual angle; police officers saw him about to enter his mother's home; he was very drunk. One of the officers began to ask him for a breath specimen, but the defendant interrupted him by shouting and swearing; he then became violent. The officer arrested him, under s 6(5)(b), Road Traffic Act 1988, for failing to provide a specimen. The defendant continued to be violent and abusive. He was not told the reason for his arrest at the time because of his behaviour. He head-butted the officer when the officer was trying to put him into the police car, and that assault formed the basis of the charge.

The magistrates found that the officers had had reasonable cause to suspect that the defendant had alcohol in his body and that he had been driving; they used reasonable force in effecting the arrest; the reason for his arrest, although not given at the time, was given as soon as was reasonably practicable; the officers did what was reasonable and there was no other reasonable and immediate alternative. They convicted the defendant of assault. He appealed.

HELD: "… The issue in this case was whether or not the constable had required the Appellant to provide a specimen for a breath test. It is not necessary for the word 'require' to be used. All that is necessary is that the constable's language could fairly be said to amount to a requirement … The Justices found as a fact that [the constable] was arresting him for this reason and that [the constable] 'had in mind to request a breath test'… The officer apparently never went beyond saying: 'I suspect you have driven this car with an alcohol level above the …'

"It follows, therefore, that [the constable] did not request or even begin to request a specimen of breath. In those circumstances, in my judgment, the arrest must be unlawful. It follows … that the police officer was not acting in the execution of his duty … ."

Appeal allowed.

Clayton v DPP

Unreported, CO/2633/97, 19 October 1998, QBD (DC)

It is sufficient for an officer to say that breath specimens cannot be taken because a breath analysis device is not available; there is no need to elaborate further.

A motorist had been charged with driving with excess alcohol, contrary to s 5, Road Traffic Act 1998. At the police station, the sergeant administering the procedure told the defendant that breath specimens could not be taken because a breath analysis device was not available, and that he required a specimen of blood or urine for a laboratory test. Blood samples were then taken and revealed excess alcohol. The motorist was convicted and appealed.

QUESTION(S) FOR THE COURT: Whether the justices were right to hold that the evidence of the sergeant complied with *DPP v Warren*, page 75.

HELD: "The simple point that is taken is that the officer … failed to give the defendant sufficient information as to the reason why … specimens of breath could not be taken by using the Intoximeter machine …

"… [The appellant] submits that it was not enough for the police officer to say that an instrument was not available, but he had to go on and give more detailed reasons as to why the machine was not available and generally to give further and better particulars of the unavailability or non-functioning of the machine. This, he submits, was necessary in order that the appellant could understand his rights and if necessary challenge the statement of the officer …

"… Lord Hutton has defined [in *DPP v Jackson; Stanley v DPP*, page 79] as a mandatory requirement in the present context only that there should be a statement of the reason under the subsection why breath specimens cannot be taken or used (in addition, of course, to the prosecution warning) … It would seem to me to be a regrettable and retrogressive step to read into what Lord Hutton has said something which he did not say …

"… the criticism made of the procedure adopted in this case is unsustainable … ."

Appeal dismissed.

Burke v DPP

[1999] RTR 387, 31 March 1999, QBD (DC)

To prove that a requirement for a specimen for laboratory testing has been made, it is not necessary to show that the officer specified that blood or urine would be required, or asked whether the driver would be willing to provide the specimen.

A motorist had been involved in a road traffic accident and, at hospital, the doctor gave an officer permission to require specimens. The motorist refused to supply a breath specimen. The officer, following a *pro forma*, then required a specimen of blood or urine; warned the motorist that refusal would make her liable to prosecution; explained that he, the officer, had the right to choose the type of specimen; and asked if there was any reason why a specimen of blood could not or should not be taken. She replied "No, no, no", questioned the legality of the request and mentioned the European Court of Justice. The officer took this as a refusal and did not put the rest of the question, in which he would have given his decision on the type of specimen and a further reminder of the consequences of refusal, and requested the chosen type of specimen.

The motorist was charged with failing to provide a specimen for analysis, contrary to s 7, Road Traffic Act 1988. At the trial, she submitted there was no case to answer because the officer had not put the second part of the question. The magistrates rejected that submission and convicted. She appealed.

QUESTION(S) FOR THE COURT: (1) Whether the procedure in s 7, Road Traffic Act 1988 is complied with if the police officer: (i) fails to specify to the defendant whether a sample of blood or urine is to be required; and (ii) fails to ask the defendant whether she is willing to give a specimen.

HELD: "… the appellant submits that a requirement is not made of the driver for the purposes of [s 7] until the officer has decided which category of specimen to ask for, communicated his decision to the driver, and then enquired of the driver whether he is willing to provide that specimen …

"… the *prima facie* evidence of a requirement, which was sufficient for the purpose of section 7, consisted of the officer's words 'I require you to provide a specimen of blood or urine for laboratory test.'

"… [The appellant's] answer: 'No, no, no' followed by the fact that she went on to question the legality of the request and to make reference to the European Court of Justice is said to constitute *prima facie* evidence of 'refusal' and therefore of 'failure' … those words, given the context in which they were spoken, were capable of amounting to *prima facie* evidence of refusal …

"… to prove the offence under section 7(6), the prosecution must prove that the driver was required to provide a specimen in pursuance of section 7. Whether the driver was so required is a question of fact. It is not essential in order to prove the making of the requirement for the police officer either (1) to specify which category of specimen, blood or urine, he required or (2) to ask the driver whether he or she was willing to provide that specimen."

Appeal dismissed.

Cawley (Stephen) v DPP

[2001] EWHC Admin 83, 24 January 2001, QBD (DC)

Although the officer had not endorsed on the pro forma his decision to require a blood specimen, the defendant had failed to provide specimens and was guilty of the offence. Where the defendant claimed he had not been driving and the prosecution did not call evidence on the point, disqualification from driving is discretionary not mandatory.

A motorist had been charged with failing to provide a specimen of blood for analysis, contrary to s 7(6), Road Traffic Act 1988. A reliable breath testing device was not available. The officer conducting the procedure therefore required a specimen of blood or urine, reading the following words from a *pro forma*: "I require you to provide me with a specimen of blood or urine which, in the case of blood, will be taken by a doctor. It is for me to decide which it will be unless a doctor is of the opinion that for medical reasons a specimen of blood cannot or should not be taken, in which case it will be of urine. If I decide the specimen shall be of blood, your only right to object and to give urine instead will be for medical reasons. You will be supplied with part of the specimen if you so require. The other part will be sent to a forensic laboratory for analysis. I warn you that failure to provide a specimen will render you liable to prosecution." He then asked, "Are there any reasons why a specimen of blood cannot or should not be taken by a doctor?" The next question on the *pro forma* was, "Could the reasons given amount to medical reasons?" Both were answered "no" on the form. The motorist refused to supply a specimen. The police officer then entered on the *pro forma*: "Detainee refused to provide any samples of blood".

The motorist was convicted by the Crown Court and appealed further.

QUESTION(S) FOR THE COURT: Whether there was any evidence: (1) upon which a reasonable bench properly directing itself could have held that the appellant had been lawfully required to supply a specimen of blood for analysis; (2) to prove that the appellant was driving.

HELD: "[On (1)] 9. … there is no requirement on the police officer to fill in [a *pro forma*] …

"11. … for there to be a conviction for failing to provide a specimen, there must have been a requirement by the police that such a specimen be provided. …

"17. … It seems … abundantly clear on the findings of fact made by the Crown Court that it was proper to infer that a proper and lawful requirement was made. In the first place, … the police sergeant read out the paragraph which did require a specimen of blood or urine and did give a warning regarding the failure to provide a specimen …

"18. … he then proceeded to ask … whether there were any medical reasons why blood could not be taken, and the reply to both questions was 'no'.

"19. … there was an election for blood and a request for blood, although that was not endorsed on the form as the sergeant was not familiar with it. The Appellant admitted in evidence that he had refused to give a sample of blood …

"21. Looking at all the circumstances … and the facts found …, it seems to me impossible to suggest that there was no lawful requirement within the meaning of the legislation. I would therefore dismiss that part of the appeal.

"[On (2)] 22. … If he was not driving the question of disqualification becomes discretionary as opposed to mandatory. The court imposed mandatory disqualification for the minimum period … If he was not proved to have been driving then the question of disqualification would have been entirely within the discretion of the court.

"23. The evidence … was: 'At the police station the Appellant was under investigation because he was suspected of driving a motor vehicle … The Appellant gave evidence that he had not been driving but another named person had. He called no evidence in support of that contention. [W]e disbelieved him.'

"24. [The prosecutor] did not call any direct evidence as to whether the defendant was driving or not and, in these circumstances, there was no evidence before the court to justify them in reaching the conclusion they did, bearing in mind the criminal burden and standard of proof … ."

Appeal allowed in part.

Beatrice v DPP

[2004] EWHC 2416 (Admin), 6 October 2004, QBD (DC)

The warning of the consequences of failure to provide must be given by the officer, not by a doctor. Where the case stated contained no finding or inference that the officer gave the warning, the conviction had to be overturned.

A motorist had been convicted of driving with excess alcohol, contrary to s 5(1)(a), Road Traffic Act 1988. Following a road traffic accident, he had refused to take a roadside breath test. He was taken to hospital, where the officer conducting the case asked the hospital doctor if the police surgeon could attend to take a blood specimen. The hospital doctor agreed. When the police surgeon arrived, the defendant at first refused to provide a specimen, but the doctor reminded him that refusal would mean an automatic ban and he consented. Analysis of the specimen revealed excess alcohol.

In the magistrates' court, the officer referred to the "drink drive hospital procedure booklet", explaining that he had worked through all the questions in it. The book would have contained the warning in s 7(7), Road Traffic Act 1988, that failure to provide may render the subject liable to prosecution. Another officer confirmed that the correct procedure had been followed.

The motorist appealed against conviction.

QUESTION(S) FOR THE COURT: Whether the court was right to hold that the appellant had been warned of prosecution on the basis of advice supplied to him by the police surgeon.

HELD: "11. … a constable must warn a suspect of the consequences of failure to provide a specimen … A doctor cannot fulfil the function in place of a constable. Thus if the justices acted on the basis that [the police surgeon] gave the necessary warning that is simply wrong in law. The requirements of the statutory procedure must be strictly observed and a failure to warn in accordance with subsection (7) would lead to inevitable acquittal …

"16. … nowhere … in the findings, nor in [the question for the court] do the justices refer to the police evidence as to the procedure and the booklet, nowhere do they suggest that they have drawn an inference from all the evidence that [the police officer] gave the necessary warning. …

"19. … the book itself was never produced in evidence …

"26. … I cannot say that on the evidence as presented a finding that the officer gave the warning would have been inevitable. If it was inevitable it is somewhat surprising that the justices did not make it. I am, therefore, driven very reluctantly to the conclusion that this conviction must be set aside."

Appeal allowed.

DPP v Coulter

[2005] EWHC 1533 (Admin), 29 June 2005, QBD (DC)

Failing to follow the guidance in the pro forma MG DD/A does not necessarily render a requirement for a specimen unlawful. See also McKeon v DPP, page 213, where the mouthpiece was not kept; Scheiner v DPP, page 296, where a mobile phone may have been on in the breath analysis room; Ivic v DPP, page 664, where a police radio was on in the breath analysis room; and DPP v Chajed, page 673, where the officer did not ask whether the suspect had brought up anything from his stomach within the preceding 20 minutes.

A motorist had been charged with failing without reasonable excuse to provide two specimens of breath for analysis, contrary to s 7(6), Road Traffic Act 1988. He had been stopped and a roadside breath test was positive. At the police station, during the breath testing procedure, he was asked whether he had eaten anything. He replied that he "might have had a tic-tac". The advice to police officers on the *pro forma* MG DD/A used in the drink-drive procedure was to wait 20 minutes before testing a suspect who has (*inter alia*) eaten anything. The officer did not wait 20 minutes. It was argued before the magistrates that this failure rendered unlawful the requirement to provide specimens. The magistrates found that the officer should have waited; that he could not prove the consumption of a tic-tac would not affect the breath test; that he had not been trained in the consequences of failing to wait 20 minutes; and that he could cite no authority that the 20-minute delay was not mandatory. They dismissed the charge. The prosecutor appealed.

QUESTION(S) FOR THE COURT: Whether the officer's failure to follow the procedure in Form MG DD/A rendered his request for a sample unlawful.

HELD: "10. There is nothing in [s 7, Road Traffic Act 1988] to indicate that a requirement is unlawful if guidance in the form … is not followed. Even in the absence of authority it would seem to me that that is the clear answer to the case.

"11. [After quoting from *DPP v Smith*, page 58] … If there is a failure to follow the guidance it is possible, in certain circumstances, that that might affect the reliability of a specimen that was, in fact, provided. There are limited circumstances in which a challenge to the reliability of a specimen that is provided can arise. That, in my view, is not relevant here. No specimen was provided. There was a failure to provide a specimen.

"12. In my judgment the Justices were wholly wrong to regard the argument that had been advanced as of any relevance. They were wrong to conclude that there was no case to answer."

Appeal allowed.

R v Bryan

[2008] EWCA Crim 1568, [2009] RTR 4, 22 July 2008, CA (Crim)

Where the judge erred in directing the jury, but the errors did not go to the point at issue, which was whether or not the motorist had been warned of the consequences of failing to provide a specimen, the errors were immaterial.

A motorist had been charged with, *inter alia*, causing death by careless driving while over the limit, contrary to s 3A(1)(b), Road Traffic Act 1988. His vehicle had overturned, killing one of his two passengers. He was taken to hospital. A police surgeon took a blood specimen, which showed excess alcohol. At his trial, the motorist said that he had not been warned of the consequences of failing to provide a blood specimen, as required by s 7(7). The hospital doctor gave evidence that he could not remember being asked, on this or any other occasion, whether a person was fit to provide specimens. On the basis of this, the defence argued that if the officer had not obtained the doctor's consent, it was likely that he had not properly followed the procedure and had not warned the motorist. Breach of s 9 was not argued. The judge directed the jury that the prosecution did not have to prove that the hospital doctor's consent was obtained before a specimen of blood was taken; while it was good practice to do so, if it was not done, it was more likely that there had been no warning. The defendant was convicted and appealed.

GROUND(S) OF APPEAL: That the judge misdirected the jury in telling them that the prosecution did not have to prove as a matter of law that the medical practitioner in immediate charge of the appellant had been notified of the proposed statutory requirement to give blood and had been asked for his consent.

HELD: "28. The judge's observation to the jury that the prosecution do not as a matter of law have to prove [the consent of the doctor having charge of the suspect], that the consent required is that of the doctor who took the sample and that obtaining the hospital doctor's consent was good practice only, was erroneous in two respects. In the first place the requirement is mandatory and not mere good practice. Secondly, what is required is not the treating doctor's consent but that he should have been notified of the proposal to take blood and not have objected. …

"29. It is implicit in the jury's verdict that they accepted the [investigating officer's] evidence; they were satisfied he complied with the requirement of s 7(7). In these circumstances, … the judge's errors were immaterial."

Appeal dismissed. Appeal against sentence also dismissed.

R (Cox) v DPP

[2009] EWHC 3595 (Admin), [2010] RTR 18, 18 November 2009, QBD (Admin)

The justices erred in law in finding that it was not necessary to give the statutory warning of liability to prosecution for failure to provide a specimen. The prosecution was not allowed to have a new trial on the basis of evidence which could and should have been deployed at the first trial.

See also Cox v DPP [2010] EWHC 3589 (Admin), 7 December 2010, QBD (DC), where the motorist's application for a costs order was rejected.

A motorist had been charged with driving with excess alcohol, contrary to s 5(1), Road Traffic Act 1988. In its closing submissions, the defence raised, for the first time, that the investigating officer had not warned the defendant that failure to provide specimens would render him liable to prosecution, as required by s 7(7), Road Traffic Act 1988, arguing that the specimens were therefore inadmissible. The prosecutor declined the justices' invitation to recall the officer, saying that there had been no need for the warning as the defendant had been fully compliant with the procedure. The justices convicted the defendant, and he appealed.

QUESTION(S) FOR THE COURT: Whether the justices had erred in law in finding that it was unnecessary to give the warning.

HELD: "15. … The justices were in error, since it is clear that s. 7(7) is in mandatory terms …

"22. There is now a very clear obligation on the defence to make its defence and the issue it raises clear to the prosecution and to the court at an early stage. …

"24. … there is nothing in the noted evidence which shows that [counsel for the defendant] raised the s.7(7) point with the police officer. However, the point was squarely, if not fairly, raised in her closing submissions. At that stage, the prosecution could have recalled [the officer], or could have asked for an adjournment to consider the position. The court, too, should have been alive to the risk that the prosecution had been taken by surprise and should have been aware of its case management powers to ensure that justice was done to both parties.

"[On the Crown's argument that there was evidence that the warning had been given and that the decision of the justices should be quashed allowing the Crown to apply for a new trial] 25. … What … was impermissible was for the prosecution to make a bad submission of law, fail to call relevant evidence, accept in this court that the decision is, for that reason, flawed, but to contend that the prosecution should nevertheless be allowed to have a new trial on the basis of evidence which could and should have been deployed at the first trial.

"[The exercise of the discretion to order a new trial] 26. … will depend on the circumstances of an individual case. It will most often be exercised where there has been some misconduct or infraction of the rules of procedure by the defence which has resulted, or may have resulted, in unfairness or injustice. However, … this is not such a case."

Case remitted to the justices to acquit.

Bielecki v DPP

[2011] EWHC 2245 (Admin), 23 August 2011, QBD (Admin)

A court may properly infer, in the absence of evidence to the contrary, that a requirement for specimens, and the statutory warning of the consequences of failing to provide, which were interpreted by an accredited interpreter, were understood by the suspect.

A motorist was charged with failing without reasonable excuse to supply specimens of breath, contrary to s 7(6), Road Traffic Act 1988. He was a Polish national who spoke little or no English. The procedure at the police station was conducted with an interpreter in the usual way. The officer conducting the procedure told the motorist that she required him to provide two specimens of breath, and warned him more than once that if he did not provide them he might be prosecuted, but did not circle "yes" or "no" at the end of A14 on MG DD/A (the requirement and warnings, and the question, do you agree?). The magistrates were satisfied that the testing procedure had been properly explained via the interpreter and that the motorist understood the requirement. They convicted; the motorist appealed.

QUESTION(S) FOR THE COURT: Whether the magistrates were entitled to find: (i) that there had been a valid requirement to provide specimens of breath for analysis; (ii) that the appellant had been given the warning required by s 7(7); and (iii) that the appellant had no reasonable excuse for failing to provide.

HELD: "22. The short issue is whether the justices were entitled … in the absence of any direct evidence from the interpreter, to infer that what was said … (they being satisfied so that they were sure that [the officer] had indeed made the relevant requests in English) had been translated properly by the interpreter and understood by the Appellant. [The appellant argues] that no such inference was permissible and that the justices needed to hear direct confirmation from the interpreter before being able to come to that conclusion. …

"27. … I do not see that there is anything in the ruling [in *R v Attard* 43 Crim App R 90, cited by counsel for the appellant] that negates the proposition that a court may draw the inference, if the evidence supports it, that someone being asked to do something in a police station by a police officer with the assistance of an accredited interpreter of the relevant language has been asked the correct question, understands it and also the consequences of not responding to it. Here there is no evidence at all that the interpreter, for example, said to the officers 'I am sorry, but he does not understand what you are asking him to do'. If that had been said, one could see that concerns might arise, but no such evidence was given and, as I have said, there was other evidence available to the justices that suggested that the Appellant knew and understood what was happening."

The answers to the questions were "yes". Appeal dismissed.

For other cases concerning the statutory warning, see *Whitfield v DPP*, page 104 – where the officer had followed the *pro forma*, justices were entitled, in the absence of challenge, to use their own knowledge of the form to find that the warning had been given; *Edmond v DPP*, page 115, where there was no need to repeat the warning when inviting further breath specimens because the analysis of the first two was not satisfactory.

11. MEDICAL REASONS WHY A BLOOD SPECIMEN CANNOT OR SHOULD NOT BE TAKEN

See s 7(4A), Road Traffic Act 1988 – a specimen of blood is not to be required if the medical practitioner who is asked to take it is of the opinion that, for medical reasons, it cannot or should not be taken, or if a health care professional who is asked to take it is of the like opinion and there is no contrary opinion from a medical practitioner. See also the cases concerning hospital patients (pages 98 to 107); Jubb v DPP, page 341 – where the suspect says there are no medical reasons for not requiring a blood specimen, the officer is entitled to require such a specimen; and DPP v Camp, page 257, on the distinction between medical reasons and reasonable excuse.

Grix v Chief Constable of Kent

[1987] RTR 193, 12 March 1987, QBD (DC)

If a driver refuses to provide a blood specimen, the officer is under no duty to investigate the reason or to call a doctor to advise whether there may be a medical reason why a blood specimen cannot or should not be taken. Offering a urine specimen in response to a requirement for a blood specimen is not a special reason not to disqualify.

A motorist had been charged with failing without reasonable excuse to provide a specimen of blood for a laboratory test, contrary to s 8(7), Road Traffic Act 1972 as substituted by s 25 and Sch 8, Transport Act 1981. At the police station, he was unable to provide breath specimens because of an injury to his mouth; he was therefore required to provide a blood specimen. He refused, saying "No, specimen of urine – no blood".

The justices found, *inter alia*, that the officer was entitled to select whether the alternative sample be of blood or urine and was not required to inquire the reason for refusing to supply blood; that since no medical reason had been mentioned, the officer was not required to call a doctor; and that the facts did not amount to special reasons for not disqualifying. They convicted the motorist, who appealed against both conviction and sentence.

QUESTION(S) FOR THE COURT: (1) Whether a police officer, when making a request for a specimen of blood under s 8(3) and (4), Road Traffic Act 1972 as likewise substituted, which was refused, was required to: (a) ask why a sample of blood was being refused; (b) arrange for a medical practitioner to attend to determine whether a sample of blood could or should not be provided. (2) Whether a defendant who was so required to provide a sample of blood but refused, offering instead a sample of urine, could contend that that was a special reason for not being disqualified under s 93(1), Road Traffic Act 1972.

HELD: "... it is perfectly apparent from the bland nature of the refusal ... that no medical issue had been raised. The officer was not put on inquiry, and I can see no basis for implying a duty on the officer to investigate whether or not the driver desired to raise such an issue.

"[A proposition that a police officer is nevertheless] under a duty in any event to arrange for the attendance of a medical practitioner ... would clearly fly in the face of the decision in *Johnson v West Yorkshire Metropolitan Police* [see page 98].

"... if it were a special reason that a driver ... offered one sample even though he maintained his refusal to provide the particular specimen which the officer was entitled to require, then it would inevitably be a special reason in every such case. This would be inconsistent with the law which provides for a conviction when, as here, the police officer, in the proper exercise of his discretion, requires a particular specimen ... ."

Appeal dismissed.

Wade v DPP

[1996] RTR 177, 6 February 1994, QBD (DC)

The driver's statement that he took tablets could amount to a medical reason why a blood specimen could not or should not be taken; the officer should have considered it. See also Davies (Gordon Edward) v DPP, page 28, where the motorist said he had "haemophiliac tendencies".

A motorist had been charged with driving with excess alcohol in blood, contrary to s 5(1)(a), Road Traffic Act 1988. At the police station, no reliable breath testing device was available and the sergeant administering the procedure therefore required an alternative specimen, under s 7(3)(b), Road Traffic Act 1988 (reliable device not available). He asked the motorist if he had any preference between giving blood or urine; the motorist preferred to give blood. The sergeant asked if there was any reason why a specimen of blood could not or should not be taken, to which the motorist replied "I do take tablets". The sergeant went on to ask if he would supply a specimen of blood; the motorist agreed; blood was taken and it revealed excess alcohol.

At the hearing, the motorist contended that the reply "I do take tablets" was a medical reason for not providing a blood specimen; that the sergeant should have asked for a urine specimen or allowed the doctor to decide whether the specimen should be of blood or urine; and that the blood analysis was therefore inadmissible in evidence.

The justices rejected this contention and convicted. The motorist appealed.

QUESTION(S) FOR THE COURT: (1) Whether the sergeant should have required urine having heard the defendant's reasons why a specimen of blood could not or should not be taken; (2) whether there was any evidence to show that the sergeant made an informed decision when he demanded blood; (3) whether the justices were right to hold that the sergeant had performed the correct procedure laid down in s 7, Road Traffic Act 1988.

HELD: "… The fact that a man may prefer to give blood is not relevant to the question whether there is a medical reason why he should not or could not give it …

"… Why should [the answer 'I do take tablets'] have been mentioned at all …, other than as a possible reason why a specimen of blood could not or should not be taken? … it must be taken as a representation as to which specimen should be taken, albeit the defendant was also saying that he would have personally preferred to give blood … there was no evidence before the justices that [the sergeant] took into account the answer given or gave consideration to whether it should be treated as a medical reason.

"… the officer had … to consider whether the reason proffered was capable of being a medical reason. On the face of it, it was … but in the absence of any medical evidence it is impossible to know."

The answer to question (1) was that the sergeant should not have required urine without consideration of the answer "I do take tablets"; the answer to questions (2) and (3) was "no". Appeal allowed.

DPP v Wythe

[1996] RTR 137, 19 July 1995, QBD (DC)

The officer should have considered whether the driver's statement that he was a diabetic could have been a medical reason why a blood specimen could not or should not be taken.

A motorist had been charged with failing without reasonable excuse to provide a specimen of blood for analysis, contrary to s 7(6), Road Traffic Act 1988. A blood specimen had been required under s 7(3)(b) of the Act (reliable device not available). The officer conducting the procedure asked the motorist if there was any reason why a blood specimen could or should not be taken. He replied that he was a diabetic and needed two injections a day; he did not want other people to use needles on him. The officer, observing that the motorist had pierced ears and tattoos, proceeded to require the blood specimen. The motorist replied, "If you take it out of my finger, yes; if it is going to come out of my arm, no". The officer did not treat that as a refusal, but referred to a medical practitioner the question whether there was a medical reason why blood could or should not be taken. No evidence was given about what ensued.

At the hearing, the magistrate accepted a submission of no case to answer and dismissed the information. The prosecutor appealed.

QUESTION(S) FOR THE COURT: (a) Whether, where a constable acting under s 7(3) and (4), Road Traffic Act 1988 heard cogent representations that a specimen of blood should not be required because of an aversion to hypodermic needles, the constable should have referred to a police surgeon the issue of whether that amounted to a medical reason why blood could not or should not have been taken; (b) if the constable, without so referring, required a specimen of blood, whether that was a lawful requirement; and (c) if the requirement was lawful but the constable, on making it, received a reply capable of amounting to a refusal but again raising the possible medical reason and at that stage referred to a police surgeon for medical guidance, whether the Crown could rely on that reply as a refusal and secure a conviction without adducing evidence of what was subsequently said to the accused.

HELD: "... The defendant had raised an objection based on his medical condition which, on its face, was not particularly convincing but should have caused the constable to delay making his request for blood until a medical practitioner had expressed an opinion under section 7(4).

"... I do not accept that the words used by the defendant were, in fact and in law, a failure without reasonable excuse to provide a specimen of blood. The defendant was advancing reasons connected with his medical condition why he should not give a specimen of blood ... it was not for the constable to substitute his opinion for that of a medical practitioner ... The case stated is silent as to what happened, if anything, after the doctor had examined the defendant ...

"Whatever actually happened, it is plain ... the requirement to provide a specimen was, in the circumstances ... an unlawful request. The defendant's claim about the medical reasons for refusal was not rejected after due fulfilment of the procedures. He was thus deprived of his rights under the Act of 1988 and no requirements 'in pursuance of this section' had been made."

Appeal dismissed.

DPP v Gibbons (Stuart Michael)

[2001] EWHC 385 (Admin), (2001) 165 JP 812, 10 May 2001, QBD (Admin)

Where a doctor said the driver's condition might be due to some drug, and the driver told the officer, "You are not going to examine me", this did not amount to a possible medical reason why a specimen of blood could not or should not be taken.

A motorist had been charged with failing without reasonable excuse to provide a specimen of blood for analysis, contrary to s 7(6), Road Traffic Act 1988. A roadside breath test was negative, but the motorist was arrested under the Public Order Act 1986 and taken to the police station. A medical examiner was called; from the motorist's obstructive attitude, the doctor formed the view that he was probably under the influence of some drug. The officer therefore required a specimen of blood, saying: "As the doctor is of the opinion that you have a condition which might be due to drugs, I require you to provide a specimen of blood or urine which in the case of blood will be taken by a doctor. It is for me to decide which it will be unless a doctor is of the opinion that for medical reasons a specimen of blood cannot or should not be taken in which case it will be urine.

If I decide the specimen shall be of blood, your only right to object and to give urine instead will be for medical reasons. You will be supplied with part of the specimen if you so require. The other part will be sent to a forensic laboratory for analysis. I warn you that failure to provide a specimen will render you liable to prosecution. Are there any medical reasons why a specimen of blood cannot or should not be taken by a doctor?" The respondent replied, "You are not going to examine me". He gave no medical reason why he should not be required to provide a specimen of blood or urine. The officer did not ask for a specimen of urine.

The justices found that the doctor's opinion that the motorist's behaviour was due to some drug, coupled with his lack of consent which precluded the taking of a blood sample, together constituted a medical reason necessitating the officer to go on to require a urine specimen. The officer had not done so and the justices acquitted the motorist. The prosecutor appealed.

QUESTION(S) FOR THE COURT: Whether, in the course of an investigation into whether a person has committed an offence under s 4, Road Traffic Act 1988, a constable, having been advised by a medical practitioner that the condition of that person might be due to some drug, and that person having failed to consent to provide a specimen of blood, is obliged by s 7(4), Road Traffic Act 1988 also to require that person to provide a specimen of urine for a laboratory test.

HELD: "21. ... The [respondent's] answer here was: 'You are not going to examine me'. Since no further examination was being requested that answer did not offer any possible medical reason as to why a specimen of blood could not or should not be taken ... Moreover, there is no attempt by the respondent to put forward any medical reason to the medical practitioner. These factors lead irresistibly to the conclusion that no medical reason was being advanced ... as to why a specimen of blood could not or should not be taken. A refusal to be examined (without more) could not possibly amount to such a medical reason ... Whether the specimen is to be of blood or urine is to be decided by the constable, and not dictated by the preference of the suspect: see *DPP v Warren* [see page 75] ... ."

The answer to the question was "no". Appeal allowed.

Kinsella v DPP

[2002] EWHC 545 (Admin), 13 March 2002, QBD (DC)

Where a motorist said there was no medical reason why a blood specimen could not or should not be taken, but had with him tablets and a spray, the officer was not obliged to seek medical advice. Abnormal alcohol metabolism is not a special reason for not disqualifying.

A motorist had been charged with driving with excess alcohol, contrary to s 5(1)(a), Road Traffic Act 1988. Blood analysis revealed 105 mg alcohol in 100 ml blood. He at first pleaded guilty, then, having changed his solicitors, sought to change his plea, and to introduce an argument that there were special reasons for not disqualifying under s 34(1), Road Traffic Offenders Act 1988 in that, unknown to him, he had an abnormal alcohol metabolism, otherwise he would have been within the limit.

It was argued that the correct procedure had not been followed at the police station; the defendant had had in this possession unidentified tablets and a mouth spray; the sergeant had recognised the spray as for use in connection with a heart condition; the sergeant did not consult a doctor on whether or not there were medical reasons for not requiring a blood specimen.

The magistrate found that the motorist had been directly asked by the sergeant if there was any medical reason why a blood specimen should not be taken and had answered "no"; and the doctor who took the specimen certified that the motorist had not put forward any reason why blood should not be taken. The magistrate did not allow the motorist to change his plea and sentenced him. He appealed.

QUESTION(S) FOR THE COURT: (1) Whether the magistrate was right to decide that an abnormal alcohol metabolism cannot be a special reason for not disqualifying; (2) whether the fact that the custody record refers to mouth spray and tablets placed on the police officer an obligation to consult the doctor before deciding that any specimen to be provided would be one of blood; (3) whether it was unreasonable to refuse to give the appellant leave to vacate his plea of guilty.

HELD: "14. … [It is submitted] that, in the light of the late appearing material as to the use of the spray, it was not open to the officer merely to rely upon the answer given by the defendant when he said that there was no medical reason. The officer should … it is said, have taken into account the fact that tablets (of an unidentified nature) and a spray were found in the defendant's possession on arrest.

"17. … the defendant specifically said that there were no [medical] reasons. He did not seek to say that the tablets or spray in his possession gave rise to a medical reason, and the actual use of the spray, in the way which he described in his written statement, was a matter which … the … District Judge was … entitled to view with scepticism when exercising his discretion …

"19. … [On (1), it is argued] that the expert evidence gave rise to a special reason by virtue of the very rare medical condition from which the defendant suffers …

"31. … the learned district judge was entirely correct … that the particular metabolic rate of the defendant was not, in a breathalyser case, capable of being a special reason."

The answer to question (1) was "yes"; the answer to questions (2) and (3) was "no". Appeal dismissed.

Joseph v DPP

[2003] EWHC 3078 (Admin), [2004] RTR 341, 24 November 2003, QBD (DC)

In the unusual circumstances of this case, the officer should have taken into account that, before he had decided whether the specimen would be of blood or urine, the motorist said he could not give blood for religious reasons; the discretion under s 7(4), Road Traffic Act 1988 is broad.

A motorist had been charged with driving with excess alcohol, contrary to s 5(1)(a), Road Traffic Act 1988. Breath analysis revealed a lower reading below 50 µg alcohol in 100 ml breath; the officer conducting the procedure therefore offered the option to provide a blood or urine specimen, under s 8(2), Road Traffic Act 1988 (lower breath reading no more than 50 – now repealed; see page v). Before the officer had decided, under s 7(4), Road Traffic Act 1988, whether the alternative specimen should be of blood or urine, the motorist said he could not give blood as it was against his religion (Rastafarianism).

The Crown Court found, *inter alia*, that religion did not constitute a medical reason for not providing a blood specimen. He was convicted on the basis of the breath specimens, and appealed.

QUESTION(S) FOR THE COURT: Whether a reasonable tribunal, properly directed, faced with the evidence adduced, could have arrived at the findings of fact.

HELD: "5. [Concerning s 7(4)] … It has been assumed that if a blood specimen can be requested, then it should be requested, unless a medical practitioner is of the opinion that for medical reasons it should not. Such an understanding of the subsection is, in my judgment, inconsistent with the language of section 7(4) …

"7. … the officer has the broadest of discretions to determine what sort of specimen should be required.

"9. The discretion of the constable may be very wide but nonetheless it is a statutory discretion … and therefore in the appropriate circumstances is to be tested in accordance with the well-known *Wednesbury* principles. The circumstances in which it will be possible to interfere with the exercise of the constable's discretion will be rare. …

"10. However … the present case is unusual. Before the officer had made his choice as to which specimen to select, the appellant had made clear that he was not prepared to give a specimen of blood. He is a Rastafarian and he said that it was contrary to his religious beliefs to give such a specimen. …

"18. … In those circumstances the officer, not having any reason not to choose urine, should have chosen urine rather than blood. … the officer had considered that if there was no medical reason for not choosing blood, he was required to choose blood … this was a misunderstanding of the position. … the appellant genuinely believed … he should not give a blood sample. That was certainly something which the officer, in exercising his discretion, should have considered before coming to his conclusion as to whether he should require a urine or blood specimen. …"

The answer to the question was "no". Appeal allowed.

See also the following cases, all based on the "statutory option" under s 8(2), Road Traffic Act 1988 (alternative specimen where lower breath reading no more than 50 – repealed, with effect from 10 April 2015, by s 52 and Sch 11, Deregulation Act 2015):

- *Johnson v West Yorkshire Metropolitan Police* [1986] RTR 167, [1986] Crim LR 64, 31 July 1985, QBD (DC): A repugnance of needles is capable of being a medical reason why a blood specimen cannot or should not be taken. Compare *DPP v Lawrence (Scott James)*, page 188, where the suspect said he was afraid of needles and this was held to be a refusal to provide.
- *Andrews v DPP* [1992] RTR 1, 1 May 1991, QBD (DC): Where a medical practitioner advised the officer (by telephone) that a fear of needles did not amount to medical reasons for not supplying a blood specimen, the procedure was correctly followed; it was not for the court to question the correctness or otherwise of the medical opinion.
- *Salisbury v CPS* unreported, CO 3412/94, 29 March 1995, QBD (DC): When the motorist was asked if there was any reason why a specimen of blood could not or should not be taken by a doctor, and unequivocally replied "none at all", there was no error in the procedure, even though he also said he was afraid of needles.
- *DPP v Joiner* [1997] RTR 387, 4 December 1995, QBD (DC): Where the officer asked whether there were any medical reasons why blood should not be provided, without saying that the only right to object and give urine instead would be determined by a medical practitioner, there was no error in the procedure.

12. HOSPITAL PATIENTS

See s 9, Road Traffic Act 1988 – protection for hospital patients. See also DPP v Wilson, page 7 – the fact that a person was arrested while at hospital as a patient did not invalidate the subsequent procedure; Kohler v DPP, page 9 – breath analysis following a breach of s 6D(3) (prohibiting the arrest of a person while at a hospital as a patient) is admissible in evidence; Russell v Devine, page 121 – where a requirement for a blood specimen is made at a police station, the specimen may be taken elsewhere than at a police station or a hospital; Cherpion v DPP, page 585, where the doctor who saw the driver at hospital was found to be the medical practitioner in charge of the case; and Jones (Vivian Mary) v DPP, page 631 – where a specimen is taken at hospital, there is no requirement to explain why a breath specimen cannot be taken.

Askew v DPP

[1988] RTR 303, 14 January 1988, QBD (DC)

In the circumstances of this case, the motorist was not a hospital patient at the time he was required to provide a breath specimen.

A motorist had been charged with driving with excess alcohol, contrary to s 6(1)(a), Road Traffic Act 1972 as substituted by s 25 and Sch 8, Transport Act 1981. He had been involved in a traffic accident and was taken to hospital. Police officers went to the hospital. A nurse told the motorist that the doctor had discharged him and that he was to get dressed; he complained of pain and was given pain-killing tablets. He dressed. The officers then asked him to step outside the hospital building; he did so and the officers began the breathalyser procedure, which led to his arrest and positive breath analyses.

The magistrates concluded that at the time of being asked for a breath sample, the motorist was no longer a patient in a hospital within s 9(1), Road Traffic Act 1972 (hospital patient not to be required to provide a specimen unless the medical practitioner in charge does not object), and convicted him. The motorist appealed.

QUESTION(S) FOR THE COURT: Whether there was any evidence sufficient to justify the finding by the justices for the purposes of s 7(2), Road Traffic Act 1972 as substituted (power to require breath specimens after accident), that the defendant was not a patient at a hospital receiving treatment at the time immediately prior to the defendant's arrest.

HELD: "The issue … is … whether … the defendant was … a patient at a hospital …

"… the commonsense approach … will involve ascertaining among other things whether or not a person has had treatment at the hospital, whether that treatment has come to an end, whether the doctor in charge of the treatment has informed the police that the treatment was at an end, or a nurse has said so … and whether … the patient has begun at least to prepare himself for making his way out of the hospital … justices need not be influenced in their conclusion by the fact that a person had not actually left the precincts of a hospital when a request by a police officer is made …

"Here, … the justices, on the facts as they found them, could only sensibly have come to the conclusion they did, namely, that this defendant was not a patient at the hospital when asked to step outside … ."

Appeal dismissed.

Whelan v DPP

Unreported, CO 24/94, 28 June 1994, QBD (DC)

Where a blood specimen was required at a hospital, but the driver was discharged and the blood specimen was then taken at the police station, the evidence of analysis was inadmissible in the absence of evidence that the procedure at the police station had been followed correctly.

A motorist had been charged, *inter alia*, with driving with excess alcohol, contrary to s 5(1)(a), Road Traffic Act 1988. He had been stopped by police; he refused to provide a specimen for a breath test and was arrested. He said he thought he was having a heart attack and needed an ambulance. At the police station, the officer in charge was concerned about his state of health and the defendant was taken to hospital. At the hospital, the arresting officer again requested a breath specimen; it was given and was positive. The officer therefore requested a blood specimen, but before the specimen could be taken, the defendant was discharged from hospital and taken back to the police station. At the police station, the breath analysis device was defective and a blood specimen was taken.

The magistrates convicted the defendant on the basis of blood analysis. He appealed.

QUESTION(S) FOR THE COURT: (a) As the defendant had already been arrested for failing to provide a specimen for a breath test, was the officer acting unlawfully in requiring a second such specimen at the hospital? (b) If so, is that illegality capable of rendering inadmissible in evidence the analysis of the blood specimen? (c) Was the officer acting unlawfully in requiring a blood specimen at the hospital? (d) If so, is such illegality capable of rendering inadmissible in evidence the analysis of the blood specimen?

HELD: "[On (a)] The present case meets the literal words of section 6(1)(b) [power to require specimen for a breath test] … But … the police constable's own evidence was that he did not think that he was acting under statutory authority … Therefore … the request at [the] hospital … was not a request made in accordance with section 6(1)(b), and to that extent was not a lawful request.

"[On (b)] … it follows from [*Fox v Chief Constable of Gwent*, see page 1, and *DPP v McGladrigan*, see page 14] that the fact that the procedure under section 6 of the 1988 Act was not properly complied with was not necessarily fatal to a conviction on the basis of the subsequent evidence of the analysis of a specimen obtained, if I may put it in this way, on the back of that procedure. The Justices could exclude such evidence as unfairly obtained under section 78 [Police and Criminal Evidence Act 1984 – discretion to exclude evidence which would have such an adverse effect on the fairness of the proceedings that the court ought not to admit it]. However, … the Justices found that the police constables had acted entirely in good faith. They accepted the evidence of [the constable] that he had requested the second test simply to be fair to Mr Whelan …

"[On (c) and (d)] In other words, was the proper procedure followed in respect of the taking of the blood specimen? … I am quite satisfied that the proper procedures were followed in respect of a patient in hospital, subject to one technical difficulty … in general terms those procedures were followed, and there is no ground for saying that there was a further illegality at the hospital stage. Therefore, the answer to question c) is No and the answer to question d) is that it does not arise.

"… [counsel for the respondent] … has very properly drawn our attention to further difficulties … The specimen of blood … was not taken at the hospital. It was taken at the police station …

"The Justices made no findings as to the procedure … at the police station … Under section 9(1)(a) … '… if the requirement is then made, it shall be for the provision of a specimen at the hospital' … it is very doubtful whether that could be extended to cover a specimen that is in fact taken outside the hospital … it may be the case that, if the patient leaves the hospital before the specimen can be taken, even though through no fault at all of the police officers, the process may have to be started again … it is evident … that that is what the police constable … thought had to be done and in fact sought to do. There are no findings on this matter, but … there is evidence that Mr Whelan was presented to the Intoximeter officer, the equipment was found to be defective, and, therefore, for that reason (although not expressly stated) blood had to be required …

"… the burden of proving compliance with [the requirements in *DPP v Warren*, see page 75] rests upon the prosecution. There is nothing in this Case … to show that compliance had been proved before the Justices. Indeed, there is every reason to believe that it had not been so dealt with. … this appeal must succeed, not on any of the grounds raised in the Case, but on the further point which … [counsel for the prosecutor] has thought it right to put before us."

Appeal allowed.

R v Burton upon Trent JJ ex p Woolley

[1995] RTR 139, [1996] Crim LR 340, 11 November 1994, QBD (DC)

Where the motorist is a patient in a hospital, the officer need not ask whether there are any medical reasons why a blood specimen cannot or should not be taken; it is sufficient to ask whether there is any reason why such a specimen cannot be taken. Nor need the officer explain why a breath specimen cannot be taken.

A motorist had pleaded guilty to, *inter alia*, driving with excess alcohol, contrary to s 5(1)(a), Road Traffic Act 1988. He had been driving while disqualified, and there was a collision; he was taken to hospital where he was required to provide breath specimens; he refused because of his injuries; the officer therefore required a specimen of blood or urine for a laboratory test and asked whether there were any matters which the motorist wished the officer to take into account in deciding which it should be; he replied that he knew of none. Blood was taken and analysis revealed excess alcohol.

The motorist was convicted. Three days later, the Crown Prosecution Service contacted the motorist's solicitor, saying that the charge of driving with excess alcohol should have been withdrawn; there had been a technical error in the procedure for requiring the specimen, in that the officer had not asked whether there were any reasons why a blood specimen should not be taken by a doctor. The motorist sought an order of *certiorari* to quash the conviction and sentence.

GROUND(S) FOR APPEAL: (1) The evidence of analysis of the blood specimen would have been inadmissible because the officer who required the specimen used a form of words which did not comply with the law.

HELD: "... the purpose of the 'medical' inquiry is to bring about the involvement of a doctor where a medical opinion is or may be required under section 7(4). But in the hospital case such a purpose is otiose. By definition, and by the specific terms of section 9 of the Act of 1988, before the requirement can be made at all it has to be positively approved by a doctor ... neither the Act of 1988 nor the speeches in *DPP v Warren* [page 75] provide justification for thinking that in hospital cases the constable must ask a separate or separately phrased 'medical' question. In such cases it is sufficient if the driver is asked simply whether there is any reason why the specimen of blood should not be taken from him ...

"I now turn to the alleged requirement that the constable should tell the driver why a specimen of breath cannot be taken ... in a hospital case the inability to take a specimen of breath is not a matter of fact but a matter of law, because of the limitations on the taking of breath specimens imposed by section 7(2). In these circumstances it is entirely supererogatory to require the constable to recite why breath cannot be taken ... no such requirement in a hospital case can be drawn either from the Act of 1988 or from *Warren*.

"... the requirements of the Act of 1988 were observed in this case ... the evidence of the specimen would have been admissible if the applicant had contested the charge, and therefore ... this application must be dismissed."

Application dismissed.

Webber v DPP

[1998] RTR 111, 4 December 1995, QBD (DC)

The requirement to provide a blood specimen is not discharged where a suspect leaves hospital after the requirement is made but before the specimen is given.

A motorist had been charged with driving with excess alcohol in blood, contrary to s 5(1)(a), Road Traffic Act 1988. She had been involved in a traffic accident; no roadside breath test was carried out; she was taken to hospital, where she refused to provide breath for a screening test. A police officer therefore required her to provide a specimen of blood for a laboratory test under s 9(1), Road Traffic Act 1988. The doctor in charge of the case had been notified and had not objected. The motorist agreed, but was discharged from the hospital before providing the specimen. She was then arrested, on the basis that she had refused to provide breath specimens and no longer had the protection afforded to hospital patients. At the police station, a blood specimen was taken and revealed excess alcohol.

At the Crown Court, the motorist argued that on discharge from hospital she was also discharged from the obligation to provide a specimen of blood; the police should have started afresh, using the breath analysis device; and that the blood specimen provided at the police station had not been provided in accordance with any lawful requirement. It was, though, agreed that the requirement for a blood specimen made at the hospital had been lawful.

The Crown Court convicted her; she appealed.

HELD: "… the officer set in train a procedure by virtue of his lawful requirement … that procedure was not in any way varied or discharged by the mere fact, before she could comply, that this Appellant, for whatever reason, left hospital. I can see nothing in the statute to drive me to the view that the *locus* at which the specimen is provided is vital, so vital that if it not be provided at hospital that specimen and the analysis thereof ceased to be admissible."

Appeal dismissed.

Butler (Michael Joseph) v DPP

[2001] RTR 28, [2001] Crim LR 580, 20 December 2000, QBD (DC)

Where the procedure began at a police station but the motorist was then taken to hospital, the officer should have told the hospital doctor that the motorist had said he had "immune system breakdown". The officer is not, though, required to tell the doctor he proposes to require a specimen in the absence of the patient.

A motorist had been charged with driving with excess alcohol, contrary to s 5(1)(a), Road Traffic Act 1988. He had been arrested and at the police station was asked whether he was suffering from any medical condition. He replied "immune system breakdown". This was recorded in the custody record; a doctor was called and saw the motorist. The breath analysis procedure was then begun, but the motorist complained of chest pains before he had given a specimen. He was again taken to see the doctor, following which the breath analysis procedure was recommenced. He again complained and asked to see the doctor. The custody officer pointed out that he had seen the doctor twice and had been found fit to carry out the procedure. The officer told him to blow into the machine, but the motorist got up and tried to leave the room, then fell to the floor. He was taken to hospital.

A police sergeant went to the hospital, and, in the presence of the motorist, asked the doctor in charge of his case if a specimen of blood or urine could be taken. The hospital doctor, who had not been told that the motorist said he suffered "immune system breakdown", or of any medication the motorist was taking, said there was no objection. Blood was taken and revealed excess alcohol. The motorist was convicted; he appealed.

QUESTION(S) FOR THE COURT: Whether the sergeant: (a) should have informed the hospital doctor that the appellant had said at the police station that he was suffering from "immune system breakdown" – a potential medical reason why a blood specimen should not be authorised; (b) should not have asked for that doctor's consent in the appellant's hearing.

HELD: "[On (a)] 16. … contrary to the justices' decision, in the unusual circumstances of this case, the sergeant was required to inform the hospital doctor that the appellant had said that he suffered from 'immune system breakdown'; and (2) there was no requirement that the notification to the doctor by the constable of his proposal to require a specimen be made in the patient's absence."

Appeal allowed.

Whitfield v DPP

[2006] EWHC 1414 (Admin), 17 May 2006, QBD (DC)

Where an officer had followed Form MG DC/C, the justices were entitled, in the absence of challenge, to use their own knowledge of the form to find that he had given the warning about the consequences of failing to provide a specimen of blood for analysis. Again in the absence of challenge, the justices were entitled to find that the person who took the specimen was a medical practitioner.

A motorist had been charged with driving with excess alcohol in blood, contrary to s 5(1)(a), Road Traffic Act 1988. He had been warned about the consequences of failing to provide specimens while in an ambulance at the scene of an accident; he gave a positive roadside breath test; at the hospital, a police sergeant explained the procedure and a doctor took the blood specimen. The sergeant followed the MG DC/C booklet. The magistrates convicted the motorist; he appealed.

QUESTION(S) FOR THE COURT: (2) whether there was any evidence upon which a reasonable tribunal could have been satisfied that the defendant was warned in hospital that he would be prosecuted if he did not provide a specimen of blood; (5) whether the magistrates were right to have accepted that the blood sample had been taken by a healthcare professional.

HELD: "9. … the justices were entitled to find on the evidence … that [the sergeant] gave the mandatory warning required by section 7(7) [Road Traffic Act 1988] as to the consequences of failing to supply a blood specimen. The relevant finding of fact is the finding that [the sergeant] followed the procedure set out in the MGDCC [*sic*] booklet and followed the checklist in that booklet. …

"13. … The booklet used in this case was disclosed to the defence. It was open to the defence to cross-examine the sergeant if the procedure set out in the booklet did not comply with the statutory requirements. The justices were entitled to conclude … in the light of their knowledge as to the law and the procedure set out in the booklet, if necessary after refreshing their memory … that the requirement was set out.

"14. … the fifth question is … stated in a wrong form. … The relevant finding of fact is … that the justices were satisfied that [the doctor] is a *bona fide* medical practitioner capable of taking blood samples." The court had adjourned to enable the doctor to give evidence; when he appeared, the defence successfully resisted the prosecution's application for him to give evidence.

"15. … the defence … did not … specify that … it was not accepted that [the doctor] was a medical practitioner. … The issue as to his qualifications was not squarely put in issue before the close of the prosecution case …. Accordingly, [the justices] were entitled to conclude, as they did, that [the doctor] was a medical practitioner."

The answers to the questions were "yes". Appeal dismissed.

Townson v DPP

[2006] EWHC 2007 (Admin), 13 June 2006, QBD (DC)

The officer should have referred to the doctor the reasons put forward for not providing a blood specimen at hospital (difficulty finding veins; pain; diabetes; high blood pressure); he should not have decided for himself that these could not amount to medical reasons.

A motorist had been charged with failing to provide a specimen of blood for analysis, contrary to s 7(6), Road Traffic Act 1988. He had had a road accident and was taken to hospital. He smelt strongly of intoxicants. The doctor in charge of his case assured the police sergeant in attendance that there was no medical objection to a breath test or to supplying blood, or to the appropriate warnings being given. The motorist refused to supply a specimen of breath, saying he was "hurting too much". The sergeant then formally required him to provide a specimen of blood. The motorist again refused because, he said: (a) he had had a lot of tests recently and there had been difficulty finding veins; (b) he was in pain; (c) he was diabetic; and (d) he had high blood pressure. The sergeant did not consider any of these reasons, singularly or cumulatively, as capable of being medical reasons excusing the appellant from providing a specimen of blood. The court agreed and convicted. The defendant appealed.

QUESTION(S) FOR THE COURT: Whether the reasons given by the appellant were capable of being medical reasons.

HELD: "18. … the sergeant was not entitled to conclude, on the material before him, that the reasons advanced by the appellant were incapable of being medical reasons to such an extent that resort to medical opinion was unnecessary. The initial reference to [the doctor] did not deal with the matter because what was being advanced by the appellant in answer to [the sergeant's] questions was not information which was already in the possession of [the sergeant]. What is envisaged by section 7(4A) [Road Traffic Act 1988] is that a medical practitioner and only a medical practitioner shall decide whether or not the specimen should be taken having regard to the reasons advanced by the suspect. … there are cases where what is put forward by the suspect is so self-evidently incapable of forming a medical reason that the officer is entitled to form his own judgment that it is so incapable and proceed accordingly. That is what [the sergeant] sought to do here.

It is clear from the evidence that he had formed the opinion that the appellant was simply playing games.

"20. It seems to me that the strength of the case for the appellant lies particularly in [the] matters of diabetes and high blood pressure. Once the sergeant had been informed of those, it was not within his reasonable powers to conclude that they were matters incapable of amounting to medical reasons. Accordingly, he ought not to have reached the decision that he did and by so doing prevent the intervention of a medical practitioner, whose better view under the statute was required to prevail.

"21. In the circumstances, I conclude reluctantly that the procedure was flawed, and that the question posed by the case stated must be answered in the affirmative."

Appeal allowed.

DPP v Tandey

[2024] EWHC 1992 (Admin), 2024 WL 02333227, 22 May 2024, KBD (Admin)

Section 9(1), Road Traffic Act 1988 requires proof that the investigating officer approached a doctor on duty in the hospital and in charge of the suspect's case and asked whether that doctor objected to a specimen of blood being obtained, and that doctor indicated that he/she did not object. There is no need to prove the identity of the doctor.

A motorist had been stopped; she had slurred speech and glazed eyes. She was asked to take a breath test but did not register a reading on the device. She was arrested for failing to provide a specimen contrary to s 7, Road Traffic Act 1988. She said she had taken diazepam and was having suicidal thoughts. She was taken to hospital. An officer asked a doctor whether there was any objection to taking samples of blood; according to the MG DD/C form, the doctor's name was Oliver Stubbs, Stubble or possibly something else. In a witness statement made some time later, the officer said that the doctor had had no objection to blood being taken. Blood was taken and revealed 185 mg of alcohol per 100 ml of blood. The motorist was charged with driving with excess alcohol contrary to s 5, Road Traffic Act 1988.

The court found that the officer's notes and the MG DD/C form were incorrect as to the name of the doctor and the time of the procedure. There was also an issue concerning third-hand hearsay, the doctor in question having since moved to Australia, and there having been a telephone conversation with him. The defence applied to exclude the MG DD/C from evidence pursuant to s 78, PACE (discretion to exclude evidence which would have such an adverse effect on the fairness of the proceedings that the court ought not to admit it). The application was granted on the basis that the officer's records could not be relied on. The Crown agreed it could not prove its case and the charge was dismissed. The prosecution appealed.

QUESTION(S) FOR THE COURT: Whether the court below was wrong in the circumstances to determine the application pursuant to s 78 where it had become apparent that the officer's notes were incorrect in one material way and highly likely in two significant ways.

HELD: "12. … As the judge correctly observed … : 'The issue in this case was whether the Crown could prove that [the officer] had spoken to a doctor' [as required by s 9(1), Road Traffic Act 1988]. … the identity of the doctor is immaterial, the question is: whether the officer approached a doctor on duty in the hospital and in charge of dealing with the respondent's case to ask whether that doctor, whoever it was, objected to a specimen of blood being obtained, and that doctor indicated that he did not. The name of the doctor is irrelevant. … It is sufficient that the doctor in charge was asked and raised no objection.

"13. The judge's second reason for excluding the MGDDC form wholesale was concern about discrepancies in timing. [After reviewing the timings recited on the form] I cannot see what the timing discrepancy is in the contemporaneous documents …

"17. … the whole basis of the decision to exclude the MGDDC form in toto was flawed. … the test under section 78 is whether the admission of the evidence would have such an adverse effect on the fairness of the proceedings that the court ought not to admit it. I am quite unable to see that there would have been anything unfair in allowing the MGDDC form to be used as a memory aid by [the officer in the case], for him to be called in the usual way and for any points such as whether there really was a hospital doctor on duty at the time who was spoken to by [the officer], to be put to the officer in cross-examination. The decision to exclude the evidence in toto was, in my judgment, so flawed that it does not fall within the bounds of the discretion given to a trial judge under section 78. … it was wrong to exclude the evidence wholesale under section 78."

Appeal allowed.

13. REPEAT REQUIREMENTS AND MULTIPLE SPECIMENS

See also Denny v DPP, page 47 – where the device proved unreliable after breath specimens had been provided, it was lawful to require further breath specimens for analysis by a different device; Hussain v DPP, page 59 – where the device had not produced a reliable indication, an officer was entitled to require further breath specimens at a different police station; Mercer v DPP, page 290, where two breath analysis cycles were necessary; Jubb v DPP, page 341 – an officer may invite, but not require, further breath specimens; and DPP v MacPhail, page 353, concerning a repeat request for a roadside breath test.

Blake v Bickmore

[1982] RTR 167, 16 November 1981, QBD (DC)

Where there was no evidence that an officer had not complied with the manufacturer's instructions for a roadside breath test, and no evidence that if those instructions had not been followed, the results would have favoured the prosecutor, there was no basis for an appeal.

A motorist had been charged with driving with excess alcohol, contrary to s 6(1)(a), Road Traffic Act 1972. At the roadside he had been required to provide a specimen of breath. At the first attempt, he did not succeed in illuminating both lights on the device. At the second, he did. The specimen was positive. He was arrested and a urine specimen showed excess alcohol.

At the trial, the officer gave evidence of having assembled the device and asking the motorist to blow into it; the manufacturer's instructions for use of the device were not adduced in evidence. The defence contended that it was for the police to show that the device had been used in accordance with the manufacturer's instructions; the prosecutor argued that it was for the defence to show that the result obtained as a result of the method of using the machine was unduly favourable to the Crown and that the defence had failed to do so.

The justices did not accept that the second test had been influenced by the first; no air from the first test went from the mouthpiece into the fuel cell and into contact with the electrodes; it made no difference that the tube was not replaced. They convicted the motorist, who appealed.

QUESTION(S) FOR THE COURT: (1) Whether, if an officer required a driver to blow into a Lion Alcolmeter SL-2 breath test device with one continuous breath and long enough to illuminate sampling lights "A" and "B" and the driver failed with the first breath to illuminate light "B", the breath test was vitiated if the constable requested the driver to blow into the device again in the same manner immediately after the first unsatisfactory sample; and (2) whether there was a valid breath test within the meaning of the Road Traffic Act 1972.

HELD: "... First, there was no evidence that the police constables ... had not followed the instructions of the manufacturers; and, secondly, there is no evidence whatever that if they had not followed the instructions of the manufacturers the result would tend to favour the Crown rather than the defence. In those circumstances I find it difficult to see how this case stated can get on."

Appeal dismissed.

Sparrow v Bradley

[1985] RTR 122, 21 February 1984, QBD (DC)

The fact that a motorist is asked to blow into a second screening device, the first apparently having malfunctioned, does not invalidate the subsequent procedure.

A motorist had been convicted of driving with excess alcohol, contrary to s 6(1), Road Traffic Act 1972. He had been asked to provide a specimen of breath for analysis by a Lion Alcolmeter S-L2 screening device. Certain lights on the Alcolmeter did not illuminate; others flashed erratically; the police provided a different Alcolmeter, into which the motorist blew, producing a positive result. The motorist contended that in requiring him to provide a second specimen the police had not correctly followed the procedure under s 8(7), Road Traffic Act 1972; he appealed.

QUESTION(S) FOR THE COURT: (1) Were the police acting lawfully in requiring the defendant to provide a second specimen of breath for a breath test at the police station? (2) In view of the evidence given was it open to the justices to find, as they announced, 'Having examined the requirements of the manufacturer and considered the evidence of the police officers administering the test we are satisfied that a satisfactory sample was not provided in the first instance and that, quite properly, the defendant was given a further opportunity to provide such sample on a different meter'?

HELD: The answers to both questions were "yes". On the evidence, "it would have been open to the justices to hold that there was something wrong with the [first] device, but ... it was also open to them to hold, as they did, that the defendant did not blow breath into the machine of sufficient length and strength to allow the instrument to function properly ... is it right ... that, if a person ... is invited to blow into a device ... and it appears to the police officer who is applying the test that the device either is or may not be operating correctly, then, if the officer gives him another opportunity – or possibly more correctly, a proper opportunity – to blow into a second device and he then blows into that device and produces a positive reading, the fact that he has been given the opportunity to blow into that second device invalidates all subsequent procedure thereafter carried out? ... one has only to state the point to realise that it must be answered in the negative."

Appeal dismissed.

Howard v Hallett

[1984] RTR 353, [1984] Crim LR 565, 4 May 1984, QBD (DC)

Where, as a result of error, three specimens of breath are provided, it is the lower of the first two which is to be used.

A motorist had been convicted of driving with excess alcohol, contrary to s 6(1), Road Traffic Act 1972 as substituted by s 25 and Sch 8, Transport Act 1981. He had given a first specimen of breath for analysis, but, in error, the police officer operating the machine had failed to ask for a second specimen within the required time. The procedure was begun afresh and two further specimens taken. The last two readings were put before the justices; the first was not, although it was the lowest of the three. The justices relied on the lower of the two readings before them. The motorist appealed.

QUESTION(S) FOR THE COURT: (A) Whether a police officer is empowered by s 8(1)(a), Road Traffic Act 1972 as substituted, to require a third specimen of breath, two proper such specimens having previously been provided; (B) if not, whether the justices were entitled to convict when the first proper specimen produced a lower reading than the second, even though there was no evidence before them of what that first reading was; (C) if the answer to (A) is "yes", whether the justices were entitled to convict when there was evidence before them of the existence of a lower, albeit unknown, reading.

HELD: "… Section 8(1)(a) … does not give the constable power to require the person concerned to provide any more than two specimens of breath; s 8(6), providing that the lower reading be used and the other disregarded, relates only to specimens taken in accordance with s 8(1)(a) … the proper course for the justices in this case would have been to conclude that the evidence before them should have been of the first two tests. Of these two, the second, which was the higher, should have been disregarded, and, only on the basis of the first should the defendant have been convicted … However, there was no evidence of that test … before the justices … the justices … should not have convicted the defendant on the evidence before them … ."

The answer to questions (A) and (B) was "no"; question (C) did not arise. Appeal allowed.

Owen v Morgan

[1986] RTR 151, 15 July 1985, QBD (DC)

The legislation does not prevent the officer repeating the request for breath specimens if the motorist has failed to provide them in response to the first request.

Magistrates had dismissed a charge, under s 6(1), Road Traffic Act 1972 as substituted by s 25(3) and Sch 8, Transport Act 1981, of being in charge with excess alcohol. The motorist had failed to provide breath specimens for analysis at the first attempt, but had done so when asked again 15 minutes later. The readings were 48 and 45 μg alcohol in 100 ml breath and she had been offered the option, under s 8(6), Road Traffic Act 1972 as likewise substituted (alternative specimen where lower breath reading no more than 50 – now repealed; see page v), of instead providing a specimen of blood; she did so and it was positive.

The justices found that the Act does not provide for the taking of specimens of breath after an initial failure; the two readings later achieved were inadmissible and the offer of an analysis of blood samples null and void. They dismissed the charge. The prosecutor appealed.

QUESTION(S) FOR THE COURT: Whether the justices were correct in considering that the evidence of the blood alcohol reading was rendered inadmissible by reason of the officer giving the defendant the opportunity to provide a second specimen of breath.

HELD: "There is nothing whatsoever in the legislation to indicate that the police are not empowered, a person having failed to provide a specimen of breath, to make a further request for the provision of such a specimen." The justices were not correct in their finding. Appeal allowed.

Chief Constable of Avon & Somerset v Creech

[1986] RTR 87, [1986] Crim LR 62, 31 July 1985, QBD (DC)

Where more than two evidential breath specimens are provided, the third and any subsequent specimens are not to be taken into account. The two specimens need not be provided in the same cycle. There is no reason why the results of the analysis cannot be proved by oral evidence.

Magistrates had dismissed an information of driving with excess alcohol, contrary to s 6(1)(a), Road Traffic Act 1972 as substituted by s 25 and Sch 8, Transport Act 1981. A first specimen produced a reading of 95 µg alcohol in 100 ml breath but the motorist failed to produce a second specimen, the Intoximeter running out of time and registering "no sample". The police decided to start the breath testing procedure afresh and two further specimens produced readings of 98 and 100 µg alcohol in 100 ml breath. As the police were empowered to require only two specimens, the prosecutor did not adduce evidence of the third, and sought to rely on the oral evidence of the police sergeant of his observations of the Intoximeter and its readings rather than on the printouts.

The magistrates dismissed the information on the ground that the two specimens should have been provided during the same operating cycle. The prosecutor appealed.

QUESTION(S) FOR THE COURT: Whether the justices were correct in: (a) deciding that they could have found that there was a case to answer on the oral evidence of the police sergeant as to the breath alcohol analysis readings notwithstanding that the printouts were not admitted in evidence; and (b) holding that the two specimens of breath must be given during the same operating cycle to constitute the approved method of obtaining the specimens.

HELD: "… Since the constable has power to require no more than two specimens [s 8(1)(a) as substituted], once he has validly required and validly obtained two specimens of breath any third and subsequent specimens provided pursuant to a purported request are not valid, and are therefore not to be taken into account …

"There is no evidence before us, and I see no reason at all to infer, that the accuracy of one operation is in any way compromised by the omission of a second [specimen in the first cycle] … the prosecutor was entitled to put in evidence the results of the first two tests …

"I can see no reason in policy to prevent [the police officer] from proving the results of the analysis by oral evidence in the ordinary way."

The answer to question (a) was "yes"; the answer to question (b) was "no". Appeal allowed.

Nugent v Ridley

[1987] RTR 412, [1987] Crim LR 640, 25 February 1987, QBD (DC)

There is nothing in the legislation to prevent a urine specimen used for evidential purposes being the third or even a later specimen.

A motorist had been charged with driving with excess alcohol in urine, contrary to s 6(1)(a), Road Traffic Act 1972 as substituted by s 25 and Sch 8, Transport Act 1981. At the police station, he had refused to provide a breath specimen, saying he had a bad cold. He also refused to supply a blood specimen, saying he was afraid of needles. A doctor was called, who was satisfied that he did have a phobia about needles, but persuaded him to produce a urine specimen. That first urine specimen was discarded. Two urine samples were then provided to the police at the officer's request. The specimen analysed proved positive.

The motorist argued that the terms of the statute had not been correctly complied with – the statute permitted only two urine specimens; the motorist had provided a total of three; it was the third which had been analysed, and that analysis was not therefore admissible. The justices found that he had in fact provided only two specimens to the police, the first having been supplied at the request of the doctor. They convicted him and he appealed.

QUESTION(S) FOR THE COURT: Whether, on the evidence before the justices, they were justified in finding that the specimen of urine had been requested and provided by the defendant in accordance with s 8, Road Traffic Act 1972 as substituted, and whether such request was lawful within the meaning of the Act.

HELD: "There is nothing in section 8(5) ['A Specimen of urine shall be provided within one hour … and after the provision of a previous specimen of urine'] to prevent the specimen which is sent for analysis being the third or even a later specimen provided by the relevant person … after the provision of a previous specimen and within an hour of the request … the view taken by the justices of the facts and the application of the relevant statutory provisions to those facts was right".

Appeal dismissed.

Durdan v Chief Officer, Metropolitan Police

Unreported, CO 285/94, 28 July 1994, QBD (DC)

If an officer requires breath specimens but the driver fails to provide them, and the officer then requires a blood specimen and the motorist again fails to provide, there is nothing to prevent the officer (in this case, following medical advice) asking again for specimens of breath.

A motorist had been charged with failing without reasonable excuse to provide two specimens of breath for analysis, and with failing without reasonable excuse to provide a specimen of blood for analysis, both contrary to s 7, Road Traffic Act 1988. At the police station, he had complained of stomach pains and ulcers; he was twice asked to provide breath specimens and did not reply. The police officer conducting the procedure took the view that there was reasonable cause to believe that for medical reasons a specimen of breath could not be provided or should not be required; he therefore asked for a specimen of blood. The motorist did not reply. The officer called the forensic medical examiner, who confirmed that the motorist was suffering from spasmodic stomach pains, but that he could provide a specimen of breath between spasms; the doctor was not asked whether the motorist was fit to provide blood. The officer again asked for a specimen of breath; the motorist said he could not do so.

The magistrates found that the motorist was capable of providing a breath specimen at the final request; the earlier requests had been negated by the request for blood; the request for blood could not relied on since the motorist was unwell and the doctor had not been asked to consider his fitness to provide a blood specimen. They dismissed the charge of failing to provide a blood specimen, but convicted him of failing without reasonable excuse to provide breath specimens. He appealed.

QUESTION(S) FOR THE COURT: (1) Whether, having been requested to provide a breath specimen for analysis and having failed to do so and … having subsequently been requested to provide a specimen of blood and having failed to do so, and following a medical examination thereafter, it was lawful to demand a further specimen of breath for analysis. (2) Whether, if the second request for a specimen of breath was lawful, the second request should be followed by a request for blood if the second request for breath is not complied with, if there is a possibility that at that time the person of whom the request is made is unable to comply with it.

HELD: "Nothing in the wording of [s 7, Road Traffic Act 1988] … in any way precludes a police officer from asking for a further specimen of breath …

"The submission … is that whilst that is so in some circumstances, it certainly cannot be made once the police officer has moved on and embarked upon the procedure of requiring a sample of blood. I can find no reason from the statutory provision to conclude that such a limitation has to be imposed … If … no specimen has been provided, I can find nothing unfair or unreasonable in a further request being made … ."

The answer to question (1) was "yes"; question (2) was irrelevant. Appeal dismissed.

Morrison (Trevor) v DPP

Unreported, CO 1156/94, 12 October 1994, QBD (DC)

Where a motorist supplied two specimens of breath but they were not analysed because the device was not ready, it was lawful to require further breath specimens.

A motorist had been charged with driving with excess alcohol in breath, contrary to s 5(1)(a), Road Traffic Act 1988. At the police station, he had been asked to provide breath specimens for analysis; he did so, but the breath analysis machine reverted to "standby" mode because of a delay since switching it on and programming it; it produced no analysis on the screen and no printout. The machine was re-programmed and the defendant provided further specimens, each revealing excess alcohol.

At the hearing, the motorist contended that he had been required to provide more than two specimens and that the court could rely on the first two only. The prosecutor contended that the only specimens which had been recognised and analysed were those which the motorist believed to have been the third and fourth specimens, and that those were admissible.

The magistrate convicted the motorist, who appealed.

QUESTION(S) FOR THE COURT: Whether a person, having already complied with a requirement to provide two specimens of breath for analysis, can lawfully be required by a constable on the same occasion to provide further specimens of breath for analysis by an approved device which is in good working order, but which did not produce an analysis of the two specimens, and whether the result of the analysis of those further specimens is admissible in evidence.

HELD: "… in the present case the first two samples were not recorded, no printout was provided and no information of the analysis appeared on the machine's screen.

"In those circumstances, the first two samples given were "no supply" or "no-go" samples. The third and fourth samples were, effectively, the first and second samples recognised by the Intoximeter. Hence, I would answer the question posed … in the affirmative."

Appeal dismissed.

Stewart (John Kimball) v DPP

[2003] EWHC 1323 (Admin), [2003] RTR 35, 12 June 2003, QBD (DC)

Where two breath specimens were analysed and the device generated the message "breath difference", the officer was not obliged to go on to require a blood specimen; he could instead offer to take, or require, further breath specimens.

A motorist had been charged with driving with excess alcohol, contrary to s 5(1)(a), Road Traffic Act 1988. He had been arrested and at the police station provided two specimens of breath. The readings were 56 and 66 µg alcohol in 100 ml breath and the device produced the warning "breath difference". The officer conducting the procedure found the readings unreliable and gave the motorist the choice of providing two more specimens of breath, or specimens of blood or urine. The motorist chose to give further breath specimens. The procedure for requiring the specimens, including the warning that failure to provide might lead to prosecution, was repeated in its entirety, and satisfactory readings were produced. The motorist was convicted. He appealed.

QUESTION(S) FOR THE COURT: (1) Where a person provides two specimens of breath into an approved machine, and the operator has reasonable cause to believe that the machine has not given a reliable indication of the proportion of alcohol in the breath of the person concerned, whether the operator is acting lawfully in either requiring or giving the person the option to provide two further specimens of breath; (2) whether the fact that the operator is acting in good faith affects whether or not he is acting lawfully.

HELD: "29. … section 7(3)(bb) [officer having reasonable cause to believe that the machine has not produced a reliable indication] deals with the circumstances in which a request for blood or urine may be made. By it, the officer is entitled to require blood or urine once the request for breath has resulted in an unreliable indication. Nothing in the section states that in such a case the officer is obliged to require blood or urine: that the option of a further breath test may not be offered. …

"30. … on any sensible interpretation of section 11(3)(b) [specimen not provided unless provided in such a way so as to enable the objective … of the analysis to be satisfactorily achieved], each of the first two specimens … did not 'enable the objective of the … analysis to be satisfactorily achieved'. It seems to me to follow that once it is accepted that effectively no specimen of breath is provided, there would be nothing to prevent the officer requiring further specimens of breath. He is not obliged to do so."

Jubb v DPP (see page 341) was distinguished on the facts.

The answer to question (1) was "yes"; it was not necessary to answer question (2). Appeal dismissed.

Edmond v DPP

[2006] EWHC 463 (Admin), [2006] RTR 18, 23 February 2006, QBD (DC)

Where an officer invited further breath specimens because the analysis of the first two was not satisfactory, it was not appropriate or necessary to impose the requirement for specimens again, or repeat the warning of prosecution for failure to provide.

A motorist had been charged with driving with excess alcohol, contrary to s 5(1)(a), Road Traffic Act 1988. He had been stopped by police; a roadside breath test was positive; he was arrested. At the police station he was asked for breath specimens and warned that failure to provide them might render him liable to prosecution. The two readings were 90 and 76 µg alcohol in 100 ml breath. Because of the variance between the two readings, the officer conducting the procedure considered they were not reliable and asked for two further specimens; he did not repeat the warning. The motorist agreed and the second readings were 89 and 86. The motorist was convicted, and appealed.

QUESTION(S) FOR THE COURT: Whether the justices were right to convict given that the officer did not formally require the second set of specimens and did not repeat the warning of the consequences of failure.

HELD: "18. … [The appellant] accepts that the officer … was entitled to invite the appellant to provide a second set of specimens of breath and to do so without, at the same time, offering the option of providing blood …

"19. … [but h]e contends … that once the officer has obtained the consent of the person concerned, he is obliged then to require that person to provide further specimens and to go through the statutory procedure again, including the giving of a warning under section 7(7). …

"21. … it was not necessary … to give the appellant a further warning under section 7(7). That subsection … obliges an officer to give a warning on *requiring* a person to provide a specimen. Such a warning was given at the outset … After the first set of specimens proved unreliable, the officer did not impose any further requirement that the appellant provide specimens, nor, as it seems to me, was he obliged to impose any such further requirement.

"22. What happened thereafter was voluntary. The officer invited the appellant to provide a further set of specimens and the appellant agreed to do so. Section 7(7) plainly does not apply in that situation. Indeed, the very purpose of the subsection is inapplicable in such a situation. As its terms make clear, the purpose is to warn that failure to provide a specimen as required may render a person liable to prosecution. But a failure to provide a specimen when invited, rather than required, to do so cannot render a person liable for prosecution. The only consequence of a failure to provide a specimen in those circumstances is that the officer may exercise his further powers to require a specimen to be given, whether that be a specimen of breath or of blood or urine.

"23. I would reject [the] contention that where an invitation has been made to provide a further specimen of breath and the motorist has agreed to do so, the officer is then obliged to go through the entire procedure of imposing a requirement on the motorist to provide such a specimen. …"

Appeal dismissed.

14. URINE SPECIMENS

See also the cases in Chapter 3 under the heading "Taking Specimens: Urine", page 123; Nugent v Ridley, page 112 – a urine specimen used for evidential purposes may be the third or even a later specimen; DPP v Baldwin (Alistair), page 126 – the results of the analysis of a urine specimen provided 15 minutes after expiry of the statutory hour are admissible; Walters (Julian) v DPP, page 205 – in calculating the one hour allowed for providing urine specimens, the court was not obliged to take seconds into account; and Robertson (Eric) v DPP, page 206, where the motorist's appeal succeeded because the officer delayed (for up to half an hour) allowing the suspect to produce the first specimen, and would not allow the second specimen to be given some 75 minutes after the initial request.

Wyllie v CPS

[1988] Crim LR 753, 10 May 1988, QBD (DC)

There is nothing to prevent an officer requiring a urine specimen following failure to provide a blood specimen. In the circumstances, there was no injustice in allowing the information to be amended to refer to a specimen of blood, rather than urine.

A motorist had been suspected of driving with excess alcohol, arrested and taken to a police station. No breath analysis device was available and the police therefore required, under s 8(3)(b) Road Traffic Act 1972 as substituted by s 25(3) and Sch 8, Transport Act 1981, a specimen of blood, which the motorist refused to provide. He was later asked for a specimen of urine; he provided one such specimen, but not the second.

The information against the motorist alleged failure without reasonable excuse to provide a specimen of urine, contrary to s 8(7), Road Traffic Act 1972 as likewise substituted. The prosecution sought to amend the information to refer to a specimen of blood; the defence objected, intending to argue that having once required a blood specimen, the police were not then empowered to require a urine specimen. The justices offered the defence an adjournment, which was declined, and permitted the amendment. The motorist was convicted on the amended information and appealed.

HELD: "The purpose of [s 8(4) – constable to decide whether specimen to be of blood or urine] is simply to allocate to the investigating police officer the decision whether blood or urine should be required as distinct from the accused driver. The terms of the subsection do not import any suggestion that the officer is entitled to ask for only one specimen and if this is not complied with, he is in no circumstances entitled to ask for another …

"[After reviewing the arguments and authorities on whether or not the justices were wrong in law to allow the amendment] The first point … is that … the same offence was charged, that is to say, an offence under the same subsection of failing to provide a specimen … It is merely the nature of the specimen which is different according to the original information as distinct from the amendment. The failure to provide either specimen would require the same evidence to be laid … particularly having regard to the point which the defence wished to submit, namely, that the police officer was not entitled to ask for a second specimen. It would be a prerequisite of that submission that evidence was adduced that he had in fact asked originally for the specimen of blood …

"… in accordance with their obligation to see that justice was done between the parties, the justices had in fact offered the defence an adjournment if they required it so that they could properly meet the case being put … there is no injustice to the defendant by the form of the amendment which was granted. …"

Appeal dismissed.

Barnes v Chief Constable of Durham

[1997] 2 Cr App R 505, 24 April 1997, QBD (DC)

In the circumstances of this case, the justices' decision on a question of identity could not be impugned. An unproductive request for one specimen does not prevent a subsequent request for another specimen from being valid. See also DPP v Garrett, page 76 – where the procedure for requiring a blood specimen was not correctly followed, but it was not then possible to obtain a blood specimen and a urine specimen was required instead, the analysis of the urine specimen was admissible.

A motorist was charged with failing without reasonable excuse to provide a specimen of urine for a laboratory test, contrary to s 7(6), Road Traffic Act 1988. He had been involved in a road traffic accident and was taken to hospital; he later discharged himself and was then arrested. He gave his name as John William Hawkins born on 10.9.64; his name was in fact John William Barnes, born on 9.10.64. At the police station, the breath analysis device was not functioning correctly and the sergeant therefore requested a specimen of blood. The motorist said he had a phobia about needles and would not provide blood. The sergeant consulted the police surgeon, then requested a specimen of urine. The motorist failed to provide it.

At the hearing, the motorist argued that there was insufficient evidence that he was the man who had been arrested and taken to the police station; and that, having required a blood specimen, the sergeant could not then require a urine specimen. The justices rejected these submissions and convicted the motorist. He appealed.

QUESTION(S) FOR THE COURT: (a) Whether there was admissible evidence which would allow the magistrates to find that the appellant was the person who had failed to give a specimen of urine; (b) whether the procedure that took place in the police station was one which would allow the magistrates to convict the appellant of failure to provide a specimen of urine for analysis.

HELD: "[On (a)] The only evidence that the defendant John William Barnes was the driver of the vehicle concerned, and was the person who was required to provide a specimen, was that of DC Gibson … [who] … was certain that the man in the dock was the man he had interviewed that night … he could remember the appearance of the defendant …

"… the man in the police station denied being the driver … There is no evidence that any identification parade was in fact ever held, nor is there any evidence that John Williams Barnes when charged, either made any admission as to his being the driver or … expressed any challenge to the allegation that he was the same man as John William Hawkins …

"… it has been customary ever since I can remember for a police officer or other witnesses to be asked 'Do you see the driver in court', and for him to identify the defendant. Absent such an identification an acquittal may well follow. If in every case where the defendant does not distinctly admit driving there has to be an identification parade, the whole process of justice in a Magistrates' Court would be severely impaired …

"Allied to the general point about dock identification it is submitted on behalf of the appellant, that given that it was now some 33 months since the police officer had the opportunity of seeing the appellant, the Justices in the exercise of [their] discretion should have rejected the evidence. That in my judgment was entirely a matter of weight for the Justices to consider and their decision cannot be impugned.

"[On (b), authorities] support the prosecution contention that an unproductive request for one specimen does not prevent a subsequent request for another specimen from being valid. One can envisage a situation … where the request is made for blood, and it then transpires that there is not available any doctor to take blood. It would be inconceivable in those circumstances that as a result of the request for blood being wholly unproductive, an officer cannot then ask for a sample of urine … the sergeant was perfectly entitled to ask for a specimen of urine after refusal to provide blood … ."

The answers to both questions were "yes". Appeal dismissed.

DPP v Taylor (Graham)

Unreported, CO-203/97, 17 June 1997, QBD (DC)

It is lawful to require a urine specimen following refusal to provide a blood specimen.

A motorist had been charged with failing without reasonable excuse to provide a specimen of urine for analysis, contrary to s 7(6), Road Traffic Act 1988. He had been stopped by police, who formed the view that he was intoxicated and requested a roadside breath sample. He refused, and was arrested and taken to the police station. The custody sergeant believed the breath analysis device was giving inaccurate readings. Section 7(3)(b), Road Traffic Act 1988 (reliable device not available) therefore applied, and the sergeant said he intended to require a specimen of blood, asking whether there were any medical or other reasons why a blood specimen should not be taken. The motorist said "Yes, there is a reason. Ask the doctor", adding that it was to do with a condition he suffered while in the army. The sergeant asked for a specimen of blood; the reply was "No comment". He then asked for a specimen of urine and received the same reply.

The stipendiary magistrate held that once the sergeant had chosen blood rather than urine, if the motorist advanced a medical reason why such a specimen should not be provided, a doctor should have been called to determine the medical issue; conversely, if the motorist's assertions were not capable of constituting a medical reason, then the sergeant could request a specimen of blood. The reply "No comment" clearly constituted a refusal; the procedure was complete and the motorist should have been charged with failing to provide a specimen of blood; the sergeant was not entitled to require a specimen of urine. He dismissed the case. The prosecutor appealed.

QUESTION(S) FOR THE COURT: Whether a police officer is entitled to ask for a specimen of urine after a failure to provide a specimen of blood without reasonable excuse.

HELD: " [After reviewing the authorities] ... an *a fortiori* argument arises that where a defendant who has refused within the context of the Act to provide one form of sample [he] should not be able to take advantage of that fact when the officer says, in effect: 'If you will not give that sample, let us consider the giving of the other sample'. In my view, that distinction simply cannot be drawn. The sergeant in this case ... having been thwarted in his attempts to obtain a sample of blood, was perfectly entitled to ask for a sample of urine, and, when that was refused, to charge the defendant with failing to provide a sample of urine and not have to relate back to charging the Respondent with failing to provide a sample of blood."

The answer to the question was "yes". Appeal allowed.

Chapter 2

Specimens for Laboratory Testing

See s 15, Road Traffic Offenders Act 1988 – use of specimens in proceedings for an offence under ss 3A to 5A, Road Traffic Act 1988.

1. TAKING SPECIMENS: BLOOD

See also Jones (Vivian Mary) v DPP, page 631 – where a specimen is taken at hospital, there is no requirement to explain why a breath specimen cannot be taken; and DPP v Carless, page 368, where, on the facts, the analysis of a blood specimen given in connection with the investigation of a possible abduction was admissible to prove driving with excess alcohol.

Russell v Devine
[2003] UKHL 24, [2003] 1 WLR 1187, [2003] 2 Cr App R 26, 8 May 2003, HL

Where a requirement for a blood specimen is made at a police station, the specimen may be taken by a medical practitioner elsewhere than at a police station or a hospital (in this case, at a health centre).

A motorist had been arrested on suspicion of driving while unfit through drink, contrary to art 15(1), Road Traffic (Northern Ireland) Order 1995 (SI 1995/2994). Article 18 of that Order is in substantially the same terms as s 7, Road Traffic Act 1988 (provision of specimens for analysis). At the police station, no officer trained to operate the evidential breath testing device was available, and the defendant was required to provide a specimen of blood. He consented. The police officer conducting the proceedings contacted a doctor. The doctor was the only doctor on duty at a nearby health centre, so he asked that the defendant be taken to the health centre for the specimen to be taken. The defendant was duly taken to the health centre, where the requirement for a specimen of blood was repeated, and the specimen was taken. Analysis of the specimen revealed excess alcohol.

CERTIFIED QUESTION: Whether it is necessary, if the requirement to provide a specimen of blood or urine has been duly made under art 18, Road Traffic (Northern Ireland) Order 1995 at a police station or a hospital, that the specimen be taken at a police station or a hospital.

HELD: "26. Section 15(4)(a)(ii) [, Road Traffic Offenders Act 1988 (as amended by s 57(3), Police Reform Act 2002), the wording of which was identical to art 18(4), Road Traffic Offenders (Northern Ireland) Order 1996 (SI 1996 No 1320)] states, in effect, that a specimen of blood may be taken by a doctor at a place other than a police station or a hospital. In my opinion section 57(3) was not intended to change the law and to remove a restriction as to where a doctor could take a specimen of blood … In Northern Ireland the road traffic legislation is based on, and is virtually identical to, the equivalent English legislation. Therefore in the light of section 57(3) I consider that the Court of Appeal were right to hold that after a requirement for a specimen of blood had been made in the police station, the specimen might be taken elsewhere by a medical practitioner …

"[On the argument that the requirement had been made not at the police station or at a hospital, but at a health centre] 27. … the requirement made … in the police station about 2 a.m. was not superseded by the requirement made … in the health centre about 2.15 a.m. When the appellant was taken to the health centre I think it was to give effect to the requirement made in the police station and his consent given there, and I consider that the specimen was provided in consequence of this requirement and that the repetition of the requirement within such a short period of time did not deprive the first requirement of its operative effect."

The answer to the question was "no". Appeal dismissed.

Afolayan v CPS

[2012] EWHC 1322 (Admin), 1 May 2012, QBD (Admin)

On the findings in this case, the procedure for taking a blood specimen was correctly followed, even though the MG DD form had not been fully completed.

A motorist had been charged with driving with excess alcohol in blood, contrary to s 5(1), Road Traffic Act 1988. The arresting officer gave evidence that he was present when the blood specimen was taken and that he packaged the specimen, gave it a unique reference number and placed it in a safe. The desk sergeant gave evidence that "all normal procedures" were correctly followed. The doctor who took the specimen did not give evidence. The MG DD/A form had not, however, been fully completed. It did not record that part of the specimen was offered to the motorist, sealed in his presence and accepted by him. The motorist did not agree that the specimens were sealed in his presence, but did accept he had been given a specimen, which he did not have analysed. The analyst of the specimen said, in an agreed statement, that she had received the specimen with the unique reference number allocated by the arresting officer and conducted a routine analysis. The magistrates were satisfied that the procedure for taking the blood specimen had been correctly followed and convicted. The motorist appealed.

QUESTION(S) FOR THE COURT: Whether the magistrates could be satisfied beyond reasonable doubt that the correct medical procedures were followed.

HELD: "21. The simple answer to that question is yes. The police officers could give evidence, as they did, about the procedure that was followed and that it was followed correctly. The magistrates were entitled to prefer that evidence to such evidence as may have been given by the appellant to opposite effect. They were entitled to rely upon the undisputed evidence of the forensic scientist that a properly sealed and bagged specimen reached her laboratory and was analysed by her. The appellant had his own opportunity to have the sample, which he admits was given to him, tested. Had it been and had it cast doubt upon the result achieved on the sample analysed by the forensic scientist, then there may well have been a difficult issue for the court to resolve. But on the evidence that they heard, the magistrates were clearly entitled to reach the conclusion they did."

Appeal dismissed.

2. TAKING SPECIMENS: URINE

See s 7(5), Road Traffic Act 1988 – a specimen of urine is to be provided within one hour of the requirement for it and after the provision of a previous specimen. See also the cases in Chapter 1 under the heading "Urine Specimens", page 116; Walters (Julian) v DPP, page 205, in calculating the one hour allowed for providing urine specimens, seconds need not be taken into account; and Robertson (Eric) v DPP, page 206, where the officer delayed allowing the driver to produce the first specimen, and disallowed a second specimen to be provided after the expiry of the hour.

Ross v Hodges

[1975] RTR 55, 1 November 1974, QBD

Where the container holding the second urine specimen was spilt, whether deliberately or not, no second specimen was provided.

A motorist had been charged with failing without reasonable excuse to provide a laboratory specimen contrary to s 9(3), Road Traffic Act 1972. He provided a first urine specimen, and then filled a jar with urine for the second specimen. The officer reached to take the jar, but it fell from the motorist's hand and the contents were spilt. The driver declined to provide a further specimen. The justices accepted that, since there was no suggestion that the jar had been deliberately dropped, the passing of the urine into the jar was sufficient provision, and that, even if there had been a failure to provide, it was not without reasonable excuse. They accepted a submission of no case to answer and dismissed the case. The prosecutor appealed.

QUESTION(S) FOR THE COURT: Whether, on the facts, the justices came to a correct determination and decision in point of law.

HELD: "In my view the second urine specimen was not provided. I am not prepared to accept that the mere passing of the urine was a provision for present purposes unless and until the police officer was given the opportunity of taking charge of it and did take charge of it. He did not have that opportunity, and it matters not … whether the jar was deliberately dropped or not. The specimen contained in the jar was not provided."

Any question of reasonable excuse would have been for the defendant to make out. Appeal allowed.

R v Coward

[1976] RTR 425, 11 March 1976, CA

To be sufficient, a urine specimen must be capable of being divided into two parts such that both parts are capable of analysis; there can be no failure to provide a urine specimen until the hour is up.

A motorist had been charged with driving with excess alcohol in urine, contrary to s 6(1), Road Traffic Act 1972. At the police station, he provided a first urine specimen which was discarded in the usual way. The second specimen was insufficient to cover the bottom of a glass jar. The station sergeant decided it was insufficient for division into two parts and discarded it. A third specimen was produced within one hour of the original request. It was divided and analysed, and revealed excess alcohol. The motorist was convicted and appealed.

GROUNDS FOR APPEAL: The prosecution had failed to establish that the second sample of urine provided by the appellant was insufficient for the purposes of division and analysis; even if the second specimen was insufficient, there was no power to require a further specimen and the motorist should have been treated as having failed to provide.

HELD: "… this appeal turns upon what is meant by a 'specimen of … urine'. There is no statutory definition. … a specimen of urine within the meaning of section 9 must be large enough to be divided into two parts by a police constable in a police station; and each part must be capable of analysis. … In this case the sergeant gave evidence that there was not enough urine for him to divide into two parts. The jury were entitled to accept his evidence and they must have done so. …

"If the appellant did not provide a specimen within the meaning of the Act at all when he made his unsuccessful try, he still had time to provide a second specimen: the request made to him was to provide two specimens within one hour. What he provided on his further try was capable of division and analysis and was so dealt with. It was a specimen within the meaning of the Act and was the second specimen. [The sergeant] would have been in error to treat the unsuccessful try as a failure to provide a specimen. A motorist ought not to be held to have failed to provide a specimen of urine until the hour is up."

Appeal dismissed.

Prosser v Dickeson

[1982] RTR 96, 16 October 1981, QBD

Where the officer directed the suspect to stop urinating, discarded the urine supplied, and then directed the suspect to resume urinating, the whole process taking no more than 2 minutes, only a single specimen was supplied.

A motorist had been charged with driving with excess alcohol in urine, contrary to s 6(1), Road Traffic Act 1972. At the police station, he provided urine. He began urinating at 2.49 am, and when the jar contained half to three quarters of an inch of urine, the officer told him to stop. The officer discarded the urine and washed the jar. At 2.50 am, the officer directed the suspect, who had not put his penis away, to continue urinating. He did and analysis showed excess alcohol. The justices were of the opinion that only one specimen had been provided, and dismissed the information. The prosecutor appealed.

QUESTION(S) FOR THE COURT: Whether, on the facts as found, the defendant in law provided one specimen of urine or two specimens of urine.

HELD: "… having regard to the fact that the entire operation occupied no more than two minutes and that the sergeant directed the defendant to stop, and then to 'continue urinating', it seems to me perfectly obvious that this was all one single operation, which was momentarily discontinued on the direction of the sergeant. In my judgment, the justices were satisfied in reaching the conclusion that here was one and not two specimens."

Appeal dismissed.

Over v Musker

[1985] RTR 84, 1 March 1984, QBD (DC)

Where there is only a short time lapse (one minute) between the giving of two urine specimens, two specimens are nevertheless provided.

A motorist had been charged with driving with excess alcohol in urine, contrary to s 6(1), Road Traffic Act 1972. He was requested to provide two specimens of urine under s 9(5)(b), Road Traffic Act 1972. The first was provided at 2.15 am and duly disposed of; a further specimen was volunteered by the motorist and provided at 2.16 am. Analysis of the second specimen revealed 155 mg alcohol in 100 ml urine.

At the hearing, the motorist submitted that there was no case to answer in that the "second" specimen was in fact a continuation of the first, in view of the very short time lapse; that, therefore, only one specimen had been given, which, under the statute, had to be thrown away; there was therefore no specimen which could be analysed. The justices accepted that argument and dismissed the charge. The prosecutor appealed.

QUESTION(S) FOR THE COURT: (i) Whether the justices were right in determining that, because of the short lapse of time between the provision of the two specimens of urine, the defendant had not provided two separate specimens;

(iii) whether the justices could properly find, in view of the evidence called that the defendant, following the provision of the first specimen of urine, put his penis away and resumed his seat and only then requested the opportunity to provide his second specimen, that the two specimens were the result of one operation momentarily interrupted.

HELD: "… the conclusion reached by the justices … was not warranted by the evidence before them. Here we have a case where the request was given in the proper form; where a first specimen was given; where the defendant then – to use the euphemism – adjusted his dress and resumed his seat. Having done so, albeit a short time afterwards, he then indicated that he was ready to give a second specimen. He then gave it.

"… it is plain that, although there was only a short time between the giving of the two specimens, nevertheless two specimens were given.

"… there is no question here of the defendant not being given a full and fair opportunity to supply a second specimen, because he of his own free will gave the second specimen. There was no question of his being told to stop and start again … ."

The answers to all three questions were "no". Appeal allowed.

DPP v Baldwin (Alistair)

[2000] RTR 314, 30 March 2000, QBD (DC)

The results of the analysis of a urine specimen provided 15 minutes after expiry of the statutory hour were admissible.

A motorist had been arrested following a positive roadside breath test. At the police station, the breath analysis device was not working. The police doctor concluded that the motorist should not be required to provide a blood specimen. The officer therefore required two urine samples. The request was made at 2.00 am. The first sample was produced at 2.15 am and duly discarded. The second sample was provided at 3.15 am and in due course revealed excess alcohol. The driver was charged with driving with excess alcohol, contrary to s 5(1)(a), Road Traffic Act 1988. He argued that the wording of s 7(5) of the Act – "A specimen of urine shall be provided within one hour of the requirement for its provision being made and after the provision of a previous specimen of urine" – meant that the results of the analysis were inadmissible in evidence because the specimen relied on had been provided more than one hour after the request.

The justices found no case to answer and dismissed the case. The prosecutor appealed.

QUESTION(S) FOR THE COURT: Whether the justices were correct in concluding that there was no case to answer by virtue of the second sample of urine which was obtained for analysis being provided 75 minutes after the initial request; that is in excess of the one hour stipulated in s 7(5), Road Traffic Act 1988.

HELD: "… The only significance of the period of one hour is to make finite the length of time available to a driver to provide the specimen required of him … If after that time the driver has failed to provide a specimen he may there and then be charged with the offence of failing to supply a specimen, but if the supervising officer permits him to provide a specimen after the hour has elapsed that does not render the evidence of the analysis inadmissible … the results of the analysis of the specimen provided 15 minutes after the expiration of the statutory hour were … clearly admissible."

The answer to the question was "no". Appeal allowed.

Ryder v CPS

[2011] EWHC 4003 (Admin), 14 April 2011, QBD (Admin)

A specimen of urine can be provided from a catheter bag; urine taken after separate emptyings of a catheter bag were separate specimens.

A motorist had been charged with driving with excess alcohol in urine, contrary to s 5(1), Road Traffic Act 1988. He had been involved in a road traffic accident and was in hospital. For medical reasons a blood specimen could not be taken, and the motorist agreed to provide a specimen of urine. He had a catheter in place. It had two chambers, the first of which collected urine, which would then drain into a second, larger chamber. When the procedure for taking the specimen began at 5.43, the upper chamber was drained to the lower chamber and allowed to refill. At 5.44 the upper chamber was drained again and when it had filled for the third time the officer took a specimen from the upper chamber at 5.50. This is the specimen which was analysed. The officer gave evidence that the flow of urine into the upper chamber was continuous throughout and he did not try to stop it. Analysis of the urine specimen showed excess alcohol. The motorist was convicted and appealed.

QUESTION(S) FOR THE COURT: Whether the justices were right to conclude that the provision of the specimen occurred at the point at which the catheter bag was emptied, rather than at the point the urine left the defendant.

HELD: "[On the argument that "providing" a specimen is the equivalent of excreting it] 22. … I cannot accept this submission. … the words of the statute … do not require in terms that a motorist should urinate. What is requested from the motorist under the statutory provisions is a specimen. What is not requested is urination as such. A specimen of urine is in my view not provided at the moment it is excreted. Provision involves the concept of provision to someone. …

"[On the argument that urine was continuously flowing and that emptying the catheter bag did not amount to providing two separate specimens] 26. … if a flow of urine is connected in a chamber and that chamber is emptied, as it was here, into another chamber, the urine which thereafter collects in the first chamber is not the same sample, not the same urine as that which has been drained away. A specimen of that second filling seems to me to constitute a second specimen of urine. In this case, there were in fact three samples, one or two specimens being disregarded before that which was taken for evidential purposes ... Given that the purpose of the provisions was to ensure that the urine ultimately sent for analysis was a fresh specimen, and properly reflected the bodily condition of the person from whom it was taken, it seems to be entirely consistent with that principle that the statutory words should be interpreted here as the Bench interpreted them, that there was here more than one specimen."

The answer to the question was "yes". Appeal dismissed.

3. DIVIDING THE SPECIMEN AND SUPPLYING PART

See s 15(5), Road Traffic Offenders Act 1988 – where the suspect asks for part of the specimen, it must be divided into two parts and one must be supplied to the suspect. See also Jones (Vivian Mary) v DPP, page 631 – putting a blood sample into the defendant's handbag which was with her personal belongings on a hospital trolley constituted supply.

Perry v McGovern

[1986] RTR 240, 18 December 1985, QBD (DC)

Where the police, in error, misled the defendant into believing that her part of the blood specimen could not be submitted for analysis, her conviction could not stand. See also Byrne (Simon David) v DPP, page 147, where, on the facts, the defendant had not been discouraged from having his specimen analysed.

A motorist had been charged with driving with excess alcohol in blood, contrary to s 6(1)(a), Road Traffic Act 1972 as substituted by s 25 and Sch 8, Transport Act 1981. She had been arrested and at the police station the breath analysis device was not functioning properly, so the police officer administering the procedure required a blood specimen under s 8(3)(b), Road Traffic Act 1972 as likewise substituted (reliable device not available). The blood specimen was taken and the motorist elected to take a part for independent analysis. The specimen was divided into two in the usual way, except that the part given to the motorist was not put into an envelope, sealed, and the flap signed by the officer and offered to the motorist for signature. The police later informed her that because of this her part of the specimen could not be submitted for analysis; therefore she did not do so. The part retained by the police was analysed and revealed 83 mg alcohol in 100 ml blood.

At the hearing, the motorist argued that s 10(6), Road Traffic Act 1972 as likewise substituted had not been complied with and she had been deprived of the right to have an independent analysis. The justices rejected that argument and convicted the motorist. She appealed.

QUESTION(S) FOR THE COURT: Whether the justices were correct in law in deciding that s 10(6), Road Traffic Act 1972 had been complied with in view of the fact that the defendant had been told by a police officer that the specimen she had selected could not be submitted for independent analysis.

HELD: "Section 10(6) … provides '… Where, at the time a specimen of blood or urine was provided by the accused, he asked to be supplied with such a specimen, evidence of the proportion of alcohol or any drug found in the specimen is not admissible on behalf of the prosecution unless (a) the specimen in which the alcohol … was found is one of two parts into which the specimen provided by the accused was divided at the time it was provided; and (b) the other part was supplied to the accused'…

"… the defendant, on the same day that she had given the specimen and been supplied with a part of it by the police, had been told by a police officer that the specimen given to her could not be submitted for analysis as the correct procedure had not been followed … the information thus given to her was never corrected …

"… the defendant here was misled by the prosecution, undoubtedly in good faith, into thinking that she did not have a specimen that could be submitted to independent analysis as contemplated and required by the statute.

On that short and narrow ground, I would allow this appeal."

Dear v DPP

[1988] RTR 148, [1988] Crim LR 316, 20 November 1987, QBD (DC)

Where two blood specimens were taken and the part provided to the motorist included blood from both, the procedure had not been correctly followed and the conviction was overturned.

A motorist had been charged with driving with excess alcohol in blood, contrary to s 6(1), Road Traffic Act 1972 as substituted by s 25 and Sch 8, Transport Act 1981. The breath analysis device was not available and accordingly a blood specimen was required. At the first attempt, only a very small amount of blood was taken. At the second attempt, a sufficient specimen was obtained. Part of this sample was retained by the police; in error, the doctor mixed the other part with the blood which had been taken on the first attempt, and it was this mixture which was handed to the motorist. The police analysis revealed 130 mg alcohol in 100 ml blood.

The justices accepted that the mixing of the two specimens did not alter or affect the fact that the defendant had been provided with half the sample properly provided on the second occasion. They convicted the motorist. She appealed.

QUESTION(S) FOR THE COURT: Whether s 10(6), Road Traffic Act 1972 (blood analysis not admissible unless specimen divided and one part supplied to the accused, etc) had been complied with in view of the facts found, and in particular, whether the justices were right to conclude that there was sufficient evidence for them to decide that s 10(6) had been complied with.

HELD: "… It is to be noted from section 10(6) that reference is made to only one sample called a 'specimen' taken upon one single occasion … It is the product of that which has to be divided …

"... what was handed to the defendant was not one half or one portion of the single sample taken from her body, but it was that and, in addition, blood taken from her body upon a previous occasion. That seems to me to be quite contrary to the plain terms of section 10(6) ... with very considerable reluctance, therefore, I have come to the conclusion that the justices were wrong ... the only evidence ... was inadmissible."

Appeal allowed.

Butler v DPP

[1990] RTR 377, 3 February 1989, QBD (DC)

The fact that a blood specimen was wrongly labelled did not mean that it was not "supplied".

A motorist had been charged with driving with excess alcohol in blood, contrary to s 6(1)(a), Road Traffic Act 1972 as substituted by s 25 and Sch 8, Transport Act 1981. He was at a hospital, and a police officer required a blood specimen for a laboratory test under s 8(3), Road Traffic Act 1972 as likewise substituted. A specimen was taken in the usual way, except that, in error, the doctor who took the specimen labelled the motorist's part of the specimen with the surname of the officer conducting the procedure, rather than that of the motorist. The motorist took his part for independent analysis; the analyst declined to analyse it because the name on the specimen was not the motorist's name. Analysis of the part retained by the police revealed excess alcohol.

At the hearing the motorist contended that the prosecution blood analysis should not be admitted because the prosecution had not complied with the requirement in s 10(6)(b) to supply part of the specimen to him. The justices rejected that and convicted the motorist. He appealed.

QUESTION(S) FOR THE COURT: Whether the justices were correct in law in admitting evidence of analysis of a blood specimen under s 10, Road Traffic Act 1972 as substituted, having regard to the fact that the defendant had been told by the analyst to whom he took his part of the specimen that he (the analyst) would not analyse it; and whether there was evidence upon which the magistrates' court could find that a specimen was properly supplied to the defendant as required by s 10(6), Road Traffic Act 1972.

HELD: "... the appropriate specimen was physically supplied to the defendant, as required by section 10(6) ... The specimen was capable of analysis. Only if it was supplied in such circumstances that the defendant would be expected to be deterred or prevented from having it analysed could there be a defence on the basis of *Perry v McGovern* [page 128]. I do not consider that the wrong surname accidentally placed on a label put the specimen into that category ... No explanation was given in evidence as to why [the analyst] declined to analyse it. There is no obvious reason why he should have declined to analyse it, and none has been suggested to us.

"… the fact that the specimen was wrongly labelled does not … mean that it was not supplied for the purposes of section 10(6)."

Appeal dismissed.

DPP v Elstob

[1992] RTR 45, [1992] Crim LR 518, 15 November 1991, QBD (DC)

A time lapse of 2 minutes between taking a blood specimen and dividing it meets the requirement to divide the specimen at the time it is provided.

A motorist had been charged with driving with excess alcohol, contrary to s 5(1)(a), Road Traffic Act 1988. He had been asked to provide a blood specimen. A doctor was called and the blood specimen was taken; the doctor then took the blood away to the cell area and placed it in two capsules. He returned some 2 minutes later.

At the hearing the motorist argued that the blood analysis was not admissible in evidence because it had not been divided "at the time it was provided", as required by s 15(5)(a), Road Traffic Offenders Act 1988. The justices found that because the specimen had not been separated "at the time" it was given and in full view of the motorist, that infringed a vital requirement and they dismissed the case. The prosecutor appealed.

QUESTION(S) FOR THE COURT: Whether the justices could properly hold that: (a) the division of the blood sample by the doctor took place other than "at the time it was provided", thus breaching s 15(5)(a), Road Traffic Offenders Act 1988; (b) the evidence of the proportion of alcohol in the defendant's blood was therefore inadmissible; (c) the information accordingly had to be dismissed.

HELD: "… The expression 'at the time' must be considered in its context. Parliament cannot have contemplated that equipment would have been available which enabled the provision of the sample and its division to take place simultaneously … It must have been contemplated that the two operations were to take place consecutively and that some passage of time is inevitable between the one and the other … the expression contemplates that the two operations must be closely linked in time and performed as part of the same event. It is a question of fact and degree. In this context it does not mean that the two things must be done simultaneously or even within seconds; hours on the other hand would clearly be too long.

"… All that is required is that the division must take place as part of the same event as the provision … it does not follow that compliance … requires the presence of the defendant … however, … it is desirable whenever possible that the division should take place in the presence of the defendant."

Appeal allowed.

DPP v Snook

[1993] Crim LR 883, 16 June 1993, QBD (DC)

The procedure for dividing a blood specimen was correctly followed even though the phial containing the defendant's part was not placed in an envelope.

A motorist had been charged with driving with excess alcohol in blood, contrary to s 5(1)(a), Road Traffic Act 1988. He had been stopped by police and breath analysis revealed 44 µg alcohol in 100 ml breath. He was therefore offered the option (alternative specimen where lower breath reading no more than 50 – now repealed, see page v) of replacing the breath specimens by a blood specimen. He did so and was given part of the specimen in a sealed container; the container was not enclosed in an envelope. An envelope was later handed to the motorist, but the blood specimen was not put into it and the envelope was not signed. The next day the motorist contacted an analyst, as a result of which he understood that any analysis would be of little value in any court proceedings because the phial containing the specimen had not been sealed in the envelope at the time. No analysis on behalf of the motorist was therefore carried out. The blood analysed on behalf of the police revealed 87 mg alcohol in 100 ml blood.

The magistrates found that the proper procedure had not been followed and acquitted the defendant. The prosecutor appealed.

QUESTION(S) FOR THE COURT: Whether the justices were correct in law in deciding that the provisions of s 15(5), Road Traffic Offenders Act had not been complied with.

HELD: "… the Act was complied with. The blood sample was divided into two parts and one part was supplied to the accused. It is perfectly true that in most, if not all, police stations there is a gloss on that basic procedure which the statute lays down, namely that envelopes are customarily, if not always, provided into which the sample is put … But what is called the 'brown envelope routine' is not part of the requirement of the statutory provision laid down. All that is required is that a person who may be accused under the Act is given his sample so that he can make up his own mind whether he throws it away, takes it to an analyst or passes it on to somebody else for analysis later on.

"… it cannot be said … that what the analyst may have told Mr Snook was anything to do with the prosecution or with the police. It is true … that analysts do not like to accept samples unless they are in brown envelopes, but that is not a matter which has been led in evidence and it is not a matter which should affect us or the Magistrates. That fact is that the sample was there; it was Mr Snook's blood; he knew that it was his blood because he had been given the requisite half sample and he chose, after speaking to the analyst, not to have his blood analysed."

Appeal allowed.

Johnson (Antony Harold) v DPP

Unreported, CO 1241/94, 13 October 1994, QBD (DC)

Where the blood specimen was taken and divided in the usual way, and the defendant's part was stored in the refrigerator at the police station, the procedure was correctly followed, the court finding that the defendant did not seek to recover his part.

A motorist had been charged with driving with excess alcohol, contrary to s 5(1)(a), Road Traffic Act 1988. A police officer stopped him while driving; he gave a false name and tried to escape. At the police station, the breath analysis device was not operating correctly, but the motorist agreed to provide a blood specimen. It was taken and divided into two parts in the usual way. The motorist was given the opportunity to choose one of the parts; he did so. Both containers were put into bags and sealed; the part selected by the motorist was handed to him, then taken by a police officer and put into the refrigerator to prevent deterioration while the motorist remained in custody pending inquiries. On leaving the police station, the motorist's property was handed to him, but not the blood specimen. He said in evidence that he had asked for the specimen but that the officer had been unable to find it. He conceded that he had returned to the police station twice more, with his legal representatives, but had not inquired after the blood specimen because his solicitors had told him to leave it to them.

The specimen analysed for the police revealed not less than 83 mg alcohol in 100 ml blood.

The justices found, *inter alia*, that the specimen had been supplied to the motorist in that it had been made available to him; that it was available to him had he requested it; the fact that he had given false details and had left the scene affected his credibility as a witness and they were not satisfied that he had requested the specimen and that the police officer had been unable to find it. The justices convicted the motorist; he appealed.

QUESTION(S) FOR THE COURT: Whether there was sufficient evidence to hold that the police had complied with s 15(5), Road Traffic Offenders Act 1988 for the admission in evidence of the result of the blood analysis.

HELD: "There is nothing … to suggest that [the appellant's] sample was taken out [of the refrigerator] again. As to the custody record, it shows that his property was returned to him and he signed for it. Underneath that, there is the entry 'Blood sample (in fridge)'. He does not sign for that.

"I am quite unable to see why the Justices should not draw the inference, as they did, from that record that it remained in the fridge, and was not taken away by him … they simply did not believe his story of having asked for it and the police having been unable to find it. He could have come back for it the next day … he gave evidence that … he told his solicitor about it and they told him to leave it to them, that, no doubt, is why he did nothing about it when he returned to the police station on two occasions, and obviously his solicitor did not do anything about it either. That does suggest that neither he nor his solicitor were interested in recovering it …

"… the Appellant was supplied with his sample of blood when it was divided and he chose the one that he wanted."

The answer to the question was "yes". Appeal dismissed.

Mokhra v DPP

Unreported, CO/1414/96, 10 December 1996, QBD (DC)

Where the police, in error, notified the defendant that no further action would be taken and the defendant then threw away his part of the blood specimen, but in any event had taken no steps to have it analysed and had not indicated that he wished to challenge the prosecution's analysis, his appeal against conviction failed. See also Byrne (Simon David) v DPP, page 147, and DPP v Snook, page 132, where, on the facts, the defendant had not been discouraged from having his specimen analysed; compare Perry v McGovern, page 128, where the defendant was so deterred.

A motorist had been charged with driving with excess alcohol, contrary to s 5(1)(a), Road Traffic Act 1988. On 16 April 1995, he had been stopped by police, cautioned and arrested, and gave a blood specimen. He took one part of the specimen home with him and put it in the refrigerator. He later received a letter, dated 24 May 1995, from the police saying, *inter alia*, that no further action would be taken. This letter was sent in error. The driver did not attempt to have his part of the blood specimen analysed and was not sure how long he intended to keep it. On receiving the letter of 24 May, thinking the case would not proceed, he threw away the blood. He was later summonsed, and told that the blood-alcohol reading was 240 mg alcohol in 100 ml blood.

The motorist sought a stay of proceedings, arguing that there had been an abuse of process. The magistrates dismissed that application on the grounds that the motorist had not been prejudiced by the letter; he had taken no steps to have his part of the specimen analysed and had not indicated that he wished to challenge the blood-alcohol level on which the prosecution intended to rely. The trial proceeded and the motorist was convicted. He appealed.

HELD: "[Counsel for the appellant submits that] … The police error which led him to throw away his blood sample deprived him of the chance to have it analysed and thus of the chance to challenge the prosecution evidence …

"… [Section 78, Police and Criminal Evidence Act 1984 – discretion to exclude evidence which would have such an adverse effect on the fairness of the proceedings that the court ought not to admit it] gives the appropriate remedy where the Prosecution seek to rely upon evidence in circumstances where it is unfair that they should do so. In the present case it would have been open to the appellant to object to the admission of the prosecution blood sample at his trial … To have any chance of succeeding it would be necessary for [the appellant] to persuade the Magistrates that had he not thrown this sample away he would have [had] it analysed in order to attempt to challenge the prosecution evidence. The agreed facts in the case stated were to the contrary which is not surprising having regard to the extent to which the prosecution sample was over the limit … the appellant had no possible basis for arguing that there was an abuse of process … ."

Appeal dismissed.

DPP v Higgins (Adam Scott)

[2001] EWHC Admin 871, 29 October 2001, QBD (Admin)

The fact that a blood specimen was wrongly labelled did not amount to a breach of art 6, European Convention on Human Rights.

A motorist had been charged with driving with excess alcohol in blood, contrary to s 5(1)(a), Road Traffic Act 1988. The lower of two breath analyses was 50 μg alcohol in 100 ml breath; the motorist was therefore offered the option of providing an alternative specimen (under s 8(2), Road Traffic Act 1988 – lower breath reading no more than 50 μg alcohol in 100 ml breath – now repealed; see page v); he elected to do so and a blood specimen was taken and divided into two. The custody sergeant inadvertently labelled both parts with the name of another prisoner. One part was handed to the motorist and the other forwarded to the laboratory for analysis. The sergeant realised his error and notified the laboratory that the specimen related to the defendant. Analysis revealed 117 mg alcohol in 100 ml blood.

The defendant sent his part of the specimen for analysis, but it was returned to him untested, the analyst having refused to analyse a specimen in someone else's name. The defendant did not take any other steps to have the specimen analysed.

The magistrates were of the opinion that the human rights issues of fair trial and abuse of process distinguished the case from that of *Butler v DPP* (see page 130). They found that the motorist had been deprived of his right to obtain and examine witnesses on the same conditions as the prosecutor; they stayed the proceedings as an abuse of process. The prosecutor appealed.

QUESTION(S) FOR THE COURT: Whether the justices were right: (1) to conclude that the wrongly labelled specimen given to the respondent prevented him from obtaining and calling independent expert analysis of the part sample; (2) to differentiate between *Butler v DPP* and this case by giving fullest effect to the art 6 right to a fair trial; (3) to conclude that the respondent could not receive a fair trial and stay proceedings on the grounds of an abuse of process.

HELD: "13. … the facts of *Butler* are indistinguishable … 14. [there] the analyst refused to analyse the sample simply upon the basis that the sample did not bear the defendant's name, precisely … as … in the present case.

"16. … The magistrates undoubtedly had a discretion, but that discretion had to be exercised upon the basis of some evidence. Here there was simply no evidence that the inadvertent error in labelling prevented the respondent from obtaining an independent analysis. There was simply one refusal by one expert, with no explanation of the circumstances beyond the fact that he had declined to analyse a sample that was not labelled with the defendant's name. There was no indication as to whether he would have persisted in that course if asked again to perform the analysis with some explanation of how the inadvertent error had occurred. There was no attempt to clarify matters with the prosecution, no attempt to see if another analyst might adopt a less unhelpful position. …

"17. Whilst article 6 undoubtedly guarantees the right to a fair trial there was simply no evidence that there could not be a fair trial in the circumstances of this case … There was no abuse of process … There was an inadvertent error. There was no question of there having been improper conduct on the part of the prosecution and, crucially, no evidence that the inadvertent error prevented a fair trial or made it in any way unfair to try the defendant."

The answers to all three questions were "no". Appeal allowed.

Campbell v DPP

[2003] EWHC 559 (Admin), 28 February 2003, QBD (Admin)

There is no requirement that the police inform a suspect of his right to request part of his blood specimen.

A motorist had been convicted of driving with excess alcohol, contrary to s 5(1)(a), Road Traffic Act 1988. He had been arrested and, at the police station, the breath analysis device was not operating correctly and the officer conducting the procedure therefore required a specimen of blood, which was given. Analysis revealed excess alcohol. The justices were satisfied that a warning of the risk of prosecution had been given; that the appellant had been advised that a blood sample was required because the breath testing device was not available; and that the appellant was told that he would be provided with a sample of blood if he so required.

QUESTION(S) FOR THE COURT: Whether a reasonable bench of justices, properly directing themselves, could have held on the evidence that: (1) the appellant had been given all the requisite information about providing a specimen of blood; and (2) that the appellant had been made aware and understood that he was entitled to be provided with part of his own blood sample if he so wished.

HELD: "9. … Neither of those questions has been advanced … in this appeal. …

"10. …The appellant is seeking to raise for the first time a matter of fact and law not raised before the justices … Nevertheless, I have proceeded to consider the merits of the argument which has been addressed to me …

"11. [It is now submitted], relying upon two decisions of the Court of Appeal decided under the Road Traffic Act 1962, that the justices were required to consider whether the information given to the appellant that he was entitled to request his own sample was still operating on his mind at the time the sample was taken. It is submitted that, notwithstanding the fact that the justices were never asked to consider such a question at the trial, they should have made a specific finding of fact about it.

"12. It is submitted that since the justices made no such finding the appeal must succeed. The submission I find is entirely misconceived.

"13. Section 2(5) of the [1962 Act] provided: 'A constable requesting any person to consent to the making of, or to provide a specimen of blood or urine for analysis, shall offer to supply him in a suitable container part of the specimen, or in the case of a specimen of blood, which it is not practicable to divide, another specimen which he may consent to have taken'.

"18. … Section 2(5) of the 1962 Act has not been re-enacted in the 1988 legislation. It is, therefore, no longer a statutory requirement for the officer to inform the suspect of his right to request his own specimen. [The appellant] submits that I should regard it as by now a settled principle of common law that such information should be provided to those against whom police officers are proceeding under section 7 of the 1988 Act.

"19. … that is a hopeless proposition. There may well be circumstances, however, when … a defendant will wish to challenge the admissibility of the analysis because he claims to have been unaware of his right to request the sample and as a result has suffered prejudice. …

"20. Here, however, no application was made to the justices to exclude the evidence of analysis on the basis of some prejudice suffered by the accused. The appellant elected not to give evidence in his own trial."

Appeal dismissed.

Jones (Elaine) v CPS

[2003] EWHC 1729 (Admin), 23 June 2003, QBD (DC)

It is for the defendant to ask to be supplied with part of the blood specimen.

A motorist had been charged with driving with excess alcohol, contrary to s 5(1)(a), Road Traffic Act 1988. At the police station, a doctor took a blood specimen and it was divided into two; the motorist was asked which part she wanted. She pointed to one of the samples but never physically took hold of it. Both samples were sealed and placed in the refrigerator. The doctor left the police station. Shortly after, the officer completed the paperwork and released the motorist. She did not ask for the specimen.

She was later convicted and appealed.

QUESTION(S) FOR THE COURT: Whether the justices were right to conclude: (1) that the appellant had in fact made a request for a blood sample; (2) that, given that she had requested a specimen, although it was not physically handed to her, but kept in the refrigerator and available for her to collect, it had been supplied to her within s 15(5)(b), Road Traffic Offenders Act 1988.

HELD: "7. … The scheme of the section is clear. At the time when the sample [of] blood is provided, it is for the accused to ask to be provided with a specimen of his or her blood. When he so asks, the specimen of blood provided by him must be divided at the time it is provided and the other part supplied to him. Failure in either respect renders the evidence of the proportion [of] alcohol or drug in the blood inadmissible. …

"13. [Counsel for the respondent] submitted that there was no evidence that the appellant had requested a specimen and the Justices were wrong in regarding acceptance [of the offer of a specimen] as … 'equivalent' to a request …

"14. Secondly, if there had been a request, there had been a supply. The appellant was offered one of two specimens and had pointed out one of them, and that was a sufficient supply and it was immaterial that the sample was then put in refrigerated storage. The onus was on her either to take hold of it at the time or collect it on release.

"15. [These] submissions are correct in both respects. There must be a request by the accused to be provided with a specimen. The scheme of the Act is clearly that this triggers the process of dividing the specimen. It may be that the specimen, as here, was divided without a request, but without a request, the provisions of section 15(5) do not engage.

"19. On the question of supply … [t]he combined effect of the offer of one of two samples and of the appellant pointing to a sample specimen amounted to a tendering of the sample to her. If she did not immediately take up the offer and take hold of her chosen specimen, or take it with her when she left the police station, or return shortly afterwards to collect it, she cannot later be heard to say that it was not supplied to her."

The answer to question (1) was "no"; the answer to question (2) was "yes". Appeal dismissed.

O'Connell v DPP

[2006] EWHC 1419 (Admin), 17 May 2006, QBD (Admin)

Where a blood specimen was taken, and the accused's part was supplied to his friend because the accused was not able to take possession of it himself, the specimen was "supplied" for the purposes of s 15(5), Road Traffic Offenders Act 1988.

A motor cycle rider had been charged with driving with excess alcohol, contrary to s 5(1)(a), Road Traffic Act 1988. There had been a collision and he was taken to hospital. Police attended the hospital; the rider was conscious but undergoing a CT scan. A blood specimen was taken and divided into two. The rider requested part of the specimen. It was handed to one of the rider's friends as he could not at the time take hold of it himself, and, being in the accident and emergency department, there was nowhere to keep the specimen safely. The specimen analysed on behalf of the prosecution revealed excess alcohol.

At the trial, it was argued that the defendant did not know his friend had been given the specimen for safekeeping and that it had not therefore been supplied to him in accordance with s 15(5), Road Traffic Offenders Act 1988. The district judge rejected that argument and convicted the accused. He appealed.

QUESTION(S) FOR THE COURT: Whether the district judge was correct to hold that the requirements of s 15(5), Road Traffic Offenders Act 1988 applied and that the prosecution certificate of analysis should be admitted.

HELD: "7. The purpose of Section 15(5) is clear. It provides a condition precedent to the admissibility of the evidence of analysis of the sample kept by the police by giving the defendant a chance to test that sample in case he wishes to challenge the evidence of the police analysis.

"8. It is agreed between the parties that the word 'supplied' is not restricted to the physical handing over of the sample. …

"14. [After reviewing the authorities] On whichever basis of fact the district judge proceeded – i.e., direct or indirect inference that the appellant must have known what was happening to the sample he requested, that it was being handed to his friend, or even if he did not – I have no doubt that the district judge was entitled to find on the evidence that a supply had taken place.

"15. Accordingly I answer the question in the affirmative and dismiss this appeal."

Lidington v DPP

[2006] EWHC 1984 (Admin), 29 June 2006, QBD (Admin)

Where a blood specimen is taken from an unconscious person under s 7A, Road Traffic Act 1988, there is no duty to offer a choice of part. Magistrates' findings expressed in the terms "we believe" are findings beyond reasonable doubt.

A motorist had been charged with, *inter alia*, driving with excess alcohol, contrary to s 5(1)(a), Road Traffic Act 1988. She had been stopped; a roadside breath test was positive; she refused to get into the police vehicle; there was a struggle; she fell motionless, claiming she was about to have a heart attack. She was taken to hospital; she was unconscious; a police surgeon took a blood specimen and divided into two parts in the usual way. Some 1½ hours later she was conscious and the police officer told her the specimen had been taken; she did not ask for part of it but the officer gave her one of the phials. He did not give her a choice which part she was to have. She consented to the testing of the specimen, which in due course revealed excess alcohol.

The magistrates convicted her; she appealed.

QUESTION(S) FOR THE COURT: (1) Whether there was any evidence on which a reasonably minded bench of justices, properly directing themselves, could have held that the correct procedure for obtaining a blood specimen had been followed. (2) Given that the appellant did not request part of the sample, whether s 15(5A), Road Traffic Offenders Act 1988 (as enacted by s 57, Police Reform Act 2002) required that she be given a choice of the part of the sample that should be given to her. (3) Whether the bench applied the correct standard of proof.

HELD: "[On (1) and (2)] 7. … [The appellant] asserts that it was a necessary requirement for the admissibility of the results of the analysis of the blood specimen provided that the appellant should have been asked if she wished to exercise a choice as to which of the two parts of the one sample she wished to have …

"12. … it is difficult to see quite what providing a choice to an accused would add to protection against the mischief at which this part of the Act is directed. It is not immediately apparent why a sample which is divided into two … should be one in respect of which the accused should have a choice as to which part he or she has for personal analysis, or whatever use he may wish to make of it.

"13. Accordingly, we see no force whatsoever in this point. We should merely add for completeness that the procedure to be adopted for a person who is, by reason of unconsciousness, unable to provide consent for the taking of a sample, is laid down by section 7A of the Road Traffic Act [1988]. That too makes no reference to there being any choice of sample.

"14. The third question as to the standard of proof arose because the Magistrates expressed themselves in open court in the terms of a note which we have in handwritten form. … Each of the paragraphs of the handwritten note begins with the two words, 'We believe.' … There is no part of the evidence which the Magistrates believed was capable of assisting the appellant. It was all an acceptance of the prosecution case.

"15. [Counsel for the appellant] argues that the words 'We believe' are words which are appropriate and appropriate only to an approach to the standard of proof which is that of proof on the balance of probabilities. It falls short, he submits, of finding a case proved beyond a reasonable doubt.

"16. We reject his argument in this respect, too. First, in the case itself, … the Magistrates give as their opinion that the prosecution case had been proved on all charges beyond reasonable doubt. … In any event, had we not been of this view, we would have been of the view that the expression 'We believe' … indicates an acceptance that the Magistrates were sure."

The answer to question (1) was "yes"; the answer to question (2) was "no"; the answer to question (3) was "yes". Appeal dismissed.

Blyth v CPS (Essex)

[2022] EWHC 2558 (Admin), 19 July 2022, QBD (DC)

Supply of part of a specimen does not connote a physical exchange between police officer and accused, but the effective transfer of control; on the facts in this case, the accused had been supplied with part of his blood specimen.

A motorist was convicted of driving with an excess of a controlled drug, contrary to s 5A(1), Road Traffic Act 1988. He had been stopped because he was wanted for questioning on certain matters. A roadside preliminary test was positive for cannabis and he was arrested for drug-driving. He was taken to a police station where a specimen of blood was taken. It was divided and sealed in the motorist's presence. He requested a part, which was placed with his property. The motorist was released under investigation for drug-driving. On other matters, he was charged, refused bail and taken to another police station to appear before court by video link. His blood sample was retained for safekeeping at the second police station. After the court appearance, he was remanded in custody. His property, including the blood sample, was returned to him and went with him to prison. It was booked in with his property, but was not refrigerated. The part retained by the police revealed an excess of delta-9-tetrahydrocannabinol (cannabis).

At trial, the motorist argued that the blood analysis was not admissible because the police had not complied with their duty to supply him with part; alternatively, the evidence should be excluded pursuant to s 78, Police and Criminal Evidence Act 1984 (discretion to exclude evidence which would have such an adverse effect on the fairness of the proceedings that the court ought not to admit it) as he had been denied the right to obtain an independent analysis. Those arguments were rejected and he was convicted. His part of the sample was eventually returned to him when he was released from custody, more than 3 months after the date of the driving offence, and after his conviction for drug-driving. He appealed against conviction.

QUESTION(S) FOR THE COURT: Whether the justices were correct to find that: (a) supply of a sample that was capable of analysis had taken place at the point when it was supplied; (b) supply had taken place at the police station, rather than when it came into the defendant's physical control; (c) supply had taken place within s 15(5), Road Traffic Offenders Act 1988; and (d) the evidence of the Crown's sample analysis should not be excluded under s 78.

HELD: "22. … supply does not connote a physical exchange of the sample between police officer and accused, but the effective transfer of control over the sample. …

"23. … [The appellant] did not request appropriate storage for the sample and there is no evidence that he alerted his solicitors to the sample or that he or his agents made any attempt to access the same. … we are satisfied the sample was available and accessible to his direction and control at all stages whilst he was on remand. …

"26. When considering [the] application to exclude the evidence pursuant to s 78 … the justices were entitled to have regard to the fact that no issue was raised as to: the procedure dictated by section 15(2) to (4) of the Road Traffic Act 1988; that the samples differed from each other in quantity or quality so as to affect the ability to make analysis; or, that the analytical procedure that had been conducted erroneously in any respect. [The appellant] had taken no steps to ensure the integrity of the sample and showed no intention to seek independent analysis. The results of analysis indicated a quantity of cannabinoids in [his] bloodstream which could not be described as borderline. His objection to the admissibility of the evidence pursuant to s.78 … may be described as 'opportunistically technical and unrealistic'. We see no basis upon which to determine that the proceedings would be adversely impacted by the admission of the evidence, legitimately obtained, and not *per se* inadmissible for procedural irregularity."

The first two questions were necessarily incorporated into the third; the answers to the third and fourth questions were "yes". Appeal dismissed.

4. ANALYSIS TECHNIQUES AND PROCEDURES

R v Coomaraswamy

[1976] RTR 21, [1976] Crim LR 260, November 1975, CA

It is sufficient to prove, on the basis of a laboratory test, that the defendant's alcohol level was above the prescribed limit; it is not necessary to establish an exact reading.

A motorist had been charged with driving with excess alcohol, contrary to s 6(1), Road Traffic Act 1972. He had provided a specimen of urine which had been divided into two in the usual way. The part analysed on behalf of the prosecutor revealed not less than 251 mg alcohol in 100 ml urine. The part analysed for the defendant revealed 156 mg, the analyst suggesting that the difference could possibly be accounted for by evaporation of alcohol from one of the samples, and that both results might indeed be too low.

The judge directed the jury that, to convict, what had to be proved was that the level of alcohol, as ascertained from a laboratory test, exceeded the prescribed limit and that it was not necessary to ascertain the degree of the excess. The defendant was convicted, and appealed on the ground that the judge had misdirected the jury.

HELD "… It is plain from the evidence in this case that no analyst would swear that his figure is absolutely right. To start with, more often than not, the figure produced by an analyst is an average of a number of different analyses; not only an average, but an average which is reduced, as it was in this case, to allow for errors in experimentation or errors in sampling. Consequently, if that is the case and if the prosecution were bound to [prove] that a particular figure was right, then no one could ever be convicted of this offence.

"… what has to be proved is that the alcohol content exceeded the permitted maximum, not that any specific figure of alcohol content was correct."

Appeal dismissed.

Lomas v Bowler

[1984] Crim LR 178, 25 November 1983, QBD (DC)

On the facts of this case, the court was correct in accepting the prosecution's analysis of a urine specimen even though it showed a far higher concentration of alcohol than the analysis carried out for the defendant.

A motorist had been convicted by magistrates of driving with excess alcohol, contrary to s 6(1), Road Traffic Act 1972. He appealed to the Crown Court. A forensic scientist for the police had made two analyses of a specimen of the motorist's urine and found it to contain 191.1 mg and 190.2 mg alcohol in 100 ml urine. The motorist said he had drunk only 2 pints of beer. A public analyst instructed by the motorist found 80 mg and 82 mg alcohol in 100 ml urine in the specimen sent to him; he said he had found no sign that the specimen had been tampered with – to do so was possible but extremely difficult; and that in a very small proportion of cases, two analyses of the same specimen do not agree but that no logical explanation could be found.

The court found that the manner of the motorist's driving was consistent with his having taken too much alcohol; the police analysis was correct; it was not satisfied that the specimen analysed on behalf of the motorist was the same specimen; the analysis carried out on behalf of the motorist would be incorrect if he had drunk 2 pints of beer and only just possible had he drunk 3 pints of beer.

The Crown Court dismissed the appeal; the motorist further appealed.

QUESTION(S) FOR THE COURT: Whether on the evidence given and the facts found the court was entitled in law to accept that the analysis made on behalf of the respondent was an accurate record of the proportion of alcohol in the appellant's urine.

HELD: "On the evidence given and the facts found the court was entitled to accept the analysis made on behalf of the respondent as an accurate record of the proportion of alcohol in the appellant's urine at the time of providing a specimen. …" Appeal dismissed.

Sophocleous v Ringer

[1988] RTR 52, [1987] Crim LR 422, 29 January 1987, QBD (DC)

In the circumstances of this case, the court was right to accept expert evidence of the alcohol concentration in blood.

A motorist had been charged with driving with excess alcohol, contrary to s 6(1)(a), Road Traffic Act 1972 as substituted by s 25 and Sch 8, Transport Act 1981. At trial, the justices accepted expert oral evidence for the prosecution of four blood analyses which had proved positive. In giving evidence, the expert referred to a computer-produced graph which was not itself put to the justices. In cross-examination, the expert accepted that it would have been possible for the alcohol level in the specimen to have increased after the specimen had been taken if the blood had contained certain antibodies, but that she knew of no recorded incident of such an occurrence. The motorist appealed against conviction.

QUESTION(S) FOR THE COURT (INTER ALIA): Whether the justices were entitled to find as a fact that the specimen of blood contained more than the prescribed limit of 80 mg alcohol in 100 ml blood.

HELD: "… It is not unknown for advocates to cross-examine scientists and suggest to them that for one reason or another it is possible that a result produced by them in a test may not be entirely accurate. In this case, with abundant caution [the expert witness said] the question put to her raised a possibility, which could not be ruled out absolutely, that there was some inaccuracy, but … the witness knew of no recorded instance … In those circumstances … the justices would have been wholly perverse to have reached any conclusion other than that which they did reach."

The answer to the question was "yes". Appeal dismissed.

Stephenson v Clift

[1988] RTR 171, 7 July 1987, QBD (DC)

Where the justices had found as a matter of fact that the prosecution's analysis was more convincing than the defendant's, the conviction would stand.

A motorist had been charged with driving with excess alcohol in blood, contrary to s 6(1)(a), Road Traffic Act 1972 as substituted by s 25 and Sch 8, Transport Act 1981. The blood specimen had been analysed by experienced analysts on behalf of both prosecutor and motorist. The analysis for the prosecution, carried out by gas chromatography, showed 91 mg alcohol in 100 ml blood; the analysis for the motorist, carried out under the ICMA system, which the analyst accepted was not as modern a technique as gas chromatography, showed 80 mg alcohol in 100 ml blood. In both cases the usual deduction of 6 mg, to allow for any error, was made. Both analysts gave oral evidence at the hearing.

The justices found the prosecution evidence to be more accurate than that of the motorist and convicted. The motorist appealed.

QUESTION(S) FOR THE COURT: Whether the justices were entitled to hold on the totality of the evidence adduced and beyond a reasonable doubt that the blood-alcohol level of the defendant exceeded the statutory limit of 80 mg in 100 ml of blood.

HELD: "… the justices … set out with sufficient clarity the basis on which they did conclude that they found the evidence of [the prosecution's analyst] more convincing than that of [the defendant's analyst] and, having concluded that, they were entitled to find as a matter of fact … that they were satisfied that the proportion of alcohol in the defendant's blood was 91 milligrammes per 100 millilitres of blood, and accordingly was in excess of the level fixed by statute.

"The question was in the end wholly one of fact for the justices, and I cannot find in their reasoning or their conclusions any flaw in law which would entitle this court to interfere."

The answer to the question was "yes". Appeal dismissed.

Yhnell v DPP

[1989] RTR 250, 5 December 1988, QBD (DC)

The prosecution is not precluded from giving evidence of breath analysis if necessary to establish the right to rely on a blood analysis, but the justices should not (and here did not) take it into account as part of the evidence on the alcohol level in the blood.

A motorist had been charged with driving with excess alcohol in blood, contrary to s 6(1)(a), Road Traffic Act 1972 as substituted by s 25 and Sch 8, Transport Act 1981. Breath analysis showed 42 µg and 43 µg alcohol in 100 ml breath and the motorist claimed to have the breath specimens replaced by blood, under s 8(6), Road Traffic Act 1972 as likewise substituted (lower breath reading no more than

50 μg alcohol in 100 ml breath – now repealed; see page v). The part of the blood specimen analysed by the police revealed 97 mg alcohol in 100 ml blood; the part analysed on behalf of the motorist showed 74 mg. The justices found that the motorist had added to his part of the specimen blood containing no alcohol, which accounted for the different results.

The motorist argued that the breath analysis readings should not have been admitted in evidence because of the words in s 8(6), "if he then provides such a[n alternative] specimen neither specimen of breath shall be used"; and because the readings were highly prejudicial. The justices rejected that argument, finding that the alcohol level in the breath specimen could have no bearing on the level in the blood specimen, and convicted on the basis of the prosecution evidence of the blood alcohol. The motorist appealed.

QUESTION(S) FOR THE COURT: Whether the justices were right to allow the prosecutor to adduce evidence of the breath readings when the defendant's reading was less than 50 μg per 100 ml of breath and he had provided a specimen of blood.

HELD: "[The judgment in *Smith v Geraghty*, see page 530] is not to the effect that] the prosecution are prohibited from giving evidence which they have to give in order to comply with the requirement that the procedure must be strictly gone through in order to establish their right to rely on the blood sample at all.

"... justices may thereafter err if they do take into account as part of the evidence of excess alcohol in the blood the reading on the Intoximeter which had previously been taken. It is submitted on behalf of the defendant in this case that the justices must ... have taken into account the Intoximeter reading in order to prefer the higher reading in the blood sample taken by the prosecution analysis, rather than the lower figure taken from the defendant's analysis. Had the justices done so I would ... have had no doubt that they had offended against section 8(6), but they state clearly that they had done nothing of the sort. They had before them evidence which they accepted, that the reason for the lower reading in the defendant's analysis was that he had deliberately falsified his sample ... thereby reducing inevitably the proportion of alcohol remaining in the sample."

Appeal dismissed.

R v Bolton Magistrates' Court ex p Scally and Other Cases

[1991] 1 QB 537, [1991] 2 WLR 239, [1991] 2 All ER 619, [1991] RTR 84, [1991] Crim LR 550, 1 October 1990, QBD (DC)

Where swabs containing ethanol, which could produce artificially high blood alcohol readings, might have been used before taking blood specimens, the resulting convictions could not stand. See also R v Bravender, page 151, where data at the laboratory which conducted blood analysis had been manipulated.

Four motorists had pleaded guilty to charges of driving with excess alcohol, contrary to s 6(1)(a), Road Traffic Act 1972 as substituted by s 25 and Sch 8, Transport Act 1981. All had provided specimens of blood which had been analysed and shown to be positive. The police later discovered that, before taking the blood samples, the skin might have been cleaned with swabs containing ethanol which would have produced artificially high blood alcohol readings. These swabs had recently been introduced in place of the type previously used. They had been widely used; many outstanding charges in such cases had been withdrawn; in other cases the Home Secretary had declined to grant free pardons. The motorists sought orders of *certiorari* to quash their convictions; the prosecution did not oppose the applications.

GROUND(S) FOR APPEAL (INTER ALIA): Breach of natural justice; irregularity in the proceedings.

HELD: [On the submission that the issue is whether a conviction is amenable to quashing by *certiorari* if it was obtained without unfairness by the tribunal or malpractice by the prosecution, and after reviewing authorities] "Grounds other than fraud or collusion can … be … regarded as irregularities …

"… A defendant has no means of knowing whether a swab the doctor uses is not fit for the purpose … Nor … can he possibly know that the analyst's certificate is based on a false premise, namely, that the sample was unadulterated. Such certificates contain hidden untruths which if known would have rendered them inadmissible … Admission of them to evidence would be akin to perjury, albeit unwittingly committed … jurisdiction enabling us to deal with these applications has been clearly established … here … the prosecutor … corrupted the process leading to conviction in a manner which was unfair … that is conduct analogous to fraud, collusion or perjury if ever there was."

Applications granted.

Gregory v DPP

[2002] EWHC 385 (Admin), 19 February 2002, QBD (Admin)

The court should not, without a rational basis, have rejected the defence expert's unchallenged evidence calling into question the procedure adopted by the prosecution's analyst.

A motorist had been charged with driving with excess alcohol, contrary to s 5(1)(a), Road Traffic Act 1988. A blood specimen was analysed and revealed 84 mg alcohol in 100 ml blood. The motorist was convicted by magistrates and appealed to the Crown Court.

The police surgeon who took the specimen gave evidence that the sample contained approximately 4 ml of blood, which she divided and placed into two vials, each containing approximately 2 ml. No other evidence was called as to the quantity of blood in either of the vials. The method of analysis used was "headspace gas chromatography".

The defence called a toxicologist, who gave evidence that if the vial is not filled to capacity (some 6 ml) then the amount of preservative in the vial is such that the eventual figure becomes distorted if headspace gas chromatography is used to analyse the sample.

The Home Office analyst gave evidence of how she had analysed the sample in question, but did not comment on the toxicologist's evidence.

The Crown Court convicted the motorist, who appealed further.

QUESTION(S) FOR THE COURT: Whether, on the evidence adduced, the finding that the appellant's blood alcohol level exceeded the prescribed limit was *Wednesbury* unreasonable particularly as no precise evidence is available in such cases as to the exact amount of blood placed in each vial.

HELD: "13. ... to the extent that the Crown Court appear to have regarded the defence toxicologist's evidence as merely theoretical, it fell into error. [His] evidence that the prosecution analysis of the appellant's blood sample was not reliable or accurate was based to a significant extent upon the following uncontroversial facts: (1) that the capacity of the sample vials was 6 millilitres; (2) that fluoride was present in the vials as a preservative; (3) that an approximate amount of 2 millilitres of blood had been placed in each sample vial; and (4) that the method of analysis which had been used to measure the alcohol content of the blood sample was headspace gas chromatography.

"14. ... [He] gave unchallenged evidence as to his scientific opinion, namely that, given the amount of blood and fluoride in the sample vial, the headspace gas chromatography method of analysis would give a reading which was about 8 per cent too high ... It was opinion evidence which seriously called into question, in the circumstances of this particular case, the reliability and accuracy of the blood alcohol analysis ...

"15. ... [the toxicologist's] opinion evidence on these critical matters was not challenged ... If the Crown Court was to reject this critical evidence, there had to be a rational basis for doing so but, ... there was no such basis or any other proper reason for rejecting his evidence."

The answer to the question was "yes". Appeal allowed.

Byrne (Simon David) v DPP

[2003] EWHC 397 (Admin), 21 February 2003, QBD (Admin)

Blood analysis by an analyst who is not authorised for the purposes of s 16(1)(b), Road Traffic Offenders Act 1988 is acceptable under s 9, Criminal Justice Act 1967. Where the specimen was identified by a code there was continuity of evidence. On the facts, the defendant had not been discouraged from having his specimen analysed; the certificate of consent to the taking of the blood was acceptable.

A motorist had been charged with driving with excess alcohol, contrary to s 5(1)(a), Road Traffic Act 1988. The breath analysis device had generated an unreliability printout, and the police officer conducting the procedure therefore requested a specimen of blood. The defendant consented, and a specimen was taken. At the trial, a video recording of a conversation between the custody sergeant and the defendant, when the sergeant handed the defendant his part of the sample, was shown. The sergeant was heard to say that if the defendant had his specimen analysed, it would probably come back three times over the limit, it would be expensive, and that no one had done so before. The prosecution adduced a statement of a blood analysis pursuant to s 9, Criminal Justice Act 1967, showing excess alcohol. That statement referred to a vial labelled with a three letter, ten digit code – the same code as appeared on the certificate of consent to taking the specimen.

QUESTION(S) FOR THE COURT: (i) Whether the person who analysed the specimen was an authorised analyst for the purposes of s 16(7), Road Traffic Offenders Act 1988; (ii) given that there was no label attached to the sample sent for analysis, whether there was continuity in this evidence; (iii) whether the appellant was discouraged from sending his own sample for analysis in view of the custody sergeant's comments; (iv) since the certificate of consent for taking blood, produced to the court, was a photocopy and there was no evidence that it was a true copy, whether the sample was taken without consent.

HELD: "[On (i)] 5. … it is conceded that [the analyst] was not authorised for the purposes of section 16(1)(b) of the Road Traffic Offenders Act 1988. It follows that a certificate signed by him for the purposes of that section would have been inadmissible in evidence. However, the evidence of the analysis of the blood in this case was … sought to be adduced … on the basis of a section 9 [of the Criminal Justice Act 1967] statement. Section 16 … is not … a comprehensive or exclusive means of evidencing that fact. Manifestly, for example, the defence may call an expert analyst who is not authorised by the Home Secretary, whose evidence may be preferred by a court to that of [an] authorised analyst called by the prosecution where there is live evidence.

"6. The statement of [the analyst] included a statement of his qualifications and experience. … Clearly he was an expert … and his evidence was, therefore, admissible as expert evidence in the form of a section 9 of the 1967 Act statement in the same way as his oral evidence would have been. …

"[On (ii)] 11. … the district judge was entitled to treat [the code on the *pro forma* booklet] as a unique code. He was similarly entitled to infer from the sticker on the doctor's certificate that it was attached to that by way of identification and to identify the certificate, and therefore the blood specimen taken, with the procedure which had been carried out pursuant to the *pro forma* booklet. When, therefore, the glass blood vial appeared at the laboratory … with Mr Byrne's name and that code on it, the district judge was entitled to infer that that vial was the one which had been so identified and labelled at the police station by the police officer. … the district judge was entitled to find continuity. …

"[On (iii)] 12. … The district judge … 'found as a fact that the appellant was given written instructions with his sample and he was not discouraged at all from sending his sample away for analysis'. … based on that finding of fact, no question of the unfairness of the prosecution or of the trial arose. … I would emphasise, however, that it is inadvisable in the extreme for police officers to give advice of the kind that was given in this case to accused persons even if what is said is true …

"[On (iv)] 13. [question 13] is whether the district judge was right to hold that the appellant's blood was taken with his consent on the basis of a photocopy of what is purported to be a doctor's certificate when there is no evidence that it was a true copy of the original or that it had been served on the appellant. … There were two aspects of the photocopy to be considered: Whether a copy had been served as required by section 16 of the 1988 Act, and the fact that it was a photocopy. …

"15. Section 16 provides for a mandatory procedure in relation to the admissibility of certificates and documents of the kind referred to in it; that is to say, they are only admissible if they have been served. … A copy of the document was served on the appellant's solicitors on 2 April 2002. Its receipt was acknowledged by them … Had objection been taken on the ground of non-service when the document was tendered, the prosecution could have cured that. … It is not a pre-requisite of prosecution for the offence now under consideration that the prosecution must give evidence of that service. They are required to do so if the issue is raised … So far as the photocopy is concerned, it is not suggested that the photocopy was not a true copy of the doctor's certificate. Had issue been taken when the document was tendered, either the original would have been produced, or the district judge could have determined how the document should be authenticated. …

"16. … the district judge was entitled to accept the photocopy of the doctor's certificate. It was a true copy of the original. A true copy had been served on the appellant's solicitors sufficiently in advance of the hearing. That photocopy and the original were evidence in accordance with section 16 that the appellant's blood was taken with his consent … ."

Appeal dismissed.

Dhaliwal v DPP

[2006] EWHC 1149 (Admin), 16 March 2006, QBD (Admin)

In the circumstances of this case, the court had evidence that the blood analysis had been correctly carried out and it was not necessary to prove that preservative had been added to the specimen.

A motorist had been charged with driving with excess alcohol in blood, contrary to s 5(1)(a), Road Traffic Act 1988. At the trial, the prosecution's forensic analyst gave evidence about the procedure in the laboratory and about the specimen in question. In response to a question put to her in cross-examination, she consulted the case file and said that her assistant had checked that the specimen contained a preservative, without which the analysis would have been unreliable.

The motorist was convicted and appealed.

QUESTION(S) FOR THE COURT: Whether, on the evidence which was admissible, the court was entitled to conclude that the prosecution had proved its case.

HELD: "29. To the extent that the evidence which was given could have been taken to have been evidence that a preservative had been added … [it] was inadmissible. … If it was necessary for the prosecution to prove that a preservative had been added, or that it had been added in any particular quantity, then the evidence which was given by the forensic scientist was inadmissible to prove that … Therefore … to the extent that the court admitted the hearsay evidence for the purposes of concluding that there had been preservative added and any quantity the preservative added, the evidence was inadmissible and hearsay evidence and incapable of proving those facts.

"30. So far as the prosecution's case is concerned … it was not necessary, having regard to the way in which the issue had been raised by the defence, for it to prove that the preservative had been added and in any quantity. The nature of the issue which had been raised by the defence merely went to whether or not the due and proper procedures had been followed at this laboratory for the purposes of the analysis being carried out professionally.

"31. … the court had the evidence of … the analyst herself, which was to the effect that she believed that all the procedures had been carried out. She had reasonable grounds for so stating."

Appeal dismissed.

Carter v DPP

[2006] EWHC 3328 (Admin), [2007] RTR 22, 8 November 2006, QBD (DC)

In the absence of challenge supported by evidence, the prosecution need not prove the presence of preservative in a blood specimen. In a case based on a blood specimen, the district judge was entitled to take into account the breath analysis when judging a defendant's credibility.

A motorist had been charged with driving with excess alcohol, contrary to s 5(1)(a), Road Traffic Act 1988. The lower of two breath analyses was 49 µg alcohol in 100 ml breath. The officer administering the procedure therefore offered the motorist the option, under s 8(2), Road Traffic Act 1988 (lower breath reading no more than 50 µg alcohol in 100 ml breath – now repealed; see page v), of replacing the breath specimen with an alternative specimen. The motorist provided a blood specimen, analysis of which revealed excess alcohol.

At the trial, expert evidence was given to the effect that if the defendant had drunk only what he claimed to have drunk, then by the time the blood was taken, there would have been no alcohol left in his body.

The district judge, taking into account, *inter alia*, the breath analysis reading, did not accept the defendant's version of the amount he had drunk. Nor, in the absence of any evidence-based challenge, did she accept an argument that the prosecution was required positively to prove that there was preservative in the blood phial. She convicted. The defendant appealed.

QUESTION(S) FOR THE COURT: (1) Whether the district judge misdirected herself as to the law in any respect. (2) Whether the decision to convict was *Wednesbury* unreasonable.

HELD: "19. Unless there is something in the material before the court to suggest to the contrary, … the court is entitled to presume that the procedures laid down for the preparation of [blood testing] kits such as the ones we are concerned with here have been carried out correctly. In those circumstances the district judge was clearly entitled to come to the conclusion that she did, having heard the evidence of [the officer who conducted the procedure] that the procedures were properly carried out at the police station and the evidence of [the analyst of the blood specimen] which did not suggest in any way that … the sample might have been contaminated or otherwise affected by any failure to place in the phials the appropriate preservatives and other substances …

"23. [It is argued that] the district judge … 'used' the reading taken at the police station as part of the evidence, and accordingly she breached the prohibition in section 8(2) which provides that such a specimen shall not be used in the course of the trial …

"26. … All she did was to add it as a third reason for concluding that she could not accept the defendant's evidence as credible. It formed no part of her conclusion as to the reliability of the analysis … of the blood sample. …

"27. … [The district judge] used it … as a means of helping her to determine whether the appellant's evidence before her was capable of belief. That seems to me to be a wholly proper use to be made of this material. It is relevant. It is admissible and it does not seem to me that Section 8(2) is worded in such a way as to preclude its use in that context. I therefore have no doubt that the district judge was entitled to take that piece of evidence into account in the way she did in coming to her conclusion as to credibility."

Appeal dismissed.

R v Bravender

[2018] EWCA Crim 723, 28 March 2018, CA Crim

Where blood analysis had been conducted in a laboratory whose accreditation for forensic testing was then suspended, the court would disregard those results and sentence on the basis of results later produced by an alternative laboratory, without regard to any deterioration of the specimen between the two testing routines.

A motorist had been convicted of causing death by careless driving while over the limit for drugs, contrary to s 3A(1)(ba), Road Traffic Act 1988. Forensic testing by Randox Testing Services – a forensic science provider with laboratories in Northern Ireland and Manchester for a number of police forces – had shown a level of delta-9-tetrahydrocannabinol (THC) of 2.5 μg per litre of blood (the limit being 2 μg), and 186 μg benzoylecgonine (BZE) per litre of blood (the limit being 15 μg). The motorist was sentenced on the basis that the amount of drugs in his system was at its highest level for the purposes of the relevant Sentencing Council guideline. An investigation began into the results of quality-controlled data produced at the Randox facility in Manchester. It revealed that an operator had manipulated some of the data relating to the quality-controlled testing used to check the drug testing process. The United Kingdom Accreditation Service then suspended accreditation of drug testing toxicology at the Randox Manchester site and, following further investigation, Randox voluntarily suspended its equivalent accreditation in Northern Ireland and advised that samples previously tested for drugs by Randox should be re-tested.

The appellant's blood specimen was re-tested by a different company. It showed a level of BZE in a litre of blood was 59 μg. The remaining blood sample was insufficient to permit testing for THC.

The motorist appealed against sentence.

GROUNDS OF APPEAL: The correct reading for the active ingredient in cocaine was 59 μg per litre of blood, just over the legal limit. Consequently the court was inadvertently misled by the prosecution to a significant degree as to the correct level of cocaine metabolites in the appellant's blood. As a result the judge applied the wrong category in assessing the starting point; the correct category should be the lowest, namely a minimum quantity of drugs.

The court was invited to proceed on the basis of the second result without consideration of any degradation.

HELD: "24. … the only reliable scientific reading now before this court as to the presence of any drugs or their metabolites in the blood of the appellant at the time of the accident is the reading of 59 micrograms of BZE in a litre of blood. No cocaine was detected. There is no reliable scientific evidence relating to cannabis. We take no account of evidence relating to any use of cannabis.

"25. … the result of the re-testing and the reading of 59 micrograms of BZE in one litre of blood is such as to place the quantity of drugs in the lowest category of the Sentencing Council Guidelines, namely a minimum quantity of drugs."

The original sentence of imprisonment (5 years and 4 months) was quashed and replaced with a shorter (2 years and 8 months) sentence accordingly.

R v Ward (Anderson Charles)

[2018] EWCA Crim 872, 13 April 2018, CA Crim

Where blood analysis had been carried out by Randox, the safety of the conviction is fact-specific; where there was overwhelming evidence against the appellant, apart from the blood analysis, his conviction would stand.

Following a road traffic collision in which the appellant's passenger was killed, the appellant had been convicted of a number of offences, including causing death by careless driving when unfit through drugs, contrary to s 3A(1)(a), Road Traffic Act 1988. Analysis of his blood specimen was carried out by Randox Testing Services, whose accreditation for drug testing toxicology had been suspended (see *R v Bravender*, above). It showed 35 ng mephedrone per ml of blood, and a level of 96 μg GHB/GBL per ml of blood. Evidence was given by other drivers, the officers who attended the scene and medical practitioners who interacted with the appellant and to whom the appellant disclosed his use of drugs about the appellant's driving on the day in question; by experts on the general effects of those drugs on ability to drive; and by Randox on the result of the analysis of the blood specimen. The jury found that the appellant was driving without due care and attention while unfit through drugs, and that his driving caused the death of the deceased. The appellant appealed against conviction.

The blood sample was later re-tested by another company, and showed a level of 97 μg GHB/GBL per ml, compared with the 96 μg reported by Randox.

GROUND OF APPEAL: Whether the appellant's conviction was unsafe given the inability to rely on the Randox evidence alone, or remained safe because of the other evidence before the court.

HELD: "3. Though … there are a significant number of cases affected by the difficulties encountered by Randox …, in each case the question of the safety of the conviction will necessarily be fact specific, hinging both on the offence or offences in question and the other evidence in the case.

"19. The issues for the jury were whether the appellant was driving without due care and attention at a time when he was unfit thorough drugs and whether [his] driving caused the death of the deceased.

"[After summarising the evidence given by the witnesses, the fresh evidence concerning Randox, and the result of the re-testing of the appellant's blood specimen] 31. … While the Crown no longer relied upon the Randox testing alone to prove the presence of the quantity of the drug … the corroboration of the results, both at the time of the original examination and subsequently means an appeal based on unreliability of the sample is not sustainable. …

"38. The failure of a forensic science laboratory is a matter of deep concern potentially going to the integrity of the criminal justice system… .

"39. … Notwithstanding the concerns as to Randox, the evidence against the appellant … is overwhelming … we entertain no doubt about the safety of the Appellant's conviction.

"40. … factual evidence from [the witnesses] amply establish the appellant's careless driving. Of itself this body of evidence pointed very strongly to the appellant's unfitness to drive being attributable to drugs.

"41. Secondly, the report from [the second company which analysed the blood specimen] puts that conclusion beyond doubt."

Appeal dismissed.

R v Senior

[2018] EWCA Crim 837, 13 April 2018, CA Crim

Where the only reliable evidence of cannabis in the blood showed a level below the legal limit, conviction for driving with an excess of cannabis could not stand, even though the appellant was a regular user of cannabis.

The appellant had been convicted of two offences, one of which was driving with an excess of cannabis over the specified limit, contrary to s 5A(1)(a) and (2), Road

Traffic Act 1988. The appellant's blood specimen was analysed by Randox; the first test did not detect any of the s 5A drugs. Apparently there had been a problem with the testing equipment. A second test found a level of delta-9-tetrahydrocannabinol (THC) above the limit. The charge was based on that second test. In the light of the problems at Randox (see *R v Bravender*, page 151), the appellant's blood specimen was tested again by another company which found THC, but at a level below the specified limit. The appellant appealed against conviction.

GROUND OF APPEAL: The Randox reports were unreliable and the conviction on the driving offence unsafe.

HELD: "22. It is plain that this appellant had used cannabis and had cannabis in his bloodstream when he was stopped by the police. That much is accepted and is demonstrated by means of reliable evidence. But this offence is only committed if the quantity of THC in the bloodstream exceeds 2 micrograms per litre of blood. Once the Randox reports are put to one side there is no scientific evidence to show that the appellant had THC in excess of that limit in his blood.

"23. We are unable to infer from the other evidence relied upon by the prosecution that THC in excess of that limit was present… . That other evidence establishes … that the appellant was a regular user of cannabis and had used cannabis in the recent past before he was stopped. But that is not enough… .

"26. We would wish to emphasise what has already been said in other cases … that each case involving Randox testing must turn on its own facts. There is no single answer to appeals against convictions based in whole or part on Randox testing. It all depends.

"27. But in the particular circumstances of this case, given the lack of reliable evidence to support the suggestion, put to the appellant in interview, that THC in excess of 2 micrograms per litre was present in his bloodstream, we conclude that this conviction is unsafe and must be quashed."

Appeal allowed.

See also *R v Wilson, Walmsley, York & Senior*, page 608.

5. THE ANALYST

Stevens v DPP

Unreported, CO/0736/92, 9 December 1992, QBD (DC)

The prosecution is not required to prove the qualification of the analyst. On the facts of this case, there was ample material from which to conclude that the sample analysed was the defendant's.

A motorist had been charged with driving with excess alcohol, contrary to s 5(1)(a), Road Traffic Act 1988. At the police station, the lower of two breath analyses revealed 41 µg alcohol in 100 ml breath, so the defendant was offered the option, under s 8(2), Road Traffic Act 1988 (lower breath reading no more than 50 μg alcohol in 100 ml breath – now repealed; see page v), of replacing the breath specimen. A blood specimen was taken and, on analysis, proved positive.

The motorist was convicted by magistrates and his appeal to the Crown Court failed. He appealed further.

HELD: "[On the appellant's submission on whether there was evidence to show that the blood analyst was qualified] First, the prosecution do not have to prove the qualification of the analyst ... Secondly, ... the certificate here proffered was appropriate for the purposes of section 16(1)(b) [Road Traffic Offenders Act 1988: admissibility of evidence of blood alcohol by production of certificate signed by an authorised analyst].

"[On the submission that the certificate of blood analysis referred to the analyst as qualified under the Road Traffic Act 1972, and that it should refer to the 1988 Act] There is ... no substance in this contention.

"[On the submission that it was not proved that the blood sample analysed was that of the appellant, that there had been no evidence of the writing on the label so that the label was hearsay] The details on the label on the specimen analysed coincide with the findings of fact by the Court, and the label itself was of course before the Court ... [I]n ... the Crown Court, the only challenge by [the appellant] was with regard to the procedures adopted in relation to the obtaining of the blood sample ... No question was asked of the officer as to whether he had written on the label or not ... I have not the slightest hesitation in concluding that there was ample material before the Crown Court to entitle them to conclude that the sample of blood analysed and certified had indeed emanated from this appellant."

Appeal dismissed.

CPS v Sedgemoor Justices

[2007] EWHC 1803 (Admin), 3 July 2007, QBD (DC)

The requirement that the analyst of a blood specimen be authorised applies only in the context of proof by means of the production of a certificate; other written, or oral, evidence may be given by an expert who is not authorised.

A motorist had been charged with driving with excess alcohol, contrary to s 5(1)(a), Road Traffic Act 1988. The prosecution proposed to rely on the evidence of an analysis of the motorist's blood carried out by a forensic toxicologist employed by a private firm of analysts, who was not an "authorised analyst" within the meaning of s 16(7), Road Traffic Offenders Act 1988 (definition of "authorised analyst"). The justices ruled her evidence inadmissible. The prosecutor sought judicial review of that decision.

QUESTION(S) FOR THE COURT: Whether the effect of s 16 is that evidence of blood analysis can be given only by an authorised analyst, or whether the effect is that a certificate of analysis, rather than oral or (if accepted) written evidence must be given by an authorised analyst only.

HELD: "[After a review of the general principle that proceedings in a magistrates' court are not generally susceptible to challenge at an interlocutory stage, and finding that, exceptionally, the court could deal with the application because the proceedings were in effect over – without the evidence of analysis, the prosecution could not proceed] 23. … Section 16(1) [Road Traffic Offenders Act 1988] is plainly permissive. It does not stipulate the only manner in which evidence of analysis can be given. Rather [it provides] for one means by which evidence of analysis [may] be given, namely by mere production of [the] certificate, provided that the analyst is authorised and subject to the right of the accused under sub-section (4) to require the attendance of the analyst. …

"24. It would be surprising if the effect of Section 16 were to limit evidence of analysis to an authorised analyst because, if it did, the accused himself would be able to have his specimen examined only by such a person. Often, of course, he may do so, but there is no reason why he should not go to a reputable analyst who has not sought authorisation from the Minister. …

"28. … the evidence which the Crown advanced of the professional toxicologist by way of statement tendered under section 9, with the witness to attend if required by the defence, was evidence which was admissible."

Case remitted to the justices to continue the hearing in the light of the judgment.

6. THE 6 mg ALLOWANCE

Walker v Hodgins

[1984] RTR 34, [1983] Crim LR 555, 24 February 1983, QBD (DC)

Magistrates were correct to make the usual 6 mg allowance in respect of the defence analysis of a blood specimen, bringing the level below the limit.

A motorist had been charged with driving with excess alcohol in blood, contrary to s 6(1), Road Traffic Act 1972. A blood specimen had been taken. The part analysed on behalf of the prosecution showed 96 mg alcohol in 100 ml blood; the usual margin of error of 6 mg had been allowed, reducing the level to 90 mg. The part analysed on behalf of the motorist showed 83 mg alcohol in 100 ml blood before making any deduction to allow for error. Both analysts had acted in good faith and their methods were unimpeachable.

At the hearing, the motorist argued that since it was normal laboratory practice to reduce the level found on analysis by 6 ml, this should be applied to his analysis, so reducing it to below the legal limit.

The justices accepted this and acquitted the motorist. The prosecutor appealed.

QUESTION(S) FOR THE COURT: Whether the justices were entitled to have regard to the normal laboratory practice of allowing a margin of 6 ml for error when determining whether they could be satisfied that the actual amount of alcohol in the defendant's blood exceeded the prescribed limit for to do so would have reduced the reading on the defendant's analysis below the legal limit.

HELD: "... the justices acted perfectly properly. The prosecutor's evidence consisted not only of the certificate, which was 10 milligrammes above the permitted limit but it also contained the evidence that in these analyses there was a potential error. They were inherently unreliable to a very small extent, and to make proper allowance for that margin of error, they always made the deduction of 6 milligrammes.

"... the justices were perfectly entitled to say that they could not, in the light of that evidence, be satisfied beyond a reasonable doubt that no deduction should be made from the figure of 83 milligrammes and no deduction which would bring it below the figure of 80 milligrammes."

Appeal dismissed.

Oswald v DPP

[1989] RTR 360, 29 June 1989, QBD (DC)

The court is not required to "round down" a blood analysis as well as applying the 6 mg allowance.

A motorist had been charged with driving with excess alcohol in blood, contrary to s 6(1)(a), Road Traffic Act 1972 as substituted by s 25 and Sch 8, Transport Act 1981. His blood specimen had been analysed on behalf of the police, producing four results varying between 86.7 mg and 89.6 mg alcohol in 100 ml blood, and averaging 88.2 mg. The defendant's part of the specimen had been separately analysed, and produced six results ranging from 85.4 mg to 87.1 mg and averaging 86.2 mg. All ten results gave readings over 85 mg; and seven of the ten, even after deducting the usual margin of error of 6 mg, were above the limit of 80 mg. The motorist argued that his average of 86.2 mg should be reduced by the usual 6 mg, and then, as is the practice of blood analysts, rounded down to 80 mg, raising a reasonable doubt whether the motorist had been over the limit. The justices rejected this argument and convicted. The motorist appealed.

QUESTION(S) FOR THE COURT: Whether the court was bound to deal with a case on the basis that as well as deducting 6 mg from the results of analysis it should disregard anything less than a whole milligramme shown in those results when given in evidence.

HELD: "... although it may be the practice of analysts to deduct 6 milligrammes from a particular result in order to allow for the margin of error which may otherwise occur, that approach is not necessarily appropriate when a whole range of results are produced by analysis. Furthermore it may not be appropriate to deduct 6 milligrammes from the figure produced as a result of averaging a whole range of analysed results.

"Whether that is so or not ... the approach of the justices was correct. The statute prohibits driving on a road when the blood alcohol level is in excess of 80 milligrammes ... The justices on the basis of the evidence which was before them, concluded that it established beyond reasonable doubt that the defendant, at the material time, did have in excess of 80 milligrammes of alcohol in 100 millilitres of blood. That was their finding of fact.

"… that finding is unassailable … the court is not bound to deal with a case on the basis of rounding down the figures after the decimal point."

Appeal dismissed.

DPP v Perkins

Unreported, 5 April 1995, QBD (DC)

The magistrates should not have proceeded on their own unsupported idea that the 6 mg allowance might be insufficient.

A motorist had been charged with driving with excess alcohol, contrary to s 5(1)(a), Road Traffic Act 1988. A blood specimen had been provided and forensic analysis showed not less than 81 mg alcohol in 100 ml blood.

At the trial before the magistrates, the forensic scientist who had analysed the blood gave evidence that he had followed normal procedures: the blood was tested four times; the results varied between 86.8 mg and 88.8 mg; a slight variation was to be expected; the four results were aggregated then divided by four to give an average, which in this case had been rounded down to 87 mg; the usual practice of deducting 6 mg to the benefit of the motorist was then followed, resulting in a minimum level of 81 mg. The analyst further said that he thought the possibility of the result being more than 6 mg out was so remote that it could be discounted. The motorist did not adduce any arguments.

The justices were of the opinion that the evidence of the allowance of 6 mg was not supported and could have been insufficient; and that, as the readings from the four tests were different and the forensic scientist had commented that perfection in testing was not possible, they were not satisfied beyond reasonable doubt that the defendant's blood alcohol content exceeded the limit. They dismissed the charge. The prosecutor appealed.

QUESTION(S) FOR THE COURT: Whether, on the facts found, the justices were entitled to dismiss the information.

HELD: "… although the Justices asserted that '… the allowance of 6 was not supported and could have been insufficient', it was supported in so far as the evidence was given by an expert, and the notion that it could have been insufficient was not itself based upon any evidence or any material of which the Justices, in this context, were entitled to take account.

"The assertion … that [the Justices] '… were not satisfied as to the accuracy of the readings …' does not appear to have stemmed from any unwillingness to accept the evidence given by [the forensic scientist], but merely to proceed upon the unsupported idea that the allowance given to cover errors and imperfections might not have been sufficient.

"… The Justices do not say that they did not accept the evidence of [the forensic scientist] and, indeed, unless for some reason they regarded him as palpably not telling the truth, there [was] no basis upon which they could refrain from accepting as fact the evidence that he gave.

"… Though the Justices asserted … that they '… relied upon the level of doubt expressed by the forensic scientist …', that has to be gauged against the statement … that [he] 'said that he thought the possibility of the result being more than 6 milligrammes out was so remote that it could be discounted'."

The answer to the question was "no". Appeal allowed.

DPP v Welsh (Eric Thomas)

(1997) 161 JP 57, 4 November 1996, QBD (DC)

The magistrates were wrong to apply the 6 mg allowance only to the lowest of four samples.

A motorist had been stopped by police; a roadside breath test was positive and he was arrested and taken to the police station. Breath analysis revealed a lower reading of 41 μg alcohol in 100 ml breath. The motorist was therefore offered the option, under s 8(2), Road Traffic Act 1988 (lower breath reading no more than 50 μg alcohol in 100 ml breath – now repealed; see page v), of replacing the breath specimens, and chose to provide a blood specimen. The analyst, in accordance with usual practice, divided the specimen into four and conducted four separate analyses, producing results of 88 mg, 86.6 mg, 87.6 mg and 88 mg alcohol in 100 ml blood, and an average mean of 87.6 mg. That was rounded down to 87 mg, and the usual allowance of 6 mg was deducted, leaving a reading of 81 mg.

The magistrates took the view that each of the four samples was equally valid, and applied the usual procedure, of rounding down and deducting 6 mg, to the lowest of the four results (86.8 mg), leading to a reading of 80 mg, which was not over the prescribed limit. They acquitted the motorist. The prosecutor appealed.

QUESTION(S) FOR THE COURT: Whether it was reasonable for the magistrates to conclude that no one sample of the four taken was more reliable than any other and to use the accepted formula to calculate the level of alcohol present in the blood with reference only to the lowest of those readings instead of applying the formula to the average of all four readings.

HELD: "The submissions that were made to the Magistrates on behalf of the Respondent really suggest that a defendant to such a charge … should have, as a matter of law, a series of factors applied for his benefit so as to ensure that he is not the victim of scientific miscalculation. Not only (it must have been suggested) should he have the benefit of the rounding down from the decimal point but he should also have the deduction of six in respect of the margin of error, and so far as the four samples are concerned, he should have the benefit of the lowest of the four.

"… that is not an approach which a defendant can require as a matter of law. The rounding down … is not a matter of law but is widely a matter of practice. The deduction of six milligrammes falls into a similar category. To build into the approach a legal condition that the lowest of the four analysed samples should be the one that is conclusive in each case in my judgment goes too far."

The answer to the question was "no". Appeal allowed.

7. BACK-CALCULATIONS

See also Chapter 7, on the assumption that the proportion of alcohol at the time of the offence was not less than in the specimen; and Smith v Geraghty, page 530 and Woodward (Mark de Maine) v DPP, page 536, on back-calculations in relation to "special reasons" arguments.

Gumbley v Cunningham

[1989] AC 281, [1989] 2 WLR 1, [1989] 1 All ER 5, [1989] RTR 49, [1989] Crim LR 297, 9 December 1988, HL

Where a blood specimen was taken over 4 hours after an incident, expert evidence of the rate of alcohol elimination, and of the blood alcohol level at the time of the incident, was admissible.

A motorist had been charged with driving with excess alcohol, contrary to s 6(1)(a), Road Traffic Act 1972 as substituted by s 25 and Sch 8, Transport Act 1981. He had been involved in a fatal accident, and a blood specimen had not been taken until more than 4 hours after the accident. Analysis of the specimen showed 59 mg alcohol in 100 ml blood – below the limit. Medical evidence on the rate of alcohol elimination had been adduced, to the effect, *inter alia*, that at the time of the accident the blood-alcohol level would have been between 120 mg and 130 mg alcohol in 100 ml blood. The motorist's contention that such evidence was inadmissible had been rejected by the justices, the Crown Court and the Divisional Court. He appealed further.

CERTIFIED QUESTION(S): Whether on a true construction of ss 6(1) and 10(2), Road Traffic Act 1972, as amended, the prosecutor is entitled to adduce evidence other than by way of the specimen of breath or blood provided by the accused in order to prove the proportion of alcohol in the accused's breath or blood at the material time.

HELD: "[The appellant's] submission in essence is that Parliament would have expressly provided for the admissibility of 'back-tracking evidence' as this is now conveniently called, if it had intended that such evidence, although undoubtedly relevant, should be considered by the courts … [but] it would be quite wrong to interpret the … statutory provisions as [excluding] evidence which is relevant to establishing the blood-alcohol concentration at a time when the defendant was driving.

"I therefore agree with the conclusion reached by the Divisional Court that those who drive whilst above the prescribed limits cannot necessarily escape punishment because of the lapse of time."

Appeal dismissed.

Benham v DPP

Unreported, CO-2293-93, 24 March 1994, QBD (DC)

Where a blood specimen was analysed for the defendant 5 months after it had been provided, it was not permissible to "back-calculate" the result to cast doubt on the prosecutor's original analysis.

A motorist had been charged with driving with excess alcohol on 14 June 1992, contrary to s 5(1), Road Traffic Act 1988. Breath analysis revealed a lower reading below 50 µg alcohol in 100 ml. The motorist was therefore offered the option, under s 8(2), Road Traffic Act 1988 (lower of two breath readings not more than 50 µg alcohol in 100 ml breath – now repealed; see page v), of providing a replacement specimen. A blood specimen was provided. It was analysed on behalf of the prosecution on 26 June and showed not less than 88 mg alcohol in 100 ml blood. The specimen was re-analysed for the prosecution on 17 December when it was found to contain some 73 mg alcohol in 100 ml blood. The part of the specimen retained by the motorist was analysed some months after it had been taken, and showed not less than 71 mg.

At the hearing, the prosecution's analyst gave evidence that the first analysis would have been the most reliable, the later analyses less so since some alcohol would be expected to have been lost from the samples; the sample analysed for the prosecution had, since the analysis in June, been kept in uncontrolled conditions which could cause the alcohol level to drop more quickly. The motorist said he had kept his part of the specimen in his domestic refrigerator; analysis was delayed because he was seeking legal aid. A statement from his analyst said that the specimen had been found to contain 77 mg alcohol, which should be converted to 71 mg under the usual practice of deducting 6 mg. A letter from that analyst largely confirmed what was said by the prosecution's analyst about the rate of loss of alcohol from specimens.

The justices convicted the motorist. He appealed.

QUESTION(S) FOR THE COURT: Whether there was sufficient evidence to satisfy the requisite standard of proof that the proportion of alcohol in the defendant's blood exceeded the prescribed limit.

HELD: "... What the evidence comes to is that the loss rate of alcohol, even if the sample is kept at a constant temperature of 4 degrees centigrade, may be anything between 0.2 and 2 mg%. There is no warrant for taking an arbitrary figure (even if it is described as an average) at halfway between those two points and using that as the basis for calculation.

"Secondly, ... there was at no time any evidence ... as to the operating temperature of the appellant's domestic refrigerator ... the [specimen analysed for the prosecution] was kept under uncontrolled conditions at ambient temperatures varying between refrigerator and room temperature over a period of five months; yet that sample also, on re-analysis after the five month interval, produced an analysis which agreed closely with that obtained by [the analyst appointed by the appellant]. Further, [the analyst appointed by the appellant] agreed that the most accurate analysis of the three was likely to be the one carried out when the sample was fresh.

"Both scientists also expressed the opinion … that the Intoximeter reading of 47 µg% … would, when suitably adjusted for the lapse of time, indicate a blood alcohol concentration of 95 mg% at [the time] the blood sample was taken …

"Finally the Magistrates had before them a copy of the document handed to the appellant with his part of the sample, which advised him that if he wished to have that sample analysed he should do so within five days and in the meantime to keep it cool, preferably refrigerated.

"… the Justices were entirely justified in concluding … that they were satisfied beyond reasonable doubt that he had driven [with excess alcohol].

"… there was no basis whatsoever for seeking to calculate back over a period of some five months … in an attempt to cast doubt upon the accuracy of the original analysis. …"

The answer to the question was "yes". Appeal dismissed.

R v Hodnitt

[2003] EWCA Crim 441, 10 February 2003, CA (Crim)

On the facts – back-calculation, no evidence that drink could not have been taken in the hour before the incident, no evidence as to how the motor cycle left the road – the offence of causing death by careless driving while over the limit was not made out.

A motor cyclist had been convicted of causing death by careless driving while over the limit for alcohol, contrary to s 3A(1)(b), Road Traffic Act 1988. Police attended the scene of an accident where they found a motor cycle jammed between a telegraph pole and bushes, the injured rider astride the cycle and his passenger on the ground nearby. The passenger died soon afterwards, while the rider suffered retrograde amnesia and could not remember what had happened. A blood specimen was taken from the rider some 3½ hours after the officers attended the scene. Back-calculation showed that, on the assumption that no drink had been taken within an hour preceding the accident, the blood alcohol level at the time of the incident would have been between 117 mg and 147 mg in 100 ml blood. The motor cyclist's argument that there was no case to answer was rejected. He was convicted and appealed.

GROUNDS OF APPEAL: The submission of no case to answer should have been accepted and the case stopped.

HELD: "7. … there was on the face of it a period of about an hour, give or take a few minutes, unaccounted for – that is on the assumption that it takes just a few minutes to get from where the appellant was last seen with his motorbike to … the place … where the accident occurred.

"8. The back calculation … depends for its validity upon there having been no drink taken by the appellant within [that hour] and so it was for the Crown to prove that no drink could have been taken within that period. … there were … no witnesses to the accident itself. Because of the tragic outcome it is quite impossible of course for any evidence to come from the victim and because of the [appellant's] amnesia … , he was unable to help. All there was was the evidence of the Morgans [a couple who lived immediately opposite the scene and called the police] and the facts … as to the position of the motorcycle, the rider and the pillion passenger and, importantly, … the absence of any marks on the road to indicate the presence or involvement of another vehicle. But then there remains the fact that according to the Morgans, … there was seemingly at least one other person present at the scene at or soon after the happening of the accident.

"9. … the two young men [the motor cyclist and the deceased] must have been occupying their time in some fashion over the period of approximately an hour and who is to say, despite the unlikelihood of such a thing, that they had not met up with another member of the party [they had attended earlier] who still had a supply of drink about him or her, and that they had by that means been able to imbibe in the period immediately preceding the accident. How is it to be proved, it is suggested, that there was not some place open where drink might be obtained …? Unless, it is said, the Crown were able to show with the necessary degree of certainty that those possibilities did not exist then it was not safe to allow the matter to proceed before the jury. Further, it is asked rhetorically: why must it be assumed that simply because the motorbike can be seen to have left the road that that was the consequence of careless driving? Why must it be thought that no other individual or agency was involved in the accident? …

"10. So how was it to be shown that no other vehicle or no other individual had been involved in the accident to allow the only safe conclusion that the motorbike belonging to the appellant had left the road by reason of his careless driving? …

"12. … the Crown are now and were at the time unable to prove both limbs of the offence as it was necessary for them to do if this charge was to be made good. They are unable to remove from consideration the real possibility that drink had been taken in the hour before the accident, or the real possibility that some other agency may have been involved in the accident which need not necessarily have come about through the appellant's careless driving. This may be one of those rare cases where the court is left with a lurking doubt. Whether for that reason or for others which we have expressed, we do not consider this conviction to be safe. …"

Appeal allowed.

8. CERTIFICATES

See s 16(1), Road Traffic Offenders Act 1988 – evidence of the proportion of alcohol or a drug in a specimen may be proved by producing a certificate signed by an authorised analyst; s 16(2) – evidence that a blood specimen was taken with the defendant's consent may be proved by production of a certificate to that effect, signed by a medical practitioner; and s 16(3) on service. See also Tobi v Nicholas, page 45 – doctor's certificate of taking a blood specimen not admissible unless properly served; Badkin v DPP, page 46, where the prosecution failed to give notice of the results of the blood analysis and to call evidence of the results of the analysis; Rathbone v DPP, page 50 – oral evidence of taking of blood specimen is sufficient; Byrne (Simon David) v DPP, page 147, where a photocopy of the certificate of consent was admissible; Williams (Alan Davies) v DPP, page 484 – for the purposes of serving the certificate of blood analysis, "hearing" means the hearing at which the evidence is to be given, not a preliminary hearing; and Steward v DPP, page 651, where the magistrates confused evidence of the taking of a blood specimen with the analyst's certificate. See also the cases in Chapter 7 under the heading "The Printout", page 302.

Anderton v Kinnard

[1986] RTR 11, 6 February 1985, QBD (DC)

Service of the certificates of consent to the taking of a blood specimen, and of the blood analysis, on the defendant's solicitor was, in the circumstances of this case, good service.

A motorist had been accused, under s 6(1)(b), Road Traffic Act 1972 as substituted by s 25(3) and Sch 8, Transport Act 1981, of being in charge with excess alcohol. The lower breath analysis reading was 50 µg alcohol in 100 ml breath and the motorist claimed, under s 8(6), Road Traffic Act 1972, as likewise substituted (lower breath reading no more than 50 µg alcohol in 100 ml breath – now repealed; see page v), that the breath specimen be replaced by a specimen of blood. The certificates of the doctor who took the specimen and the analyst who analysed it were not served on the defendant himself under s 10(5) (certificate admissible if served on the accused no later than 7 days before the hearing), but his solicitors had asked for and received them, and said they did not require the doctor or the analyst to appear at the trial.

At trial, at the close of the prosecution case, the defendant objected to the admissibility of the certificates on the basis of failure properly to serve them. The justices agreed, and dismissed the charge. The prosecutor appealed.

QUESTION(S) FOR THE COURT: Whether the justices were correct in law to rule: (1) at the close of the prosecution case, that the prosecutor had failed to establish a case to answer and to refuse an adjournment and thereupon to dismiss the information; (2) that the certificates were inadmissible on the ground that the provisions of s 10(5) as to service had not been complied with.

HELD: "Two points arise; 1, was service of the ... documents ... upon the solicitors good service within section 10(5)? 2 If it was not, was good service waived by either (a) the letter [in which the motorist's solicitors said they did not require the witnesses to attend] or (b) the fact that no objection was taken until the prosecution evidence had been completed.

"[Quoting from the judgment in *R v Bott* [1968] 1 WLR 583, [1968] 1 All ER 1119], '... it is sufficient that a copy of the written statement to be tendered in evidence is given to the solicitor of the other party to the proceedings ...' ... there was ... good service ... That is not to suggest that in all cases, service may be effected on people other than the parties themselves ... I am satisfied that there was good service. If I were wrong about that, I would also hold that there had been a waiver in this case on both grounds [(a) and (b) above]... in almost all circumstances the objection [to the admissibility of evidence] must be taken when the evidence is tendered. If not then taken, the objection or defect is waived."

The justices were wrong to rule at the close of the prosecution case that the prosecutor had failed to establish a case to answer; the question of adjournment did not therefore arise. The answer to question (2) was "no". Appeal allowed.

Penman v Parker

[1986] 1 WLR 882, [1986] 2 All ER 862, [1986] RTR 403, 11 April 1986, QBD (DC)

Service of the certificates of consent to the taking of a blood specimen, and of the blood analysis, on defence counsel, he being the only person in court at the relevant time dealing with the case, was good service.

A motorist had been charged with driving while unfit, contrary to s 5(1), Road Traffic Act 1972. At the first court appearance, a police officer had served a doctor's certificate of taking a specimen of blood from the motorist, and an analyst's certificate showing that the proportion of alcohol in the blood exceeded the prescribed limit, on counsel for the motorist, the motorist and his solicitor having left court. The motorist was later also charged with failing without reasonable excuse to provide a specimen of breath for analysis, contrary to s 8(7), Road Traffic Act 1972 as substituted by s 25 and Sch 8, Transport Act 1981, and with driving with excess alcohol, contrary to s 6(1)(a), Road Traffic Act 1972 as likewise substituted. The justices ruled the two certificates inadmissible and dismissed all charges. The prosecutor appealed.

QUESTION(S) FOR THE COURT: Whether, on the facts, the justices were correct in deciding that the provisions of s 10(5), Road Traffic Act 1972 (certificate admissible if served on the accused no later than 7 days before the hearing) had not been complied with.

HELD: "... the provisions of section 10(8) (evidence of the proportion of alcohol to be served personally or sent by registered post or recorded delivery) ... do not necessarily require service to be upon the defendant himself. Service upon an authorised agent in appropriate circumstances may be valid service for the purposes of the section … particularly in the magistrates' court counsel has this limited authority at least, that his client having generally through the solicitor entrusted him with the conduct of the case he has authority to accept, or in his discretion to decline to accept, documents relevant to the matter in issue … Since [counsel] was the only person present in court at the relevant time, still dealing with the matter in issue, I would hold that in the limited sense I have described he did have authority to receive service of the documents.

"[On whether the documents were admissible in respect of the two charges laid after the documents had been given to counsel, these charges] arise out of the same incident and indeed the only reason why the second and third charges were laid later was because the driving with excess alcohol charge could not be laid until the analyst's certificate had been received … ."

The answer to the question was "no". Appeal allowed.

Hawkins v DPP

[1988] RTR 380, 26 June 1987, QBD (DC)

On the facts of this case, there was prima facie evidence of service of the certificates of consent to the taking of a blood specimen, and of the blood analysis, which the appellant failed to displace.

A motorist had been charged with driving with excess alcohol in blood, contrary to s 6(1)(a), Road Traffic Act 1972 as substituted by s 25 and Sch 8, Transport Act 1981. The certificate of the medical practitioner who took the specimen and a copy of the analyst's certificate showing the blood alcohol level had been sent to the defendant by recorded delivery post to his usual address.

At the hearing, the prosecutor sought to establish good service in the form of the sender's endorsements of posting marked on the certificates, in accordance with r 67(2), Magistrates' Courts Rules 1981 (SI 1981/552) (proof of service, etc by a certificate signed by the person by whom service was effected or the letter posted or registered) and s 7, Interpretation Act 1978 (service deemed effective by properly addressing, pre-paying and posting, etc).

The defendant said he had not received the documents, and that they were therefore inadmissible in evidence since they had not been served on him as required by s 10(5), Road Traffic Act, as likewise substituted (certificate admissible if served on the accused no later than 7 days before the hearing). The recorded delivery letter in question had not been returned by the Post Office. The prosecutor did not produce the postman's record of delivery. An adjournment notice sent to the defendant by recorded delivery had been returned by the Post Office marked "not called for"; the defendant had attended court in response to another adjournment notice posted by recorded delivery.

The justices found that there was sufficient proof of service and convicted the motorist. He appealed.

QUESTION(S) FOR THE COURT: Whether the justices were correct in law to find that the certificates were admissible under s 10(5), Road Traffic Act 1972 by proof of service of those documents not later than 7 days before the hearing, by production of the certificate of posting under r 67(2), Magistrates' Courts Rules 1981 by recorded delivery, despite the defendant's denial of receipt.

HELD: After reviewing the provisions of s 10(8), Road Traffic Act 1972 (certificate to be served personally or sent by registered post or recorded delivery), r 67(2), Magistrates' Courts Rules 1981 and s 7, Interpretation Act 1978, "There was before the justices *prima facie* evidence of service of the certificates in the usual way. It was open to the defendant to satisfy the justices that the certificates had not been served. He tried to do so but he failed."

Appeal dismissed.

Ramsey (Jennifer) v DPP

Unreported, CO/1268/96, 17 July 1996, QBD (DC)

Where the certificates of consent to the taking of a blood specimen, and of the blood analysis, contained errors but were re-served in corrected form, service was good.

A motorist had been involved in a road traffic accident; a roadside breath test was positive; she was arrested and taken to the police station. The breath analysis device was not working and the motorist was therefore required to provide a specimen of blood for analysis. Blood was taken and analysis revealed 169 mg alcohol in 100 ml blood.

At the hearing, the prosecution tendered in evidence the doctor's statement of having taken the specimen and the analyst's certificate. The motorist argued that neither was admissible. Some 10 months before the hearing, the motorist's solicitors had declined to accept as evidence the two certificates because the doctor's statement was illegible in part and the analyst's certificate mis-recited the analyst's forenames. The Crown Prosecution Service said it would therefore call the witnesses, but, 4 months before the hearing, re-served the statements in corrected form. The motorist's solicitors acknowledged receipt of the statements, but did not comment on their admissibility or suggest that they still required the witnesses to be called.

The justices held that the two documents had been properly served and convicted the motorist. She appealed.

QUESTION(S) FOR THE COURT: Whether the justices were entitled to hold that the written statement of the doctor and the certificate of the analyst were admissible in evidence.

HELD: "In the light of the Justices' finding [that] there was a proper re-service of these two statements … they were entitled to find that [they] were admissible. In the first place the doctor's statement was clearly admissible under section 9 of the Criminal Justice Act. No notice had been given after the re-service of the statement of [the doctor]. It was the first time that that particular statement had been served. It was made clear that it was served under the appropriate statutory provisions. Accordingly the Appellant's solicitors must have known that if they were to require the attendance of the witness they had within seven days, after the service, to give notice that they required the witness to attend.

"... The [certificate of analysis] had been served on the Appellant well before seven days before the hearing ... [but no notice requiring the attendance of the person who signed the statement] was, in fact, served, and [the appellant's] argument rests upon the much earlier statement in correspondence to the Crown Prosecution Service before ... these two documents had been properly re-served. It must ... have been abundantly clear to the Appellant's solicitors why the Crown Prosecution were re-serving these documents. In any event they would have to have been re-served because of the defects in the original documents ... ."

The answer to the question was "yes". Appeal dismissed.

Louis v DPP

[1998] RTR 354, 9 June 1997, QBD (DC)

The fact that the certificate of service of the blood analysis was unsigned did not affect the admissibility of the certificate of analysis.

A motorist had been charged with driving with excess alcohol, contrary to s 5(1)(a), Road Traffic Act 1988. Breath analysis was positive but revealed less than 50 µg alcohol in 100 ml breath. The motorist was therefore offered the option, under s 8(2), Road Traffic Act 1988 (lower breath reading no more than 50 µg alcohol in 100 ml breath – now repealed; see page v), of providing an alternative specimen. He gave blood which was taken in the usual way. Analysis for the prosecutor revealed 94 mg alcohol in 100 ml blood.

The certificate of service of the analyst's certificate of the blood analysis had not been signed, but the certificate of analysis was admitted in evidence and the motorist was convicted. He appealed.

QUESTION(S) FOR THE COURT: Whether the analyst's certificate was admissible in evidence.

HELD: "[I]t is a necessary requirement of the law that for the certificate [of analysis] to be placed in evidence it must have been served not later than seven days before the hearing ...

"What happened here ... is that it was discovered that there was no signature to the certificate of service. Indeed, it is now argued that it was not filled in at all. However, it is apparent from the case stated and from the Stipendiary's affidavit that there was no submission to the Stipendiary that the certificate was not admissible by reason of failure to comply with the provisions of section 16 [Road Traffic Offenders Act 1988, documentary evidence as to specimens].

"[In *Tobi v Nicholas*; see page 45] [t]here had been no service. Service was a statutory requirement and that statutory requirement could not be waived. Here, however, the Stipendiary Magistrate was dealing with the certificate of service.

He was not dealing with whether there had been, in fact, service, but with the fact that the certificate of service had not been signed, perhaps had not been filled in.

"… All that was in issue here was the certificate of service and not service itself."

Appeal dismissed.

Whyte v DPP

[2003] EWHC 358 (Admin), 20 February 2003, QBD (Admin)

Where the only evidence of service of the analyst's certificate was that of a police officer who had not been present at the time at which service was said to have taken place, that evidence was hearsay and the magistrates were not entitled to conclude that the certificate had been properly served. It was therefore inadmissible in evidence.

A motorist had been convicted of driving with excess alcohol in blood, contrary to s 5(1)(a), Road Traffic Act 1988. A police officer gave evidence that the analyst's certificate (of the alcohol content of the blood specimen) had been served on the defendant when he returned to the police station from which he had been bailed following the taking of the specimen. The police officer, however, had not been present at the police station on that date.

The motorist was convicted and appealed.

QUESTION(S) FOR THE COURT: Whether there was any evidence upon which a reasonable bench, properly directing itself, could have found: (1) (as reformulated in the judgment) that the certificate had been served on the appellant; (2) that the blood purportedly analysed by the forensic service was that of the appellant.

HELD: "3. … the only evidence of service was hearsay. Hearsay being inadmissible, in effect there was no admissible evidence before the bench.

"4. Section 16 of the Road Traffic Offenders Act 1988 makes service of the certificate on the accused not later than seven days before the hearing a precondition of its admissibility in evidence. It follows that the magistrates were not entitled to come to the conclusion that the certificate had been served as required by section 16, and it equally follows that the contents of the certificate were not admissible in evidence.

"9. [Question (2)] arises because, although the certificate correctly identified the time and place when the sample had been taken, the officer in question, the doctor in question and, presumably, the identity of the container in question, all by reference to information contained on the label of the container of blood, there was no evidence before the magistrate[s] as to whether, and if so, that label had been affixed on the sample at the police station. The common sense inference, of course, is that the information on the container matching precisely the evidence as to the taking of the sample came from information applied to a label at the time the sample was taken. However, even that information, coming as it does from a certificate, depends on the admissibility of the certificate itself and, of course … the certificate itself was inadmissible before the magistrates."

The answers to both questions were "no". Appeal allowed.

Wooldridge v DPP

[2003] EWHC 1663 (Admin), 19 June 2003, QBD (Admin)

Reading the certificate of consent to the taking of a blood specimen at the trial is not good service. A witness statement signed below the opening declaration rather than at the end was admissible.

A motorist had been charged with driving with excess alcohol in blood, contrary to s 5(1)(a), Road Traffic Act 1988. At the trial, the prosecutor produced to the court witness statements; a blood analysis certificate; and a medical practitioner's certificate of consent to the taking of the specimen. The prosecutor read the certificates and the first witness statement, following which the defendant's solicitor objected that none of the documents had been received in his office; the witness statement and analyst's certificate had been supplied to him informally, but he had never seen the medical practitioner's certificate and argued that it was therefore inadmissible. The magistrates ruled it admissible. They also accepted in evidence a police officer's witness statement which had not been signed at the end but had been signed below the opening declaration, finding that the omission was a matter of form not substance. They convicted the defendant. She appealed.

QUESTION(S) FOR THE COURT: Whether the magistrates were correct: (i) to admit the medical practitioner's certificate under s 16(2), Road Traffic Offenders Act 1988, given that no prior objection was taken to it by the defence under s 16(3) or (4); (ii) to admit the statement of the police officer under s 9, Criminal Justice Act 1967, even though it had not been signed at the end; (iii) to convict.

HELD: "[On (i), after quoting s 16(2), (3) and (4) – evidence that a specimen of blood was taken with consent by a medical practitioner may be given by the production of a certificate signed by the medical practitioner; such a certificate is admissible only if handed to the accused when produced or served not later than 7 days before the hearing.] 11. If the medical certificate … is not served on the accused at least seven days before the hearing, that is a bar to its reception in evidence. The absence of service is a defect which cannot be waived by the defendant or his advisers [quoting the authorities]. On the other hand, it is possible for the defendant to waive the requirement that service be formally proved …

"12. The magistrates took the view that … the appellant had waived the requirement of proof of service. … the magistrates can only be referring to the fact that [the appellant's solicitor] waited for a minute or two after the certificate was read out before making his objection. … a pause of that length of time cannot possibly give rise to a waiver. [The solicitor] was taken by surprise when the certificate was read out. He had never seen it before and was previously unaware of its existence. …

"13. … the first question … includes the … phrase, '… given that no prior objection was taken to it by the defence under section 16(3) or section 16(4) of that Act.' This is a somewhat odd comment. No prior objection could be taken to the certificate, since neither the appellant nor her solicitor was in possession of it until the trial … was in progress. …

"14. … the medical certificate was not served at the appropriate time. There was no relevant waiver by the appellant or her solicitor, and that certificate was inadmissible in evidence.

"[On (ii)] 15. … the statement … was correctly received in evidence for the reasons given by the magistrates. In relation to question (iii), [the appellant] submitted that the conviction cannot stand. [The prosecutor], however, points out that there might have been other evidence which was before the magistrates and which established that … [the doctor] took a specimen of blood from the appellant with her consent. On the other hand, … no such evidence appears in the stated case.

"16. This court cannot uphold a conviction on the basis of speculation about what other evidence, not mentioned in the stated case, might show. Furthermore, if such speculation were permissible, I would come to the opposite conclusion."

The answers to the questions were: (i), "no"; (ii), "yes"; (iii), "no". Appeal allowed.

Jeffreys v Director of Public Prosecutions

[2006] EWHC 1377 (Admin), 19 May 2006, QBD (Admin)

On the facts, there was evidence on which the court below could find that the certificate of analysis of a specimen had been served.

A motorist had been charged with driving with excess alcohol, contrary to s 5, Road Traffic Act 1988. At his trial, his counsel contended, in her closing speech, that the certificate of analysis of the blood specimen had not been served at least 7 days before the trial as required by s 16(3)(b), Road Traffic Offenders Act 1988. The defence had not raised the matter at any time before the hearing. The prosecution handed up the certificate of analysis at the hearing. Its admissibility was not disputed at that stage. The defendant gave no evidence about it. The trial judge was satisfied that the certificate of analysis had been posted to the defendant and that the issue being raised concerned the certificate of service rather than service itself; and that lack of proof had been waived by implication. The motorist was convicted and appealed.

QUESTION(S) FOR THE COURT: Whether there was any evidence upon which the court below could have found that the certificate of analysis had been served on the defendant.

HELD: "7. It is clear from *Tobi v Nicholas* [see page 45] that this service requirement of the certificate of analysis is mandatory. If the certificate is not served, the fact of the analysis is not admissible in evidence. Service cannot be waived. …

"17. ... the facts as found … are as follows … in reality the Appellant was putting in issue the certificate of service and not service itself since the Appellant had never claimed that the certificate of analysis had not been served on him but indeed had founded his defence on attempting to displace the statutory assumption created by the certificate of analysis. …

"20. … The cross-examination by the appellant related solely to the issue of post-accident consumption, and the issue surrounding the service of the certificate was not raised until the closing speeches … the issue relating to proof of service and the issue not being raised until the closing speeches was waiver of the need for proof."

The answer to the question was "yes".

DPP v Stephens

[2006] EWHC 1860 (Admin), 22 June 2006, QBD (DC)

A doctor's witness statement of taking a blood specimen was validly served under s 9, Criminal Justice Act 1967, even though it was not served in accordance with s 16, Road Traffic Offenders Act 1988, but the certificate of analysis must be served as required by s 16.

A motorist had been charged with driving with excess alcohol, contrary to s 5(1)(a), Road Traffic Act 1988. The lower breath analysis reading was 41 μg alcohol in 100 ml, and the motorist accepted the option under s 8(2) (lower of two breath readings not more than 50 μg alcohol in 100 ml breath – now repealed; see page v) to provide a blood specimen instead. Blood was taken and analysis showed excess alcohol. The witness statement of the doctor who took the blood specimen, and the certificate of analysis of the specimen, were posted to the defendant but he did not receive them. They were served personally on him 6 days before the trial.

At the trial, the prosecution sought to prove the taking of the blood specimen by witness statement under s 9, Criminal Justice Act 1967, and to prove the proportion of alcohol under s 16(1)(b), Road Traffic Offenders Act 1988. The justices found that neither document had been served as required by s 16, refused a prosecution application to re-serve the documents or to call live evidence and dismissed the case. The prosecutor appealed.

QUESTION(S) FOR THE COURT: (a) Whether the justices were correct to rule that the statement and certificate were inadmissible because they had not been served by registered post or recorded delivery in accordance with s 16(6), Road Traffic Offenders Act; (b) whether their decision not to grant an adjournment to the prosecution was *Wednesbury* unreasonable, where neither the doctor's evidence nor the contents of the certificate of analysis were not in dispute and the defence did not require the attendance of the doctor or of the maker of the certificate.

HELD: "5. … [the doctor's] witness statement was validly served under section 9(8)(a) of the Criminal Justice Act 1967 … as was admitted. Section 16 of the Road Traffic Offenders Act 1988 provides an alternative method of service of a witness statement which complies with the requirements of section 9. Hence the word 'may' in section 16(1) and the reference to a statement being admissible 'in pursuance of this section' in section 16(3)(a). Section 16 does not purport to exclude service of a section 9 witness statement under that section. Nor does it. [The] witness statement was validly served under section 9(8)(a), and no counter-notice having been served under section 9(2)(c), the justices were wrong to refuse to admit it.

"6. That was however not enough to prove the prosecution case. The certificate also had to be admitted. It was not in the form of a section 9 statement and so could only be admitted under section 16 of the 1988 Act. Section 16(6) provides exclusively for methods of service: personally or by registered post or by recorded delivery service. The word 'may' in this subsection permits any one of those three methods of service to be adopted. It does not permit any other method. No other method is prescribed by any other provision of any other statute or by the common law. The analyst's certificate is only admissible under section 16 of the 1988 Act. Because it was not served by one of the means specified in section 16(6) not later than seven days before the hearing as required by section 16(3)(b), the justices were right to rule it inadmissible…

"8. … Given the facts … the refusal to grant an adjournment did cause substantial unfairness to the appellant. It was irrational and cannot be upheld."

Appeal allowed.

Brett v DPP

[2009] EWHC 440 (Admin), [2009] 1 WLR 2530, 16 March 2009, QBD (Admin)

A certificate of analysis could be admitted under s 116, Criminal Justice Act 2003 even though notice had been given under s 16(4), Road Traffic Offenders Act 1988 that the attendance of the analyst was required. There was here a change of circumstances for the purposes of s 8A, Magistrates' Courts Act 1980 such that a pre-trial ruling by justices did not bind the trial court.

A motorist had been convicted of driving with excess alcohol in blood, contrary to s 5(1)(a), Road Traffic Act 1988. At a pre-trial hearing, the prosecutor successfully applied for the evidence of the analyst of the blood specimen to be given under the hearsay provisions in s 116, Criminal Justice Act 2003 (admissibility of hearsay evidence – witness unavailable), on the grounds that she was living abroad, had not been warned, and that it was not practicable to secure her attendance. The trial was listed for the following week, but did not take in fact place until some months later. At the trial, the deputy district judge considered himself bound by the decision of the magistrates on the question of hearsay and refused to hear further argument on the point. The motorist was convicted and appealed.

QUESTION(S) FOR THE COURT: (1) Whether it was correct to admit in evidence a certificate of analysis served under s 16, Road Traffic Offenders Act 1988 when notice had been given under s 16(4) that the attendance of the analyst was required; (2) whether the district judge was bound by the decision of the justices on this point.

HELD: "[On (1)] 10. … The possibility that the certificate might be admitted through some [route other than pursuant to s 16] is underlined by the words of section 16(1) … which is permissive rather than obligatory and section 16(4) which does no more than provide that if appropriate notice is given, … the certificate is not … admissible by this route …

"11. … I would reject the contention that section 16 … provides an exhaustive process for the proof of the proportion of alcohol … the justices were entitled to admit [the certificate] through the mechanism provided by the CJA 2003 notwithstanding that notice had been given pursuant to section 16(4) … requiring the analyst to attend.

"[On (2)] 12. … section 8A of the Magistrates' Courts Act 1980 provides that a pre-trial ruling is binding … unless there has been a material change of circumstances since the ruling was made such that … it is in the interests of justice to discharge or vary the earlier ruling …

"14. … When the case came before the justices the trial … was due to take place six days later. The justices found that the appellant had failed to comply with the directions of the court and failed sufficiently to identify the issues relating to the analyst's evidence. … there was simply insufficient time to make those enquiries and to consider arrangements for the attendance of the analyst …. After that trial had been adjourned, however, the position was different and it is unarguable that there was a material change of circumstances. A period of some months were available when it was open to the prosecution to make enquiries of the analyst … or otherwise discover what could be done to secure the evidence other than the use of section 116. …

"15. … there is no question of the decision in August binding the deputy district judge in relation to a trial in December and no basis upon which he should have prevented [counsel] from arguing the question of admissibility."

Conviction quashed.

Clarke v CPS

[2024] EWHC 704 (Admin), 26 March 2024, KBD (DC)

MG DD forms attached to the investigating officer's statement were exhibits for the purposes of s 9(7), Criminal Justice Act 1967 and therefore admissible in evidence; and, on the facts, were admitted by agreement to hearsay as part of the evidence; consent to the taking of a blood specimen given to the investigating officer was sufficient.

A motorist had been charged with driving with an excess of cocaine, contrary to s 5A(1)(a) and (2), Road Traffic Act 1988; and with an excess of benzoylecgonine, contrary to the same provisions. At the police station, he consented to provide a specimen when required to do so by the investigating officer; he again consented when, in the presence of the health care professional who was to take the specimen, he was asked if he still consented. He pleaded not guilty and, at trial, argued that the prosecution had failed to prove that he had consented to his blood being taken as required by the statutory provisions.

The magistrates found that the MG DD forms were exhibited to the investigating officer's statement; his evidence had been agreed during case management at the first hearing; and his statement and the "attached" MG DD forms stood as "unchallenged admissible" evidence at trial. They further found that s 11(4), Road Traffic Act 1988 was satisfied as the accused had consented to the taking of the specimen from him and it was taken by a registered health care professional, as set out in the MG DD forms; and that s 15(4), Road Traffic Offenders Act 1988 was also satisfied as the blood specimen was taken from the accused by a health care professional with his consent (given to the officer). He was convicted and appealed.

QUESTION(S) FOR THE COURT: Whether the magistrates were correct: (1) to admit as evidence the contents of the MG DD forms; and (2) to determine that giving consent to the taking of the blood sample to the police officer alone was sufficient to satisfy the requirements concerning consent in s 11(4), Road Traffic Act 1988 and s 15(4), Road Traffic Offenders Act 1988.

HELD: "28. As to the first question … section 9(7) Criminal Justice Act 1967… defines an exhibit as a 'document' referred to as an exhibit and 'identified in a written statement tendered in evidence'. The documents were identified in the statement. The Forms used were identified by name and it was made clear that they had been marked with Mr Clarke's name. There was no doubt on the facts below that the MGDD Forms concerned Mr Clarke. [The investigating officer] referred to the MGDD forms in his statement and attached them to that statement. On the facts as found, the Magistrates were entitled to conclude that he referred to them as part of his evidence of the sample-taking procedure concerning this specific person and a specific occasion. They were entitled therefore to conclude that the Forms were exhibits to the statement and so were admissible under section 9(7) of the 1967 Act. …

29. Further, we consider that the findings of the Magistrates establish that these Forms were admitted by agreement to hearsay as part of the evidence. The Forms were being put forward to establish the truth of their contents: the issue at trial had become solely the matter of consent which was recorded in the Forms. … the Magistrates expressly found that [the officer's] evidence was '… agreed at the case management hearing by the applicant. His statement and the attached MGDD Forms stood as unchallenged admissible evidence at trial' … the Magistrates found that [his] evidence comprised the statement and the MGDD Forms and it was that evidence which was agreed.

31. The second question … is not entirely clear. …

32. It may be that the question was intended to ask whether the consent given to the police officer … when the medical professional was not present … was sufficient or whether it was only the later consent, given … to the police officer … but in the presence of the medical [practitioner] … that satisfied the relevant statutory requirements. …

33. … if the Magistrates correctly admitted the MGDD Forms as evidence, on the facts found by the Magistrates this question does not arise. That is because the Forms show that there was consent given at 17.29 hours by Mr Clarke to the taking of his blood in the presence of a medical professional. That was, on the Appellant's own case, satisfactory consent for the purposes of Section 11(4) of the 1988 Act and Section 15(4) of the RTOA.

34. … the issue as to whether consent of the type given … in the presence of the police officer alone would be sufficient should be determined in a case where it would affect the outcome. Each case will be fact specific. …"

The answer to question (1) was "yes"; the answer to question (2) was, on the facts, "yes". Appeal dismissed.

9. THE PROVENANCE OF THE SPECIMEN

See also Taylor v DPP, page 62 – on the facts (matching names, matching police station, but a minor discrepancy in transcribing the serial number), the justices were right to find that the blood specimen analysed was that taken from the defendant; Byrne (Simon David) v DPP, page 147, where the specimen was identified by a code; Stevens v DPP, page 154, where, on the facts, there was ample material from which to conclude that the sample analysed was the defendant's; Whyte v DPP, page 169, where there was no proof of service of the analyst's certificate and therefore no proof that the blood analysed was that of the defendant; Bentley v Northumbria Police, page 260, where there was no evidential link between the specimen taken and the specimen analysed; MacDonald v Skelt, page 647, where there was no evidential link between the blood specimen taken and the specimen analysed; and Khatibi v DPP, page 652, where the magistrates were entitled to find that the blood analysed was that of the appellant.

Tremlett v Fawcett

The Times, 9 October 1984, 4 October 1984, QBD (DC)

The fact that there was no evidence of how a specimen had been transported from the police station to the laboratory was not of itself sufficient to cast doubt on its provenance.

A motorist had been charged with driving with excess alcohol. At the police station, he provided a urine specimen for a laboratory test; it was divided and sealed in the usual way. One part was given to the motorist; the other was placed in the refrigerator at the police station. A specimen labelled with the name of the appellant, the police force, division and station, the date and time, and the name of the officer in the case, was received at the Home Office Forensic Science Laboratory a few days later. Analysis revealed 271 mg alcohol in 100 ml urine.

At the hearing, the motorist submitted that there was no case to answer because the prosecution had failed to prove that the specimen had been properly taken from the refrigerator at the police station and delivered to the laboratory. The justices rejected that submission and convicted the motorist. He appealed.

HELD: "… The submission made to this court … was that … the justices could not have been satisfied … that the specimen taken from the appellant was in fact that which was analysed at the forensic science laboratory there having been no evidence as to how it had been transported from the police station to the laboratory …

"… there was ample evidence upon which the justices could be satisfied that the sample analysed was that which was taken from the appellant … It would be coincidence upon coincidence upon coincidence that the sealed container should be labelled with the details which corresponded precisely with that which the officers had given as to the procedure at the police station. They included not only the name (correctly recorded) of the appellant, the police force, the division, the station, the date, the time … and the officer in the case.

"… the justices were entitled to draw the inference that the sample analysed by the scientist was that which was taken."

Appeal dismissed.

Gregson v DPP

Unreported, CO-102-93, 10 June 1993, QBD (DC)

Where the usual labelling procedure had been carried out and the specimen despatched to the laboratory by recorded delivery, the court was correct to accept that the sample analysed was the sample taken from the motorist. The court was also correct to assume that a reference in the custody record to two specimens was a reference to the two parts into which the single specimen had been divided.

A motorist had been arrested and, at the police station, was required to provide specimens of breath for analysis. The lower reading was 41 µg alcohol in 100 ml breath, entitling the motorist to provide an alternative specimen under s 8(2), Road Traffic Act 1988 (lower breath reading no more than 50 µg alcohol in 100 ml breath – now repealed; see page v). He elected to give blood and the specimen was taken by a doctor. A sergeant labelled each of two containers with the motorist's name, the police force, division and station, the time and the name of the officer in the case. The doctor also signed the labels. One container was put in a bag for transmission to the laboratory, and the sergeant said in oral evidence that he had labelled the bag with the initials "JVR". The *pro forma* record of the proceedings recited that the sergeant had marked the bag with his initials; the officer who, the next day, sent the specimen for analysis, said the bag had been marked "JVR 1". Analysis revealed 91 mg alcohol in 100 ml blood.

The motorist appealed against conviction.

QUESTION(S) FOR THE COURT (INTER ALIA): Whether the justices erred in concluding that: (a) there was sufficient evidence that the blood analysed was that provided by the appellant; … (c) only one specimen of blood had been provided by the appellant at the police station, divided thereafter into two samples, one of which was forwarded to the analyst.

HELD: "[On (a)] … there was … overwhelming evidence that the sample examined by the Forensic Science Laboratory was indeed the sample which had been taken from Mr Gregson. It had the label on it which bore his name on the face of it. It had been transmitted from [the] police station to [the] Forensic Science Laboratory under cover of a recorded delivery service which had the identical number, and the coincidence between 'JVR' and 'JVR 1' is also something which points … in the same direction …

"[On (c)] … nothing was asked of [the sergeant] as to how it appeared in the custody record that there was a reference to two specimens, whereas …both he and the doctor were saying only one was in fact taken. But had he been asked, it seems … that the answer he would have given is obvious, namely that, the sample having been taken by the doctor, it was divided, as it always is, into two parts so that the person who was accused of having committed an offence could be provided with one of those parts. That is the inference which obviously the magistrates were prepared to draw … ."

The answers to the questions were "no". Appeal dismissed.

McGinty v DPP

Unreported, CO 4135/95, 18 March 1996, QBD (DC)

The court was entitled to find that the specimen analysed was the specimen taken from the motorist despite the fact that his first names had been deleted from the covering form by the analyst.

A motorist had been charged with driving with excess alcohol in blood, contrary to s 5(1)(a), Road Traffic Act 1988. The lower of two breath analyses was 46 µg alcohol in 100 ml breath. The officer administering the procedure therefore offered the motorist the option, under s 8(2), Road Traffic Act 1988 (lower breath reading no more than 50 µg alcohol in 100 ml breath – now repealed; see page v), of replacing the breath specimen with an alternative specimen. He did so; blood was taken and the specimen was divided into two containers, identically labelled with the motorist's name in full. One part was given to the motorist. The other part was put into a Jiffy bag together with a form giving the motorist's particulars. The particulars on the form and on the container labels were identical. The Jiffy bag was taken to the forensic science laboratory where the form was taken out and signed by the person who took it there; he was given a photocopy. The original form was later returned to the police station, when it was discovered that the motorist's first names had been deleted, presumably by the forensic scientist dealing with the specimen. Analysis of the blood by the forensic scientist revealed excess alcohol.

The magistrates found sufficient evidence that the blood sample taken from the motorist was the blood sample taken to the forensic science laboratory and convicted him. He appealed.

QUESTION(S) FOR THE COURT: Whether the justices were entitled to find on the evidence the blood sample analysed was the same blood sample as that provided by the defendant.

HELD: "… Since the form was the form put into the Jiffy bag with the Appellant's specimen of blood and since there was no evidence about why the first names of the Appellant were deleted on that form, the Magistrates were … entitled to find that the specimen analysed was the Appellant's specimen … ."

Appeal dismissed.

Rawal (Sushil) v DPP

Unreported, CO/156/2000, 21 March 2000, QBD (DC)

In the circumstances of this case, the court was entitled to find that the specimen analysed was the specimen taken from the motorist, despite inconsistencies in the record; and that the defendant was sufficiently informed of the reasons why breath specimens could not be taken.

The defendant had been required to provide specimens of breath for analysis, but the breath analysis device was found not to be working properly. He was then required to provide a specimen of blood or urine, and agreed to provide a specimen of blood. A doctor was called and took the specimen. The officer conducting the procedure marked the specimen "SPR 1", SPR being his initials. When the specimen was taken for analysis, the driver who collected it noted that the specimen bearing the defendant's name "Rawal" was marked "JWT/1", JWT being the initials of the doctor who had taken the specimen. Analysis revealed that the specimen marked "Rawal" contained 198 mg alcohol in 100 ml blood. The label on this specimen referred to a police station other than the one to which the defendant had been taken.

The defendant was convicted of driving with excess alcohol, and appealed.

QUESTION(S) FOR THE COURT: (1) Whether a reasonable bench, properly directing themselves, could have held that there was evidence which enabled them to find that the blood analysed was the defendant's blood taken by the doctor. (2) Whether the defendant was properly informed of the reason why the Lion Intoxilyser was not going to be used.

HELD: "[On 1] 11. Here the evidence … was that a specimen of blood was taken from the appellant at Hall Lane police station at 4.19 am on 24th November 1998 by Dr Tankel. Two days later a specimen was collected from that same police station by a civilian driver and taken to the laboratory. The detail shown on the label accompanying that specimen had the name of the appellant. The specimen analysed at the laboratory was labelled with the surname and initial of the appellant. The date and time on that label coincided precisely with that at which [the officer] said the appellant had provided the specimen. The label also recorded the correct police force and the name of the arresting officer.

"12. … whilst there were plainly some inconsistencies in the record relating to the specimen as it passed through the system, … there was sufficient evidence to entitle the Justices to conclude that the specimen analysed had been provided by the appellant …

"[On 2] 14. … the Justices found … that the appellant was unable to provide two satisfactory specimens of breath because the device was not working properly. After being handed the printout that showed the device to be not working properly, the appellant was informed that as it was not practicable to use a breath testing device he was required to provide either a specimen of blood or urine …

"16. It is submitted by the appellant that the procedure was fatally flawed because the appellant was not told precisely why he was required to provide blood or urine …

"21. … The Justices were satisfied that the appellant knew the reason why he was being asked to provide a specimen of blood, namely because the [Intoxilyser] was not working properly. He was, on any view, told that it was not practicable to use the [Intoxilyser]. If the machine was not working, it was not practicable to use it …

"22. … the appellant was sufficiently informed of the reasons why the breath specimens could not be used to satisfy the requirements of the Section 7(3)."

Appeal dismissed.

Mills v DPP

[2003] EWHC 1451 (Admin), 21 May 2003, QBD (DC)

The circumstances of this case (a labelling error and other matters) gave rise to significant doubt that the specimen analysed was the motorist's and his appeal against conviction succeeded.

A motorist had been charged with driving with excess alcohol, contrary to s 5(1)(a), Road Traffic Act 1988. He had been arrested, and at Skelmersdale police station he was required to provide a specimen of blood. The specimen was taken and divided into two; the officer conducting the procedure sealed the samples and marked them with the letters "ERP" (evidence related property) and the figures 2100. A driver took a specimen from the ERP refrigerator, marked "CJ/210/01" and delivered it to the laboratory, where it was analysed and revealed excess alcohol. The sample analysed was marked with the defendant's name; the name of the police force and the division; the name Chorley police station; the date 2/3/01; the time 01.53; and the name of the officer in the case.

The motorist was convicted and appealed.

QUESTION(S) FOR THE COURT: Whether there was evidence upon which a reasonable bench properly directing itself could have held that the blood analysed was the appellant's blood.

HELD: "7. … the evidence established that [the officer] wrote on the specimen, … 'ERP 2100'. At some unspecified later time, [the courier] removed from the fridge at the police station a specimen differently labelled, and took it to the Forensic Science Services in Chorley. Ten days later, [the analyst] examined the sample, which contained a label on which further details had been written. The station at which [the appellant's] sample was taken was not Chorley, as recorded on that label, but Skelmersdale. Otherwise, the details were certainly consistent with the taking of the specimen from the appellant at a police station at 01.53 am on 2nd March 2001 …

"8. … the court gave no explanation as to the process by which it purported to reach the conclusion that it was satisfied that the sample analysed … was the same sample which had been taken from the appellant on the night of 2nd March 2001 …

"10. There were … at least four unsatisfactory aspects of the chain of evidence. First, [the police officer] labelled the specimen, but there was no evidence that he placed it in the fridge. Second, his marking of the specimen did not, on the face of the evidence, match the marking on the specimen recovered by the courier from the fridge. Third, the incorrect origin of the specimen was subsequently placed on yet another label. Fourth, there was no evidence as to who the source of the information ultimately written on the label of the specimen analysed was, and no evidence that the specimen labelled was indeed that taken from the appellant.

"11. These circumstances must, in my judgment, raise significant doubt … whether the sample analysed was the appellant's. It would have been contrary, of course, if the prosecutor had been in a position to prove that the specimen had been placed by [the officer], or another officer, in an empty fridge, and that no other such cases were dealt with at Skelmersdale Police Station before [the courier] removed the specimen and took it to the laboratory. In the absence of evidence from which the appropriate inference could have been drawn … the court should not have reached the conclusion that it did."

The answer to the question was "no". Appeal allowed.

Chapter 3

Failing without Reasonable Excuse to Co-operate or to Provide Specimens

See s 6(6), Road Traffic Act 1988 (failing without reasonable excuse to co-operate with a preliminary test), and s 7(6), Road Traffic Act 1988 (failing without reasonable excuse to provide specimens for analysis). See also Chapter 4, on reasonable excuse; and Culleton v Palmer, page 402, on oral evidence of failing to provide.

1. THE MEANING OF "FAILING"

See also Burke v DPP, page 83, where the defendant's words in response to the requirement amounted to failure to provide; DPP v Byrne (David Stephen), page 201 – providing a single breath specimen amounts to failing to provide; DPP v Radford, page 202 – a motorist who held the mouthpiece to his mouth but the device registered no breath provided, failed to provide; and DPP v Fountain, page 248 where the words "In view of the danger of AIDS, I'd rather not give blood", amounted to refusal to provide.

Smith v Hand

[1986] RTR 265, 19 May 1986, QBD (DC)

In the circumstances of this case – the motorist asked to speak to his solicitor before deciding whether or not to provide breath specimens, the police gave him permission to do so, the motorist spoke to his solicitor and then provided the specimens – the motorist did not refuse to provide specimens. Compare the cases in Chapter 4 under the heading "Conditional Agreement", page 216.

A motorist had been charged with failing without reasonable excuse to provide a specimen of breath for analysis, contrary to s 8(7), Road Traffic Act 1972 as substituted by s 25 and Sch 8, Transport Act 1981. Having been asked to provide specimens, he indicated that he wished to consult his solicitor first. The police permitted this; the motorist did so, and then provided the specimens. The justices dismissed the charge, finding that there had been no refusal. The prosecutor appealed.

QUESTION(S) FOR THE COURT: (1) Whether the defendant's request to speak to a solicitor first before agreeing to provide specimens amounted in law to a failure to provide a specimen of breath; (2) whether on the facts as found, if it was considered that there was a failure in law on the part of the defendant to provide a specimen of breath, such failure was with reasonable excuse in law.

HELD: "[Quoting from *Pettigrew v Northumbria Police Authority* [1976] RTR 177, [1976] Crim LR 259 (DC)] 'the motorist … refuses to comply with the request if he gives an acceptance which is subject to a condition … in practice there will be many cases in which the motorist will wish not immediately to give a specimen. Sometimes it is because he wants a solicitor … a distinction must be made between the motorist who says "I will not unless –" and the motorist who says "I will but may I do so-and-so beforehand?" In the second instance there is no refusal …'

"… I … have not found it entirely easy to decide which of those is the right interpretation to give to that sentence ['We resolved that his conversation with the police only amounted to a request to speak to his solicitor before deciding whether to give a specimen'] in the findings of fact. But, left as I am in some doubt, I feel it right to give the benefit of the doubt to the defendant and decide this case on the basis that he requested to speak to his solicitor before deciding whether to give a specimen … The police gave him that permission and, therefore, there is no question of estoppel here."

Appeal dismissed.

Campbell v DPP

[1989] RTR 256, 11 November 1988, QBD (DC)

A motorist was guilty of the offence of failing to provide breath specimens for analysis even though the requirement was made in a room where there was no breath analysis device, and no breath analysis device was presented to him.

A motorist had been charged with failing without reasonable excuse to provide a specimen of breath for analysis, contrary to s 8(7), Road Traffic Act 1972 as substituted by s 25 and Sch 8, Transport Act 1981. He had been arrested and cautioned. The requirement for breath specimens was made at the police station in a room other than the room where the breath analysis machine was installed. The motorist made no reply to the request, or to two more requests.

The magistrates convicted. The motorist appealed.

QUESTION(S) FOR THE COURT: Whether, the defendant, having been cautioned that he need not say anything, his silence amounted to a failure to provide a breath specimen without reasonable excuse if the approved device was not presented to him for use.

HELD: "The question … is … whether the principle applies that a person cannot fail to do something unless he is enabled to do it by the production immediately before him of the equipment. In *R v Ferguson* [[1970] RTR 395 (CA)] it was held that the opportunity was provided, even though a device was not presented to the defendant and even though a fresh request was not made when the situation arose in which the defendant had previously said he would supply a specimen. If the defendant had an opportunity in those circumstances, the defendant in the present case had an opportunity … He was asked to provide the specimen at a police station where a device was in fact present and the defendant could reasonably be expected to know that a device was present and readily available … it was not necessary actually to show the defendant the device in order to establish that the opportunity was provided.

"… the fact the failure to reply followed a caution [has no] bearing upon whether the defendant met the statutory requirements under s 8(7)."

Appeal dismissed.

DPP v Shuker

Unreported, CO 2822/94, 7 March 1995, QBD (DC)

In the circumstances of this case (feigned attack; saying "bronchitis"; demanding a doctor, etc), the motorist failed without reasonable excuse to provide breath specimens.

A motorist had been charged with failing without reasonable excuse to provide two specimens of breath for analysis, contrary to s 7(6), Road Traffic Act 1988. A roadside breath test had been positive; he had been arrested and, at the police station, agreed to provide specimens of breath for analysis. When taken to the breath analysis device, he clutched his chest as though having an attack. When asked if there was any medical reason why he could not provide specimens, he replied "Bronchitis". The police officer administering the procedure thought he was feigning the attack because he had already provided a sample for a roadside breath test, he refused to make any effort to provide the specimens, and the attack did not take place until the precise moment when he was to give the specimens. The police surgeon arrived at the police station nearly an hour later; the defendant was taken to the police surgeon, where he immediately said he would blow into the machine but only if the doctor gave him a certificate saying he was fit to do so. He then demanded his solicitor and an ambulance. He provided no specimen for analysis.

The magistrates accepted the defendant's submission that the procedure had been suspended pending medical advice and should have been restarted when the doctor said the motorist was fit; they concluded that the motorist had not been required to provide a breath specimen, and dismissed the information. The prosecutor appealed.

QUESTION(S) FOR THE COURT: (1) Was the court right to decide that the respondent had not failed to provide a specimen without reasonable excuse? (2) Was the court right to conclude that the procedure should have been restarted and the defendant required to provide two specimens of breath following the defendant's failure to give specimens of breath and the pronouncement that he was fit to do so?

HELD: "… in the case stated the Magistrates set out … an incontrovertible statement that the Respondent had been required … to provide a breath sample and failed to do so …

"… if the decision of the Magistrates … was correct, it gives virtually a charter to recalcitrant motorists to play the system to the best of their ability. At the very least they could succeed in getting some sort of delay …

"The section is quite clear; it is quite simple. Once you are required to provide specimens of breath for analysis, as this Respondent was, you are guilty of an offence if, without the reasonable excuse, you fail to provide a specimen … this Respondent did fail to provide the specimen. He did not seek to raise by way of his defence … any reasonable excuse, and that seems … to be the end of the matter."

The answers to both questions were "no". Appeal allowed.

Smyth v DPP

[1996] RTR 59, 18 May 1995, QBD (DC)

Where a motorist at first refused to provide breath specimens but within 5 seconds changed his mind, the offence of failing to provide specimens was not made out.

A motorist had been charged with failing without reasonable excuse to provide two specimens of breath for analysis, contrary to s 7(6), Road Traffic Act 1988. At the police station, he was asked to provide breath specimens for analysis; he said "no", but within 5 seconds, said "Can I change my mind? I want to change my mind".

The justices found that his refusal was unequivocal and convicted him. The motorist appealed.

QUESTION(S) FOR THE COURT: Whether the justices were correct in their finding that the defendant had failed to provide specimens.

HELD: "… it is a matter of fact for decision by the tribunal of fact … whether the defendant's words and conduct amount to a refusal …

"… the justices [must have] ignored the defendant's words 'Can I change my mind?' and 'I want to change my mind', which followed as little as five seconds after his 'No', and must be relevant words and conduct to be taken into account …

"… the only conclusions that could reasonably be arrived at, having regard to all the words and conduct of the defendant, was that he was not proved to have failed to provide the specimen."

Appeal allowed.

Hingley-Smith v DPP

[1997] EWHC 952 (Admin), 31 October 1997, QBD (DC)

A motorist who provided a single breath specimen was liable to prosecution for failing to provide specimens even though offered a second chance to do so. On the facts, the information was sufficient and the court was entitled to accept that there was no defect in the breath analysis device.

A motorist had been charged with failing without reasonable excuse to provide two specimens of breath for analysis, contrary to s 7(6), Road Traffic Act 1988. She had been arrested following a positive roadside breath test and taken to the police station. At 12.15 am she was asked to provide two specimens of breath for analysis. She agreed, and provided a first sample at 12.19 am, and that was recorded by the sergeant conducting the procedure. The record went on to say "Machine aborted at 00.20". The reading was 134 µg alcohol in 100 ml breath. At 12.34 am the sergeant offered the motorist a chance to provide another specimen; she did not and the machine again shut down. At 12.38 am she was asked to provide a specimen of blood or urine; she declined.

The motorist was convicted in the magistrates' court and appealed to the Crown Court. The sergeant gave evidence that he was not aware that the breath analysis device was supposed to allow 3 minutes for the two specimens to be given; he thought it was usual for it to allow about 2 minutes; he believed the machine had been working correctly. He was not challenged about his record of timings. The motorist adduced expert evidence to the effect that the Home Office had specified that an approved breath analysis device should allow 3 minutes for the two specimens to be given; and that if the machine in question had aborted after one minute, as the record showed, there must have been something wrong with it. The prosecutor adduced expert evidence from an experienced engineer employed by the manufacturers of the machine, that he saw no indication on the printouts of any malfunctioning; he had never known a machine allow anything other than the prescribed 3 minutes.

The Crown Court accepted that the machine had been operating correctly and dismissed the appeal; the motorist appealed further.

QUESTION(S) FOR THE COURT: (1) Was r 100, Magistrates' Courts Rules 1981 (SI 1981/552) (sufficiency of the information) complied with by the prosecutor? (3) Was it perverse to find as a fact that the Intoximeter was working correctly and had allowed the appellant 3 minutes to provide her specimen; and in reaching that finding were the Bench, as a matter of law, entitled not to take into account any fact that occurred after the commission of the *actus reus* at 00.19 hours? (4) Can a court take a point against a defendant in a criminal case and if it does so, should it call evidence itself on that point or allow the parties to do so? (5) If a constable allows a driver a second chance to blow into the machine after he has failed to do so satisfactorily on the first attempt, can he still be guilty of a failure in relation to the first attempt? (6) In deciding whether the Intoximeter was working correctly, could the court have taken into account the engineer's evidence that he had never come across such a fault in the 12 years he had worked for its manufacturer?

HELD: "(1) [Counsel for the appellant] submits that the information … was defective because it did not state which failure to provide a specimen was relied upon, the failure at 12.19 am or that at 12.35 am … This appellant knew perfectly well the case she had to meet … She was not in any way embarrassed by lack of particularity … The first question … should be answered 'yes'. …

"(3) [Counsel for the appellant] submits that [the sergeant's] forms show that at 12.19 and 12.34 the machine only allowed the appellant one minute or so to give a second specimen before it closed down … [and] the Crown Court should have accepted [the officer's] timings … [T]he Crown Court found itself sure that there was no mechanical defect and recognised that in making that finding it necessarily had, at any rate to some extent, to reject the evidence of the Police Sergeant …

"(4) The whole substance of this submission … is that it was not put to [the sergeant] that his timings were wrong … If it was thought appropriate to put it … it was possible for the defence to have put it … the court was entitled to make the finding that it did, insofar as that was a finding that it was sure that the explanation of what occurred was that there was no mechanical defect and that in some way or another the Sergeant's record was in error.

"(5) [Counsel for the appellant] submits that if the driver provides a satisfactory sample at a second attempt, he cannot be guilty of the first failure. That … I have no difficulty in accepting. He goes on to submit, however, that if the police officer affords the driver a chance to make a second attempt, he thereby jettisons the right of prosecution to rely upon the first failure as the basis of a charge. There is no authority for that proposition which does not find any support in the statute and I … do not accept it.

"(6) [Counsel for the appellant] submits that the evidence of [the engineer] was inadmissible because it was simply evidence about the generality of such machines … in *DPP v Charles* [[1996] RTR 247] … it is quite clear that this court said that such evidence was *prima facie* admissible, and I … can see no reason why in the circumstances which arose in the present case it should not be admissible."

Appeal dismissed.

DPP v Lawrence (Scott James)

[1998] COD 361, 1 July 1998, QBD (DC)

Where a motorist refused to provide a specimen of blood but changed his mind 35–40 minutes later, he was guilty of the offence of failing to provide. In the absence of any medical reason there could be no reasonable excuse, nor could thinking he had a choice between giving a blood or a urine specimen amount to a reasonable excuse. See also Procaj v Johnstone [1970] RTR 49 – failure to provide a specimen is complete upon first refusal; it is immaterial that the suspect later changes his mind.

A motorist had been charged with failing to provide a specimen of blood for a laboratory test, contrary to s 7(6), Road Traffic Act 1988. He had been stopped and arrested. At the police station, the breath analysis device was not working. A doctor was called and a blood specimen was required. The defendant said he would not give blood as he was afraid of needles. The procedure was halted, the doctor being called away to examine someone else who needed urgent medical attention. The doctor returned to the defendant some 17 minutes later, examined him in private and found him fit to give blood. He then agreed to do so.

The defendant contended before the justices that he had not failed to provide a specimen of blood as, once the doctor had explained to him that he was fit to do so, he agreed. The justices found, *inter alia*, that the defendant thought he had a choice between giving blood or urine; and that his agreeing to give a blood specimen after a private examination by the doctor did not amount to a refusal. They found him not guilty. The prosecutor appealed.

QUESTION(S) FOR THE COURT: Whether the justices were wrong in law in finding that there was (no) failure without reasonable excuse to provide a specimen of blood.

HELD: "The first issue raised was … was there a failure or refusal to provide a specimen? …

"The respondent's response to the question of whether there was a reason why a specimen of blood could or should not be taken from him was that there was a reason: he did not like needles … This was at about 1.00 am, the procedure under section 7(4) having started at 0.57 am … There was … therefore a clear refusal by the respondent at the time that the constable had gone through the procedure required under section 7(4). The subsequent opportunity to allow the respondent to talk to the doctor did not detract from that refusal …

"… if at the end of the procedure which the constable is required to follow … the respondent's refusal was clear (as indeed the respondent's refusal was at about 1.00 am), then the offence is complete … There can, of course, be circumstances where the change of mind follows so quickly that, looking at the responses as a whole at the end of the procedure the constable is required under section 7(4) to follow, the tribunal of fact can properly conclude there was no refusal …

"In the instant case … [it] was not until … some 35 to 40 minutes later that he changed his mind …

"I turn to consider the second issue: was there a reasonable excuse? It is a question of law whether something put forward is capable of being a reasonable excuse … [Applying the test in *R v Lennard*; see page 220] … there was, in fact, no medical reason and none was, in fact, advanced as to why a specimen of blood could not be given. Furthermore, the fact that the respondent thought he had a choice of providing blood or urine cannot amount to a reasonable excuse … Moreover the respondent was not entitled to delay his response and discuss the matter with a doctor unless he had raised an objection on medical grounds, which the constable was bound under the provisions of section 7(4) to refer to a doctor."

Appeal allowed.

May v DPP

[2000] RTR 7, 19 October 1998, QBD (DC)

Where it was unclear whether the officer had decided that the motorist had refused to provide a second breath specimen, or had decided that there were medical reasons why breath could not be provided or should not be required, the case was remitted to the justices for rehearing.

A motorist had been charged with failing to provide two specimens of breath for analysis, contrary to s 7, Road Traffic Act 1988. Officers had approached a stationary car on a public road; the defendant was sitting in the driver's seat; it was his car; the key was in the ignition which was in the auxiliary position so that the electrical system was engaged. The officers noticed that he smelt of alcohol and his eyes were glazed. A roadside breath test was positive; the motorist was arrested and taken to the police station where he was required to provide two specimens of breath. He provided one specimen which gave a reading of 78 µg alcohol in 100 ml breath, but failed to give a second specimen. When invited again to provide the second specimen, the defendant said the reading was caused not by alcohol but by drugs he was taking for Crohn's disease. He was given further opportunities to provide a second breath specimen but failed to do so, saying that he wished blood to be taken. A doctor took a specimen of blood. No evidence from the doctor or of the result of the blood analysis was adduced in evidence.

The justices found that the defendant had had no problem in providing the first specimen and was physically and mentally capable of providing the second specimen, but chose not to do so. They convicted him; he appealed.

HELD: "Had the matter ended with the refusal of the appellant to provide a second specimen of breath it may very well have been that there was no answer whatever to this information against him … [but] the matter did not end there and that blood was taken. The power to require the taking of blood or urine is strictly governed by subsection (3) of section 7 … the officer … must have been relying on [s 7(3)](a), namely that he had reasonable cause to believe that for medical reasons a specimen of breath could not be provided or should not be required. If, however, he was of that opinion then he may not have regarded the conduct of Mr May as a refusal and must or may have formed the opinion that there were medical reasons why a specimen of breath could not be provided or … should not be required.

"These matters were not explored … That … places this court in an impossible position because it leaves … unanswered … whether the officer did form the judgment that there was a refusal or whether he, in fact, took the view that there were medical reasons why a sample of breath should not be required, therefore initiating the medical procedure … I would … order that the case be remitted to the justices to be reheard … so that in particular any appropriate evidence may be heard concerning the circumstances in which a sample of blood came to be required (if it was required) and given."

Appeal allowed in part.

DPP v Swan

[2004] EWHC 2432 (Admin), 21 October 2004, QBD (Admin)

The offence of failing to provide may be committed even if the officer does not produce the roadside breath testing device to the motorist; rude and aggressive behaviour, delaying tactics and demanding to have a photograph taken amounted to refusal to provide breath specimens.

A motorist had been charged with failing without reasonable excuse to provide a specimen for a breath test, contrary to s 6(4), Road Traffic Act 1988; and with failing without reasonable excuse to provide two specimens of breath for analysis, contrary to s 7(6), Road Traffic Act 1988. He had been stopped by police; he was agitated; he was required to provide a specimen of breath but the officer did not proffer or produce the device. He was hand-cuffed and arrested. At the police station, he was abusive and preoccupied with his wrists. He said he would provide breath specimens only if the officer would confirm that he had marks on his wrists, and guarantee to take a photograph of them. The breath analysis device timed out without specimens having been given.

The magistrates dismissed both charges. The prosecutor appealed.

QUESTION(S) FOR THE COURT: (a) Whether the officer at the roadside had to produce the device for the requirement to be lawful, or whether the spoken words of the requirement sufficed; (b) whether the respondent's rude and aggressive behaviour and delaying tactics at the roadside amounted in law to a failure, and then to a failure without reasonable excuse; (c) whether by his admitted conduct of shouting and swearing in the custody area, dropping his trousers in plain view, constantly shouting over the officer trying to administer the test and saying he would not take it unless photographs were taken of alleged injuries to his wrists was sufficient to constitute failure and then, the failure without reasonable excuse.

HELD: "[On the events at the roadside] 9. … the physical production of the breath test device is … clearly [not necessary]. All that is needed to constitute a proper request for a breath specimen, and to give the opportunity, is that the driver is told that he is required by the officer to provide a specimen of breath. If his conduct then shows that he is not willing to provide that specimen, or he imposes, by what he says or by his conduct, unacceptable terms upon which, and only upon which, he will provide the specimen, then a failure may well be made out.

"10. The first question, therefore, must be answered in the negative. …

"11. So far as question (b) is concerned, whether the admitted rude and aggressive behaviour, combined with the admitted delaying tactics, amounted to a failure, the only answer [is] yes … . The justices were wrong … in concluding … that there was no failure. …

"[On (c)] 34. … What the justices clearly had to do was to look at the conduct as a whole. … The manner in which the respondent was behaving would have led any police officer reasonably to take the view that he was being thoroughly uncooperative and that he was evincing a clear intention that he was not going to co-operate in any way unless his requirements were met. There could be no reasonable excuse, if I may move on to that, in requesting that a photograph be guaranteed before there was any agreement to take the breath test."

Appeal allowed.

Plackett v DPP

[2008] EWHC 1335 (Admin), 15 May 2008, QBD (DC)

Where a suspect had initially refused to provide breath specimens then changed his mind, and the investigating officer led him to believe he would be allowed another opportunity, a full 3-minute cycle should have been allowed.

A motorist had been charged with failing without reasonable excuse to provide two specimens of breath for analysis, contrary to s 7(6), Road Traffic Act 1988. A police officer had found him sitting in his car in a car park; he refused to take a roadside breath test and was arrested. At the police station, he at first refused to provide specimens of breath for analysis; he then left the room to speak by telephone to the duty solicitor, and while he was out of the room, the investigating officer began the operating cycle of the breath analysis device. The suspect returned to the room and indicated that he now wished to provide specimens. There was about one minute of the cycle left. At the first attempt to provide specimens, the mouthpiece came off; at the second, the amount of breath provided was insufficient. No further opportunity to provide specimens was given. The justices convicted the accused; he appealed.

QUESTION(S) FOR THE COURT: (1) Whether the justices were entitled to convict when the officer had begun the operation in the absence of the appellant; (2) whether the justices were right to find that the appellant had a proper opportunity to provide a specimen given that the officer allowed him only one minute instead of the usual three.

HELD: "17. … it may well be that the appellant having refused to provide a specimen of breath and left the room, albeit with the permission of the officer, to speak to the duty solicitor, the officer would have been entitled to treat the refusal as the commission of the offence and not to offer any further opportunity to the appellant to provide a specimen. However … he chose not to do that, and, having commenced the operating cycle … whilst the appellant was out of the room, for whatever purpose, gave the appellant the opportunity to provide a specimen when the appellant returned to the room and indicated that after taking advice he wished to take the breath test. …

"18. … the officer having decided that he would give the appellant the opportunity, it was incumbent on him to give an opportunity to take the test in the normal way, using a full cycle …

"19. … the justices were of the view that the appellant was given the expectation by the officer that he would be able to take the breath test and that what occurred within the remainder of the cycle of the machine satisfied that expectation. In my judgment, it did not."

"[On (1)] 20. I do not consider that the fact that the officer administering the test began the operation of the machine in the absence of the appellant would necessarily be a bar to conviction. But in the circumstances of this case, where the appellant subsequently expressed the wish to take the test and the officer by his conduct agreed to the request, the offence was not … made out where the normal procedure with the approved machine running full cycle was not carried out."

The answer to question (2) was "no". Appeal allowed.

2. THE SUFFICIENCY OF THE SPECIMEN

On the sufficiency of specimens and the manner in which they are to be provided, see s 11(3) and (4), Road Traffic Act 1988. See also Denny v DPP, page 47, and Stewart (John Kimball) v DPP, page 114, both to the effect that breath specimens must be capable of analysis; Hussain v DPP, page 59 – where the device did not produce a reliable indication, the specimens were unreliable for the purposes of s 11(3)(b); R v Coward, page 124 – a urine specimen must be capable of being divided into two parts such that each part is capable of analysis; Gregory v DPP, page 146, concerning the volume of a blood specimen; and DPP v Byrne (David Stephen), page 201 – a single breath specimen is insufficient to enable the analysis to be carried out.

Teape v Godfrey

[1986] RTR 213, 14 February 1985, QBD (DC)

The production of the printout showing a breath specimen to have been insufficient is not an essential prerequisite for a conviction. A suspect who makes no effort to blow has no reasonable excuse for failing to provide.

The defendant had been convicted under s 7(4), Road Traffic Act 1972 as substituted by s 25(3) and Sch 8, Transport Act 1981, of failing without reasonable excuse to provide a specimen of breath for a breath test; and, under s 8(7) as likewise substituted, of failing without reasonable excuse to provide a specimen of breath for analysis. On both charges, the justices found that the defendant had deliberately failed to provide specimens; his asthmatic condition did not render him incapable of providing a sufficient specimen; he had not told the police of his condition, nor did the police have any reasonable cause to believe that for medical reasons specimens could not or should not have been provided.

The defendant appealed.

QUESTION(S) FOR THE COURT: (a) Whether, in the absence of a printout indicating that the specimen provided was insufficient for a proper analysis, the justices were right to conclude that the defendant had failed to provide a specimen; (b) whether, having established that the defendant may have had a valid reason for not being able to give specimens, it was right to convict him.

HELD: The production of a printout is not an essential prerequisite for a conviction. The defendant "on each occasion deliberately failed to provide the specimen … He blew round the tube rather than into it. In those circumstances, … no question of reasonable excuse in fact arose. He did not get to the stage of casting on to the prosecution … the burden of discharging an onus of proof … the justices were right in their decision to convict … in relation to both informations." Appeal dismissed.

Anderton v Waring

[1986] RTR 74, 26 February 1985, QBD (DC)

Where no sample was recorded, the justices should not, in the absence of evidence, have assumed that the breath analysis device would have shown the word "Aborted".

Justices had dismissed a charge of failing without reasonable excuse to provide a specimen of breath for analysis, contrary to s 8(7), Road Traffic Act 1972 as substituted by s 25 and Sch 8, Transport Act 1981. The motorist put the mouthpiece of the breath analysis device to his mouth and blew, but no sample was recorded. The justices found that if the machine had recorded that no sample had been provided, the visual display would have shown "Aborted" – no evidence on this point was adduced; that the defendant had made a proper and full attempt to blow; and that he had not failed to provide a specimen; alternatively, that, by acting to the best of his ability, he had not acted without reasonable excuse. The prosecutor appealed.

QUESTION(S) FOR THE COURT: (1) Whether on the evidence the prosecution proved that the defendant had failed to provide a specimen; (2) if the prosecution had proved such a failure, whether on the evidence the issue of reasonable excuse arose; and (3) if it did so arise, whether the prosecution had proved beyond reasonable doubt that there was no reasonable excuse for not providing a specimen.

HELD: "I have some sympathy with the justices because they clearly preferred the defendant to the police sergeant as a witness … Nevertheless, … the Intoximeter ought to have been assumed … to have been in good working order unless the contrary was proved … they were not entitled to make use of their experience of these machines nor to draw any inference from the absence of evidence that the visual display on the Lion Intoximeter 3000 showed the word 'Aborted', at least without raising the point in the course of the trial … I do not think that [the justices] can have taken the provisions of s 12(3) [specimen must be sufficient to enable the analysis to be carried out, etc] into account, nor … was there any material on which the justices could properly have concluded in the alternative that, if the defendant had failed to provide a specimen, he had had a reasonable excuse … ."

On (1), the prosecutor did prove failure to provide a specimen; on (2), the issue of reasonable excuse did arise; on (3), there was no evidence on which the justices were entitled to find reasonable excuse.

Appeal allowed.

DPP v Heywood

[1998] RTR 1, 8 July 1997, QBD (DC)

Blowing with insufficient force amounts to failing to provide a breath specimen.

A motorist had been charged with failing without reasonable excuse to provide a specimen for a breath test, contrary to s 6(4), Road Traffic Act 1988. She had been stopped by police and was asked to provide a specimen for a breath test. On two occasions she blew into the device but not with sufficient force to illuminate either of the two lights. She blew twice more, both times illuminating only light "A". At no time did the officer press the "Read" button. The motorist was arrested for failing to supply a specimen.

It was accepted that had the officer pressed the "Read" button when light "A" had been illuminated the device would have analysed the breath provided and it might have given a positive reading which would have been reliable; a negative reading would not have been reliable.

It was argued that since the constable had not pressed the "Read" button, it had not been established that the motorist had failed to provide a specimen and that her arrest was unlawful. The magistrate accepted that submission and dismissed the case. The prosecutor appealed.

QUESTION(S) FOR THE COURT: Whether the defendant provided a specimen of breath which was sufficient to enable the test to be carried out and which was provided in such a way as to enable the objective of the test to be satisfactorily achieved.

HELD: "… To that question there is … only one possible answer, which is 'No'. The objective of the test was to establish reliably whether a sample of the defendant's breath was or was not positive when tested for alcohol. The defendant gave a specimen in such a quantity or in such a way that it could not be established reliably whether a sample of her breath was or was not positive when tested for alcohol. The specimen she gave enabled a reading to be obtained, but the reading might or might not be reliable. [It] was reliable if it was positive, but not reliable if it was negative … ."

The answer to the question was "no". Appeal allowed.

Chand v DPP; DPP v Chand

Unreported, CO/321/98; CO/320/98, 19 October 1998, QBD (DC)

Blowing for too short a time amounts to failing to provide a roadside breath specimen. On the facts of this case (the officer having failed to say that he had decided the specimen would be of blood), the motorist had not been required to provide a specimen for laboratory testing.

In the first appeal, a motorist had been charged with, *inter alia*, failing without reasonable excuse to provide a specimen for a breath test, contrary to s 6(4), Road Traffic Act 1988. He had been asked to provide a roadside specimen and the procedure was explained to him, but the sample was of such short duration that no light illuminated on the testing device. The police officer did, though, obtain a positive reading when he pressed the "Read" button. The motorist submitted that in these circumstances there was no case to answer. The justices rejected the argument and convicted, finding that the motorist deliberately did not blow long and hard enough to illuminate the lights on the device and so had not complied with the requirement. The motorist appealed.

In the second appeal, the same motorist was charged with, on the same occasion, failing to provide a specimen of blood for a laboratory test, contrary to s 7, Road Traffic Act 1988. He was arrested and taken to the police station; the breath analysis device was unavailable due to a defect. The officer, referring to a *pro forma*, said "By virtue of section 7 of the Road Traffic Act 1988 I require you to provide a specimen of your blood or urine for a laboratory test. You have the opportunity to make representations as to which it may be but it is my entitlement to decide which specimen it shall be. Your refusal to provide this specimen may make you liable to prosecution. Will you give such a specimen?" The motorist agreed to provide a specimen, but only if he could speak to a solicitor first. The officer did not take that as a refusal and went on to say: "Do you have any representations as to why it should not be blood?" Mr Chand replied: "I don't want nobody taking blood off me when I could use a machine. I am not giving blood. No." There was no further conversation. The justices accepted a submission of no case to answer in that the officer did not inform the respondent that he had decided that the specimen to be provided should be one of blood; in other words, the officer had never required a specimen of blood to be provided. They acquitted; the prosecutor appealed.

HELD: On the first appeal, "the justices were entirely correct to reach the decision which they did. This was a very obvious case of a driver deliberately failing to blow into the device in such a way as to give a reliable reading, and it does not avail him to rely on the fact that a positive reading was obtained.

"We have been referred to *DPP v Heywood* [above] … the same approach should be taken to the present case … The driver deliberately blew into the device for an insufficient period. There is no finding that the reading which the officer obtained was reliable, and certainly the driver did not comply with the … instructions which had been explained to him. Had the result been negative it seems clear that it would have been totally unreliable …

"[On the prosecutor's appeal], Whether a requirement has on the facts of a given case been made or not depends very much on all the circumstances … In my judgment the justices were fully entitled in this case to find as a fact, and to conclude, that the officer did not require Mr Chand to provide a specimen of blood for a laboratory test … and accordingly was not in breach of the section."

Appeals dismissed.

DPP v Darwen

[2007] EWHC 337 (Admin), 24 January 2007, QBD (Admin)

A motorist is guilty of failing to provide breath specimens for analysis if the specimens are insufficient to enable the analysis to be carried out, or provided in such a way that the objective of the analysis cannot be satisfactorily achieved.

A motorist had been charged with failing to provide specimens of breath for analysis, contrary to s 7(6), Road Traffic Act 1988. He had blown into the breath analysis device eight times, over two cycles, each time providing insufficient breath and removing the mouthpiece. The device recorded that the specimens were insufficient, but nevertheless analysed them, showing excess alcohol.

The magistrates found that the motorist had provided specimens and dismissed the charge. The prosecutor appealed.

QUESTION(S) FOR THE COURT: Whether the magistrates were correct in deciding that the specimens which were rejected as incomplete were nonetheless sufficient to meet the requirements of s 11(3), Road Traffic Act 1988 (a person does not provide a specimen of breath for analysis unless the specimen is sufficient to enable the analysis to be carried out, etc), and so were specimens as required by s 7(1)(a), Road Traffic Act 1988.

HELD: "7. If a full and proper specimen is not provided even though some of the readings may exceed the prescribed limit those are not readings which can be used as admissible evidence for an offence under section 4 or 5 of the Road Traffic Act 1988…

"11. [On the argument, based on *Zafar v DPP* (page 439), that], as 'breath' has [its] ordinary dictionary definition then … the respondent had provided breath; that had been analysed and there was no offence committed …

"13. I cannot accept that argument … the issue … turns essentially upon the meaning of section 11(3) …

"14. … reading section 11(3) and asking … 'had a specimen of breath been provided in accordance with it?' the answer is plainly 'no'. The respondent did not provide a specimen for the analysis to be carried out and he did not provide it in such a way that the analysis could be satisfactorily achieved. There were two reasons: first, the respondent did not provide a specimen of breath as directed, and secondly, the machine itself made clear that the amount of air produced was insufficient for its purposes.

"15. … was the breath to be provided, taking the ordinary definition of that words as set out in *Zafar*, sufficient for the purposes set out in section 11(3)? The answer is plainly 'No'."

The answer to the question was "no". Appeal allowed.

Rweikiza v DPP

[2008] EWHC 386 (Admin), 30 January 2008, QBD (Admin)

The case of DPP v Darwen (above) was properly decided, and was applied in this case.

A motorist had been charged with failing without reasonable excuse to provide specimens of breath for analysis, contrary to s 7(6), Road Traffic Act 1988. He had been arrested and, at the police station, at each of four attempts, he provided less than the 1.2 litres of breath required by the breath analysis device to produce a satisfactory analysis of deep lung air. The partial specimens were analysed but the printout showed the words "specimen incomplete". He was convicted by magistrates and his appeal to the Crown Court failed. He appealed further.

QUESTION(S) FOR THE COURT: (i) Whether a reasonable bench, on the evidence adduced, could have held that the appellant had failed to provide two specimens of breath for analysis. (ii) Whether it was *Wednesbury* unreasonable to have held that the appellant had failed to provide two specimens of breath, when he had provided four specimens of breath, all of which had been accurately analysed. (iii) Whether the meaning of "breath" as defined in *Zafar v DPP* (page 439) has any effect on the meaning of "specimen" as defined by s 11(3), Road Traffic Act 1988.

HELD: "9. … the present case is not distinguishable from the case of *Darwin* (*sic*). [Counsel for the appellant] does not suggest otherwise. His submission is that *Darwin* was wrongly decided. This court will generally follow previous decisions of the Divisional Court, unless satisfied that they were plainly wrong. In my judgment, *Darwin* was not plainly wrong; … it was plainly right. Section 5 defines the offence. Section 11(3) [a person does not provide a specimen of breath for analysis unless the specimen is sufficient to enable the analysis to be carried out, etc] is concerned with the way in which the offence may be proved. It was not a prerequisite to the commission or proof of the offence that the excess alcohol found in the sample had come from deep lung air. It was not a prerequisite that the police used a device that concentrated on deep lung air. However, that is the device that they chose to use. That was a lawful choice. The device was one of the type approved by the Secretary of State. …

"11. Plainly the purpose of the test, through the operation of the [Intoxilyser] 6000 machine, is to measure a minimum volume of breath – 1.2 litres – and to continue to measure it until the reading reaches a plateau and produces a complete specimen. … this appellant, having been properly instructed on how to activate the machine, and having had the method demonstrated to him, deliberately failed to comply with the instructions. He chose not to cooperate, but deliberately to frustrate the objectives of the test."

The answer to question (i) was "yes"; the answer to questions (ii) and (iii) was "no". Appeal dismissed.

3. SINGLE SPECIMEN PROVIDED

See also Hingley-Smith v DPP, page 186, and May v DPP, page 189 – providing a single breath specimen amounts to failing without reasonable excuse to provide; Cracknell v Willis, page 270 – a person may not be convicted on the basis of a single breath specimen; and the cases in Chapter 1 concerning multiple specimens – page 107 et seq.

Stepniewski v Commissioner of Police of the Metropolis

[1985] RTR 330, [1985] Crim LR 675, 29 April 1985, QBD (DC)

Providing only one breath specimen for analysis amounts to failing to provide specimens.

Magistrates had convicted a motorist of failing without reasonable excuse to provide a specimen of breath for analysis, contrary to s 8(7), Road Traffic Act 1972 as substituted by s 25 and Sch 8, Transport Act 1981. The motorist's first breath specimen produced a reading of 34 μg alcohol in 100 ml breath, although he was unaware at the time that the test had shown him to be below the limit. He failed to provide a second specimen, leading to the charge of which he was convicted. His appeal to the Crown Court failed, that court finding that the motorist had been obliged to provide two specimens and had no reasonable excuse for failing to provide the second. The motorist further appealed.

QUESTION(S) FOR THE COURT: (a) What was the proper construction of s 8(7) of the Road Traffic Act 1972 as substituted; and (b) was the defendant obliged by s 8(7) to provide a second specimen of breath?

HELD: "… By the statutory provisions, a person is to be required, under section 8(1) … to give two specimens. If he only gives one and fails to give a second, then subject to the defence of reasonable excuse or special facts, that failure is … an offence under section 8(7)." Appeal dismissed.

Oldfield v Anderton

[1986] RTR 314, [1984] Crim LR 189, 4 October 1985, QBD (DC)

Several short blows instead of one long continuous blow amounts to failing to provide specimens.

A motorist been charged with failing without reasonable excuse to provide a specimen of breath for analysis, contrary to s 8(7), Road Traffic Act 1972 as substituted by s 25 and Sch 8, Transport Act 1981. He had provided one specimen which produced a reading of 75 μg alcohol in 100 ml breath; he then failed to blow as directed so that a second specimen was not provided. The magistrates rejected the argument that the reading should not be admitted since it was prejudicial, and the defence that the motorist had indeed provided a second specimen but that the breath analysis device must have been faulty. They convicted. The motorist appealed.

QUESTION(S) FOR THE COURT: Whether: (a) the justices correctly admitted in evidence the value of the reading of the first specimen of breath; (b) on all the admissible evidence, a reasonable tribunal properly directed could have found that the defendant had failed to supply a specimen of breath; (c) the justices were correct in convicting the defendant of failing without reasonable excuse to provide a specimen of breath.

HELD: "... The justices made it abundantly clear ... that the only importance they attached to the first specimen was as evidence that the defendant was capable of providing a specimen ... it would have been better ... if the value of the first reading had been excluded, [but] there was here no such material irregularity as would justify us in allowing the appeal or in quashing the conviction ... The police officer gave evidence that the defendant made several short blows into the machine instead of one long, continuous blow. The defendant gave evidence to the contrary. The justices were entitled to accept the police officer's evidence and to convict on the strength of that evidence without supporting evidence of the printout or as to what the officer saw on the visual display unit. The answer to question (a) is as set out; the answers to questions (b) and (c) were 'yes'."

Appeal dismissed.

Sykes v DPP

[1988] RTR 129, 4 November 1987, QBD (DC)

The facts that a motorist provided only one breath specimen and failed to provide a second, and the officer then in error required a blood specimen, did not render inadmissible the evidence of the first breath specimen or the failure to provide the second.

A motorist had been charged with driving with excess alcohol, contrary to s 6(1)(a), Road Traffic Act 1972 as substituted by s 25 and Sch 8, Transport Act 1981; and with failing without reasonable excuse to provide a specimen of breath for analysis, contrary to s 8(7), Road Traffic Act 1972 as likewise substituted. He provided one breath specimen which produced a reading of 93 μg alcohol in 100 mg breath; he then deliberately failed to provide another breath specimen. The police then required a specimen of blood, which the motorist refused to supply.

The motorist argued before the justices that the requirement for a specimen of blood had been unlawful and that that rendered the evidence relating to the specimen of breath inadmissible. The justices rejected that and convicted the motorist on both matters. The motorist appealed.

QUESTION(S) FOR THE COURT: Whether the justices were right to regard the evidence of the prosecutor in so far as it related to the requirement to provide a specimen of blood as irrelevant or whether they should have taken the view that in requiring a specimen of blood the prosecutor had been acting unlawfully thus vitiating the validity of any readings obtained on the approved device.

HELD: "None of the three conditions [in s 8, Road Traffic Act 1972 as likewise substituted – medical reasons for not providing breath; device or reliable device not available or not practicable to use such a device] was in fact satisfied, and consequently the officer was not in a position to require the defendant to provide a specimen of blood or urine …

"… there was ample evidence that this defendant failed to provide a second specimen of breath …

"Does the making of [the] requirement [for a blood specimen] in any way render inadmissible the evidence in relation to the specimen of breath? I cannot … see why it should do so … the justices were entirely right … ."

Appeal dismissed.

DPP v Byrne (David Stephen)

Unreported, CO/2175/90, 1 October 1991, QBD (DC)

A motorist who provided only a single breath specimen was guilty of failing to provide.

A motorist had been charged with failing without reasonable excuse to provide two specimens of breath for analysis, contrary to s 7(6), Road Traffic Act 1988. He had been arrested and taken to a police station where the breath testing procedure was begun. At the first attempt, he did not blow sufficiently hard; the second attempt produced a reading of 91 µg alcohol in 100 ml breath; at the third attempt, the machine closed down and the printout recorded "no sample" in respect of the last attempt. The motorist did not know that the machine operated on a 3-minute cycle. He was not given another opportunity to provide a specimen although he offered to do so.

At the close of the prosecution case before the magistrates, the motorist submitted there was no case to answer on the grounds, *inter alia*, that he had appeared to be blowing reasonably; he had agreed to provide a third specimen; and he had begun to blow into the machine when it shut down. The justices accepted the submission and dismissed the case.

The prosecutor appealed.

QUESTION(S) FOR THE COURT: Whether the respondent had failed to provide the specimens as required; whether the respondent should have been advised of the 3-minute time cycle.

HELD: "… Section 11 makes it clear that a specimen is not a specimen unless it is sufficient to enable the test or the analysis to be carried out. Two specimens were required here. Only one … was provided … there was no room for argument about it. There was evidence that the respondent had failed to produce more than one specimen of breath."

The answer to the first part of the question was "yes"; it was not necessary to say whether or not there was an obligation to inform the respondent that the machine operated on a cycle of 3 minutes. Appeal allowed.

DPP v Thomas (Elwyn Kenneth)

[1996] RTR 293, 11 June 1992, QBD (DC)

A motorist who provided only a single breath specimen was guilty of failing to provide. The officer was not obliged to explain that the device allows 3 minutes.

A motorist had been charged with failing without reasonable excuse to provide two specimens of breath for analysis, contrary to s 7(6), Road Traffic Act 1988. At the police station he provided a first specimen, which produced a reading of 52 µg alcohol in 100 ml breath. He was asked for a second specimen, but questioned the purpose when he had already given a specimen showing a reading of 52 µg. The motorist then commenced to give a second specimen, but the breath analysis device ran out of time and aborted before he had done so.

The justices found that during the conversation after the first specimen had been provided, the officer did not clearly indicate the necessity to provide a second specimen within 3 minutes, with the result that the motorist did not have a proper opportunity to provide the second specimen; inaccuracies in the record completed by the officer indicated confusion at the time of the investigation, and cast doubt on the reliability of the prosecution evidence. They acquitted the motorist. The prosecutor appealed.

QUESTION(S) FOR THE COURT: Whether, having heard only the police evidence, which was not contradicted by any evidence given for the defendant, the justices were correct in finding that the case was not proved.

HELD: "… there is no obligation upon a police officer who is conducting a breath test … to explain to the person undergoing the test that it is necessary for him to provide the second specimen within three minutes or any other period of time.

"… the constable complied with his duty in requiring the defendant to provide two specimens. The only reason why the defendant did not provide two specimens was that he chose, instead of providing the second specimen within a reasonable period, to argue that the second test was unnecessary … I fail to see how any doubt expressed by the justices as to the reliability of the evidence of [the constable], unparticularised as that expression of view was, could have affected their judgment in this matter … ."

Appeal allowed.

DPP v Radford

[1995] RTR 86, 10 March 1994, QBD (DC)

Where a motorist held the mouthpiece to his mouth but no breath was registered by the breath analysis device, he was guilty of failing to provide specimens.

A motorist had been charged with failing without reasonable excuse to provide two specimens of breath for analysis, contrary to s 7(6), Road Traffic Act 1988. He had been involved in a road accident, and a roadside breath test was positive. The motorist was taken to hospital for treatment, released, then arrested. At the police station, analysis of a first breath specimen revealed excess alcohol;

the motorist then failed three times to provide a second specimen, each time putting the mouthpiece to his mouth, but the machine registering that no breath was provided.

At the hearing, there was agreed expert evidence that if a person gives a specimen of breath on the roadside screening device he would be able to give one on the breath analysis device, which requires less breath. The motorist adduced medical evidence but it did not address any physical incapacity of the motorist or why he could give the roadside specimen and the first specimen at the police station, but not a second.

The justices found that the motorist was unable to provide the second specimen because he was suffering pain; he had not failed to provide a specimen. They acquitted him. The prosecutor appealed.

QUESTION(S) FOR THE COURT: (a) Whether the justices were correct in law in acquitting the defendant on the basis that the prosecution had not proved that he refused to provide a specimen of breath; and (b) whether there was evidence to support a finding that the defendant had not failed without reasonable excuse to provide such a specimen when required to do so.

HELD: "… this was a perverse decision by the justices because (1) they ignored the agreed expert evidence; (2) having found [that the defendant held the mouthpiece to his mouth but no breath was registered as having been provided, and that this was repeated twice more] failed to give that any proper weight; (3) they had no proper ground for saying that this defendant was unable to provide the second specimen at the police station due to pain … and (4) … they failed to give any weight at all … to the fact that there was no answer to the question of why the other specimens had been given but not the vital one."

The answers to the questions were "no". Appeal allowed.

4. TIME FOR PROVIDING SPECIMEN

See also DPP v Baldwin (Alistair), page 126, where the results of the analysis of a urine specimen provided 15 minutes after expiry of the statutory hour were admissible; DPP v Byrne (David Stephen), page 201, where it was not necessary to decide whether there was an obligation to inform the suspect of the 3-minute cycle; DPP v Thomas (Elwyn Kenneth), page 202 – the officer is not obliged to explain that the device allows 3 minutes; and DPP v Coyle, page 254 – the fact that the 3-minute time limit was not explained did not afford a reasonable excuse for failing to provide.

Cosgrove v DPP

[1997] RTR 153, 19 March 1996, QBD (DC)

The investigating officer is not obliged to allow the full 3 minutes for the motorist to provide two breath specimens. See also Watson v DPP, page 392, to the same effect.

A motorist had been convicted by magistrates of failing without reasonable excuse to provide two specimens of breath for analysis, contrary to s 7(6), Road Traffic Act 1988. His appeal to the Crown Court had been dismissed. At the police station, he was asked to provide specimens of breath for analysis by a device which allows 3 minutes for the provision of specimens before closing down. At the first attempt, he blew past the mouthpiece. At the second, he blew hard enough but not long enough. The officer administering the procedure asked if there was any medical reason why he had failed to provide the specimens; there was not. The motorist was not given another opportunity to provide a specimen; there were still 2 minutes of the 3-minute cycle remaining. Some hours later, before his release from custody, he was able to provide two specimens of breath sufficient for analysis. The motorist appealed further.

QUESTION(S) FOR THE COURT: (1) Whether the defendant was entitled to provide a sample at any time within the 3 minutes; or whether the Crown Court was entitled to treat him as having failed to provide a sample if at his first or second attempt he did not provide sufficient breath for analysis, even though after his second attempt there were 2 minutes left before the Intoximeter closed itself down; (2) whether, when he had provided an inadequate specimen for analysis and there were still 2 minutes left, the officer should have informed him that he could still have a further attempt to provide a sample; (3) whether a reasonable bench properly directing itself could have held, on the evidence, that the prosecutor had proved that the defendant had no reasonable excuse for not providing a breath specimen; and (4) whether a reasonable bench properly directing itself could have convicted the defendant on the evidence before it.

HELD: "… there is no principle of law that the person required to … give a specimen must necessarily be allowed the full three minutes, nor has he to be told that he has three minutes at any stage of the procedure. If … the administering officer concludes that the person required to provide a specimen is not making proper attempts to [do so], then he is entitled so to conclude part-way through the three minute period. Of course, … if the officer does take that course, then he takes a risk [in that] the justices … may conclude that the defendant did have a reasonable excuse … for failure to give a sample …

"… the court … was perfectly entitled to reach [the] conclusion [that the defendant was deliberately avoiding giving a specimen] … The fact that the defendant had once blown past the mouthpiece and the second time had only blown for a very short period of time, coupled with the fact that later on he did blow for a sufficient period to register on the machine, were facts of themselves which entitled the court so to conclude."

The second proposition in question (1) was correct; the answer to question (2) was "no"; the answer to questions (3) and (4) was "yes". Appeal dismissed.

Walters (Julian) v DPP

Unreported, CO 4250/96, 18 March 1997, QBD (DC)

In calculating the one hour allowed for providing urine specimens, the court was not obliged to take seconds into account, seconds not having been referred to in the evidence.

A motorist had been charged with failing without reasonable excuse to provide two specimens of breath for analysis, contrary to s 7(6), Road Traffic Act 1988. He had refused to provide a breath specimen at the roadside and had been arrested. At the police station, the breath analysis device was out of order, so he was asked to provide a specimen of blood or urine. He said, falsely, that he was a Muslim, and the officer therefore asked, at 2.10, for two specimens of urine. By 3.10, the specimens had not been provided and the procedure was abandoned. The motorist was convicted, and appealed.

QUESTION(S) FOR THE COURT: Whether on the evidence that the appellant was requested to provide a specimen of urine at 2.10 and was informed at 3.10 that the time for providing a specimen had expired (and he was not then permitted to provide a specimen which he then offered to do), he failed to provide a specimen of urine within one hour of the requirement for its provision being made.

HELD: "… it is submitted that the request to provide a urine sample at 2.10 could have been made as late as 2.10 and 59 seconds, whereas the abandonment of the procedure at 3.10 could have been made on the dot of 3.10 or a second or so thereafter, thereby limiting the power from a full 60 minutes to 59 minutes and a few seconds, and if that possibility remains, it is submitted [that the requirement in s 7(5), Road Traffic Act 1988 (urine specimen to be provided within one hour of the requirement, etc)] has not been wholly carried out … It is perfectly right to say that the subsection does specifically say one hour, but the findings of fact by the magistrates make it clear that they found that the request was made at 2.10 and the abandonment was at 3.10. If there had been evidence before them that indicated that seconds had been referred to in evidence it would have been perfectly open to them to have referred to that and made a finding as to whether or not the full hour had in fact elapsed, but … on their findings the full hour elapsed."

Appeal dismissed.

Oberoi (Yash) v DPP

Unreported, CO/936/1999, 23 November 1999, QBD (DC)

Refusing to blow until after the motorist had spoken to a solicitor amounted to failing to provide breath specimens.

A defendant had been lawfully required to provide a specimen of breath for analysis. On arrival at the police station, he asked to speak to a solicitor. The sergeant administering the breath analysis procedure told him that the breathalyser procedure would not be delayed for that purpose. The defendant repeated that he could not supply a specimen until after he had spoken to a solicitor. The sergeant started up the machine but the defendant declined to blow into it. The machine closed down. The defendant was then allowed to speak to the duty solicitor by telephone; the duty solicitor told him that the law required him to blow into the breath analysis device and that he could not choose to give a blood or urine sample instead. The defendant then offered to provide specimens of breath but was told it was too late; the machine had closed down and the procedure finished. The sergeant believed he had no discretion to allow another attempt.

The defendant was convicted by the magistrates' court of failing without reasonable excuse to provide a specimen of breath for analysis, contrary to s 7(6), Road Traffic Act 1988. His appeal to the Crown Court was dismissed. He appealed further.

QUESTION(S) FOR THE COURT: Whether it was right to have held that the appellant had failed to provide a specimen of breath.

HELD: Following argument that, pursuant to s 78, Police and Criminal Evidence Act 1984, it would be unfair to admit the evidence of the appellant's refusal because, if the sergeant had known the law, he might, in the exercise of his discretion, have allowed another opportunity to blow into the Intoximeter, "It is clear from … *Billington* [see page 216] and *Ward* [*DPP v Ward (Jack Evan)* [1999] RTR 11] that the police sergeant … was entitled to take the view that he would not delay the breathalyser procedure to enable the appellant to speak to a solicitor. After he had embarked upon that procedure by setting up the Intoximeter, the appellant continued to refuse to blow into it until he had seen a solicitor. That state of affairs continued until the Intoximeter had closed down. After the Intoximeter had closed down, the officer was entitled to take the view that the procedure had finished and that the appellant had failed or refused to provide a specimen of his breath … the offence was complete … ."

The answer to the question was "yes". Appeal dismissed.

Robertson (Eric) v DPP

[2004] EWHC 517 (Admin), 11 February 2004, QBD (DC)

Where a motorist was required to provide a specimen of urine, but the officer then delayed (for up to half an hour) allowing him to produce the first specimen, and would not allow the second specimen to be given some 75 minutes after the initial request, the procedure for requiring urine specimens had not been complied with and the breath analysis was not admissible. Software changes and the fact that it could not detect mouth alcohol did not take the breath analysis device outside the scope of the approval order.

A motorist had been charged with driving with excess alcohol, contrary to s 5(1)(a), Road Traffic Act 1988. He had been arrested and at the police station breath analysis revealed 50 µg alcohol in 100 ml breath. He was therefore offered the option to provide a blood or urine specimen, under s 8(2), Road Traffic Act 1988 (lower of two breath readings not more than 50 μg alcohol in 100 ml breath – now repealed; see page v). He accepted, but it transpired he had a fear of needles, so the officer asked for a specimen of urine. There was some delay – possibly up to half an hour – before the motorist was permitted to provide the first specimen, and he was unable to provide a second specimen until 15 minutes after the expiry of one hour following the requirement; the officer rejected this as too late.

At the trial, the defendant argued that he had not been allowed the full hour to provide the urine specimen. The district judge did not accept his evidence of timing. He found that if the procedure was not carried out in accordance with ss 7(4) and (5) and 8, Road Traffic Act 1988, the prosecution could rely instead on the breath analysis. The district judge also rejected argument as to the approval status of the breath analysis device. He convicted the defendant, who appealed.

QUESTION(S) FOR THE COURT: (b) Whether ss 8(2) and 7(4) and (5), Road Traffic Act 1988 had been complied with so that the prosecution could rely on the specimens of breath; (c) whether the officer should have allowed the defendant to provide a second specimen of urine when he was able to do so.

HELD: "10. [on (b)] … I … proceed on the basis that there was a delay between the request to provide urine and the first urination and that this delay might have been as long as half an hour. …

"22. In the normal case … [o]nce the requirement has been made the clock starts to tick. Normally the driver will then provide the first specimen which is the one to be discarded since it is not the effective urine specimen for analysis. He has an hour from the time of the requirement in which to provide the second specimen, which is the effective one. …

"24. The problem in the present case … is that no sooner had the constable made the requirement than he effectively countermanded it for a period of time. … [The appellant] was not permitted to provide the first specimen, the one to be discarded, until some part of that hour, which may have been as much as half an hour, had passed. … a person cannot be under a requirement to provide a urine sample during a period when he is not being permitted by the police officer to do so. …

"27. … If once the procedure for providing a urine specimen has been embarked upon the driver is not given the proper opportunity to provide an effective specimen, and it is for this reason that no effective specimen is provided, then the driver is deprived of the very safeguard which section 8(2) affords him. In these circumstances it seems to me that the prosecution cannot fall back to rely upon the specimens of breath.

"28. … Question (c) only arises on the basis that there was a finding that the appellant did tell the officer that he was able to provide a second specimen. If he did so then my answer to that question is 'yes' so long as the time at which the appellant was able to provide the second specimen was within an hour after the time at which he was permitted to urinate for the first time."

Appeal allowed on point (b).

5. WHETHER REQUIREMENT MADE UNDER SECTION 6 OR SECTION 7

DPP v Karamouzis

[2006] EWHC 2634 (Admin), 10 October 2006, QBD (DC)

Where a roadside breath test was carried out using a mobile device which gives a reading of the breath alcohol level and showed excess alcohol, and the suspect was then arrested and required to provide specimens at the police station, the roadside breath test was a preliminary test under s 6, Road Traffic Act 1988, not a requirement under s 7(6) (provision of specimens for analysis).

A motorist had been charged with failing to provide two specimens of breath for analysis, contrary to s 7(6), Road Traffic Act 1988. A roadside breath test, using a recently introduced mobile device with a digital read-out, showed 111 μg alcohol in 100 mg breath. The motorist was arrested and taken to the police station where she refused to provide breath specimens for analysis. She did not give evidence at the hearing, but was acquitted. The prosecutor appealed.

QUESTION(S) FOR THE COURT: Whether the justices were right to acquit the respondent on the basis that the conditions in s 7(2D), Road Traffic Act 1988 (as inserted by s 154, Serious Organised Crime and Police Act 2005) had not been complied with when the test in issue was one under s 6, Road Traffic Act 1988.

HELD: "5. … Until July 2005, tests under section 7 could only be carried out at a police station, but section 154(5) of the Serious Organised Crime and Police Act 2005 amends that to allow breath tests under section 7 to be carried out at the roadside. However, by subsection (2D) of section 7, where a roadside breath test on an approved device has been carried out, a requirement to take a further breath test at the police station may only be made if a device or reliable device of the type mentioned in section 7(1)(a) was not available; or it was, for any other reason, not practicable to use it at the roadside; or the constable who carried out the roadside test has reasonable cause to believe that the device used there has not produced a reliable indication …

"6. There are thus two quite different types of roadside breath test: (a) the section 6 preliminary test which, if positive, may lead to the arrest of the suspect and his or her being taken to a police station for a section 7 test; (b) alternatively, since July 2005, a section 7 roadside test on an approved device. This has the advantage that if it is carried out and there is no reason to believe the reading was unreliable, there is no need, and arguably no power, to take the suspect to the police station for further tests. …

"7. In the present case, the Justices acquitted because they accepted a defence submission that they could not be sure that the roadside test was not a section 7 test. The only witness giving evidence of what happened at the roadside was [the officer] …

"12. … The question which the Justices had to decide, once the point had been taken, was whether the roadside breath test had been a section 6 preliminary test, or a section 7 approved device test pursuant to the 2005 legislation. In my view, on the facts … the only possible answer was that it had been a section 6 preliminary test. This is both because of the answer given by [the police officer] that the digital read out was not accurate as a roadside test, and also because the whole point of the section 7 test is to make it unnecessary for the defendant to be taken to the police station.

"13. The justices should have asked themselves … why on earth should or would [the officer] have bothered to take the respondent to the police station under arrest when he had, if the defence submission is right, all the evidence required by the Act? In fact, we have been told that no approval has been given to any device for the purposes of the new section 7 as inserted by section 154 of the 2005 Act. Even without that information, my reading of the case stated is that the Justices could only reasonably have found that this was a section 6 preliminary test."

The answer to the question was "no". Appeal allowed.

6. CAUSING DEATH BY CARELESS DRIVING HAVING FAILED TO PROVIDE

R v Coe (Christopher Steven)

[2009] EWCA Crim 1452, [2010] RTR 37, 14 July 2009, CA (Crim)

Where the offence under s 3A(1)(c), Road Traffic Act 1988 (causing death by careless driving having failed without reasonable excuse to provide specimens required under s 7) is charged, the prosecution needs prove only driving without due care and attention and failure without reasonable excuse to provide specimens; there was no need to prove excess alcohol.

A motor cyclist had been convicted of causing death by careless driving, contrary to s 3A(1)(c), Road Traffic Act 1988, on the basis that he had failed without reasonable excuse to provide specimens for analysis. He had hit and killed a pedestrian who was crossing a dual carriageway at a pelican crossing. The motor cyclist was injured and was taken to hospital. Blood specimens were taken for medical purposes. The doctor in charge of the case told police that there was no reason why the motor cyclist could not give specimens. A police officer required the motor cyclist to provide a specimen for a preliminary breath test, but he did not reply, and did not react when the mouthpiece of the device was place against his lips. The doctor said that the motor cyclist might have been "in and out of consciousness", so the officer decided to proceed under s 7A (specimens of blood from persons incapable of consenting) and called for a police surgeon. When the police surgeon arrived, the motor cyclist opened his eyes and refused to provide a specimen, despite being warned that it would be an offence to refuse without a reasonable excuse. The police later obtained an order for production of a blood specimen taken by the hospital, which showed 210 mg alcohol in 100 ml blood. The blood analysis was admitted in evidence. The motor cyclist appealed against conviction.

HELD: "28. … Given that the offence charged was contrary to section 3A(1)(c), the prosecution had to prove only that the defendant was driving without due care and attention (it not being disputed that the impact caused [the victim's] death) and that the appellant had no reasonable excuse for his failure to provide specimens of breath and blood. The prosecution did not have to prove that the appellant had taken drink or how much drink he had taken, as they would have had to do if the charge had been contrary to section 3A(1)(a) or (b) ….

"29. … there was ample evidence of both … matters … independently of the blood sample analysis. In relation to driving without due care and attention there was clear evidence … the appellant did not see [the victim] until he was some 20 feet away. The appellant clearly failed to keep a proper lookout and braked far too late. In relation to failing to provide the specimen, there was evidence … from which the jury was perfectly entitled to conclude that the appellant was conscious at all relevant times, was doing his best to avoid giving a specimen, and that he had no reasonable excuse for failing to do so.

"30. It follows that had the evidence of the analysis of the blood sample been admitted in error, it would not … have affected the safety of the conviction."

Appeal dismissed.

Chapter 4

Reasonable Excuse

See s 6(6), Road Traffic Act 1988 (failing without reasonable excuse to co-operate with a preliminary test) and s 7(6), Road Traffic Act 1988 (failing without reasonable excuse to provide specimens for analysis). See also the cases in Chapter 3 under the heading "The Meaning of 'Failing'", page 183.

1. THE BURDEN OF PROOF

Neale v DPP

Unreported, CO/1333/88, 11 October 1988, QBD (DC)

Where the court rejected the defence evidence of reasonable excuse for failing to provide, there was nothing for the prosecution to negate.

A motor cyclist had been charged with failing without reasonable excuse to provide a specimen for a breath test, contrary to s 7(4), Road Traffic Act 1972 as substituted by s 25 and Sch 8, Transport Act 1981; and with failing without reasonable excuse to provide a specimen of breath for analysis, contrary to s 8(7), Road Traffic Act 1972 as likewise substituted.

At the hearing the motor cyclist adduced evidence, including medical evidence, in support of an argument that he had a reasonable excuse for failing to provide the specimens. The justices rejected that evidence, finding that since the defence of reasonable excuse had not been raised by any evidence which they believed, there was no burden on the prosecution to negate such a defence. They convicted the motor cyclist. He appealed.

QUESTION(S) FOR THE COURT: Whether the justices were able, on the evidence and having the benefit of seeing the appellant's demeanour before them, to come to the conclusion that he was lying and therefore had failed to raise the defence of reasonable excuse.

HELD: "I would answer that question unhesitatingly in the affirmative. [The justices] were clearly entitled to come to the conclusion, as a matter of fact, that the appellant had been lying when giving evidence before them, and that consequently … there was no issue raised before them as to there being in existence a reasonable excuse … They rejected the evidence provided by the defence, and accordingly there was … nothing for the prosecution to negate."

Appeal dismissed.

DPP v Crofton

[1994] RTR 279, 24 February 1994, QBD (DC)

Where the defendant said (but did not adduce medical evidence) that he could not provide breath specimens because he was depressed, suicidal and shaking, and the justices applied the correct test but were not satisfied that the prosecutor had negatived the defence of reasonable excuse, the acquittal of the motorist was upheld.

A motorist had been charged with failing without reasonable excuse to provide two specimens of breath for analysis, contrary to s 7(6), Road Traffic Act 1988. He had been arrested following a positive roadside breath test. At the police station, he was polite and co-operative. He tried three or four times to provide a specimen, but each time just failed to provide sufficient breath.

At the hearing, the motorist submitted that he had a reasonable excuse for failure to provide the specimens. He had been depressed, felt suicidal, and was shaking. Depression caused him to be breathless. He did not call any medical evidence.

The justices found him an honest witness; his evidence of depression had been wholly convincing and supported by the evidence of police officers; his breathlessness was not self-precipitated; it had prevented him from blowing hard or long enough to provide a satisfactory specimen. Despite the absence of medical evidence, they accepted that he had a reasonable excuse and dismissed the charge. The prosecutor appealed.

QUESTION(S) FOR THE COURT: Whether the evidence entitled the justices to find that the defendant had a reasonable excuse for failing to provide two specimens of breath for analysis.

HELD: "It was clear … that the justices did direct their minds to the three important matters that they had to consider: (i) the need for evidence of physical or mental incapability to provide the specimen; (ii) that medical evidence would normally be required to support such a claim …; and … (iii) the necessary causative link between the physical or mental conditions and the failure to provide the specimen … the justices were not satisfied that the prosecutor had negatived the defence of reasonable excuse.

"… the findings of fact are unimpeachable once the justices believed the defendant on the three issues … and … the justices clearly did go through the necessary steps … before reaching their decision … ."

The answer to the question was "yes". Appeal dismissed.

McKeon v DPP

[2007] EWHC 3216 (Admin), [2008] RTR 14, 19 December 2007, QBD (DC)

On the facts of this case, discarding the mouthpiece did not amount to an abuse of process, but the justices applied the wrong standard of proof in respect of "reasonable excuse". See also Longstaff v DPP, page 237, where, again, the defendant was not prejudiced by failure to keep the mouthpiece.

A motorist had been charged with, *inter alia*, failing without reasonable excuse to provide two specimens of breath for analysis, contrary to s 7(6), Road Traffic Act 1988. He had provided incomplete specimens. He was asked if there was any medical reason why he could not provide a specimen and he replied that he had "no more puff". The officer administering the procedure concluded that he was not trying. The breath testing instrument prompted the officer to keep the mouthpiece for forensic examination, but he did not do so, because he had seen the suspect's breath go through the mouthpiece and had seen it working properly.

The magistrates convicted the motorist, who appealed.

QUESTION(S) FOR THE COURT: (1) Whether it was *Wednesbury* unreasonable to refuse to stay the case as an abuse of process because the mouthpiece had not been retained; (2) whether it was *Wednesbury* unreasonable to have found the defendant guilty; (3) whether the reasons given for convicting the defendant were adequate, or whether they contravened art 6, European Convention on Human Rights.

HELD: "[On (1)] 6. … The justices held … that the appellant had not shown on the balance of probabilities that [the absence of the mouthpiece] has caused prejudice to his right to a fair trial … [the officer] had felt the appellant's breath go through the mouthpiece and had seen that the mouthpiece was working properly. This is to be combined with the fact that the appellant did not blow for any long periods but only for the very short periods recorded. This would not have been caused by the mouthpiece being faulty. Thirdly, the appellant had called medical evidence that he had a chest condition which could have caused him not to blow for longer. That is in reality inconsistent with a faulty mouthpiece being to blame. [The justices'] approach to the issue of abuse of process was correct as a matter of law … .

"[On (2)] 10. …the burden under section 7(3) as to reasonable excuse is on the defendant to raise the issue on the evidence and once that is done it is for the prosecution to prove the absence of reasonable excuse to the criminal standard. Here the appellant had raised the issue by the medical evidence … .

"11. … the sentence in the case stated 'We were of the opinion that the appellant had failed to make out a reasonable excuse …' … clearly suggests that the justices considered there was a burden on the appellant to make out, that is to prove, a reasonable excuse … by reason of this, the decision to convict the appellant should be quashed.

"[On (3)] 13. … [the justices' reasons] were not so inadequate as to leave the appellant in doubt as to why the justices had found against him on the main points."

Appeal allowed.

Piggott v DPP

[2008] EWHC 305 (Admin), [2008] RTR 16, 8 February 2008, QBD (DC)

There is no requirement that a suspect communicate a reasonable excuse for failing to provide a breath specimen, although failure to do so may lead the court to conclude that an excuse belatedly proffered was not a reasonable one because in reality there was a wilful refusal or failure to provide. Compare DPP v Lonsdale, page 230, where the officer conducting the evidential breath testing did not know that the motorist had told the arresting officer that he suffered from bronchitis, and that he had a prescription in his pocket.

A motorist had been charged with failing without reasonable excuse to provide specimens of breath for analysis, contrary to s 7(6), Road Traffic Act 1988. She had been arrested and, at the police station, failed to provide a satisfactory breath specimen after four attempts. When asked if there were any medical reasons, she replied "no". At her trial, a medical report was adduced, in which it was said she suffered from asthma and hyperventilation syndrome. That report was accepted. She also said she had told the arresting officer she suffered from asthma but did not think it necessary also to tell the investigating officer.

She was convicted and appealed.

QUESTION(S) FOR THE COURT: (i) Whether the justices were correct to find that it was essential for the motorist to inform the officer requiring the specimens of breath whether she suffered from any medical condition which could prevent her providing the specimens; or (ii) should the justices have found that the motorist informing another officer who witnessed the breath test procedure was sufficient.

HELD: "11. [After a discussion of the contents of the case stated] it is clear that the justices did not convict the appellant because they believed that there was no medical reason for her failure or because they believed that she had not genuinely tried to give a sample. She was convicted because she had told the wrong officer, … the arresting officer, rather than … the officer responsible for obtaining the specimens, about the medical problem that was the reason for her failure to give a specimen. …

"14. … the statutory question is whether there was a reasonable excuse for the failure, not whether that reasonable excuse has been communicated to the officer requiring the provision of a specimen or indeed to anybody else. A failure to mention an excuse at the time when the specimen is required will be a highly relevant, and may well be a decisive factor against the defendant, when the justices are deciding whether or not the excuse belatedly proffered for the failure was a reasonable one. If a defendant says nothing about a medical condition of which he or she is well aware, it is highly likely that the justices will reach the conclusion that the failure to produce the specimen was wilful and that the defendant had not made a genuine attempt to provide a specimen. However, that is a matter of evidence to be considered on a case by case basis and I can see no justification for importing an additional legal requirement that there should be notification into subsection (6)."

The answer to question (i) was "no"; the answer to question (ii) was "sufficient, yes, but not necessary". Appeal allowed.

R (Cuns) v Hammersmith Magistrates' Court

[2016] EWHC 748 (Admin), 4 March 2016, QBD (Admin)

It is for the appellant to provide an evidential basis for asserting reasonable excuse (in this case needle phobia).

A motorist had been convicted of failing without reasonable excuse to provide a specimen of blood for a laboratory test, contrary to s 7(6), Road Traffic Act 1988. The justices found that, although needle phobia had been mentioned as a reasonable excuse, there was no evidence to support it. They convicted him, and refused his application to state a case. The driver sought judicial review of their refusal.

HELD: "4. The law is clear that it is for the Crown to prove that there was no reasonable excuse but that does not mean that they have to discover reasonable excuses and then set about disproving any which might apply. They only have to disprove a reasonable excuse if there is some evidential basis provided by the claimant so that the issue is in play. If the issue has been raised with some evidential basis it is then for the prosecution to disprove it. …

"13. … It is for the claimant to provide some evidential basis for the asserted reasonable excuse, in this case needle phobia. It does not begin to be enough for a claimant to say at the police station 'I have needle phobia' and then to cause the CPS to have to disprove that through a process of accessing his records and requiring a medical examination. It is for the defendant in the Magistrates' Court to provide some evidence, whether from him himself or from family or from a doctor, so as to provide an evidential basis of needle phobia, and of needle phobia to such an extent that it overcomes his power to grant consent to the taking of the specimen.

"14. The mere fact of asserting at the police station immediately or otherwise that you have needle phobia cannot possibly constitute a basis for the police to have to disprove it. Whatever happens in the procedure at the police station, there has to be evidence at the Magistrates' Court that requires them to disprove it. There was none … .

"15. Accordingly, the justices were entirely right to refuse to state a case; permission to apply for judicial review refused."

2. CONDITIONAL AGREEMENT

See also Smith v Hand, page 183, and Plackett v DPP, page 192, where the investigating officers permitted the suspects to speak to a solicitor before deciding whether or not to provide specimens; DPP v Swan, page 190, where the suspect would provide specimens only if photographs of his wrists were taken; Oberoi (Yash) v DPP, page 205, where a motorist who refused to blow until he had spoken to a solicitor was guilty of failing to provide; Hudson v DPP, page 348, where the suspect believed he need not provide breath specimens until he had received legal advice; Watson v DPP, page 392, where the defendant wished to use the lavatory before providing a second breath specimen; and the cases in Chapter 7 under the heading "Legal Advice", page 377 et seq.

DPP v Billington; Chappell v DPP; DPP v Rumble; Corywright v East

[1988] 1 WLR 535, [1988] 1 All ER 435, [1988] RTR 231, [1987] Crim LR 772, 20 July 1987, QBD (DC)

The procedure for taking breath specimens for analysis is not an interview and the provisions of the Police and Criminal Evidence Act 1984 do not allow a suspect to delay the procedure while he speaks to a solicitor; the right to consult a solicitor does not afford a suspect a reasonable excuse for failing to provide specimens.

In each case a motorist had been charged with failing without reasonable excuse to provide a specimen of breath for analysis, contrary to s 8(7), Road Traffic Act 1972 as substituted by s 25 and Sch 8, Transport Act 1981. Each had refused to provide a specimen until he had consulted a solicitor, and, at trial, contended that this amounted to a reasonable excuse. Two had been convicted and two acquitted. There was an appeal in each case.

QUESTION(S) FOR THE COURT: The questions concerned the effect on the procedure under s 8, Road Traffic Act 1972 as substituted (power to require specimens, etc), of s 58, Police and Criminal Evidence Act 1984 (a person arrested and in custody entitled to consult a solicitor, etc) and PACE Code C, paragraph 6.3 of the Codes of Practice under s 66, Police and Criminal Evidence Act 1984 (a person who asks for legal advice may not be interviewed or continued to be interviewed until he has received it).

HELD: After summarising the principles applying before the Police and Criminal Evidence Act 1984, and on the argument that s 58 confers an unconditional right to a person who has been arrested and is in custody to consult a solicitor privately at any time, "All that the Act of 1984 requires is that the defendant be permitted to consult a solicitor as soon as practicable. There is nothing in the Act of 1984 which requires the police, whether expressly or by implication, to delay the taking of a specimen under section 8 of the Act of 1972 in the meantime … Under the Code a person who has asked to consult a solicitor … may not be interviewed until he has received that advice, save in certain circumstances … the section 8 procedure of the Act of 1972 is not in any sense an interview … there is nothing in the Act of 1984 itself, nor in the Code, to change or affect in any way the section 8 procedure … the right to consult a solicitor … does not furnish a defendant with a reasonable excuse for not providing a specimen when requested."

Prosecutors' appeals allowed; motorists' appeals dismissed.

See also *DPP v Verity*, unreported, CO/1495/87, 9 December 1987, QBD (DC); *DPP v Skinner; DPP v Cornell* [1990] RTR 254 QBD (DC); *DPP v Rous and Davis*, page 459; *Salter v Chief Constable of Wiltshire* [1992] RTR 386 QBD (DC); *DPP v Varley* [1999] Crim LR 753 QBD (DC); and *DPP v Noe* [2000] RTR 351 QBD (DC), in which the principles in *DPP v Billington* were applied. See also the earlier cases of *Chief Constable of Avon & Somerset v O'Brien* [1987] RTR 182 QBD (DC), *Grennan v Wescott* [1988] RTR 253 QBD (DC) and *Francis v Chief Constable of Avon and Somerset* [1988] RTR 250 QBD (DC), all to the effect that a suspect who declines to provide specimens before speaking to a solicitor or doctor had no reasonable excuse. Compare *Prouse v DPP*, page 354, *Ortega v DPP*, page 355, *Charles v DPP*, page 371 and *CPS v O'Shea*, page 458, where interviews took place; and *R (Ridehalgh) v DPP*, page 460 and *Sneyd v DPP*, page 461, where questioning did not amount to an interview.

DPP v Whalley

[1991] RTR 161, [1991] Crim LR 211, 17 October 1990, QBD (DC)

The motorist's belief that he was entitled to consult the PACE Codes of Practice before providing breath specimens for analysis was not a reasonable excuse for failing to provide.

A motorist had been charged with failing without reasonable excuse to provide a specimen of breath for analysis, contrary to s 8(7), Road Traffic Act 1972 as substituted by s 25 and Sch 8, Transport Act 1981. At the police station, he was told, *inter alia*, that he could consult the Codes of Practice under s 66, Police and Criminal Evidence Act 1984, either then or later. He also read certain documents on the rights of detained persons, which were given to him by the police. He was then asked to provide breath specimens, but said he wanted to read the PACE Codes of Practice first. The police interpreted this as a refusal to provide specimens.

The justices found that the motorist mistakenly believed that he was entitled to read the PACE Codes of Practice before supplying specimens; that the police had made no attempt to correct the mistake; that that belief had arisen directly as a consequence of reading the notices supplied to him by the police, which were misleading. They found that he had had a reasonable excuse, and dismissed the charge. The prosecutor appealed.

QUESTION(S) FOR THE COURT: Whether the justices were correct in finding that the defendant's belief that he was entitled to consult the PACE Codes of Practice before complying with a request to provide breath specimens constituted a reasonable excuse for failing to provide a breath specimen.

HELD: "… the motorist understood perfectly well what was being asked of him. In such a situation there can be no reasonable excuse for not complying … unless …, as was said in *R v Lennard* [see page 220], … there is a physical or mental reason which would entail a substantial risk to health [for] the refusal …

"It does not … avail the defendant … that he claimed to have been confused or misled by anything the officer may have said as to his right to see Codes of Practice … *R v Lennard* must be strictly followed by justices."

Appeal allowed.

DPP v Kirk

[1993] COD 99, *The Times*, 2 December 1992, 17 November 1992, QBD (DC)

Where a detainee refused to supply breath specimens until he had spoken to his solicitor, and taken medication, and said the breath analysis would be distorted by medication he had taken earlier, he had no reasonable excuse for failing to provide.

A motorist had been charged with failing without reasonable excuse to provide two specimens of breath for analysis, contrary to s 7(6), Road Traffic Act 1988. At the police station he had asked for his solicitor; the police explained that the breath test would not be delayed pending advice from a solicitor. When asked to provide breath specimens he said he would do so on condition that his solicitor was present. He was informed that such a condition amounted to a refusal. He then asked to be allowed to take medication, and was told he could do so after the test. He refused to provide specimens because he thought the reading would be distorted because he had taken medication before his arrest.

The magistrates found that he had had a reasonable excuse for failure to provide specimens in that he was of a highly nervous disposition; he had twice been refused access to his solicitor; he had not been allowed to take his medication; and because of the brusque nature of his treatment at the police station and the undue haste of the procedure. They dismissed the information. The prosecutor appealed.

QUESTION(S) FOR THE COURT: Whether on the evidence it was open to the court to dismiss the information on the basis that the respondent had a reasonable excuse for failing to provide a specimen of breath.

HELD: "It is … quite clear on authority that refusal to provide a sample of breath, pending the arrival of, and advice from, a solicitor is a refusal without reasonable excuse …

"The fact … that the respondent was not allowed, it seems, to take his medication before submitting to a breath test cannot … amount to reasonable excuse here. The medication was not immediately necessary, nor did it affect his respiratory function. Nor is there a reasonable excuse constituted by any fear that he may have had, that the test might be distorted by his having taken medication before his arrest.

"... the test for reasonable excuse has been clearly laid down ever since *R v Lennard* [see page 220] [physical or mental inability, or substantial risk to health] ... the facts ... in the present case are incapable of disclosing a reasonable excuse in accordance with that objective test."

Appeal allowed.

DPP v Smith (Alan Robert)

The Times, 1 June 1993, 11 May 1993, QBD (DC)

Where the suspect said he would provide a blood specimen only if it were taken by his own doctor, that amounted to refusal to provide the specimen. See also Pettigrew v Northumbria Police Authority [1976] RTR 177 and Solesbury v Pugh [1969] 1 WLR 1114, [1969] 2 All ER 1171, where conditional agreements were also found to amount to refusal.

A motorist had been charged with failing without reasonable excuse to provide a specimen of blood for a laboratory test, contrary to s 7(6), Road Traffic Act 1988. At the police station, the breath analysis device was not operating correctly, and the police sergeant administering the procedure therefore required a specimen of blood or urine, under s 7(3)(b) Road Traffic Act 1988 (reliable device not available). The motorist replied, "Blood with my own doctor". The sergeant told him the police surgeon would take the specimen and asked if there was any medical reason for refusing to give blood. The motorist said, "... I am not refusing ... I want my own doctor". The sergeant explained that as a general rule personal GPs were not called out. The motorist said, "I still refuse to give it to the police surgeon".

The justices found that the motorist's request to have the blood taken by his own doctor did not amount to a refusal, and dismissed the charge. The prosecutor appealed.

QUESTION(S) FOR THE COURT: Whether the respondent's statement that he wanted his own doctor to take the specimen of blood for analysis amounted to a refusal to provide such a sample in circumstances where the police took no action to contact his doctor at his request.

HELD: "It is ... clear that the imposition of a condition by a defendant may in the circumstances of a particular case be taken as a refusal. This would be the case if the condition is unreasonable. Likewise, consent to provide a sample, coupled with prevarication and delay, may amount to a refusal.

"It is conceded that the Respondent had no right to his own doctor. The question here was whether the Respondent was insisting on having his own doctor and no one else. If he was, then ... that was the imposition of an unreasonable condition which amounts to a refusal. Any other conclusion was not one which a Bench properly directed could reasonably have reached.

"... on the facts found the Respondent was insisting on having his own doctor and no one else ... ."

Appeal allowed.

3. MEDICAL REASONS

Compare "Medical Reasons Why Breath Specimens Cannot Be Provided or Should Not Be Required", page 25, and "Medical Reasons Why a Blood Specimen Cannot or Should Not Be Taken", page 91. See also DPP v Lawrence (Scott James), page 188 – in the absence of medical reasons, there can be no reasonable excuse for failing to provide.

R v Lennard

[1973] 1 WLR 483, [1973] 2 All ER 831, [1973] RTR 252, [1973] Crim LR 312, 8 March 1973, CA (Crim)

An excuse for failing to provide a specimen is reasonable only if the person from whom it is required is physically or mentally unable to provide the specimen, or if providing it would entail a substantial risk to health.

A motorist had been charged, under s 3(3), Road Safety Act 1967, of failing without reasonable excuse to provide a specimen for a laboratory test. There had been a road traffic accident and police were called. The motorist told the police that he had just drunk a bottle of brandy, and refused to take a breath test. He was arrested and taken to the police station where he again refused to take a breath test or provide a specimen of blood or urine. He argued that the fact that he had drunk alcohol since the accident was a reasonable excuse for not providing specimens. He was convicted by the Crown Court and appealed.

HELD: "… A state of affairs which does not affect ability to take a breath test or supply a specimen does not seem, on the authorities, to amount to a reasonable excuse … no excuse can be adjudged a reasonable one unless the person from whom the specimen is required is physically or mentally unable to provide it or the provision of the specimen would entail a substantial risk to his health … excuses which do not arise out of an inability to provide evidence, or a substantial risk to health by providing it, are not reasonable ones."

Appeal dismissed.

R v Harding

(1974) 59 Cr App R 153, [1974] RTR 325, [1974] Crim LR 481, 23 May 1974, CCA

Where fear of a needle might truly incapacitate a driver from submitting to the taking of a blood specimen, that could amount to a reasonable excuse.

A motorist had been charged with failing without reasonable excuse to provide a specimen of blood for a laboratory test, contrary to s 9(3), Road Traffic Act 1972. At the police station, he had twice refused to provide a blood specimen. He argued that he had a reasonable excuse on the grounds that, since he had been a child, he had been afraid of hypodermic needles, having fainted on being vaccinated and having since refused injections. The recorder decided that there was no reasonable excuse and did not put the matter to the jury. The motorist appealed against conviction.

HELD: "... there was ... evidence from which the jury might have inferred that [the appellant] was truly incapacitated by fear of a needle from submitting to the necessary insertion. It might have been difficult, if not impossible, for a jury to have accepted, in the absence of any medical evidence, that because he shared the common experience of adolescents in fainting at injections or at the thought of them this grown man genuinely suffered from an invincible repugnance to any use of the needle ... and that he could not overcome this irrational fear however hard he tried. But that was what the appellant was at times asking the jury to believe; and we have reluctantly come to the conclusion that the recorder was wrong to deny them the opportunity of saying whether they believed it or not, and that therefore their verdict cannot stand.

"... our decision does not mean that the appellant had a reasonable excuse or that other motorists can hope to avoid conviction ... by the simple expedient of claiming that they were too frightened of the needle to give a specimen of blood, without any medical evidence as to their mental state. The law expects responsible adults to overcome their fears, whether rational or irrational, in order to comply with it. The mental condition or the physical injuries of one who refuses to provide a specimen 'must,' as Lord Parker C.J. said in *Rowland v. Thorpe* [1970] 3 All E.R. 195, 196G, 'be of a very extreme character to constitute a reasonable excuse'; and that applies, in our judgment, to a mental condition alleged to result from a nervous constitution or from a traumatic experience in the past. No fear short of a phobia recognised by medical science to be as strong and inhibiting as, for instance, claustrophobia can be allowed to excuse failure to provide a specimen for a laboratory test, and in most if not all cases where the fear of providing it is claimed to be invincible the claim will have to be supported by medical evidence."

Appeal allowed.

Woolman v Lenton

[1985] Crim LR 516, 28 February 1985, QBD (DC)

Where a motorist refused to provide breath specimens without reasonable excuse, the provisions on requiring a specimen for laboratory testing were irrelevant.

A motorist had been convicted by magistrates of, *inter alia*, failing without reasonable excuse to provide a specimen of breath for analysis, contrary to s 8(7), Road Traffic Act 1972 as substituted by s 25 and Sch 8, Transport Act 1981. He appealed to the Crown Court. The motorist said he had told police that, in the past, he had had difficulties in breathing through his nose owing to some malformation or other physical defect. The police evidence was that they had no recollection of this. The motorist called medical evidence that he had undergone an operation for nasal congestion some 4 years earlier; the doctor also said that in his opinion any partial blockage of the nose would lead to discomfort but would not be painful on inhalation through the nose; thus, breathing into the breath analysis device might cause discomfort, but would not be painful.

The Crown Court found that the motorist had had no reasonable excuse for failure to provide specimens, but that it was incumbent on the officer carrying out the procedure to take account of any observation made by the motorist about his medical condition which might have afforded at least reasonable cause to believe that for medical reasons alone a specimen of breath could not or should not be provided. The Crown Court therefore found that the continued request for breath specimens was unlawful and allowed the appeal.

The prosecutor appealed further.

QUESTION(S) FOR THE COURT: Whether the Crown Court's ruling was correct.

HELD: "… The only relevant question which the Crown Court could and should have asked themselves was whether this respondent had a reasonable excuse for not providing a specimen of breath. They did ask themselves that question and answered it by concluding that he did not have a reasonable excuse. That being the only relevant question, it follows that they should have dismissed the appeal …

"Unfortunately the Crown Court went on to ask themselves another and … wholly inappropriate question. They seem to have thought that on the facts section 8(3)(a) [constable having reasonable cause to believe that for medical reasons a breath specimen cannot be provided or should not be required, when requiring a specimen for laboratory testing] was of relevance.

"… That was not in issue here at all. No such specimen had been asked for … the ruling of the Crown Court was wrong."

Appeal allowed.

DPP v Boden

[1988] RTR 188, 15 October 1987, QBD (DC)

A motorist could properly be found guilty of failing to provide breath specimens when the officer had gone on to require a blood specimen, having decided there might be medical reasons, and thus a reasonable excuse, for the refusal to supply breath specimens. See also Pattison v DPP, page 235, to the same effect.

A motorist had been charged with failing without reasonable excuse to provide a specimen of breath for analysis, contrary to s 8(7), Road Traffic Act 1972 as substituted by s 25 and Sch 8, Transport Act 1981. On a request for a breath analysis he had said, "… No I won't. There is a medical reason for this". He had declined to say what the medical reason was. The officer administering the test then required a blood specimen under s 8(3)(a), Road Traffic Act 1972 as likewise substituted (constable having reasonable cause to believe that for medical reasons a breath specimen cannot be provided or should not be required). The motorist refused to supply a blood specimen.

The charge was based on the failure to supply breath specimens, the Crown Prosecution Service having taken the view that the requirement to supply blood was unlawful. The magistrate found that, since a specimen of blood had been required, the motorist could not then be convicted of failing to provide a specimen of breath, and dismissed the charge. The prosecutor appealed.

QUESTION(S) FOR THE COURT: Whether on the evidence the defendant can properly be found guilty of failing to provide a specimen of breath when he was given the option of supplying a specimen of blood, the sergeant having decided that there might be medical reasons and thus a reasonable excuse for his refusal to supply a specimen of breath.

HELD: "The word 'option' is an unhappy word in the context, because a requirement under section 8(3) is not a requirement which is describable as putting an option …

"… The matter has … to be looked at solely in relation to the issue of breath … The test … is an objective test … I can see no reason at all why a request for blood should eliminate penal consequence for a refusal to give breath without reasonable excuse … It seems … that the magistrate did not address … the point whether there was in fact a reasonable excuse. He treated the sergeant's request for blood as of itself determinant on the question of reasonable excuse. He should … have asked himself … have the prosecution made me satisfied so as to be sure that no reasonable excuse existed for refusing to supply breath? If he had so asked himself he might well have reached the same conclusion as in fact he did, but I could not be sure that he would have done."

The answer to the question was "no". Appeal allowed.

DPP v Judge

Unreported, CO/669/88, 27 October 1988, QBD (DC)

On the facts of this case (no finding of physical inability to provide specimens), the defendant did not have a reasonable excuse for failing to provide specimens of breath.

A motorist had been charged with failing without reasonable excuse to provide a specimen for a breath test, contrary to s 7(4), Road Traffic Act 1972 as substituted by s 25 and Sch 8, Transport Act 1981; and with failing without reasonable excuse to provide specimens of breath for analysis, contrary to s 8(7), Road Traffic Act 1972 as likewise substituted. At the police station he had been asked if there was any medical reason for his inability to provide specimens; the motorist replied that there was none, and gave no other reason.

The justices found that the motorist suffered from medical conditions which affected his respiratory system and which could have caused difficulty in blowing; and that this amounted to a reasonable excuse. They acquitted on both charges. The prosecutor appealed.

QUESTION(S) FOR THE COURT: Whether there was evidence on which the justices could properly have determined that the respondent had a reasonable excuse for failing to provide a specimen of breath contrary to s 7(4) and/or failing to provide two specimens of breath for analysis contrary to s 8(7).

HELD: "[After quoting from *R v Lennard*, see page 220], There is no finding of fact that the respondent was physically unable to provide the specimen or, to put it another way, that he was prevented by his medical condition from providing a specimen … It was found that the condition of the respondent's respiratory system would have caused him difficulty … blowing … It was also found that it would not have prevented him from doing so.

"… [T]he respondent deliberately failed to breathe into the machine … he has failed to lay the factual basis on which it might have been possible for him to invoke [reasonable excuse]."

The answer to the question was "no". Appeal allowed.

DPP v Daley

[1992] RTR 155, 9 May 1991, QBD (DC)

Where a driver failed to provide breath specimens at the roadside, and at the police station, but said there was nothing wrong with his lungs, he did not have a reasonable excuse.

A motorist had been charged with failing without reasonable excuse to provide a specimen for a breath test, contrary to s 6(4), Road Traffic Act 1988; and with failing without reasonable excuse to provide two specimens of breath for analysis, contrary to s 7(6), Road Traffic Act 1988. At the roadside, he blew twice into the screening device but no light appeared on either occasion. At the police station, he twice blew into the breath analysis device and twice there was no reading. When asked if there was any reason why he could not provide a specimen of breath, he replied that there was nothing wrong with his lungs.

At the hearing, the motorist said he could not account for his failure to provide breath specimens. The justices found that he had been physically unable to do so and dismissed the charge. The prosecutor appealed.

QUESTION(S) FOR THE COURT: Whether the evidence entitled the justices to find that the defendant had a reasonable excuse for failing to provide the specimens sought: (i) at the roadside; and (ii) at the police station; (iii) whether in dismissing the charges the justices came to a correct determination and decision in law.

HELD: "… No evidence was provided … that [the respondent] was medically incapable, at any time, of blowing into the devices which were proffered to him both at the roadside and at the police station. There was nothing to suggest, in fact, that he was any other than a perfectly fit, normal human being … he told the police officers that there was nothing wrong with his lungs. There was, accordingly, before the justices no evidence which entitled them to assume or to infer that he was incapable of providing a specimen of breath."

Appeal allowed.

DPP v Curtis

[1993] RTR 72, 7 July 1992, QBD (DC)

Where there was no evidence of a risk to the motorist's health, the magistrates were not entitled to go beyond the evidence to make a finding of reasonable excuse for failing to provide.

The defendant had been acquitted on a charge under s 7(6), Road Traffic Act 1988 of failing without reasonable excuse to provide two specimens of breath for analysis. The first specimen had produced a reading of 86 µg alcohol in 100 ml breath, but the defendant failed to provide a second specimen; she said she had a cold; she appeared nervous and anxious; the officer conducting the procedure saw nothing to indicate that she was suffering any medical condition which might prevent her providing a specimen. The defendant had a "low anxiety threshold" and had suffered from "anxiety related complaints"; she had been treated for asthma, which could prevent a person from providing a specimen. There was no medical evidence of her condition at the time of the alleged offence. The prosecutor appealed.

QUESTION(S) FOR THE COURT: (1) Whether breathing difficulty, caused by nervous asthma created by the stress and anxiety of arrest, and being required to undergo the breath testing procedure could amount to a reasonable excuse in the absence of any obvious physical inability to provide a specimen; (2) whether the justices were correct in taking into account as capable of amounting to a reasonable excuse the facts: (a) that the defendant did try to provide specimens, (b) was nervous, and (c) had difficulty breathing caused by nervous asthma, rather than an asthma attack, sufficient to prevent her providing a specimen; (3) whether a reasonable tribunal, properly directed, could have reached the conclusion that the defendant was physically or mentally unable to provide a specimen.

In reply to questions by the Divisional Court concerning the case stated, the justices said "… We believe that the defendant who was nervous anyway … was subject to an asthma attack brought about by fear and anxiety … We did not find symptoms of nervous asthma, but found there were signs … We all have experience or knowledge of the medical condition … ."

HELD: "… there are in many cases signs of stress of one kind and another which could … be attributed to the fact that the motorist is in a police station … What justices are not entitled to do is to act upon material beyond the evidence which is before them … justices should beware of using whatever knowledge they possess of some physical or mental condition so as to come to a decision one way or another as to precisely what is affecting a motorist when asked to provide a specimen …

"[Quoting the test in *R v Lennard* (see page 220)] There is no evidence … that to have provided a specimen would have entailed a risk to the health of the defendant. As to evidence … that she was physically or mentally unable to provide it, the justices in fact had the evidence of the inspector [that she was not at the time undergoing an asthma attack] which … they … accepted … [the justices'] decision was wholly unreasonable."

Appeal allowed.

DPP v Szarzynski

[1993] RTR 364, 5 November 1992, QBD (DC)

Where the motorist adduced medical evidence that he suffered from hyperventilation, which he had not known about at the time of failing to provide specimens, and the prosecution failed to negative that evidence, the prosecutor's appeal against acquittal failed. Compare DPP v Furby, page 228, where, again, the defendant was unaware of an incapacity which would have prevented him from providing breath, but made no attempt to do so.

A motorist had been charged with failing without reasonable excuse to provide two specimens of breath for analysis, contrary to s 7(6), Road Traffic Act 1988. A roadside screening test had been positive; he was arrested but escaped from the police car while en route to the police station. He was re-arrested some half hour later. At the police station, he failed to blow sufficiently hard or continuously to operate the breath analysis device, although he appeared to be breathing normally and showed no sign of illness.

The motorist was convicted by justices, and appealed to the Crown Court, where he adduced medical evidence that he suffered from a medical condition known as hyperventilation but had not known that at the time of the alleged offence. The Crown Court found, *inter alia*, that hyperventilation might prevent a sufferer from operating the breath analysis device; that stress was likely to bring on an attack; and that stress arising out of the escape would explain why the defendant could provide the first but not the second specimen. The Crown Court concluded that the prosecutor had not disproved that the motorist suffered from hyperventilation; and that it was not safe to infer that the defendant knew he suffered from hyperventilation or that his escape would bring on the condition. The Crown Court quashed the conviction. The prosecutor appealed.

QUESTION(S) FOR THE COURT: Whether the Crown Court was correct in law in holding that the defendant could rely on his medical condition as reasonable excuse for failing to provide a specimen of breath.

HELD: "… I cannot be satisfied that the Crown Court did make a positive finding that the hyperventilation was caused by the defendant's unlawful act [of escaping from police custody].

"… my conclusion must be that the [Crown Court] was not satisfied … that the prosecution had negatived the reasonable excuse, namely, the hyperventilation on which the defendant relied. I would therefore dismiss the appeal because there is no ground for interfering with the Crown Court's decision to quash the conviction … ."

Appeal dismissed.

DPP v Hammond

Unreported, CO-2004-93, 4 March 1994, QBD (DC)

Where magistrates gave insufficient weight to medical evidence that the motorist had been fit to provide a blood specimen, his defence of reasonable excuse could not be upheld.

A motorist had been charged with failing without reasonable excuse to provide a specimen for analysis, contrary to s 7(6), Road Traffic Act 1988. There had been an accident and the motorist's head hit the windscreen of the car; he went home, where he telephoned the police; he swooned during the conversation; he had chest pains. Later he was taken to hospital; there, a doctor told the police officer that for medical reasons a specimen of breath should not be required, but authorised the officer to ask for blood or urine. The motorist refused.

At the hearing, medical evidence was adduced that the motorist had been fully oriented and was fit enough to provide the specimens; that he had rational and clear thinking; that his condition deteriorated and fluctuated significantly during the night. The defendant's wife gave evidence that he had been totally irrational, loud and aggressive, and "was not him". The justices found that the motorist had produced sufficient evidence to raise the defence of reasonable excuse and the prosecution had not negatived it. They dismissed the charge. The prosecutor appealed.

QUESTION(S) FOR THE COURT: Whether any bench of justices properly directed upon the facts and upon the law could have acquitted the respondent.

HELD: "1. At [the respondent's] first meeting with the police a coherent conversation took place … 2. At the hospital there was evidence that the respondent had a rational conversation with his wife … 3. The respondent was asked by a woman police officer present at the hospital to give her his telephone number … and to sign her notes … The respondent refused … 6. … there was positive medical evidence before the Justices from two doctors that the respondent at all material times was not afflicted by any lack of understanding. No contrary medical evidence was before the Justices. … 7. There was … the evidence of the respondent's wife … that the respondent was acting in various ways … but … the Magistrates put too much weight upon it …

"8. … Justices should be wary of rejecting medical evidence on this sort of topic where there is no medical evidence which is contrary … ."

The answer to the question was "no". Appeal allowed.

DPP v Furby

[2000] RTR 181, *The Times* 23 March 2000, 14 March 2000, QBD (DC)

A person who is unaware of an incapacity which would prevent him from providing breath specimens, but who makes no attempt to provide specimens, does not have a reasonable excuse for failing to provide.

The defendant had been required to provide specimens of breath for analysis. He first blew round the mouthpiece of the breath analysis device. The sergeant conducting the procedure repeated the instruction on how to provide a sample. The defendant then held the mouthpiece in his hand so that the officer could not see where he was blowing. The device completed its cycle without any specimen having been provided. The defendant was charged with failing without reasonable excuse to provide specimens of breath for analysis contrary to s 7(6), Road Traffic Act 1988.

At the hearing, a consultant chest physician satisfied the court that at the time the defendant did not have the lung capacity to provide the specimens of breath. The defendant had not known this and so could not tell the sergeant about it.

The magistrate found that the defendant had deliberately refused to provide a specimen, but that because of his reduced lung capacity, which he did not know about at the time, he could not have provided a specimen; he therefore had a reasonable excuse for failing to provide a specimen. The defendant was acquitted. The prosecutor appealed.

QUESTION(S) FOR THE COURT: (1) Whether a motorist, having lawfully been required by a constable to provide two specimens of breath by means of an approved device, who deliberately fails to provide any specimen, has a reasonable excuse for failing to provide any specimen if it is later found, for medical reasons unknown to him, that his vital lung capacity was inadequate for the purposes of such device. (2) Whether the magistrate was right to acquit the defendant.

HELD: "… The way the statute is worded using the present tense is such as to make it clear that there must be a direct relationship between the excuse relied upon and the failure to provide a sample. So that a man whose lung capacity is impaired to such an extent that he is incapable of providing a specimen, but who is unaware of that impairment, cannot rely upon it as an excuse unless he makes a genuine attempt to provide the specimen. If he knows of his incapacity he may prefer to explain why it is not even worth making the attempt. If he is unaware of his incapacity and has made no genuine attempt, he cannot at the time of his failure have had any reasonable excuse for it … the fact that he subsequently discovered that had he made a genuine attempt he would not have been able to provide a specimen is, for the purposes of the statute, irrelevant."

The answers to both questions were "no". Appeal allowed.

Falzarano v DPP

[2001] RTR 217, 27 October 2000, QBD (DC)

The appellate court could not go behind the lower court's finding, on medical evidence, of a causative link between the physical/mental condition of the respondent and her failure to provide breath specimens.

A motorist had been charged with failing without reasonable excuse to provide two specimens of breath for analysis, contrary to s 7(6), Road Traffic Act 1988. She had been arrested and at the police station agreed to provide the specimens. She blew around the tube but not into it; she said she was doing her best; she did not say she was on medication and gave no reason why she could not properly provide a specimen.

At the hearing she gave evidence of certain medication she was taking; that on the day in question her boyfriend had ended their relationship; that the police had been aggressive; that she was in a state of panic; and that she got very upset when short of breath. She adduced medical evidence that the slightest stress could bring on extremes of agitation; that she suffered "panic attacks" and that she had been prescribed drugs for several years.

The court accepted there was a reasonable excuse and acquitted. The prosecutor appealed.

HELD: "[After reviewing the authorities] 18. … the justices … correctly applied their minds to the need for evidence of physical or mental incapability to provide a specimen. Further, they had in mind that medical evidence would normally be required to support this defence. They carefully considered the evidence of [the doctor] that during a panic attack there would be nothing physical or mental to prevent the defendant providing breath specimens. That evidence was considered in the light of the legal advice given. But the justices found that: 'The demeanour of the defendant whilst giving her evidence … led us to accept her evidence that when she gets upset she gets very short of breath.'

"19. And [they] found as a fact that the defendant did her best to provide a breath specimen, and that shortness of breath brought on by the panic attack prevented the defendant from providing breath specimens.

"20. … these findings of fact disclose a causative link between the physical/mental condition of the respondent defendant and the failure on her part to provide a specimen. This court cannot go behind those findings. They were findings that the justices were entitled to reach on the evidence."

Appeal dismissed.

DPP v Lonsdale

[2001] RTR 444, [2001] Crim LR 659, 6 February 2001, QBD (DC)

Where the officer conducting the evidential breath testing did not know that the motorist had told the arresting officer that he suffered from bronchitis, and that he had a prescription in his pocket, and the motorist did not mention those matters, the motorist could not later invoke them as a reasonable excuse for failing to provide specimens. Compare Piggott v DPP, page 214 – there is no requirement that a suspect communicate a reasonable excuse, although failure to do so may lead to the conclusion that an excuse belatedly proffered was not a reasonable one.

A motorist was charged with failing to provide two specimens of breath for analysis, contrary to s 7(6), Road Traffic Act 1988. He had been stopped and he told the officer he was suffering from bronchitis. The officer asked him to blow as hard as he could and the motorist provided a positive roadside sample. He was arrested and at the police station the arresting officer did not tell the sergeant who conducted the breath testing procedure of the motorist's bronchitis. The motorist failed to provide breath specimens; he was searched and a prescription was found on him. On the custody record, a question whether the detainee had a medical condition was answered "no" and "see below". The magistrates accepted an argument that the sergeant should have taken into account the motorist's medical condition and should have considered whether alternative samples should be taken. They acquitted; the prosecutor appealed.

QUESTION(S) FOR THE COURT: (2) Whether the fact that the arresting officer did not communicate to the custody sergeant the respondent's contention at the roadside that he suffered from bronchitis could amount to a reasonable excuse for not providing specimens of breath. (3) Whether the justices were right to acquit the respondent.

HELD: "12. … *Teape v Godfrey* [see page 193] and *DPP v Furby* [see page 228] … make it clear that if a police officer requires the motorist to take a breath test in the police station and the motorist makes no effort at all to blow … then he cannot, subsequently, contend that he has a reasonable excuse for failing to do so.

"… 14. [On the submission that] if the constable making the requirement had reasonable cause to believe that for medical reasons a specimen of breath should not be required then he should not require the specimen of breath … on the facts as found by the Justices, [the sergeant] did not know that Mr Lonsdale was suffering from bronchitis and did not know at the time that he made the relevant requirement that he had a prescription in his pocket.

"15. … [On the argument that] in reliance on the decision of this court in *Horrocks v Binns* [see page 25], … one should test [the sergeant's] state of mind objectively and say that any objective observer would be of the view that he had reasonable cause to believe that for medical reasons a specimen of breath should not be required because Mr Lonsdale had already told a different police officer at the roadside that he had bronchitis …

"16. … this approach to statutory construction is very farfetched …

"17. … [If the sergeant] did not know of the bronchitis, and Mr Lonsdale did not tell him about the bronchitis, then no objective observer could say that he had reasonable cause to believe that for medical reasons a specimen of breath should not be required."

The answers to the questions were "no". Appeal allowed.

McMahon v CPS

[2001] EWHC Admin 180, 27 February 2001, QBD (DC)

Where the motorist refused to provide a specimen because he had a sore ear, but the medical examiner found there was no reason why he could not give a breath specimen, the motorist did not have a reasonable excuse for failing to provide specimens.

A motorist had been convicted of failing without reasonable excuse to provide two specimens of breath for analysis, contrary to s 7(6), Road Traffic Act 1988. He appealed to the Crown Court. He had been arrested and at the police station he complained of a pain in his ear; the forensic medical examiner was called. Meantime the sergeant conducting the procedure continued; the motorist refused to provide breath because he had a sore ear. The sergeant took the view that he would be charged with failing to supply, subject to what the medical examiner might say. The doctor duly arrived; he found the motorist's ear swollen but said there was no reason why he should not give a breath specimen. Shortly afterwards, the motorist was charged with failing to provide a specimen.

At the hearing the motorist adduced medical evidence of a history of disorder of the ear; and that on the day in question his condition was such that forced expiration might increase his pain a little. The court found that had the motorist been truly concerned about the risk of damage to his ear he would have mentioned it to the medical examiner; it found he had no reasonable excuse for failing to provide specimens and convicted him. He appealed further.

QUESTION(S) FOR THE COURT: (A) Whether the Crown Court was entitled to find that in the circumstances of the case the appellant did not have a reasonable excuse for failing to provide a specimen of breath. (B) Whether the reason given for the appellant failing to provide a specimen of breath gave the custody sergeant reasonable cause to believe that for medical reasons a specimen of breath should not be required under s 7(1)(a) and whether he ought then to have required a specimen of blood or urine.

HELD: "[12] … Whether the Appellant had a reasonable excuse for failing to provide a breath specimen was a question of fact for the Crown Court to determine …

"[23] [After reviewing the authorities, in particular *R v Lennard* (see page 220)], [it was] submitted that it could be said that the Appellant was physically or mentally unable to provide a specimen because of his fear. That submission is not tenable in the light of the Court's finding [that it]

"[24] ' … was quite satisfied that there was no physical bar to the provision of the specimen as had been confirmed by the [medical examiner]'.

"[25] Although the Court accepted that the Appellant was, 'in some pain from his ear condition, it did not accept that fear of such pain made him mentally unable to provide a specimen'.

"[27] Would the giving of a specimen have entailed a substantial risk to the Appellant's health? The short answer to that question is 'no'…

"[29] … the Appellant had been able to provide a specimen of breath in the street. If there was any credible medical reason why he could not supply a further specimen, it was open to him to explain that to [the medical examiner]. He did not do so. …

"[30] Turning to the second question [the sergeant] was not obliged to accept the Appellant's contention that a painful ear prevented him from giving a breath specimen. …

"[31] … [The medical examiner] said … the Appellant would come to no harm. Therefore, the sergeant, on the court's findings of fact, did not have reasonable cause to believe, that for medical reasons a specimen of breath should not be required."

The answer to question (A) was "yes"; the answer to question (B) was "no". Appeal dismissed.

Martiner v DPP

[2004] EWHC 2484 (Admin), 11 October 2004, QBD (Admin)

The provisions of s 7(6) apply whatever type of specimen is required; where the defendant failed to mention at the time a condition which might have amounted to a medical reason, he did not have a reasonable excuse for failing to provide a blood specimen. Compare Piggott v DPP, page 214 – there is no requirement that a suspect communicate a reasonable excuse, although failure to do so may lead to the conclusion that an excuse belatedly proffered was not a reasonable one.

A motorist had been charged with failing without reasonable excuse to provide two specimens of breath for analysis, contrary to s 7(6), Road Traffic Act 1988. He had been stopped and a roadside breath test was positive. At the police station, the officer administering the procedure was not satisfied that the breath analysis device was working properly. He therefore required a blood specimen; the motorist refused. When asked if there was any medical reason for refusing, he replied that it was "his human right to say no".

At the trial, the defendant adduced expert evidence that he suffered a needle phobia, which he had not disclosed to the police officer, and "anxious avoidant personality disorder". He was convicted and appealed.

QUESTION(S) FOR THE COURT: (1) When a motorist has been lawfully required to provide a specimen of blood for analysis and deliberately fails to provide it, whether he has a reasonable excuse for so failing when he suffers from a medical condition which might have prevented him from doing so but which he did not mention to the police constable requiring the specimen; (2) whether it was right to convict.

HELD: "[On the argument that the requirement to inform the officer of a medical reason for inability to provide a specimen applies in respect of breath specimens only, and after reviewing the authorities], 29. … Section 7(6) applies to the entirety of section 7 and relates to the failure to provide a specimen as required under that section: that is to say specimens of breath or blood samples or urine samples. I can see absolutely no consideration of policy or sense which might give rise to a different argument depending … upon whether the specimen sought to be provided, but refused to be or failed to be provided … is breath on the one hand, or blood or urine on the other hand. …

"32. … if no attempt is made to provide the specimen requested and no reasonable excuse is advanced, particularly where the defendant knows of such excuse but deliberately chooses not to avail himself of it, then the position is … no different with regard to requests for specimens of blood (or urine) to that applicable (as established by authority) in the case of requests for specimens of breath. … There can, after all, be no hardship on a defendant in a case such as this, if he knows of a reason as to why he cannot even attempt to supply a blood specimen, [in] frankly saying so. The … reason why he should do so, is that it then enables the police officer in question to consider taking alternative steps, such as seeking a medical opinion or considering requiring a urine sample or something like that. It does not seem to me to be right that, in effect, defendants in this position can subsequently seek to take advantage of their own deliberate failure to advance an excuse known to them for not attempting to provide the requested specimen."

The answer to question (1) was "no"; the answer to question (2) was "yes". Appeal dismissed.

DPP v Mukandiwa

[2005] EWHC 2977 (Admin), [2006] RTR 304, 21 October 2005, QBD (DC)

Claiming "spiritual reasons" and asserting that the sight of blood might cause the motorist to go into a trance and become violent did not amount to a substantial risk to health so that the motorist did not have a reasonable excuse for failing to provide a blood specimen.

A motorist had been charged with failing without reasonable excuse to provide a specimen of blood for a laboratory test, contrary to s 7(6), Road Traffic Act 1988. He had been arrested on suspicion of being unfit to drive. At the police station, the breath testing procedure was not completed, the officer in charge having been satisfied that there were good medical reasons. He went on to require a specimen of blood, giving the appropriate warning and asking if there was any medical reason for not giving blood. The motorist said he could not give blood "for spiritual reasons". He failed to provide a specimen.

In the magistrates' court, the defendant said he originated from Zimbabwe and was a licensed healer and spirit medium or *mhondoro*; he had to avoid situations which drove him into a trance; the sight of blood was one such situation, which would cause him to go into a trance, become violent, and create a risk of injury to himself and others.

The district judge found that, although the defendant had used the word "spiritual" when refusing to provide a specimen of blood, it was primarily a health concern and acquitted him. The prosecutor appealed.

QUESTION(S) FOR THE COURT: Whether, without a finding that the respondent would have gone into a trance, the court was entitled to conclude that to give a specimen of blood would cause a substantial risk to the respondent's health.

HELD: "12. … there is a material difference – and it is highly relevant for the purposes of this case – between, on the one hand, the sight of blood and, on the other hand, the taking of blood. But the District Judge does not appear to have had in mind this distinction. …

"20. The court in deciding whether the respondent had a reasonable excuse for not providing a specimen of blood had to make findings on the evidence about what would or was likely to happen if the respondent was required to do so. The District Judge did not properly undertake that exercise. Had he done so, he would have identified, accepting the whole of the respondent's evidence as he did, that it was the sight of blood that was the problem – the problem that in my judgment could, on the face of it, easily have been avoided by the respondent shutting his eyes or looking away. Secondly, the District Judge made no finding that a trance would in the event have followed the sight of blood. Thirdly, even if the respondent went into a trance, the District Judge conducted no real analysis of the likely consequences, other than to conclude that the respondent might be violent to himself or to others.

"21. All this seems to me to be a far cry from the evidence showing that to give a sample would entail a substantial risk to the respondent's health.

"22. The District Judge decided the case on the basis that there was a substantial risk to the respondent's health, and in my view that finding was not open to him on the facts that were found."

The answer to the question was "no". Appeal allowed.

Pattison v DPP

[2005] EWHC 2938 (Admin), [2006] 2 All ER 317, [2006] RTR 13, 15 December 2005, QBD (Admin)

Where a police officer reluctantly accepted that a motorist who said he had asthma had a medical reason for not supplying breath specimens, and went on to require a blood specimen, but the motorist refused, his conviction for failing to provide a breath specimen was upheld. See also DPP v Boden, page 222, to the same effect.

A motorist had been charged with, *inter alia*, failing without reasonable excuse to provide two specimens of breath for analysis, contrary to s 7(6), Road Traffic Act 1988. At the police station, he did not provide breath specimens, saying he could not blow as instructed because he had asthma. The officer, although not convinced, accepted that for medical reasons breath could not be provided or should not be required, and so requested a specimen of blood. The motorist refused, saying "No one is sticking any needles in me, it's against my religion to give blood … I am a Christian, a Gypsy Christian".

The magistrates convicted him; he appealed.

QUESTION(S) FOR THE COURT (INTER ALIA, THE PRINCIPAL QUESTION CONCERNING PROOF OF DISQUALIFICATION FROM DRIVING): Whether the justices, upon the facts and the law, could properly convict the defendant for the offence of failing to provide specimens of breath.

HELD: "34. … The appellant's case is that since [the officer] accepted asthma as a medical reason at the time, it was not open to the magistrates to go behind that contemporaneous conclusion. It is said the appellant could have been charged with refusing to supply a specimen of blood.

"35. … the Justices were entitled to come to the conclusion they did for at least the following reasons:

(i) It is conceded that [the officer] had endorsed on the *pro forma* that he had accepted asthma as a medical reason for the failure, that the breath test procedure had not been used because a medical reason had been believed and that he had reasonable cause to believe that, for medical reasons, a specimen of breath could not be provided or should not be required. However, this was based entirely on the word of the appellant at the stage [at] which [the officer] wrote those endorsements.

(ii) [The officer] had made these endorsements before the appellant went on to refuse to supply a specimen of blood. The Justices were entitled to consider all of the evidence including the overall behaviour of the appellant. Having done so, they were entitled to conclude that what the appellant had originally told [the officer], namely that he had asthma, was incredible.

(iii) [The officer] gave evidence which the Justices must have accepted that he had not been convinced that the appellant was unable to blow into the [Intoxilyser] machine, but had accepted his word at the time.

(iv) Given the later behaviour of the appellant and, in particular, his stated reasons for refusing a specimen of blood, the Justices were entitled to conclude that [the officer] had simply given the appellant the benefit of the doubt and to conclude '… that he had no intention of providing any form of specimen'."

The answer to the question was "yes". Appeal dismissed.

Oladimeji v DPP

[2006] EWHC 1199 (Admin), 11 May 2006, QBD (DC)

On the facts of this case (nothing to suggest an asthma attack at the time; no difficulty providing breath for roadside test or for first evidential cycle, etc), the court was entitled to find that the motorist had no medical reason for not supplying breath specimens and that he therefore had no reasonable excuse for failing to provide them.

A motorist had been charged with failing without reasonable excuse to provide two specimens of breath for analysis, contrary to s 7(6), Road Traffic Act 1988. He had been stopped by police and a roadside breath test was positive. At the police station, he provided a specimen of breath which produced a reading of 72 μg alcohol in 100 ml breath. Despite three attempts he failed to provide a second specimen. He was asked whether there was any medical reason for this failure but did not reply. When asked about medication, he said he was taking *Amoxicillin* for an eye infection. He had suffered from asthma in the past, but had shown no signs of an asthma attack on the day in question.

At the trial, the defendant's general practitioner gave evidence that she had, a week before the incident, prescribed antibiotics for a throat infection; he was not being treated for asthma at the time; and there were no concerns about his breathing on the date in question. Medical evidence for the prosecution was that, given there were only 5 minutes between the first breath specimen and the final failure, it would be unlikely that a person's asthma could deteriorate in that time without it being obvious to a lay observer. Medical evidence for the defendant was to the contrary effect. The magistrates found no evidence of an asthma attack on the day in question and convicted the defendant. He appealed.

QUESTION(S) FOR THE COURT (INTER ALIA): Whether the justices were right to conclude that there was no evidence to support the conclusion of the defendant's medical witness that the defendant may have been suffering from a narrowing of the airways.

HELD: "[After criticism that the case stated did not comply with rule 64.6, Criminal Procedure Rules 2005 (SI 2005/384)] 17. … the finding of the justices was that there was no evidence of signs that on the day in question [the appellant] was suffering from an asthma attack and consequential narrowing of the airways … That seems to me to have been a finding open to the justices, given the evidence that the appellant had not had difficulty in providing a roadside breath specimen; that he had successfully provided a first one at the police station; that he did not suggest at the time that there was any medical reason for his subsequent failure to provide a second one; that he had not been coughing at the time; and all that against the background of evidence that he had not had any asthma problems for a number of years, and that there had not been any concerns about his breathing when he was seen by [his general practitioner the week before].

"18. That being so, the Bench was … entitled to conclude … that they were sure that the appellant was not suffering from an asthma attack and a narrowing of the airways on [the date in question], or indeed any medical condition which caused a failure on his part to be able to provide a specimen of breath."

Appeal dismissed.

Longstaff v DPP

[2008] EWHC 303 (Admin), [2008] RTR 17, 31 January 2008, QBD (DC)

A motorist failed to provide a breath specimen, saying he could not breathe properly because of back pain; the officer therefore required a blood specimen, but the doctor found no medical reason for not supplying a breath specimen and the requirement for a blood specimen was abandoned. The motorist's conviction for failing to provide a breath specimen was upheld. On the facts, the motorist was not prejudiced because the mouthpiece had not been kept. See also McKeon v DPP, page 213, where, again, the defendant was not prejudiced by failure to keep the mouthpiece.

A motorist had been charged with, *inter alia*, failing without reasonable excuse to provide specimens of breath for analysis, contrary to s 7(6), Road Traffic Act 1988. He had been arrested and, at the police station, failed to provide a satisfactory breath specimen after three attempts. When asked if there was a medical reason why he could not provide a breath specimen, he said he was unable to breathe properly because of back pain. The officer conducting the procedure therefore required a blood specimen and a doctor was called. The officer and the doctor agreed that the doctor should ascertain whether there was a medical reason for the failure to provide a breath specimen; the doctor examined the motorist and said there was not. The officer therefore told the doctor he did not require him to take a blood specimen. The motorist was convicted of failing to provide a specimen of breath and appealed.

QUESTION(S) FOR THE COURT: (1) Whether it was wrong in law not to complete the procedure and take a blood specimen; whether the fact that a blood specimen was not taken caused prejudice to the motorist and deprived him of a fair trial. (2) Whether the motorist was deprived of a fair trial because the mouthpiece used on the breath analysis device was not retained by the police. (3) Whether the case should have been stayed on the ground that it was an abuse of the court's process.

HELD: "10. … It [was] said that, once the [procedure to require a specimen of blood commenced], the sample of blood should have been obtained. …

"11. … Nothing in the Act states that this conclusion follows from the premise. …

"14. … it was said that … there could be no reliance on the failure to provide breath when the provision for taking blood was engaged. … I do not see anything in the statute to suggest that the mere fact that the officer later sought a blood test debars the prosecution from asserting that there was a failure to provide a specimen of breath without reasonable excuse.

"19. … The mere fact that at a time after the failure to provide a specimen of breath the procedure for obtaining a blood sample had been put in motion does not give rise to a legitimate expectation that no complaint would be made about the failure to supply a specimen of breath. …

"20. … I would answer question 1: 'The failure to complete the procedure for taking a specimen of blood was not wrong in law, did not cause prejudice to the appellant and did not deprive him of a fair trial. Even if it had been wrong in law, that would have had no bearing on the question whether the appellant was guilty of an offence under section 7(6).'

"[On (2) and (3)] 21. The starting point … is that Form [MG DD/A] states that the mouthpiece should be retained … where there is to be a charge of failing to provide a specimen where an attempt to use the device was made in case there is a need for forensic examination. In the present case, … the mouthpiece appears to have been lost. That gave rise to a submission … that the case against the appellant should be dismissed for abuse of process. …

"22. There may well be cases where it is important to have the mouthpiece available for forensic examination. In my view this case is not one of them. The Magistrates accepted the custody officer's evidence that the appellant was deliberately failing the breath test. There had been no suggestion by the appellant that there was anything wrong with the mouthpiece. … Moreover, the appellant gave his reason at the time for failing to provide a satisfactory specimen, namely that he suffered from back pain. …

"23. Accordingly, I would answer question 2: 'The appellant was not deprived of a fair trial; in the particular circumstances of this case, there was no need to have the mouthpiece available for inspection by the defence'. My answer to question 3 would be: 'No'."

Appeal dismissed.

Atkinson v DPP

[2011] EWHC 706 (Admin), 10 March 2011, QBD (Admin)

The time at which a medical reason must be shown to exist is the time the procedure is being carried out. A motorist who feigned having banged his head had no reasonable excuse.

A motorist had been charged with failing without reasonable excuse to provide specimens of breath, contrary to s 7(6), Road Traffic Act 1988. At the police station, the motorist asked to go to the lavatory. He was allowed to do so, accompanied by an officer who could see the motorist through a window in the door of the lavatory. As the motorist came out of the lavatory, he gave an exaggerated groan, fell to his knees in a controlled way and lay with his head in his hands. He was moaning and saying he had banged his head. The officer was sure he had not. The procedure was started again, and again the motorist fell to the floor in a controlled manner, saying he had banged his head. Both the officer conducting the procedure and the officer who had taken the motorist to the lavatory took the view that this was a pretence. The motorist refused to get to his feet and remained on the floor while the statutory questions were asked. He did not provide specimens.

A custody nurse saw the suspect about an hour later. The nurse gave evidence that the motorist knew where he was and why, but that he again complained of having fallen and having banged his head. His blood pressure and pulse were high and an ambulance was called. The ambulance arrived, but the motorist decided not to go to hospital. The nurse gave evidence that a panic attack could not be ruled out. A psychiatrist also gave evidence that the blood pressure and pulse readings were consistent with a head injury, heart attack or panic attack and that, while on the floor, the motorist would not have understood what was said to him.

The motorist was convicted and appealed.

QUESTION(S) FOR THE COURT: Whether a reasonable bench, properly directing itself, could have found that the case was proved.

HELD: "12. … [the possibility of a heart attack and a head injury having been ruled out] … There is no dispute that a panic attack can, but will not necessarily, mean that a person suffering one is unable to appreciate what he is being told or what he is being asked to do.

"13. … the timing is of considerable importance. The time at which the relevant pulse and blood pressure readings were taken was shortly after or at about 2 am. That was after the procedure had been carried out. There was clear evidence … that the appellant had pretended he had suffered a head injury … Both the police officers … [were] of the view that the appellant was, when the procedure was being carried out, clearly pretending not to understand. …

"14. … The crucial time is when the procedure was being gone through …

"15. … [the justices'] conclusion that he was feigning a condition which disabled him from understanding what was going on at the time the procedure was being carried out is a conclusion that they were reasonably entitled to reach ….".

The answer to the question was "yes". Appeal dismissed.

4. "TRYING HARD"

See also DPP v Coyle, page 254 – "doing one's best" is not a reasonable excuse.

Grady v Pollard

[1988] RTR 316, 3 February 1988, QBD (DC)

Evidence that the defendant had tried as hard as he could, unsuccessfully, to provide a breath specimen was not of itself a reasonable excuse for failing to provide the specimen. See also DPP v Comber, unreported, CO/361/91, 24 June 1992, QBD (DC) and DPP v Simpson (Ian William), unreported, CO/991/1999, 18 January 2000, QBD (DC), in which the principle in Grady v Pollard was applied.

The defendant had failed to provide a specimen of breath for analysis; he had made every effort to do so, although he had been argumentative; he gave no reason for his failure and adduced no medical evidence of inability. Magistrates convicted him of failing without reasonable excuse to provide a roadside breath test contrary to s 7(4), Road Traffic Act 1972 as substituted by s 25(3) and Sch 8, Transport Act 1981, and of failing without reasonable excuse to provide two specimens of breath for analysis, contrary to s 8(7), Road Traffic Act 1972 as likewise substituted.

His appeal to the Crown Court failed, that court finding no medical evidence to show why he should have been unable to provide specimens, and that there was no evidence to suggest that the breath test devices were faulty; he therefore had no reasonable excuse. The Crown Court had not considered whether he would have had a defence had it been satisfied he had tried as hard as he could to provide a specimen. The defendant appealed further.

QUESTION(S) FOR THE COURT: Whether the Crown Court had been mistaken in law in failing to consider whether or not they were satisfied that the defendant had tried as hard as he could to provide a specimen of breath in each case.

HELD: "[U]nless there is some evidence that the defendant is physically or mentally unable to provide the specimen, or that providing it would entail a substantial risk to his health, then there is no question of there being a reasonable excuse for failure to provide the specimen. Such evidence will normally be the evidence of a medical practitioner, but it need not be, and one can envisage situations in which there is other evidence; indeed, in some circumstances, the evidence of the defendant himself, which would suffice to justify the court in concluding that, within the dictum of Lawton LJ in *R v Lennard* [see page 220], they were not satisfied that there was no reasonable excuse and thus acquit … Albeit the court did not consider the question, the simple evidence that the defendant had tried as hard as he could to provide the specimen … did not of itself … provide, even if it was accepted, a reasonable excuse … ."

Appeal dismissed.

DPP v Eddowes

[1991] RTR 35, [1990] Crim LR 428, 18 January 1990, QBD (DC)

Where a motorist "tried hard", but failed, to provide a second breath specimen, he did not have a reasonable excuse for failing to provide the specimen.

A motorist had been charged with failing without reasonable excuse to provide two specimens of breath for analysis, contrary to s 8(7), Road Traffic Act 1972 as substituted by s 25 and Sch 8, Transport Act 1981. The first specimen produced a reading of 126 µg alcohol in 100 ml breath. The motorist attempted but failed to provide a second specimen. He was acquitted, on the grounds that he had been ready and willing to provide a second specimen, and had tried as hard as he could to provide it, but was unable to do so. The prosecutor appealed.

QUESTION(S) FOR THE COURT: Whether the evidence which had been properly adduced before the justices entitled them to find that the defendant had a reasonable excuse for failing to provide two specimens.

HELD: "… the justices … were wholly wrong and mistaken in their approach to the case and should, on the facts which were in front of them, have come to the conclusion that there was no excuse whatsoever, certainly not a reasonable one for the failure … to provide a second specimen."

Appeal allowed.

DPP v Ambrose

[1992] RTR 285, 29 October 1991, QBD

Trying to provide a breath specimen but failing because of distress does not amount to a physical or mental inability to provide the specimen and is not therefore a reasonable excuse. Medical evidence is usually necessary for a finding of physical or mental inability to provide.

A person had been charged with failing without reasonable excuse to provide a specimen of breath for analysis, contrary to s 7(6), Road Traffic Act 1988. She had been a passenger in a car, but the police mistakenly believed her to have been the driver. She was arrested and taken to a police station, where she failed to provide breath specimens for analysis.

The justices found that, on each of three occasions when she blew into the machine, due to her distressed state she failed, having tried her best, to provide sufficient breath for analysis. They found this was a reasonable excuse and dismissed the charge. The prosecutor appealed.

QUESTION(S) FOR THE COURT: Whether the justices were correct in law in finding that the defendant had a reasonable excuse for failing to provide a specimen of breath for analysis.

HELD: "… where reasonable excuse by reason of some medical or mental infirmity has not been raised, it is not for the justices to embark on an investigation of their own …

"… [after quoting from *R v Lennard*, see page 220] … The finding of physical or mental inability is a finding which is achievable only on evidence. That evidence will, in almost all imaginable cases, be evidence of a medical character …

"… the evidential basis on which the justices reached their finding that the inability to give a specimen was 'due to her distressed state' [does not appear in the case stated]. Certainly it was not a conclusion founded on any medical evidence."

The answer to the question was "no". Appeal allowed.

5. OTHER REASONABLE EXCUSE ARGUMENTS

See also Hartland v Alden, page 3 – unlawful arrest was not a reasonable excuse; DPP v Lawrence (Scott James), page 188 – suspect thinking he had a choice between giving a blood or a urine specimen was not a reasonable excuse; Cracknell v Willis, page 270 – the defendant's belief that he had not drunk enough to take him over the limit was not a reasonable excuse; DPP v McKeown, DPP v Jones (Christopher), page 294 – the fact that the printout showed the wrong time was not a reasonable excuse; Daniels v DPP, page 350 – failure to tell a motor cyclist that he was no longer suspected of stealing the motor cycle was not a reasonable excuse; and R v Downey [1970] RTR 257, [1970] Crim LR 287 (CA) – the fact that the suspect did not agree that he had committed a traffic offence was not a reasonable excuse.

See also the Scottish cases of McGregor v Jessop 1988 SLT 719 – a suspect who was unable to provide a second urine specimen within the time limit had a reasonable excuse which the prosecution failed to negate; and Mcguckin v O'Donnell 2001 SLT 768 – there could be no question of reasonable excuse because the suspect had made no attempt to provide the second urine specimen.

R v John

[1974] RTR 332, 15 March 1974, CA

A personal religious belief precluding a person from allowing a blood specimen to be taken did not amount to a reasonable excuse.

A motorist was accused of failing without reasonable excuse to provide a specimen of blood for a laboratory test, contrary to s 3(3)(a), Road Safety Act 1967. He had a genuine and sincerely held belief that he was "possessed of certain faith-healing powers derived from the presence in his blood of divinely given gifts", and that these beliefs precluded him from allowing blood to be taken. His argument that this amounted to a reasonable excuse for failing to provide was rejected and he was convicted. He appealed.

QUESTION(S) FOR THE COURT: Whether it was a reasonable excuse to say, "My personal religious belief or faith or tenet does not allow me to comply with that request, albeit it is one which you properly make to me in accordance with your duty under the statute".

HELD: "[Referring to *R v Lennard*, page 220,] for an excuse to be capable of being a reasonable excuse, it must be an excuse which is related to the capacity of the person concerned to supply a sample, be it of urine or be it of blood. It is not related to his belief whether or not he ought because of his personal faith or belief, to be required to supply a sample of urine or blood. There is, in the view of this court, this very marked difference between the two positions. One depends on whether or not, for example, he is in a mental or physical condition which enables him physically to give the sample. It may be in some cases that he will not be in that condition. Such facts, if proved, may at least be capable of affording a reasonable excuse for not giving the sample. But it is not enough for someone to come along and say 'True others are obliged to comply with the law, but my personal faith or belief frees me from the obligation which rests upon others'.

"That, with all respect to the appellant and to the sincerity of his beliefs, is what he is seeking to say in this court. This court must reject that argument."

Appeal dismissed.

Beck v Sager

[1979] RTR 475, [1979] Crim LR 257 (DC), 26 January 1979, QBD (DC)

A motorist who failed to provide breath specimens, because he had only very limited English and did not understand the requirement, had a reasonable excuse for failing to provide.

A motorist had been charged with failing without reasonable excuse to provide a specimen for a laboratory test, contrary to s 9, Road Traffic Act 1972. He was a student air pilot and had been in England for only a month or two at the time in question, and his command of English was strictly limited. He was stopped by police and a roadside breath test was positive. At the police station, the procedure for requiring a specimen was followed, but the motorist did not provide a specimen. He did not ask for an interpreter, and the police honestly believed he understood what was said to him.

The magistrates heard evidence on the standards of English of students in the same position as the defendant, and, having seen and heard the defendant, found that he did not have a sufficient grasp of English to allow him to understand the nature of the request to give samples or why the requirement was being made. They therefore found his refusal to provide a specimen reasonable and dismissed the charge. The prosecutor appealed.

QUESTION(S) FOR THE COURT: Whether a failure resulting from a lack of understanding of English to understand for what purpose a request had been made under s 9(1), Road Traffic Act 1972 and the consequences of such failure to provide a specimen could amount to a reasonable excuse for such failure.

HELD: "… the answer … [is] plainly 'yes'. Parliament has … imposed a clear requirement on the police … to bring it home to the suspect that a failure … to provide a specimen … will involve … severe penal consequences …

"… it does not seem … very difficult to bring the circumstances of this case at all events within the spirit, if not within the letter, of the principle enunciated by Lawton LJ in [*R v Lennard*, see page 220] in that … where there has been a substantial failure of communication, with the result that the defendant at the police station has not understood what is being required of him, or has not understood the penal consequences which may flow from his failure to comply … he is … mentally unable to provide the specimen …

"… there was here evidence on which the justices could properly conclude that the failure of understanding was sufficiently significant to amount to a reasonable excuse … ."

Appeal dismissed.

McGrath v Vipas

[1984] RTR 58, [1983] Crim LR 628, 12 May 1983, QBD (DC)

The fact that the suspect believed the request for a breath specimen was invalid did not give her a reasonable excuse for failing to provide.

A person had been charged with failing without reasonable excuse to provide a specimen of breath for a breath test, contrary to s 8(2) (accident; power to require breath specimen from person whom a constable has reasonable cause to believe was driving) and s 8(3), Road Traffic Act 1972; and with failing without reasonable excuse to provide a specimen for analysis, contrary to s 9(3), Road Traffic Act 1972. There had been an accident. Ten minutes later, a police officer went to the defendant's address; the defendant was drunk, and was wearing a dressing gown. The officer required a breath sample; the defendant denied she had been driving and refused to take a breath test.

At the hearing, the defendant had argued that the way in which the procedure was conducted led her to believe, albeit mistakenly, that the police had no reasonable or genuine belief that she had been the driver and had acted *mala fides*; she therefore had a reasonable excuse. The justices made no finding as to whether or not the defendant in fact held such a belief; they rejected the argument and convicted her. She appealed.

QUESTION(S) FOR THE COURT: Whether a genuine but mistaken belief that a police officer was not acting *bona fide* and had no honest belief that the accused had driven a motor vehicle could constitute a reasonable excuse for failing to supply a sample of breath and a laboratory specimen.

HELD: "… a request [for a specimen under s 8(2)] is valid if (i) an accident has occurred …; (ii) the request is made by a constable in uniform; and (iii) the constable has reasonable cause to believe that the person to whom the request is addressed was driving or attempting to drive the motor vehicle at the time of the accident.

"A defendant may challenge any one or more of the preconditions to a request … However, a person who declines a request because he believes one or more of the preconditions is not satisfied does so in the peril of being wrong. Where, as in the present case, the preconditions are satisfied, then the only remaining question is whether the defendant 'without reasonable excuse (failed) to provide a specimen of breath' … That the defendant at the time of the request believed that it was an invalid request is not material. The defendant's only concern at this second stage can be to show a 'reasonable excuse' for not complying with that request. That which can be a 'reasonable excuse' … centre upon mental or physical inability … ."

The answer to the question was "no". Appeal dismissed.

Dawes v Taylor

[1986] RTR 81, 3 May 1985, QBD (DC)

Where a motorist was required to take a breath test while seated in the back of a police car, unable to see the lights on the device, in the absence of evidence that he was physically unable to provide a specimen, he had no reasonable excuse for failing to provide.

A motorist had been convicted by magistrates, under s 7, Road Traffic Act 1972 as substituted by s 25(3) and Sch 8, Transport Act 1981, of failing without reasonable excuse to provide a specimen of breath. He had been given a single opportunity to provide a specimen; at the time, the motorist was sitting in the back of a police car; the officer administering the test was in the front of the car. The motorist was told to "blow long enough and hard enough so that the lights come on and stay on"; he leaned forward, blew, but did not illuminate the lights on the device. He was in such a position that he could not see those lights.

His appeal to the Crown Court was dismissed on the grounds that neither the difficulty of operating the device at first attempt, nor the circumstances of the test, including the defendant's position in the car and the instructions, which might have been difficult to follow, amounted to a reasonable excuse. The motorist appealed further.

QUESTION(S) FOR THE COURT: Whether, on the facts found, the Crown Court came to a correct determination and decision in point of law.

HELD: "… In order to provide a specimen of breath when required to do so a person must first of all understand what is required of him, and that means not only that the information must be properly given to him, but also that he must be capable of performing it. Secondly, he must be capable of performing the physical act … In the present case, there is no evidence to suggest that the defendant was physically unable to provide the necessary sample … ." Appeal dismissed.

Spalding v Paine

[1985] Crim LR 673, 13 May 1985, QBD (DC)

Inability to understand the requirement, caused by emotional distress, is capable of constituting a reasonable excuse for failing to provide breaths specimens.

Magistrates had found a motorist not guilty of, *inter alia*, failing without reasonable excuse to provide a specimen of breath for analysis, under s 8(7), Road Traffic Act 1972 as substituted by s 25 and Sch 8, Transport Act 1981. Police had found the motorist in the driving seat of a car parked on a double yellow line, her head on the steering wheel and the hazard lights flashing. There was some whisky in a bottle beside her; she admitted she had been drinking.

The motorist failed to provide breath specimens at the police station; her eyes were glazed and her speech slurred; in response to questions by police she said "I want to die"; she was in an emotionally disturbed state. The justices were not satisfied that she had been aware of or heard the request for specimens, and that was a reasonable excuse for failure.

The prosecutor appealed against both acquittals.

QUESTION(S) FOR THE COURT: Whether, in the circumstances, it was a reasonable excuse for failing to give samples of breath that the respondent did not understand what was being required of her because of emotional distress.

HELD: "… the justices had come to the conclusion that because of the emotional condition of this lady she was not in a condition to go through the mental processes which the statute contemplated. In those circumstances, … the case comes within the decision on *Beck v Sager* [see page 243] in that there was a failure to communicate of a material kind … her emotional distress was capable of providing a reasonable excuse."

Appeal dismissed.

Foster v Bentley

Unreported, CO/211/85, 1 November 1985, QBD (DC)

Where a defendant said that he could not provide a second breath specimen because of nervousness, and there was no medical evidence in support, he did not have a reasonable excuse for failing to provide.

A motorist had been convicted of failing without reasonable excuse to provide a specimen of breath for analysis, contrary to s 8(7), Road Traffic Act 1972 as substituted by s 25 and Sch 8, Transport Act 1981. He had provided one specimen which produced a reading of 54 μg alcohol in 100 ml breath; he failed to provide a second specimen because he was extremely nervous. His appeal against conviction to the Crown Court failed; he appealed further.

HELD: "No medical evidence supported this appellant either in the magistrates' court or in the Crown Court. He relied, simply and solely, upon the fact … that he was, at the time he attempted to provide the second specimen, extremely nervous. [Referring to *R v Harding*, page 220,] it was always a matter of fact and degree, whether embarrassment, physical injuries or mental condition could provide a reasonable excuse … it is always a matter of fact and degree for the tribunal to decide upon the given facts whether the prosecution has negated the defendant's attempt to establish that he had a reasonable excuse … on the facts the defendant had no reasonable excuse."

Appeal dismissed.

Kemp v Chief Constable of Kent

[1987] RTR 66, 14 January 1986, QBD (DC)

Having already supplied a blood specimen for medical purposes does not amount to a reasonable excuse for failing to provide a blood specimen for laboratory analysis.

A motorist had been charged with failing without reasonable excuse to provide a specimen for laboratory analysis, contrary to s 8(7), Road Traffic Act 1972 as substituted by s 25 and Sch 8, Transport Act 1981. He had been driving and had had an accident; he was injured and taken to hospital. The doctor told police he had no objection to their taking a specimen of blood. When asked to provide such a specimen, the defendant replied that he had already given blood, declined to give a further specimen and said he was not prepared to listen to them at that time of night. He had given a blood specimen for medical purposes.

At the hearing, he submitted he had a reasonable excuse for not providing a specimen in that, *inter alia*, he had already provided a specimen of blood for the hospital authorities. The justices found that this excuse did not relate to his physical or mental capacity to supply a specimen of blood. They convicted him. He appealed.

QUESTION(S) FOR THE COURT: (2) Whether as a matter of law the provision of a sample of blood to hospital authorities given by a person whilst in that hospital as a patient constitutes a reasonable excuse for subsequently failing to provide a specimen of blood when required to do so by a constable under s 8, Road Traffic Act 1972.

HELD: "[On (2)] … this … involves no question of law at all. Whether circumstances are capable of providing a defendant with a reasonable excuse under section 8(7) is of course a question of law. But whether those same circumstances do in fact provide him with an excuse is a pure question of fact for the justices and not something on which this court should pronounce.

"… the defendant was not … physically incapable of providing a further specimen … there was no medical objection to his doing so. … the justices were plainly entitled to reach the conclusion which they did."

Appeal dismissed.

DPP v Fountain

[1988] RTR 385, 9 October 1987, QBD (DC)

Neither fear of AIDS, nor the fact that the motorist had been drinking non-alcoholic lager, was a reasonable excuse for failing to provide a blood specimen.

A motorist had been charged with failing without reasonable excuse to provide a specimen of blood for a laboratory test, contrary to s 8(7), Road Traffic Act 1972 as substituted by s 25 and Sch 8, Transport Act 1981. He declined to give a breath specimen, saying he had only one lung. He then refused to give a blood specimen, in view of the danger of AIDS.

The justices acquitted him, finding that he had not refused to provide a specimen in that if the procedure for taking blood had been explained he would almost certainly have complied; and that even if he had refused, his fear of AIDS and the failure of the police to allay that fear amounted to reasonable excuse. The prosecutor appealed.

QUESTION(S) FOR THE COURT: (c) Did the defendant's reply, "In view of the danger of AIDS, I'd rather not give blood" amount to a refusal to supply a specimen? (d) If it did amount to a refusal, was there any reasonable excuse for it? (e) If the defendant, as he claimed, had been drinking non-alcoholic lager would this have been a reasonable excuse for not providing a specimen?

HELD: "[On (c)] What is or is not a refusal is a question of fact … the defendant's reply to the sergeant's request was indeed a refusal.

"[On (d)] … whether the facts before the tribunal are capable of constituting a reasonable excuse is a matter of law … the defendant's belief … was not capable of constituting a reasonable excuse … ."

The answer to question (e) was "no". Appeal allowed.

Smith (Nicholas Paul) v DPP

[1992] RTR 413, 28 April 1989, QBD (DC)

In the absence of medical evidence, nervousness or stress is unlikely to be accepted as a reasonable excuse for failing to provide breath specimens.

A motorist had been charged with failing without reasonable excuse to provide a specimen of breath for analysis, contrary to s 8(7), Road Traffic Act 1972 as substituted by s 25 and Sch 8, Transport Act 1981. On being asked to provide breath specimens, he had done his best, making four attempts before the machine aborted and registered no sample. He had told the police there was no medical reason why he could not complete the procedure.

At the hearing, he argued that his failure had been due to the stress of the moment, which amounted to a reasonable excuse. The prosecutor contended that there could be no reasonable excuse unless the motorist could adduce evidence that he was mentally or physically unable to provide the specimen. The magistrates found him guilty. The motorist appealed.

QUESTION(S) FOR THE COURT: Whether the justices were right in finding that the fact that the motorist had done the best he could to provide a specimen could not amount to a reasonable excuse.

HELD: "... in the vast majority of cases ... it will be necessary to have some medical or other expert evidence to say that the observations made of nervousness are, in the context of the appellant concerned, at least a possible explanation for the failure to provide the breath specimen. In the absence of such evidence it will be rare indeed, if indeed it could ever exist, that a condition of nervousness would be sufficient to explain a failure to be able to provide the breath test.

"... the magistrates had nowhere found that the nervousness and stress exhibited by the appellant was the explanation for his failure ... ."

The answer to the question was "yes". Appeal dismissed.

Dickinson v DPP

[1989] Crim LR 741, 26 May 1989, QBD (DC)

Being advised by a solicitor not to provide breath specimens for analysis does not amount to a reasonable excuse for failing to provide. Since the motorist did not adduce sufficient evidence that that advice had deprived him of the defence of consuming alcohol after driving, without which the alcohol level would not have exceeded the limit, there were no special reasons for not disqualifying.

A motorist had been charged with failing without reasonable excuse to provide two specimens of breath for analysis, contrary to s 8(7), Road Traffic Act 1972 as substituted by s 25 and Sch 8, Transport Act 1981. He had had his solicitor with him at the police station; the solicitor advised him to refuse to supply specimens, and he refused.

At the hearing, the motorist argued that he was entitled to assume that a qualified solicitor, acting in his professional capacity, would advise him correctly and that in following that advice, there was: (a) a reasonable excuse; and (b) the motorist had been deprived by the solicitor's advice of the opportunity to plead the "hip-flask" defence, and that this was a special reason for not disqualifying under s 93(1), Road Traffic Act 1972. He gave evidence that he had consumed a quantity of drink between the time of driving and his arrest.

The justices convicted and disqualified the motorist. He appealed.

HELD: On reasonable excuse, applying *R v Lennard* [see page 220] and *Grady v Pollard* [see page 240], in the absence of evidence of physical or mental inability to provide a specimen, there was no reasonable excuse.

On special reasons, "... there was no basis ... for saying that there were special reasons. The justices ... adverted to the possibility that the appellant might have had a defence on the lines indicated and they found ... as a fact that the appellant had not adduced sufficient evidence to show that he had been deprived of a defence ... The burden was upon the appellant to establish special reasons. It is clear that if he gave evidence of having consumed a substantial amount of alcohol after he had finished driving and only a very small amount beforehand the justices did not accept that evidence."

Appeal dismissed.

DPP v Beech

[1992] RTR 239, [1992] Crim LR 64, 4 July 1991, QBD (DC)

Being too drunk to understand the instructions for providing breath specimens or the consequences of failing to provide them was not a reasonable excuse for failing to provide. Compare Young (Paula) v DPP, page 30 – intoxication can amount to a medical reason why breath cannot be provided or should not be required.

A motorist had been charged with failing without reasonable excuse to provide a specimen of breath for analysis, contrary to s 7(4), Road Traffic Act 1988. The police had been called to a house where it was alleged a domestic dispute was in progress. There they found the motorist, who admitted he had driven his car and that there had been an accident. He was arrested on suspicion of having driven with excess alcohol; at the police station he refused to provide breath specimens.

At the hearing, he contended that he did not understand the procedure, or the consequences of failure to provide a specimen, because he was confused and agitated. The justices found that the breath test procedure had been explained but that he was too drunk to understand it; that constituted a reasonable excuse for failure to provide a specimen and they dismissed the charge. The prosecutor appealed.

QUESTION(S) FOR THE COURT: Whether it could amount to a reasonable excuse for failing to provide a specimen of breath for analysis under s 7, Road Traffic Act 1988 that the defendant was so intoxicated, such intoxication being self-induced, that he was unable to understand the procedure under s 7 and the consequences of his refusal.

HELD: "… what the police constable said was capable of giving the respondent the necessary information to comply with the statute. It was the respondent's self-induced drunkenness which rendered him incapable of understanding what was said …

"… It would … defeat the object of the legislation, which is intended for the protection of the public, to hold that the fact that the defendant was too drunk to understand what was said to him could provide him with a reasonable excuse. It would also be an abuse of language so to describe it."

Appeal allowed.

DPP v Pearman

[1992] RTR 407, 23 March 1992, QBD (DC)

On the facts of this case, intoxication and distress, rendering the defendant physically incapable of providing a breath specimen, were held to amount to a reasonable excuse for failing to provide.

A motorist had been charged with failing without reasonable excuse to provide two specimens of breath for analysis, contrary to s 7(6), Road Traffic Act 1988. On the evening in question, she and her husband had been to a party and had intended to walk home, but they were attacked by a number of rowdy youths; there were other unpleasant incidents before the car was stopped by police. At the police station, the motorist provided a first breath specimen, which produced a reading of 92 µg alcohol in 100 ml breath. She then began to lose composure, was shocked and/or drunk and unable to provide a second specimen although she blew audibly round the tube; she sobbed and tried unsuccessfully to calm down.

The justices found she had been physically unable to supply a breath specimen; that was a reasonable excuse which the prosecutor had not negated. They dismissed the charge. The prosecutor appealed.

QUESTION(S) FOR THE COURT: (i) Whether evidence of inebriation combined with a distraught, deeply emotional state, which rendered the defendant physically incapable of providing a breath specimen, could ever amount to a reasonable excuse under s 7(6), Road Traffic Act 1988; (ii) in the light of the foregoing, whether the justices were right to dismiss the charge.

HELD: "… it was open to the justices to reach the conclusion that [the respondent] was physically incapable of providing the second specimen. But the fact that she succeeded in providing the first specimen means that the case must have been very near the border line …

"In the present case the connection [between the condition of the defendant and the inability to provide a specimen] is made …

"… Normally medical evidence will be required. But I am not persuaded that the justices were not entitled to act on the defendant's own evidence in this case.

"… Although the finding that the defendant was 'shocked and/or drunk' is imprecise, other findings show that the state of shock was a substantial factor in the defendant's inability to provide a specimen. The justices … were clearly impressed by the quality of [the] evidence."

The answers to both questions were "yes". Appeal dismissed.

De Freitas v DPP

[1993] RTR 98, [1992] Crim LR 894, 22 June 1992, QBD (DC)

A fear of contracting AIDS from contact with the mouthpiece of the breath analysis device, amounting to a phobia, was a reasonable excuse for failing to provide.

A motorist had been charged with failing without reasonable excuse to provide two specimens of breath for analysis, contrary to s 7(6), Road Traffic Act 1988. He had provided a roadside sample by cupping his hands over the mouthpiece but not putting his lips on it; that test had been positive. At the police station, he wished to provide breath specimens for analysis in the same way, having an obsessive fear of AIDS, but the police found this unacceptable and he was charged with the offence under s 7(6).

He was convicted by magistrates, and on appeal to the Crown Court called medical evidence that he had a genuine fear of contracting AIDS from any kind of contact with a receptacle such as a glass, cup or mouthpiece – a fear that amounted to a phobia and had been part of his mentality for a number of years. The Crown Court accepted that he had a phobia, but not that it amounted to a reasonable excuse; it was not an incapacity and did not entail any substantial risk to health. They therefore upheld the conviction. The motorist appealed further.

QUESTION(S) FOR THE COURT: Whether it availed a defendant charged with failing to provide requisite specimens that he had a genuine but unreasonable phobia against their provision by means that presented no substantial risk to his health.

HELD: "… it must be rare that anyone will succeed in persuading a court that he had a reasonable excuse … because he claims to have phobia that, if he does, he might catch … AIDS …

"Clearly the court not only accepted the entire medical evidence going to the presence of the phobia in the mind of the defendant and the genuineness of that condition but also that the reason why and the only reason why the defendant … would not breathe into the device at the police station was because he could not use his own method of doing that …

"… having expressed … such positive findings … [the Crown Court] could not go on later permissibly to emasculate those findings by *inter alia* expressing the view that the phobia was 'an obstinate and absurd belief', such as to justify rejecting the defendant's excuse for not providing a specimen of breath …

"… here [there] was uniquely … an occasion when the excuse which was advanced by the motorist was genuine."

Appeal allowed.

DPP v Brodzky

[1997] RTR 425, 16 December 1994, QBD (DC)

Where there was no causal connection between the motorist's anguish and his failure to provide breath specimens for analysis, the motorist did not have a reasonable excuse for failing to provide.

A motorist had been charged with failing without reasonable excuse to provide two specimens of breath for analysis, contrary to s 7(6), Road Traffic Act 1988. He had been arrested and, at the police station, while waiting for the breath testing procedure to be administered, he was subjected to what the justices found to be threatening behaviour by the sergeant in charge – *inter alia*, he was required to move along the bench where he was sitting to a place where there was blood, and to sign a document about his rights without being given the opportunity to read it, both under threat of being charged with failure to provide specimens. When required to provide specimens, he did not give sufficient breath.

At trial, he said he was relatively fit, had no current medical problems, but had been in a state of mental anguish; he did not know why he had failed to provide a specimen save for the mental anguish caused him by the sergeant's threatening him.

The justices accepted that there was a reasonable excuse and dismissed the charge. The prosecutor appealed.

QUESTION(S) FOR THE COURT: (1) Whether the evidence entitled the justices to find that the defendant had a reasonable excuse for failing to provide specimens of breath; (2) whether, in dismissing the charge, the justices came to a correct determination in law.

HELD: "The justices in the present case needed … first, to look for evidence of physical or mental incapacity to provide the specimen. The only such evidence was the evidence of the defendant in cross-examination, that he did not know why he could not provide a sample, save for the mental anguish which was caused to him due to the sergeant threatening him. There was no medical evidence to support such a claim. There is no doubt that medical evidence will not be necessary in every case … Perhaps the most important reason for the need for such evidence is to enable the justices to answer the third question, which is: whether there is a proper link established between the physical or mental condition alleged and the failure to provide a specimen.

"… the material which was before the justices was wholly insufficient to justify the conclusion that they reached, that there was such a causative link. The defendant was said to be, on his own admission, a relatively fit man with no current medical problems. There was no doubt that he was perfectly able to understand all the instructions that he was given. The state of anguish which is described is not described in terms which enables, or would enable, a bench of justices, properly directing their minds to that evidence, to conclude that there was a causal connection between the anguish and his failure to provide a specimen … ."

The answers to both questions were "no". Appeal allowed.

DPP v Coyle

[1996] RTR 287, 23 June 1995, QBD (DC)

The fact that the 3-minute time limit was not explained to the motorist did not afford him a reasonable excuse for failing to provide breath specimens; neither is "doing one's best" a reasonable excuse.

A motorist had been charged with failing without reasonable excuse to provide two specimens of breath for analysis, contrary to s 7(6), Road Traffic Act 1988. He had tried twice to provide a specimen but had failed; as he began the third attempt, the machine's 3-minute cycle came to an end. He had been told of the time limit only after the first attempt. There was no explanation for his failure; he was not obstructive or deliberately delaying.

At the hearing, the motorist adduced no expert or medical evidence. The justices accepted his submission that the constraint imposed by the 3-minute time limit should have been explained, together with an indication of when it commenced; they found he had done all he could to comply with the procedure and deserved to be acquitted. They dismissed the charge. The prosecutor appealed.

QUESTION(S) FOR THE COURT: Whether the justices were correct in deciding: (i) that the lack of prior references to a time limit for completion of the breathalyser procedure could amount to a reasonable excuse for not providing a specimen; (ii) that the defendant had a reasonable excuse for failing to supply two adequate specimens of breath without any evidence to explain the failure other than the defendant's assertions that he followed the officer's instructions to the best of his ability.

HELD: "… it is not a reasonable excuse in law simply that the motorist was doing his best, or trying as hard as he could, without succeeding to provide a specimen …

"… [the justices] were not correct in deciding that the lack of prior reference to a time limit could amount to a reasonable excuse. [Quoting from *DPP v Thomas (Elwyn Kenneth)*, see page 202] '… there is no obligation upon a police officer … to explain to the person who is undergoing the test that it is necessary for him to provide the second specimen within three minutes of any other period of time … .'"

The answers to both questions were "no". Appeal allowed.

DPP v Meller

[2002] EWHC 733 (Admin), 11 April 2002, QBD (Admin)

Where the motorist was anxious and agitated, but capable of providing specimens and understood the requirement, she did not have a reasonable excuse for failing to provide a blood specimen.

A motorist had been charged with failing without reasonable excuse to provide specimens of breath for analysis, contrary to s 7(6), Road Traffic Act 1988. She had been involved in an accident and left the scene. The police found her at home; she appeared drunk; denied the accident; was arrested and taken to the police station. The officer formed the view that for medical reasons breath could not or should not be provided; he therefore required a specimen of blood or urine and a doctor was called. The motorist refused to provide a specimen of blood.

At the hearing the motorist said she did not remember being asked for blood; she had felt harassed and in no fit state to comprehend the situation. The doctor said she had been anxious and agitated, but capable of providing breath or blood; she understood the requirement; she smelt of alcohol and her speech was slurred but she appeared orientated and able to answer questions appropriately. The justices acquitted the motorist. The prosecutor appealed.

QUESTION(S) FOR THE COURT: (ii) Given the unchallenged evidence of [the sergeant] that he had given the statutory warning of the consequences of a failure to provide a specimen for analysis, as required by s 7(7), Road Traffic Act 1988 and the evidence of the doctor that although anxious and agitated the respondent was capable of providing the specimens and understood the requirement, was it perverse of the justices to acquit the respondent, on the basis that they were not satisfied that the respondent understood the statutory warning?

HELD: "7. The justices had found that because the breath test procedure was incomplete, in that the second warning was not given … the subsequent request for a specimen of blood was invalid, and it seems to me that that was the basis for the justices' decision to acquit the respondent. The real issue on this appeal has, however, been this. Assuming a valid request for blood, were the justices perverse in concluding they were not satisfied the respondent understood the statutory wording; which in effect means, contends the respondent, a reasonable excuse for not providing a specimen …

"16. … This defence can only be sustained if as a result of extraneous matters – that is, not matters of a self-induced nature, such as the consumption of drink – the respondent's ability to understand the warning was impaired. The doctor's evidence about the [respondent's] being orientated and able to answer questions appropriately, which does not appear to have been rejected by the justices, is quite inconsistent with a defence of this nature …

"17. … there was no material that justified a finding by the justices of a reasonable excuse defence."

The answer to the question was "yes". Appeal allowed.

DPP v Grundy

[2006] EWHC 1157 (Admin), 3 May 2006, QBD (Admin)

On the facts of this case, there was no causative link between the defendant's distress and her failure to provide a specimen; she therefore did not have a reasonable excuse for failing to provide.

A motorist had been charged with failing without reasonable excuse to provide two specimens of breath for analysis, contrary to s 7(6), Road Traffic Act 1988. She had failed to provide a sample for a roadside breath test; at the police station she failed to provide specimens for analysis. At the trial she argued that she had a reasonable excuse in that she had been so distressed that she could not provide the specimens.

The magistrates found that she was distressed upon arrival at the police station; that she was placed in a cell which would have caused her distress; that although medical evidence is normally required to establish a defence of reasonable excuse, they had an element of doubt whether the prosecution had negated the defence. They acquitted the defendant. The prosecutor appealed.

QUESTION(S) FOR THE COURT: Whether the magistrates were wrong to acquit on findings of fact made without reference to any medical evidence on the issue of distress and its effect on the defendant's capability of providing a specimen of breath.

HELD: "[After quoting from *DPP v Brodzky*, page 253, and after referring to the three requirements – (i) for evidence of physical or mental incapacity to provide; (ii) that medical evidence would normally be required and (iii) for a causative link between the condition and the failure to provide], 8. [It is] submitted that on the facts as found, the magistrates were not entitled to find that the defence of reasonable excuse had been sufficiently or properly raised by the respondent so as to render it necessary for the prosecution to negative that defence. [Counsel for the DPP] submitted that there was no evidence upon which the magistrates could properly conclude that there was a causative link between the condition of distress from which the respondent was suffering and her failure to provide a specimen.

"9. [He] acknowledged that medical evidence is not an absolute requirement in cases such as this, but submitted that it was clear from cases such as *Brodzky* that such evidence will invariably be required when addressing the issue of the causative link between the physical or mental condition in question and the failure to provide the specimen. I agree with that submission … the material before [the magistrates] was wholly insufficient to justify the conclusion that there was any such causative link between the defendant's distressed state and her inability to provide a specimen.

"11. … Since the evidence lacked that essential ingredient … there was insufficient evidence of the defence of reasonable excuse to make it necessary for the Crown to call any evidence to negative it."

The answer to the question was "yes". Appeal allowed.

DPP v Camp

[2017] EWHC 3119 (Admin), 15 December 2017, QBD (DC)

Self-induced intoxication does not amount to a reasonable excuse for failing to provide; distinction between reasonable excuse and medical reasons; once the failure to provide breath is complete, there is no duty to proceed to require an alternative specimen.

A motorist was charged with failing without reasonable excuse to provide specimens of breath for analysis, contrary to s 7(6), Road Traffic Act 1988. He understood the instructions to provide the specimens, and was given a number of opportunities to do so, but was too drunk to comply. The investigating officer was of the view that he did not have a medical reason why breath specimens could not be provided or should not be required. The district judge in the magistrates' court accepted that he had a reasonable excuse for failing to provide and acquitted him. The prosecutor appealed.

QUESTION(S) FOR THE COURT: (a) Whether the fact that the respondent was so intoxicated, such intoxication being self-induced, that he was physically unable to provide a breath specimen for analysis can amount to a reasonable excuse for failing to provide; (b) whether the officer should have aborted the procedure for breath, and required a blood or urine specimen instead.

HELD: "18. … the scope of a 'reasonable excuse' … will always be a question of fact for the court on the evidence before it. … The fact that voluntary intoxication may sometimes, perhaps often, explain a person's inability to provide a specimen does not mean that that person will therefore have a 'reasonable excuse' for not doing so.

"19. … it is important to distinguish between, on the one hand, the concept of 'medical reasons' in section 7(3) and, on the other, the concept of a 'reasonable excuse' in section 7(6). …

"20. … That the police are given an alternative method of obtaining a relevant specimen, whether of blood or urine, does not of itself render reasonable a defendant's failure or refusal to provide a specimen of breath where such failure or refusal is based on, or sought to be justified by, his own self-induced intoxication. There is no logical connection between the two. …

"22. … it is quite clear that the respondent understood what was being required of him, either when he had been stopped by the police or later at the police station. … The fact … that in [the investigating officer's] view the respondent was so drunk that he could not physically provide a specimen of breath, and … was struggling to understand what was happening, did not preclude a finding that the respondent had no 'reasonable excuse' for failing to provide a specimen of breath. Indeed, such evidence would generally go to support that finding …

"23. … To qualify as a 'reasonable excuse', the proffered excuse must be, in the circumstances, inherently 'reasonable'. And, on the face of it at least, the evidence before the district judge, and in particular the evidence of the respondent's level of intoxication and the absence of any particular feature in the evidence that might have sustained a defence of 'reasonable excuse', left it open to him to conclude that that defence was not available here – because in the circumstances the excuse was not a 'reasonable' one."

The answer to question (a) was "no", at least in the circumstances of the case.

"[On (b)] 30. … once the respondent had failed to provide a specimen of breath, it was open to the officers to take the view that an offence under section 7(6) had been committed and that he should be charged with that offence. They were entitled to abandon the procedure for obtaining a specimen of breath when they did, and there was nothing in section 7, or elsewhere in the 1988 Act, to compel them to proceed to require a specimen of blood or urine. …"

The answer to question (b) was that the officers were entitled to abandon the procedure for obtaining a specimen of breath as and when they did, and that they were not then under a duty to require a specimen of blood or urine.

Appeal allowed.

Chapter 5

Challenging the Breath Testing and Breath Analysis Devices

1. TYPE APPROVAL

See also Wright (Andrew James) v DPP [2005] EWHC 1211 (Admin), based on the "statutory option" under s 8(2) Road Traffic Act 1988 (now repealed – see page v), where it was not open to the motorist to adduce evidence to show that the breath analysis device was not an approved device; DPP v Memery [2002] EWHC 1720 (Admin), [2003] RTR 18, also based on the "statutory option": courts may not rule on the approval of the device; Grant v DPP, page 16 – it was not open to the defendant to assert that the device should not have been approved; Robertson (Eric) v DPP, page 206 – software changes and the fact that the device did not detect mouth alcohol did not take it outside the scope of the approval order; Parker v DPP, page 293 – the Secretary of State had not acted ultra vires in approving a device which timed readings in GMT only; DPP v McKeown, DPP v Jones (Christopher), page 294 – the fact that the printout showed the wrong time did not take the device outside its approval; DPP v Brown, DPP v Teixeira, page 297 – there is a presumption of law that an approved device is reliable; Fearnley v DPP, page 426 – it was for the appellant to adduce evidence that the software was other than the specified software before the prosecution came under a burden to prove the software; DPP v Wood, DPP v McGillicuddy, page 428 – disclosure of material concerning reliability or type approval of the breath analysis device should not have been ordered where the defence statement did not raise either of those issues; and Murphy (Gerard) v DPP, page 666 – where there was no evidence to the contrary, the device was assumed to be type approved; the approval order does not constitute expert evidence. See also the Scottish case of Brown (Gary) v Procurator Fiscal, Falkirk High Court of Justiciary [2003] RTR 17 on the Breath Analysis Devices (Scotland) (Approval) Order 1998.

Bentley v Northumbria Police

[1984] RTR 276, 31 October 1983, QBD (DC)

A court may take judicial note of the approval of a breath testing device. On the facts of this case (blood specimen identified by the defendant's surname and accompanied by a form giving a sample number), there was no evidential link between the blood specimen taken and the specimen which was analysed.

A motorist had been charged with driving with excess alcohol in blood, contrary to s 6(1), Road Traffic Act 1972. A roadside breath test was positive; at the police station, a second screening test, using an "Alcolyser" device was also positive. A blood specimen was provided; analysis revealed 247.6 mg alcohol in 100 ml blood.

At the hearing, the analyst gave oral evidence confined to the facts that he had analysed blood from a phial marked "Bentley" which had been accompanied by a form showing a sample number, and the alcohol level found; the prosecution did not put a certificate of analysis in evidence.

The motorist submitted that there was no evidence that the Alcolyser was an approved device and that the justices were not entitled to infer that it was; nor was there any reliable evidence that the sample of blood analysed was that taken from the defendant. The justices rejected these submissions and convicted the motorist, who appealed.

QUESTION(S) FOR THE COURT: (a) Where there was no evidence that the breath test device used in the second breath test under s 9, Road Traffic Act 1972 was an approved device but only that it was an "Alcolyser" device, whether the court could infer that it was an approved device; (b) where the evidence of the analysis of blood was provided by the analyst in person rather than by means of a certificate of analysis, whether the evidence from the analyst that the name "Bentley" was on the phial of the blood analysed was sufficient evidence to identify the sample of blood taken from the defendant as the sample of blood analysed.

HELD: "[On (a)] … the use of the Alcolyser was in fact approved by the Breath Test Device (Approval) (No 1) Order 1979 … [the justices] were entitled to take judicial note of the fact that it was an approved device …

"[On (b)] … [the justices] knew, simply, that a sample of blood had been taken from the defendant … on the day … when the offence was alleged to have been committed and that a sample of blood bearing the name of 'Bentley' was analysed … the question [is] whether that evidence was sufficiently cogent to establish that the sample analysed was none other than that taken from the body of the defendant.

"… it was not open to the justices upon such tenuous material to reach such a conclusion. There was no evidential link between the sample taken and the sample analysed … the sample taken may have become mixed up with other samples. There may have been more than one by the name of Bentley from whom a blood sample had been taken … A number of possible reasons can be envisaged why the sample taken may not have been the sample analysed, none of which is fanciful."

Appeal allowed.

Hayward v Eames; Kirkpatrick v Harrigan
[1985] RTR 12, 9 October 1984, QBD (DC)

The Secretary of State acted within his powers when approving the Lion Intoximeter 3000 for the purposes of analysing breath specimens, and therefore evidence obtained by using the device is admissible.

Motorists had been charged with driving with excess alcohol, contrary to s 6(1), Road Traffic Act 1972 as substituted by s 25 and Sch 8, Transport Act 1981. Both had been tested on a Lion Intoximeter 3000 which showed excess alcohol. Section 8(1)(a), Road Traffic Act 1972 as substituted by s 25(3) and Sch 8, Transport Act 1981 authorises a constable to require breath specimens for analysis by means of a "device of a type approved by the Secretary of State". The Breath Analysis Devices (Approval) Order 1983 stated that the Lion Intoximeter 3000 was approved for the purposes of s 8(1). In *Hayward v Eames* the motorist had been convicted and appealed; in *Kirkpatrick v Harrigan* the charge had been dismissed and the prosecutor appealed.

QUESTION(S) FOR THE COURT: Whether the Secretary of State was empowered to approve the device by virtue of s 8(1)(a) and, if so, whether there was proper evidence of the defendant's breath alcohol exceeding the prescribed limit (*Hayward v Eames*); whether the Home Secretary was acting within his power – administrative or legislative – in giving his approval to the Lion Intoximeter 3000 and accordingly whether the magistrate was right in refusing to admit evidence relating to the machine (*Kirkpatrick v Harrigan*).

HELD: "The wording of section 8 states plainly, and without any ambiguity, that a device of a type approved by the Secretary of State may be used for gauging the proportion of alcohol on the subject's breath. The Lion Intoximeter was so approved. The fact that the approval was given before the coming into force of that particular part of the Act does not mean … that the approval is any the less real or any the less effective."

The Secretary of State was empowered to approve the device by virtue of s 8(1)(a) and there was proper evidence of the defendant's breath alcohol content exceeding the prescribed limit (*Hayward v Eames*).

The Home Secretary was acting within his power in giving his approval to the Lion Intoximeter 3000, and the magistrate should not have refused to admit evidence relating to that machine (*Kirkpatrick v Harrigan*).

The answers to both questions were "yes". Appeal in *Hayward v Eames* dismissed. Appeal in *Kirkpatrick v Harrigan* allowed.

Chief Constable of Northumbria v Browne

[1986] RTR 113, 30 October 1985, QBD (DC)

A drafting error in the description of a company which manufactures a breath analysis device did not invalidate the approval order.

A motorist had been charged with driving with excess alcohol, contrary to s 6(1), Road Traffic Act 1972 as substituted by s 25 and Sch 8, Transport Act 1981. Breath analysis by a Camic Breath Analyser showed excess alcohol. In the Breath Analysis Devices (Approval) Order 1983 (approving devices for the purposes of s 8(1), Road Traffic Act 1972 as likewise substituted), the maker of the device had been referred to as "Camic Car and Medical Instrument Company Limited"; the name of the company was in fact "Car and Medical Instrument Company Limited". The justices found that the words describing the manufacturer were an integral and vital part of the Order and therefore doubted whether the device was an approved device; they dismissed the charge. The prosecutor appealed.

QUESTION(S) FOR THE COURT: Whether the justices were wrong: (a) "in ruling that the name of the manufacturer … was an integral and vital part of the said Order; and (b) … in coming to the conclusion that, as there had been no manufacturing company by the name of 'Camic Car and Medical Instrument Company Limited' as cited in the said Order, the Camic Breath Analyser and Camic Simulator were not therefore approved devices … ."

HELD: The misdescription was a mistake by the draftsman. "… It was wholly unnecessary for the draftsman to have included the names of the manufacturing companies of these devices and accordingly a mistake by him in the description of one of them does not invalidate the approval.".

Appeal allowed.

Young v Flint

[1987] RTR 300, 28 April 1986, QBD (DC)

Defence counsel is entitled to cross-examine an expert witness for the prosecution to discover whether modifications to the breath analysis device could take it outside the approval order.

A motorist had been charged with driving with excess alcohol, contrary to s 6(1), Road Traffic Act 1972 as substituted by s 25 and Sch 8, Transport Act 1981. The breath testing procedure had been conducted in the normal way and two breath analyses using a Lion Intoximeter 3000 each revealed 76 μg alcohol in 100 ml breath.

At the trial, the prosecutor adduced expert evidence that the manufacturers had made certain modifications to Lion Intoximeter 3000 machines. Counsel for the defendant sought to cross-examine the witness, with a view to eliciting whether or not the modification might have rendered the device no longer an approved device. The justices refused to allow such cross-examination. They were of the opinion that the device was an approved device and convicted the motorist, who appealed.

QUESTION(S) FOR THE COURT: Whether the justices were right to hold that the defendant could not cross-examine the prosecutor's expert witness.

HELD: "It is fundamental to the proper conduct of a defence that counsel [for] a defendant be permitted to cross-examine a witness for the prosecution on any relevant matter. No application in that behalf is required. It is a right enjoyed by the defence which a defendant cannot be denied [unless] the court is satisfied that cross-examination is directed to inadmissible matters …

"The defence was entitled … to cross-examine that witness about the modifications for the purpose of discovering whether or not the kind of modification and its effect upon the device had the further effect of taking that device outside the approval order."

Appeal allowed.

Richardson v DPP

[2003] EWHC 359 (Admin), 20 February 2003, QBD (Admin)

The approval of the breath analysis device may be challenged only on the basis that modifications are such that it is no longer an approved device. Where, following a positive breath analysis, the police refused to allow the motorist to give a blood specimen, there was no breach of art 6, European Convention on Human Rights. See also DPP v Camp, page 257 – once the offence of failing without reasonable excuse to provide a breath specimen is complete, there is no duty on the investigating officer to require an alternative specimen.

A motorist had been charged with driving with excess alcohol, contrary to s 5(1)(a), Road Traffic Act 1988. The lower of two breath analysis readings was 93 μg alcohol in 100 ml breath. The motorist asked to give a sample of blood, but the police refused.

At trial, the defendant sought an adjournment to seek disclosure of the service history of the breath analysis device used; the application was refused on the ground that the approval of the device was a matter solely for the Secretary of State and no useful purpose would be served by the disclosure of information calculated to suggest that the device should not continue to enjoy that approval. The defendant was convicted; he appealed.

QUESTION(S) FOR THE COURT: (a) Whether the magistrates were correct in ruling that the approval of the device could not be challenged in their court, and that the request for an adjournment should therefore have been refused; (b) whether the refusal of the blood option amounted to a denial of the right to a fair trial.

HELD "13. … If the only contention on behalf of the accused … was that the modifications to the Intoximeter device had been such that it was no longer in the same condition as it had been when the Secretary of State's approval was given, that could not amount to a defence. They had to be able to go further and show that the modifications were such that it was no longer an approved device. It is not clear from the case stated that the matter was put in that way to the magistrates. Moreover … the magistrates would have been perfectly entitled to refuse the adjournment on the ground of its lateness, and the fact that there was no evidential basis put before them as to there being documents going to … whether there had been such modifications as took the Intoximeter out of the description in the schedule to the approval order. … the magistrates would have been perfectly entitled to reject the application for an adjournment in the exercise of their discretion, having regard to (a) the fact that it was to a significant extent … a fishing expedition … and (b) because of the lateness of the raising of the issue …

"The second [argument] 26. … is that the refusal by the officer to permit blood to be taken was an infringement of the appellant's rights under Article 6 of the European Convention on Human Rights [right of a person charged with a criminal offence … to have adequate time and facilities for the preparation of his defence]. …

"34. The provisions of Article 6 are, of course, mandatory, but in an area such as [that in] question, it is well established that the European Court accepts that national legislatures, and indeed national courts, have a measure of discretion as to what is to be considered adequate, what is necessary, and what goes beyond the adequate and is unnecessary. That margin of appreciation applies to the provisions of section 8(2) of the Road Traffic Act 1988. … There is nothing in the present case … to indicate that there was any risk of a denial of the right to a fair trial in the circumstances where the 50 microgrammes of alcohol limit had not simply been exceeded, but exceeded by a very substantial margin.

"35. … the refusal of a blood specimen option to the appellant did not amount to a denial of a right to a fair trial."

Appeal dismissed.

Kemsley v DPP

[2004] EWHC 278 (Admin), (2005) 169 JP 148, 4 February 2004, QBD (DC)

Where the device used to analyse breath was found not to be an approved device, the motorist's conviction could not stand.

A motorist had been charged with driving with excess alcohol, contrary to s 5(1)(a), Road Traffic Act 1988. Breath analysis, using an Intoximeter EC/IR, was positive. At the trial, expert evidence was adduced that, since approval, the EC/IR Intoximeter had been modified to such an extent that it was no longer of the same type as the approved device. It was not suggested that the Intoximeter had been malfunctioning. The district judge apparently accepted that evidence but convicted the defendant. She appealed.

QUESTION(S) FOR THE COURT: Whether the district judge was entitled to convict on the evidence before him.

HELD: "21. … Was the judge entitled to convict … on the basis of the evidence that he had accepted? We are driven to conclude that he was not. The reason he was not is that he has to be interpreted as accepting that the device used to breathalyse her was not an approved device. That was fatal, rightly or wrongly, to the admissibility of the evidence that that device produced; irrespective of the reading it gave, which was very high; irrespective of the fact that it was substantially like an approved device. Therefore we have to say that this appeal must be allowed and the conviction quashed.

"22. It is important to emphasise what this case does not decide. This case turns solely and only on the form of the case stated (which, at this stage, the matter having already been before this court, this court cannot go behind) and upon the district judge's acceptance, as he sets out, of the account that he gives of [the expert's] evidence, whether or not that was right or wrong. It does not decide anything about breathalyser cases in general. It does not decide anything about whether the EC/IR machine in general is in fact a device approved by the Home Secretary. All that it does is say that on the evidence before the court in this case the court is obliged to proceed on the basis that in this case it has been found as a fact that the machine was not such a device."

Appeal allowed.

Skinner v DPP

[2004] EWHC 2914 (Admin), [2005] RTR 207, 29 November 2004, QBD (DC)

In the absence of evidence to the contrary, it could be assumed that the Intoximeter EC/IR, being an approved device, was operating with the correct type-approved software and was operating correctly. The conduct of the trial was essentially a matter within the discretion of the district judge.

A motorist had been charged with driving with excess alcohol, contrary to s 5(1)(a), Road Traffic Act 1988. Breath analysis was carried out using an Intoximeter EC/IR, and revealed excess alcohol. The case was one of several in which the reliability of the device in question was being challenged, and at a pre-trial hearing it was ordered that the case be joined for trial with those of two other defendants.

The three cases were heard separately but together, so as to avoid the repetition of evidence; the defendants were not joined as co-accused. The evidence lasted 7 days, given on 14–16 July 2003, 17–19 November 2003 and 2 February 2004. The first adjournment was to await the decision of the High Court in relation to a relevant case; the second was caused by the ill-health of a witness.

The motorist was convicted and appealed.

QUESTION(S) FOR THE COURT: (2) Whether the district judge was entitled to conclude, as a matter of law, that in the absence of any admissible evidence to the contrary, the prosecution was entitled to rely on a presumption that the EC/IR, being an approved device, was operating with the correct type-approved software. (3) Whether the district judge was entitled, as a matter of law, to rule that there was a presumption that, in the absence of sufficient evidence to challenge its reliability, a machine found to be an Intoximeter EC/IR and an approved device, was operating correctly (including operating with the correct software) at the time the specimens were provided. (4) With regard to the conduct of the trial, whether the district judge was entitled to: (a) commence the trial knowing that it would have to be adjourned; (b) continue with the trial part-heard in November 2003 and again in February 2004; (c) interpret the decision to "join" the three cases as a direction that they be "heard together" rather than legally joined; (d) continue to hear the informations together to avoid the need for similar expert evidence to be repeated in separate trials, albeit that the cases were in fact concluded separately; (e) refuse to allow cross-examination of an expert witness not called on behalf of the appellant where no advance statement of evidence from that witness had been served on the Crown and where that evidence would not be taken into account in determining her case; (f) refuse to allow the defendant to call a second expert whose evidence was the same as the expert called on behalf of the appellant and who would not give any new evidence that was materially different from that already given; (g) continue with the case against the appellant having concluded the case against one of the other defendants.

HELD: "32. … [The Crown] submits, in relation to questions 2 and 3, that, there being a presumption that this was the right sort of machine, a matter which is not in dispute, it could be assumed that it contained the right software. Such an assumption is, he submits, within the reasonable limits of assumptions which Lord Bingham [in *Sheldrake v DPP; Attorney General's Reference (No 4 of 2002);* [2004] UKHL 43, [2004] 3 WLR 976, page 502] indicated are permissible. It would … be absurd to dismantle the machine to see what was inside it, unless there was some evidence to suggest that the machine might be affected. It would be proper to assume that it contained the correct software. The District Judge, having heard the cross-examination of the prosecution expert …, was entitled to conclude that there was no evidence to suggest that the software might be unreliable or not approved. …

"33. As to question 4 and the questions raised as to the conduct of the trial, … [t]he conduct of this trial was essentially a matter within the discretion of [the] District Judge … within the parameter of the direction previously given … She was entitled to interpret that earlier ruling in the way she did and there was no injustice or prejudice resulting to the appellant from the way in which her case was conducted. Furthermore, the conclusion which the District Judge reached as to what could permissibly be assumed in relation to the software within the approved device was correct, in the absence of any evidence at all suggesting that the software was not that which it ought to have been."

Appeal dismissed.

Breckon v DPP

[2007] EWHC 2013 (Admin), [2008] RTR 8, 22 August 2007, QBD (DC)

The motorist's arguments that the breath analysis device was not an approved device, and that the result of the roadside breath test should be before the court, were rejected. See also Smith (Stephen John Henry) v DPP, page 344 – the prosecution is not obliged to disclose a breath alcohol reading obtained from a preliminary breath test, although it is good practice to do so; Murphy (Gerard) v DPP, page 666 – where the roadside breath testing device generates and stores analysis figures, the prosecutor is not required to adduce those figures.

A motorist had been charged with driving with excess alcohol, contrary to s 5(1)(a), Road Traffic Act 1988. The district judge rejected his arguments concerning the type approval of the breath analysis device, and that the reading from the roadside breath test should have been put before the court, and convicted the defendant. He appealed.

QUESTION(S) FOR THE COURT: Whether the district judge erred in law in holding: (1) that the breath analysis device was an approved device; (2) that the prosecutor did not have to adduce the alcohol level revealed by the breath test carried out at the roadside.

HELD: "[On the argument that the breath analysis device was not an approved device because it had a manual change-over valve rather than an automatic change-over valve as specified in the Home Office's *Guide to Type Approval Procedures*, referred to in an agreement between the Home Office and the manufacturers of the device] 29. The device which is approved is set out in the Schedule to the Approval document dated 25 February 1998. There is no reference, express or implied, in this schedule to either the Agreement with the manufacturer or to the Guide, and I see no reason why those documents should be incorporated within the Approval or why the Approval should be read as being subject to them. …

"31. The device must receive Type Approval but that is precisely what the Schedule to the Approval achieves. … there must be room to make sensible modifications without having to seek a new approval every time this is done. The test must be whether after such modification or alteration the machine remains one to which the description in the schedule still properly applies. If it does not, then the device is no longer an approved device; but if the description does still properly apply to the device it will remain an approved device even though modifications or alterations have been made. Thus the removal of one cylinder, which did not affect the operation of the device, did not take it out of the Approval. Nor in my judgment, would the supply of a device with a manual change-over valve, rather than an automatic change-over valve when the machine had two cylinders, render it no longer an approved device. It remained an Intoximeter EC/IR with a gas delivery system. …

"[On (2)] 34. Section 15(2) of the Road Traffic Offenders Act 1988 does not … apply to preliminary tests under section 6 of the Road Traffic Act 1988 or indeed to preliminary breath tests under its amendment by virtue of section 6A. The purpose of the preliminary test is to obtain an indication of whether the proportion of alcohol was likely to exceed the prescribed limit. It is not to determine whether the limit has in fact been exceeded, which is the function of the specimens taken for analysis under section 7. The latter part of section 15(2) clearly applies to section 7 specimens … and there is no basis for believing that the earlier part of the section refers to a different type of specimen. It cannot have been intended that the roadside breath test, which does not determine whether an offence has been committed, and is not subject to safeguards for the accused such as warning of the risk of prosecution, could be the specimen which has, under the assumption, to determine the lowest level of alcohol in the accused's breath or urine.

"35. It would in many instances … be to the serious disadvantage of the Defendant that the roadside breath test figures are adduced. They will often be greater than those later obtained."

The answers to both questions were "no". Appeal dismissed.

Rose v DPP

[2010] EWHC 462 (Admin), 11 March 2010, QBD (Admin)

The decision in Zafar v DPP (page 439) does not make a difference to whether or not an attack on type approval can be made. The prosecution is not required to disclose breath readings obtained at the roadside (see also Murphy (Gerard) v DPP, page 666 – where the roadside breath testing device generates and stores analysis figures, the prosecutor is not required to adduce those figures). On the facts, delay was not such as to deprive the defendant of a fair trial.

A motorist had been charged with driving with excess alcohol, contrary to s 5(1)(a), Road Traffic Act 1988, his breath alcohol having been nearly three times the limit.

The Crown Court heard evidence that the evidential breath analysis device used did not always detect mouth alcohol. The defendant submitted that, as the court in *Zafar v DPP* (page 439) defined breath so as to include air which might be mixed with alcohol from the mouth, a device that did not reliably detect mouth alcohol may produce a falsely high reading and should therefore be regarded as outside type approval.

During the trial before the justices it was discovered that the roadside device stored breath alcohol readings, but that they were retrievable only by the manufacturers of the device. The motorist argued that it was an abuse of process for the prosecution not to have provided the figures from the roadside device; the prosecution had a duty to disclose them by virtue of s 3, Criminal Procedure and Investigations Act 1996; and, by virtue of s 15(2), Road Traffic Offenders Act 1988, was bound to put the figures in evidence.

The offence took place in 2001. The defendant was convicted in 2004 and the Crown Court heard an appeal in 2008. The defence sought a stay of proceedings on the grounds of delay.

The Crown Court dismissed all these arguments and the motorist appealed further.

QUESTION(S) FOR THE COURT: (1) Whether, on the facts, a reasonable bench, properly directed, could have held that the device was approved. (2) Whether it was *Wednesbury* unreasonable to have held that there was no abuse of process or prejudice to the appellant because the prosecution did not disclose the digital reading of the roadside test and whether a fair trial could take place. (3) Whether the court erred in law, or it was *Wednesbury* unreasonable, to have held that delay did not prevent a fair trial.

HELD: "[On (1)] 16. … [*DPP v Memery* [2002] EWHC 1720 (Admin), [2003] RTR 18]] made clear … that a public law challenge to the approval was not available, but it left open a challenge to the reliability of the particular device. …

"17. … The fact that giving evidence of the possible presence of 'mouth alcohol' does not provide a defence since breath includes all that is exhaled, does not in any way limit the giving of that evidence to support a case that the device is unreliable if there is other evidence which would support that case. There was … no such evidence in this case. Indeed the evidence was overwhelming that the device had recorded accurately that the appellant was well in excess of the limit.

"[On (2)] 34. … At no stage was there any duty on the prosecution to disclose, even if the figures could have assisted the defence. In any event, on the evidence, it is inconceivable the figures would have assisted the appellant's defence.

"[On (3), after reviewing all the circumstances (case originally joined with four others, the availability of experts, technical evidence, discovery that the roadside device stored readings, awaiting decisions in other cases),] 55. … the question is whether [the defendant] can have a fair hearing. … A fair hearing was possible."

The answer to question (1) was "yes"; the answer to questions (2) and (3) was "no". Appeal dismissed.

Coxon v Manchester City Magistrates' Court

[2010] EWHC 712 (Admin), 11 March 2010, QBD (DC)

On the facts, there was nothing to suggest that a Lion Intoxilyser 6000, to which had been connected a LIBIS computer, was not an approved device. Type approval is a matter of description, and separate from reliability.

A motorist had been charged with driving with excess alcohol, contrary to s 5(1)(a), Road Traffic Act 1988. His breath had been analysed using a Lion Intoxilyser 6000 connected to a LIBIS computer system, which took over the keyboard functions of the Intoxilyser. The defendant argued that this meant that the device was no longer approved, the reading might be affected, and the device could not be considered reliable. The district judge rejected his expert evidence to this effect as speculative, and convicted the defendant. He applied for judicial review of the refusal of his application for a case stated.

HELD: "21. … The issue is whether a device meets the description set out in the schedule [to the type approval order]. That is a separate issue from reliability or quality. Description means the essence or identity of the device. That is a broad common sense test. It will turn very much on the build and function of a device and the circumstances in which type approval is given. The issue then arises whether collateral attributes of the device go to its description affecting, in other words, its essence or identity so that the device can no longer be regarded as of that description. … That demands a common sense judgment as to whether the build and function of the device is such that it still has, in fact, the essence or identity of the device specified in the type approval.

"25. … the District Judge … found as a matter of fact that there was no direct evidence that the Lion [Intoxilyser] 6000 UK was altered so significantly as a result of the LIBIS connection to take it outside its description. … He found that there was no change of function as a result … and that the device still met the description in the type approval order. …

"28. … the District Judge applied the correct test in law. He concluded that the claimant had not raised any evidence that the device was not of an approved type."

The application for judicial review was refused.

2. THE AMOUNT SAID TO HAVE BEEN CONSUMED

See also the cases in Chapter 6, on the assumption that the alcohol level at the time of the offence was not less than in the specimen; DPP (Blakeley) v Manchester and Salford Magistrates' Court; DPP (Whyte) v Manchester and Salford Magistrates' Court, page 605; and DPP (Thaiss) v Lincoln Magistrates' Court, page 609.

Cracknell v Willis

[1988] AC 450, [1987] 3 WLR 1082, [1987] 3 All ER 801, [1988] RTR 1, 5 November 1987, HL

The offences of driving with excess alcohol and failing to provide a specimen of breath for analysis are alternatives and mutually exclusive. A person may not be convicted on the basis of a single breath specimen. A defendant may adduce evidence of the amount he has drunk to challenge the assumption that the breath analysis device is reliable. A defendant's belief that he had not drunk enough to take him over the limit is not a reasonable excuse for failing to provide breath specimens.

A motorist had been charged with driving with excess alcohol, contrary to s 6(1)(a), Road Traffic Act 1972 as substituted by s 25 and Sch 8, Transport Act 1981; and with failing without reasonable excuse to provide a specimen of breath for analysis, contrary to s 8(7), Road Traffic Act 1972 as likewise substituted. He had provided one breath specimen which revealed excess alcohol. He made attempts to provide a second specimen but the machine aborted, the motorist allowing air to escape from the mouthpiece. The justices found the breath analysis device to have been working correctly, refused to allow the motorist to adduce evidence of the amount he had drunk, and convicted him on both charges. His appeal to the Divisional Court was dismissed and he appealed further.

CERTIFIED QUESTION(S): "(1) Whether it is open to a court to convict a defendant both of an offence contrary to s 6(1)(a) and an offence contrary to s 8(7) of the Road Traffic Act 1972 as substituted … where, pursuant to a request by a constable for two specimens of breath the defendant supplies only the first [or one] specimen; and (2) whether the court should permit a defendant charged with an offence contrary to s 6(1)(a) or s 8(7) of the Act of 1972 to adduce evidence (from whatever source) of the amount of alcohol actually consumed by the defendant, prior to the giving of or the failure to provide as the case may be, the specimen which founds the prosecution."

HELD: "… the two offences were intended to be alternatives and … the Act should be construed so as to provide that they are mutually exclusive … If only one specimen of breath has been taken it is not to be relied upon for the purposes of a conviction, and is not a specimen which the magistrates are entitled to take into account under section 10(2). [*Duddy v Gallagher* [1985] RTR 401 (DC) and *Burridge v East* [1986] RTR 328, [1986] Crim LR 632 (DC) overruled] … in assessing the penalty for refusing to provide a specimen of breath the magistrates are entitled to take into account any evidence that indicates the motorist's consumption of alcohol and this would include the result of the analysis of the first breath specimen if he unreasonably refuses to provide a second specimen …

"I am unable to agree … that the wording of section 10(2) gives any support for the view that Parliament intended any challenge to the reliability of a device to be limited to a particular type of evidence. In the case of a breath specimen there is of course a presumption that the machine is reliable but if that presumption is challenged by relevant evidence the magistrates will have to be satisfied that the machine has provided a reading upon which they can rely before making the 'assumption'. …

"Suppose that a teetotaller after dining with people of the highest repute, two bishops if you will, forgets to turn on his lights and is stopped by the police. He is asked to take a roadside breath test and indignantly but inadvisedly refuses. He is arrested and taken to the police station. There he thinks better of his refusal. He agrees to supply two specimens of breath and the machine to his astonishment shows very high readings. He asks to be allowed to prove the machine wrong by supplying a blood or urine specimen. The police agree and he gives a blood specimen. An analysis shows no alcohol in the specimen. It is virtually certain that the police would accept the analysis and he would not be prosecuted. But if he were prosecuted it is equally certain that the magistrates would prefer the analysis and he would be acquitted. But now suppose that the police refused his request to supply a blood or urine specimen because the reading on the machine was over 50 microgrammes. Is he to be convicted without the opportunity of calling the two bishops as witnesses to the fact that he had drunk nothing that evening …

"... it would require the clearest possible wording to show that Parliament intended such an unjust result. If Parliament wishes to provide that either there is to be an irrebuttable presumption that the breath testing machine is reliable or that the presumption can only be challenged by a particular type of evidence then Parliament must take the responsibility of so deciding and spell out its intention in clear language.

"Until then I would hold that evidence which, if believed, provides material from which the inference can reasonably be drawn that the machine was unreliable is admissible ... ." *Hughes v McConnell* [1986] 1 All ER 268, [1985] RTR 244 and *Price v Nicholls* [1986] RTR 155, [1985] Crim LR 744 (DC) overruled.

Appeal against conviction under s 6(1)(a) allowed. Appeal against conviction under s 8(7) upheld: "Although the magistrates erred in refusing to admit ... evidence, it provides no ground for quashing the ... conviction ... The fact that a motorist does not believe that he has drunk more than the prescribed limit does not provide a reasonable excuse entitling him to refuse to provide a specimen."

DPP v Hill

[1991] RTR 351, 20 December 1990, QBD (DC)

On the findings in this case (glazed vision, half a pint of lager consumed), the justices were wrong to conclude that the breath analysis device had not been reliable.

A motorist had been charged with driving with excess alcohol, contrary to s 6(1)(a), Road Traffic Act 1972 as substituted by s 25 and Sch 8, Transport Act 1981. The roadside breath test had been positive and the lower of two Intoximeter readings was 46 μg alcohol in 100 ml breath.

The justices found that the defendant's vision had been glazed, but accepted evidence that he had drunk only one half pint of lager, and therefore were not satisfied that the Intoximeter had been reliable. They dismissed the charge. The prosecutor appealed.

QUESTION(S) FOR THE COURT: Whether the justices' decision to acquit was perverse in that no reasonable bench could have reached such a decision on that evidence.

HELD: "... if the defendant were to be believed, however credible ... he appeared to be ... it would involve three very surprising consequences: one that the Intoximeter itself was faulty; two that not only was that faulty, but that the Draeger Alert [the roadside breath testing device] device also was faulty and, finally, that there was some explanation other than drink to account for the evidence of glazed vision ...

"... [the justices] may have misinterpreted the effect of the decision in *Cracknell v Willis* [see above] and have thought that, because it was possible as a matter of law to rebut the presumption [that the breath analysis device is reliable] by evidence, that meant that might be a comparatively easy thing to do.

"On the facts of this particular case it really was quite impossible to come to the conclusion that the justices reached … ."

Appeal allowed.

Lafferty v DPP

Unreported, CO 1884 93, 27 April 1994, QBD (DC)

Where a defendant challenges the reliability of the breath analysis device by asserting he had not drunk enough to take him over the limit, the prosecution may rebut that assertion by any relevant evidence, including the result of the roadside breath test.

A motorist had been charged with driving with excess alcohol, contrary to s 5(1)(a), Road Traffic Act 1988. The roadside breath test had been positive; the lower of two Intoximeter readings was 62 µg alcohol in 100 ml breath.

At the hearing, the motorist said he had drunk insufficient to produce such a reading and adduced expert evidence to the effect that if he had drunk only what he claimed, such a reading would not have resulted. He also submitted that evidence of a positive roadside breath test was inadmissible to support the charge under s 5(1)(a).

The magistrates rejected these submissions and convicted the motorist. He appealed.

QUESTION(S) FOR THE COURT: Whether the justices were correct to hold that evidence as to the administration of a roadside breath test under s 6, Road Traffic Act 1988 was admissible where two specimens of breath were lawfully obtained under s 7, Road Traffic Act 1988.

HELD: Where a "defendant seeks to challenge the reliability of an Intoximeter reading by asserting that he had drunk only a particular quantity of alcohol, it is open to the prosecution to seek to rebut that assertion by any relevant evidence … the result of the roadside breath test is admissible for [this] purpose, even though … [its] accuracy, compared to the Lion Intoximeter, [is] relevant to the weight to be given."

The answer to the question was "yes". Appeal dismissed.

DPP v Spurrier

[2000] RTR 60, 21 July 1999, QBD (DC)

Where there was no expert evidence, yet nothing to indicate why the court below had attached sufficient weight to the motorist's evidence of consumption to acquit her, the prosecutor's appeal failed.

A motorist had provided a positive roadside breath test and was arrested. Breath analysis revealed 143 µg of alcohol in 100 ml breath, although the motorist had displayed no signs of erratic driving, was not unsteady on her feet, nor were her eyes glazed. She co-operated throughout. But for the smell of alcohol there were no observable signs that she had consumed alcohol.

She was charged with driving with excess alcohol, contrary to s 5(1), Road Traffic Act 1988. At the hearing, the magistrates accepted that on the day before her arrest, between 8.30 pm and 11.30 pm, she had consumed two cans of lager and shared a half bottle of whiskey equally with her husband; and that she had consumed no alcohol between 11.30 pm the day before and her arrest at 11.45 am the following day. On that evidence the magistrates concluded that the amount she had consumed was not compatible with the very high reading from the breath analysis device; nor was her observable behaviour and condition compatible with that high reading. They acquitted her. The prosecutor appealed.

QUESTION(S) FOR THE COURT: (1) Whether the justices' decision to acquit the defendant was perverse in that no reasonable bench could have reached such a decision on that evidence; (2) whether, to rebut the statutory presumption of reliability of the breath analysis device, it is necessary for a defendant who gives evidence of consumption of a certain quantity of alcohol to also adduce expert evidence of the reading that would be produced by the consumption of that amount of alcohol by that defendant in the circumstances stated by the defendant.

HELD: "... the submission is that in this case the magistrates could not properly reach the conclusion they came to namely that the device was unreliable, absent medical or scientific evidence.

"The evidence the submission contemplates ... would relate to absorption rates for alcohol and opinion evidence as to whether having regard to the size, condition and health of the defendant and other relevant considerations, the reading shown by the device was consistent with the amount said to have been consumed ...

"... on the basis of the evidence accepted by the magistrates, namely no consumption since 11.30 pm the prior night, no consumption other than the amount claimed, and no observable signs of inebriation, all taken against a very high reading, I am not persuaded that the inference drawn by the magistrates is one [to] which no reasonable bench properly directing themselves could come ... other magistrates may well not have come to the same conclusion and properly so.

"... there is nothing in the case [explaining] the reasons for the weight which the magistrates must have attached to the respondent's evidence ... this appeal must be dismissed and the case is to be distinguished from the case of *Hill* [page 272]."

The answers to both questions were "no". Appeal dismissed.

Williams (John Robert) v DPP

[2001] EWHC Admin 932, 16 November 2001, QBD (DC)

Magistrates are entitled to reject a defendant's evidence of the amount he has drunk and to rely on the presumption that the breath analysis device is reliable.

A motorist had been charged with driving with excess alcohol, contrary to s 5(1)(a), Road Traffic Act 1988. A roadside breath test was positive and at the police station breath analysis revealed a lower reading of 60 μg alcohol in 100 ml breath.

At the hearing, the motorist argued that he had not drunk enough to be over the limit, adducing expert evidence that if he had consumed the amount of alcohol he claimed, then his breath alcohol limit at the time he provided the specimens would have been below the limit; in fact, it would have been zero.

The magistrates found that he had consumed sufficient alcohol to exceed the prescribed limit and convicted him; he appealed.

QUESTION(S) FOR THE COURT: Whether the magistrates were entitled on the evidence to find as a fact that the defendant had consumed sufficient alcohol to exceed the prescribed limit.

HELD: "11. Before this Court [counsel] for the respondent submitted as follows. Had the magistrates accepted the appellant's evidence, and the evidence of the expert witnesses, his breath alcohol concentration would have been zero. The magistrates found that the appellant's eyes were glazed, his breath smelt strongly of alcohol, the roadside breath test was positive and a reading of 60 microgrammes of alcohol in 100 millilitres of breath was obtained. In making these findings, in the circumstance of this case, the magistrates must have rejected the evidence of the appellant. The magistrates were entitled on the evidence to find as a fact that the defendant had consumed sufficient alcohol to exceed the prescribed limit.

"12. I refer to my analysis of the relevant statutory provisions and the relevant legal principles in my judgment in *DPP v Brown* and *DPP v Teixeira* [see page 297]. In the case of a breath specimen there is a presumption that the device is reliable, but if that presumption is challenged by relevant evidence the magistrates will have to be satisfied that the machine has provided a reading upon which they can rely before making the assumption …

"13. Mr. Williams gave evidence before the magistrates that on [the date in question] he had been in a London restaurant between 1 p.m. and 5.30 p.m. and between 7 p.m. and 9 p.m. and had consumed 4–5 glasses of red wine, one glass of beer and one bottle of beer. … It does not follow … that the magistrates were accepting the accuracy of his evidence as to when he consumed the alcohol. When the magistrates' reasons are carefully examined it is clear that they did not accept the whole of Mr. Williams' evidence. … it was open to them to point out … that taking the quantities Mr. Williams said he had consumed (but not accepting his evidence as to time of consumption) the breath test sample would have been over the prescribed limit. …"

The answer to the question was "yes". Appeal dismissed.

Santos v Stratford Magistrates' Court

[2012] EWHC 752 (Admin), 1 March 2012, QBD (DC)

Where evidence of the correct functioning of the device was not given, and there was no submission on the point in the court below, a challenge on appeal could not be entertained.

A motorist had been charged with driving with excess alcohol, contrary to s 5(1), Road Traffic Act 1988. When the trial opened, defence counsel identified as one of the issues the accuracy of the device, on the basis that the motorist had not consumed enough to put him over the limit. The sergeant who conducted the breath analysis procedure gave evidence, but, possibly because of an interruption, did not give evidence that the device was working correctly at the relevant time. Defence counsel cross-examined the officer, but the district judge did not allow her to put questions relating to the accuracy or proper functioning of the device, on the ground that there was no issue concerning the functioning of the device, and that in any event the officer was not an expert.

The motorist gave evidence suggesting he had consumed insufficient alcohol to account for the reading, and on that basis it was submitted that the evidence of the Intoximeter should not be relied on. There was no submission based on the absence of evidence that the device was functioning properly. At the end of the case, the defence did not submit that there was no case to answer.

The motorist was convicted and appealed.

QUESTION(S) FOR THE COURT: (1) Whether the district judge was right to prevent counsel from asking the officer whether the device was correctly functioning at the material time; (2) whether there was any admissible evidence, and if so, sufficient evidence that the breath alcohol level was above the prescribed limit.

HELD: "6. … the District Judge was in error [in disallowing the questions about the correct functioning of the device]; there had been indicated a *Cracknell v Willis* [see page 270] challenge to the accuracy of the functioning of the intoximeter, and [the sergeant] would have been entitled to give evidence, based on the print out and his use of the machine, that it was working normally.

"12. … What became clear subsequently … was that the applicant was contending that because no positive evidence was given by [the officer] to the effect that the intoximeter was working correctly, the prosecution's case is fatally flawed. It is well established that there must not only be evidence of the analysis, which can be given orally, but also evidence of the reliability of the device used … Such evidence was not given … Had the point been raised in the court below by means of a submission of no case to answer, or indeed in a properly formulated closing submission, it seems to me inevitable that the court would have acceded to a prosecution application to reopen this case in the interests of justice. … the accuracy of the intoximeter would then have been demonstrated by the evidence of the custody officer, and/or by the production [of] the print out, which on its face shows a normally functioning machine … .

"16. … I do not consider that the District Judge's error in preventing cross-examination of the officer as to the accurate functioning of the intoximeter had any material effect on the fairness of the proceedings. … It is abundantly clear that if the question had been permitted, it would only have served to put evidence of the correct functioning of the intoximeter before the court. The effect would have been that the point which has now been taken before us would not have arisen …

"17. … the failure to raise the present issue at the time of the trial on the point of what is, in reality, pure technicality, is highly material to the issue as to whether we should grant relief. … the technical defect in the prosecutor's case now relied on should not avail this applicant. … the conviction should remain undisturbed."

Appeal dismissed.

CPS v Cipriani

www.judiciary.uk/wp-content/uploads/2016/09/cps-v-cipriani-judgment.pdf, unreported, 24 June 2016, Westminster Magistrates' Court

This decision is not a binding authority. The precise nature of a challenge to the investigative procedure should be spelt out at the case management stage. "Reliability of breath alcohol readings" was insufficient to identify the matter in dispute. Summary trials must concentrate on the real contested issues, and not descend into a game of smoke and mirrors.

A motorist was charged with driving with excess alcohol, contrary to s 5, Road Traffic Act 1988. Numerous points were raised in his defence. On the principal issue – whether the evidential breath analysis device was working correctly – the district judge rejected argument that the defendant had not drunk enough to take him over the limit. In view of the length of time the trial had taken and the large number of matters raised (reliability of breath alcohol readings; whether procedure correctly followed; whether there was a *bona fide* investigation; admissibility of 'verbals'; sufficiency of evidence of driving; procedure unduly delayed; non-disclosure; abuse of process; exclusion of evidence pursuant to s 78, Police and Criminal Evidence Act 1984; insufficient evidence of calibration of the breath alcohol device), District Judge Howard Riddle made the following points.

HELD: "… the defence has at one stage or another argued almost every conceivable defence that there might be to a charge under section 5 of the Road Traffic Act 1988. [The real issue was whether the evidential breath analysis device was working correctly.] … Either Mr Cipriani is wrong about the amount of alcohol he consumed, or the reading is wrong. … [g]iven the reliance of [counsel for the defence] on passages from judgments that do not directly apply and given the way that this case was conducted over a number of days, I believe the following points need to be made.

"a. There is a presumption that the [evidential breath machine] is working accurately. That was so at the time of *Cracknell v Willis* [[1988] AC 450, see page 270] and is indeed a common law principle. The cases [quoted by the defence] took place in the early days of the breath testing machines. Since then a second generation of machines has been introduced. They have been in operation every day for many years. They have gained an enviable reputation for accuracy. They self-calibrate (or more accurately they check calibration) so that the operator can see if a fault has developed, and the motorist is given a copy of the print out so it can be checked by his own experts, as happened here.

"b. The common law presumption and the statutory assumption are both rebuttable. They can be rebutted by evidence of consumption by the defendant.

"c. The defence can also directly challenge the reliability of the reading produced by the machine. In this case the print-out was provided to the defendant and was available to the experts and at the time of trial. The officer could have been cross-examined about the reliability of the machine, calibration or indeed any other matter of concern. I am suggesting that it is appropriate for the experts to be present in court during this cross-examination. The experts can later be called to say why the machine was unreliable, normally after the defendant has given evidence of consumption or other relevant issues. Without a challenge to the prosecution witness, the presumption that the machine works will on this point take the case beyond 'no case', and indeed may lead to the question of admissibility of the defence expert, as not relevant to an issue raised.

"d. In this case there was express evidence that the evidential breath machine was working and reliable, and there was evidence of calibration. … However, absent an express challenge to the machine, direct evidence of reliability and calibration is unnecessary. The presumption and assumption will suffice. The defendant's protection is that he can challenge reliability, operator competence, and calibration by clear and direct cross examination (and advance notice in the case management form) so that these matters can be properly and fully considered by the trial court.

"e. There is no principle of law that the Crown must adduce evidence of calibration. …

"f. The Criminal Procedure Rules have effected a sea change to the way cases are to be conducted. The parties are required to abide by the Rules. This case, where almost everything was challenged or put to proof (even the identity of the driver), has an antique air about it.

"g. In future, drink driving cases cannot be conducted in the way that this one was. All parties, including the court, have an obligation to ensure that only relevant and contested issues require evidence. Here, this court acknowledges its own failings. It should have ensured that the precise nature of the challenge to the MGDDA procedure was spelt out at the case management stage. Similarly, the 'reliability of breath alcohol readings' was insufficient to identify the matter in dispute. If it was radio, then that should have been made clear. Similarly, if the question was calibration then that should have been made clear. If the issue was that the operator failed to detect an error on the face of the print out, then that should have been made clear.

"h. Where the Crown is put to proof, for example as to the identity of the driver, then it might have been more appropriate for that evidence to be given in statement form, rather than requiring a witness to attend when his evidence on this point was not in dispute. Indeed, while it remains the case that a defendant can put the Crown to proof generally, the practice of single issue 'putting to proof' may well be inconsistent with the Criminal Procedure Rules.

"i. … I am concerned that colleagues, especially those not trained in the law, should not be faced with the type of arguments that have been put before me. Drink drive cases should be far simpler than this. If the issue is that the defendant's consumption of alcohol shows that the machine is unreliable, then that is a straightforward matter of fact and does not need to be accompanied by a large number of law reports of early cases. If the issue is that the statutory warning has not been given, then this should be spelled out in the case management form and dealt with in cross examination. If the issue is that the machine was not properly calibrated, then again this should be spelled out in advance and dealt with directly by cross examination and possibly expert evidence. If the issue is operator error, so that the operator should have noticed that the machine had not properly completed its cycle and produced a certificate then I venture to suggest this can be dealt with very early on by producing the relevant printout to the Crown Prosecution Service and demonstrating the error. In those circumstances I doubt that a trial would be necessary.

"j. It is essential that the bench has and retains confidence in the advocates who appear before it. In those circumstances I trust [counsel for the defence] to bring the above comments … to the attention of a bench trying cases such as these. He can of course point out why he disagrees, and it is clear that these comments are not a binding authority. However, it is in the interests of all that summary trials concentrate on the real contested issues, and do not descend into a game of smoke and mirrors. I find the case proved."

R (Hassani) v West London Magistrates' Court

[2017] EWHC 1270 (Admin), [2017] Crim LR 720, [2017] ACD 73, [2017] 3 Costs LR 477, 5 April 2017, QBD (DC)

In the absence of specific evidence which indicates that there is a problem with the evidential breath analysis device, extensive exploration of technicalities is normally a waste of time; the district judge was right to practise firm case management. Criminal courts have a duty of active case management using Criminal Procedure Rules

A motorist had been convicted of driving with excess alcohol, contrary to s 5, Road Traffic Act 1988. He had not given evidence or contradicted the Crown's case; he did not appeal to the Crown Court. Belatedly, he sought judicial review. The application was refused, then renewed, and finally (having been advised by fresh counsel) withdrawn.

HELD: "5. … it is clear … that the application for permission for judicial review was totally without any merit.

"6. The trial was marred by an excessive number of technical points being raised on Mr Hassani's behalf. There were complaints about disclosure. There were attempts to lengthen the trial without advance notice being given. The Applicant's solicitors had confirmed in writing that they were 'trial ready'. [Counsel for the appellant] claims that he made an application for an adjournment of the hearing. [The district judge in the court below] has stated that he has no memory and no note of such an application. The notes of the legal advisor present contain no record of such an application. There was an application to exclude evidence under section 78 of the Police and Criminal Evidence Act 1984 on the ground that the evidence had not been seen by the defence, and thus a defence expert had not been fully instructed.

"7. … [The MG DD/A form] had been completed at the police station. The officer in the case … had properly completed it. He brought a copy to the court. [Counsel for the appellant] objected to the use of the copy as a breach of the 'best evidence' rule. The officer gave evidence that the relevant equipment was in proper working order and that the statutory requirement of two successive samples of breath had been taken. The lower reading was 57 micrograms per 100 millilitres of breath. … Mr Hassani never claimed that he had not been drinking; he never claimed that he was not the driver; … he never gave evidence.

"8. Not only was every imaginable point taken below, but [counsel for the appellant] settled grounds of appeal with seven grounds. Upon a reading of the papers, it appears to me that they are, and were, all without foundation.

"9. The criminal law is not a game to be played in the hope of a lucky outcome, a game to be played as long and in as involved a fashion as the paying client is able or prepared to afford.

"10. [The district judge] practised firm case management in this case. He was absolutely right to do so. Other courts faced with this kind of approach must do the same, whether the court is constituted by a professional district judge or by lay magistrates. Courts must consider the Criminal Procedure Rules, which are there to be employed actively so as to preclude game-playing and ensure that the courts only have to address real issues with some substance.

"11. … Time wasting, extension of hearings and taking hopeless points in the hope of wearing down an opponent or the court are neither proper nor legitimate ways in which to conduct a case, for a party or for a party's lawyers. Courts must be aware of such behaviour and employ firm case management to prevent it. …

"13. Critical rules affecting all parties … are rules 3.2, 3.3 and 3.11. …

"14. In the absence of some specific evidence which indicates that there is a problem with the Intoximeter EC/IR machine … extensive exploration of technicalities will normally be a waste of time.

"15. It is perfectly open to a court to ask if a defendant intends to give evidence to the effect that he or she had not been drinking or had drunk so little that the excess alcohol reading cannot properly be explained. If the answer is no, then the court can properly question what may be the evidential basis for a challenge to the reading produced by the testing equipment, provided the proper procedures have been followed.

"16. Lawyers advising defendants on the conduct of such a case as this should routinely remind clients that these cases are criminal proceedings, that their evidence will be given on oath or following affirmation, and that lying in such evidence will be perjury.

"17. On 24 June 2016, Senior District Judge Riddle, as he then was, gave a decision in *R v Cipriani*. He was sitting in the Westminster Magistrates' Court on 24 June 2016. It was a case of a similar nature. His written judgment deals authoritatively with many aspects of such litigation as this and will be helpful for those addressing such cases. [Passages from that decision are annexed to the judgment, to be read in conjunction with this ruling; see page 276.]

"18. This judgment is an intentional reminder to criminal courts that active case management using the Criminal Procedure Rules is their duty. Increased rigour and firmness is needed. This judgment can be cited pursuant to the Practice Direction (Citation of Authorities) [2001] 1 WLR 1001. Counsel and solicitors acting in motoring cases, for the prosecution or defence, should cite this judgment when appropriate. Indeed it will be the professional obligation of those with the conduct of such cases, to cite this judgment when issues of adjournment or case management arise. Likewise, legal advisers to magistrates should draw this judgment to the attention of the Court and the parties when applications arise. I direct that a copy of this judgment and the annex be sent to [counsel for the appellant] of counsel, for his attention and future citation.

"19. This application having been withdrawn, permission to appeal is refused."

3. CALIBRATION

See also the cases in Chapter 1 under the heading "Breath Analysis Device Unreliable, Unavailable, or Not Practicable to Use", page 34, and in Chapter 7 under the heading "Oral Evidence", page 402, for cases on the admissibility of oral evidence of calibration; Waite v Smith, page 37 – where a calibration check is outside the manufacturer's specified range, the device is unreliable; Sneyd v DPP, page 461, where unchallenged oral evidence was sufficient to establish the calibration and reliability of the device; Hasler v DPP, page 338, where the printout was not adduced and there was no oral evidence of calibration; and Leeson v Haringey JJ and DPP, page 339, where failure to produce the printout to prove calibration was simply an oversight.

R v Kingston upon Thames JJ ex p Khanna

[1986] RTR 364, 6 November 1985, QBD (DC)

Where the calibration check showed the breath analysis device to be unreliable but this was not noticed until after the defendant had been convicted, an order of certiorari was available to quash the conviction.

A motorist had been charged with driving with excess alcohol, contrary to s 6(1)(a), Road Traffic Act 1972 as substituted by s 25 and Sch 8, Transport Act 1981. He had provided specimens of breath for analysis and the lower reading was 81 µg alcohol in 100 ml breath. The calibration check on the breath analysis device had gone beyond the limits of tolerance, registering "38 high" against the maximum reliability figure of 37.9, rendering the device unreliable, but neither the motorist nor the police officer conducting the analysis realised that at the time. The motorist's solicitor was told by the police, on the day of the hearing in the magistrates' court, that the device had been in order; the solicitor advised the motorist to plead guilty; he did so and was sentenced. The printout had not been before the court and the calibration checks had not been mentioned by the prosecutor. The motorist later discovered that the device had been unreliable and appealed to the Crown Court; that court found his plea equivocal and remitted the case to the justices for rehearing. The justices then declined to hear the matter further, holding themselves to be *functus officio*. The applicant applied, by way of judicial review, for an order of *certiorari* quashing the conviction.

QUESTION(S) FOR THE COURT: Whether there had been a breach of natural justice.

HELD: "… there was clearly no error … on the part of the tribunal … but there was … a gross irregularity in the proceedings stemming from the very initiation of them, the commencement of which, as the prosecution is only too anxious to concede, was unjustifiable and indefensible. True it is that the printout was in the hands of the applicant and expert assistance could have enabled him to contest the admissibility of the only evidence against him, namely the analysis … the overwhelming wrong here … was the bringing of a prosecution of an offence in respect of which there was simply no evidence … the ambit of *certiorari* does exist so as to enable this court to exercise its supervisory role in circumstances such as this."

Application granted; conviction quashed.

R v Ealing JJ ex p Wheeler

Unreported, CO/1713/85, 12 May 1986, QBD (DC)

The magistrates were entitled to find that the breath analysis device was working correctly despite evidence of data corruption within the 2 months spanning the date in question.

A motorist had been charged with driving with excess alcohol, contrary to s 6(1)(a), Road Traffic Act 1972 as substituted by s 25 and Sch 8, Transport Act

1981. The breath analysis device had produced a lower reading of 49 µg alcohol in 100 ml breath; there was nothing to suggest that the machine was not operating correctly; it self-calibrated normally. At the hearing, the motorist adduced expert evidence that, *inter alia*, the test carried out by the device before it analysed the motorist's breath checked only certain parts of the mechanism; he could not give a definitive answer as to the effects of a data corruption which had occurred within the 2 months spanning the date in question; and that, since a data corruption had occurred, he could not rule out the possibility that this had affected the accuracy of the machine. On cross-examination, the expert said, *inter alia*, that he could not claim expert knowledge of the internal workings of the machine; that the printouts showed no evidence of malfunction on the day in question; and that the reading could not be reconciled with the applicant's claim to have consumed only 2 pints of lager.

The magistrates found that the device had been working correctly on the evening in question and convicted. The motorist applied to them to state a case; they refused. The motorist sought an order of *mandamus* requiring the magistrates to state a case.

HELD: "… the magistrates … were perfectly entitled to reach the conclusion that they did … Their basic finding was that they were satisfied that the … equipment was working correctly on the evening in question. They could find no evidence to suggest otherwise. They were of the view that the isolated evidence of data corruption at other times did not lead them to consider that the machine was defective on the evening in question."

Application dismissed.

Mayon v DPP

[1988] RTR 281, 4 February 1988, QBD (DC)

The breath analysis device must be shown to have been working properly by proof that the calibration was within proper limits.

A motorist had been charged with driving with excess alcohol, contrary to s 6(1), Road Traffic Act 1972 as substituted by s 25 and Sch 8, Transport Act 1981. The motorist provided a first specimen of breath for analysis and the reading was 75 µg alcohol in 100 ml breath; he breathed into the machine a second time and it registered "abort". The device was accidentally unplugged before it could perform its calibration check and produce a printout. A second cycle of tests was begun; the first specimen produced a reading of 74, and the machine aborted on the second specimen; it provided a printout relating to this second cycle.

The justices found that the motorist had provided two valid specimens of breath and convicted. The motorist appealed.

QUESTION(S) FOR THE COURT: Whether, upon the findings of fact, the justices came to a correct determination and decision in point of law.

HELD: "… It may perhaps be assumed that at the beginning of the first cycle the machine showed that it was calibrating itself properly, though the case stated does not say so. What we do know is that it did not calibrate itself at all at the end of the first cycle because somebody pulled the plug out. As to the second cycle, there is no evidence in the case stated as to whether the machine calibrated itself correctly either at the beginning or at the end of that cycle. Such evidence could have been given, if it were recorded on the printout, by the production of the printout, or … by oral evidence … the pre-condition that the machine must be proved to have been working properly by proof that the calibration was within proper limits is not shown by this case stated to be satisfied."

Appeal allowed.

DPP v Parkin

[1989] Crim LR 379, 24 November 1988, QBD (DC)

It is not necessary to prove the purging of the breath analysis device as long as the calibration is proved.

A motorist had been charged with driving with excess alcohol, contrary to s 6(1)(a), Road Traffic Act 1972 as substituted by s 25 and Sch 8, Transport Act 1981. The breath testing procedure had been carried out normally and certain figures logged, but the printout had been lost. At the hearing, the officer who had conducted the testing gave oral evidence of the positive results and of the calibration of the Intoximeter, but not of the purging process of the machine.

At the close of the prosecution case, the defence submitted that there was no case to answer on the basis of the absence of a printout and of other full and accurate evidence of the complete mechanical process conducted by the device, particularly the purging exercises; and the results of calculations given orally were either impermissible and/or insufficiently reliable.

The justices accepted the submission and dismissed the charge. The prosecutor appealed.

QUESTION(S) FOR THE COURT: Whether the absence of the printout, and of oral or other evidence of the purging processes, is such that a court cannot be satisfied that the Intoximeter was a reliable device within the meaning of s 8(1)(a) and (3), Road Traffic Act 1972.

HELD: "… The phrase 'a reliable device' is taken from section 8(3), which is not directly in point …

"It is now plain that oral evidence may be given in lieu of the printout.

"[After reviewing the authorities] … in none of the cases … is it requisite that the purging process be demonstrated. What is, however, required is evidence of the calibration. That evidence was here given. Once that evidence is given, the device … is to be regarded as a reliable device unless there is some evidence of malfunction … It may be added that the calibration figures themselves may be able to show that the machine was purging itself properly … the justices were wrong to find that there was no case to answer."

Appeal allowed.

DPP v Deveney

Unreported, CO-467-94, 28 June 1994, QBD (DC)

Where a defendant is prosecuted for failing to provide breath specimens for analysis it is not necessary to prove that the breath analysis device was calibrated.

A motorist had been charged with failing without reasonable excuse to provide specimens of breath for analysis. He had refused to provide a specimen when stopped by police; he was arrested and, at the police station, refused to provide specimens for analysis. The breath analysis device was calibrated some time after the refusal, and found to be in working order.

At the hearing, the defendant submitted there was no case to answer, on the grounds that the prosecutor must show that at the time of the requirement of the specimen the breath analysis device was working properly; and that since the device was calibrated 2 hours after the refusal there was no evidence that the machine was reliable. The magistrates accepted that submission and dismissed the case. The prosecutor appealed.

QUESTION(S) FOR THE COURT: (i) Whether the magistrates were correct in ruling that the prosecution must adduce evidence that there was available at the time of the requirement to provide the specimen a properly calibrated device. (ii) Whether on the facts found the magistrates were correct in ruling that the respondent had no case to answer.

HELD: "… in a case of this kind where there has been refusal of breath there is no need for the machine to be calibrated at all because the machine has simply not come into play. In any event, as a belt and braces exercise, in this case the machine was calibrated and was found to be in order … ."

The answers to both questions were "no". Appeal allowed.

Prince v CPS

[1996] Crim LR 343, 26 July 1995, QBD (DC)

The requirement to prove the calibration of the breath analysis device does not arise where the prosecution is based on a blood specimen.

A motorist had been charged with driving with excess alcohol in blood, contrary to s 5(1)(a), Road Traffic Act 1988. The lower of two breath analyses was 47 µg alcohol in 100 ml breath. The officer administering the procedure therefore offered the motorist the option, under s 8(2), Road Traffic Act 1988 (lower breath reading no more than 50 µg alcohol in 100 ml breath – now repealed; see page v), of replacing the breath specimen with an alternative specimen. The motorist opted to provide a blood specimen, which was duly taken and analysis revealed 91 mg alcohol in 100 ml blood.

The magistrates convicted the motorist on the basis of the blood analysis. He appealed.

HELD: "… the requirement to prove the proper calibration of the Intoximeter does not arise in a case where the prosecution rely not on the specimen of breath but upon a specimen of blood … if the driver elects to provide blood and does so the specimen of breath ceases to have any probative value in proving the offence of driving with excess alcohol.

"… The positive specimen of breath was no more than the prerequisite for the supply of a specimen of blood … ."

Appeal dismissed.

DPP v Schon

Unreported, CO/481/97, 27 June 1997, QBD (DC)

Evidence of calibration is evidence of reliability. Where, because the breath analysis device used GMT and it was BST, the printout showed the date as 6 July but it was in fact 7 July, but the officer had noted on a certificate under s 69, Police and Criminal Evidence Act 1984, that it was 6/7 July, the printout was admissible.

A motorist had been charged with driving with excess alcohol, contrary to s 5(1)(a), Road Traffic Act 1988. Breath analysis revealed 68 µg alcohol in 100 ml breath. The printout showed the times of the two tests as 23.27 and 23.31 Greenwich Mean Time on 6 July; it was in fact British Summer Time. A certificate under s 69, Police and Criminal Evidence Act 1984 (since repealed), signed by the sergeant who had administered the procedure, referred to the "test record dated 7/7" and was annotated at the end, "6/7 GMT".

The magistrates dismissed the charge. The prosecutor appealed.

QUESTION(S) FOR THE COURT: (2) Whether the justices were right, where the operator of the breath analysis device had given evidence as to the correct calibration thereof to find that they were not satisfied beyond reasonable doubt that the device was operating properly. (3) Whether the justices were right, where the printout recorded the date as 6 July1995 and times in Greenwich Mean Time, to find that the certificate under s 69, which covered an automatically produced test record dated 7 July 1995, was not proved to their satisfaction to certify the said printout.

HELD: "[On (2), the sergeant] gave evidence as to the correct calibration of the machine … There was no evidence before the Magistrates that it was not operating correctly … In those circumstances, the calibration evidence was conclusive evidence that it was operating correctly …

"[On (3)] The test record referred to … was dated 6th, but the entry '6/7 GMT' … clearly identifies it as being the document, at least in the absence of any evidence suggesting that there was any other reading on 7th … the certificate clearly did identify the document."

The answer to question (2) was "not on the facts of this case where there was no evidence to set in the scales against the evidence that the machine itself was self-calibrating correctly and within permitted tolerance and the first and second readings were exactly the same"; the answer to question (3) was "no". Appeal allowed.

Dunwoodie v DPP

Unreported, CO/442/98, 23 March 1998, QBD (DC)

Where a police officer gave evidence that he was a trained operator of the breath analysis device and had complied with the procedure and completed the paperwork, that was capable of giving rise to the inference that the device had correctly self-calibrated.

A motorist had been convicted by magistrates of driving with excess alcohol, contrary to s 5(1)(a), Road Traffic Act 1988, and appealed to the Crown Court.

At the Crown Court, the printout was not produced in evidence; the court was not told what the calibration figures were. The motorist argued that there was no evidence that the breath analysis device had correctly self-calibrated. The court found that the officer who performed the procedure was a fully trained Intoximeter operator and that he complied with the procedures and completed the necessary paperwork; and that the breath analysis device had correctly self-calibrated.

The Crown Court dismissed the appeal; the motorist appealed further.

QUESTION(S) FOR THE COURT: Whether a reasonable bench properly directing themselves could have held that there was any evidence of correct calibration.

HELD: "… The question … is one of construction. The officer having said that he was fully trained in Intoximeter procedures as an Intoximeter operator, was it open to the Court properly to conclude that, when he said that he had gone through the Intoximeter process, complied with the Intoximeter procedures properly, and completed the necessary paperwork, that embraced checking that the calibration was correct?

"For my part, I have no doubt that it was proper so to conclude. It would clearly have been preferable …, in order to avoid matters of this kind troubling this Court, had the officer been specifically asked: 'Was the calibration working properly'? However, I have no doubt that that which the officer did say was capable properly of giving rise to the inference which the Crown Court drew … ."

Appeal dismissed.

Derham v DPP

Unreported, CO/4122/95, 19 May 1998, QBD (DC)

Where the printout was before the court and no point was taken as to calibration, the matter could not later be raised.

A motorist had been charged with driving with excess alcohol, contrary to s 5(1)(a), Road Traffic Act 1988. Breath analysis had shown 64 µg alcohol in 100 ml breath.

At the hearing, the motorist argued, *inter alia*, that the breath analysis device had not been working properly because, on the uncontradicted evidence of the sergeant who conducted the procedure, the time recorded by the device was accurate only to plus or minus 4 minutes; and that the device was not therefore an approved and reliable device for the purposes of s 7, Road Traffic Act 1988. The justices convicted the motorist, who appealed.

QUESTION(S) FOR THE COURT (INTER ALIA): Whether a reasonable bench properly directing themselves could have held on the evidence that the machine used in this case was an approved and reliable device.

HELD: "To that question I would answer 'Yes'. The only basis upon which it is now suggested that any other answer could be given is that there was no evidence before the lower court that the machine was properly calibrated. The position, as clearly explained by Glidewell LJ in *Mayon v DPP* [see page 283] is that if oral evidence is given then it is necessary for the witness to establish that the machine has been properly calibrated, but that if the prosecution are in a position to rely on a printout, and that printout contains all the evidence it should, then such oral evidence is not called for.

"The plain fact in this case is that no point was raised before the justices as to … calibration … for the very obvious reason that the printout was before the justices and no point was taken that it did not contain the information it should relating not only to the readings of breath, but to the purges of the machine and to its two calibrations … ."

Appeal dismissed.

Melia v DPP

Unreported, CO/1492/98, 5 June 1998, QBD (DC)

Where the printout showed calibration checks of 32 to 37, against correct calibration readings of 33 to 36, it was not irrational for the justices to find the device reliable.

A motorist had been charged with driving with excess alcohol. The breath analysis procedure had been conducted in the usual way, and the officer who conducted the procedure gave evidence. In cross-examination, she said that to be correct the calibration checks would be 33 to 36; the printout showed 32 to 37.

The magistrates found, *inter alia*, that they were entitled to conclude the device was dependable. They convicted the motorist, who appealed.

QUESTION(S) FOR THE COURT: (b) Whether there was any evidence on which a reasonable bench properly directing themselves could have held the Intoximeter to be reliable and its results admissible in evidence. (c) Whether the magistrates were right in law to convict.

HELD: "… it is submitted that having heard evidence that the calibration reading was 32 to 37 and that the correct reading would be 33 to 36, it was irrational for the Justices to conclude that the Intoximeter was unreliable … Although the point had not been argued, the court, of course, found the Intoximeter to be dependable. There is insufficient material in the stated case for this court to conclude that the evidence about the calibration checks makes this finding irrational and in any event it is now far too late to take this point."

Appeal dismissed.

Gibson v DPP

[2001] EWHC Admin 131, 20 February 2001, QBD (DC)

Where the printout was before the court, the court had evidence of calibration and was entitled to conclude that the breath analysis device was working correctly. Where the court permitted cross-examination on the reliability of breath analysis devices in general, but was satisfied that the device in question was working correctly, there was no error, even if art 6, European Convention on Human Rights applied.

A motorist had been convicted of driving with excess alcohol in breath, contrary to s 5(1)(a), Road Traffic Act 1988 and appealed to the Crown Court. He challenged the reliability of the breath analysis device, claiming that hydrocarbons naturally occurring in the body could adversely affect the reading. A forensic officer from the manufacturers of the device gave evidence on reliability; he had not examined the machine in question, although he had examined the service records and the printout in the case. The Crown Court erroneously understood the motorist to have told the police that he believed he was over the limit; in fact he had said the opposite.

The Crown Court dismissed the appeal; the motorist appealed further.

QUESTION(S) FOR THE COURT: (1) Was there any admissible evidence on which a reasonable bench, properly directing themselves, could have held that the defendant's breath alcohol concentration exceeded the legal limit? (2) Was there any admissible evidence upon which a reasonable bench, properly directing themselves, could have held that the breathalyser had correctly calibrated itself? (3) Was the court right not to consider the European Convention on Human Rights in reaching its decision? (4) Did the court's mistake over what the appellant said to the Intoximeter operator in any way impeach or undermine the court's decision to dismiss the appeal?

HELD: "14. … The material on which the expert witness … based his opinion was placed before him without objection by [counsel for the appellant]. If it was thought that that material … was inadmissible, [counsel] ought to have taken a point as to admissibility when the Crown invited [the witness] to look at the material and express a view upon it. In any event, … [the witness] relied on the printout which the defendant had signed and which the Justices found the defendant had signed … There was … evidence of correct calibration before the court, and the Justices were entitled to conclude … that the breathalyser was working correctly …

"16. [The human rights point] has to be understood in the light of the decisions in this court, of which the *DPP v Charles* [1996] RTR 247] is one, that, generally speaking, a defendant has no right to cross-examine ... about the reliability of machines of the type in question in cases such as this. But ... the Crown Court permitted [counsel] to cross-examine generally about the unreliability of the Lion Intoximeter 3000 in general ... Having considered all the evidence, the Crown Court found that the breathalyser was working correctly. Therefore, on the facts found, and even assuming that the provisions of Article 6 of the Convention on Human Rights applied, it cannot be said that the Crown Court in any way fell into error. ...

"17. As to the ... misapprehension on the part of the court as to what the appellant said to the police about his condition, ... the Crown Court was fully entitled to take the view that their error was not a fundamental feature of their final decision ... In any event, the opinion of the appellant as to what he considered his alcohol level to be was irrelevant."

The answer to questions (1), (2) and (3) was "yes"; the answer to question (4) was "no". Appeal dismissed.

Mercer v DPP

[2003] EWHC 255 (Admin), [2004] RTR 8, 3 February 2003, QBD (Admin)

Where two cycles were necessary to analyse two breath specimens, then as long as the Lion Intoxilyser was operating in conformity with its operating procedures, it mattered not that it did not self-calibrate when it terminated the first cycle on detecting an interfering substance.

A motorist had been charged with driving with excess alcohol, contrary to s 5(1)(a), Road Traffic Act 1988. He had been arrested; at the police station; the breath analysis procedure was conducted using a Lion Intoxilyser 6000. On analysing the second specimen, the instrument displayed the words "interfering substance" and recorded "unsatisfactory specimen 2". The officer conducting the procedure took the view that the machine was not defective but that there had been something wrong with the second specimen. He decided to conduct the breath analysis again and the second cycle was carried out satisfactorily. Thus three specimens were provided. It was accepted that if the Lion Intoxilyser detects an interfering substance it ceases the cycle without recalibrating itself; the Lion Intoximeter 3000 (the forerunner of the Lion Intoxilyser 6000) would complete the cycle and recalibrate.

The defendant was prosecuted on the basis of the lower of the first reading from the first cycle and the first reading from the second cycle (52 μg and 53 μg alcohol per 100 ml breath). He argued that, to establish two valid readings, the prosecution was required to prove that the readings were taken in a cycle in which the instrument self-calibrated before the first and after the second reading; it had self-calibrated before the first reading, at the commencement of the cycle before the second reading and after the third reading at the conclusion of the second cycle, but not after the first reading.

The justices rejected the argument and convicted the defendant. He appealed.

QUESTION(S) FOR THE COURT: Whether the justices were correct to admit the evidence of the first two readings notwithstanding that no calibration took place at the end of the first cycle producing the first reading.

HELD: "34. [After reviewing the authorities] all of which reinforce the principle stated … in *Creech* [*Chief Constable of Avon & Somerset v Creech*, page 111] that 'the ascertainment by means of an approved device of the proportion of alcohol in a specimen must be performed in conformity with the operating procedures of the device in question'. …

"37. [The prosecutor] submits that the operating procedures … were followed satisfactorily; the instrument was simply not designed to recalibrate after an interfering substance result. In this regard the facts are indistinguishable, he submits, from *Creech*, in which the instrument did not recalibrate because the cycle simply ran out of time. Here, that result was produced by the second specimen of breath introduced to the instrument during the first cycle.

"38. [The prosecutor] submits that that did not imply that the reading from the first specimen of the first cycle was unreliable or invalid. The instrument had only moments before calibrated itself satisfactorily. As to the second cycle, the instrument calibrated before the first specimen and after the second. Since it was not necessary for both specimens to be taken during the same cycle, provided that the instrument was functioning properly at the time both were recorded, the requirements of the statute were, he submitted, met.

"39. I accept the submissions made on behalf of the prosecutor … the test described … in *Creech* was in this case met on the evidence and upon the findings made by the justices … the results from both specimens relied upon by the prosecutor in the court below were valid and admissible."

Appeal dismissed.

Haggis v DPP

[2003] EWHC 2481 (Admin), [2004] 2 All ER 382, 7 October 2003, QBD (DC)

The fact that the officer did not know the calibration limits for the breath analysis device could not be taken to mean that she was not properly trained or that the device was not working properly.

A motorist had been charged with driving with excess alcohol, contrary to s 5(1)(a), Road Traffic Act 1988. He had given a positive roadside breath test and was arrested. At the police station, breath analysis revealed 43 μg alcohol in 100 ml breath.

At the trial, it was argued that the officer who conducted the procedure was not properly trained since she did not know the calibration limits of the breath analysis device, and that the court could not be satisfied that the machine was operating properly and that its analysis was accurate. The deputy district judge rejected those arguments and convicted the defendant. He appealed.

QUESTION(S) FOR THE COURT: (1) Since the officer did not know the correct calibration limits for the machine, whether a reasonable bench properly directing themselves could have been satisfied on the criminal burden of proof that the machine was operating properly and that its analysis was accurate; (2) in view of the officer's evidence that she was a trained operator of the device in question, whether it was *Wednesbury* unreasonable to hold that she was a trained operator, i.e. a person who understood the process of calibration and recognised that unless the result of that process lies within accepted limits, the machine is not calibrating as it should and is therefore reliable.

HELD: "[On (2)] 10. … Save for the fact that [the officer] did not know the correct calibration limits of the machine, there is nothing to indicate that there was any other challenge to her knowledge and expertise. There was no challenge to her evidence that she was a trained operator … nor to the details that she gave of her training. It was not, for example, suggested that her training had been inadequate. She knew that the machine was self-calibrating. She stated that it was working properly, that it produced a print out with appropriate readings … It was not unreasonable for [the district judge] to conclude that [the officer] was a trained operator. …

"[On (1), distinguishing *Mayon v DPP*, page 283] 13. There was nothing to gainsay [the officer's evidence that the machine] was 'working properly'. …

"14. … beyond eliciting that [the officer] did not know the correct calibration limits of the machine, there was no attempt to challenge her evidence that the machine was working properly, that it had produced a printout and that the readings appeared … to be appropriate … ."

The answer to question (1) was "yes"; the answer to question (2) was "no". Appeal dismissed.

4. THE DATE AND TIME

See also Kneale v DPP, page 56 – relying on an inspector's written note that if the clock on the device was more than one minute wrong was reasonable cause to believe that the device was unreliable; and Mace v Dean, page 404 – oral evidence is admissible to explain an apparent discrepancy in the dates on the printout.

Fawcett v Gasparics

[1986] RTR 375, [1987] Crim LR 53, 24 June 1986, QBD (DC)

The fact that the printout contained an error in the day of the week might go to the weight to be given to it, but does not render the printout inadmissible in evidence.

A motorist had been charged with driving with excess alcohol, contrary to s 6(1)(a), Road Traffic Act 1972 as substituted by s 25 and Sch 8, Transport Act 1981. Breath specimens produced positive readings, but the printout showed the date as "Sat Oct 14, 1984"; in fact 14 October was a Sunday. The police officer gave evidence that the Intoximeter had correctly self-calibrated, but the magistrate accepted the motorist's contention that the machine had been unreliable and dismissed the charge.

The prosecutor appealed.

QUESTION(S) FOR THE COURT: Whether the magistrate was "right to reject, as evidence of the proportion of alcohol in the defendant's specimen of breath, the statement automatically produced by the Lion Intoximeter 3000, on the grounds that the statement contained an error about the day or date".

HELD: "... while the failure of the machine to give the correct combination of day of week and date may go to the weight or the value to be placed upon that which is set out in the printout – and in particular as to the proof and identification of the occasions when the samples were taken – such an error cannot undermine the admissibility in evidence of the printout ...

"... provided the machine functions and produces that which purports to be a statement together with a certificate it should be ... admitted, subject to any criticism or argument which may be advanced as to the weight to be attached to it ...

"It is of prime significance ... that the section itself allows the admission of a document 'purporting' to be a statement relating to a specimen provided by the accused at the date and time shown in the statement. The actual date, 14 October, was correct. The wrong day of the week was 'attributed' to that numerical date. But any ambiguity, and there was indeed such ambiguity here, could be and was remedied by the evidence of the constable."

Appeal allowed.

Parker v DPP

[1993] RTR 283, 16 March 1992, QBD (DC)

Where the device timed readings in GMT even though BST was in operation, the printout was reliable; the Secretary of State had not acted ultra vires in approving the device. See also DPP v Schon, page 286, again concerning a device which registered time in GMT only.

A motorist had been convicted of driving with excess alcohol, contrary to s 6(1), Road Traffic Act 1972 as substituted by s 25 and Sch 8, Transport Act 1981. Two specimens of breath had been analysed and were over the limit. Although it was British Summer Time, the Intoximeter timed the readings according to Greenwich Mean Time, which was also shown on the printout. The motorist appealed.

QUESTION(S) FOR THE COURT (INTER ALIA): Whether the times expressed as Greenwich Mean Time on the printout accorded with the times given as British Summer Time by the prosecutor; and whether the printout was reliable.

HELD: "The document itself makes it perfectly plain that it is timed according to Greenwich mean time … The justices were very well aware that it was in fact summer time at the material time and that, therefore, the times recorded on the document … had to be advanced one hour to comply with summer time … I can see nothing wrong with that at all …

"[On the argument that the Secretary of State had acted *ultra vires* in approving the Intoximeter for the purposes of the Road Traffic Act because it recorded time according to Greenwich Mean Time instead of British Summer Time] … I cannot accept the submission for one moment … It is quite plain that a document can, on its face, specify the time and date upon which it is made. If it does so with clarity and accuracy in that respect, I … can see nothing wrong with it whatsoever."

Appeal dismissed.

DPP v McKeown, DPP v Jones (Christopher)

[1997] 1 WLR 295, [1997] 1 All ER 737, [1997] 1 Cr App R 155, [1997] RTR 162, [1995] Crim LR 69, 20 February 1997, HL

The fact that the printout showed the wrong time does not take the breath analysis device outside its approval, nor does it amount to a reasonable excuse for failing to provide breath specimens for analysis. The case also concerned s 69, Police and Criminal Evidence Act 1984, now repealed.

Ms McKeown had been convicted of driving with excess alcohol, contrary to s 5(1)(a), Road Traffic Act 1988; Mr Jones had been convicted of failing without reasonable excuse to provide two specimens of breath for analysis, contrary to s 7(6), Road Traffic Act 1988. In both cases, the convictions had been based on printouts from the same breath analysis device, which, at the material times, showed the wrong time.

The convictions had been quashed on appeal to the Divisional Court. The prosecutor appealed further.

CERTIFIED QUESTION: "… (3) Is a Lion Intoximeter 3000 device to be regarded as no longer approved and reliable for the purposes of prosecution under section 5(1)(a) of the Road Traffic Act 1988 when it is not accurately recording the time of day even though the evidence shows that in all other respects it is operating satisfactorily?"

HELD: "… section 7(1) [Road Traffic Act 1988] says only that a constable may require a person under investigation to 'provide two specimens of breath for analysis by means of a device approved by the Secretary of State'. There is nothing about the approved device having to have an accurate clock. The Lion Intoximeter was an approved type of device and it seems to me impossible to argue that, by reason of the inaccuracy of its clock, the device … could no longer be described as a Lion Intoximeter … ."

"[On the argument that the inaccuracy of the clock was a reasonable excuse] The difficulty about this argument is that Mr Jones never claimed to have the slightest notion that there was anything wrong with the time on the clock … I do not say that an excuse must be something which the accused had in mind when he failed or refused to provide the specimen … There must have been some causal connection between the excuse and the failure to provide … even if Mr Jones had noticed that the clock was slow, I do not think that this would have been an excuse."

Appeals allowed.

DPP v Bateson

Unreported, CO/470/98, 3 June 1998, QBD (DC)

It did not matter whether or not the breath analysis device was accurately recording the time, or whether its clock had been accurately set. On the facts of this case, there was nothing to suggest data corruption.

A motorist had been charged with driving with excess alcohol. He had been stopped by police. His breath smelt of alcohol. He was arrested and taken to the police station, where breath analysis showed that he was over the prescribed limit. According to the officer who conducted the procedure, and according to the form she completed at the time, she requested two specimens of breath at 2.17 British Summer Time; the first test was performed at 2.18 and the second at 2.20. In evidence the officer said her watch was accurate and confirmed that the readings on the screen were the same as the readings on the printout from the breath analysis device. The printout showed that the first calibration check took place at 1.15 Greenwich Mean Time; that at 1.16 a purge took place; that the two tests took place at 1.18 and 1.20 Greenwich Mean Time; and that at 1.21 a further calibration check confirmed that the device was operating within acceptable limits. The officer signed a certificate as to the accuracy of the device. There was no evidence that the clock in the breath analysis device was either accurate or inaccurate.

The defendant called expert evidence to the effect that there could be only three explanations for the discrepancy in the timings: the officer's watch was wrong; the clock in the breath analysis device was wrong; or that data corruption had occurred. The magistrate was of the opinion that the first and second possibilities were more probable, but had no assistance from the Crown to overcome the doubt raised by the third possibility. He acquitted the defendant. The prosecutor appealed.

QUESTION(S) FOR THE COURT: Whether there was any or sufficient evidence of data corruption such that a reasonable doubt was cast upon the reliability of the Lion Intoximeter.

HELD: "[After referring to *DPP v McKeown*, above] It did not matter whether the Intoximeter clock was accurately recording the time or whether the Intoximeter clock had been accurately set …

"… Two calibration tests were conducted which showed that the Intoximeter, in so far as it was analysing, storing and reproducing the results of the analysis, was working properly. There were two readings of the specimens of breath provided by the Respondent and they gave figures which were closely related, namely 84 and 89. As the officer confirmed, the readings on the screen were the same as the readings on the printout. If data corruption had occurred it would be a most extraordinary coincidence that the Intoximeter was still able to produce the internally consistent print-out which it produced."

The answer to the question was "no". Appeal allowed.

5. MOBILE TELEPHONES AND RADIOS

See also Ivic v DPP, page 664 – the fact that a police radio was on in the breath analysis room did not render the breath analysis inadmissible.

Scheiner v DPP

[2006] EWHC 1516 (Admin), 13 June 2006, QBD (DC)

The fact that a mobile telephone may have been in the room and switched on when the breath analysis was carried out does not render the analysis inadmissible or unreliable.

A motorist had been charged with driving with excess alcohol, contrary to s 5(1)(a), Road Traffic Act 1988. He had been arrested and at the police station breath analysis revealed excess alcohol. The manufacturer's instructions for the use of the breath analysis device included the words "As a precaution all radio sets and mobile telephones in the room where the evidential breath testing instrument is in use should be switched off".*

The officer conducting the procedure gave evidence that he probably had his mobile telephone with him and that, if so, it would have been switched on. The defendant argued that the test had not therefore been conducted in accordance with the manufacturer's instructions and was not valid.

The defendant was convicted. He appealed to the Crown Court, which accepted expert evidence that there was no evidence that the result of the analysis was inaccurate; it dismissed the appeal. The motorist appealed further.

QUESTION(S) FOR THE COURT: Whether the court erred in law in holding that there had been a valid breath analysis when the operator testified that he probably had his mobile telephone with him during the carrying out of the analysis, in which case it would have been switched on.

HELD: "9. [Quoting from *DPP v Carey*, page 72] … 'provided that [the officer] acts *bona fide* in the conduct of the test and in the evaluation of its result, it matters not that it may subsequently be proved … that through inadvertence or ignorance of some relevant circumstances the instructions were not fully complied with'.

"10. [Quoting from *Cracknell v Willis*, page 270], 'In the case of a breath specimen, there is of course a presumption that the machine is reliable. But if that presumption is challenged by relevant evidence, the magistrates will have to be satisfied that the machine has provided a reading upon which they can rely before making the assumption'.

"11. The Crown Court was satisfied that the device … provided a reading upon which it could rely … Having so found, it was right – and indeed … bound – to reject the appeal … there was no evidence that the operation of the device was impaired by the possibility that the operator's mobile telephone was switched on and was with him.

"12. … Evidence is required at least to raise the realistic possibility that the device … may have malfunctioned and produced a false reading. Assertions based merely on an alleged failure to comply with manufacturer's recommendations do not amount to such evidence."

The answer to the question was "no". Appeal dismissed.

* *Editor's note: It is understood that these instructions in fact appear on the DD form, not the manufacturer's instructions.*

6. MOUTH ALCOHOL

See also DPP v Memery [2002] EWHC 1720, [2003] RTR 18, based on the "statutory option" under 8(2), Road Traffic Act 1988 (now repealed; see page v) – the fact that the device did not detect mouth alcohol did not make it unreliable; Robertson (Eric) v DPP, page 206 – the fact that the device did not detect mouth alcohol did not take it outside the scope of the approval order; Zafar v DPP, page 439 and Woolfe v DPP, page 440, both concerning the possibility of breath specimens being affected by alcohol regurgitated from the stomach.

DPP v Brown; DPP v Teixeira

[2001] EWHC Admin 931, [2002] RTR 23, 16 November 2001, QBD (DC)

The fact that the breath analysis device did not detect mouth alcohol did not make it unreliable.

In both cases motorists had provided breath specimens into a breath analysis device; the results were positive and they were charged with driving with excess alcohol, contrary to s 5(1)(a), Road Traffic Act 1988. Experts had examined the devices in question and performed experiments on them, as a result of which it was argued that the machines were unreliable, their failure always to detect mouth alcohol taking them outside the relevant technical specification.

In both cases the magistrates found the device unreliable and acquitted; in *Teixeira*, the magistrates also took into account evidence of how much the motorist said he had drunk. The prosecutor appealed.

QUESTION(S) FOR THE COURT: *Brown*: Whether the magistrates were entitled to find that the breath analysis device in question was defective in its material function and unreliable, and to dismiss the information.

Teixeira: (1) Whether, in all the circumstances, the magistrates were right in law to determine that the breath testing device was not functioning to the same standard as the device approved by the Home Office and therefore could not be relied upon to provide accurate evidence upon which a conviction could be based; (2) whether the magistrates were entitled to accept the defence evidence of three witnesses as to the level of alcohol consumed and on the basis of decided authority to reject the evidence of the breath specimen reading as incompatible with the defence witnesses.

HELD: *Brown*: "50. … The challenge by the defence to the technical reliability of the particular device was confined to expert evidence as to its ability to detect mouth alcohol or alcohol vapour in the dead-space of the upper respiratory tract. No other technical defect was alleged. It was not suggested that there was any link between the alleged deficiency and any wider technical deficiency. It did not follow that because the device did not meet a specification standard in one respect, it was unreliable on the facts of Mr. Brown's case. The magistrates should have asked themselves at the conclusion of the evidence (i) has the presumption that the device is reliable been challenged by relevant evidence? If no, they would convict. If yes, they should ask themselves (ii) are we satisfied that the device provided a reading upon which we can rely? If yes, they would convict, if no, they would acquit.

"… I am inclined to think … that the magistrates should have concluded that on the facts of Mr. Brown's case that the presumption was not challenged by relevant evidence [but] I would hear further submissions as to whether there should be a re-hearing."

Teixeira: "51. … The correct approach was as follows. The Intoximeter … was an approved device … There was thus a presumption of law that the device was reliable … The defence challenged the presumption. No question of mouth alcohol or alcohol vapour arose on the facts of Mr. Teixeira's case. The challenge by the defence to the technical reliability of the particular device was (as in Mr. Brown's case) confined to expert evidence as to its ability to detect mouth alcohol or alcohol vapour in the dead-space of the upper respiratory tract. No other technical defect was alleged. It was not suggested that there was any link between the alleged deficiency and any wider technical deficiency. The magistrates should have asked themselves at the conclusion of all the evidence … are we satisfied that the device provided a reading upon which we can rely? If yes, there would be a conviction; if no, an acquittal.

"The magistrates' approach … was in error … I would direct a re-hearing in Mr. Teixeira's case."

O'Sullivan v DPP

[2005] EWHC 564 (Admin), 25 February 2005, QBD (DC)

In the circumstances of this case (consistency and closeness of readings; unlikelihood of regurgitation), the court was entitled to conclude that mouth alcohol had not affected the specimen.

A motorist had been charged with driving with excess alcohol, contrary to s 5(1)(a), Road Traffic Act 1988. At the roadside, he was asked if he had consumed alcohol within the preceding 20 minutes; he answered that he had not. The roadside breath test was positive. At the police station, some 41 minutes after the roadside test, breath analysis readings were 71 and 73 µg alcohol in 100 ml breath. He was convicted and appealed to the Crown Court.

At the Crown Court, he sought to argue that the specimens of breath could have been affected by mouth alcohol. He said he suffered from indigestion, heartburn and a chesty cough but had not sought medical help for it. The court rejected the argument on the grounds that he had given a positive roadside breath test at 0.45; the closeness of the two readings meant that regurgitation would have had to have taken place to virtually the same degree at regular intervals; he had not stated in evidence that he had experienced indigestion or heartburn or reflux or regurgitation; a "Quick Test" reading at 3.55 showed 53.9 µg alcohol, which, given the average elimination rate, was consistent with the earlier readings. The motorist appealed further.

QUESTION(S) FOR THE COURT: (1) Whether it was *Wednesbury* unreasonable to have held that mouth alcohol was not the cause of the appellant's breath analysis showing that he had a level of alcohol which exceeded the prescribed limit; (2) whether the Crown Court, as a matter of law, was entitled to take account of the result of the Quick Test carried out by the Intoximeter prior to the appellant's release from custody.

HELD: "10. [The appellant] submits that the Crown Court erred in law in taking into account … the roadside breath test; the closeness of the two readings; the Quick Test results; and the appellant's evidence about his medical condition. …

"11. The device used in a roadside breath test cannot detect mouth alcohol. … the test had been given after enquiry had been made as to whether 20 minutes had elapsed since his last drink. The positive result of the test would therefore have pointed towards the appellant being over the prescribed limit without mouth alcohol having contributed to that excess. …

"12. … it was relevant as a factor, particularly since there was evidence of the enquiry as to when the last drink had been taken and an answer in the negative. It was a matter for the Crown Court to attach such weight to it as it thought proper. …

"[The prosecution's expert gave evidence that] the closeness of the readings meant that if the presence of mouth alcohol by regurgitation had occurred it would have had to have been regurgitated from his stomach into his mouth or upper respiratory tract in very similar concentration and at similar intervals prior to the provision of each specimen. Further, he would have had to have blown into the Intoximeter at a similar rate on each occasion. In his view that would be very unlikely.

"15. … the Crown Court has carefully recited the nature of the evidence given by each of the experts. It is clear that it accepted the evidence of [the prosecution's expert] as to the significance of the closeness of the readings of 71 and 73 …

"[On the Quick Test] 24. By reason of the time at which the test was conducted it could not be disputed that it had probative value, not to prove the Crown's case based upon the specimens taken at 01.26 and 01.29, but to rebut the suggestion that they were affected by mouth alcohol.

"30. … there was ample evidence upon which the Crown Court was entitled to rely which was capable of leading it to the conclusion that it was not possible that mouth alcohol had affected the specimen."

The answer to question (1) was "no"; the answer to question (2) was "yes". Appeal dismissed.

7. POSITIVE BREATH ANALYSIS FOLLOWED BY NEGATIVE SCREENING TEST

See also O'Sullivan (Sarah) v DPP, page 305 – the burden of proving the reliability of the breath analysis device is on the prosecutor; it is not for a defendant to disprove it.

Snelson v Thompson

[1985] RTR 220, 29 October 1984, QBD (DC)

Where a screening test, taken 66 minutes after positive breath analysis, was negative, the court was entitled to convict on the basis of the breath analysis.

A motorist had been convicted, under s 6(1), Road Traffic Act 1972 as substituted by s 25(3) and Sch 8, Transport Act 1981, of driving with excess alcohol. He had tested positive on a Lion Intoximeter 3000 at 1.31 am and at 1.36 am. Shortly before leaving the police station at 2.42, he was tested on a Lion Alcolmeter S-L2 screening device; that test proved negative.

The motorist adduced expert evidence on the rate of loss of alcohol in breath, contending that the inconsistent results pointed to the Intoximeter's having been defective.

The magistrates, however, accepted the Intoximeter results, finding that the S-L2 was not as accurate as the Intoximeter and that the medical evidence was not of sufficient probative value. The motorist appealed.

QUESTION(S) FOR THE COURT: Whether a reasonable bench of justices could have been satisfied beyond reasonable doubt that the Lion Intoximeter analysis was accurate and reliable.

HELD: "… the Lion Alcolmeter S-L2 is but a screening device … whereas the Lion Intoximeter 3000 … is an instrument for which the designers claim a level of precision which permits of almost no, or very little, error … not very long before the defendant blew into the Lion Intoximeter 3000, he had blown into either a Lion Alcolmeter S-L2 at the roadside or something like it … and had failed that test … In these circumstances, it is quite impossible to say that the justices were disentitled from coming to the conclusion that they could not safely rely on the Lion Intoximeter 3000."

Appeal dismissed.

Parish v CPS

[2000] RTR 143, 1 November 1999, QBD (DC)

On the facts of this case (negative screening test 12 minutes after a blood specimen was taken which transpired to be positive; expert evidence on both sides), the magistrates were wrong to refuse the defence application for an adjournment to consider the prosecution's expert evidence and for further tests to be carried out.

A motorist was taken to a police station where he provided a blood specimen. Twelve minutes later, he was tested on the Alcolmeter which showed that he was not over the limit, and he was released. Subsequent analysis of the blood specimen, however, showed not less than 100 mg alcohol in 100 ml blood and he was charged with driving with excess alcohol.

The defence provided the prosecution with reports from two experts whom the motorist intended to call. The first was to say, *inter alia*, that the type of Alcolmeter used was very accurate. The second expert (Dr Rose) had prepared a report to the effect that it was impossible for anyone to have a rate of alcohol metabolism compatible with the difference between the blood analysis and the breath test. Although at the time of the hearing the Crown Prosecution Service had been in possession of the latter report for over 6 months, it disclosed for the first time at the hearing a report from its own expert disputing Dr Rose's report and saying that the Home Office Forensic Service could carry out further tests on the point in dispute. The motorist was agreeable to undergoing such tests.

Counsel for the motorist applied for an adjournment to enable Dr Rose to consider the Crown Prosecution Service expert's report and for the further tests to be carried out. The justices refused the application because "the results of the pre-release test could not, as a matter of law, impugn the results of an analysis of a specimen of blood". They convicted the motorist. He appealed.

QUESTION(S) FOR THE COURT: (1) Whether the justices were right in law to refuse the adjournment. (2) Whether the justices were right to rule that they were bound by *Snelson v Thompson* (above) to hold that the appellant could not contradict the evidence of the analysis of alcohol in the blood specimen by the evidence of the result of a breath test on an Alcolmeter device taken 12 minutes later.

HELD: "… *Snelson v Thompson* does not say that it is impossible to contradict the findings of an Intoximeter by evidence of the kind that the Appellant sought to call in this case. It is for the Justices to consider all the evidence and to decide whether or not the defence have cast doubt upon the accuracy and reliability of the evidence relied upon by the prosecution. There is nothing in the case which says that such evidence as the Appellant sought to call in this case was inadmissible or, if admissible, should be ignored. Each case depends upon its own facts.

"In this case the Justices thought that the evidence which the appellant sought to call would be of no value and that is the basis upon which they refused the adjournment. In that I am quite clear that they were wrong. The evidence was evidence which was admissible and was evidence which they could and should have considered before deciding whether the prosecution had proved their case. In failing to allow the adjournment to enable that evidence to be called, … they erred in law."

The answers to both questions were "no". Appeal allowed.

8. THE PRINTOUT

See also the cases in Chapter 1 under the heading "Breath Analysis Device Unreliable, Unavailable, or Not Practicable to Use", page 34; and in Chapter 7 under the heading "The Printout", page 335.

Burditt v Roberts

[1986] RTR 391, [1986] Crim LR 636, 13 May 1986, QBD (DC)

Spelling mistakes on the printout did not render the breath analysis device unreliable.

A motorist had been charged with driving with excess alcohol, contrary to s 6(1)(a), Road Traffic Act 1972 as substituted by s 25 and Sch 8, Transport Act 1981. Breath analysis was positive; the procedure had been correctly carried out, but on the printout the word "Station" erroneously appeared as "Sation" and the defendant's name, which was Roger Patrick Burditt, erroneously appeared as "ROGERPBUIURDITTTT". The justices rejected an argument that the breath analysis device had been unreliable, accepted the printout as admissible, and convicted the motorist. The motorist appealed.

QUESTION(S) FOR THE COURT: Whether the justices' decision was wrong in law in that, having found as a fact that the statement produced by the Lion Intoximeter 3000 contained the word "Sation" instead of "Station", and the name of the defendant was printed as "ROGERPBUIURDITTTT": (a) the device remained reliable for the purpose of proving the proportion of alcohol in the defendant's breath; and (b) the statement produced by the device was admissible in evidence and was conclusive proof of the proportion of alcohol in the defendant's breath.

HELD: "... The justices found that the evidence as to the self-calibration and analysis were evidence of analysis and reliability. Where the machine shows that the self-calibrating exercise has properly been gone through and produced readings of alcohol, those readings, in the absence of some evidence of malfunction in the machine, are admissible ... The only evidence of malfunction is the mis-spelling and the justices state that that was produced as a result of human input. It does not go to the reliability of the machine, rather does it go to the fallibility of the operator ... the findings of the justices make it quite impossible to say that this machine was unreliable so as to render the evidence of the proportion of alcohol in the specimen inadmissible ... ."

The answers to both questions were "yes". Appeal dismissed.

Reid (Sheena) v DPP

[1999] RTR 357, 19 February 1998, QBD (DC)

The court was entitled to find that the breath analysis was accurate despite abnormalities in the printout.

A motorist had been charged with driving with excess alcohol, contrary to s 5(1)(a), Road Traffic Act 1988. At the police station she was required to provide two specimens of breath for analysis. The procedure, including the calibrations and purges of the breath analysis device, was correctly carried out and revealed excess alcohol. The sergeant administering the procedure observed that the readings displayed on the screen were the same as those on the printout. There were, however, two abnormalities on the printout: on all three, the second half of the first character and the second character in every line were omitted; and one of the printouts had the top line printed in smaller type than the rest of the printout. The sergeant's opinion was that the most likely cause was a broken printer pin.

The magistrates convicted the motorist; her appeal to the Crown Court was dismissed; she appealed further.

QUESTION(S) FOR THE COURT: Whether the court, on the evidence, was entitled to find that the results of the analysis of the appellant's breath were accurate.

HELD: "The decision of the House of Lords in *McKeown* [see page 294] has made it far more difficult for unmeritorious and unattractive appeals of this kind to succeed. ...

"... it seems clear beyond doubt that the Crown Court was entitled to conclude that the computer part of the Intoximeter was operating and functioning properly. The necessary calibration checks and purges had been properly carried out and the readings displayed on the screen after the appellant had provided specimens of breath were the same as those on the printout subsequently produced ... the Crown Court was entitled to conclude that the abnormalities in the printout were unconnected to the operation of the computer part of the Intoximeter and that the abnormalities of parts of the typeface of the printout were not related to the storage, processing and retrieval of information by the computer … ."

Appeal dismissed.

DPP v Barber (David Anthony)

(1999) 163 JP 457, 19 May 1998, QBD (DC)

The defendant should not have been acquitted because of a printer malfunction when there was evidence from the operator that the device was reliable. Expert evidence on reliability should, on the facts of this case, have been admitted.

A motorist had been charged with driving with excess alcohol, contrary to s 5(1)(a), Road Traffic Act 1988. He had been arrested, and at the police station breath analysis revealed 86 μg alcohol in 100 ml breath. The breath analysis device printed out the results in such a way that the first two characters of each line were missing, but the record of the calibration of the machine, the purges and the breath analyses were complete.

At the hearing, the motorist submitted, *inter alia*, that the device was not reliable and the evidence of the printout was inadmissible. The magistrate accepted that contention. The prosecutor sought to call as a witness the service engineer who had later examined the device, but the magistrate ruled such evidence inadmissible on the ground that he was not an expert on the workings of the computer and that his observations would not be relevant to the workings of the machine at the material time. He dismissed the charge. The prosecutor appealed.

QUESTION(S) FOR THE COURT: (1) Whether the magistrate was right to regard the breath analysis device as not working properly where the printout failed to print the first two letters on the left hand side of each column, when there was evidence from a trained operator that it was reliable. (2) Whether the magistrate was right to rule that the evidence of a service engineer who remedied a fault to the printer on 14 August 1995 was irrelevant and inadmissible as to its working on 27 July 1995. (3) Whether the magistrate was right to acquit the respondent.

HELD: "[On whether the service engineer's evidence should have been admitted] An expert is a person who is qualified by education, training or experience to express an opinion which, if based on that education, training or experience, has an authority greater than an opinion expressed by one not so qualified. While the qualifications of this witness have not been fully explored, on the face of it he was singularly well qualified to examine the machine and ascertain whether the defect in the printout was the result of a defect in the printer or whether it indicated some malfunctioning of that part of the computer which had the role of processing, storing or retrieving the information used to generate the statement tendered in evidence … There can be no rule of law that a lapse of days or weeks between first evidence of a malfunction and an inspection renders evidence derived from the inspection inadmissible or irrelevant. It may or may not affect its weight and acceptability, but that will depend on the effect of the evidence and the answers given by the witness under cross-examination …

"… The question whether the … device was not working properly … where the printout failed to print the first two letters on the left-hand side of each column of the printout when there was evidence before the court from a trained operator of such a device that it was reliable … is a question to be decided on all the evidence before the court bearing in mind the guidance given by the House of Lords in *DPP v McKeown* [see page 294] and by this court in *Reid v DPP* [see page 303] … the magistrate … was not in all the circumstances right to acquit the respondent at the stage when he did."

Appeal allowed.

9. THE BURDEN OF PROOF

O'Sullivan (Sarah) v DPP
Unreported, CO/3306/1998, 27 March 2000, QBD

On the facts of this case, documentary medical evidence of alcohol elimination rate was admissible but the court was entitled to conclude that it should not be admitted. The burden of proving the reliability of the breath analysis device is on the prosecutor; it is not for a defendant to disprove it.

A motorist had been arrested and required to provide specimens of breath for analysis. The breath analysis device appeared to be operating correctly and at 1 am produced readings of 57 μg and 56 μg alcohol in 100 ml breath. The motorist remained at the police station until her alcohol level fell to below the prescribed limit. At between 2.30 am and 2.45 am, a further specimen was analysed by the same device and produced a reading of 23 μg.

The motorist was charged with driving with excess alcohol and convicted. On appeal to the Crown Court, it was argued that the court could not be sure that the breath analysis was reliable in view of the difference between the readings, which indicated a rate of fall in alcohol level of 43 μg an hour. The defendant called expert evidence that, *inter alia*, such a rate could be found in only 1% of the population and only among heavy drinkers. She also adduced evidence that, when tested some 11 months later by the same expert, her own blood alcohol level fell at a rate of 24 μg per hour.

The prosecution adduced evidence that over 1,000 of about 100,000 drivers arrested each year had rates of decline of alcohol level similar to or higher than the one in this case, but that such a rate occurs only among heavy drinkers.

The defendant sought to introduce in evidence medical records so that her expert could say whether there was anything in them to suggest that she should have a rapid rate of decline in alcohol level. The court refused to admit them, holding that evidence of past visits by the appellant to her doctors should come from the notes of the doctors and be subject to cross-examination.

The appeal was dismissed. The appellant appealed further.

QUESTION(S) FOR THE COURT: (1) Whether the Crown Court erred in law in refusing to permit the appellant to adduce in evidence her medical records without calling the doctors who made the records. (2) Whether the Crown Court erred in law in dismissing the appeal because: (A) it did not accept that the difference in readings proved the machine was unreliable; (B) it did not accept that the expert evidence proved that the difference in readings was impossible in the sense that no human being could show such results; (C) the appellant's test 11 months after the incident did not persuade the court that the machine must be wrong.

HELD: "[On (1)] 15. … the Crown Court was clearly entitled to conclude … that the records of the appellant's general practitioner fell within the definition of business documents contained in section 24(1) of the Criminal Justice Act 1988. The court then had to apply the principles set out in section 25 [Criminal Justice Act 1988] in determining whether to permit the records to be admitted …

"16. Three of the four specific areas set out in section 25(2) are plainly satisfied: the documents were authentic; they went to a relevant issue; there could be no unfairness to the accused since she sought their admission. The remaining matter … was the extent to which the … notes appeared to supply evidence which would not otherwise be readily available … The evidence of past visits by the appellant to her doctors, and their findings consequent upon those visits, was readily available from the doctors themselves.

"17. … the Crown Court was entitled to conclude that in the interests of justice the general practitioners' records, whilst admissible, should not be admitted …

"[On (2)] 21. Three separate reasons for dismissing the appeal are thus given; in each reason advanced the burden of proof is reversed. It was not for the appellant to prove that the machine was unreliable …

"22. … the prosecution must prove affirmatively that the Intoximeter device was reliable.

"23. As to the second reason advanced: it was not for the appellant … to prove that the difference in readings was impossible. It was for the respondent to prove that the difference in readings gave rise to no reasonable doubt about the reliability of the results …

"25. … it is … quite impossible to disregard the way in which the court's conclusions have been phrased … the Crown Court … clearly misdirected itself on the burden of proof. There was something surprising, to say the least, and very unusual about the results produced by the Intoximeter … ."

The answer to question (1) was "no"; the answer to question (2) was "yes". Appeal allowed.

Ali v DPP

[2020] EWHC 2864 (Admin), 13 October 2020, QBD (Admin)

Once an accused has adduced relevant evidence that a breath analysis reading may be unreliable, it is for the prosecution to prove, to the criminal standard, that the reading is reliable.

A driver had been convicted of driving with excess alcohol in breath, contrary to s 5(1)(a), Road Traffic Act 1988. Breath analysis had produced a lower reading of 46 µg alcohol in 100 ml breath. The driver claimed he had drunk only a single glass of wine and adduced evidence that the evidential device should therefore have returned a reading of zero; that the device in question should have been serviced every 6–7 months but had last been serviced 10 months before; and that he suffered reflux which caused mouth alcohol to be present in his breath. The deputy district judge found that the presumption of reliability had not been rebutted on the balance of probability and that the device had been working correctly. The submissions concerning servicing and reflux were rejected. The driver was convicted and appealed.

QUESTION(S) FOR THE COURT: Whether the deputy district judge: (1) was entitled to accept the evidence of the investigating officer that the machine was operating correctly and to reject the evidence of the defendant's expert that the machine may not have been reliable; (2) erred in law to find that there was a legal burden on the defendant to rebut the presumption of reliability on the balance of probabilities.

HELD: "… 23. In the context of driving with excessive alcohol, there are two presumptions or assumptions which are relevant. The first is the common law presumption of regularity that breath specimen machines are reliable. The second is the statutory assumption … that the proportion of alcohol in the relevant specimen was not less than the proportion of alcohol at the time of the offence…

"26. It is … common ground between the parties that:

(1) There is a presumption that a … reading is reliable;

(2) The presumption is rebuttable;

(3) If evidence that the reading is not reliable is adduced, the burden is on the prosecution to establish, to the criminal standard of proof, that the reading is reliable.

"27. … It follows that the answer to the … second question is that [the deputy district judge] did err in finding that there was a legal burden on the Appellant to rebut the presumption of reliability of the evidential breath machine on the balance of probabilities. A defendant may adduce 'relevant' evidence that the … reading was not reliable. Once a defendant does that, it is necessary for the prosecution then to prove, to the criminal standard, that the reading was reliable, notwithstanding the evidence adduced by the defendant.

"28. In the present case, however, the Judge did go on to find, to the criminal standard of proof, that the reading was reliable. Unless the Appellant can show that this finding was flawed, the Judge's error that there was a legal burden on the Appellant to rebut the presumption of reliability is of no effect …

"30. Ultimately, however, the Judge's conclusion that the … reading was reliable was a factual assessment based on the evidence that was before her. The evidence that the reading was unreliable consisted of:

(1) The evidence [of the appellant's expert] that the [evidential breath machine] had not been calibrated within the required time period;

(2) The evidence of the Appellant as to the quantity of drink he had imbibed.

"31. … [The appellant's expert] had not examined the [evidential breath machine] in question or its calibration records. [His] evidence was based on a Quality Framework document that the Judge found was 20 years old and did not refer to a specific device. As against that, there was direct evidence from [the investigating officer] that the machine was within its calibration dates …

"35. … the Judge found that the Appellant was an unreliable witness; he had not been forthcoming; his evidence was self-serving; and his evidence was inconsistent with the evidence of the police officers (which the Judge accepted).

"42. … it is quite clear that the Judge was entirely satisfied (indeed, 'certain') on the evidence that the [evidential breath machine] reading was reliable and that the case against the Appellant was proved 'beyond reasonable doubt', *i.e.* to the criminal standard …

"43. … the [deputy district judge] was entitled to make the findings of fact that she did and, accordingly, to convict the Appellant."

The answers to the questions were "yes". Appeal dismissed.

Chapter 6

The Assumption that the Proportion of Alcohol or a Drug at the Time of the Offence Was Not Less Than in the Specimen

1. THE STATUTORY ASSUMPTION

See s 15(2), Road Traffic Offenders Act 1988, on the assumption that the proportion of alcohol or of a drug in the accused's breath, blood or urine at the time of the alleged offence was not less than in the specimen. See also the cases referred to in Chapter 2 under the heading "Back-Calculation", page 160; the cases in Chapter 5 under the heading "The Amount Said to Have Been Consumed", page 270; and R v Ash [1999] RTR 347 where the Court of Appeal held that s 15(2) is specific to the offences under s 3A, s 4 or s 5 where the taking of drink or the quantity of drink is a constituent of the offence itself; s 15(2) does not apply to an offence under s 1 (causing death by dangerous driving).

Beauchamp-Thompson v DPP

[1989] RTR 54, [1988] Crim LR 758, 15 June 1988, QBD (DC)

Justices were right not to allow evidence to rebut the statutory assumption. Where the motorist made no inquiry about what wine he was drinking, but later claimed he was drinking stronger wine than usual, he did not have a special reason for not disqualifying.

A motorist had been charged with driving with excess alcohol in blood, contrary to s 6(1)(a), Road Traffic Act 1972 as substituted by s 25 and Sch 8, Transport Act 1981.

At the hearing, he sought to adduce expert evidence that, although he had been over the limit when the blood specimen was taken, he was or may have been below it at the time of driving. The justices declared such evidence inadmissible on the basis of s 10(2), Road Traffic Act 1972 as likewise substituted (assumption that proportion of alcohol at time of offence not less than in the specimen unless ...); and on the ground that *Gumbley v Cunningham* (see page 160) did not extend the admissibility of evidence of "back-tracking" to a defendant. The motorist was convicted.

The motorist then sought to adduce special reasons for not disqualifying under s 93(1), Road Traffic Act 1972. He said he had unknowingly drunk a stronger wine than he usually did; the justices found, *inter alia*, that he had made no inquiry into what wine he had been drinking and that he should have known he was drinking Chardonnay rather than Riesling, which were distinctly different. They found no special reason, and disqualified.

The motorist appealed.

QUESTION(S) FOR THE COURT: Whether the justices should have: (i) allowed the defendant to adduce expert evidence to show the blood alcohol level at the time of driving; and (ii) whether on the facts before the justices they were entitled to determine there were no special reasons.

HELD: "[On (i), and on whether s 10(2) gives rise to a rebuttable or an irrebuttable presumption] I can detect no ground for construing that as a rebuttable rather than irrebuttable presumption, if presumption is the right word, bearing in mind that the word in the section is 'assumption' … The fact that there is an exception … seems to me to support [that] conclusion … the justices were correct to decide that it was not open to them to receive evidence designed to show that, notwithstanding at the moment the test was taken … the blood-alcohol level exceeded the prescribed limit, it may have been lower at the moment when the defendant was driving.

"[On (ii)] … there was no question of the defendant having been in any way misled … This was simply a case where he failed to make any inquiry or take any precautions in relation to the quality of the alcohol which he was consuming, and, accordingly, it was not capable of being a special reason … Quite apart from that, the justices [found] that the defendant should have known that the wine he was drinking … was different and heavier from the Riesling which he said he was accustomed to drink, and on that ground also they were entitled … to find that there were no special reasons."

Appeal dismissed.

DPP v Williams

[1989] Crim LR 382, 14 November 1988, QBD (DC)

The assumption applies regardless of the time between the driving and the breath analysis; it is for the defendant to prove having consumed alcohol after driving.

A motorist had been charged with driving with excess alcohol, contrary to s 6(1)(a), Road Traffic Act 1972 as substituted by s 25 and Sch 8, Transport Act 1981. At 3.50 am police officers located a car they had been looking for; without examining the car, they then found the driver in a nearby home. He admitted he had driven the car; the police detected alcohol on him; he said he had last had a drink some 5 hours earlier. He was taken to the police station, where breath analysis was positive.

At the close of the prosecution case, the motorist submitted there was no case to answer on the grounds that the only evidence of his having driven the car was his own admission to the police; and that the prosecution had failed to prove that the motorist had been over the prescribed limit at the time of driving. The magistrates accepted the submission and dismissed the charge. The prosecutor appealed.

QUESTION(S) FOR THE COURT: Whether on the undisputed evidence, the justices were required to make the assumption in s 10(2), Road Traffic Act 1972 as substituted (proportion of alcohol at time of offence not less than in the specimen unless defendant proves consumption of alcohol after ceasing to drive which took him over the limit), notwithstanding that they heard no evidence of the alleged offence or of when the respondent had driven his car in relation to his consumption of alcohol, and thought that the investigating officer should have made more inquiries than he did.

HELD: "… the officers had reasonable cause to suspect that the driving had taken place when the respondent had alcohol in his body, and that there was still alcohol in his body so as to enable them to require him to provide a specimen of breath under section 7 of the Act …

"Where a breath sample that has properly been taken is found on analysis to be positive, then it is for the defendant, if he is to raise the question of drink having been taken after driving, to discharge the obligations that are set out in section 10(2). It is not for the prosecution to seek to prove a precise period of time of driving, or bracket of time of driving, before that reversal of the burden of proof provided under the section comes into effect.

"Here, the evidence … was a clear admission by the respondent that he had been driving … that he had taken his last drink … at 11 p.m., and … that, when samples were taken at about 4 am, the proportion of alcohol in his breath exceeded the prescribed limit. It is the very type of case for which the assumption in section 10(2) and the reversal of the burden of proof in that provision is aimed."

The answer to the question was "yes". Appeal allowed.

Millard v DPP

[1990] RTR 201, [1990] Crim LR 601, 17 February 1990, QBD (DC)

Evidence of alcohol consumed before driving is inadmissible to rebut the presumption; the presumption is irrebuttable.

A motorist had been charged with driving with excess alcohol, contrary to s 6(1), Road Traffic Act 1972 as substituted by s 25 and Sch 8, Transport Act 1981. He had driven to a public house, parked his car and drunk almost all of a large whisky; he then moved the car to another parking place, went back to the public house and drank almost a pint of beer. Police officers spoke to him, as a result of which the breath testing procedure was commenced; breath specimens proved positive. A blood specimen was also provided, which was, again, positive.

At the hearing, the motorist submitted that the justices should admit expert evidence for the purpose of calculating retrospectively the effect of the whisky drunk before driving and of the beer drunk after driving, with a view to establishing that at the time of driving his alcohol level had been below the limit.

The justices held they could hear such evidence only in respect of the alcohol taken after driving, i.e. the beer; the motorist did not adduce such evidence.

The justices convicted. The motorist appealed.

QUESTION(S) FOR THE COURT: Whether, on a charge of driving with excess alcohol, a defendant may adduce evidence: (i) of his consumption of alcohol prior to driving his motor vehicle; and (ii) of a medical and scientific nature to explain the effect of such alcohol consumption on the proportion of alcohol in his breath, blood or urine at the time of driving, for the purpose of establishing that at the time of driving the level of alcohol concentration was below the prescribed limit, notwithstanding that at the time the specimen for analysis was provided, the proportion of alcohol exceeded the prescribed limit.

HELD: "The evidence sought to be admitted … was designed to destroy what justices, under section 10 of the Act [assumption that proportion of alcohol at time of offence not less than in the specimen unless defendant proves consumption of alcohol after ceasing to drive which took him over the limit] must in certain circumstances assume …

"… the assumption in section 10(2) when it comes to be made is irrebuttable … the justices … were entirely right."

Appeal dismissed.

Parker (Lee Christopher) v DPP

[2000] EWHC Admin 429, [2001] RTR 240, 7 December 2000, QBD (DC)

The irrebuttable statutory assumption does not infringe the right to a fair trial or the presumption of innocence.

A motorist had been convicted of driving with excess alcohol, contrary to s 5(1)(a), Road Traffic Act 1988. The lower of two breath readings was not more than 50 µg alcohol in 100 ml breath and the motorist exercised the option under s 8(2) (lower breath reading no more than 50 µg alcohol in 100 ml breath – now repealed; see page v), to provide a specimen of blood. Analysis of the blood revealed 81 mg alcohol in 100 ml blood.

The motorist instructed an expert, who concluded that the motorist's blood alcohol analysis was consistent with his stated consumption of alcohol, namely two pints of lager; and that the blood alcohol level at the time of driving, more than an hour earlier, was unlikely to have exceeded the statutory limit.

The magistrates convicted the motorist and his appeal to the Crown Court was dismissed. He appealed further.

HELD: "16. … [It is submitted on behalf of the motorist] that the Convention rights which have been infringed in this instance are under Article 6 [right to a fair trial] or more particularly Article 6(2) [presumption of innocence].

"19. It is [submitted] that it was unfair to prevent a defendant calling evidence to establish the fact that, whilst he was driving or in charge of a motor vehicle, the proportion of alcohol in his blood was lower than the prescribed limit … It was unfair in that the prosecution had the right to calculate back in order to demonstrate guilt and there was not equality of arms unless the defendant had the same right. Furthermore, the distinction drawn between the motorist who had consumed alcohol after driving and thus brought himself within s 15(3) placed the motorist who had merely consumed alcohol before driving in an unfair position.

"20. … accordingly [it is] submitted that … the court should strive to construe s 15 in accordance with s 3 of the Human Rights Act 1998 as not containing an irrebuttable assumption …

"26. … The language of the section … provides for an irrebuttable assumption … there is no infringement of Convention rights by providing for such an irrebuttable assumption in the context of this legislation as a whole. In those circumstances s 15 can be read in accordance with its natural meaning compatibly with Convention rights."

Appeal dismissed.

Griffiths (Richard Stephen) v DPP

[2002] EWHC 792 (Admin), (2002) 166 JP 629, 18 April 2002, QBD (Admin)

The statutory assumption is not rebuttable, and does not infringe the right to a fair trial. The fact that a motorist hoped to complete his journey before his breath alcohol level reached the prescribed limit was not a special reason for not disqualifying.

A motorist had been charged with driving with excess alcohol, contrary to s 5(1)(a), Road Traffic Act 1988. He had failed a roadside breath test at 8.30 pm At the police station, breath specimens given at 9.15 pm and 9.16 pm both revealed 47 µg alcohol in 100 ml breath. The motorist was therefore offered the option, under s 8(2), Road Traffic Act 1988 (lower of two breath readings not more than 50 µg alcohol in 100 ml breath – now repealed; see page v), of providing an alternative sample. He provided a blood specimen which, when analysed, showed 106 mg alcohol in 100 ml blood.

The motorist was convicted by magistrates and at the Crown Court contended that s 15(2), Road Traffic Offenders Act (assumption that the proportion of alcohol in the breath, blood or urine at the time of an alleged offence not less than in the specimen) does not create an irrebuttable presumption where there is clear evidence to the contrary; alternatively, to treat the assumption as irrebuttable contravenes arts 6(1) and (2) of the European Convention on Human Rights. The motorist also adduced expert evidence that, since the last sample of breath and the sample of blood were taken approximately an hour apart, and since it is general experience that it will take a period after the consumption of the last alcohol before the blood- or breath-alcohol proportion peaks, the proportion of alcohol in the breath or blood was still rising at the time the breath specimen was taken, and so must have been lower than the figure recorded; by backwards extrapolation, it could be proved to have been lower than the prescribed limit at the time of driving.

This argument was also advanced as a special reason for not disqualifying under s 34(1), Road Traffic Offenders Act 1988.

The Crown Court convicted the motorist and rejected the plea of special reasons; he appealed.

QUESTION(S) FOR THE COURT: (1) Whether the presumption under s 15(2), Road Traffic Offenders Act 1988 is irrebuttable; is the fact that contrary evidence is ignored an infringement of a defendant's right to a fair trial under arts 6(1) and (2), European Convention on Human Rights? (2) Whether the expert evidence, which had been ruled out as a defence to the charge, could be used as a special reason not to disqualify.

HELD: "[After reviewing the authorities] 30. … section 15(2), read, as it must be, with section 5(1), is a fair compromise between the considerations, first, that anyone who takes any alcohol before driving will to some extent expose the public to risk and that the level at which an offence is created … is artificial. Parliament, while preserving the right of any person to take a drink before driving, expressed itself in such a way that if such a person is then subjected to a breath, blood or urine test which shows an excess proportion of alcohol the person who has provided that specimen is, by section 15(2), assumed to have had no less a proportion of alcohol in his breath at the time when he was driving … it was not competent to the court to receive evidence from an expert which would have undermined or contradicted the statutory assumption created by section 15(2). Moreover, that statutory assumption [is] wholly proportionate to the situation where a person having taken drink then proceeds to drive a motor vehicle on a road. There is, therefore, no infringement of a defendant's right to a fair trial under Article 6.1 and 6.2.

"[On (2)] 32. … The answer, in my judgment, is a plain 'No' …

"33. … the evidence is unequivocal. Before setting out on his journey [the motorist] had consumed alcohol in such quantity that in time his alcohol-blood or alcohol-breath proportions would have exceeded the statutory limit. The mere fact that [he] hoped to have completed his journey (if this was in truth his thinking) before his breath or alcohol-blood levels exceeded the prescribed amount does not help him at all … the circumstances … were … special to the offender and not to the offence … there was no basis upon which the court below could have found special reasons … ."

The answer to questions (1) and (2) was "no". Appeal dismissed.

2. CONSUMING ALCOHOL AFTER CEASING TO DRIVE

See s 15(3), Road Traffic Offenders Act 1988 – the assumption in s 15(2) is not to be made if the defendant proves he consumed alcohol after the time of the alleged offence, but for which the defendant would not have been over the limit or unfit – the "hip flask" or "post-incident consumption" defence. *See also the cases under the heading "Laced Drinks", page 528.*

Thynne v Hindle; R v Newcastle upon Tyne JJ ex p Hindle

[1984] 1 All ER 770, [1984] RTR 231, 8 August 1983, QBD (DC)

It is for the defendant to adduce evidence of drinking after driving. See also Patterson v Charlton, page 627 and DPP v Williams, page 310 – the burden is on the defendant to displace the assumption.

A motorist had been charged, *inter alia*, with driving with excess alcohol in blood, contrary to s 6(1), Road Traffic Act 1972. There had been an accident; the motorist left his car, but returned some time later, by which time the police had arrived at the scene. The motorist admitted he had been the driver, and told the officers he had consumed alcohol since the accident. A breath test, taken 20 minutes later, was positive. The motorist told the officer that he believed the test would have been negative but for the alcohol he had consumed since the accident.

At the police station, a blood specimen was taken and revealed 101 mg alcohol in 100 ml blood. The motorist told police he had had a double and a single brandy since the accident; that it had not occurred to him that the police might wish to take a breath test, but that if he had, he might not have returned to the car; and that he had had very little to drink before the accident. He denied drinking after the accident to conceal having drunk before it.

At the hearing, the prosecution adduced evidence of the words spoken between the motorist and the police. The motorist then argued there was no case to answer, on the ground that the prosecutor had introduced evidence that he, the motorist, had taken alcohol between the time of the accident and the time of the testing, and that the prosecutor had not established the admissibility of the blood analysis. The justices accepted that argument, finding that the police officer had been satisfied that the motorist had consumed alcohol since the accident; they dismissed the charge. The prosecutor appealed.

QUESTION(S) FOR THE COURT: Whether, on the facts of the case, it was necessary for evidence on whether the defendant had consumed alcohol after the accident and before being required to take a breath test to be called on behalf of the defence.

HELD: "If evidence was placed before the court – nearly always by the defence, but possibly through witnesses called by the prosecution – to show that the accused consumed alcohol after ceasing to drive but before the test, then the prosecution had to discharge the burden which rested upon them to negative that fact … [I]f … the tribunal concluded that the accused might have so consumed alcohol then they had to acquit him.

"… neither the defendant's statement [to the police officer that he taken alcohol since the accident], nor his acceptance of it, nor the fact that the defendant had the time and opportunity to consume alcohol, could constitute the necessary evidence.

"… there was … no basis for the justices' acceptance of the defence submission … it was necessary for evidence on the issue of drinking after the accident to be called on behalf of the defence … ."

Appeal allowed.

Dawson v Lunn

[1986] RTR 234 (note), 30 November 1984, QBD (DC)

An extract from the British Medical Journal was insufficient to establish the defence.

Magistrates had dismissed a charge, under s 6(1), Road Traffic Act 1972 as substituted by s 25(3) and Sch 8, Transport Act 1981, of driving with excess alcohol. The motorist had invoked the defence in s 10(2), Road Traffic Act 1972 (consumption of alcohol after ceasing to drive which took him over the limit). He adduced in evidence an extract from the *British Medical Journal*, on alcohol concentrations and rates of removal, from which the justices concluded that a third pint of beer, drunk after ceasing to drive, had been sufficient to take the motorist over the limit. The prosecutor appealed.

QUESTION(S) FOR THE COURT: Whether the justices were right in dismissing the charge having regard to the provisions of s 10(2), Road Traffic Act 1972 as amended by the Transport Act 1981, having regard to the evidence given by the defence which did not include any medical or other expert evidence.

HELD: "… the document [the extract from the *British Medical Journal*] provides no basis for the conclusion which [the justices] drew … there was no evidence on which the justices could reach the conclusion which they reached … they misconstrued and misunderstood the document …

"… the case … provides the most vivid illustration of the need of guidance of that kind [expert evidence] in these cases, to prevent justices struggling with the unequal tasks of themselves interpreting scientific documents without the aid of those who are qualified to assist them in that interpretation."

The justices were not right in dismissing the charge. Appeal allowed.

Lloyd v Knight

The Times 13 February 1985, 8 February 1985, QBD (DC)

On the facts of this case (an expert report concerning breath alcohol levels after drinking certain amounts of alcohol) it was not possible to say that the magistrates could not have concluded that the defence was made out.

A motorist had been charged, *inter alia*, under s 6(1), Road Traffic Act 1972 as substituted by s 25(3) and Sch 8, Transport Act 1981, with driving with excess alcohol. The charge was dismissed, the justices finding that the defence under s 10(2), Road Traffic Act 1972 (consumption of alcohol after ceasing to drive, which took the motorist over the limit) had been made out. The defence was based on an expert report, the admission of which had not been questioned by the prosecutor, concerning breath alcohol levels after drinking certain amounts of alcohol. The prosecutor appealed.

QUESTION(S) FOR THE COURT: (i) Whether the court considered the correct standard of proof because, when it stated that the case would be dismissed, it added that the prosecution had not proved its case beyond reasonable doubt; (ii) whether the defence had provided sufficient relevant, admissible and reliable evidence to establish the defence.

HELD: "It may be that if the report had not been agreed and the forensic scientist had been examined and cross-examined, some doubt could have been thrown on the validity of his report … I cannot see that it is possible to say that this bench of magistrates could not have come to the conclusion that the defence had been made out. It may well be that in the light of other evidence that existed from what the respondent herself said, they could have come to another conclusion."

The answers to both questions were "yes". Appeal dismissed.

Rynsard v Spalding

[1986] RTR 303, [1985] Crim LR 795, 19 July 1985, QBD (DC)

The justices were wrong to decide this case on whether or not the defendant was still in charge of the vehicle when he consumed alcohol.

The defendant had been charged with driving with excess alcohol contrary to s 6(1)(a), Road Traffic Act 1972 as substituted by s 25 and Sch 8, Transport Act 1981. He had been driving on a car park and collided with a number of other vehicles. He had had two double whiskies after the accident; between the accident and the arrival of the police, the driver of one of the other vehicles involved in the collision had taken the defendant's car keys to ensure he did not leave the scene. Blood analysis revealed 133 mg alcohol in 100 ml of the defendant's blood.

At the trial the defendant sought to establish the defence under s 10(2), Road Traffic Act 1972, as likewise substituted (consumption of alcohol after ceasing to drive which took him over the limit). The justices found that the defendant had not shown that at the time he consumed the two double whiskies he had ceased to be in charge of the vehicle, despite the fact that he had been divested of the keys; they convicted him of being in charge with excess alcohol. He appealed.

QUESTION(S) FOR THE COURT: Whether in the circumstances it could be said that the defendant was in charge of his vehicle whilst the proportion of alcohol in his blood exceeded the prescribed limit.

HELD: "… the defendant … contended that … section 10(2)(a) had to be construed [to the effect that] if a person is charged with 'driving' he must show that he consumed alcohol after he ceased to drive. If he is charged with 'attempting to drive', he must show that he consumed alcohol after he had ceased to attempt to drive. If he is charged with being 'in charge', he must show that he consumed alcohol after he ceased to be in charge …

"… the justices proceeded upon an assumption which is flawed … in proceeding as they did [they] were concerned with whether the defendant remained in charge of his motor vehicle after he had consumed alcohol …

"Upon … the correct approach and upon the basis that there was no suggestion that the defendant drove after consuming either of the double whiskies, I would set aside the justices' adjudication … I would answer the justices' posed question 'this question did not arise'."

Appeal allowed.

Oxford v Fairhurst

Unreported, CO/1992/85, 21 May 1986, QBD (DC)

Expert evidence is normally required to establish the defence.

A motorist had been charged with driving with excess alcohol, contrary to s 6(1)(a), Road Traffic Act 1972 as substituted by s 25 and Sch 8, Transport Act 1981. He argued that he had a defence under s 10(2), Road Traffic Act 1972 as likewise substituted (consumption of alcohol after ceasing to drive which took him over the limit). There had been an accident; the police arrived at the motorist's home some time later and saw there half a bottle of wine, a glass containing wine, and a corkscrew; the motorist had been drinking since arriving home. The justices found the defence made out and acquitted the motorist. The prosecutor appealed.

HELD: "… [the] authorities … are to the effect that generally speaking a motorist … who sets out to establish that he would have been below the limit were it not for the amount of drink he took after driving, cannot accomplish that task unless he calls an expert to give evidence on such matters as how quickly alcohol disappears from breath and blood …

"There may be rare circumstances in which, no expert evidence being provided, Justices would be permitted to use their common sense, and in so doing accept that a motorist has accomplished his task of discharging the burden of proof imposed upon him. But … the apparent failure of the Justices to be clear in their own minds as to just how much alcohol they accepted the respondent had actually drunk at his home before the arrival of the police … did not permit them to do [so] without expert evidence and rely simply upon common sense, if that is what they did."

Appeal allowed.

DPP v Singh

[1988] RTR 209, 17 March 1988, QBD (DC)

Where the justices had no means of knowing whether drink consumed before driving would have taken the defendant over the limit, and there was no expert evidence, the defence was not made out.

A motorist had been charged with driving with excess alcohol, contrary to s 6(1), Road Traffic Act 1972 as substituted by s 25 and Sch 8, Transport Act 1981.

There had been a collision with another vehicle, following which the defendant had changed places with his passenger and both vehicles were then driven to a place where the drivers could exchange details. On the way, the defendant drank two plastic cups of whisky. Breath analysis revealed 127 μg alcohol in 100 ml breath.

The motorist gave evidence that he had drunk 1½ pints of beer before the accident, but adduced no expert evidence. He invoked the defence under s 10(2), Road Traffic Act 1972 as likewise substituted (consumption of alcohol after ceasing to drive which took him over the limit), and was acquitted. The prosecutor appealed.

QUESTION(S) FOR THE COURT: Whether there was evidence to support the finding that the defendant had proved, pursuant to s 10(2), that he had consumed alcohol after he had ceased to drive and before he provided a specimen of breath; and that had he not done so the proportion of alcohol in his breath would not have exceeded the prescribed limit; and whether the justices were right to dismiss the information.

HELD: "… it is by no means clear that the justices were alive to the necessity for the defendant to prove not only that what he had consumed after driving was sufficient to account for his exceeding the prescribed limit, but also that what he had consumed before would not have had that result …

"… even if … I am wrong as to this … the facts of this case come nowhere near to bringing it within that class of case where justices can, without expert evidence and relying simply upon common sense, reliably and confidently conclude that the defendant has accomplished the task of discharging the onus upon him. … They had no means of knowing whether the one and a half pints would have resulted, without more, in raising the defendant's alcohol level above the permitted limit … the evidence of the defendant himself was not capable of supporting the justices' finding."

Appeal allowed.

DPP v Lowden

[1993] RTR 349, 2 April 1992, QBD (DC)

Where the magistrates accepted the defendant's claim that he had drunk minimally more since driving than he had first indicated, and there was expert evidence, the prosecutor's appeal against acquittal failed.

A motorist had been charged with driving with excess alcohol, contrary to s 5(1)(a), Road Traffic Act 1988. There had been an accident, and the police went to the home of the driver. At the police station, breath analysis revealed a lower reading of 67 μg alcohol in 100 ml breath. The motorist told the police he had drunk gin between the time of driving and the police arriving at his home; he had returned home with the police and showed an officer the glass from which he had drunk, agreeing with the constable's indication of the level to which the glass had been filled.

At the hearing, the motorist raised the defence under s 15(3), Road Traffic Offenders Act 1988 (consumption of alcohol after ceasing to drive which took him over the limit). The prosecutor adduced expert evidence to the effect that if he had drunk the amount of gin he claimed to have drunk, the reading would have been 53 μg and therefore still over the limit. The defendant submitted that he had actually drunk more than first indicated, and that the amount he had in fact drunk wholly accounted for his having been over the limit. Expert evidence was given on the amount of alcohol that would have had to have been consumed to reduce the reading to the limit.

The justices found the difference between the amounts of gin said to have been consumed minimal, and dismissed the information. The prosecutor appealed.

QUESTION(S) FOR THE COURT: Whether, on the evidence, the justices were entitled to find that the defence had proved the quantity of alcohol in the defendant's breath would not have exceeded the prescribed limit.

HELD: "… The defence depended … wholly on the oral evidence of the defendant … the decision made by the justices was open to them on the evidence. They had adequate expert assistance as to the amounts involved, and … in the end, they merely had to decide whether the evidence given by the defendant was to be believed on a balance of probabilities in the light of the expert evidence … I cannot … say that the decision was perverse or that there was any error in law …

"… I cannot see how the difference in quantities in the gin could be regarded as minimal. But … I am not persuaded that this vitiates the justices' overall conclusion."

Appeal dismissed.

R v Wells Street JJ ex p Hobbs

Unreported, CO-1923-92, 25 March 1994, QBD (DC)

On the evidence adduced by the motorist in this case, the magistrates were entitled to find that the statutory assumption had not been displaced.

The defendant had been charged with driving with excess alcohol contrary to s 5, Road Traffic Act 1988. He had been involved in a minor accident with a taxi, but did not stop. The taxi driver followed him to the next traffic lights, which were red. The taxi driver spoke to the defendant, who at first denied there had been an accident; he got out of his car and, according to the taxi driver, he was supporting himself on the car door and smelling of alcohol. The driver disappeared. The taxi driver stopped a passing police car. Later that evening, the driver went to the police station and reported the accident; he said he had had to leave the scene of the accident to attend a meeting; he had had some drink there. The officers who had been at the scene later went to the driver's home, where he admitted driving, but denied the accident or that he had run away. A breath test was positive; at the police station, the lower breath analysis revealed 78 μg alcohol in 100 ml breath.

At the hearing, the taxi driver gave evidence. The defendant gave evidence that he had had a glass of wine at lunchtime and nothing until the meeting, where he had two whiskies; he had a third whisky after arriving home but before going to the police station, and a fourth after he returned. He then had two glasses of white wine with supper, before the police officer arrived. Four statements were put before the justices under s 9, Criminal Justice Act 1967. Two were from persons who had been at the meeting and confirmed that the defendant had had two whiskies there. One was from his wife and concerned, *inter alia*, what he had drunk at home. The fourth was from a forensic scientist, saying that, assuming a normal blood:breath alcohol ratio and a normal elimination rate, the lunchtime glass of wine would have been entirely eliminated by 6 pm and that the reading of 78 μg was fully accounted for by the drink said to have been consumed after the accident but before the breath analysis.

The magistrates accepted the evidence of the taxi driver in preference to that of the defendant, and convicted. The defendant wished to appeal, but the magistrates refused to state a case on the basis that the application was frivolous. He sought an order of *mandamus* requiring them to state a case.

HELD: "… the Justices … found that the applicant had not discharged the burden of proof which was upon him by virtue of section 15 of the 1988 Road Traffic Offenders Act [assumption that proportion of alcohol at time of offence not less than in the specimen unless defendant proves consumption of alcohol after ceasing to drive which took him over the limit] …

"[It was] open to the Justices to weigh up the evidence that had been put to them [in the statements] against the other evidence … and to decide whether or not they found it convincing. They plainly did not …

"… the … statements … proved little or nothing about the precise quantities of drink that had been consumed … The forensic scientist's report assumed that the applicant's elimination rate was what is generally regarded as the standard … This may well not have been so … perhaps even more remarkably, the scientist assumed that each whisky amounted to 80 ml of spirit …

"… If the forensic scientist was right, or anything like right, then at the time when this incident happened the concentration of alcohol in the applicant's blood would have been at, or about, the zero mark. Such a conclusion was wholly inconsistent with the evidence given by the taxi driver, who described … a man who appeared to be very considerably under the influence of alcohol and who behaved in a somewhat bizarre manner …

"… the Justices were fully entitled, as a question of fact, to treat the evidence that had been put before them … with very considerable reserve … ."

Application refused.

DPP v Sangha

Unreported, CO/2900/97, 28 January 1998, QBD (DC)

The motorist's own statement of the amount he drank after ceasing to drive is insufficient to establish the defence.

A motorist had been charged with driving with excess alcohol, contrary to s 5(1)(a), Road Traffic Act 1988. He had been involved in a road traffic accident; he left his vehicle and went to a petrol station where he telephoned for a taxi to take him to the home of relatives. There was an opportunity for him to consume alcohol at their home before the police arrived. Police officers duly arrived; breath analysis revealed a lower reading of 112 µg alcohol in 100 ml breath. When interviewed by the police, the motorist said he had drunk 4 or 5 glasses of Bacardi since driving. At the hearing, the statement of a forensic scientist for the motorist was admitted in evidence; it concluded that the amount of drink the motorist said he had taken after driving was consistent with the breath test result and that if he had not drunk after driving, the breath test result would have been approximately zero.

The justices accepted a submission of no case to answer and dismissed the case. The prosecutor appealed.

QUESTION(S) FOR THE COURT: (a) Whether the court on the evidence before it could justify the finding that the respondent consumed alcohol after his driving ceased on the basis of the statement; (b) whether the justices had correctly applied the law as stated in *Patterson v Charlton* (see page 627); (c) whether the justices were correct in law in allowing a submission of no case to answer when no evidence was given by the respondent as to his alleged post-accident consumption.

HELD: "… Central to this appeal are subsections (2) and (3) of section 15 of the Road Traffic Offenders Act [assumption that proportion of alcohol at time of offence not less than in the specimen unless defendant proves consumption of alcohol after ceasing to drive which took him over the limit)] …

"… was there sufficient evidence before the Justices upon which they could properly conclude that the Respondent had discharged the burden upon him to establish, on the balance of probabilities, that all his drinking had followed rather than preceded his driving …?

"That issue in turn raises this factual question: were the justices satisfied that the respondent was probably telling the truth in what he said at interview with the police merely because (a) he had said it; and (b) his breath alcohol analysis was consistent with it being the truth? …

"[Counsel for the respondent] seeks to pray in aid … that the petrol attendant to whom the respondent spoke after this accident had not smelt any alcohol on his breath, and that there had indeed been the opportunity post accident for him to have consumed the drink that he claimed to have consumed. With the best will in the world, however, these additional threads of evidence do not add significantly to the material in support of the Justices' conclusions …

"The reality here ... is that these Justices accorded far too great weight to the assertions in the Respondent's police interview which were of course totally self-serving and which without the support of sworn testimony were effectively worthless ...

"... the only issue was whether, on the material before them ... the respondent could properly be held to have discharged the burden undoubtedly by then lying upon him. In my judgment, the answer was plainly no."

The answers to all three questions were "no". Appeal allowed.

DPP v Ward (Kevin William)

Unreported, CO/2605/98, 2 October 1998, QBD (DC)

The defendant must adduce evidence of drinking after driving; the justices were wrong to infer it.

A motorist had been charged with driving with excess alcohol, contrary to s 5(1)(a), Road Traffic Act 1988. He had been seen driving a car which did not belong to him; on being challenged, he got out of the car and proceeded in a direction which would take him past a public house which he regularly frequented. The police arrested him some 45 minutes later; breath analysis revealed 66 μg alcohol in 100 ml breath.

He failed to attend court for his trial, and the case proceeded in his absence. The justices considered it "likely or possible" that the motorist had gone to the public house after driving, and felt it unsafe to convict since the first breath test was not taken until more than 45 minutes after the incident in question. They acquitted him on the basis that he could have consumed alcohol after driving. The prosecutor appealed.

QUESTION(S) FOR THE COURT: Whether the justices were right: (a) to acquit the respondent in circumstances when he failed to appear at his trial and had not presented any evidence as to post-driving consumption of alcohol; (b) to dismiss the information without inviting the prosecutor to address them as to whether or not there was a case to answer; (c) to acquit the respondent.

HELD: "... the answer to [question (a)] is clearly 'no'... [s 15(2), Road Traffic Offenders Act 1988] sets out a statutory assumption that if the proportion of alcohol in a specimen of breath exceeds the prescribed limit, it should be assumed that it exceeded the prescribed limit at the time he was driving the car unless he can prove the matters set out in subsection (3). He is required to prove that he consumed alcohol before he provided the specimen and after he had ceased to drive on the road, and he must prove that had he not done so, the proportion of alcohol in his breath would not have exceeded the prescribed limit.

"On the facts found by the justices there was no evidence at all of the matters set out in subsection 3(b) ... the statutory assumption therefore applied ...

"[On (b)] This was a summary trial, and in the ordinary way the prosecutor would be allowed one speech at the start of the trial ... however, it would not have been reasonable for the prosecutor … to forecast that reliance might be placed on section 15(3) of the Act …

"In those circumstances … justice clearly required the justices to put a point of law which was liable to influence them to enable the prosecutor to address submissions of law to them on that point … ."

The answers to all three questions were "no". Appeal allowed.

R v Drummond

[2002] EWCA Crim 527, [2002] Cr App R 25, [2002] RTR 21, 7 March 2002, CA (Crim)

Section 15(3) imposes on the defendant a persuasive burden of proof (that is, on the balance of probabilities) rather than an evidential burden (that is, to raise a reasonable doubt which the prosecution must then negative). The legislative interference with the presumption of innocence is no greater than is necessary.

A motorist had been charged with causing death by careless driving while under the influence of drink, contrary to s 3A, Road Traffic Act 1988. He had struck a scooter, killing the passenger and injuring the driver; he did not realise what had happened and continued home. When he saw the damage to his car, he telephoned the police, saying he thought he had fallen asleep at the wheel and hit somebody. Police went to his home; he said he had had two quarter bottles of wine before driving and had had gin since arriving home. A breath test was positive and he was arrested. Breath analysis revealed excess alcohol.

At the Crown Court, the judge ruled that the reverse burden of proof under s 15(3), Road Traffic Offenders Act 1988 (assumption that proportion of alcohol at time of offence not less than in the specimen unless defendant proves consumption of alcohol after ceasing to drive which took him over the limit) was a persuasive burden. The defendant was convicted and appealed.

QUESTION(S) FOR THE COURT: It was argued for the appellant: (2) that, if the burden is on the defendant to prove that he had taken a drink or drinks after the accident and that, but for that drink, his specimen would not have been over the limit, that would be an infringement of the presumption of innocence in art 6(2), European Convention on Human Rights; and (3) that therefore the provision should be read to mean that the defendant had only an evidential burden; that would mean the defendant would have to produce some evidence that he had drunk alcohol after the accident and that the amount he had had to drink "would have made a difference".

HELD: "1. This appeal concerns section 3A of the Road Traffic Act 1988 dealing with causing death by careless driving while the proportion of alcohol in the body exceeded the prescribed limit but the point equally arises under sections 4 and 5 of the Act which deal with offences of driving while under the influence of drink and with breathalyser offences tried in the magistrates' courts. …

"31. … First, the offence of driving while over the legal limit is not an offence which requires the court to ascertain the intent of the accused at all. Conviction follows after a scientific test which is intended to be as exact as possible. Second, in most cases such test is exact or, to the extent it is less than exact, the inexactness will work in favour of the accused. Thirdly, it is the accused himself who, by drinking after the event, defeats the aim of the legislature by doing something which makes the scientific test potentially unreliable. There is a distinct danger that in many (perhaps the majority of cases) the accused will have taken alcohol after the event for the precise purpose of defeating the scientific test. Fourthly, the relevant scientific evidence to set against the result ascertained from the specimen of breath or blood is all within the knowledge (or means of access) of the accused rather than the Crown. This evidence will include:- (1) the amount which the accused had to drink after the incident; (2) what is called his 'blood-breath ratio', important for calculating the rate at which his body absorbs alcohol; (3) the rate at which his body eliminates alcohol over time; (4) the accused's body weight.

"These are all matters correctly mentioned by the judge in his ruling in this particular case and also in his summing-up to the jury.

"34. For the reasons [given] above … the legislative interference with the presumption of innocence in section 15 of the Road Traffic Offenders Act 1988 amounts to an imposition of a persuasive burden on the defendant and … such interference is not only justified but is also no greater than necessary. It hardly needs to be said that driving while over the limit and causing death by driving in such circumstances are both social evils which Parliament sought to minimise by this legislation."

Appeal dismissed.

Lonergan v DPP

[2002] EWHC 1263 (Admin), [2003] RTR 12, 29 May 2002, QBD (Admin)

Magistrates were wrong to reject a motorist's evidence of the amount he had drunk on the basis that they would have expected a higher reading if it had been true.

A motorist had been charged, *inter alia*, with driving with excess alcohol, contrary to s 5(1)(a), Road Traffic Act 1988. He had been involved in a road accident at 11.10 pm on the day in question; shortly afterwards he went to a public house where he remained for over 1½ hours. He then walked home. At about 1.30 am police officers went to his home where a breath test was positive. He was arrested and breath analysis, at 2.21 am, revealed 51µg alcohol in 100 ml breath.

At trial, the motorist said he had had half a bottle of lager before the accident, and after the accident had had a number of drinks at the public house, which explained the breath test reading. Two witnesses gave evidence that he had been at the public house drinking.

The magistrates did not accept the evidence about the consumption of alcohol at the public house; they would have expected a much higher reading at 2.21 am if the evidence was accurate; there was no scientific evidence; the motorist had failed to discharge the burden under s 15(3), Road Traffic Offenders Act 1988 to establish that had he not drunk alcohol after ceasing to drive, his breath alcohol would not have exceeded the limit. They convicted him; he appealed.

QUESTION(S) FOR THE COURT: Whether the evidence justified the magistrates' finding that at the time of driving the alcohol in the appellant's breath exceeded the prescribed limit.

HELD: "15. … [It is argued] that the justices were not entitled to act on the basis that, had his story been true as to how much he had drunk in the pub, then the reading taken at 2.21 would have been much higher. [It is submitted] that that is not factual evidence which the justices are entitled to take into account; it is expert evidence which goes beyond that which can properly be considered as evidence of which they are entitled to take judicial notice.

"19. … justices … may be entitled to say on occasions that this finding is so outrageous and so contrary to the evidence that it is not sustainable. But I do not accept that this evidence can properly be put into that category …

"20. It seems to me in this case that this was a matter which weighed heavily in the reasoning of the magistrates … they were using it as a factor against which to test credibility, but … from the way in which the case is stated … but for this factor, they may well have reached a different conclusion on the issue of credibility … there was other evidence from which they could have doubted the credibility of the appellant, but I would have expected those factors to have been expressly referred to in [the case stated] if they carried any material weight. This particular matter loomed large in their reasoning and I do not think it is the kind of matter that they could take judicial notice of. …

"[On the question posed] 22. The evidence … may well have justified that finding, had [the justices] approached the matter in the appropriate way. But the evidence on which they relied, and in particular the specific assessment which they themselves made as to what would be an appropriate reading on the intoximeter at 2.21 a.m., was not evidence they could properly rely upon … ."

Appeal allowed.

DPP v Chambers

[2003] EWHC 2142 (Admin), (2004) 168 JP 231, 25 July 2003, QBD (Admin)

Magistrates were in error to overlook the defendant's admission, and to prefer expert evidence based on instructions from the motorist over expert evidence based on the police record; the defence was not made out.

A motorist had been charged with driving with excess alcohol, contrary to s 5(1)(a), Road Traffic Act 1988. A Mr Morris had parked his car outside a newsagent; when he came out, it had been damaged. He went to the defendant's home; there was an argument and he called the police. The defendant refused to provide a breath specimen and was arrested; at the police station, breath analysis revealed excess alcohol. She said she had drunk about two glasses of wine since the time of the alleged offence. She was interviewed the next day, and said that she had drunk wine and vodka, then driven to the newsagent, but did not remember a collision; she had drunk alcohol after the accident, but believed she would have been over the limit when she drove. The police record (Form TF7) was that she had had three large glasses of wine before driving, and a glass of wine and a vodka with orange juice afterwards.

Both the prosecutor and the defendant instructed expert witnesses, one of whom gave agreed evidence at the hearing. The evidence was based on two scenarios: that set out in the written police record, and the other on instructions from the motorist, to the effect that she had taken a greater amount of wine and vodka after the accident. On the basis of the expert evidence, the magistrates found no evidence that the motorist had been over the limit when she drove. They dismissed the case. The prosecutor appealed.

HELD: "26. … when [the magistrates] were considering whether the respondent had discharged the burden of proving on a balance of probabilities that which must be proved under section 15(3) (consumption of alcohol after ceasing to drive which took the driver over the limit), their first error was to consider the evidence only by reference to the expert evidence …

"27. They … did not consider … the fact that the respondent had admitted at an earlier stage the consumption of vodka as well as wine prior to the incident.

"29. The second error was to have regard … to the final scenario, the provenance of which was what the respondent had told her expert … that scenario had no evidential basis whatsoever. It was merely a hypothesis. As such, it was no more evidence than would be a hypothesis put to a witness by counsel in cross-examination.

"32. The third reason why … this appeal must be allowed is that … it was irrational for the Magistrates to conclude that there was no case to answer on the basis of the drinking pattern outlined in form TF7 and the expert evidence upon it. In relation to section 15(3), the burden was and remained upon the respondent.

"35. For those three reasons, taken both separately and cumulatively, I conclude that the submission of no case to answer ought to have been rejected."

Appeal allowed.

DPP v Ellery

[2005] EWHC 2513 (Admin), 14 July 2005, QBD (DC)

There were no grounds for revisiting the decision in R v Drummond (page 324); under s 15(3), Road Traffic Offenders Act 1988 the defendant bears a legal burden of proof on the balance of probabilities.

A motorist had been charged with driving with excess alcohol, contrary to s 5(1)(a), Road Traffic Act 1988. He had been drinking the evening before, and on the afternoon of, the day in question. The police, acting on information received, went to his home, where a breath test was positive. He was arrested and analysis of a blood specimen revealed excess alcohol. It appeared he had drunk a can of lager since driving. The justices acquitted him. The prosecutor appealed.

QUESTION(S) FOR THE COURT: Whether the justices were correct in law and on the evidence in acquitting the defendant.

HELD: "9. … [The defendant argues] that section 15(3) [Road Traffic Offenders Act 1988 – assumption that proportion of alcohol at time of offence not less than in the specimen unless defendant proves consumption of alcohol after ceasing to drive which took him over the limit], or at least some part of that subsection, should be read as imposing merely an evidential burden by virtue of the Human Rights Act 1988 … [In] *R v Drummond* [page 324] [t]he court … held that the legislative interference with the presumption of innocence arising from the imposition of a legal burden of proof, in relation to section 15(3), was not only justified but was also no greater than necessary.

"14. … [On the argument that *R v Drummond* should be revisited following *DPP v Sheldrake* (page 502) where it was said that] the Convention did not outlaw presumptions of fact or law, but required that these should be kept within reasonable limits and should not be arbitrary … the substance and effect of any presumption adverse to a defendant must be examined and must be reasonable.

"15. Relevant to any judgment on reasonableness or proportionality will be the opportunity given to the defendant to rebut the presumption, maintenance of the rights of the defence, flexibility and application of the presumption, retention by the court of a power to assess the evidence, the importance of what is at stake and the difficulty a prosecutor may face in the absence of a presumption. It is here argued that the approach in *Drummond*, by not adopting these distinctions, lacked flexibility. …

"17. I can see no basis for suggesting that there is any such lack of flexibility as should lead this court to conclude that the decision in the case of *Drummond* should be revisited. … it is, as a matter of practical reality, entirely appropriate for the statutory regime to take all four of the factors [mentioned in the judgment in *Drummond*] together so that both on the scientific aspect, and on the amount which the accused actually had to drink after the incident, it is for the accused to bear a legal burden of proof. That burden of proof will, of course, only be on the balance of probabilities.

"18. … it is impossible, on the facts found by the Justices, to suggest that there was here any satisfaction by the respondent of a burden of proof on the balance of probabilities."

Appeal allowed.

DPP v Tooze

[2007] EWHC 2186 (Admin), 24 July 2007, QBD (DC)

The magistrates applied the wrong burden of proof in respect of s 15(3), which is on the defendant.

A motorist had been charged with driving with excess alcohol, contrary to s 5(1)(a), Road Traffic Act 1988. He had driven home, where he had been drinking; there was a gap of 2½–2¾ hours between the time he drove and the time his breath was analysed. The lower reading was 90 µg alcohol in 100 ml breath.

The magistrates found that, although it was likely the motorist had been over the limit when he drove, the assumption in s 15(2), Road Traffic Offenders Act 1988 (that the proportion of alcohol in the breath, blood or urine at the time of the offence was no less than in the specimen) should not be made because of the large amount of alcohol consumed since driving, together with the considerable length of time before the breath analysis; and that the analysis could not be an accurate reflection of the alcohol in the defendant's system at the time of driving. They concluded that they were not sure beyond reasonable doubt that the motorist had been over the limit and acquitted him, but later accepted that this was the wrong standard of proof. The motorist was acquitted and the prosecutor appealed.

QUESTION(S) FOR THE COURT (AS REPHRASED IN THE JUDGMENT): Whether the justices applied the incorrect burden of proof when assessing the application of s 15(2).

HELD: "12. Clearly, first of all, the assumption would have been applicable … by virtue of section 15(2). And also in view of the nature of the defence the assumption required the accused to prove the matter set out in Section 15(3), in other words, the burden of proof passed to him. …

"15. … the justices simply … had the burden of proof wrong. There can therefore be no doubt that an error of law was made and that the appeal must succeed. …"

The answer to the question was "yes". Appeal allowed. Case remitted to the magistrates' court with a direction to convict.

DPP v Bolton

[2009] EWHC 1502 (Admin), 4 June 2009, QBD (Admin)

Expert evidence is normally required to establish the exception in section 15(3), Road Traffic Offenders Act 1988.

A motorist had been charged with driving with excess alcohol in blood, contrary to s 5(1)(a), Road Traffic Act 1988. The analysis showed 155 mg alcohol in 100 ml blood. He was unrepresented at his trial. He said he had drunk 3 pints of lager topped up with lemonade over a period of almost 6 hours before driving, and 1½ pints of cider, and a cup of tea with a small whiskey in it, after driving. He argued that it would be obvious that the amount drunk before driving would not be sufficient to put him over the limit when he ceased driving, and that the matter was so obvious that medical evidence was not necessary. The justices accepted this argument and acquitted him. The prosecutor appealed.

QUESTION(S) FOR THE COURT: Not recited in the judgment.

HELD: "9. … the Crown contended before the Magistrates that the evidence given by the accused could not, on its own, make out the defence on the balance of probabilities under section 15 … [I]t is submitted [that the magistrates] fell into error in that they did not examine the defendant's evidence against the background of scientific evidence which would have either supported or worked against the … defendant; in particular the key questions as to whether he had taken alcohol after he had finished driving and whether the alcohol he took after he had finished driving had taken him over the prescribed limit.

"10. I find the submissions of the Crown persuasive and hold that the magistrates did fall into error in jumping to the conclusion they did."

Case remitted to the magistrates' court with a direction that they allow the unrepresented respondent the opportunity to re-open his case and call further evidence, failing which, the magistrates were to convict.

DPP v Dukolli

[2009] EWHC 3097 (Admin), 30 October 2009, QBD (DC)

Where the credibility of the defendant is in question, expert evidence concerning alcohol said to have been taken after driving is essential.

A motorist had been charged with driving with excess alcohol, contrary to s 5(1)(a), Road Traffic Act 1988. He had been driving and police found him at 3.15 am, standing by his car in a lay-by. He said he had had a lager at 11 pm. A preliminary test was positive and, at the police station, breath analysis showed excess alcohol. When giving the breath specimens, the motorist said he had not had a drink after he had stopped driving. In interview, he said he had had a shot of vodka at 6 pm the previous evening, and a bottle of lager at about 11 pm, and repeated that he had not drunk since he stopped driving. At the trial, he gave evidence that, in addition to the first shot of vodka and the lager, he had a second shot of vodka after stopping in the lay-by and getting out of the car. He swallowed it as the police approached. He said he had been afraid to admit this earlier. The justices found that it was the alcohol consumed after the defendant stopped driving that had caused him to be over the limit. They dismissed the charge. The prosecutor appealed.

QUESTION(S) FOR THE COURT: (1) Whether a reasonable bench, properly directing itself, could have concluded that the defendant had discharged the burden of proof in s 15(3), Road Traffic Offenders Act 1988 (consumption of alcohol after ceasing to drive which took him over the limit) in the light of the evidence, and in particular the lack of scientific evidence. (2) Whether magistrates have a discretion to find the statutory assumption in s 15(2), Road Traffic Offenders Act 1988 (assumption that the proportion of alcohol in the breath, blood or urine at the time of an alleged offence not less than in the specimen) discharged as per s 15(3) without the benefit of scientific evidence?

HELD: "[On (1)] 11. … except in rare cases where it is unnecessary, it has been the standard practice for many years for defendants to call medical or scientific evidence when running [the defence under s 15(3)] if they are to stand any real chance of success.

"12. … there was a real issue whether the defendant was a credible witness, not least because what he said in court contradicted what he said to the police officer at the time of his arrest, at the time of giving the breath test and indeed in interview. In addition, aspects of his account, such as swallowing a mouthful of vodka as the policeman approached, seemed inherently unlikely. This is … precisely the kind of case where expert evidence is important. Expert evidence would, or certainly may have, enabled the justices to test whether the readings given were consistent with the defendant's account, and may very well have led to the conclusion that they were not. Furthermore, even if they accepted his story of having a mouthful of vodka, it is not at all obvious to me that a lay person would have found that that mouthful explained or even could have explained the excess. For these reasons … in the absence of medical or scientific evidence called to support his version, the magistrates were wrong to find that the defendant had discharged the burden of proof."

The answer to question (2) was "15. … yes, but only in the comparatively rare case where a layman can reliably and confidently say that the alcohol taken after the driving must explain the excess which was not the position here". Appeal allowed.

Goldsmith v DPP

[2009] EWHC 3010 (Admin), [2010] RTR 20, 4 November 2009, QBD (DC)

A person guilty of driving with excess alcohol who drank after driving, but who cannot establish that it was that drink which took him over the limit, is nevertheless entitled, for sentencing purposes, to adduce evidence that the reading at the time of driving was lower than that shown on the printout.

A motorist had been charged with driving with excess alcohol, contrary to s 5(1)(a), Road Traffic Act 1988. He had been drinking in a pub. He then drove his car, but drove it into a ditch. He abandoned it, was collected by friends and went back to the pub where he resumed drinking. Police later arrested him and breath analysis showed 71 μg alcohol in 100 ml breath. The police made enquiries to establish how much he had drunk after the accident, and then sought expert evidence of the likely level at the time of driving. The expert's opinion was that that would have been 46 μg. The defendant was charged on the basis of 46 μg, but the Crown Prosecution Service later amended the charge to 71 μg, as shown in the printout.

The defendant then appointed his own expert, who said that, on the basis of what the defendant had told him about how much he had drunk, the likely reading at the time of driving would have been no more than 57 μg. The defendant pleaded guilty, but on the basis that the reading was no more than 57 μg. He argued that he should be sentenced on that basis, so that penalty would be lower than for a reading of 71 μg. The court found that the assumption in s 15(2), Road Traffic Offenders Act 1988 (evidence of the proportion of alcohol in a specimen of breath to be taken into account) applied and could be rebutted only under section 15(3) (consumption of alcohol after ceasing to drive which took driver over the limit). The defendant was accordingly sentenced on the basis of the reading of 71 μg. He appealed.

QUESTION(S) FOR THE COURT: Whether it was correct to find that the assumption in s 15(2) prevented the court from sentencing on the basis of a reading lower than that provided by the evidential test, where there had been post-driving consumption of alcohol.

HELD: "16. … The appellant … has argued … that the assumption in section 15(2) applies … only to trials, and has no relevance once guilt is established … when … the court can, and indeed should, come to its own conclusions on the evidence available, taking account of, even giving weight to, the readings, but ready to come to some other conclusion if the evidence plainly establishes that the reading must have been wrong. …

"17. Let us take an example. Let us say that there is clear evidence that someone left work without having had a drink. He then goes to the pub and has one and a half pints of beer before driving off, sufficient, perhaps, just to put him over the limit, but not by very far. Then, like the appellant, he has an accident. Like the appellant, he leaves his car and goes back to the pub with his friends, where he has, say, four or five pints, or even more, before the police arrive.

"18. The reading on the certificate … would be very high indeed. The appellant would have to plead guilty because he could not establish that he was not over the limit when he was driving. To put it another way, he could not displace the assumption under section 15(2) because he could not prove the exception in section 15(3) applied. If the prosecution are right, he must be sentenced on the basis that he was driving with that very high reading, rather than the modest excess which the evidence establishes must have been the position.

"19. This is not just. It is not fair. I do not accept that it is the law. The court should not be compelled to sentence upon a factual basis which is demonstrably false.

"20. Furthermore, … there are certain linguistic signposts within section 15 which make clear that the presumption applies only to contested trials. Section 15(1): this section applies 'in respect of proceedings for an offence' under section 5. This is apt to describe a trial, but not apt to describe a hearing after a plea to determine sentence.

"21. Furthermore, the assumption in subsection (2), although it says it applies 'in all cases', is subject to the exception in subsection (3) which allows the defendant to set aside the assumption if he proves that he consumed alcohol after he ceased to drive and it was the alcohol taken after he ceased to drive which pushed him over the limit. The exception in subsection (3) is plainly relevant to trials, and only to trials, which strongly suggests that the presumption in subsection (2) also applies only to trials."

The answer to the question was "no"; the case was remitted to the justices for a *Newton* hearing.

DPP v Ridings

[2024] EWHC 498 (Admin), 6 March 2024, KBD (Admin)

The magistrates did not apply the correct reverse burden of proof under s 15(3), Road Traffic Offences Act (consumption of alcohol after ceasing to drive which took the driver over the limit).

A motorist had been charged with driving with excess alcohol contrary to s 5(1)(a), Road Traffic Act 1988. She had been involved in a road traffic accident and left the scene. At the police station, and later at trial, she claimed to have had two vodkas and coke after the accident but before police found her at a friend's home. She said she would not have been over the limit but for those drinks. The magistrates found (among other matters) that the prosecution had not proved its case beyond reasonable doubt, and that there was insufficient evidence to show that the respondent had been over the limit at the time of the alleged offence or before consuming alcohol at her friend's home. They acquitted her and the prosecution appealed.

QUESTION(S) FOR THE COURT: Whether the magistrates misdirected themselves as to the reverse burden of proof under s 15(3), Road Traffic Offenders Act 1988 requiring the defendant to rebut the presumption in s 15(2) on the balance of probabilities.

HELD: "2. Where, as in this case, the issue arises whether a defendant has consumed alcohol after the alleged offence but before providing a specimen, sections 15(2) and (3) of the [Road Traffic Offenders Act 1988] impose on the defendant a legal (persuasive) burden of proof, to the civil standard: see *R v Drummond* [2002] EWCA Crim 527 [2002] 2 Cr App R 25 [see page 324]. …

"21. … the Magistrates … state, in terms, that 'there was insufficient evidence to prove beyond reasonable doubt that the [respondent] was over the limit at the time of the offence or prior to the consumption of alcohol at the home of [her friend]'. This reasoning can mean only one thing. The Respondent was being given the benefit of the doubt. The Magistrates were not satisfied so that they were sure. The finding of not guilty and the dismissal of the case against the Respondent were arrived at 'consequently' on those conclusions. That, in and of itself, establishes a material misdirection in law. …

"25. … nowhere do the Magistrates describe themselves as having been satisfied by the Respondent and by the evidence adduced by her that, on the balance of probabilities, the excess alcohol was attributable to post-driving consumption. … Read fairly and as a whole, the Magistrates' reasoning is consistent – and only consistent – with their not having been satisfied to the criminal standard by the prosecution, on the issue in the case. It is not consistent with having been satisfied to the civil standard by the defence. The final reinforcement is the Acknowledgment. … in … the Stated Case … [where the Magistrates said that] 'the court is aware that it was in error in terms of the standard and burden of proof applied'. This reflects the substance of what the Magistrates said and did."

The answer to question (1) was "yes"; it was not necessary to answer a second question. Appeal allowed; case remitted for re-trial before a differently constituted bench.

Chapter 7

Evidence

See s 16(1), Road Traffic Offenders Act 1988 – evidence of the proportion of alcohol or a drug in a specimen may be given by producing a printout from the breath analysis device or a certificate signed by an authorised analyst; s 16(2) – evidence that a blood specimen was taken with consent may be given by production of a certificate to that effect, signed by a medical practitioner or registered health care professional; and s 16(3) – the printout or certificate is admissible if a copy has been handed to the accused when produced or a copy served no later than 7 days before the hearing. See also the cases in Chapter 2 under the heading "Certificates", page 164.

1. THE PRINTOUT

See also the cases under the heading "Oral Evidence", page 402, on the admissibility of oral evidence of the contents of the printout.

Gaimster v Marlow

[1984] QB 218, [1984] 2 WLR 16, [1985] 1 All ER 82, [1984] RTR 49, [1984] Crim LR 176, 8 December 1983, QBD

A test result and certificate produced by a breath analysis device constituted a statement within s 10(3)(a), Road Traffic Act 1972 and were to be taken together, not compartmentalised. An officer may give evidence to interpret the record.

A motorist had been charged with driving with excess alcohol, contrary to s 6(1), Road Traffic Act 1972 as substituted by s 25 and Sch 8, Transport Act 1981. The magistrates dismissed the charge on the basis that the test record produced by the Lion Intoximeter was not a "statement within the meaning of s 10(3)(a) of the Road Traffic Act 1972 as amended", and was therefore inadmissible as evidence. Their reasons were, *inter alia*, that a statement must be understandable by an ordinary person; the test record in question was not understandable without explanation; a statement under s 10(3)(a) had to contain all the facts to prove the entire matter in s 10(3); evidence by the police officer who conducted the test was inadmissible hearsay.

The prosecutor appealed.

QUESTION(S) FOR THE COURT: Whether it was correct to treat the test record as inadmissible as evidence in that it was not a statement within s 10(3)(a), Road

Traffic Act 1972; whether it was correct to exclude the evidence of the police officer who conducted the test to explain or interpret the meaning of the contents of the document.

HELD: "… It was not clear from the case stated whether the justices had seen the whole of the document produced by the Intoximeter; they should have done. The document is not to be compartmentalised into the part containing the test result (the statement) and the part containing the explanation (the certificate), so that only the first part is admissible. The one document contains in its second part the explanation and meaning of the first part … The fact that to some people, or even to most people, it may not be immediately intelligible without explanation does not prevent it being a statement.

"… if the officer is shown to be a trained operator of the machine and knows what the meaning of these signs is, and that is proved by way of evidence, then it seems to me there is no reason why he should not give evidence."

The justices were incorrect on both points. Appeal allowed.

Chief Constable of Surrey v Wickens

[1985] RTR 277, 14 November 1984, QBD (DC)

Where the copy printout handed to the motorist had not been signed by the officer, the copy was nevertheless served.

Magistrates had dismissed a charge, under s 6(1), Road Traffic Act 1972 as substituted by s 25(3) and Sch 8, Transport Act 1981, of driving with excess alcohol. The copy of the breath analysis test record and certificate handed to the motorist had been signed by the motorist but not by the officer conducting the breath test. The justices concluded that that document was not a "copy" and not therefore admissible in evidence under s 10(5), Road Traffic Act 1972 as likewise substituted (printout admissible only if a copy of it has been handed to the accused when produced, etc). They found the police officer's own evidence of the Intoximeter reading unreliable. The prosecutor appealed.

QUESTION(S) FOR THE COURT: (a) Whether the prosecution has failed to comply with the requirement in s 10(5) to serve a "copy"; (b) whether the prosecution was prohibited from giving evidence of the proportion of alcohol in breath by calling oral evidence from a trained operator of the Intoximeter as to the reading given on the visual display unit, without relying on the printout.

HELD: "We would answer the first question in the negative … An unsigned copy is a copy, and that is all that subsection (5) requires. If the legislature had intended that the copy as well as the original of the document must be signed, it would have said so." The second question did not, in the light of that, need to be answered. Appeal allowed.

Walton v Rimmer

[1986] RTR 31, 4 February 1985, QBD (DC)

Leaving a copy of the printout on the counter at which the defendant was standing did not constitute handing it to him.

Magistrates had dismissed a charge, under s 6(1), Road Traffic Act 1972 as substituted by s 25(3) and Sch 8, Transport Act 1981, of driving with excess alcohol. Analysis of two breath specimens was positive, but the magistrates found that the Intoximeter printout could not be relied on in evidence by the prosecutor because a copy had not been handed to or served on the motorist in accordance with s 10(5), Road Traffic Act 1972 as substituted. The printout had been produced in triplicate; the motorist had signed two copies; the third had simply been left on the counter at the police station. The prosecutor appealed.

QUESTION(S) FOR THE COURT: Whether the printout was admissible in evidence on behalf of the prosecution as having been "handed to the accused when the document was produced" if, when the document was produced in triplicate by the approved device, all three copies thereof, duly certified by a constable, were placed on a counter at which the defendant was standing, and the contents thereof having been explained to him he then and there signed at least two of them.

HELD: "… the Act of 1972 should not and cannot be so construed that a defendant can render the evidence inadmissible by refusing to take a document … which is handed to him. But it does not follow that if he signs a document it must previously have been handed to him … What happened in this case was that the documents were put down on a counter at which [the driver] was standing, and he was asked to sign them. There is no finding that it was indicated to him in any way that one of those copies was for him to take away … [The printout] should be either handed – that is to say, tendered to – the defendant at the time of production, or served thereafter. In this case … the facts as found … did not show that the document had been handed to the defendant."

Appeal dismissed.

R v Tower Bridge Magistrates' Court ex p DPP

[1988] RTR 193, [1987] Crim LR 693, 13 May 1987, QBD (DC)

Where the defendant had pleaded guilty, the court's insistence on the production of the printout was an improper exercise of discretion.

A motorist had been charged with driving with excess alcohol in breath, contrary to s 6(1)(a), Road Traffic Act 1972 as substituted by s 25 and Sch 8, Transport Act 1981. He had appeared before the justices unrepresented and pleaded guilty. After hearing the facts, the justices adjourned the case for 24 hours for the original breath analysis printout to be put before the court. At the resumed hearing, the original printout was still not available; the magistrate invited the motorist to change his plea to not guilty, which he did. The magistrate then invited the prosecutor to proceed; he was unable to do so and the magistrate dismissed the case for want of prosecution.

The prosecutor applied, by way of judicial review, for orders of *certiorari* to quash the dismissal of the case, and *mandamus* to direct the magistrate to hear the case; and for declarations that the decision to insist on the original printout was an improper exercise of discretion, and that the decisions to order a change of plea, refuse an adjournment and dismiss the charge were improper exercises of discretion.

GROUND(S) FOR THE APPLICATION: That the magistrate acted in breach of natural justice, exceeding his jurisdiction by requiring the original printout to be produced upon an unequivocal plea of guilty.

HELD: "… it is the practice at Tower Bridge Magistrates' Court, where an offence is charged against section 6 … to inspect the printout … in order to check that the calibration is accurate and the readings correct, and to see whether there is any vast discrepancy between the higher and lower readings and so on … There was no need for the original document, since there had been a plea of guilty. The court on the first day – or on the second – could and should have proceeded to sentence … the decision to insist upon production of the original printout … was an improper exercise of discretion in the circumstances … the decisions to order a change of plea, to refuse an adjournment and to dismiss the charge were improper exercises of the magistrate's discretion … ."

Order of *certiorari* granted.

Hasler v DPP

[1989] RTR 148, [1989] Crim LR 76, 17 May 1988, QBD (DC)

Where the printout was not adduced and there was no oral evidence of matters such as the calibration of the device and of the breath alcohol reading, the magistrates should not have rejected the submission of no case to answer.

A motorist had been charged with driving with excess alcohol, contrary to s 6(1)(a), Road Traffic Act 1972 as substituted by s 25 and Sch 8, Transport Act 1981. At the hearing, the police officer who had administered the breath testing procedure gave oral evidence that the breath analysis printout was available in court should the justices wish to see it; he did not adduce it as evidence; and gave no oral evidence concerning calibration.

The defence submitted there was no case to answer, on the ground that there was nothing before the justices which established the reading other than such reference as had been put by the police officer; nor was there evidence of other essential matters, particularly of correct calibration.

The justices rejected that submission; at that point they were handed the printout. They convicted the motorist, who appealed.

QUESTION(S) FOR THE COURT: Whether the justices were correct in finding that the prosecution had produced evidence of the reliability of the breath analysis device on which the defendant gave a specimen of breath, and therefore, whether they were correct in rejecting the defendant's submission of no case to answer.

HELD: "It is quite plain that [the printout] was not produced in evidence … It is the task of the prosecution to adduce all necessary evidence … It would … have been open to them to have adduced evidence in another way – indeed, to some extent, in the way they did, by calling [the police officer]. But … it would have been necessary for the officer to give evidence not only of the reading … but that he was familiar with the instrument, that he knew how to take the appropriate reading and that the instrument was working properly in the sense that it was properly calibrated.

"None of those matters was proved before the justices and so … at the end of the prosecution case … they had not established the case against the defendant. …"

The answer to the question was "no". Appeal allowed.

Leeson v Haringey JJ and DPP

[2000] RTR 385, 26 July 1999, QBD (DC)

On the facts of this case (failure to produce the printout was simply an oversight and defence counsel did not take the point at the time), the magistrates were entitled to take into account the printout handed up after the prosecution had closed its case and the defence had begun.

A motorist had provided a positive roadside breath test and was arrested. Breath analysis revealed 53 µg alcohol in 100 ml breath and he was prosecuted for driving with excess alcohol, contrary to s 5(1)(a), Road Traffic Act 1988. At the hearing, the sergeant who had conducted the procedure at the police station gave evidence, but he was not cross-examined about the reliability of the breath analysis device and there was no challenge concerning the calibrations of the machine.

At the end of the case, counsel for the defendant submitted that there was no evidence that the device was correctly calibrated. Certain items, including the printout from the breath analysis device, were then handed to the court's legal adviser and retained in the court file, but they were not formally exhibited. The magistrates were advised that the Crown's case had not shown that the device was properly calibrated. They went on to decide that, in view of the oral evidence of the sergeant, and the fact that the test record had been produced, the device had been correctly calibrated.

They convicted the defendant; he appealed.

HELD: "… From time to time … the prosecution as an oversight neglect to do that which is incumbent upon them to do. In this instance to produce the printout in evidence which is held in court by a witness who has given oral evidence. Without the printout establishing the results of the breath specimens and the self-calibration of the machine to establish its reliability the case will not be proved …

"If the failure to adduce that evidence … is simply an oversight … in that the prosecution has not adduced evidence of that which they are in a position to call that day, either by producing the document or calling the witnesses, in my judgment particular considerations do apply …

"It must always be a matter for the magistrates to consider anxiously … [counsel] in this instance made no submission to the magistrates, for example urging upon them that it would be wrong for them, for any particular reasons which he could have advanced, to exercise their discretion to admit the documents.

"… whether the magistrates wrongly exercised their discretion to permit the evidence to be called … should have been taken as a point at the time."

Appeal dismissed.

McCormack v DPP

[2002] EWHC 173 (Admin), [2002] RTR 20, 7 February 2002, QBD (Admin)

The fact that a motorist declines to take a printout does not mean that it has not been handed to him.

A motorist had been charged with driving with excess alcohol, contrary to s 5(1)(a), Road Traffic Act 1988. A roadside breath test was positive; he was arrested and taken to the police station, where he provided breath specimens. The lower reading was 79 μg alcohol in 100 ml breath. The breath analysis device produced three copies of a printout of the reading; both the motorist and the police officer signed all three copies. One of the copies was offered to the motorist but he declined to take it.

Before the magistrates, the defendant argued, *inter alia*, that the printout should be excluded because it had not been served in accordance with s 16(3), Road Traffic Offenders Act 1988 (statement admissible only if a copy had been handed to the accused when the document was produced or served on him not later than 7 days before the hearing).

The magistrates convicted the motorist. He appealed.

QUESTION(S) FOR THE COURT: Whether s 16(3)(a), Road Traffic Offenders Act 1988 was complied with by offering the printout to the appellant when there was no physical transfer of possession of the document.

HELD: "[After considering the Scottish case of *McDerment v O'Brien* 1985 SLT 485, which was decided differently from *Walton v Rimmer* (see page 337) on similar facts, and the argument that the legislation should be interpreted in the same way in England and Wales as in Scotland, and quoting from the judgment in *Walton v Rimmer*] 22. … I accept entirely that the Act of 1972 should not and cannot be so construed that a defendant can render the evidence inadmissible by refusing to take a document of the correct nature which is handed to him. …

"33. … the interpretation … in *Walton v Rimmer* is indeed correct and … should not be departed from."

The answer to the question was "yes". Appeal dismissed.

Jubb v DPP

[2002] EWHC 2317 (Admin), [2003] RTR 19, 25 October 2002, QBD (Admin)

The requirements of s 16(1), Road Traffic Offenders Act 1988, on the production of printouts from the breath analysis device, do not apply where the printout is in evidence only to show that the officer had reason to believe that the device had produced an unreliable indication. Nor does s 16(3) require the printout to be produced where the prosecution is based on a blood specimen. An officer may invite, but not require, further breath specimens. Where the suspect says there are no medical reasons for not requiring a blood specimen, the officer is entitled to require such a specimen.

A motorist had been charged with driving with excess alcohol in blood, contrary to s 5(1)(a), Road Traffic Act 1988. At the police station, he said he occasionally suffered from asthma for which he had medication. He provided two specimens of breath; the readings were 52 µg and 63 µg alcohol in 100 ml breath and the printout included the words "breath difference". The sergeant conducting the procedure took the view that this was not because the machine was unreliable but because the specimens of breath were of uneven volume. The printout was not signed or given to the motorist and no copy was served on him. The sergeant offered the motorist the opportunity to repeat the breath testing procedure, stressing that he was not obliged to do so. The motorist declined. He was therefore required to provide a specimen of blood; when asked if there was any medical reason why a blood specimen should not be taken, he said there was none. The specimen was analysed and revealed excess alcohol.

At his trial, the defendant argued that the printout from the breath analysis device was not admissible in evidence since it had not been served as required by s 16, Road Traffic Offenders Act 1988 (handed to him at the time it was produced or served at least 7 days before the hearing); that, as the officer believed the device was reliable, he should have required two further breath specimens; and that the requirement for a blood specimen was invalid because the defendant had said he was on medication. The magistrates rejected these arguments and convicted the defendant. He appealed.

QUESTION(S) FOR THE COURT: (1) Whether the printout from the breath analysis device was admissible in evidence when a copy had not been served at the time it was produced nor 7 days in advance of the hearing; (2) whether the officer was entitled to require a specimen of blood or urine or whether he had to require two further specimens of breath; (3) if the officer was entitled to require a specimen of blood or urine, whether he was entitled to require a specimen of blood rather than of urine.

HELD: "32. ... the prosecution did not seek to adduce the printout as evidence of the proportion of alcohol in the specimen of breath. ... it was the offence of driving with excess alcohol in the blood that was charged. The print-out was adduced in the present case for two purposes: first, ... as evidence that, when the accused provided his two specimens of breath, the device produced a printout which stated ‘breath difference’, thereby indicating an unreliable indication of breath alcohol had been recorded; and, secondly … as evidence that the sergeant had reasonable cause to believe that the approved device had not produced a reliable indication of the proportion of alcohol in the breath … Thus … section 16(1) was of no relevance …

“[On a submission that the prosecution should have adduced evidence of the print-out, after compliance with s 16(3), to meet the requirements of s 15(2) – evidence of the proportion of alcohol etc in all cases to be taken into account] 40. … I cannot think that the principal ground for [the decision in *Badkin v DPP*, see page 46] was … that evidence of the relevant proportion of alcohol in breath was required to be given in addition to the blood sample by provision of a print-out which, under the same statutory scheme, the officer had already reasonably decided might be unreliable. Such a contention seems to me precisely contrary to the reasoning … in that case.

“[On 2] 44. The officer was lawfully entitled to invite the appellant to give further specimens of breath … but he could not *require* them … in the circumstances found by the Justices he was also entitled to require a specimen of blood or urine. … The concluding passage of section 7(3) clearly indicates that the requirement of blood or urine can be made notwithstanding that the accused has already provided or has been required to provide specimens of breath.

“45. There is no authority to support a contention that a suspected person must be required to provide a second set of breath specimens in circumstances such as arose in the present case. …

“[On 3, on the submission that an accused cannot be lawfully required to provide a specimen of blood if he has stated that he is on medication] 49. … the [appellant] was specifically asked whether there were any medical reasons for not giving blood, and the appellant said there were none. Thus, the officer … addressed his mind to the relevant question at the relevant time and had no reason to question the information supplied by the defendant himself.”

The answer to question (1) was “yes, for the purposes for which that evidence was adduced”; the answer to question (2) was that the officer was entitled to require a specimen of blood or urine, and he did not have to require the defendant to provide two further specimens of breath; the answer to question (3) was “yes”. Appeal dismissed.

Hawke v DPP

[2011] EWHC 1345 (Admin), 10 May 2011, QBD (Admin)

Where there was no evidence before the court that an accused was over the limit, his conviction could not stand.

A motorist had been convicted of driving with excess alcohol, contrary to s 5(1), Road Traffic Act 1988, despite the fact that no evidence of his having been over the limit was before the court. He appealed.

HELD: "2. … It is acknowledged, on behalf of the Crown, that if there was no admissible evidence at the close of the prosecution case that he was over the limit, he was entitled to be acquitted. His representatives … at the hearing before the Justices perfectly properly requested … the attendance at trial of an officer whose evidence was crucial to establishing that the intoximeter used was accurate and had been properly self-calibrated.

"3. … without his attendance there was no admissible evidence on this crucial issue. … the officer was apparently not available to give evidence when required and an application, as I understand it, was made by the prosecution for an adjournment, but that was rejected.

"4. No further application was made to treat the relevant computer printout as hearsay evidence, and thus possibly admissible by that route. … It is accepted now that the justices should have acceded to the submission of no case and should have acquitted the appellant. Since that was not done he is now entitled to be acquitted and that is the order that I make."

Appeal allowed.

R (Olajide) v Stratford Magistrates' Court

[2018] EWHC 2159 (Admin), 19 July 2018, QBD (Admin)

The procedure under s 16(3), Road Traffic Offenders Act 1988 – handing or service of the printout – is permissive only; other evidence of the readings from the evidential breath analysis is equally admissible. Judicial review may deal only with matters in relation to which permission has been given.

A driver had been convicted of driving with excess alcohol contrary to s 5(1), Road Traffic Act 1988. His argument that he had not been the driver of the vehicle in question was rejected at trial and he was refused permission for judicial review of that aspect of his case. It was also argued at trial that the statement under s 16(1)(a) had not been served in accordance with s 16(3). It was served by the prosecutor at the trial. This argument was rejected on the ground that s 16(3) is permissive and other methods of proving the level of alcohol may be used. One of the police officers dealing with the case had given evidence of the breath analysis process and the readings. The applicant sought judicial review of the magistrates' decision to convict.

HELD: "15. The argument is that [the] statement produced by the device was not provided either at the time it was printed off by the machine or at any time prior to the day of the hearing and therefore, it was not admissible in evidence. …

"17. … Section 16 does not provide an exhaustive process for the proof of level of alcohol in breath. … There are other routes.

"18. The evidence served on the claimant and adduced before the court included the evidence of a Police Constable Cooper … [which] read as follows, insofar as was relevant: 'I have been present whilst Olajide has blown into the evidential breath analyser and given two samples of 87 milligrams and 90 milligrams.'

"19. There is a presumption that a machine of the type the officer was speaking of works correctly. His evidence as to what the machine indicated was and is admissible. That evidence, without any more, proved that the level of alcohol in breath was in excess of the legal limit. ..."

Application dismissed.

2. ADMISSIBILITY OF A READING FROM A PRELIMINARY BREATH TEST

See also Breckon v DPP, page 267, where the court rejected an argument that the result of the roadside breath test should be before the court; Rose v DPP, page 268 – the prosecution is not required to disclose breath readings obtained at the roadside; Lafferty v DPP, page 273 – the prosecution may rebut a defendant's assertion that he had not drunk enough to be over the limit by any relevant evidence, including the result of the roadside breath test; Murphy (Gerard) v DPP, page 666 – where the roadside breath testing device generates and stores analysis figures, the prosecutor is not required to adduce those figures; and Kang v DPP, page 63 – a roadside breath reading may be taken into account as confirming the procedure at the police station.

Smith (Stephen John Henry) v DPP

[2007] EWHC 100 (Admin), [2007] 4 All ER 1135, [2007] RTR 36, 30 January 2007, QBD (DC)

The prosecution is not obliged to disclose a breath alcohol reading obtained from a preliminary breath test, although it is good practice to do so.

A motorist had been charged with driving with excess alcohol, contrary to s 5(1)(a), Road Traffic Act 1988. He had been stopped and required to undergo a preliminary breath test using a device which is capable of providing a breath alcohol reading in figures, although such a reading was not obtained. At the police station, breath analysis showed excess alcohol.

At the trial, it was contended that, pursuant to s 15(2), Road Traffic Offenders Act 1988 (evidence of the proportion of alcohol in a specimen of breath to be taken into account) the prosecution was obliged to adduce in evidence the results in figures of the roadside breath test. The district judge dismissed the argument, finding that the word "specimen" in s 15(2) referred only to a specimen taken at a police station for evidential purposes. He convicted the motorist, who appealed.

QUESTION(S) FOR THE COURT: Whether it was right to hold that the prosecution did not have to adduce in evidence the result in figures of the roadside breath test.

HELD: "9. [The appellant] submits that the prosecution were obliged to adduce in evidence the breath/alcohol reading obtained at the roadside breath test in figures. Alternatively, he submits that, on a request from the defence, they are obliged to disclose the figure. Had the figure been disclosed, it may have supported the case that the device used at the police station was not working satisfactorily so that the figure on which the conviction was based was unreliable.

"26. As a matter of statutory construction, I cannot accept that submission. The specimens of breath which establish whether or not a defendant has committed an offence under Section 5(1) of the 1988 Act, are those which may be required of a defendant at the police station under Section 7 of the Act, the two specimens of breath mentioned in Section 7(1)(a) …

"27. … the use in the current Section 6 and 6A of the Act of the expressions 'preliminary test' and 'preliminary breath test' confirm the purpose of the roadside test. The roadside procedure, as Section 6A provides, is a procedure by which an 'indication' whether the prescribed limit is likely to be exceeded is obtained, and the specimen has no greater status.

"28. Further, the assumption in the last part of Section 15(2) [that the proportion of alcohol in the breath, blood or urine at the time of the offence was no less than in the specimen] plainly applies to the Section 7 specimens which provide the evidence for the Section 5 offence. It would defeat the scheme of the Act (often to the detriment of defendants) if the assumption were to be based upon the roadside breath test.

"29. When the 1988 Acts took effect, the device used in the roadside test provided only a threshold test. Technology has advanced and a reading in figures can, with modern equipment, readily be obtained. That change in technology has not, in my view, affected the statutory procedure to the extent that the prosecution are obliged to put that figure in evidence in every case.

"31. I would, however, consider it to be good practice, where equipment is in use which permits it easily to be done, for the reading in figures obtained from the roadside breath specimen to be disclosed to the defence. We are told that that has become general practice. It is a sound practice and one which may be required by Section 3 of Criminal Procedure and Investigations Act 1996, which deals with the prosecution's duty to disclose material. While in most cases, the evidence, if adduced, is likely to support the prosecution case, there may be cases in which it can provide a basis for a challenge to the accuracy of the Section 7 specimens obtained."

The answer to the question was "yes". Appeal dismissed.

3. THE RECORD OF THE PROCEDURE

For the non-statutory status of the contemporaneous record, see DPP v Smith (Robert James), page 58; McNeil v DPP, page 60; DPP v Rous and Davis, page 459; and DPP v Chajed, page 673.

R v Pydar JJ ex p Foster

(1996) 160 JP 87, 12 May 1995, QBD (DC)

Once the record of the procedure has been produced to the court, the court may call for and examine the printout even after the close of the prosecution case.

A motorist had been convicted of driving with excess alcohol, contrary to s 5(1)(a), Road Traffic Act 1988. The officer who administered the breath analysis procedure gave evidence and formally produced the document, Form RTA 2, in which the procedure had been contemporaneously recorded; the officer gave evidence of two readings of 52 µg alcohol in 100 ml breath, but was not questioned about the calibration or functioning of the breath analysis device. At the close of the prosecution case, the motorist's solicitor submitted there was no case to answer on the ground that the printout from the breath analysis device, contained in the Form RTA 2, had not been admitted in evidence. The justices then called for the Form RTA 2 and found it to contain all the relevant information on the breath alcohol reading, the operator's familiarity with the machine, and its proper calibration and functioning.

The motorist sought to appeal by way of case stated, but the justices refused to state a case on the ground that the application was frivolous. He then sought judicial review to compel them to do so.

HELD: "[Counsel for the applicant submits that] even though the document here was formally produced, the Justices did not actually have it before them or examine it before the close of the prosecution case, and, accordingly at that stage had no knowledge of its contents.

"I regard this as a quite impossible argument; once an exhibit is produced, the court has jurisdiction over it. It is available to the court and the court can examine it and derive from it all that it contains, whenever they please.

"It only became necessary here actually to examine the document once the defence made the submission of no case with regard to it.

"... the applicant's argument in the present case is impossible."

Application dismissed.

Williams v DPP

Unreported, CO/670/95, 4 December 1995, QBD (DC)

Where the officer gave oral evidence of the procedure, using the record to refresh his memory, the court was entitled to see the document, and indeed should have done so.

A motorist had been convicted of, *inter alia*, failing without reasonable excuse to provide two specimens of breath for analysis, contrary to s 7(6), Road Traffic Act 1988. At the trial, the officer who had administered the procedure gave evidence; he used the record of the procedure to refresh his memory, and the court had sight of the document. The document was, according to the judgment of the Divisional Court, "a combination of *pro forma* and adjunct to a proper procedure".

The motorist's appeal to the Crown Court was dismissed. He appealed further.

HELD: "[Counsel for the applicant submits that the fact that the court saw the record of the procedure] was totally erroneous as a matter of law. It is conceded that if it were contemporaneous the officer could, in the familiar way, refresh his memory from it. He would, I think, further concede that for that purpose the court is able to have a look at the document to make sure that he is in fact refreshing his memory from a contemporaneous document which said what he purported to say that it said … But [counsel argues] … it must not be put in, as it were, as part of the evidence in chief …

"… The critical matter was as to whether the course taken was within the reasonable discretion of the court, with a view to doing justice to both parties. For my part, I have found it difficult even to understand the merits of this matter. One is familiar for many years with witnesses utilising a document to refresh their memory. Had that document not been seen by the court, I, for one, would have been critical, not on grounds of law but critical on grounds of practice, that they were not properly checking the use of the form for the purposes for which the officer was seeking to utilise it. So far from being a matter for criticism that they saw the form, for my part, it would have been a matter for criticism if they had not seen the form."

Appeal dismissed.

4. THE DISCRETION TO ADMIT OR EXCLUDE EVIDENCE: UNFAIRNESS

See s 78, Police and Criminal Evidence Act 1984 – discretion to exclude evidence which would have such an adverse effect on the fairness of the proceedings that the court ought not to admit it. See also Twigg v R [2019] EWCA Crim 1553, 13 September 2019, CA (Crim), page 70.

DPP v Godwin

[1991] RTR 303, 22 April 1991, QBD (DC)

On the facts of this case (routine stop check; officer having no reasonable cause to suspect that the defendant had alcohol in his body before requiring breath test; unlawful arrest), there were no grounds for interfering with the justices' decision to exclude the evidence of breath analysis.

A motorist had been charged with driving with excess alcohol, contrary to s 5(1)(a), Road Traffic Act 1988. The police had been carrying out routine traffic stop checks and stopped the motorist; they asked if he had been drinking; he said he had not; he did not provide a roadside breath sample and was arrested. At the police station he provided breath specimens for analysis, which showed excess alcohol.

The justices found that, in the absence of evidence to the contrary, the constable had no reasonable cause to suspect that the defendant had had alcohol in his body before requesting a breath test and that the arrest was unlawful; although that would not automatically exclude the breath analysis evidence, and although lawful arrest is not an essential prerequisite to a request for a specimen, the justices chose to exercise their discretion under s 78, Police and Criminal Evidence Act 1984 (to exclude evidence which would have such an adverse effect on the fairness of the proceedings that the court ought not to admit it) to exclude the breath analysis evidence. They accordingly dismissed the charge. The prosecutor appealed.

QUESTION(S) FOR THE COURT: (1) Whether the justices were correct in finding that the arrest of the defendant was unlawful; (2) If so, whether their discretion to exclude the results of the police station procedure was correctly exercised.

HELD: "... it is not necessary for justices to be satisfied that the police or the prosecuting authorities have acted in bad faith or oppressively for the discretion under section 78 to be exercised ...

"... The justices were entitled to conclude that the substantial breach by the constable of the protection afforded to members of the public by section 6 [Road Traffic Act 1988 – reasonable cause to suspect, etc] was denied to the defendant, that as a result the prosecutor obtained evidence which he would not otherwise have obtained, and that as a result the defendant was prejudiced in a significant manner in resisting the charge against him.

"... the justices were entitled to exclude the evidence ...

"This court is entitled to intervene only if it shown that that discretion had been exercised in a manner which is legally challengeable. On the facts here the justices have directed themselves accurately and correctly so far as the law is concerned."

Appeal dismissed.

Hudson v DPP

[1992] RTR 27, 20 May 1991, QBD (DC)

On the facts of this case (motorist believing he need not provide breath specimens until he had received legal advice; delay in and suspension of procedure), it was open to the court below to exercise its discretion to exclude the evidence of failing to provide.

A motorist had been charged with failing without reasonable excuse to provide two specimens of breath for analysis, contrary to s 8(7), Road Traffic Act 1972 as substituted by s 25 and Sch 8, Transport Act 1981. He had been arrested and taken to a police station, where he was given documents (one of which was Form 300) explaining his right, under s 58, Police and Criminal Evidence Act 1984, to consult a solicitor. He asked for legal advice and the police took a number of steps to contact a solicitor. When asked to provide breath specimens, some 50 minutes after his arrival at the police station, the motorist at first agreed, but then asked for the duty solicitor; the procedure was suspended, but the duty solicitor declined to go to the police station because the motorist had not given his name and address. The breath testing procedure was begun again at 01.20, 19 minutes after the first request for breath specimens. The motorist declined to give specimens until he had consulted a solicitor. At 01.38 the motorist's solicitor spoke to him by telephone and advised him to co-operate. At 02.00 the motorist was told he would be charged with failing to provide specimens.

The justices convicted him. The motorist appealed to the Crown Court on the grounds, *inter alia*, that the documents given to him at the police station gave rise to a belief that he was entitled to consult a solicitor before any further steps were taken by the police and that that amounted to a lawful excuse for failure to provide a specimen; and that in any event the evidence of refusal should have been excluded under s 78, Police and Criminal Evidence Act 1984 (discretion to exclude evidence which would have such an adverse effect on the fairness of the proceedings that the court ought not to admit it). That appeal failed. The motorist appealed further.

QUESTION(S) FOR THE COURT: Whether the Crown Court was right to conclude: (i) that the defendant had no reasonable excuse for failure to provide a breath specimen; (ii) that evidence of the failure to supply a specimen of breath was admissible and should not have been excluded under s 78, Police and Criminal Evidence Act 1984.

HELD: "… when one looks at the two forms in the context of what happened … and in the time scale and events which occurred, it does not seem possible to say that there was not material upon which a court could have exercised its discretion under section 78 … from the time of [the defendant's] arrival at the police station nothing was done about activating the breathalyser procedure for very nearly an hour, … in looking at what the defendant's state of mind was at 01.20 hours when the admitted refusal took place, [it is important] to consider with some care that which … appears on the Form 300. Certainly between 01.00 hours and 01.20 hours the defendant would have had his belief in his rights reinforced by the apparent acceptance of his request.

"… therefore, I am not able to say that there were no circumstances … which ruled out any exercise of discretion under section 78 by the court."

Appeal allowed.

Daniels v DPP

[1992] RTR 140, 18 November 1991, QBD (DC)

Where police suspected the defendant both of having stolen a motor cycle and of having taken alcohol, and were then satisfied he had not stolen the cycle but did not tell him so and went on to require breath specimens, it was not unfair to admit evidence of failure to provide. The circumstances could amount to a special reason for not disqualifying.

The defendant had been charged with failing without reasonable excuse to provide a specimen of breath for analysis, contrary to s 8(7), Road Traffic Act 1972 as substituted by s 25 and Sch 8, Transport Act 1981. He had been helping another to "bump start" a motor cycle on the car park of a public house; the engine suddenly fired and the defendant decided to drive it into the road and turn it to keep the engine running. He was stopped by police because he was not wearing a helmet; they questioned him about the ownership of the cycle; they suspected him of having taken alcohol but did not require a roadside breath test; they could not locate the owner of the cycle and arrested the defendant for theft. Some time after his arrival at the police station, the police were satisfied that he had not stolen the cycle, but did not tell him so. He was then asked to provide specimens of breath for analysis, but refused.

He was convicted by magistrates; he appealed to the Crown Court, arguing, *inter alia*, that the evidence of the breathalyser procedure should have been excluded under s 78, Police and Criminal Evidence Act 1984 (discretion to exclude evidence which would have such an adverse effect on the fairness of the proceedings that the court ought not to admit it); and that the unusual factual circumstances amounted to special reasons for not disqualifying and endorsing the licence under s 93(1), Road Traffic Act 1972 as likewise substituted.

The Crown Court dismissed the appeal, finding no reasonable excuse and no special reasons. The motorist appealed further.

QUESTION(S) FOR THE COURT: Whether the Crown Court was correct: (ii) in refusing to exclude the evidence of the requirement; and (iii) to hold that none of the circumstances could amount to a reasonable excuse within s 8(7), or a special reason within s 93.

HELD: "[On (ii)] … the police did not behave in a manner in which they should have; in coming to their conclusion that the defendant was not responsible for the theft of the motor cycle, they failed to inform him of that fact before they embarked upon the breath analysis procedure … section 78 … is not confined to circumstances of *mala fides* … the Crown Court were clearly not confining themselves to considering whether there was a question of *mala fides*. They did not merely state that there was here no impropriety. They went on to add … that they did not consider that it would be unfair to the defendant to receive the evidence … they took into account all the relevant circumstances and came to the conclusion … that in this case it was not unfair to admit the evidence …

"[On special reasons] … the fact that [the defendant] refused to provide a breath specimen and there had been no reasonable excuse … does not mean inevitably that there will be no special reasons … While he understood the request that was being made to him, he was distracted from the request because of his concern about being charged with theft. He regarded it as a much more serious offence – an offence of dishonesty … if he had been told [the charge of theft] was no longer being explored, he might have taken a different view of providing a specimen. That … is something which a court is entitled to take into account as possibly providing special reasons. It would not provide a reasonable excuse, but it is … capable of providing a special reason."

Appeal allowed in part.

Brown (Kevin Mark) v DPP

Unreported, CO/583/93, 26 October 1993, QBD (DC)

Even if, on the facts (questioning before caution), there had been a breach of PACE Code C, it was not such as to lead to the exclusion of the defendant's admission that he had driven.

A person had been convicted of driving with excess alcohol, contrary to s 5(1), Road Traffic Act 1988. He had attended the police station in connection with another matter and, in conversation with a police officer, was asked how he had got to the police station so quickly. He replied that he drove there. The officer smelled intoxicating liquor; the person then denied he had said he had driven, saying that he had walked to the police station.

It was argued that there had been breaches of PACE Code C of the Codes of Practice under s 66, Police and Criminal Evidence Act 1984, and that the justices should consider excluding the evidence in question, under s 78(1), Police and Criminal Evidence Act 1984 (discretion to exclude evidence which would have such an adverse effect on the fairness of the proceedings that the court ought not to admit it). In particular, it was said that the justices should infer from the nature of the evidence given that the police officer had grounds to suspect an offence and should have administered the caution, either before asking the suspect how he had got to the police station so quickly, or before he answered that question. It was further argued that the whole passage amounted to an interview under the Code.

The defendant appealed.

HELD: "… I see no ground at all to impugn that decision [that the officer was making preliminary inquiries so that cautioning was not required] by the Justices. There is no indication that the circumstances were such that before putting that first question the police officer had grounds to suspect that the criminal offence was committed, and in those circumstances I see no basis to hold that there was a breach of para 10.1 [of PACE Code C] …

"I find it impossible to fault the finding of the Justices that this was not an interview. This was, indeed, simply questioning to obtain information; in essence making preliminary inquiries, which themselves might or might not lead in turn to circumstances in which a caution should be given, and in which further questioning became an interview within the terms of the Code.

"... were I persuaded there were breaches of the Code ... I could not be satisfied that those breaches were of such substance that any Court taking them into account pursuant to s 67(11), must have been driven to the view that this evidence should be excluded pursuant to s 78(1) of the Act ... ."

Appeal dismissed.

Worsley v DPP

Unreported, CO-1679-92, 11 November 1994, QBD (DC)

The fact that a motorist was not warned that failure to provide a roadside breath specimen would be an offence was not grounds for excluding evidence of failure to do so. The reference in the information to breath/blood/urine was not duplicitous; s 7(6), Road Traffic Act 1988 creates a single offence.

A motorist had been convicted of failing without reasonable excuse to provide a specimen for a breath test, contrary to s 6(4), Road Traffic Act 1988; and, "... having been required to provide a specimen of breath/blood/urine for analysis ...", with failing without reasonable excuse to do so, contrary to s 7(6), Road Traffic Act 1988. He had simply refused to give the breath, both at the roadside and at the police station. He appealed.

QUESTION(S) FOR THE COURT: (2) Whether the appellant had a reasonable excuse for not supplying a breath sample; (3) whether the justices were entitled on the evidence to convict.

HELD: "[On the contention that the appellant should have been warned at the roadside that refusal would be an offence and that the magistrates should have excluded it under s 78, Police and Criminal Evidence Act 1984 (discretion to exclude evidence which would have such an adverse effect on the fairness of the proceedings that the court ought not to admit it)] ... there is no statutory provision that such a warning is mandatory ... I would not have found that a warning was strictly necessary in the absence of a statutory direction, but where the Act spells out expressly that it is in certain circumstances and does not do so in others, that conclusion seems to me to be inevitable.

"The question [is] whether the magistrates reached a decision which no reasonable magistrate could have reached as a matter of discretion. I have no hesitation in rejecting that submission.

"[On (2)] ... the debate on that question had really been because it had been suggested that the appellant had been taking some pills ... The magistrates' findings indicate that was not made out; ... the appellant had no reasonable excuse."

The answer to question (3) was "yes".

"But [counsel for the appellant] takes another point, which is that one of the charges was bad for duplicity … a point of duplicity [may] be taken on appeal, albeit for the first time …

"… one offence only is created by section 7(6). It is an offence of failing to provide a specimen. It might be a specimen of blood, breath or urine, but only one offence is created … the reference in the information to breath/ blood/urine is not duplicitous in the sense that it charges three or even two separate offences … the information was not duplicitous."

Appeal dismissed.

DPP v MacPhail

Unreported, CO/1084/97, 8 July 1997, QBD (DC)

Magistrates were not wrong in law to find that a police officer had acted male fide in requiring a second roadside breath test after a first negative test and before 20 minutes had expired; nor were they wrong in law to exclude evidence of the subsequent breath analysis.

A motorist had been charged with driving with excess alcohol, contrary to s 5(1)(a), Road Traffic Act 1988. He had been stopped by police, who smelt alcohol on his breath and asked for a roadside screening test. What then happened was disputed. The officer said he asked the motorist to wait 20 minutes before he could administer the test, as required by the instructions provided with the breath testing equipment; the motorist refused to wait and the officer therefore administered the test before the 20 minutes had elapsed; there was only one test. The respondent, on the other hand, said he had blown twice into the device; the first sample illuminated a red and an amber light; the second illuminated two red lights. He said that on the first breath, the officer looked at the device and said the test was not correct. The motorist contended that the officer had acted in bad faith in that he did not tell the motorist that he should wait 20 minutes before taking the test, and that, having provided a negative sample by means of the first test, the officer had nevertheless detained him at the roadside and required a further sample without explanation.

The respondent was then taken to the police station where breath analysis revealed 56 μg alcohol in 100 ml breath.

The magistrates found that, at the roadside, two breath tests had been taken within a short time; the first had been negative, the second positive; both were conducted before 20 minutes had elapsed since the time of the motorist's last drink. They found that the officer had acted *mala fide* in requiring a second test after a first negative test before the 20 minutes had elapsed; even if they were wrong in that, they would exercise their discretion under s 78, Police and Criminal Evidence Act 1984 (to exclude evidence which would have such an adverse effect on the fairness of the proceedings that the court ought not to admit it) to refuse to admit the evidence of the breath analysis at the police station.

They acquitted the motorist. The prosecutor appealed.

QUESTION(S) FOR THE COURT: (1) Was the court's finding of fact that the respondent had provided a negative breath test perverse in the circumstances? (2) Was the court right as a question of law to find on the evidence adduced that the arresting officer at the roadside acted with *mala fides*? (3) Was the court right in exercising its discretion to exclude evidence of breath analysis under s 78, Police and Criminal Evidence Act 1984? (4) Was the court right to acquit the respondent?

HELD: "[Section 78 confers] a power to exclude evidence if [the court thinks] that its admission would have an adverse effect on the fairness of the proceedings … In the instant case the magistrates heard the witnesses giving conflicting accounts and made clear findings that they accepted the evidence given by the respondent. That is a matter that this court cannot go behind … It is not necessary to establish *mala fides*, oppression or conduct of that sort before a court can exercise its discretion under section 78 … Their decision is … only reviewable if it can be said that it is either perverse or based upon no evidence … the magistrates' view cannot be said to be such."

The answer to question (1) was "no"; question (2) did not arise; question (3): "the question for this court is not whether the magistrates were right, but whether the magistrates were wrong in law in taking that view, to which reformulated question the answer is 'no'". On question (4), "there is no error of law reviewable by this court in the decision to acquit the respondent". Appeal dismissed.

Prouse v DPP

Unreported, CO/157/99, 7 July 1999, QBD (DC)

Given the breaches of the Police and Criminal Evidence Act 1984 which occurred in this case, it was correct to exclude evidence of three interviews, but to admit evidence of a fourth interview which had been conducted in accordance with the Police and Criminal Evidence Act 1984.

The defendant had been arrested on suspicion of driving with excess alcohol and taken to a police station. He was offered legal advice by telephone and spoke to the duty solicitor. He was breath-tested, the lower reading showing 68 μg alcohol in 100 ml breath. He was then detained until he was fit to be interviewed, and was interviewed at 12.30 am the following morning.

Before arriving at the police station he had been spoken to three times; once before arrest and before caution in his home, once after arrest and caution at his home, and once in the car on the way to the police station. Those three conversations revealed that he had been to a funeral that day; he had taken alcohol after the funeral; he had last had "a couple of cans" at about 4.00 pm; he had last driven his car at about 5.00 pm; and that he had not had a drink since he arrived home. At the police station the custody sergeant found that the defendant was not fit to be interviewed, and detained him to be interviewed later when he was fit. The final interview, at 12.30 am the next day, was properly conducted; the defendant was offered further legal advice, but declined it.

On appeal against conviction for driving with excess alcohol, it was conceded that the first three conversations were interviews within PACE Code C of the PACE Codes of Practice and that the defendant had not been in a fit state to be properly interviewed. It was said that there were further breaches of the PACE Codes of Practice and, in particular, PACE Code C. The Crown Court considered the most important breach was the breach of paragraph 6, the appellant not having been offered any opportunity to take legal advice before conversations, i.e. interviews, took place. The court held that the earlier interviews should not be admitted in evidence because they would have an adverse effect on the fairness of the trial, and so excluded them under s 78, Police and Criminal Evidence Act 1984 (discretion to exclude evidence which would have such an adverse effect on the fairness of the proceedings that the court ought not to admit it), but admitted evidence of the fourth interview.

The Crown Court dismissed the appeal; the appellant appealed further.

HELD: "… Whether or not a later interview should be excluded where the earlier interviews have been excluded on the grounds of unfairness, is essentially a matter of fact and degree … The only question which arises is whether or not the Appellant had an opportunity to form an independent and sensible judgment as to how he should conduct himself in the course of that interview unaffected by the breaches which had occurred earlier … the Crown Court was right to conclude that the opportunity the Appellant had had to take legal advice at that stage in the proceedings, although he declined to have the advantage of a solicitor, during the interview was sufficient … the later interview was perfectly properly conducted and therefore admissible … the Crown Court were entirely right to conclude that interview four was properly admitted."

Appeal dismissed.

Ortega v DPP

[2001] EWHC Admin 143, 26 February 2001, QBD (DC)

On the facts of this case (doorstep interview – no grounds to suspect offence; police station interview conducted fairly), the decision to admit evidence of both interviews was not improper.

The appellant had been convicted of driving with excess alcohol in breath, contrary to s 5(1)(a), Road Traffic Act 1988 and appealed to the Crown Court. A Ministry of Defence police officer, Constable Stewart, had received information about a drunken male who was about to drive a vehicle from Lakenheath Air Base. The officer went, with a colleague, to the address of the registered keeper of the vehicle. The car was in the drive and the engine was warm.

The appellant answered the officers' knock, and said either that he resided at the address alone or that he was at the address alone at that time. Constable Stewart asked the appellant if he was the owner of the car; he replied "yes". Constable Stewart did not believe that there were, at that stage, grounds to suspect that the appellant had driven the car, and so believed that he was not required to administer a caution before asking further questions. He asked the appellant if he had just driven from RAF Lakenheath, and he replied "yes".

The officer then asked if he had been drinking alcohol, to which the answer was "yes", and the appellant said that his last alcoholic drink had been about 20 minutes previously, when he left RAF Lakenheath. A breath sample was positive. The appellant was arrested, cautioned and taken to the police station. No contemporaneous record had been made of the conversation up to this point.

At the police station, a breath specimen was provided and the lower reading was 55 µg alcohol in 100 ml breath. The appellant was interviewed. The interview was recorded on tape; in the interview, the officer reminded the appellant of the doorstep conversation, including his admission that he had driven the vehicle, and the appellant agreed with the constable's account of what had been said on the doorstep, except for one detail. Throughout the interview, the appellant expressed uncertainty whether or not to have a solicitor present, but he was given every opportunity to have one present if he wanted.

The Crown Court found that Constable Stewart did not have grounds to suspect the appellant of having committed an offence prior to asking him on the doorstep of his house if he had just driven from RAF Lakenheath, and so found the admission that he had driven to be admissible.

The court also found that the interview at the police station had been conducted fairly and the answers not obtained by oppression; nothing was said or done which could possibly have made the answers unreliable, and nothing caused the admission of the interview in evidence to have an adverse effect on the fairness of the proceedings. They convicted the appellant, who appealed further.

QUESTION(S) FOR THE COURT: (A) Was the finding that PC Stewart had no grounds to suspect the appellant of an offence contrary to s 4 or s 5, Road Traffic Act 1988 before asking him if he had just driven from RAF Lakenheath a finding which no reasonable court could have made? (B) If so, was the decision to admit in evidence the "doorstep interview" a decision which no reasonable court could have made? (C) If so, was the decision to admit the evidence of the taped interview at the police station a decision which no reasonable court could have made?

HELD: "18. [The appellant submits that under Code C of the Codes of Practice under s 66, Police and Criminal Evidence Act 1984 he] should have been cautioned because … the officers had grounds to suspect an offence of driving while adversely affected by drink; … 19. [that] the doorstep conversation … amounted to an interview and there should have been … a contemporaneous record of it; [that] the evidence should have been excluded under section 78 of the Police and Criminal Evidence Act because of the consequential unfairness in view of the breaches of the Code …; 20. that the … police station interview was tainted by the breaches which had occurred on the doorstep. The defendant, although offered legal advice, did not know whether he ought to accept it, and he had not been given a sufficient opportunity to exercise an informed and independent choice as to whether he should repeat or retract what he had said in the first interview or say nothing. …

"25. … the finding … that Constable Stewart did not have grounds to suspect the appellant of the offence prior to asking him if he had just driven from RAF Lakenheath is, in the light of the evidence which was before the Crown Court, a conclusion which they were entitled to reach …

"26. The justices did not go on specifically to consider … whether, in the light of the failure thereafter to caution the appellant, and to make a contemporaneous record of what was said, those matters ought to have been excluded in the exercise of the court's discretion under sections 76 and 78 of the Police and Criminal Evidence Act. [Had they done so, it would] have been open to them to conclude that, despite those breaches of the Code, the evidence should properly be admitted.

"27. In any event, so far as the further interview at the police station, which again contained an admission of driving at the crucial time, is concerned, it seems … quite impossible to contend that there was any tainting of that interview or any other circumstance which could give rise to characterising the justices' decision to admit the terms of that interview under section 78 of the Police and Criminal Evidence Act as perverse."

Appeal dismissed.

Porceddu v DPP

[2001] EWHC Admin 597, 4 July 2001, QBD (Admin)

On the facts of this case, it was fair to admit identification evidence even though there had been no identification parade.

The appellant had been charged with, *inter alia*, driving with excess alcohol, contrary to s 5, Road Traffic Act 1988. His vehicle had collided with a stationary car in a well-lit street. An independent witness, who lived in the street, said there was only one occupant of the car and that he saw him get out, look back at the vehicle and stagger towards the end of the street before returning to the vehicle. The witness telephoned the police, giving a description of the man he had seen. Two other vehicles arrived; the occupant of one helped the motorist push his car to the side of the road. The police asked the witness to come out of the house to see if he could identify the driver. He identified the appellant as he was being led from his car to the police car, having been arrested.

The justices accepted the identification evidence of the witness and acknowledged that where identification is an issue, an identification parade should be held (PACE Code D2 of the Codes of Practice under s 66, Police and Criminal Evidence Act 1984), but found that the breach of the Code was not sufficiently significant and substantial so as to exclude the evidence.

They convicted; the appellant appealed.

QUESTION(S) FOR THE COURT: (1) Whether the justices were correct to admit evidence of identification of the appellant; and (2) if not, whether, properly directed, they could convict.

HELD: “18. … the significance of the breach [of PACE Code D2] is an important issue in a case such as the present. …

“19. … there were only two conceivable candidates for who was the driver of the vehicle: either it was the defendant, or … it was a second person in the vehicle, [the witness] having given evidence that there was in fact only one occupant. Furthermore, the present case is very much a recognition case rather than a true identification case because [the witness] had had a clear view of the appellant in good light and over a significant period of time shortly before he made the identification.

“20. … that the appellant was already in the hands of the police having been arrested … would, in my judgment, be of more significance if the identification was of the appellant as against the population generally rather than the appellant in the circumstances of this case, when there were, at most, only two possible candidates for the person who drove the vehicle.

“21. In my judgment, the Justices correctly held that there had been a breach of the Code, albeit that it was a breach that fell towards the rather more technical end of the scale, as it were. They then had a discretion to exercise. Whether they specifically had section 78 [Police and Criminal Evidence Act 1984 – discretion to exclude evidence which would have such an adverse effect on the fairness of the proceedings that the court ought not to admit it] in mind or not does not, in my judgment, matter because it is perfectly plain that anyone exercising a section 78 judgment on the facts of this case would inevitably have been driven to the conclusion that it was perfectly fair to admit, as an exercise in discretion, the evidence of identification.”

The answer to the first question was “no”; the second question did not therefore arise. Appeal dismissed.

Harper v DPP

[2001] EWHC Admin 1071, 5 December 2001, QBD (Admin)

On the facts of this case (unlawfulness of arrest a matter of form not substance), it was not unreasonable for the Crown Court to allow the prosecutor to adduce evidence of what occurred at the police station.

A motorist had been charged with, *inter alia*, failing without reasonable excuse to provide specimens of breath for analysis, contrary to s 7(6), Road Traffic Act 1988. A witness, and police officers, had seen a trail being left by a damaged car; police followed the trail to the defendant’s house where they saw the car, parked. There was a smell of alcohol in the car and the airbag was inflated. They suspected the driver might have been drinking and knocked on the door of the house. One of the officers saw a person duck down and the lights went off. No one answered the door. The police shouted that they were going to use force. They did so, calling to the occupants to identify themselves. The defendant appeared. The officers concluded from his appearance that he had been drinking; he was cautioned and admitted that he was the owner of the car and that he had been driving. One of the officers then said "I am arresting you on suspicion of driving a motor vehicle on the road whilst over the prescribed limit through drink or drugs". He was taken to the police station where he refused to undergo the breath testing procedure.

At the hearing, the officer said that when he used those words he had in mind s 4, Road Traffic Act 1988, although the words were not entirely appropriate to that section.

At the Crown Court it was argued that the entry of the police into the house was unlawful because the police did not have reasonable suspicion at that time that someone in the house had driven whilst unfit; and entry by force was inappropriate because it had not been shown that there was a need to use force – the back door could have been checked. It was further submitted that if the entry was lawful, the arrest was unlawful because the words used suggested that the ground for arrest was the non-arrestable s 5 offence, rather than the arrestable s 4 offence.

The Crown Court found that the police did have reasonable suspicion that someone in the house had committed the arrestable offence of driving whilst unfit; and that they had power to force entry. They convicted the defendant; he appealed.

QUESTION(S) FOR THE COURT: (a) On the facts found did the Crown Court err in law in holding that the police were not trespassers in the appellant's residence? (b) On the facts found did the Crown Court err in law in holding that the police lawfully arrested the appellant? (c) If the answer to either of the above questions is "yes", was it *Wednesbury* unreasonable for the Crown Court to have exercised its discretion under s 78, Police and Criminal Evidence Act 1984 (to exclude evidence which would have such an adverse effect on the fairness of the proceedings that the court ought not to admit it) in favour of the respondent and allow him to adduce evidence of what had occurred at the police station.

HELD: "[On (a)] 50. … the Crown Court did not err in holding that the police were not trespassers in the appellant's residence. The principles to be applied are not in doubt. Entry may be obtained by force but only 'if need be'…

"51. In the present case, the appellant was not on the other side of the door, indeed quite to the contrary he was doing his very best to hide from the police, switching off the upstairs lights and ducking down. He gave no response to the knock on the door and no response to the shouted warning that force was to be used …

"[On (b), the officer] 54. … was not obliged to use technical or precise language … [his] words are a perfectly adequate summary of an offence under section 5. They are not an adequate summary of an offence under section 4. This is not simply a technicality. It was lawful … to arrest the appellant under section 4. Parliament, for whatever reason, has not conferred a power of arrest in respect of offences under section 5 …

"56. … the appellant was told, in effect, that he was being arrested for an offence under section 5. He was perfectly entitled to resist being arrested upon that ground. The fact that the officer may have had section 4 in his mind is … nothing to the point.

"57. … the Crown Court did err in law in holding that the police lawfully arrested the appellant.

"[On (c)] 59. … for whatever reason, the appellant … was required to provide a specimen at the police station and failed to do so. …

"62. But the position, in my judgment, is quite different when it comes to the exercise of a discretion under section 78 as to the admission of evidence. There the court is concerned with substantive questions of fairness and unfairness. The position is no different under the European Convention on Human Rights, which is concerned with substance rather than form. The unlawfulness of the arrest in the present case was a matter of form not substance. There was absolutely no unfairness in allowing evidence of what occurred at the police station to be admitted. Thus, I conclude that the answer to the third question posed by the Crown Court is: no, the Crown Court did not exercise its discretion in a manner that was *Wednesbury* unreasonable."

Appeal dismissed.

Davis (Karl) v DPP

[2001] EWHC Admin 1129, 18 December 2001, QBD (Admin)

On the facts of this case, there was no injustice in admitting identification evidence even though there been no identification parade.

A motorist had been charged with failing without reasonable excuse to provide a specimen of blood for analysis. A vehicle had collided with a wall and street light; three separate witnesses saw a man near the vehicle; he was seen to use his mobile telephone and then leave the scene. Police attended the scene and the three witnesses gave them descriptions of the man. The police examined the vehicle and found the ignition to be intact; a document in the vehicle led them to the defendant. A police officer telephoned the defendant, who admitted that he was the owner of the car. He said he had given no one permission to drive it, and that it had been parked some distance from the point at which the accident took place. The police took the appellant to the scene, where one of the police officers directed the attention of the witnesses to the defendant with a nod of the head.

The magistrates accepted the evidence of the three witnesses that the defendant was the same man they had seen previously, even though he was differently dressed. Some 2 weeks later he was charged with other driving offences arising out of the same incident.

At the hearing, the defendant argued, *inter alia*, that since an identification procedure pursuant to PACE Code D of the Codes of Practice under s 66, Police and Criminal Evidence Act 1984 had not been held, the identification evidence should be excluded under s 78, Police and Criminal Evidence Act 1984 (discretion to exclude evidence which would have such an adverse effect on the fairness of the proceedings that the court ought not to admit it). The magistrates rejected the argument and convicted the defendant. He appealed.

QUESTION(S) FOR THE COURT: Whether the magistrates were correct in law not to exclude the evidence of identification pursuant to s 78, Police and Criminal Evidence Act 1984 in concluding that the appellant was the driver of the vehicle in question.

HELD: "[After reviewing the requirements of PACE Code D where identification is disputed, and assuming that the defendant did in fact dispute that he had been driving, and after reviewing the authorities] 21. … It is plain that … the defence placed some reliance [on] the fact that the officer in charge at the scene had 'directed the attention of the witnesses to the defendant with a nod of the head'… the Court should keep its feet firmly on the ground. The scene was some time after 12.30 at night; it would have been a surprising thing if, despite the fact that an accident had occurred, the scene of the accident at that hour was that of a milling crowd.

"33. … there was no material upon which the Justices … could have come to the conclusion that the admission of the evidence from the identifying witnesses would have had such an adverse effect on the fairness of the proceedings that it ought not to have been admitted."

The answer to the question was "yes". Appeal dismissed.

DPP v Davies

[2002] EWHC 1110 (Admin), 13 May 2002, QBD (Admin)

In the circumstances of this case (breach of PACE Code C in respect of a conversation), the justices were entitled to exclude evidence of the conversation.

A person had been charged with driving with excess alcohol, contrary to s 5(1)(a), Road Traffic Act 1988. Police had been called to his home; he smelled of alcohol; his eyes were glazed; he was drinking tea. One of the officers asked if he had had anything else to drink since getting home; he replied "no", and, in answer to a further question, that he had been home for about 20 or 25 minutes. The officer cautioned him and told him he suspected he had driven his car home; the respondent admitted he had driven; the officer required a sample of breath.

At the hearing, it was argued that the evidence of the conversation at the defendant's home should be excluded under s 78, Police and Criminal Evidence Act 1984 (discretion to exclude evidence which would have such an adverse effect on the fairness of the proceedings that the court ought not to admit it), because PACE Code C, paragraph 11.13 of the Codes of Practice under s 66, Police and Criminal Evidence Act 1984 had not been met (written record to be made of any comments made by a suspect outside the context of an interview but which might be relevant; record to be timed and signed by the maker; if practicable, suspect to be given the opportunity to read and sign record).

The justices found there had been a significant and substantial breach of the Code: the record was not timed or signed; the defendant had not been given an opportunity to read the record and sign it as correct or indicate any respects in which he considered it inaccurate. They exercised their discretion under s 78(1) to exclude the evidence in question. After hearing the rest of the case, they concluded there was no evidence that the defendant had been driving the car and acquitted him. The prosecutor appealed.

HELD: "19. … The whole purpose … of C 11.13 is to avoid the very kind of dispute of fact that there would have been had the evidence been admitted …

"23. This court … is loathe to interfere with exercises of discretion under section 78 and will only do so if the lower court has taken into account matters that are irrelevant, or has failed to take into account matters that are relevant, or otherwise has come to a conclusion that no reasonable bench of magistrates properly directed could have reached. I am not persuaded in this case that the magistrates have failed in any of those regards.

"30. … There was a very clear breach of the Code … and the justices were entitled to conclude that the effect on the fairness of the proceedings was such as to require them not to admit the evidence."

Appeal dismissed.

R (DPP) v Evans (Brychan Gethin John)

[2002] EWHC 2976 (Admin), (2003) 167 JP 144, 13 December 2002, QBD (Admin)

Although there had been a breach of PACE Code C (appropriate adult not called), the magistrates were wrong to exclude the evidence of the subsequent breath analysis. See also Francis v DPP, page 31, where the driver had been detained under the Mental Health Act 1983; and Miller v DPP, page 375, where the failure to call an appropriate adult did lead to the exclusion of evidence.

A minor aged 16 had been charged with driving with excess alcohol, contrary to s 5(1)(a), Road Traffic Act 1988. A roadside breath test was positive. At the police station, he was read his rights; he declined a solicitor. The custody officer did not contact a person to act as an appropriate adult pursuant to PACE Code C, paragraph 3.9 of the Codes of Practice under s 66, Police and Criminal Evidence Act 1984 (in the case of a juvenile, custody officer to inform an appropriate adult as soon as possible of the grounds for detention and the juvenile's whereabouts and ask the adult to come to the police station). It was not possible to contact his parents and he did not contact the local social services department because the time was close to the time at which their shifts changed. He made a note to contact an appropriate adult. Breath analysis revealed 43 μg alcohol in 100 ml breath; the officer conducting the procedure therefore offered the option to provide a blood or urine specimen, under s 8(2), Road Traffic Act 1988 (lower of two breath readings not more than 50 μg alcohol in 100 ml breath – now repealed; see page v). The youth declined.

The magistrates found that the reasons for not contacting an appropriate adult were inadequate and insubstantial; they exercised the discretion under s 78, Police and Criminal Evidence Act 1984 (to exclude evidence which would have such an adverse effect on the fairness of the proceedings that the court ought not to admit it) to exclude the evidence of the breath analysis and acquitted the youth. The prosecutor appealed.

QUESTION(S) FOR THE COURT: Whether the magistrates were entitled to find: (a) that the failure of the custody officer to contact an appropriate adult was a breach of PACE Code C; (b) that in the light of any such breach, they had a discretion to exclude the evidence of the breath analysis under s 78; and (c) whether they were right to exercise that discretion so as to exclude the evidence.

HELD: "15. ... there is a consistent theme running through the authorities ... It is that in relation to section 7 [provision of specimens for analysis] and section 8 [choice of specimens of breath], time is of the essence. ... It is not ... necessary to delay section 7 or section 8 proceedings in order to allow the detainee time to read the Codes or to obtain brief telephone advice, or to await the arrival of a solicitor. In my judgment, it would be contrary to the theme established by those authorities to require the attendance of an appropriate adult prior to proceeding to the section 8 stage and putting the detainee to his election. I have considered whether the specific circumstances of a juvenile require that matters be delayed either generally or in relation to the circumstances of this case. In my judgment they do not. ... whilst the magistrates were correct to identify a breach of section C3.9, they were wrong to exclude the evidence obtained pursuant to section 7 procedure because of that breach."

The answer to question (a) was "yes"; the answer to question (b) was, technically, "yes"; the answer to question (c) was "no". Appeal allowed.

DPP v Preston

[2003] EWHC 729 (Admin), 20 March 2003, QBD (Admin)

On the facts (no evidence of breach of the PACE Codes of Practice or that the motorist did not understand the procedure), the magistrates were unreasonable to exclude evidence of blood analysis.

A motorist had been charged with driving with excess alcohol, contrary to s 5(1)(a), Road Traffic Act 1988. He had been stopped; he said he was a chronic asthmatic and would not be able to provide a breath specimen; he was arrested. At the police station, it was obvious to the custody sergeant that the motorist was asthmatic, and he therefore required a specimen of blood, which was taken shortly afterwards. Analysis revealed excess alcohol.

In evidence, the sergeant said he was aware that the defendant had had breathing difficulties; that he suffered asthma, bronchitis and diabetes; and took medication and used a nebuliser. The sergeant did not ask the doctor to examine the defendant. Medical evidence confirmed chronic obstructive airways disease, asthma, diabetes and manic depressive illness.

The magistrates found that the custody sergeant had breached PACE Code C, paragraphs 1.4 (circumstances in which a person is to be treated as mentally disordered or mentally handicapped and an appropriate adult called), 9.2 (medical attention for person suffering from physical illness or mental disorder) and 9.6 (advice of police surgeon to be obtained if a detained person has in his possession or claims to need medication relating to certain conditions) of the Codes of Practice under s 66, Police and Criminal Evidence Act 1984; and that the breaches were significant and substantial. They also found that the sergeant had correctly followed the drink-drive procedure, but that the defendant had not understood the procedure. They excluded the evidence of the blood analysis under s 78, Police and Criminal Evidence Act 1984 (discretion to exclude evidence which would have such an adverse effect on the fairness of the proceedings that the court ought not to admit it) and dismissed the charge. The prosecutor appealed.

QUESTION(S) FOR THE COURT: (1) Whether the breaches of the Police and Criminal Evidence Act 1984 found to have occurred entitled the magistrates to exclude the evidence of the blood analysis; (2) in view of the magistrates' finding that the custody sergeant had followed the breath testing procedure correctly, whether they were right to exclude the evidence under s 78.

HELD: "34. … there was no evidence before the Magistrates to justify the conclusion that Code C1.4 was breached. Even if I am wrong about that and the attendance of an appropriate adult should have been arranged, that breach of itself is not material. …

"38. … there is not a word of evidence … to justify [the] finding [that the defendant did not comprehend the drink drive procedure].

"49. It is clear that Mr Preston … had diabetes, asthma and was manic depressive. There was no evidence … that he was suffering from any symptoms at the material time, save for his breathing difficulties, which were clearly symptomatic of his asthma. The material time … was short. It began with his arrival at the police station at 5.08 in the morning and ended very shortly after the taking of the blood sample at 5.28 that same morning. There was, accordingly, a breach of paragraph 9.2 if a doctor was not called to the police station.

"50. However, either … a doctor was already at the police station, or one was called there because…, at 5.28 [the doctor] took the blood specimen. …

"51. What is not made clear is at what stage and for what reason the doctor was called. Certainly, the Justices did find as a fact that [the doctor] was not asked to, and did not, examine the respondent.

"52. … however, even assuming a breach of paragraph 9.2, that breach can hardly be characterised as substantial and significant. After all, the doctor saw Mr Preston. Mr Preston could speak and he could have told the doctor that he required medical attention if in truth he did. There was no evidence before the Magistrates that he did.

"54. … there is no evidence … to warrant the finding that there had been, or may have been, a substantial and significant breach of [paragraph 9.6]. Indeed, in my view, there is no evidence to suggest that there may have been even a breach, let alone a serious one.

"55. … [The justices'] decision to exclude the evidence which proved that Mr Preston had been driving with an excess quantity of alcohol in his blood, was unreasonable. …

"56. … because there was in truth no evidence before them to justify the conclusion that there was, or may have been, any material, let alone substantial and significant breach of code C, nor was there any evidence to justify the conclusion that Mr Preston did not comprehend, or may not have comprehended, what the Justices termed 'the drink drive procedure'."

The answers to the questions were "no". Appeal allowed.

Watson v DPP

[2003] EWHC 1466 (Admin), 11 June 2003, QBD (DC)

Where a motorist's admissions (of being the owner and having driven) were not noted and dealt with as required by the Police and Criminal Evidence Act 1984, they were nevertheless admissible in the circumstances.

A motorist had been charged with driving with excess alcohol, contrary to s 5(1)(a), Road Traffic Act 1988. Police arrived at the scene of a road traffic accident. The driver of the vehicle was no longer there. They went to the defendant's home; an officer asked the defendant if he was the owner of the vehicle in question; he replied yes and the officer cautioned him before asking him if he had been the driver. He again admitted it. A breath test was positive and he was arrested. En route to the station, the arresting officer was called to another incident; he took the defendant to the police station and booked him in. He did not write up his notes of the incident until he returned, by which time the breath analysis procedure had been completed and the defendant had been charged.

The defendant argued that his admission that he had been the driver should have been noted and dealt with as required by PACE Code C, paragraph 11.10 of the Codes of Practice under s 66, Police and Criminal Evidence Act 1984 (unless impracticable, interviewee to be given the opportunity to read the interview record and sign it as correct or indicate the respects in which he considers it inaccurate); that had not been done and the magistrates should therefore exclude that evidence pursuant to s 78, Police and Criminal Evidence Act 1984 (discretion to exclude evidence which would have such an adverse effect on the fairness of the proceedings that the court ought not to admit it).

The magistrates rejected that argument and convicted the defendant. He appealed.

QUESTION(S) FOR THE COURT: (A) Whether the magistrates were correct in holding that the defendant's alleged confession, i.e. his admission that he owned the vehicle in question, and that he was driving at the time of the accident, was not obtained in circumstances where anything said or done by the police would make it unreliable; (B) whether the magistrates correctly exercised their discretion to admit the record of the defendant's answers to questions notwithstanding that the record was not made contemporaneously and was not submitted to the defendant to sign as a true record.

HELD: "10. [The prosecution] submits that … it cannot be said that this appellant was deprived of any reasonable opportunity to deny he was the driver. He was, of course, taken to the police station, and the whole breathalyser procedure gone through. At the police station … he had a series of opportunities to deny that he was the driver. … there is no suggestion of bad faith in this case. [It is accepted] that that is only one element in assessing admissibility, but here there cannot have been any question of error arising. Had the appellant said that he was not the driver, the officer would have remembered that, and any officer acting honestly in that situation would plainly have asked who the driver was. In practical terms, there is, he submits, no possibility of a mistake.

"12. … In this case … the appellant had ample opportunity to put his apparently different version of events, if he wished to do so. It also seems to me that the justices are entitled to have regard to the fact that the police officer was, as they found, called away in an emergency. I do not accept that invariably in a situation such as this, an [ad]mission must be excluded."

The answers to the questions were "yes". Appeal dismissed.

DPP v Kennedy

[2003] EWHC 2583 (Admin), (2004) 168 JP 185, 24 October 2003, QBD (DC)

Where the mouthpiece on the roadside breath testing device was not changed between attempts to provide specimens, the magistrates were wrong to conclude that the device was not correctly assembled and that the test had not been properly carried out; they were also wrong to exclude the evidence of what followed at the police station.

A motorist had been charged with driving with excess alcohol, contrary to s 5(1)(a), Road Traffic Act 1988. He had been stopped by police; an officer smelt intoxicants and required him to take a roadside breath test. The motorist blew at least twice, at first failing to provide sufficient breath to test. On a later attempt, he provided a positive sample and was arrested. The police officer did not change the mouthpiece on the device between attempts. At the police station, breath analysis was positive.

The justices found that failure to change the mouthpiece constituted incorrect assembly of the device and that there had therefore been no roadside breath test, and that the arrest was, as a result, unlawful. They refused to admit the evidence of the breath analysis at the police station, and dismissed the charge. The prosecutor appealed.

QUESTION(S) FOR THE COURT: (1) (as re-worded in the judgment) Whether, because no fresh mouthpiece was fitted after the first effort to provide a sample, there was a failure to comply with the manufacturer's instructions, and if so whether that failure was of such significance as to render the test invalid; (2) whether there was any basis on which a bench of justices properly directed on the facts and the law could have exercised the discretion under s 78, Police and Criminal Evidence Act 1984 (to exclude evidence which would have such an adverse effect on the fairness of the proceedings that the court ought not to admit it) to exclude the evidence of the specimens of breath provided for analysis.

HELD: "[After referring to the instructions for the roadside breath testing device and the police officer's evidence, the officer having agreed that he should have changed the mouthpiece, although the manufacturer's instructions did not bear that out] 12. … it seems surely obvious that, first of all, where the mouthpiece is used for a second time by the same suspect there is no danger of disease transmission and, secondly, if the second attempt to provide a sample is made straight after the first there is no realistic possibility that any residue will distort the result because the device is measuring concentrate. …

"13. … there was no sound basis for the magistrates' conclusion that the device was not correctly assembled and, therefore, [their conclusion that] the roadside test was not properly carried out …

"16. … Even if the justices were not mistaken, they patently failed to consider whether the failure to change the mouthpiece could have had any significant effect upon the test result … If they had considered that question, they would inevitably have concluded that it could not have done so … That is sufficient to dispose of the case. …

"However, I do propose to go on to consider the use of section 78 …

"17. … it is clear from the authorities that if effect is to be given to the change in the law which made proof of lawful arrest no longer a condition precedent to the admission of evidence as to tests administered at a police station, there must be something more than simply proof of unlawful arrest before a court is entitled to rely on section 78 to exclude that evidence, that is to say the evidence of what took place at the police station. It may be proof of bad faith or oppression, the list is not closed, but it is clear … in the present case that what was accepted here was simple proof of unlawful arrest; that was all there was."

The answers to both questions were "no". Appeal allowed.

R (Forde) v DPP

[2004] EWHC 1156 (Admin), 6 May 2004, QBD (Admin)

Where a police officer did not relay the suspect's request to speak to a solicitor until 20 minutes after the request, the justices were nevertheless entitled to admit evidence of failure to provide specimens.

A motorist had been charged with failing without reasonable excuse to provide a specimen of blood for a laboratory test, contrary to s 7(6), Road Traffic Act 1988. He had been arrested and at the police station the officer conducting the procedure was of the opinion that the breath analysis device was not reliable; he therefore required a blood specimen. The motorist refused, saying he wanted to speak to a solicitor. He was charged with failure to provide a specimen. Twenty minutes later the officer relayed the motorist's request to speak to a solicitor.

At the trial, the defence sought to exclude the police evidence pursuant to s 78, Police and Criminal Evidence Act 1984 (discretion to exclude evidence which would have such an adverse effect on the fairness of the proceedings that the court ought not to admit it). The magistrates rejected the application and convicted the defendant. He appealed.

QUESTION(S) FOR THE COURT: Whether the justices were correct in law to refuse the application to exclude the evidence, given the appellant's failure to provide a specific reason to the officer at the time, and the officer's failure to consider or enquire whether a consultation with a solicitor would be feasible within a timescale that did not cause unnecessary delay to the procedure.

HELD: "[After reviewing the authorities, in particular *Kennedy v CPS*, page 378] 41. … the failure at that stage [i.e. when the defendant said he wanted to speak to a solicitor] to provide an opportunity to enable the appellant to contact a solicitor did not … involve any infringement of section 58 [Police and Criminal Evidence Act 1984 – right to legal advice when under arrest and in custody at a police station] or indeed of the code of practice. I appreciate that here the failure was even to consider the matter, but since the officer would plainly have been entitled, in the light of the decision in *Kennedy*, to have refused access at that stage I do not think it assists the appellant, even if it were the case that the policeman gave no express consideration to the matter.

"42. There is the additional point that the justices may have taken the view that there was a breach of section 58 by the failure to contact the solicitor for some 20 minutes after the request had initially been made by the appellant. … it cannot possibly be said that the justices would have been required to reject the evidence on that ground. That delay was a very limited one and it caused no prejudice to the appellant. It was not, to use the language of the authorities, either a significant or substantial failure and it could not be said to have impinged in any way on the attitude of the appellant to the statutory procedures.

"43. Accordingly, to the extent that it is necessary to look at the exercise of discretion under section 78, I am satisfied that the justices were fully entitled in this case, assuming there to have been … a breach of either section 58 or the Code, to have concluded that fairness did not require them to exclude this evidence, but entitled them to admit it."

The answer to the question was "yes". Appeal dismissed.

DPP v Carless

[2005] EWHC 3234 (Admin), 13 April 2005, QBD (DC)

Analysis of a blood specimen, given in connection with the investigation of a separate offence (abduction), before the suspicion of drink driving arose, was admissible to prove driving with excess alcohol.

A motorist had been charged with driving with excess alcohol in blood, contrary to s 5(1)(a), Road Traffic Act 1988. There had been a road traffic accident, from which he walked away. When police arrived at the scene, they took samples of blood from splatters on the inside of the roof of a car and on a compact disc cartridge. Some hours later, the motorist was found by a police officer; he appeared confused and suffering from a head injury; he said he had been abducted the previous evening. He was taken to hospital and police officers began investigating the alleged abduction. As part of that investigation, they asked for specimens of blood and urine to ascertain if the alleged abductee had been drugged; he also gave a mouth swab for DNA elimination. The urine sample was cold and cloudy and the investigating officer suspected it had been diluted. The blood sample from the car matched the person's DNA, connecting the alleged abductee and the road traffic accident. The procedure for obtaining specimens under s 7, Road Traffic Act was not followed, but analysis of the blood specimen given in the course of investigating the possible abduction revealed excess alcohol; analysis of the urine sample did not.

The magistrates accepted an argument that evidence of the blood sample should be excluded pursuant to s 78, Police and Criminal Evidence Act 1984 (discretion to exclude evidence which would have such an adverse effect on the fairness of the proceedings that the court ought not to admit it) and acquitted. The prosecutor appealed.

QUESTION(S) FOR THE COURT: (1) Whether a sample of blood (or urine or breath) which is obtained with consent, by a medical practitioner before a defendant is suspected of committing a driving offence, is admissible to prove that the level of alcohol present at the time of driving exceeded the prescribed limit; (2) whether the magistrates were correct to exclude the evidence of the analysis of the blood.

HELD: "4. … Section 15(2) of the [Road Traffic Offenders Act 1988 has been amended by the Road Traffic Act 1991, which inserted] certain words, which are critical for the Crown's argument … In its current and relevant form section 15(2) reads:

'Evidence of the proportion of alcohol or any drug in a specimen of breath, blood or urine provided by or taken from the accused shall, in all cases (including cases where the specimen was not provided or taken in connection with the alleged offence), be taken into account …'.

"5. The Crown submit that, by force of the added words in section 15(2), 'including cases where the specimen was not provided or taken in connection with the alleged offence,' the blood sample … was … properly admissible under section 15(2). In my judgment that is right. The specimen was undoubtedly provided otherwise than in connection with the alleged offence, and therefore necessarily in a manner or in circumstances at variance with the statutory procedure now contained in section 7 of the Road Traffic Act 1988. The propriety of relying on it, in contrast to the position arising in *Howard v Hallett* [see page 109], is saved by the words which have been added in section 15(2).

"6. … this view may be thought to lead to the conclusion that the circumstances in which a specimen may be obtained and later used in an excess alcohol prosecution are left vague and indeterminate. But it is important to have in mind that in any case where the specimen is provided in connection with the alleged offence, then the full discipline of all the procedural requirements of the 1988 Act apply and those requirements must be strictly complied with. In those circumstances *Howard v Hallett* remains the applicable principle. Moreover, any potential injustice arising on the facts of any other case may … be averted by the vigilant use of section 78 of the Police and Criminal Evidence Act 1984. It seems to me, in short, inescapable that the words added in section 15(2) of the 1988 Act have created a new set of circumstances in which samples may be admitted in prosecutions for excess alcohol offences."

The answer to question (1) was "yes"; the answer to question (2) was "no". Appeal allowed.

R (Marsh (Ian)) v DPP

[2006] EWHC 1525 (Admin), 8 May 2006, QBD (Admin)

In the circumstances of this case, identification evidence was admissible even though, contrary to the Police and Criminal Evidence Act 1984, no note of the witness's description had been taken before the witness identified the accused.

A motorist had been charged with, *inter alia*, driving with excess alcohol, contrary to s 5(1)(a), Road Traffic Act 1988. A witness had seen, from the window of his flat, a man driving a car in a car park; he appeared drunk and the witness called the police; when they arrived they detained two people. They asked the witness to identify the person he had seen driving the motor car and he pointed out the accused.

At the trial, it was argued that the identification evidence should be excluded pursuant to s 78, Police and Criminal Evidence Act 1984 (discretion to exclude evidence which would have such an adverse effect on the fairness of the proceedings that the court ought not to admit it), because PACE Code D, paragraph 3.1 of the Codes of Practice under s 66, Police and Criminal Evidence Act 1984 had not been complied with, in that the officer had not first asked the witness for, and made a note of, a description of the person he had seen driving. The witness's statement was taken later, after the informal identification.

The magistrates admitted the evidence and convicted the accused; he appealed.

QUESTION(S) FOR THE COURT: Whether the magistrates were correct to admit the evidence.

HELD: "11. … a highly material circumstance … is that [when] the police … came to the car park they saw two men who, by reason of their behaviour and independently of what the appellant himself said, gave them every reason to suspect that one or other of them had been driving the vehicle. The explanation which had been put forward for going to the vehicle, namely, in order to collect sunglasses was one which any officer was likely to regard as absurd. The vehicle door was open, the keys were in the ignition and the internal light on. The circumstances called for the [two men] to explain their behaviour … The next matter to be considered is whether or not the breach which did occur was [a] serious breach or not. It was obvious from the evidence that, although there had not been a statement taken from [the witness], or a record made of his description, the mischief which such a record is designed to avoid was substantially repaired by a statement which was taken and which was available to the appellant and his legal advisers when subsequent interrogation and questioning took place.

"13. … I am entirely satisfied, from all the circumstances of this case, that the evidence could be admitted because the Magistrates were entitled to conclude that the admission of the evidence would not have such an adverse effect on the proceedings that they ought not to admit it."

Appeal dismissed.

Charles v DPP

[2009] EWHC 3521 (Admin), [2010] RTR 34, 26 November 2009, QBD (DC)

An admission of driving made during the course of an interview conducted in breach of the Police and Criminal Evidence Act 1984 and without caution should not have been admitted in evidence.

The defendant had been charged with driving with excess alcohol, contrary to s 5(1)(a), Road Traffic Act 1988. Police found him slumped over the steering wheel of a parked car. The parking lights were on, the keys were in the ignition and he was asleep. He was arrested for being in charge of a motor vehicle while unfit through drink or drugs. At the police station, the lower of two breath specimens showed 74 μg alcohol in 100 ml breath. He was informed that he would be charged. He was, however, then interviewed, in breach of PACE Code C, paragraph 16.5 (detainee not to be interviewed about an offence after being charged with it, or having been told that he may be prosecuted for it, unless the interview is necessary). He was not cautioned. Nor was he told, at the outset of that interview, for what offence he was being investigated. During the interview he was asked if he had been driving and he admitted that he had. At the end of the interview, he was charged, not with being in charge, but with driving with excess alcohol, rendering him liable to compulsory rather than discretionary disqualification.

The prosecutor conceded that in the absence of the admission, there was no case against the defendant that he had been driving. The justices found the admission admissible under s 78, Police and Criminal Evidence Act 1984 (discretion to exclude evidence which would have such an adverse effect on the fairness of the proceedings that the court ought not to admit it) on the basis that it had been voluntary and that the defendant must have known he would then be charged with driving with excess alcohol. They convicted him of driving with excess alcohol. He appealed.

QUESTION(S) FOR THE COURT: Whether the justices were right in law in ruling the evidence of the interview was admissible.

HELD: "12. There were … two breaches, admittedly not in bad faith, but they showed scant regard for the clear requirements in a case such as this. They had the unfortunate result that the appellant cannot have been aware that the switch in questioning half-way through the interview would lead to far more serious consequences. Although the magistrates found that he would know the consequences that would most likely follow, there is no finding, and there could not be any finding, that he was aware of what offence was being investigated in the course of that evening because he was simply not told."

The answer to the question was "no". Appeal allowed.

Moore v Preston Crown Court

[2011] EWHC 3780 (Admin), 30 November 2011, QBD (DC)

Officers' failure to make contemporaneous notes, and their inability, at trial, to remember all the details of the incident in question did not of itself render their evidence inadmissible.

A motorist was charged with driving with excess alcohol, contrary to s 5(1), Road Traffic Act 1988. Two officers had been on patrol in connection with investigating burglaries in the area. Neither was familiar with the area or knew the names of the roads. They followed a black Peugeot which stopped at a T junction. The driver, who was stumbling and was intoxicated, got out and approached the officers, asking why they had followed him. A roadside breath test was positive and in due course breath analysis revealed excess alcohol.

The officers' evidence was that they had followed the motorist until his car stopped and he got out. The motorist admitted he had been drinking, in a nearby pub, but said he had simply got into the car and gone to sleep. He denied having driven. The officers did not make their notes until some time after the incident and at the trial, they had difficulty recalling details of the roads. The court rejected the motorist's version of events and convicted him. His appeal to the Crown Court was dismissed and he appealed further.

QUESTION(S) FOR THE COURT: Whether the lack of contemporaneous notes and the inability of the constables to remember all the details of the incident should have rendered some parts of the evidence inadmissible.

HELD: "25. … the Crown Court recognised that there were some inconsistencies and variation in the police officers' accounts. However, they accepted the core evidence of the officers … that they had followed the appellant's vehicle for some considerable distance before the appellant came to a stop. Crucially, the officers were adamant and consistent that the vehicle which they had followed was the same vehicle in which they found the appellant. The Crown Court … rejected the appellant's wholly different version of events as implausible and untrue. On the material before it that conclusion … cannot be considered without foundation or perverse, even if there be force in some of the criticisms … of the coherence and consistency of the officers' overall evidence. …

"27. As a matter of good practice, it is perhaps regrettable that no such note was made and that the initial statements were made so long after the date of the offence because, if notice had been made or statements obtained early on, some of the inconsistencies and vagueness in the evidence might then have been avoided. However, there is no requirement in the Police and Criminal Evidence Act 1984 or the codes of practice requiring the police to make contemporaneous notes of incidents that they deal with. …

"28. … there were no … grounds for excluding any part of the officers' evidence under section 78 [Police and Criminal Evidence Act 1984 – discretion to exclude evidence which would have such an adverse effect on the fairness of the proceedings that the court ought not to admit it]. … the absence of any contemporaneous notes was relevant only to the weight and not to the admissibility of the evidence. The Crown Court was fully aware of the lack of notes and took that absence into account in weighing the oral evidence of the officers."

Appeal dismissed.

Stanesby v DPP

[2012] EWHC 1320 (Admin), 1 May 2012, QBD (Admin)

Where the absence of an appropriate adult caused the motorist no unfairness, evidence of breath analysis remained admissible.

A motorist was charged with driving with excess alcohol, contrary to s 5(1), Road Traffic Act 1988. The police station procedure was recorded on CCTV which was viewed by the Crown Court. The Crown Court found that the appellant appeared to understand and respond coherently to questions. The custody sergeant also gave evidence that the motorist was coherent and understood what was being asked. The motorist said he was taking medication for depression (a mental illness). Under PACE Code C, paragraph 1.4 (circumstances in which a person is to be treated as mentally disordered or otherwise mentally vulnerable) an appropriate adult should therefore have been called to advise and assist, but was not. The Crown Court found that there was no unfairness as a result. Even if an appropriate adult had been present, the breath testing procedure would have gone ahead anyway and it would have made no difference.

The motorist was convicted and appealed.

QUESTION(S) FOR THE COURT: Not recited in the judgment.

HELD: "14. … the court [below] concluded: 'Even if an appropriate adult had attended, no comfort or advice provided by such a person could have involved any justifiable interference with the breath test procedure undertaken. Accordingly, we declined to exclude the evidence.'

"15. That was a conclusion which the court was entitled to reach. Furthermore, given the facts which it found, it was one which was clearly right. This was a case in which the breach of the Code made no difference. Accordingly, in those circumstances the court was right to conclude under section 78 [Police and Criminal Evidence Act 1984 – discretion to exclude evidence which would have such an adverse effect on the fairness of the proceedings that the court ought not to admit it] that the admission of the result of the breath test procedure would not have such an adverse effect on the fairness of the proceedings that the court ought not to admit it."

Appeal dismissed.

R v Ashworth

[2012] EWCA Crim 1064, 3 May 2012, CA (Crim)

On the facts, evidence of the consumption of cocaine was admissible as relevant to the standard of driving and was not unfairly prejudicial.

A motorist had been involved in a fatal collision and was charged with causing death by careless driving when over the prescribed limit for alcohol, contrary to s 3A(1)(b), Road Traffic Act 1988. The issue at trial was whether the victim's death was caused at least in part by driving which fell below the standard of a careful and competent driver, which turned on whether or not he had been keeping a proper lookout and should have seen the victim in time to avoid the collision. A police officer who attended the scene gave evidence that the motorist was slightly unsteady on his feet, his speech was slightly slurred; he fell asleep. Analysis of a urine specimen showed not only excess alcohol, but also benzoylecgonine (BZE), signifying that the appellant had consumed cocaine. In interview, the appellant had initially denied having taken any illegal substances, but when interviewed again when the results of the analysis were available, said he had used cocaine 2 days before the incident. The motorist was convicted and appealed.

GROUNDS OF APPEAL: The judge in the court below wrongly admitted as relevant evidence that the appellant had in the recent past consumed cocaine; alternatively, if the evidence was relevant, its prejudicial effect outweighed any probative value it had and so should have been excluded under s 78, Police and Criminal Evidence Act 1984 (discretion to exclude evidence which would have such an adverse effect on the fairness of the proceedings that the court ought not to admit it).

HELD: "13. … had it not been open to the jury to conclude that the appellant was indeed under the influence of cocaine on the night of the accident, evidence of the presence of BZE in the appellant's urine should not have been admitted either because it had no probative value or because such probative value as it possessed was tenuous and was outweighed by the prejudice resulting from mere speculation. However, … this appellant had lied about his cocaine consumption in interview with the police, and then in evidence placed his latest consumption a sufficient distance of time before the accident as enabled him to claim that he was unaffected by cocaine in any way at the time of the accident.

"14. … on the facts … the evidence was admissible and is not demonstrated to have been unfairly prejudicial. It was for the jury to resolve the issue whether they were sure that the appellant was lying about the consumption of cocaine two days before in order to avoid the consequences of an admitted consumption during the night [in question]. … the ultimate issue was for the jury, namely whether he was under the influence of cocaine. If so, … such a finding would be plainly relevant to the question whether the reason the appellant failed to see the deceased well before the collision was because he was not keeping a proper lookout. As we have indicated, there was other evidence going to the same effect which the jury was entitled to consider, namely his condition on arrival of the police and the fact that he had consumed a little over the legal limit for alcohol."

Appeal dismissed.

Miller v DPP

[2018] EWHC 262 (Admin), 15 February 2018, QBD (DC)

On the facts (suspect with learning difficulties and in distress, appropriate adult not informed), the court was wrong to admit evidence of failing to provide.

Police stopped a driver on suspicion of driving under the influence of drugs. He was arrested and, at the police station, behaved erratically and aggressively. It seemed he was known to police as a person with learning difficulties and autism, and an appropriate adult had assisted on earlier occasions when the suspect had been interviewed by police. The custody record recited that he was a suicide risk, had mental health issues and learning difficulties, and had himself said that he suffered from Asperger's Syndrome. He asked for solicitors and an appropriate adult (under PACE Code C: Code of Practice for the detention, treatment and questioning of persons by Police Officers). He said he was not 'feeling well in the head'. No appropriate adult was contacted. The detainee refused to provide a blood specimen, and was charged with failing without reasonable excuse to provide such a specimen contrary to s 7(6), Road Traffic Act 1988. The justices agreed that there had been a breach of PACE Code C, but declined to exclude the evidence of the police station procedure under s 78, Police and Criminal Evidence Act 1984; the driver appealed against that decision.

QUESTION(S) FOR THE COURT: Having found that the failure to contact an appropriate adult whilst the appellant was in custody constituted a breach of PACE Code C, in all the circumstances, whether the justices were wrong in law in not exercising their discretion to exclude the evidence of the drug-drive procedure under s 78, Police and Criminal Evidence Act 1984.

HELD: "[Having found that the court had jurisdiction to hear the appeal, and having rejected an application to amend the stated case, and distinguishing *R (DPP) v Evans (Brychan Gethin John)* [2002] EWHC 2976 (Admin) (page 362)] 38. … the issue … is whether, in the light of that breach [of PACE Code C], the magistrates lawfully exercised their discretion to exclude the evidence of the drug drive procedure that then took place. …

"45. … there is a clear distinction … between the role that an appropriate adult might play in a case resulting in a charge of refusing to provide a sample, and that role in a case where a sample has been found to contain excess alcohol leading to a charge of drink driving.

"46. Amongst the reasons behind Code C requiring the presence of an appropriate adult is that he or she is independent of the police authorities, and is able both to safeguard the welfare of the detained person and to provide him with an independent perspective. The appropriate adult is likely to have a significant role to play in providing a calming influence on a minor or vulnerable adult who may have become, as in the present case, distressed and agitated as a consequence of finding himself confronted with a particularly stressful and pressured situation in custody. … the essence of the charge of refusing to provide a specimen involves the person under investigation understanding the nature of the request involved in requiring a sample and also, importantly, an insight into the consequences of the failure to allow the police to take an evidential sample. The appropriate adult is likely to play a key role in the process of both explaining the purpose of obtaining the evidential sample, and also the consequences of a failure to permit the police doing so.

"47. That is very different from the role which an appropriate adult might have played in circumstances where a freely given sample demonstrates an alcohol reading in excess of the legal limit giving rise to a drink driving charge, as was the case in [*Evans*]. In [*Evans*], the court understandably found that the breach of the Code was immaterial; because, even if an adult had been informed and had attended, in the absence of any evidence that the course of events would have been different, the result would have been the same, i.e. if the appropriate adult had arrived on time, a sample would have been given which would have shown excess alcohol. Given that the defendant was freely willing to give a sample, and there were no grounds for him not doing so, the delay in summoning an appropriate adult would merely have made the forensic result less reliable. The breach was thus legally immaterial.

"48. The situation here was very different. … The Appellant was clearly very exercised whilst being detained, and there is a very real possibility that the presence of an appropriate adult would have calmed him, and led him to behave differently and make different choices from those he in fact made.

"49. … The circumstances made it more, rather than less, necessary for an appropriate adult to be obtained …

"50. … the presence of an appropriate adult was an important procedural safeguard for the Appellant in circumstances where he could face a charge of refusing to provide a specimen. The failure to inform and summon an appropriate adult in breach of the Code therefore, in our view, had a clear adverse impact on the fairness of permitting the evidence of the drug drive procedure to be admitted."

The answer to the question was "yes". Case remitted to the magistrates' court with a direction to acquit.

5. LEGAL ADVICE

See s 58, Police and Criminal Evidence Act 1984, on the right to legal advice when under arrest and in custody at a police station. See also DPP v Billington, page 216 – the procedure for taking breath specimens for analysis is not an interview and the provisions of the Police and Criminal Evidence Act 1984 do not allow a suspect to delay the procedure to take legal advice; the cases in Chapter 5 under the heading "Conditional Agreement", page 216; Oberoi (Yash) v DPP, page 205 – refusing to blow until after the motorist had spoken to a solicitor amounted to failing to provide; R (DPP) v Evans (Brychan Gethin John), page 362 – the procedure was not to be delayed for the attendance of an appropriate adult; R (Forde) v DPP, page 367, where a 20-minute delay before relaying a request for a solicitor caused no prejudice. Compare Smith v Hand, page 183, where the officer permitted the suspect to speak to a solicitor before deciding whether or not to provide specimens; and Hudson v DPP, page 348 – where the suspect's belief that he need not provide specimens until he had received legal advice was reinforced by police delay.

Campbell v DPP

[2002] EWHC 1314 (Admin), [2004] RTR 5, 31 May 2002, QBD (Admin)

The fact that a suspect may not wait for legal advice before providing specimens does not breach s 58, Police and Criminal Evidence Act 1984 or art 6(3), European Convention on Human Rights, and does not give grounds for excluding evidence of failing to provide.

A motorist had been charged with failing to provide two specimens of breath for analysis, contrary to s 7, Road Traffic Act 1988. He had been arrested and, at the police station, when told of his rights, he asked for a duty solicitor. The breath testing procedure was then begun. Some 7 minutes after the motorist had first asked for a solicitor, an officer telephoned the duty solicitor service. The motorist refused to supply breath specimens.

It was argued before the justices that the evidence of the breath testing procedure should be excluded under s 78, Police and Criminal Evidence Act 1984 (discretion to exclude evidence which would have such an adverse effect on the fairness of the proceedings that the court ought not to admit it) on the ground that the motorist had the right to legal advice before being required to provide a breath specimen, under both s 58, Police and Criminal Evidence Act 1984 (person held at a police station entitled to consult a solicitor privately at any time) and under art 6(3), European Convention on Human Rights (right to legal assistance).

The justices rejected that argument and convicted the motorist. He appealed.

QUESTION(S) FOR THE COURT: (1) Whether, in the absence of evidence on the issue, the court was correct in determining there had been no breach of s 58 or art 6(3). (2) Whether the court was correct not to exclude the evidence under s 78.

HELD: "35. … there must be a proper balance between the protection of the interests of the individual on the one hand and the interests of the community at large on the other. The interests of the individual may only be curtailed to the extent necessary to pursue the community's legitimate aims. In other words, the restriction on any right in relation to Article 6(3) must be proportionate to the aim sought to be achieved …

"36. Here … the interests of the community are self-evident: the suppression of drink driving in order to save lives and prevent serious injury to its members … [It is] entirely proportionate to that aim to permit a police officer … to require a member of the community to provide a specimen, albeit the member of the community may have requested legal advice and not received it …

"38. Moreover, when considering the issue of proportionality, account can be taken of the protections that exist for the individual within the procedure for taking and requiring a specimen …

"42. Additionally, on the facts, the appellant has difficulties. Any obligation to secure legal advice was to do so without delay. The duty solicitor was contacted within 7 minutes. That … was sufficient compliance with the obligation. When the procedure started the appellant did not ask that it be stopped to wait for the arrival of the solicitor. He did not suggest he needed to consult as to whether he may have had a reasonable excuse for not providing a specimen … it was perfectly reasonable for the officer to go through the process of seeking to obtain a specimen. It was not necessary for him to wait for an uncertain time for a solicitor to be spoken to on the telephone or to arrive.

"43. … *DPP v Billington* [see page 216] and the authorities based upon it are still good law. Article 6(3) has not changed their effect."

The answers to the questions were "yes". Appeal dismissed.

Kennedy v CPS

[2002] EWHC 2297 (Admin), [2004] RTR 4, 6 November 2002, QBD (DC)

On the facts of this case, a breach of s 58, Police and Criminal Evidence Act 1984 (solicitor not contacted immediately) was neither significant nor substantial; the custody officer informed the defendant, by giving him a notice to detained persons, that he could not delay the procedure; and the justices were right to admit the sergeant's evidence.

A motorist had been charged with failing to provide two specimens of breath for analysis, contrary to s 7(6), Road Traffic Act 1988. He had been arrested and arrived at the police station at about 3.00 am. At about 3.20 am, he was brought to the custody desk and was told his rights; he refused to give details and was unco-operative, but, when asked if he required a solicitor, replied "yes". He was given, but did not read, a notice saying that the right to legal advice does not entitle a person to delay the drink drive procedures. The breath testing procedure began at 3.30 am and was completed at 3.40 am. The motorist twice refused to provide specimens of breath. At 3.41 am, a police officer contacted the duty solicitor call centre, and at 4.40 am a solicitor spoke to the motorist.

The justices found that there had been a breach of s 58, Police and Criminal Evidence Act 1984 (right to legal advice when under arrest and in custody at a police station) and the PACE Codes of Practice in that a solicitor was not contacted immediately; that the breath test procedure cannot be delayed while waiting for a solicitor; that the police contacted a solicitor at the first reasonable opportunity; that the delay in so doing was not significant or substantial; and that the evidence concerning the breath testing procedure would not be excluded pursuant to s 78, Police and Criminal Evidence Act 1984 (discretion to exclude evidence which would have such an adverse effect on the fairness of the proceedings that the court ought not to admit it). On art 6, European Convention on Human Rights (right to a fair trial), they found that the appellant's right to legal advice was restricted but that the restriction was proportionate. They convicted the motorist; he appealed.

QUESTION(S) FOR THE COURT: (1) Whether the justices were correct in finding the breach of s 58, Police and Criminal Evidence Act 1984 and the PACE Codes of Practice neither significant nor substantial; (2) whether the custody sergeant should have informed the defendant that he could not delay the procedure to seek legal advice; (3) whether the justices were correct in refusing to exclude the evidence of the custody sergeant.

HELD: "[After reviewing authorities] 31. … the right to a fair trial enshrined in Article 6 of the Convention can be said to be in play from the outset of a police investigation, but that right does not spell out a right to legal advice at any particular stage. For that it is necessary to go to domestic legislation which … fully satisfies the requirements of Article 6. Section 58(1) of the [Police and Criminal Evidence Act 1984] entitles a person arrested and held in custody at a police station to consult a solicitor if he asks to do so, and where a request is made (as it was in this case, albeit in response to an invitation) he must be permitted to consult a solicitor *as soon as is practicable* (section 58(4)). The custody officer, it is said in the Code [of Practice] at C:6.5 'must act *without delay*' to secure the provision of legal advice. … Having asked the question on the charge sheet in relation to legal advice is the custody officer entitled to go on with the remaining questions, or must he at once, as soon as the suspect indicates that he would like to have legal advice pick up the telephone and ring the call centre? Plainly, as it seems to me, it is a question of fact and degree in any given case whether the custody officer has acted without delay to secure the provision of legal advice, and whether the person held in custody has been permitted to consult a solicitor as soon as is practicable. Where the matter under investigation is a suspected offence contrary to section 5 of the Road Traffic Act 1988 … the public interest requires that the obtaining of breath specimens … cannot be delayed to any significant extent in order to enable a suspect to take legal advice. That, to my mind, means this – that if there happens to be a solicitor in the charge office whom the suspect says that he wants to consult for a couple of minutes before deciding whether or not to provide specimens of breath he must be allowed to do so.

Similarly, if the suspect asks at that stage to speak on the telephone for a couple of minutes to his own solicitor or the duty solicitor, and the solicitor in question is immediately available. But where, as here, the suspect does no more than indicate a general desire to have legal advice, I see no reason why the custody officer should not simply continue to take details, and alert the solicitors' call centre at the first convenient opportunity. That will probably mean that, as the justices in this case found, the call centre should be alerted before the next stage of the investigation, but in this case if a call had been made at 3.30 am it is inconceivable that the appellant would have received any legal advice prior to committing the offence contrary to section 7(6) of the 1988 Act. The breach of the statutory requirement was, as the justices found, neither significant nor substantial, and could not properly lead to any exclusion of evidence pursuant to section 78 of the 1984 Act."

The answers to the questions were: (1) "yes"; (2) he did so by the notice to detained persons, and that was sufficient; and (3) "yes". Appeal dismissed.

Myles v DPP

[2004] EWHC 594 (Admin), [2004] 2 All ER 902, [2005] RTR 1, 24 March 2003, QBD (DC)

That the process for breath testing should not be delayed "to any significant extent" is a full and sufficient explanation of the law.

A motorist had been charged with, *inter alia*, failing without reasonable excuse to provide a specimen of blood for a laboratory test, contrary to s 7(6), Road Traffic Act 1988. He had been arrested and at the police station indicated that he did not require a solicitor. The breath analysis device indicated mouth alcohol, and the motorist was therefore lawfully required to provide a specimen of blood for analysis. He was warned of the consequences of failure, but refused, maintaining that he required "further advice" or "legal advice".

He appealed to the Crown Court against conviction. The Crown Court found that the motorist had been properly required to give a specimen of blood, that he understood his rights and had declined the services of a solicitor; while the court had to consider the principles of art 6(3)(C), European Convention on Human Rights (the right for a person charged with a criminal offence to defend himself in person or through legal assistance of his own choosing), domestic law was clear and bound the Crown Court. It dismissed the appeal; the motorist appealed further.

QUESTION(S) FOR THE COURT: (1) In interpreting art 6(3)(C), European Convention of Human Rights, whether the Crown Court was right in finding that the clear, emphatic and repeated domestic law outweighed any persuasive authorities from foreign jurisdictions; (2) whether the Crown Court was right to dismiss the appeal.

HELD: "[After reviewing the domestic cases and Commonwealth authorities] 22. [Counsel for the appellant] accepts that … he cannot contend for an unlimited right to delay the procedure in order to obtain advice. The reason for this is obvious and needs no support from evidence; specimens must be taken as close to the time of the alleged offence as possible, and the default position is there should be no delay. Hence he argues for some defined short period – he says 15 minutes – for which it should be permissible to hold up the sample-taking process for the purpose of obtaining advice. This runs counter to the clear views of this Court, that the process should not be delayed 'to any significant extent'. This in my view is a full and sufficient explanation of the position in law, and will also serve as a practical guide to those who have to deal with such matters on the ground.

"23. The law is therefore clear. The questions asked should both be answered in the affirmative."

Because of delay in the proceedings on appeal, which were not attributable to the appellant or his advisers, the fine imposed in the court below was quashed, and the appeal allowed to that limited extent.

Kirkup v DPP

[2003] EWHC 2354 (Admin), (2004) 168 JP 255, 3 October 2003, QBD (DC)

A 7-minute delay in contacting a solicitor "only just" breached s 58, Police and Criminal Evidence Act 1984, and was of such a nature that it was not appropriate to exclude evidence of the request for breath specimens.

A motorist had been charged with failing to provide two specimens of breath for analysis, contrary to s 7(6), Road Traffic Act 1988. He had been arrested and taken to a police station, arriving there at 10.30 pm. While waiting to be taken to the custody sergeant, at about 10.45 pm, the motorist told the arresting officer he wanted legal advice. At 11.03 pm the custody sergeant told the motorist his rights and he asked to consult the duty solicitor. At 11.10 pm the breath testing procedure began, and at the same time the custody sergeant telephoned for a duty solicitor. The motorist refused to provide specimens of breath. At 11.29 pm the duty solicitor spoke to the motorist.

The magistrates found the delay in securing legal advice was a breach of s 58, Police and Criminal Evidence Act 1984 (right to legal advice when under arrest and in custody at a police station) but that the breach was neither significant nor substantial. They convicted the motorist; he appealed.

QUESTION(S) FOR THE COURT: (1) Having found a breach of s 58 and the PACE Code of Practice, whether the justices were correct in refusing to exercise the discretion (under s 78, Police and Criminal Evidence Act 1984 – to exclude evidence which would have such an adverse effect on the fairness of the proceedings that the court ought not to admit it) to exclude the evidence of the request for a specimen of breath; (2) whether they were correct to convict.

HELD: "32. … the period of delay which the prosecution conceded, and the magistrates accepted, gave rise to a breach of the statute and the Code was the 7 minute delay … between 11.03 p.m. and 11.10 p.m.

"33. … a delay of 7 minutes is so short … that it only just constitutes a breach of section 58 of the Police and Criminal Evidence Act 1984 and paragraph 6 of the Code.

"39. … In the light of authority, in particular *Kennedy v CPS* [see page 378], there was no duty on the police to delay taking a specimen of breath until the appellant had obtained legal advice. The police were fully entitled to commence that procedure at 11.10 p.m. Furthermore, [the] delay of 7 minutes in telephoning the Duty Solicitor Call Centre was neither a significant delay nor a substantial one.

"40. … the magistrates' exercise of discretion under section 78 of the Police and Criminal Evidence Act 1984 cannot be faulted. There was indeed a breach of section 58 of the Police and Criminal Evidence Act and of section 6.5 of the Code. However, that breach was of such a nature that it was not appropriate to exclude [the] evidence concerning [the] request for two specimens of breath."

The answers to both questions were "yes". Appeal dismissed.

Whitley v DPP

[2003] EWHC 2512 (Admin), (2004) 168 JP 350, 13 October 2003, QBD (DC)

On the facts of this case (delay – suspect taken to hospital before being removed to the police station), a time lapse of 13 minutes between the suspect's request for a solicitor and contacting a solicitor was a breach of the Police and Criminal Evidence Act 1984 but was insignificant and insubstantial; it was right not to exclude evidence of the breath testing procedure.

A motorist had been charged with failing to provide two specimens of breath for analysis, contrary to s 7(6), Road Traffic Act 1988. He had been found at the scene of a traffic accident; he failed to provide a roadside breath specimen and was arrested at 5.30 am. He was taken to hospital by ambulance, but the doctor there could see no serious injury and he was removed to a police station, where he arrived at 7.25 am. At 7.40 am the appellant signed a *pro forma* to the effect that he wished to speak to a solicitor. He was told that breath testing could not be delayed, and the procedure was begun at 7.40 am. The defendant refused to provide specimens. At 7.53 am, the duty solicitor call centre received a request for a solicitor; the duty solicitor spoke to the defendant at 8.00 am.

At the trial, the district judge found no breach of s 58, Police and Criminal Evidence Act 1984 (right to legal advice when under arrest and in custody at a police station), but that there had been a breach of the PACE Code C, paragraph 6.5, although that was an insignificant and insubstantial breach; he declined to exclude the evidence of the breath testing procedure under s 78, Police and Criminal Evidence Act 1984 (discretion to exclude evidence which would have such an adverse effect on the fairness of the proceedings that the court ought not to admit it). The motorist was convicted and appealed.

HELD: "27. Each case will turn upon its own individual facts. If there had not already been significant delay, if another officer had not been available to commence the breath test procedure immediately, if the appellant had asked specifically, 'Please may I speak to a solicitor before he begins', if the custody officer knew that the duty solicitor was at the police station, and had just finished giving advice to another detained person, then the judge's conclusion might well have been different.

"29. … it is important, given the enormous variety of circumstances which may confront a custody officer, that he should be given the flexibility to respond to the demands of the particular case. Given the particular circumstances of this case the judge was entitled to conclude, on the evidence before him that: 'The procedure had already been seriously delayed and the police were right to have made arrangements to ensure that the evidential breath specimens could be recorded as soon as possible'.

"30. For the same reasons he was entitled to conclude that the breach of Code C6.5 was insignificant and insubstantial. If the custody officer was right, in all the circumstances described by the judge, to ensure that the procedure began as soon as possible, any delay thereafter was rightly described as not significant."

Appeal dismissed.

CPS v Rice

[2004] EWHC 508 (Admin), 8 March 2004, QBD (DC)

Magistrates were wrong to find that a suspect's solicitor should have been contacted in the 4 minutes between her request for her solicitor and beginning the breath testing procedure.

A motorist had been charged with driving with excess alcohol, contrary to s 5(1)(a), Road Traffic Act 1988. She had been arrested on suspicion of drink driving and taken to the police station. It was a busy Saturday night. At 1.28 am, she asked for legal advice. The breath testing procedure began at 1.32 am; she declined the option to provide a blood specimen under s 8(2), Road Traffic Act 1988 (lower of two breath readings not more than 50 µg alcohol in 100 ml breath – now repealed; see page v), and the procedure was completed at 2.00 am. At 2.59 am, the police contacted her solicitor; after consultation, the defendant asked to provide a replacement specimen; the custody sergeant refused.

On a submission of no case to answer, the justices found that, in not contacting the solicitor before the breath testing began, the police had breached s 58, Police and Criminal Evidence Act 1984 (right to legal advice when under arrest and in custody at a police station), and that the breach was of such gravity as to justify excluding the evidence of the breath testing procedure under s 78, Police and Criminal Evidence Act 1984 (discretion to exclude evidence which would have such an adverse effect on the fairness of the proceedings that the court ought not to admit it). They dismissed the charge. The prosecutor appealed.

QUESTION(S) FOR THE COURT: (1) Whether, on the facts, the justices were right to conclude that it was reasonably practicable for the police to have contacted the defendant's solicitor between the time of her request that they do so and the time the breath testing procedure started.

HELD: "17. It would have been difficult perhaps to interfere with a conclusion by the justices that there had been a breach over the period of between two o'clock and three o'clock, but that is not a question which is before this court. Here it was concluded that it was reasonably practicable to arrange legal advice in the few minutes before the [breath testing] procedure was carried [out], or indeed up to 2 am. The argument before the justices turned upon the criticism made on the applicant's behalf, which was confined to the period after the … procedure was finished at 2 am. Therefore it follows that the reasoning which led to the exclusion of the evidence cannot be sustained either."

Appeal allowed.

Causey v DPP

[2004] EWHC 3164 (Admin), (2005) 169 JP 331, 11 November 2004, QBD (DC)

A 14-minute delay in contacting a firm of solicitors was not a significant or substantial delay and s 78, Police and Criminal Evidence Act 1984 did not require that evidence of failing to provide be excluded.

A motorist had been charged with failing to provide two specimens of breath for analysis, contrary to s 7(6), Road Traffic Act 1988. He had been arrested and arrived at the police station at 1.07 am. At 1.11 am he was asked if he wanted to speak to a solicitor; he declined, but when asked to sign the custody record in confirmation, he changed his mind and said he wanted to consult a lawyer. He was told the breath testing procedure could not be delayed and warned of the consequences of refusal. He refused to provide specimens. At 1.26 am the custody sergeant attempted to contact a firm of solicitors nominated by the motorist, but there was no reply; at 1.45 am the motorist asked for a representative from another firm and spoke to that person at 2 am.

He was convicted and appealed to the Crown Court which dismissed the appeal; he appealed further.

QUESTION(S) FOR THE COURT: Whether the court was correct in concluding that the breach of s 58, Police and Criminal Evidence Act 1984 (right to legal advice when under arrest and in custody at a police station) and the PACE Codes of Practice was neither significant nor substantial.

HELD: "[After reviewing *Kennedy v CPS*, page 378, *Kirkup v DPP*, page 381, *Whitley v DPP*, page 382, *and Myles v DPP*, page 380] The following propositions are to be derived from those four decisions:

(i) There is no general duty on the police to delay taking a specimen at the police station until the detainee has obtained legal advice.

(ii) Whether in contacting a solicitor, having been requested to do so, the custody sergeant has 'acted without delay' and 'has permitted the detainee to consult a solicitor as soon as is practicable' will always be a question of fact and degree depending on the circumstances of the case.

(iii) Particularly at night time, there is no way for a custody officer to know how long it would take to receive a response from the duty solicitor or public defender service after the scheme or service has been contacted.

(iv) If the custody officer knows a solicitor is immediately available, and particularly if there have been no other significant delays in the procedures up to that point, if there is a request from a suspect, he should be allowed to consult with his lawyer before deciding whether or not to provide specimens. ... However, specimens must be taken as close to the time of the alleged offence as possible, and the default position is there should be no delay. Moreover, that process should not be delayed 'to any significant extent'.

(v) A short and unwarranted delay in contacting a solicitor when requested may constitute a breach of section 58 of the Police and Criminal Evidence Act and the Code such as not to merit excluding the evidence of the detainee's refusal. ...

"... the sergeant was entitled not to delay the second breath test until legal advice had been received. The 14 minute delay in ringing [the first firm] was neither a significant delay nor a substantial one on the findings of fact made by the court below. ... the appellant had a straightforward choice and he had had carefully explained to him the consequences of non-co-operation. This procedure was not an interrogation or an interview, but the application of a simple breath test. ... a solicitor could have done no more than repeat what the sergeant had already explained to the appellant, 'take it [the test] or be done for the refusal'.

"... the court below was right to conclude that the fairness test laid down in section 78 of the Police and Criminal Evidence Act 1984 [discretion to exclude evidence which would have such an adverse effect on the fairness of the proceedings that the court ought not to admit it] did not require the exclusion of this evidence. Nothing that occurred was causative of any unfairness in the sense that the appellant had been deprived of a material and operative safeguard."

The answer to the question was "yes". Appeal dismissed.

Gearing v DPP

[2008] EWHC 1695 (Admin), [2009] RTR 7, 16 June 2008, QBD (DC)

A 22-minute delay in contacting the duty solicitor call centre breached s 58, Police and Criminal Evidence Act 1984; the fact that it then took 23 minutes to obtain legal advice did not provide grounds for excluding evidence of refusal to provide.

A motorist had been charged with failing without reasonable excuse to provide two specimens of breath for analysis, contrary to s 7(6), Road Traffic Act 1988. She failed a roadside breath test and was taken to the police station. On a number of occasions, she said she wished to speak to a solicitor before providing breath specimens. Some 18 minutes after her first request, she declined to provide specimens, and 4 minutes later an officer telephoned the duty solicitor call centre.

The duty solicitor spoke to the suspect and, 23 minutes after the call centre had first been contacted, told the officer that the motorist was willing to provide specimens. She was not given a further opportunity to do so. She was convicted of failing to provide. She appealed, seeking an extension of time for filing notice of appeal.

QUESTION(S) FOR THE COURT: (1) Whether the court below was entitled to conclude that there had been no breach of s 58(4), Police and Criminal Evidence Act 1984 (right to consult a solicitor as soon as is practicable, etc); (2) whether the court below was entitled to exercise the discretion to refuse to exclude the evidence of the breath test procedure pursuant to s 78, Police and Criminal Evidence Act 1984 (discretion to exclude evidence which would have such an adverse effect on the fairness of the proceedings that the court ought not to admit it).

HELD: "19. … there is a breach of section 58 here by the failure to deal with the matter as soon as was practicable once the request had been made at 1.31, when the procedure then continued without the call being made.

"[On the argument that the evidence of the refusal to provide should therefore be excluded under s 78] 21. … The important features are the public interest … the fact that the procedure carried with it its own safeguards, the practicability of obtaining prompt legal advice, the extent of the delay, and whether it is significant … This appellant knew that she had been drinking. … She knew she had failed the roadside breath test …

"23. … the delay … between first seeking a solicitor at the call centre and the receiving and giving of advice on the decision made was some 23 minutes … a substantial period when set against the need for prompt testing in the public interest, and one which on these particular facts in the circumstance would certainly persuade me that it was the correct decision to say that the evidence of the breath test conclusion taken at the police station should not have been excluded."

The answer to question (1) was "no"; the answer to question (2) was "yes". The appellant's application for an extension of time to file notice of appeal was refused; the appeal itself would also have been refused.

Cowper v DPP

[2009] EWHC 2165 (Admin), 18 March 2009, QBD (DC)

The advent of the Criminal Defence Service Direct telephone advice service did not make any difference to the principle that a suspect may await legal advice before providing specimens.

A motorist had been convicted of failing without reasonable excuse to provide two specimens of breath for analysis, contrary to s 7(6), Road Traffic Act 1988. At the police station, he asked to speak to a solicitor. About 3 minutes later the custody sergeant telephoned the Defence Solicitor Call Centre, which referred the case to the Criminal Defence Service Direct telephone service. The motorist was taken into the Intoximeter room and the testing procedure began 5 minutes after his request to speak to a solicitor. The Criminal Defence Service solicitor telephoned the police station just after the motorist had gone into the Intoximeter room and was told he could not speak to the suspect; the solicitor telephoned a number of times and finally spoke to the suspect some 44 minutes after the initial request. The justices found that he had received legal advice as soon as practicable and that there had been no breach of s 58(1) (person held at a police station entitled to consult a solicitor privately at any time) and (4) (right to consult a solicitor as soon as is practicable etc), Police and Criminal Evidence Act 1984. The motorist appealed against conviction.

QUESTION(S) FOR THE COURT: Whether the justices were correct in concluding that there had been no breach of s 58, Police and Criminal Evidence Act 1984 in the light of the commencement of the Criminal Defence Service Telephone Advice Service.

HELD: "21. The appellant's case seems to be that because of the advent of the new Criminal Defence Service Direct Line Telephone Advice Scheme, the custody officer should have waited for the return call, as [that] should not cause a significant delay because it is a dedicated computerised legal advice service.

"23. The alternative submission … is that when the solicitor did phone some two minutes later, … the custody officer should have interrupted the … procedure …

"26. … Whilst it may be true that the new phone advice system is more efficient than the previous system, at the time of the request to that service, it was not known how long it would take for a solicitor to be available …

"28. As is clear from the authorities, there is no duty on the police to delay the taking of a specimen of breath pending a suspect receiving legal advice.

"29. The justices found that it was (a) not practicable to delay or interrupt the procedure … when the duty solicitor phoned and (b) not in the public interest for the procedure to be interrupted for legal advice. … they were … entitled to reach those conclusions." Appeal dismissed.

CPS v Chalupa

[2009] EWHC 3082 (Admin), 30 October 2009, QBD (DC)

On the facts (20-minute delay in contacting duty solicitor, duty solicitor replying within 2 minutes), the rule that the provision of breath specimens may not be delayed pending legal advice applied; the exception where a solicitor is immediately available did not arise.

A motorist was charged with failing without reasonable excuse to provide two specimens of breath for analysis, contrary to s 7(6), Road Traffic Act 1988. He had been arrested and, at the police station, confirmed that he required legal advice. The police called the duty solicitor 20 minutes later. In the meantime, the breath analysis procedure was started. The motorist would not provide specimens even though he was told he could not delay for legal advice. He was charged with the offence under s 7(6). When the duty solicitor was called, he returned the call within 2 minutes, but was told, in error, that the motorist was then undergoing the breath analysis procedure.

The Crown Court found a breach of s 58, Police and Criminal Evidence Act 1984 (person held at a police station entitled to consult a solicitor as soon as practicable), but that this did not justify excluding the evidence under s 78 (discretion to exclude evidence which would have such an adverse effect on the fairness of the proceedings that the court ought not to admit it). The defendant was convicted. He appealed.

QUESTION(S) FOR THE COURT (AS REFORMULATED IN THE JUDGMENT): Whether, notwithstanding the breach of section 58, the court was entitled to exercise its discretion so as to refuse to exclude the evidence of the breath test procedure.

HELD: "[After reviewing the authorities] 26. … this is not … one of those exceptional cases where a solicitor was immediately available, such that it could be said that any delay would necessarily have been minimal. I do not accept that the exception identified in *Kennedy* [*Kennedy v CPS*, page 378 – if there happens to be a solicitor in the charge office, etc] applies here. The appellant submits that it does on the basis that … the duty solicitor did respond within two minutes of being contacted. That may be true in this case, but there is plainly no guarantee … that there will always be such a speedy response. Moreover, he would not necessarily have been in a position to respond so promptly had he been contacted earlier. …

"27. It follows that we are not in the territory where Section 78 is properly engaged in the sense that there is no arguable basis at all for excluding the evidence. The authorities establish that the right to prompt legal advice and any breach of that right will, in general, have no bearing whatsoever upon the obligation to provide a specimen of breath. It is not a reasonable excuse to refuse to provide a specimen until advice has been received. … Accordingly, there is nothing unfair or improper with the police insisting on a specimen being provided before advice is obtained. …

"30. The second reason for rejecting the appeal is that even if Section 78 was potentially engaged on the grounds that the response was in fact very speedy from the duty solicitor, then the court below is, in any event, plainly entitled to refuse to exclude the evidence. There was, in truth, no prejudice resulting from the breach of Section 58."

The answer to the question was "yes". Appeal dismissed.

Ambrose v Harris; HM Advocate v M; HM Advocate v G

[2011] UKSC 43, [2011] 1 WLR 2435, 6 October 2011, SC

Adducing evidence obtained in response to police questioning conducted under caution at the roadside, the suspect having had no access to legal advice, did not breach the right to a fair trial or the presumption of innocence.

In *Ambrose v Harris*, the defendant had been charged, in Scotland, with being in charge of a motor vehicle after consuming excess alcohol, contrary to s 5(1)(b), Road Traffic Act 1988. Officers found him sitting in the passenger seat of a car parked at the roadside. They thought he had been drinking. They cautioned him and asked three questions – where were the keys; whether he had driven; whether he was going to drive. He gave incriminating answers. Breath analysis revealed excess alcohol. The answers to the questions were led at trial in the sheriff court and the defendant was convicted. He appealed, arguing that his rights under art 6(1) (the right to a fair trial) and art 6(3)(c) (the presumption of innocence), European Convention on Human Rights had been breached. (The conjoined cases did not concern road traffic law and are not dealt with here.)

QUESTION(S) FOR THE COURT: Whether the act of leading and relying on evidence obtained in response to police questioning conducted under common law caution at the roadside and without the appellant having had access to legal advice was incompatible with the appellant's rights under art 6(1) and art 6(3)(c), European Convention on Human Rights.

HELD: "34. … The privilege against self-incrimination is not an absolute right … A person is therefore free to speak to the police and to answer questions if he is willing to do so, even after he has been cautioned. He can provide them with self-incriminating answers if he is willing to do this, and his answers will be admissible if they are truly voluntary. So long as [this approach] is applied the fundamental right under article 6 to a fair trial will be guaranteed. The test is whether the will of the person to remain silent, if that is his will, has been respected. Answers cannot be extracted from him by unfair means, and he must be protected against the risk that they may be forced out of him.…

"62. The correct starting point, when one is considering whether the person's Convention rights have been breached, is to identify the moment as from which he was charged for the purposes of article 6.1. … The moment at which the individual is no longer a potential witness but has become a suspect provides as good a guide as any to when he should be taken to have been charged for the purposes of article 6.1. …

"67. … Applying [that] test … I would hold that Ambrose was charged for the purposes of article 6 when he was cautioned and that the police officer had reason to think that the second and third questions were likely to elicit an incriminating response from him. … The context in Ambrose's case was that, when he was approached by the police, he was drunk and sitting in the car. Suspicion that he was committing an offence fell on him as soon as he told the police that the keys were in his pocket.

"68. But … it would be to go further than Strasbourg has gone to hold that the appellant is entitled to a finding that this evidence is inadmissible because, as a rule, access to a lawyer should have been provided to him when he was being subjected to this form of questioning at the roadside. This leaves open the question whether taking all the circumstances into account it was fair to admit the whole or any part of this evidence. There may, perhaps, still be room for argument on this point."

The answer to the question was "no".

Thomas (William Morgan) v DPP

[2024] EWHC 3259 (Admin), 19 December 2024, KBD (Admin)

On the facts, the decision of the court below not to exclude evidence of the Intoxilyser procedure following a breach of s 58, Police and Criminal Evidence Act 1984 was upheld.

The appellant had been convicted of failing without reasonable excuse to provide a specimen of breath for analysis, contrary to s 7(6), Road Traffic Act 1988. He had been arrested and, at the police station, asked the police to contact a particular firm of solicitors. The police refused to delay the procedure to allow the suspect to speak to a solicitor. The appellant continued to ask for his solicitor, then purported to agree to provide a specimen. He blew with insufficient force and failed to provide a specimen. Police contacted the Defence Solicitor Call Centre approximately 51 minutes after the appellant's first request for his solicitor.

At trial, the appellant argued that the evidence of the breath analysis procedure should be excluded because his right under s 58, Police and Criminal Evidence Act 1984 (person arrested and held in custody entitled to consult a solicitor privately at any time) had been breached and that this would result in an unfair trial within s 78, Police and Criminal Evidence Act 1984 (discretion to exclude evidence which would have such an adverse effect on the fairness of the proceedings that the court ought not to admit it). That argument was rejected and the appellant appealed against conviction.

QUESTION(S) FOR THE COURT: (i) Whether the effective denial of the appellant's entitlement to legal advice pursuant to s 58, Police and Criminal Evidence Act 1984 rendered unfair the admission of the evidence of the Intoxilyser procedure; and (ii) whether, in accordance with the appellant's entitlement pursuant to s 58, the police ought to have made enquiries as soon as reasonably practicable to determine whether the defendant's legal representative of choice was immediately accessible.

HELD: "[After reviewing the authorities] 33. … in neither *Kennedy* [*Kennedy v CPS*, see page 378] nor *Gearing* [*Gearing v DPP*, see page 385] was it either held or suggested that a breach of section 58 would necessarily or even probably lead to a conclusion that evidence of the procedure should be excluded pursuant to section 78. The main thrust of all the cited authorities is that, in the absence of confusion, anxiety or mental stress, it is not a reasonable excuse for not providing a sample promptly that the defendant either wishes to receive or does in fact receive advice from a solicitor. The reference to delaying for a very few minutes where a solicitor is immediately available goes to the application of section 58; it says little or nothing about whether, if there is a breach of section 58, such a breach may trigger exclusion of evidence pursuant to section 78.

"37. We accept that the failure by the police to call the solicitor promptly constituted a breach of section 58. …

"38. …[the District Judge's] decision not to exclude the evidence of the procedure was both justifiable and clearly right in the light of the consistent line of authority … . While we do not exclude the possibility that there might be a case where the *obiter dicta* of Kennedy LJ [in *Kennedy*] and Nelson J [in *Gearing*] might lead to a conclusion that the failure to call a solicitor who happens to be available is capable of triggering a decision to exclude evidence of a breathalyser procedure that was otherwise properly conducted, we are not persuaded that this comes close to being such a case. Furthermore, … the dicta should be treated with considerable caution as potentially distracting from the questions to be asked pursuant to section 78 of PACE in the context of the powerful public interest in the prompt giving of samples.

"39. On the contrary, this seems to us to be an entirely routine case where there is a duty solicitor in the background but it is not clear how long it would have taken between the duty solicitor being called and advice being given. It is clear on the authorities … that neither asking for a solicitor nor even relying upon a solicitor's advice provide a reasonable excuse for not complying with the Intoxilyser procedure. … Adopting an approach that is consistent with them leads to the conclusion that the District Judge was entitled to exercise his discretion pursuant to section 78 as he did.

"41. … the critical period was the period between when the appellant asked to speak to a solicitor and the end of the Intoxilyser procedure. Once it is accepted that (a) neither waiting for advice from a solicitor nor refusing to take the test on the basis of a solicitor's advice would amount to a reasonable excuse for refusing to provide a specimen, and (b) the appellant was warned of the consequences of not providing a specimen, it is not reasonably arguable that evidence of the appellant's informed refusal to take the test renders the proceedings unfair. … the admission of the evidence had no materially adverse effect on the fairness of the proceedings."

The answer to question (i) was "no"; the answer to question (ii) was "yes", but their failure to do so does not affect the answer to the first question.

Appeal dismissed.

6. HEARSAY

See also Dhaliwal v DPP, page 149, where hearsay evidence was wrongly admitted; Whyte v DPP, page 169, where the evidence of service of the analyst's certificate was hearsay; Brett v DPP, page 173, where a certificate of analysis was admitted under s 116, Criminal Justice Act 2003; Leong v DPP, page 410, where oral evidence of what was on the screen of the breath analysis device was not hearsay; and Clarke v CPS [2024] EWHC 704 (Admin), page 174, where MG DD forms were admitted by agreement to hearsay.

Watson v DPP

[2006] EWHC 3429 (Admin), 8 November 2006, QBD (DC)

On the facts of this case (including an earlier appeal to the Administrative Court), prosecution evidence was not unfairly admitted. The investigating officer is not obliged to allow the full 3 minutes for the motorist to provide two breath specimens.

A motorist had been charged with, *inter alia*, failing without reasonable excuse to provide two specimens of breath for analysis, contrary to s 7(6), Road Traffic Act 1988. There had been a road traffic accident. He had left the scene but was later arrested. At the police station he provided a first specimen of breath, but declined to provide a second, saying he needed to use the lavatory. He was warned that the procedure could not be delayed, but persisted in refusing to provide a second specimen.

The trial was set for 1 March 2004. On 27 February 2004, the prosecution sought an adjournment on the grounds that two of its witnesses (Ms Bulman, an employee of the defendant's insurance company, who was to give evidence about an insurance claim made by the defendant, in which he stated he was the driver of the vehicle on the occasion in question), and a police officer (PC Hall) would not be available. The application was refused on 27 February, but renewed on 1 March, when it was allowed. The defendant challenged the latter decision. In May 2005, the Administrative Court quashed the decision to allow the adjournment, ruling that the prosecution could adduce evidence of the two witnesses under ss 117 and 134, Criminal Justice Act 2003 but could not call them to give oral evidence, and that the prosecution should not be unjustly fettered.

At the trial (in October 2005), the magistrates' court admitted hearsay evidence of the insurance claim. They found that while no warning of the consequences of failure to provide specimens had been given before the first specimen, the warning was given before the defendant failed to provide the second specimen and that that satisfied s 7(7), Road Traffic Act 1988. They further found that he had no reasonable excuse for failing to provide the second specimen and convicted him. He appealed.

QUESTION(S) FOR THE COURT: Whether the justices were correct: (1) in rejecting as frivolous arguments that the hearsay should not have been admitted, and that there was a reasonable excuse; (2) in finding that s 7(7) had been met by giving the warning after the first specimen had been given and the second refused.

HELD: "[On an argument that evidence which had not been available in March 2004 should not have been admitted at the trial in October 2005,] 16. [t]he only limitation [imposed by the Administrative Court in its judgment on the first appeal] on the evidence that the prosecution could call was … that they should be denied the opportunity of calling live evidence from Ms Bulman and PC Hall. That limitation aside, the judge made it clear that no greater restriction should be placed on the evidence that the respondent could introduce …

"17. … during the trial … the Crown called Linda Wilson, a claims superintendent from the insurers, although the justices had indicated that the relevant documents which she produced were admissible hearsay evidence. She was cross-examined … for the appellant … previously the appellant had declined to agree the statement of Ms Bulman. In those circumstances counsel for the respondent had concluded the fairest approach … was … to call this witness, who could be cross-examined about the documents the prosecution were seeking to rely on and which they had permission to introduce.

"18. Those factors reveal the appellant's arguments in this regard to be without merit. The prosecution did not breach the restrictions that this court in the earlier appeal had indicated should be imposed; they gained the justices' consent to introduce the documents as hearsay under Section 117 of the Criminal Justice Act 2003; and thereafter, in a spirit of fair play, they called a relevant witness who could be questioned by the appellant about this area of the case.

"19. I reject, therefore, the suggestion that natural justice, the ingredients of a fair trial or 'general fairness' – still less the earlier judgment of this court – required the justices to restrict the respondent in the case they could present at trial to the evidence available to them on 1 March 2004.

"[On (2)] 24. Essentially [the appellant] is seeking to reverse … *Cosgrove v DPP* [, page 204, in which] this court held there was no principle of law that a person must necessarily be allowed the full three minutes to provide the breath specimen … if the administering officer concluded that a person was failing to provide a specimen before the three minutes expired, he was entitled, as a matter of law, to stop the procedure. … there is no basis for us to depart from the decision of this court in *Cosgrove* …

"25. In this case, given the appellant had already provided the first breath specimen and was insisting that rather than give a second specimen, which would have taken less than a minute, he wanted first of all to use the lavatory, the administering officer indicated – in my view wholly sustainably – that if he did not immediately provide the second specimen, his refusal to do so would constitute a failure to complete the test. That decision of the officer and the subsequent endorsement of it by the justices … were unimpeachable."

Appeal dismissed.

7. BAD FAITH

Compare R v Fox, Fox v Chief Constable of Gwent, page 1, where there was no evidence of bad faith. See also R v Bolton Magistrates' Court ex p Scally, page 145, where swabs containing ethanol had been used before taking blood specimens; and DPP v MacPhail, page 353, where police required a second roadside breath test.

Matto v Wolverhampton Crown Court

[1987] RTR 337, [1987] Crim LR 641, 20 May 1987, QBD (DC)

Where officers acted mala fides in requiring a screening test, it was open to the court to consider exercising its discretion to exclude evidence of what later occurred at the police station.

A motorist had been convicted of driving with excess alcohol, contrary to s 6(1), Road Traffic Act 1972 as substituted by s 25 and Sch 8, Transport Act 1981. The police had pursued the motorist because of the speed at which he was travelling; by the time they caught up with him, he had turned into private property. The police asked for a breath sample; the defendant replied "This is private property"; you can't do this". The police officer said, "We know what we're doing; if I wrongfully arrest you, you can sue me, OK?" The motorist then provided a positive screening sample. He was arrested and taken to the police station, where breath analysis revealed excess alcohol.

The Crown Court dismissed the motorist's contention that the breath analysis evidence should have been excluded under s 78(1), Police and Criminal Evidence Act 1984 (discretion to exclude evidence which would have such an adverse effect on the fairness of the proceedings that the court ought not to admit it): although the officers were knowingly acting in excess of their powers and were therefore acting *mala fides*, the defendant had given the sample voluntarily. The motorist appealed further.

QUESTION(S) FOR THE COURT: Whether: (1) following the finding that at the time the defendant provided a specimen of breath the police officer was acting illegally and *mala fides*, the Crown Court was entitled to exercise its discretion against the defendant even though it found that he had provided the sample of breath voluntarily; (2) it was open to the Crown Court on the evidence to find that the defendant had voluntarily given the sample of breath.

HELD: "… in this case exceptionally there could be circumstances where if the Crown Court had properly directed themselves, they could or might have exercised a discretion to refuse to admit the breath alcohol analysis in evidence. I emphasize that I come to the conclusion because of the finding … of *mala fides* [and] because … the finding of the Crown Court that the evidence of the first breath test under section 7 was voluntary was wholly inconsistent with the finding … they made as to the circumstances in which it was obtained. It is quite clear that the officers at the relevant time were behaving in an oppressive manner …

"… it was at least open to the Crown Court … to have come to a conclusion that what happened at the house was still affecting the fairness of what happened in the police station, and would in turn give rise to an argument as to the admissibility of the evidence under section 78 … ."

Appeal allowed.

Thomas (Frank George) v DPP

[1991] RTR 292, 13 October 1989, QBD (DC)

Where a motorist was, in error, arrested without the roadside breath test having been administered, justices were right not to exclude evidence of his subsequent failure to provide specimens at the police station.

A motorist had been charged with failing without reasonable excuse to provide a specimen for a breath test, contrary to s 7(4), Road Traffic Act 1972 as substituted by s 25 and Sch 8, Transport Act 1981; and with failing without reasonable excuse to provide a specimen of breath for analysis, contrary to s 8(7), Road Traffic Act 1972 as likewise substituted. He had been stopped by police who suspected he had been drinking. The police required him to provide a sample for a roadside breath test, and said that the equipment was being brought. The motorist neither agreed nor refused to provide a sample. A sergeant arrived soon after, and, misunderstanding what might or might not have happened, arrested the motorist and took him to the police station, where the motorist refused to provide specimens for analysis.

The justices found that the arrest was unlawful because of the failure to follow the requirements of s 7(4), but that that was not of itself evidence of *mala fides*; they acquitted on the s 7(4) charge but convicted on the s 8(7) charge. The motorist appealed.

QUESTION(S) FOR THE COURT: (i) Whether in the light of the justices' dismissal of the s 7(4) charge, they were nonetheless entitled to find that the defendant had no reasonable excuse for refusing to provide two specimens, contrary to s 8(7); (ii) whether they were entitled to find that there was no misconduct or whether they should have inferred misconduct or *mala fides* on the part of the police and excluded the evidence of the defendant's subsequent refusal to supply a specimen at the police station under s 78, Police and Criminal Evidence Act 1984 (discretion to exclude evidence which would have such an adverse effect on the fairness of the proceedings that the court ought not to admit it).

HELD: "There is abundant authority to show that … it is not necessary for the prosecution to prove a lawful arrest … It follows that an unlawful arrest and nothing more cannot … vitiate subsequent procedures carried out at a police station …

"… a discretion to exclude the procedures at the police station was open to the justices on a finding of *mala fides* … [but t]here is an express finding by the justices that the sergeant misunderstood what may or may not have happened before he arrived … which negatives misconduct at any time …

"[On the] alternative argument that the unlawful arrest provided the defendant with a reasonable excuse for failing to provide a specimen,] the short answer … is that the previous unlawful arrest is irrelevant to the subsequent procedures and cannot amount to a reasonable excuse …

"The justices were right not to exclude the evidence of the defendant's subsequent refusal to supply a specimen at the police station under section 78 of the Act of 1984."

Appeal dismissed.

DPP v Wilson

[1991] RTR 284, [1991] Crim LR 441, 31 January 1991, QBD (DC)

Where an officer acted on a "tip-off", waiting for a vehicle to move off and then stopping it without there having been a moving traffic offence, magistrates were wrong to find that the officer had acted mala fides and to exclude evidence of breath analysis. See also the Scottish case of Thomson v Ritchie 2000 SLT 734.

A motorist had been charged with driving with excess alcohol, contrary to s 5(1), Road Traffic Act 1988. A police officer had received an anonymous telephone call telling him of a place at which the police "would catch a drink driver". The information was passed to another officer, who went to that place, identified the car which had been mentioned, waited for it to move off, then stopped it, although there had been no moving traffic offence. The officer smelled alcohol on the driver and set in motion the breath testing procedure, which showed excess alcohol.

The justices found that the police officer had laid a trap for the defendant, that his suspicions had been founded on facts wholly unconnected with the defendant's driving, and that he had acted *mala fides*. They therefore exercised their discretion under s 78, Police and Criminal Evidence Act 1984 (to exclude evidence which would have such an adverse effect on the fairness of the proceedings that the court ought not to admit it) to exclude evidence of the breath alcohol analysis. They dismissed the information. The prosecutor appealed.

QUESTION(S) FOR THE COURT: Whether, in law, there was evidence upon which the court could properly conclude that the arresting officer's conduct amounted to malpractice such as would entitle the court properly to exercise its discretion under s 78, Police and Criminal Evidence Act 1984 to exclude all evidence following arrest.

HELD: "There is ample authority that a police officer may act on information given, even anonymously, by a third party … the finding [that the constable noticed a strong smell of intoxicating liquor on the defendant's breath] would plainly justify the conclusion that there was a reasonable cause to suspect that the defendant had alcohol in his breath and that that state of suspicion arose in connection with the defendant's driving … the decision … that [the officer's] suspicion was founded upon facts wholly unconnected with the defendant's driving is one which in law and in fact cannot stand.

"[On the question of malpractice] The constable has a duty to act on information which has been passed to him and when an offence is committed he has the duty to act appropriately. There … is no duty [as the prosecutor suggested the officer should have done in this case] on a constable to warn a potential offender of a potential offence nor … is it oppressive if a constable does not do so … There was no evidence upon which the justices could conclude that the arresting officer's conduct amounted to malpractice such as would entitle them to exclude evidence under section 78 … ."

The answer to the question was "no". Appeal allowed.

Ogden v DPP

[1992] COD 314, 6 February 1992, QBD (DC)

Where police followed a speeding motorist to his home and into his house and no mala fides was found, the justices properly considered their discretion under s 78, Police and Criminal Evidence Act 1984, exercising it so as not to exclude evidence of the alcohol testing procedures.

A motorist had been charged with failing without reasonable excuse to provide a specimen for a breath test, contrary to s 7(4), Road Traffic Act 1972 as substituted by s 25 and Sch 8, Transport Act 1981; and with driving with excess alcohol, contrary to s 6(1)(a), Road Traffic Act 1972 as likewise substituted. Police had seen him speeding; they followed him to the drive of his house, where the motorist told them he had not been drinking. Two officers then followed him into the house; they had neither been invited in nor asked to stay outside. One of the officers arrested the motorist for failing to supply a breath sample; breath and blood analyses were positive.

The motorist submitted that the police had acted *mala fides* and that the justices should therefore exclude the evidence of the alcohol testing procedure under s 78, Police and Criminal Evidence Act 1984 (discretion to exclude evidence which would have such an adverse effect on the fairness of the proceedings that the court ought not to admit it).

He was acquitted of failing to provide a specimen on the ground that he had not been asked to provide one; but convicted of driving with excess alcohol, the magistrates having found no bad faith on the part of the police, and having exercised their discretion to admit the evidence. He appealed against conviction.

QUESTION(S) FOR THE COURT: Whether the magistrates were correct in law not to exclude the evidence, pursuant to s 78, Police and Criminal Evidence Act 1984, as having been obtained in such circumstances as would have had an adverse effect on the fairness of the proceedings.

HELD: "… the absence of *mala fides* does not preclude the exclusion of evidence pursuant to section 78 … this was not a case in which the justices took the view that, once *mala fides* had been excluded, no question of favourable exercise of the discretion under section 78 arose. The justices considered their discretion and they exercised it deciding that they would not exclude the evidence … The justices had a discretion to exercise. They exercised it in a way they were entitled to and there is nothing to show that the exercise of that discretion was based upon any wrong approach to the evidence before them."

Appeal dismissed.

Sharpe v DPP

[1993] RTR 392, 3 February 1993, QBD (DC)

Justices did not properly exercise the discretion under s 78, Police and Criminal Evidence Act 1984 where they failed to consider the nature of the police behaviour before deciding to admit evidence of breath analysis, and refused to issue witness summonses against persons who might have shed light on that behaviour.

A motorist had been charged with driving with excess alcohol, contrary to s 5(1)(a), Road Traffic Act 1988. Police officers had seen him, *inter alia*, driving on the wrong side of the road and causing an oncoming vehicle to brake hard; they followed him home; one officer pursued him into his driveway, smelt alcohol on him and heard that his speech was slurred. The defendant made clear the police were unwelcome and were trespassers. He was then led or dragged back to the road, where he failed a breath test. He was arrested and taken to the police station, where breath analysis revealed 111 μg alcohol in 100 ml breath.

At the hearing, it was accepted that the officers were trespassers. It was contended on behalf of the motorist that since the officers had been acting illegally, the justices should exercise their discretion under s 78, Police and Criminal Evidence Act 1984 (discretion to exclude evidence which would have such an adverse effect on the fairness of the proceedings that the court ought not to admit it) to exclude the breath analysis evidence. The defence also applied for witness summonses against two neighbours of the defendant, whom it was said could give evidence of the officers' alleged oppressive behaviour in the driveway.

The justices admitted the breath analysis evidence and refused the application for witness summonses. They convicted the defendant, who appealed.

QUESTION(S) FOR THE COURT: (i) Whether the justices were entitled to refuse to issue witness summonses in respect of potential defence witnesses who were likely to be able to give evidence as to an allegedly illegal arrest pursuant to s 6, Road Traffic Act 1988, when there was other unchallenged evidence which in the opinion of the court justified a requirement for specimens to be provided, where such unchallenged evidence concerned events which preceded the disputed arrest; (ii) whether, having refused to issue such witness summonses, the justices were entitled to rule that the potential evidence outlined in an application for such witness summonses was immaterial to the case; (iii) whether the justices were entitled to convict the defendant.

HELD: "… the justices [did not exercise] their discretion at all. They are in fact saying that, whatever the witness might have said, however bad the behaviour of the police officers may have been … they would still not have excluded the evidence of the breath analysis at the police station … the conduct of the officers in stopping and arresting the defendant and their conduct in his driveway is something which is relevant to the exercise of their discretion under section 78 of the Act of 1984 … What the two witnesses might have said might have thrown further light … and certainly would have been a factor that the justices should have considered before exercising the discretion."

The answers to all three questions were "no". Appeal allowed.

R v Dolgellau JJ ex p Cartledge; R v Penrith JJ ex p Marks

[1996] RTR 207, [1996] Crim LR 337, 31 July 1995, QBD (DC)

On the facts of these cases (errors in procedure for providing specimens, guilty pleas), the conduct of the prosecutors was not analogous to fraud and certiorari was not available. See also R v Bolton JJ ex p Khan (Zafer Alli), page 615, where, again, there was no conduct analogous to fraud.

Motorists had pleaded guilty to driving with excess alcohol in blood, in one case contrary to s 6(1)(a), Road Traffic Act 1972 as substituted by s 25 and Sch 8, Transport Act 1981, and in the other, contrary to s 5(1)(a), Road Traffic Act 1988. In neither case had the procedure set out in *DPP v Warren* (see page 75) for requiring specimens of blood been fully followed. The motorists sought orders of *certiorari* to quash their convictions. The prosecution did not deny that the correct procedure had not been followed, but argued that the Divisional Court had no discretion to order *certiorari* in the circumstances.

GROUND(S) FOR APPEAL: That there had been an error of law, as on the evidence the applicant could, as a matter of law, never have been convicted as the correct procedure for taking blood had not been followed (*Cartledge*). That the wrong procedure had been followed by the police (*Marks*).

HELD: "Normally, *certiorari* will not lie where an applicant has entered an unequivocal plea of guilty … But there are a number of cases where notwithstanding the plea of guilty complaint has been made in relation to the conduct of the prosecution and *certiorari* was granted …

"We respectfully adopt [the analysis of Beldam J in *R v Burton upon Trent JJ ex p Woolley*, see page 101] and … answer the … question [whether the Divisional Court has jurisdiction to quash a conviction following an unequivocal plea of guilty where the conduct of the prosecution cannot fairly be categorised as analogous to fraud] in the negative … there is no suggestion that the crucial evidence of the analysis of the blood samples … was in any way open to doubt. There was a procedural error in the obtaining of such evidence. In the case of Mr Cartledge we do not think the prosecutor can possibly be criticised for failing to foresee that the House of Lords in *Warren* would declare the law different from what it was generally thought to be … In the case of Mr Marks, *Warren's* case had been reported … but … we know nothing of the circumstances in which the matter was dealt with … We do not think that the conduct of the prosecution in either of these cases is analogous to fraud … there is no injustice to the applicants. Unlike those cases where evidence that might cast doubt on guilt is suppressed, there is no doubt of it in these cases …

"Even if we are wrong on this, we do not consider that this is a case where discretion should be exercised so as to quash the convictions."

Applications dismissed.

·Braham v DPP

[1996] RTR 30, 19 December 1994, QBD (DC)

Where the discretion under s 78 was not invoked before the justices, the point could not be raised on appeal. Where there had been no cross-examination of the police officer who gave evidence of the breath analysis procedure, the justices were entitled to conclude that the defendant had been properly warned of the consequences of failing to provide specimens.

A motorist had been charged with driving with excess alcohol, contrary to s 5(1)(a), Road Traffic Act 1988. Her car had been parked; one of the doors opened and struck the side of another passing vehicle. The driver of that vehicle stopped and called the police. By the time the police arrived, the defendant had gone into a nearby flat, her home. The police went to the flat and required a breath specimen for a roadside test. She refused and was arrested; at the police station, the breath testing procedure revealed excess alcohol.

At the hearing, the justices were satisfied that the police had had reasonable cause to believe she had been driving or attempting to drive with alcohol in her body and so had been entitled to enter the flat; they restricted cross-examination on the point. They were also satisfied that the police had given the appropriate warning of the consequences of failing to supply a specimen. They convicted her; she appealed.

QUESTION(S) FOR THE COURT: Whether the justices were right: (1) to restrict cross-examination as to the entry of the police constables into the defendant's home; (2) to conclude that the defendant had been warned that she would be liable to prosecution if she failed to provide specimens of breath for analysis; …

HELD: "[On (1)] … the submission … [before the justices] was directed to the lawfulness of the arrest … the justices cannot be criticised for deciding the matter on that basis, since that was the way that the matter was put to them … if justices are not asked to exercise their power under section 78 [Police and Criminal Evidence Act 1984 – to exclude evidence which would have such an adverse effect on the fairness of the proceedings that the court ought not to admit it] … it is not for this court to criticise [their] decision which was directed to a different point on the basis that they might have decided it in a different way had section 78 been put before them. In those circumstances, I do not consider that the defendant can rely on that point today …

"[On (2)] What in fact happened … was that the custody sergeant gave evidence to the effect that the procedures in Book 116 had been followed. The justices describe that … as a *pro forma* document which includes a warning to the suspect that, if a specimen of breath is not supplied, the suspect will be liable to prosecution … they indicated that they were of the opinion that the defendant had been warned at the police station of the consequences of refusing … the justices were entitled to come to the conclusion they did, irrespective of the fact that the *bona fides* of the police had been called into question. The issue was one which could and should have been raised, if it was a proper issue, by questioning the police officer … No such cross-examination took place … ."

The answers to questions (1) and (2) were "yes". Appeal dismissed.

DPP v Corthine

Unreported, CO/1438/99, 25 November 1999, QBD (DC)

Where justices erred in finding that the police had acted mala fides, their decision to exclude evidence pursuant to s 78, Police and Criminal Evidence Act 1984, was unlawful.

A motorist had been charged with driving whilst unfit, contrary to s 4(1), Road Traffic Act 1988, and with driving with excess alcohol, contrary to s 5(1)(a) of the 1988 Act. Two police officers had seen the defendant and another man, in a drive at the gates of a building site. They spoke to the men and established that they were lawfully on the site and were locking it; they had been drinking; they were going to Slough after locking the site. Both officers could tell by the defendant's appearance and demeanour that he had been drinking but neither officer warned him not to drive, although a Renault 5 was in the driveway with its lights on, doors open and engine running. Following the conversation, the police returned to their car and drove away, but then turned round and followed the Renault 5. They stopped it and arrested the driver for driving whilst unfit. At the police station he was examined by a doctor and declared unfit. Breath analysis revealed a lower reading of 77 µg alcohol in 100 ml breath.

At the hearing, the justices disbelieved evidence given by the police officers to the effect that they had not seen the Renault; that they did not suspect the defendant would be getting into a car and driving off; that they did not make a deliberate decision to go off in the opposite direction, return and arrest the defendant; and that they did not know the defendant was the driver of the car they followed until they actually stopped him. The justices accepted the defence submission of *mala fides* on the part of both police officers and exercised their discretion under s 78, Police and Criminal Evidence Act 1984 (to exclude evidence which would have such an adverse effect on the fairness of the proceedings that the court ought not to admit it) in favour of the defendant to exclude the evidence of the medical examiner and the statement produced by the breath analysis device. They dismissed the charges. The prosecutor appealed.

QUESTION(S) FOR THE COURT: (i) Whether on the evidence and the findings, a reasonable tribunal could conclude that the police officers' actions were *mala fides*. (ii) Whether in law there was evidence upon which the court could properly conclude that the arresting officer's conduct amounted to a malpractice such as would entitle the court properly to exercise its discretion under s 78 to exclude all evidence following arrest.

HELD: "… Although two questions are posed, they raise but a single issue: could the justices conclude on the facts found that the police officers acted in bad faith or were guilty of malpractice? …

"The effect of the justices' conclusion in the case is … that the officers were to be regarded as being under a duty to inform the respondent and/or his colleague of the consequences of driving or attempting to drive after they had consumed alcohol.

"That, essentially, was the basis of another justices' decision, overturned by this court in *DPP v Wilson* [see page 396] …

"… it is plain that the sole basis of the justices' exercise of discretion here was their erroneous conclusion, in the face of the decision in *DPP v Wilson*, that the officers' conduct here evinced bad faith and thus constituted malpractice. That was not a permissible view of the matter. Accordingly, the decision to rule out the all-important evidence as to what occurred following arrest was, in my judgment, unlawful."

The answers to both questions were "no". Appeal allowed.

8. ORAL EVIDENCE

See also Morgan v Lee, page 36 and Chief Constable of Avon & Somerset v Creech, page 111 – the results of breath analysis may be proved by oral evidence; and Sneyd v DPP, page 461 – unchallenged oral evidence was sufficient to establish the breath alcohol level and the calibration and reliability of the breath analysis device.

Culleton v Palmer

Unreported, CO/467/84, 29 June 1984, QBD (DC)

Where the printout was not in evidence, justices were nevertheless right to convict on the basis of the officer's oral evidence that the motorist made no attempt to blow into the breath analysis device.

A motorist had been charged with failing without reasonable excuse to provide a specimen of breath for analysis, contrary to s 8(7), Road Traffic Act 1972 as substituted by s 25 and Sch 8, Transport Act 1981. The justices found that the testing procedure had been properly carried out, but that the motorist had made no attempt to blow into the machine; he merely "puffed his cheeks" round the mouthpiece. They did not accept the breath analysis printout in evidence, but heard evidence from the police officers who had witnessed the procedure; they convicted the motorist. The motorist appealed.

QUESTION(S) FOR THE COURT: Whether, having excluded the Lion Intoximeter 3000 printout, there was any or sufficient evidence upon which the court could find that the appellant failed to provide a specimen of breath.

HELD: "It is sufficient for present purposes to say that there was ample evidence on which the justices could conclude so as to be sure that no specimen had been provided … and were … perfectly right in convicting … ."

Appeal dismissed.

Owen v Chesters

[1985] RTR 191, [1985] Crim LR 156, 14 November 1984, QBD (DC)

Where the printout had not been served, in the absence of evidence of calibration, justices could not instead rely on the officer's oral evidence of the breath alcohol reading.

Justices had dismissed a charge, under s 6(1)(a), Road Traffic Act 1972 as substituted by s 25(3) and Sch 8, Transport Act 1981, of driving with excess alcohol. The Intoximeter printout had not been served on the motorist; there was no evidence of whether or not he had been given a copy of it at the police station. The justices found that the oral evidence of a police sergeant as to the Intoximeter reading was inadmissible on the grounds that the test record had not been served on the defendant. The prosecutor appealed.

QUESTION(S) FOR THE COURT: Whether, in view of the provisions of s 10(3), Road Traffic Act 1972 (evidence by means of a printout) as substituted, evidence of the proportion of alcohol can be given by way of evidence on oath by the police officer who conducted the test on the Lion Intoximeter 3000, without the production of the printout, or whether the production of that document is essential to prove the level of alcohol.

HELD: "It was clearly the intention of the legislature, in enacting [s 10] subsection (5) [requiring the printout to be handed to the defendant or served on him if it is to be admissible], that the defendant should be provided in advance of the hearing with the information recorded … This information includes not only the results of the measurement effected by the instrument … but also, … the results of the self-calibrating exercise which the instrument carries out … If the measurement produced by the instrument is to be relied on by the prosecution, it is clearly vital for the prosecution to establish that the instrument was properly calibrated …

"We would not regard the evidence of the police sergeant as inadmissible under the hearsay rule: it was direct evidence of what he had seen recorded on the instrument. The ground upon which we would uphold the decision of the justices is that the oral evidence of the police sergeant did not, and could not, come up to the standard of proof required by the legislation."

Appeal dismissed.

Chief Constable of Kent v Ellis

Unreported, CO/1146/84, 15 May 1985, QBD (DC)

Magistrates were wrong to refuse to admit the printout into evidence on the ground that it would be hearsay, the officer being unable to give expert evidence about the working of the machine; the presumption of reliability applies until displaced.

Magistrates had dismissed a charge, under s 8(7), Road Traffic Act 1972 as substituted by s 25 and Sch 8, Transport Act 1981, of failure without reasonable excuse to provide a specimen of breath for analysis. The motorist had blown into the Intoximeter three times; on the third occasion he was cut short by the machine's in-built time limit. Some breath had gone into the tube on each occasion. The magistrates accepted the defendant's submission of no case to answer, on the ground that the Intoximeter printout ought not to be admitted in evidence because it would be hearsay, since the officer was unable to give expert evidence about the internal workings of the machine. The prosecutor appealed.

QUESTION(S) FOR THE COURT: (i) Were the magistrates correct in holding that evidence of the indications by the machine of breath insufficiency was inadmissible unless its workings were admitted, proved or judicial notice taken thereof? (ii) Were the magistrates correct in declining to take judicial notice of the internal workings of the machine?

HELD: "[Quoting from *Castle v Cross* [1984] 1 WLR 1372, [1985] 1 All ER 87, [1985] RTR 62, [1984] Crim LR 682 (DC)], 'this printout was admissible and … the … sergeant ought to have been permitted to give evidence as to what he had observed and as to the result of what he observed …'. [Quoting from *R v Skegness Magistrates Court ex p Cardy*, see page 421], 'although … there is a presumption that the device was in order when used it is open to the defendant to rebut that presumption by calling evidence …' … [The motorist] submits that [in applying at the outset for production of the memory roll] he raised the issue of malfunction, and that thereafter the prosecution was not allowed to rely upon the presumption. I do not agree. The application had no evidential significance. The presumption applied until it was displaced by evidence … ."

Appeal allowed.

Mace v Dean

Unreported, CO/455/86, 14 November 1986, QBD (DC)

Oral evidence is admissible to explain an apparent discrepancy as to dates in the printout, and to establish reliability.

A motorist had been charged with driving with excess alcohol, contrary to s 6(1)(a), Road Traffic Act 1972 as substituted by s 25 and Sch 8, Transport Act 1981. Two specimens of breath had been provided for analysis by a Lion Intoximeter 3000; the machine correctly self-calibrated and the readings showed excess alcohol. The first specimen was analysed just before midnight, the second just after midnight, but the printout showed the whole test as having been carried out on Friday, 14 September; in fact, it had been begun on Friday, 13 September and completed on Saturday, 14 September. The police officer who conducted the test gave oral evidence of the Intoximeter readings which had appeared on the visual display and of the date and time the procedure had begun and ended.

An expert gave evidence that the Intoximeter operates at Greenwich Mean Time throughout the year; and that if a breath test is begun just before midnight, it is recorded as begun on the day of the week upon which it was begun (Friday in this case), and the second reading is recorded as the date upon which it was completed (14 September, in this case). That evidence was not challenged.

The magistrates found the machine unreliable and the printout inadmissible; they dismissed the charge. The prosecutor appealed.

HELD: "… the result of *Fawcett v Gasparics* [see page 292, not reported at the time of the justices' decision] was that if there is an apparent discrepancy of the kind which we are concerned with in this case and provided oral evidence explains the mistake there is no need for an implication or condition suggesting that the machine is not a reliable machine. The question as to its reliability, which is certainly there when one looks at the printout, is explained by the external evidence and that case is almost entirely upon all-fours with the instant case … ."

Appeal allowed.

Will v DPP

Unreported, CO/1087/88, 6 October 1988, QBD (DC)

Oral evidence of readings from a breath analysis device must be given by an officer familiar with the workings of the machine. The fact that the officer said in cross-examination that he might not have checked the second calibration did not mean that the justices could not be satisfied on the entirety of his evidence.

A motorist had been charged with driving with excess alcohol, contrary to s 6(1)(a), Road Traffic Act 1972 as substituted by s 25 and Sch 8, Transport Act 1981. At the hearing, she alleged that the officer conducting the breath testing procedure was not as well versed in the working of the machine as he claimed, in that he did not get her to sign the printout; did not hand her or serve on her a copy of it; and did not know by heart the calibration limits. Before going into court, the officer had refreshed his memory from the printout. In evidence in chief, he said the second calibration reading was 34; but on cross-examination, agreed that it was possible he had not checked the second calibration test, because he had not recorded it.

The justices found the case proved. The motorist appealed.

QUESTION(S) FOR THE COURT: Whether the justices' finding was one which a reasonable bench of magistrates, properly directing themselves, could have reached.

HELD: "… The fact that the printout had not been served as required by the Act, and was therefore not evidence …, meant that the prosecution had to rely upon the officer's oral evidence. Previous decisions of this court have made it clear that where the Intoximeter markings are sought to be proved by oral evidence, they must be proved by a witness who is familiar with the working of the Lion Intoximeter, who is aware of the necessity to carry out the necessary calibrations … and who is generally familiar with his task … Whether [the officer had disqualified himself as such a person] was a matter for the justices …

"… in cross-examination [the officer] conceded the possibility that he had not done the second calibration … to say that because he gave that answer the justices could not themselves be satisfied so as to be sure that he had checked the final calibration is to misunderstand the position. The triers of fact are not constrained within the precise words of a particular answer. They have to look at the entirety of a witness's evidence … There is nothing to suggest that the justices … did not apply their minds correctly to the question which they were required to answer. They expressly found that [the officer] was an honest and credible witness, and that he would have and did make the necessary second calibration check and observe it."

The answer to the question was "yes". Appeal dismissed.

Thom v DPP

[1994] RTR 11, 20 January 1993, QBD (DC)

Where the printout is not produced, the prosecutor may prove by oral evidence both the calibration and the breath alcohol readings.

A motorist had been charged with driving with excess alcohol, contrary to s 5(1), Road Traffic Act 1988. Two breath specimens had been analysed and showed 97 μg and 96 μg alcohol in 100 ml breath.

At the hearing, police witnesses gave evidence that, *inter alia*, the Intoximeter had correctly self-calibrated and that the motorist had been given a copy of the printout from the Intoximeter and did not query the readings. The printout was not produced in court. The motorist submitted that there was no case to answer on the ground that the printout had not been produced and that there was therefore insufficient evidence on which to proceed. The justices were satisfied that there was sufficient evidence to find that the Intoximeter had been functioning correctly, and saw no need for the prosecution to re-open the case to admit the printout. They found a case to answer and went on to convict the motorist. The motorist appealed.

QUESTION(S) FOR THE COURT: Whether the justices were correct in finding that the prosecution had produced sufficient evidence of the reliability of the Intoximeter device and the readings from it, and whether they were therefore correct in rejecting the submission of no case to answer.

HELD: "… there was evidence, first, that the Intoximeter was calibrated properly and was working properly, and, second, what the Intoximeter readings were … I can see no distinction in principle between evidence by a witness that he looked at his watch and read the time … and evidence from a witness that he looked at the Lion Intoximeter and that he read the proportion of alcohol ... there is no reason whatever to think that the readings were not accurate ...

"[Applying *Owen v Chesters*, see page 403] the prosecution proved by admissible oral evidence both the proportion of alcohol in the breath and that the Intoximeter was properly calibrated and working."

The answer to the question was "yes". Appeal dismissed.

Greenaway v DPP

[1994] RTR 17, 3 February 1993, QBD (DC)

Where an officer gave unchallenged oral evidence that all the readings showed the breath analysis device was working properly, that was sufficient to show the machine was calibrating correctly. The magistrates did not, in this case, exercise their discretion to admit the printout after the close of the prosecution case.

A motorist had been convicted of driving with excess alcohol in breath, contrary to s 5(1)(a), Road Traffic Act 1988. At the hearing, the police officer who had conducted the breath testing procedure gave oral evidence, using his contemporaneous statement to refresh his memory, of the procedure, leading to breath analysis of 51 μg alcohol in 100 ml breath. The printout from the breath analysis device was attached to the statement and was visible to the magistrates, but was not given to them before the close of the prosecution case.

The motorist then submitted that there was no case to answer because there was not sufficient evidence of the proper calibration of the machine. The justices asked to see the printout, which was handed to them. They rejected the submission of no case to answer and went on to convict the motorist. He appealed.

QUESTION(S) FOR THE COURT: Whether the justices were correct in finding that the prosecution had produced evidence of the reliability of the Intoximeter, and in rejecting the defendant's submission of no case to answer.

HELD: "... A document used to refresh memory in the course of giving evidence clearly is not, without more, formally in evidence ... It may be a formality, but it does need to be produced by the witness and exhibited if it is to become evidence in the case. There is no dispute that it was not so here.

"The next question is whether on the facts found, it is clear or sufficiently clear that the magistrates exercised their discretion to admit the document after the close of the prosecution case ... I am not satisfied ... that the magistrates did exercise a discretion ... on balance it seems that they took the view that the document was already in evidence.

"... the question then remains whether [the officer] who gave evidence gave sufficient evidence to support the conviction ... He must, of course, give the evidence of the actual reading ... But he must also give evidence that the machine is working properly and is therefore reliable ... The relevant paragraph in the case [recites that he] '... stated that at the time of the test all of the readings showed the machine was working properly. This evidence was not challenged by the defence.' … I would accept that as clearly sufficient evidence, albeit perhaps in shorthand, that he had considered the calibration readings, amongst others, and was telling the court that the machine was reliable … The time for the defendant to challenge that … was then."

The answer to the question was "yes". Appeal dismissed.

Van Flute v DPP

Unreported, CO-3118-93, 9 June 1994, QBD (DC)

Oral evidence of the contents of the printout is admissible. Where the officer mis-stated the calibration range by 1 µg, that did not reflect on his competence to give evidence on reliability. Failure to give evidence of the date and time of the readings is not a flaw in the evidence proving reliability.

A motorist had been charged with driving with excess alcohol, contrary to s 5(1)(a), Road Traffic Act 1988.

At the hearing, the printout from the breath analysis device was not produced in evidence, but the police sergeant who had administered the breath testing procedure gave oral evidence, *inter alia*, that the device had to calibrate in the range 32–38 µg alcohol in 100 ml breath; that it calibrated at 33 µg; and that he was satisfied that the device was operating correctly. The motorist contended that no evidence of the date and time of the test had been given; the prosecutor submitted that it had.

The magistrates found that the police evidence contained sufficient detail of time, date, calibration and readings for them to convict. They did so, and the motorist appealed.

QUESTION(S) FOR THE COURT: Whether the justices were right to convict.

HELD: "… Ordinarily, it is right that, if possible, the written record produced by the machine should be produced in court … [but i]t is by no means improper for the officer to give oral evidence of what might otherwise have been established by producing the written record.

"[On the point that the relevant calibration range was said by the sergeant to be 32 to 38 µg, but is in fact 32 to 37 µg, and that because of that error, the officer may not have understood the purging aspect and so may not have been a competent person to operate and report on the reliability of the machine] I see no strength in that argument … since 33 [the actual calibration reading] was comfortably within the proper bracket, there is no flaw in his evidence which can reflect … upon [his] competence generally …

"[On the argument that were was no evidence of the date and time on which the test was taken] It is … true that there was no direct evidence that the sergeant said to the magistrates that he saw on the visual display the date … and a particular time when the breath test was in fact taken … But … the failure to give those exact readings from the machine cannot be fatal to the conviction … It is not …

a flaw in the evidence proving the reliability of the machine that the evidence was not given *ipsissima verba* … ."

Appeal dismissed.

Perkins v DPP

[2004] EWHC 255 (Admin), 6 February 2004, QBD (DC)

A court was entitled to accept part but not all of a police officer's evidence, without discussing it with the witness or counsel; where a suspect had failed to provide breath specimens, it was irrelevant that the officer later refused the suspect's request to provide a blood specimen. Article 6, European Convention on Human Rights, was not engaged.

A motorist had been charged with failing without reasonable excuse to provide specimens of breath for analysis, contrary to s 7(6), Road Traffic Act 1988. He had provided a roadside breath specimen, but at the police station failed to provide breath specimens for analysis. He then asked to provide a blood specimen, but the police did not allow him to do so. He was convicted by magistrates and appealed.

At the Crown Court, the officer who conducted the procedure referred to his record of the procedure and gave evidence that he had encouraged the motorist to keep blowing; the printout, however, showed that insufficient breath had been given. There was expert evidence that the device was functioning correctly. The court found that there was nothing wrong with the device and that there was no medical reason why the motorist could not have provided breath. It also found that the officer's evidence that he had encouraged the motorist to blow was inconsistent with the printout. It decided that the officer's recollection was wrong and upheld the conviction. The motorist further appealed.

QUESTION(S) FOR THE COURT: (1) Whether it was *Wednesbury* unreasonable to have found that the officer's recollection of events could not be relied upon; (2) whether it was a breach of art 6, European Convention on Human Rights (right to a fair trial) to have reached that decision when the point had not been raised by one of the parties and without having put it to the officer; (3) whether it was correct to find that the officer was entitled to refuse to allow a blood specimen to be provided.

HELD: "[On (1), it is submitted that] 18. … the court accepted part of [the officer's] evidence and … rejected part of his evidence. That is the function … of the Crown Court … and to attack it as an improper process is frankly unfortunate. There is no merit in the complaints made under [this] head.

"[On (2)] 16. … I know of no rule of law or practice … whereby the court, having discussed matters … would have to return to court to discuss their reasoning with the witness or counsel calling the witness, whose evidence may not be preferred by the court. Of course it is obvious that the court must not surprise litigants by taking a major point without warning to the parties, … [in the present case] the court had to choose between these two conflicting pieces of evidence, that is to say the sergeant's and the evidence that resulted from what [the expert witness] said about a malfunction.

"[On (3)] 23. … First, it is the failure to provide the breath sample which is the offence: a blood sample below the permissible level is not a defence to a charge of failing to provide a specimen of breath. Second, on the facts of this case … Article 6(3)(b) does not engage. The sequence of events here, of not providing a specimen by the expedient of not trying to do so, when he had no reasonable excuse for not providing it, and for no known reason, does not cause the Article to engage. There is nothing, in my opinion, in the facts of this case, that has any relevance to the requirement of the Article that he should have 'adequate time and facilities for the preparation of his defence'."

Appeal dismissed.

Leong v DPP

[2006] EWHC 1575 (Admin), 12 June 2006, QBD (Admin)

Oral evidence of what was on the printout was admissible where the printout had not been served; there is no difference between what is on the printout and what is on the screen.

A motorist had been charged with driving with excess alcohol, contrary to s 5(1)(a), Road Traffic Act 1988. He had been arrested and breath analysis revealed excess alcohol.

At the trial, the officer who conducted the proceedings gave oral evidence of the breath analysis procedure and of the contents of the printout. The defendant argued that the evidence was not admissible because the printout had not been served as required by s 16(3)(a), Road Traffic Offenders Act 1988; and that the officer had simply read the printout without giving any independent evidence of what he had seen on the display.

QUESTION(S) FOR THE COURT: Whether the justices were entitled to rely on the officer's evidence of the contents of the printout without making the printout an exhibit and given that the appellant objected that it had not been served on him.

HELD: "9. … section 16 does not seek to set out an exhaustive and comprehensive statement of how the prosecution can prove that a defendant had more than the prescribed amount of alcohol in his blood, his breath or his urine. … There are indeed no provisions which limit the form of admissible evidence which can be adduced relating to the requisite amount of alcohol in the blood, breath or urine of a driver.

"13. [Counsel for the appellant submits that the decision in *Sneyd v DPP*, page 461] was wrong because the court there were admitting hearsay evidence. She relies on a number of cases, such as *Denneny v Harding* [1986] RTR 350, [1986] Crim LR 254], in which the police officer had read off the screen and that evidence was inadmissible. It is significant that none of the judgments in any of those cases state or even imply that the only way in which the level of blood alcohol can be proved is on the basis of what the officer reads from the result on the visual display. In my view, there is no difference between what is on the visual display and what is seen on the print-out, provided, as was the case here, that the machine was working properly.

"14. … the correct approach was that set out [in] *Sneyd* … 'I see no problem of oral evidence of the results shown on the print-out and no difference in principle between that and oral evidence of the results on the screen of the machine. These are just two different ways by which the machine displays its results. The same thing appears on both. In neither case, in my judgment, is oral evidence inadmissible hearsay.'

… that is a proper and correct analysis because what [the officer] was doing in this case was merely saying what he had seen; that is not hearsay evidence. Where, as in the present case, there is evidence that the machine is working properly, there is no reason why the police officer concerned cannot give admissible evidence of what he saw in the print-out. There is no difference between that and what was seen on the screen. So the justices were correct."

Appeal dismissed.

Cummings v CPS

[2016] EWHC 3624 (Admin), 15 December 2016, QBD (Admin)

An officer may refresh her memory from an MG DD form where she witnessed the breath analysis procedure and completed the form jointly with the officer who conducted the procedure.

A motorist had been convicted of, among other matters, failing to provide a specimen of breath for analysis, contrary to s 7(6), Road Traffic Act 1988. A police sergeant conducted the breath analysis procedure at the police station in the presence and hearing of a police constable. The two officers together completed the Form MG DD/A, although the constable did not countersign it. The sergeant did not appear at the trial. Instead, the constable gave evidence, and was allowed to refresh her memory from the form. The motorist appealed against conviction.

QUESTION(S) FOR THE COURT: Whether the justices wrongly acceded to the prosecution's application to allow a police officer to refresh her memory pursuant to s 139, Criminal Justice Act 2003 from Form MG DD/A.

HELD: "11. Section 139(1) provides:

'A person giving oral evidence in criminal proceedings about any matter may, at any stage in the course of doing so, refresh his memory of it from a document made or verified by him at an earlier time if –

(a) he states in his oral evidence that the document records his recollection of the matter at that earlier time, and

(b) his recollection of the matter is likely to have been significantly better at that time than it is at the time of his oral evidence.'

"[On the argument that the constable did not make or verify the document] 18. … verification involves a question of fact as to whether witness A has at the earlier time satisfied himself that a record of his recollection has been made and that it is accurate. Evidence of verification may typically include A's signature to the relevant document, but that is simply one form of evidence. …

"19. … the justices made findings of fact that [the constable] was present throughout the whole procedure and heard all the questions and answers. … they must be taken implicitly to have accepted [her] evidence that she and [the sergeant] completed each page of the form together. Having completed the form together with [the sergeant], [the constable] must be taken to have been entirely satisfied as to the accuracy of its contents. That is the essence of verification …

"21. Section A25 [of the form] records that [the constable] was a witness to all sections of the procedure. True it is that the signature box is blank. However, the combination of the other entries in A25 and [the constable's] evidence, as accepted by the justices, can leave … no doubt that [the constable] had verified the form as an accurate record of what she saw and heard in the course of the breath test procedure. For the same reasons, the form records her recollection on that day of what she had witnessed. This was not hearsay evidence, but her direct evidence.

"22. Given the blank signature box, it is not clear how the justices concluded that [the constable] had signed the form. … However, given the evidence which they did accept, in my judgment, they were bound to reach the same conclusion even without the signature.

"23. For all these reasons, I do not accept the Appellant's core submission that [the constable] was simply giving the evidence that only [the sergeant] could have given. On [the] contrary, she was giving her evidence of what she had witnessed and was properly entitled to refresh her memory for that purpose. …

"25. The case stated records that before being given leave to refresh her memory, [the constable] gave evidence that the Appellant had refused to undertake the breath test procedure. She evidently needed to refresh her memory from the form in order to recall the precise details of the procedure and what was said by [the sergeant] and the Appellant. That is just the sort of point of precision which justifies resort to section 139.

"26. On the basis of the justices' implicit acceptance of [the constable's] evidence that she and [the sergeant] had completed each page of the form together, I also consider that they would have been entitled to conclude that she had jointly made the form within the meaning of section 139. However, since the justices did not so conclude, I would limit this decision to the issue of verification."

Appeal dismissed.

DPP v Sugden

[2018] EWHC 544 (Admin), 20 March 2018, QBD (Admin)

Subject to verification under s 139, Criminal Justice Act 2003, a copy of Form MG DD/A may be used to refresh the memory.

A motorist had been charged with driving with excess alcohol, contrary to s 5(1), Road Traffic Act 1988. He pleaded not guilty, raising issues of the reliability of the evidential breath testing instrument; whether the statutory requirements under s 7, Road Traffic Act 1988 had been met; and whether the guidance in Form MG DD/A had been followed. At trial, the prosecution was unable to produce the original Form MG DD/A which had been used by the investigating officer, or the printout, but did have copies. The district judge refused the prosecution's application, pursuant to s 139, Criminal Justice Act 2003, to allow the officer to refresh his memory from the copy documents. The defence submitted that there was no case to answer; the prosecution was unable to prove its case and the motorist was acquitted. The Crown appealed.

QUESTION(S) FOR THE COURT: Whether the district judge had erred in law in: (1) applying the "best evidence" rule to the document on which the officer wished to rely, under s 139, Criminal Justice Act 2003, to refresh his memory; and (2) refusing the application for the officer to be allowed to refresh his memory from a document purporting to be a copy of a Form MG DD/A.

HELD: "17. … it is necessary to consider the best evidence rule separately from the body of law which allows a witness to refresh his or her memory from a document not itself adduced in evidence. The two are conceptually distinct. The best evidence rule, or what remains of it, goes to the admissibility of a document as evidence. The law on refreshing of a witness's memory does not turn on the admissibility of the document from which the witness's memory is refreshed; that document is not adduced in evidence at all. …

"50. … the district judge ought to have applied the tests set out in section 139(1), which includes the test of verification in turn derived from the earlier common law authorities considered by this court in *R. v. Cummings* [see page 411].

"51. … If he had done so, it is likely that he would have acceded to the Crown's request if it turned out that [the officer] had 'verified' either the missing original form or the copy on the court file. It is not clear from the case stated that [the officer] was ever asked the necessary questions to establish whether the requirements of section 139(1) … were satisfied. Furthermore, … there was no specific evidence from the defence, as distinct from mere assertion, that there were likely to be discrepancies between the original form MG DD/A and the copy before the court.

"52. I therefore consider that the district judge erred in the manner in which he dealt with the request for [the officer] to refresh his memory from the copy document. I think it likely, subject to asking him the necessary questions arising under section 139(1), that the correct course would have been to allow him to refresh his memory and to allow the defence to explore with him in cross-examination, and subsequently in submissions, the likelihood or risk of any discrepancy between the copy and the original.

"53. … this judgment should not be taken either as an indication to prosecutors that a lax approach to production of original documents of this kind is to be encouraged, nor as any encouragement to defendants to seek the exclusion of memory refreshing documents on flimsy grounds, where by there is no reason to suppose that they differ from their original counterparts. …

"54. I do not think the advent of Better Case Management and the Digital Case System makes any difference to the analysis one way or the other. The parties will very often find it unnecessary to go beyond the electronic versions of documents disclosed using that medium; but any shortcomings in transcription, formatting, the reproduction of coloured inks and the like, can be addressed in the case of a particular document whenever that proves necessary.

"56. … [The answer to question (1) was] that the best evidence rule was not the correct starting point and that the words of section 139(1) ought to have been applied.

"57. [The answer to the second question was] … the judge did so err and … on a retrial the court is likely, applying the words of section 139(1), to permit recourse to the copy MG DD/A if the original has not by then been found."

The verdict of not guilty was set aside and a re-trial ordered.

9. EVIDENCE OF UNFITNESS TO DRIVE

See ss 3A(2) and 4(5), Road Traffic Act 1988 – a person is unfit to drive if his ability to drive properly is impaired; and R v Richards [1975] 1 WLR 131, [1974] 3 All ER 696, [1974] RTR 520, 59 Cr App R 288, 16 July 1974, CA – "fitness to drive may depend upon all sorts of circumstances. The amount of alcohol which will make one man unfit to drive does not necessarily make another man unfit."

Leetham v DPP

[1999] RTR 29, 25 March 1998, QBD (DC)

On the facts of this case (eyes red and glazed, speech slurred, answers slow), the justices were entitled to find unfitness to drive without medical evidence.

A motorist had been charged with driving when unfit through drugs, contrary to s 4(1), Road Traffic Act 1988. He was stopped by police because of the dangerous manner of his driving; there was no smell of intoxicating drink. He volunteered that he had smoked cannabis. At the police station he was examined by a police surgeon who took a blood sample. Analysis of the sample revealed no alcohol, but a chemical compound arising from cannabis or cannabis resin.

Before the justices, a police officer gave evidence that the defendant's eyes had been red and glazed, his speech slurred and his answers slow. The scientist who had analysed the blood specimen gave evidence of the effects of cannabis. For the defence, it was argued, *inter alia*, that, to establish unfitness to drive, it was necessary to call expert medical evidence, in particular, that of the police surgeon who had examined the motorist. The justices found that there was ample evidence of unfitness to drive without any medical evidence; they convicted. The motorist appealed.

QUESTION(S) FOR THE COURT: Whether the justices were entitled to convict on the basis of the evidence of the police officer and of the forensic scientist.

HELD: "… The crucial question in this case is whether there was material, despite the fact that no doctor was called, which justified the Justices in concluding that drugs had impaired the Defendant's ability properly to drive.

"In my judgment, they were entitled to look at all the evidence in the case in relation to the way in which the car was driven, the consumption of cannabis which the Defendant admitted, the presence of cannabis in his blood on subsequent analysis, the effects of that drug, in particular, in relation to 'feelings of relaxation and possible drowsiness, loss of coordination and reduced concentration,' and to put all that evidence with the evidence from the police officers as to the slurred and slow character of the Appellant's speech. For my part, therefore, I would answer both the questions posed by the Justices in the affirmative and I would dismiss this appeal."

Hurst v DPP

Unreported, CO/2733/97, 6 May 1998, QBD (DC)

On the facts of this case, the justices were not wrong in law to find unfitness to drive on the basis of police and expert evidence, there having been no expert evidence the other way.

The defendant had been charged, *inter alia*, with driving when unfit through drink or drugs. He had visited friends before going to Henley Regatta; he left his car at the friends' home. At the Regatta, he was with a group of others; another in the group was deputed to drive everyone home, and the defendant consumed champagne and wine. On leaving the Regatta, he was driven back, with others, to his friends' home; they stopped on the way and the defendant drank a pint of beer. After arriving back at the friends' home, he then drove their daughters to see their horses. There was an accident.

The magistrates accepted police evidence that, immediately after the accident, the defendant's breath smelt reasonably strongly of alcohol; they also accepted evidence that his actions and speech were slow; and that this, and his slurred speech, were consistent with alcohol rather than with his injuries; that alcohol had contributed to his losing control of the car. The road in question had recently been resurfaced leaving loose grit on the surface, but the justices rejected an argument that the accident had been caused by an unforeseen hazard; other drivers had given evidence that they had experienced no difficulty from the resurfacing.

They convicted the defendant of driving when unfit and of driving without due care and attention. He appealed.

QUESTION(S) FOR THE COURT: Whether the verdicts which the justices reached were verdicts to which they could properly come in the light of the facts they found proved by the evidence.

HELD: "… [The appellant submits] that the [mother of the children] did not find his voice to be slurred; … that the Justices should have given no or extremely little weight to the fact that the appellant's breath smelt of alcohol; … that the [appellant's] injuries … could well explain [his] behaviour after the accident and [the slurring of his voice]. [There was expert evidence that] '… Slurring is more likely to indicate intoxication whilst inconsistent illogical reasoning with clear but slow diction is more likely to result from concussion'; and 'that the road, which had recently had a new surface, had become an unforeseen hazard'.

"I … do not accept … that Justices … are not entitled to reject an explanation by an expert when there is no expert evidence the other way. The evidence is … always a matter for the court to consider …

"… whereas it is obviously perverse and an error of law to make a finding of fact for which there is no evidential foundation, it is not perverse, even though it may be mistaken for a court to prefer the evidence of A to B or to accept some of the evidence of A but not all of A's evidence. If a court comes to that conclusion … that gives rise, in the absence of special and unusual circumstances which do not exist here, to no error of law challengeable before this court … It may give rise to an error of fact. But, if that is the case, then the proper forum would be the Crown Court … ."

Appeals dismissed.

Willicott v DPP

[2001] EWHC Admin 415, (2002) 166 JP 385, 11 June 2001, QBD (DC)

Magistrates were wrong to take into account readings from partial breath specimens when determining whether or not a person was driving whilst unfit. Compare R v Ashworth, page 374.

A motorist had been charged with failing without reasonable excuse to provide two specimens of breath for analysis, contrary to s 7(6), Road Traffic Act 1988; and with driving while unfit, contrary to s 4(1), Road Traffic Act 1988. He had been seen driving by two police officers. His driving seemed erratic and he went through two sets of red traffic lights. The officers stopped him, and noticed that his breath smelled of alcohol, his speech was slurred and his eyes were glazed. A roadside breath test was positive; the motorist did not mention any medical condition while at the roadside.

At the police station he was required to give a breath specimen. He made four attempts, but each time failed to provide a proper specimen, although the readings, each of which exceeded the prescribed limit, were noted, as were the times of each reading. The appellant told the officer he was suffering from asthma and that he had tried as hard and as long as he could; he was not aware of any other reason why the tests did not register; he said that stress may have made him short of breath, although the police officer did not note any signs of distress or any appearance of physical discomfiture.

The justices convicted him of both offences. He appealed.

HELD: "8. [The appellant submitted] … that the Magistrates were wrong as a matter of law to have had regard to [the breath analysis] readings. They undoubtedly took those into account when determining whether or not the appellant was driving whilst unfit through drink … There was no evidence before the Magistrates which could have entitled them to come to any conclusion as to the reliability of those readings and their relevance to the issues before them.

"12. … Nonetheless, [the prosecutor] submits, firstly, that does not infect the charge relating to the failure to provide a breath test; secondly, he submits that there was ample material before the Justices to conclude that the appellant was driving whilst unfit through drink from the conclusions that they reached on matters which were essentially matters relating to the credibility of the police officers and not of the appellant.

"13. … The evidence which was inadmissible was undoubtedly used by the Magistrates and can only have been used in order to test the appellant's credibility. In those circumstances, the conclusions that they reached on credibility will be clearly relevant to both charges. It follows that since their conclusions as to credibility must have been at least in part dependent upon the receipt of that inadmissible evidence, then the conclusions that they reached in relation to both charges are infected by that error of law.

"14. … although there are undoubtedly arguments for saying that there was [other] material before the Justices … as to the appellant's credibility which could justify the convictions, it would be inappropriate for this court to conclude that that was material which would have inevitably resulted in the appellant's conviction … ."

Appeal allowed.

R v Irvine

[2002] EWCA Crim 827, 19 March 2002, CA (Crim)

On the facts, the jury was entitled to take into account evidence on the general effects of ecstasy in deciding whether or not consumption of that drug had caused impairment.

A driver had been charged with causing death by driving without due care and attention when under the influence of drink or drugs, contrary to s 3A(1), Road Traffic Act 1988. He had been to a rave, was driving home, but stopped in a lay-by and slept for a couple of hours before resuming driving. After overtaking another vehicle, he continued towards the kerb and then down the embankment, killing the front-seat passenger. The driver remembered nothing; the inference was that he had fallen asleep at the wheel. His heart rate became high, which could have been caused by drugs or by shock. A blood specimen was taken and showed 0.2 µg of MDMA (ecstasy) per ml. Back-calculation showed that, at the time of the accident, the concentration would have been 0.6 µg, which the analyst described as a high level. Both the hospital doctor and the analyst gave evidence about the general effects of ecstasy – an initial stimulant phase followed by a secondary phase of fatigue and sleepiness. The driver was convicted and appealed.

HELD: "17. … It is not in doubt or in dispute that the prosecution must prove that alcohol or drugs – in the present case drugs – is the real effective cause of a defendant's impaired ability to drive. …

"[After referring to *R v Millington*, page 420] 24. This is a case in which there was evidence from two doctors [the hospital doctor and the analyst of the blood specimen] as to the general effects of ecstasy – that is to say, evidence as to both its stimulant and to its secondary rebound stages – and we think that the jury was entitled to use that evidence, in the exercise of its own common sense on all the facts of the case, to consider whether this appellant was guilty of the offence charged and whether the drugs which he had consumed had been the effective cause of an impaired ability to drive."

The appellant's arguments, based on criticism of the judge's summing-up to the jury in the court below, were rejected. Appeal dismissed.

R v Mohamed (Ahmed)

[2018] EWCA Crim 596, [2020] 4 WLR 1, 21 February 2018, CA (Crim)

The sentencing guideline for the s 3A offences applies to an offence under s 3A(1)(ba) – causing death by careless driving when over the prescribed limit for a specified controlled drug, even though the guideline predates subs (1)(ba). It is not necessary to prove impairment to establish the offence under s 3A(1)(ba), although the level of impairment is relevant to sentencing.

The appellant had pleaded guilty to causing death by careless driving when over the prescribed limit for a specified controlled drug, contrary to s 3A(1)(ba), Road Traffic Act 1988. Blood analysis showed a level of cannabis more than three times the limit. The sentencing judge accepted that the level of cannabis was not to be seen as any accurate measure of the extent to which, if at all, the appellant's ability to drive was impaired, and proceeded to sentence him by reference to the sentencing guideline for the offence of causing death by careless driving when under the influence of drink or drugs contrary to s 3A. The appellant appealed against sentence.

GROUNDS FOR APPEAL (INTER ALIA): Since the judge had declined to find that the appellant's ability to drive had been impaired by drugs, he should have based the sentence on the guideline for causing death by careless or inconsiderate driving (which carries a maximum sentence of 5 years' imprisonment) rather than on the guideline for causing death by careless driving when under the influence of drink or drugs (which carries a maximum of 14 years' imprisonment).

HELD: "22. … the judge was correct to apply the guideline for causing death by careless driving when under the influence of drink or drugs. That is the guideline for an offence contrary to section 3A of the 1988 Act, and the defendant fell to be sentenced for an offence contrary to section 3A …

"23. Prior to the most recent amendment adding sub-paragraph (ba), which applied in this case, there were at the time the guideline was introduced in 2008 four circumstances in which the offence could be committed: (a) that at the time of driving, the offender is unfit to drive through drink or drugs; (b) that the offender has consumed so much alcohol that the proportion of it in his breath, blood or urine exceeds the prescribed limit; (c) that within 18 hours after the time of the driving the offender is required to provide a specimen but fails without reasonable excuse to do so; and (d) that the offender is required by a constable to give permission for a laboratory test for a specimen of blood, but without reasonable excuse fails to provide it.

"24. The amendment introduced by sub-paragraph (ba) puts controlled drugs on a par with alcohol by making it an offence to drive when 'he has in his body a specified controlled drug and the proportion of it in his blood or urine at that time exceeds the specified limit for that drug' … only sub-paragraph (a), driving when unfit through drink or drugs, requires proof of actual impairment. The other sub-paragraphs are, in effect, proxies for impairment based either on the quantity of alcohol or drugs in the body, or on deliberate action by the defendant to avoid providing such evidence. Parliament has thus provided that, as an alternative to proof of actual impairment, the offence will equally be committed by driving with alcohol or drugs in the body in excess of the prescribed limit. Actual impairment is not a prerequisite for the commission of the offence. It follows that the guideline must be taken to apply to all offences contrary to section 3A, although the extent of any actual impairment will still be a relevant consideration."

Appeal dismissed.

See also *R v Myers* [2018] EWCA Crim 1974; *R v Adebisi* [2020] EWCA Crim 1446; *R v Redding* [2021] EWCA Crim 1502; and *R v Keilan Roberts* [2023] EWCA Crim 1023, following *Mohamed*; and *R v Roberts (Karl Junior)* [2018] EWCA Crim 2965.

10. EVIDENCE OF CARELESS DRIVING

R v Millington

[1996] RTR 80, 26 April 1995, CA

Where the issue was whether the accused had driven without due care and attention, evidence of the consumption of alcohol was admissible; it was for the jury to decide whether or not that affected his ability to drive carefully.

A driver had been charged with causing death by driving without due care and attention having consumed alcohol such that he was over the limit, contrary to s 3A(1), Road Traffic Act. He had drunk six vodkas and 2 pints of beer. He collided with a pedestrian, who died. The driver admitted driving with excess alcohol but denied driving without due care and attention, arguing that he had not been in any way adversely affected by the drink. He was convicted and appealed against conviction and sentence.

HELD: "In cases of careless driving the court is entitled … to consider the circumstances: those include evidence that a driver is adversely affected by drink or that the amount of drink taken was such as would adversely affect a driver.

"… the appellant was within some 18 per cent of having a breath test reading twice the legal limit for driving. He had been in a public house for some two hours, consuming … six vodkas and two pints of beer. What evidence did the jury need in order to make an assessment of the likely effect upon the driver of so much alcohol? No doubt expert evidence could have been given. But is this court to hold that a jury is not capable of assessing for itself, as a matter of common sense and general experience, the likely effect upon a driver of consuming alcohol to that extent?

"… Expert evidence was not required. The jury was perfectly capable of assessing the evidence of drink and its likely effect upon a driver. …

"Whilst it is true that no causal connection need be shown between the act of driving that amounts to carelessness and the consumption of so much alcohol as to exceed the limit … it is not a corollary that evidence of a level of alcohol is irrelevant to the issue as to whether the defendant's driving fell short of the standard of the reasonably prudent driver. The … offence requires the prosecution to prove both aspects of the offence. Inevitably the judge will have to direct the jury on their relationship and at least to warn them that it does not necessarily follow that because a driver is over the limit they should conclude that he was therefore driving carelessly. … Whether the amount taken in an individual case has had that effect and where the particular driving in question was influenced by the excess of alcohol in the body, is a question of degree and of fact for the jury to decide. It follows that the judge was right to admit evidence of the level of alcohol in this case and to direct the jury about its significance. … his directions cannot be faulted."

Appeal dismissed. The appellant's appeal against sentence was also dismissed.

11. WITNESS SUMMONSES AND DISCLOSURE

See s 97, Magistrates' Courts Act 1980, on witness summonses, and Sharpe v DPP, page 398, where magistrates were wrong to refuse to issue witness summonses.

R v Coventry Magistrates' Court ex p Perks

[1985] RTR 74, 19 July 1984, QBD (DC)

Witness summonses to produce the log of a breath analysis device, the defendant wishing to examine it before entering a plea, were quashed.

A motorist had been charged with driving with excess alcohol. The Intoximeter printout showed his date of birth incorrectly. The motorist successfully applied to magistrates for witness summonses, under s 97(1), Magistrates' Courts Act 1980, against police officers, requiring production of the Intoximeter log covering a period of one month; his intention was to examine the log before entering a plea. Section 97(1) authorises the issue of such a summons where a justice is satisfied that a person "is likely to be able to give material evidence, or produce any document or thing likely to be material evidence, … and that that person will not voluntarily attend as a witness or will not voluntarily produce the document or thing …". The police sought an order of *certiorari* to quash the witness summonses.

HELD: "It is the foundation of that statutory power [in s 97(1)] that the evidence or document shall be material … I cannot … see how a record of a Lion Intoximeter 3000 over a period of a month can be material to the hearing of a charge related to a particular incident on a particular date … It would have no probative value so far as the charge is concerned. Its only potential use at the trial, if after disclosure it was thought to have any value, would be for the purpose of cross-examining … It is plain on authority that the power under section 97 is not to be exercised where the document sought is simply for the purposes of cross-examination … there is no right to general discovery in the magistrates' court … these summonses were … a fishing expedition … ."

Application granted.

R v Skegness Magistrates' Court ex p Cardy; R v Manchester Crown Court ex p Williams

[1985] RTR 49, [1985] Crim LR 237, 21 December 1984, QBD (DC)

Technical documents relating to breath analysis devices in general are unlikely to be material evidence; "fishing expeditions" by way of witness summonses are not to be permitted.

In both cases a motorist had been charged under s 6(1), Road Traffic Act 1972 as substituted by s 25(3) and Sch 8, Transport Act 1981, with driving with excess alcohol. In both cases it was sought to challenge the reliability of the breath analysis device.

In *Ex p Cardy*, the defendant's solicitors had been granted a witness summons requiring the Chief Superintendent of Police to produce certain documents relating to the device used to test the defendant's breath. The case had not yet been heard.

In *Ex p Williams*, the motorist had been convicted and was appealing. His solicitors were granted a witness summons requiring a director of the company which manufactures the Lion Intoximeter to produce a quantity of technical specifications concerning Lion Intoximeters in general, and certain other documents relating to the device used in the case in issue.

Both witnesses applied for orders of *certiorari* to quash the summonses.

GROUND(S) FOR THE APPLICATION: In *Ex p Cardy*: the documents sought would not be admissible or relevant at the trial; the applicant was not likely to be able to give material evidence or produce any document or thing likely to be material evidence; disclosure of one of the documents sought would involve disclosure of information in relation to other cases and was privileged, and/or disclosure would be against the public interest.

In *Ex p Williams*: The appropriate forum was the Divisional Court because, *inter alia*, the Divisional Court had ruled on matters involving similar principles; other such witness summonses had been issued and it was in the public interest that the Divisional Court make a ruling; the legislation under which evidential breath-testing machines were used would be unworkable if such witnesses summonses were issued.

HELD: "The crucial question … is … whether the documents … are likely to be material evidence … [In *Ex p Williams*:] … the first five sets of documents listed in the witness summons, although expressed to be related to Lion Intoximeter No 4680, by which the samples [in question] were tested, are in reality technical documents relating to Lion Intoximeters generally. In our judgment, it is impossible to say that any of these documents is likely to be 'material evidence' … this witness summons is misconceived. It simply does not relate to documents likely to be material evidence at the hearing of the appeal.

"[In *Ex p Cardy*:] There is … no reason to suppose that any of these documents is likely to be material evidence at [the] trial. This is … a pure fishing expedition. It is once again an attempt to misuse the witness summons procedure in order to obtain discovery of documents, in the hope that … they may reveal some possible points which could be used at the trial … ."

Applications granted.

R v Teesside JJ ex p Payne

Unreported, CO/1132/84, 21 December 1984, QBD (DC)

The witness summons procedure is not to be used as a means of obtaining discovery of documents.

A motorist had been charged with driving with excess alcohol, contrary to s 6(1)(a), Road Traffic Act 1972 as substituted by s 25 and Sch 8, Transport Act 1981. Justices had granted a witness summons requiring the attendance of a police officer and the production of the logbook of the breath analysis device used in the case. The motorist's solicitors wished to know if the device had been operating satisfactorily and sought the log for the 7 days before and the 7 days after the date in question. The justices granted the witness summons having found that machines can and do break down; that s 8(3), Road Traffic Act 1972 permitted a constable to exercise his discretion and require a blood or urine specimen if a reliable device is not available; and that the Home Secretary had agreed to monitor the performance of breath analysis devices by extending the option of having specimens of blood or urine tested. The police sought an order of *certiorari* to quash the witness summons.

HELD: "… For the witness summons … to fall within [s 97(1), Magistrates' Courts Act 1980], it must require [the officer] to produce a document 'likely to be material evidence' at the trial … the log for the Camic Breath Analyser in question was not such a document.

"In the first place, the log could not itself be evidence of a test carried out on the analyser. It is simply a document in which certain persons at certain times recorded certain observations concerning tests carried out by the analyser …

"… In truth, the purpose of the witness summons was not to obtain the production of evidence, but to obtain discovery of a document which the defendant's solicitor thought might contain information which could be useful to the defence … There is … no formal process of discovery in the magistrates' courts … It is certainly a misuse of the witness summons procedure … to use it … as a means of obtaining discovery of documents.

"… the defence must rely upon the prosecution to fulfil its duty to disclose to the defence material evidence of which it is aware and which might be of assistance to the defence. There is no reason to suppose that, in the present case, the prosecution has failed to perform their duty; indeed, there was not even the slightest evidence in the present case that there had been any malfunctioning of the machine in question. This was, to use a time-honoured phrase, a pure fishing expedition."

Certiorari granted quashing the witness summons.

R v Kingston-upon-Hull JJ ex p Walton

Unreported, CO/1280/84, 17 May 1985, QBD (DC)

There is no general right of discovery in a magistrates' court; witness summonses are not available for the production of documents to be used for the purposes of cross-examination.

A motorist supplied two samples of breath for analysis by a Lion Intoximeter 3000; the readings were 88 μg and 70 μg alcohol in 100 ml breath and showed a high acetone level. The motorist's solicitors, with a view to challenging the reliability of the machine, were granted a witness summons against the police, under s 97, Magistrates' Courts Act 1980, requiring the production of "Record of routine daily checks carried out during the month of February 1984 in respect of Intoximeter 3000 machine number 1390 installed at [the police station in question]". The witness summons was granted on the basis that the discrepancy between the two Intoximeter readings was material and that the application did not constitute a "fishing expedition". The police applied for an order to set aside and quash the issue of the summons by way of *certiorari* or otherwise.

HELD: "[Referring to *R v Coventry Magistrates' Court ex p Perks, R v Skegness Magistrates' Court ex p Cardy*, page 421; *Cardy; R v Manchester Crown Court ex p Williams*, page 421; and *R v Teesside Justices ex p Payne*, page 423, and dismissing argument that the large variation between the two readings and the large acetone result distinguish this case from the earlier cases] All those cases demonstrate and underline that there is no general right of discovery in a magistrates' court. Secondly, they underline the point that a person making an application under section 97 is not entitled to the production of documents which he may wish to use for the purpose of cross-examination ... I am unable to find any valid distinction to take the case outside the principles which were applied in those cases ... the documents mentioned in this witness summons, the 'record of routine daily checks' are not likely to be material evidence at the trial."

Order of *certiorari* granted.

R v Pirehill North JJ ex p Stoddard

Unreported, CO/124/85, 24 July 1985, QBD (DC)

"Fishing expeditions" by way of witness summons are not permitted.

A motorist had been charged, *inter alia*, with driving with excess alcohol, contrary to s 6(1), Road Traffic Act 1972 as substituted by s 25 and Sch 8, Transport Act 1981. Analysis of two breath specimens had produced readings of 103 μg and 95 μg alcohol in 100 ml breath; the Lion Intoximeter 3000 used self-calibrated normally. The justices granted a witness summons against the police, under s 97, Magistrates' Court Act 1980, for the production of the repair log, service repair record and memory roll relating to the device in question. The police appealed by way of judicial review, seeking an order of *certiorari* to quash the witness summons.

HELD: "[Following *R v Skegness Magistrates' Court ex p Cardy*; *R v Manchester Crown Court ex p Williams*, page 421] The position here is that [the motorist] has no reasonable grounds for suspecting that this device was working otherwise than properly at the material time. He has truly embarked upon what in the civil process is called a 'fishing expedition', hoping in other words that something might turn up, so as to put in the hands of those who represent him at the hearing which is to come some material which might challenge the reliability of this machine. That, in my judgment, is impermissible … although there may be an indulgence, for it can be no more, shown by the police in certain parts of the country to reveal the records of the Intoximeter 3000 device, there is no right in a defendant to demand those records."

Order of *certiorari* granted; witness summons quashed.

R v Tower Bridge Magistrates' Court ex p DPP

(1988) 86 Cr App R 257, [1989] RTR 118, 21 April 1988, QBD (DC)

The facts of this case again amounted to a "fishing expedition" and a witness summons was quashed.

A motorist had been charged with driving with excess alcohol, contrary to s 6(1), Road Traffic Act 1972 as substituted by s 25 and Sch 8, Transport Act 1981. The device had correctly self-calibrated, but the motorist believed it had not been working properly before or during the breath analysis; a number of police officers had been "tinkering" or "fiddling" with it and saying it was not functioning properly.

On the hearing date, before the prosecution opened its case, defence counsel applied for, and was granted, under s 97, Magistrates' Courts Act 1980, a witness summons requiring the attendance at court of the relevant police officer and the production of the service record and machine log of the device in question.

The prosecutor sought an order of *certiorari* to quash the witness summons on the grounds that no valid reason to indicate that the application was other than a "fishing expedition" had been given; in granting the witness summons, the magistrate was in breach of clear authority and/or acted in excess of jurisdiction; and that the documents required were not admissible in, and/or had no relevance to, the proceedings in question.

HELD: "… it was clearly upon the defence at the conclusion of the prosecution case, and in the normal course of events, to call evidence which of itself tended to suggest that … the evidence provided by the printout was unreliable because the machine was not working correctly … It may be that, having heard the evidence, the prosecution would come to the conclusion that it was necessary to call evidence as to the reliability of the machine … That again would be a matter to be decided at the appropriate time towards the conclusion of the hearing.

"It was not a matter … to be decided by the magistrate at the outset on an application for a witness summons, because such an application, as is clear from the authorities, … made at that stage can only be regarded in reality as a fishing expedition which it is hoped may lead to some information being disclosed which would be of assistance to the defence."

Application granted.

Fearnley v DPP

[2005] EWHC 1393 (Admin), (2005) 169 JP 450, 10 June 2005, QBD (DC)

In the circumstances of this case, the magistrates were wrong not to issue a witness summons, but correct in other decisions on the admissibility of evidence.

A motorist had been charged with driving with excess alcohol, contrary to s 5(1)(a), Road Traffic Act 1988. He had been arrested and, at Ealing police station, gave breath specimens which were analysed by an Intoximeter EC/IR and revealed excess alcohol.

The prosecution served on the defence a statement by an expert (Mr Rudrum) employed by the Forensic Science Service, describing the system of approval for evidential breath testing instruments, dealing with manufacturers' proposals for changes and the circumstances in which a new approval order is required; it confirmed that certain changes which had been made to machines of the type used in the case did not require a new approval order.

The defence statement averred that the appellant had not drunk enough to put him over the limit; disputed the breath analysis on the grounds that the device used ("the Ealing device") could not detect mouth alcohol; stated that tests showed that Intoximeter EC/IRs gave higher readings than other types; and that the Ealing device was not an approved device because alterations had been made to it since type approval.

At the trial, the defence applied for a witness summons to be served on Mr Rudrum (who could not, as a civil servant, attend unless a witness summons was issued). The prosecution did not oppose the application, but the justices refused it on the ground that it was made so late.

The defence also sought to have admitted letters from Mr Rudrum, and from a representative of the company which manufactures the EC/IR, concerning an EC/IR device used at Banbury police station. The magistrates refused on the basis that the letters were not relevant to the machine in question.

The prosecution then adduced expert evidence to the effect, *inter alia*, that the EC/IR prints a warning if it detects mouth alcohol; and that the machines are regularly tested for compliance with type approval requirements.

The defendant adduced expert evidence that, *inter alia*, the EC/IR could not consistently detect mouth alcohol; given the time since the defendant's last drink, alcohol might have been present in his stomach when he was tested; if the defendant had suffered reflux (regurgitation of the stomach contents into the mouth), and if the EC/IR had failed to detect mouth alcohol, the reading could have been higher than it should have been. In reply, the prosecution successfully applied to adduce the service engineer's report on the Ealing device, showing that it had been tested some 4 months earlier and found to be fully operational.

The magistrates found that the Ealing device was of an approved type; there was no evidence of mouth alcohol when the specimens were taken; there was no evidence that the defendant had suffered reflux; the device showed no malfunction and was reliable. They convicted the defendant; he appealed.

QUESTION(S) FOR THE COURT (INTER ALIA): Whether the magistrates were wrong: (1) to refuse to issue a witness summons in respect of Mr Rudrum; (2) to refuse to admit the two letters concerning the device used at Banbury; (3) to allow the respondent to adduce rebuttal evidence during the appellant's case; (4) and (5) to admit the service engineer's report under ss 24 and 27, Criminal Justice Act 1988.

HELD: "[On (1)] 24. … the decision … to refuse the application … was plainly wrong. The application was not opposed by the prosecution. The case was going to last two days in any event and [defence counsel's] instructions were that Mr Rudrum was willing to give evidence and could attend the following day. …

"26. The fact that the Justices were wrong not to issue a witness summons does not necessarily mean that the appellant's conviction should be set aside. …

"[On (2)] 29. … it is clear from Cresswell J's observations [in *DPP v Brown; DPP v Teixeira*, page 297] that the Justices were entitled not to look at the two letters *de bene esse* and to refuse to admit them on the ground that they did not deal with the Ealing device but with the Intoximeter EC/IR in use at the Banbury police station in November 2003. …

"[On (3), (4) and (5)] 34. … it was for the appellant to adduce some evidence that the software was otherwise than the specified software before the prosecution came under a burden to prove the software. At no stage did the appellant raise or adduce such evidence …

"36. Even if the report was not strictly rebuttal evidence, the Justices had a discretion to allow the prosecution to adduce evidence after the close of its case so long as they had proper regard to interests of justice overall and the risk of prejudice to the appellant. In my judgment, the Justices' exercise of discretion in this case cannot be successfully challenged. Their conclusion that to admit the evidence would not prejudice the appellant was plainly right. …"

Appeal dismissed.

DPP v Wood; DPP v McGillicuddy

[2006] EWHC 32 (Admin), (2006) 170 JP 177, 19 January 2006, QBD (Admin)

Disclosure of material concerning reliability or type approval should not have been ordered where the defence statement did not raise either of those issues. The manufacturer of the device is a third party, not a prosecutor. Third party material is not "prosecution material". The correct procedure in these cases was to have applied for witness summonses.

Motorists had been charged with driving with excess alcohol, contrary to s 5(1)(a), Road Traffic Act 1988. In both cases the breath analysis device used was an Intoximeter EC/IR.

In *Wood*, there were issues concerning the type approval and reliability of the device, leading to a contested application for disclosure under s 8, Criminal Procedure and Investigations Act 1996; the district judge ordered the disclosure of certain material in the possession of the manufacturer, Intoximeters UK; the manufacturer disclosed some, but declined to disclose the remainder on the grounds of commercial confidentiality. The district judge found that the manufacturer was part of the "investigating authority"; non-compliance with the order meant that the case could not be fairly tried; the prosecution would be based entirely on a reading from a machine which "had a significant potential for inaccuracy" which the defendant was entitled to investigate; he stayed the proceedings as an abuse of process.

In *McGillicuddy*, the defendant was charged on 8 June 2003; on 23 June 2003 the Crown Prosecution Service wrote to him saying that there was no prosecution material requiring disclosure to him; on 17 September 2003, the Crown Prosecution Service sent a schedule of unused material, and on 26 September the defence statement was provided. The defendant then sought disclosure, under s 8, Criminal Procedure and Investigations Act 1996, of certain documents concerning the breath analysis device used in his case. An order was made and the Crown Prosecution Service requested the documents from Intoximeters UK, whose response was the same as in *Wood*. Again, the proceedings were stayed.

The prosecutor appealed in both cases.

QUESTIONS FOR THE COURT: *McGillicuddy*: (b) whether the court exceeded its jurisdiction by ordering disclosure; (c) whether the court was *Wednesbury* unreasonable to hold that Intoximeters UK Ltd was "the prosecutor" for the purposes of ss 7 and 8, Criminal Procedure and Investigations Act 1996 and therefore required to disclose material in their possession; (d) if the court was correct in holding that Intoximeters UK was "the prosecutor", whether it erred in finding that the company was not entitled to make decisions about disclosure of material in its possession; (e) whether the court was entitled to rule that the material which it ordered to be disclosed could reasonably be expected to assist the respondent's case as set out in the defence case statement; (f) whether the court was in any event entitled to rule that the non-disclosure of the material resulted in an abuse of process such that the respondent was denied a fair trial.

Wood: (a) Whether Intoximeters UK was a third party; (b) whether the s 8 order on disclosure of material in the possession of Intoximeters UK was wrong in law; (c) whether the court's refusal of the prosecution's application to vary the disclosure order was wrong in law; (d) whether the decision to stay proceedings was wrong in law.

HELD: "27. … disclosure of the material ordered by the DJ, if otherwise justified, should have been refused on the grounds that the defence statement, which was silent as to whether the defendant was the driver or had consumed alcohol or enough to be in excess of the prescribed limits, did not raise an issue to which reliability or type approval was relevant. Those matters had no free-standing relevance. The request for disclosure … raised no issue to which the items of which disclosure was sought could be relevant. …

"36. … the material of which disclosure is sought must have some potential for bearing on the issue in respect of which is raised. The nature and degree of an alleged unreliability has to be such that it might be able to throw doubt on the excess in the reading to such an extent that the level of alcohol in the breath might have been below the level at which a prosecution would have been instituted. … In considering disclosure applications based on a claim about a particular machine's unreliability, and its possible basis for a defence, the DJ needs explicitly to consider the effect of the safeguards provided by the taking of two specimens, the intervening clearances of the device and the evidential use of the lower specimen of the two, together with the opportunity to give specimens of blood or urine and the fact that there is leeway above the breath limit before prosecution takes place. They are relevant to whether the alleged unreliability could possibly advance the stated defence. Similarly the nature and extent of the possible changes to type had to be so fundamental that it could no longer be said that this was a type approved machine; that was the issue to which the disclosure material had to be addressed. …

"[On whether the material sought was 'prosecution material' within s 8(3) (material to be disclosed must be in the possession of the prosecutor) and (4) of the Act] 43. … The only basis upon which it could be said that the material in question satisfied the requirement that it be in the possession of the prosecutor, was if the prosecutor was or at least included Intoximeters UK. That is an impossible contention. The prosecutor was the CPS. Intoximeters UK is not part of the CPS. …

"52. Intoximeters UK … was a third party in relation to the material which it alone retained in its possession. …

"56. The Attorney-General's Guidelines … deal with the obligations on the prosecutor and investigator in relation to third party material in a way which again makes it clear that third party material is not 'prosecution material' … If the third party refuses to disclose it, and its production is still thought reasonable and the statutory requirements of the relevant Act are met, here s 97 Magistrates' Courts Act 1980, the prosecutor should seek a witness summons for its production. …

"59. This means that much of the disclosure should not have been ordered in the first place and the orders should have been varied [to omit commercially sensitive material] as sought by the CPS. …

"62. Neither DJ considered whether the prosecutor had failed to … seek a summons … This was the mechanism for obtaining material in the hands of a third party. Had such an application been made, it would have had the effect of permitting the interests of the third party in the confidentiality of the material to be raised as a reason for the refusal of the summons or as a 'just excuse' and the true materiality of the documents in question to be more fully explained. …

"63. The DJs were wrong … to find an abuse of process and to stay proceedings because a fair trial was impossible. They should each have considered the need for the prosecutor to use and the value in its using s 97, Magistrates' Courts Act 1980."

The answers to the questions were, in *McGillicuddy*: (b) did not arise in the way assumed by the question. The defence case statement did not raise issues justifying the disclosure sought; (c) "yes" and it involved misinterpretation of CPIA 1996; (d) does not arise; (e) "no"; (f) "no". In *Wood*, the answers to all questions were "yes". Appeals allowed.

R (Cunliffe) v West London Magistrates' Court; R (Cunliffe) v Ealing Magistrates' Court; R (Cunliffe) v Hastings Magistrates' Court

[2006] EWHC 2081 (Admin), 7 July 2006, QBD (DC)

Witness summonses under s 97, Magistrates' Courts Act 1980 should be issued only when both limbs of s 97 (the materiality and interests of justice tests) are satisfied.

Motorists had been charged with driving with excess alcohol, contrary to s 5(1)(a), Road Traffic Act 1988. Their defences included arguments that the breath analysis devices used had lost their type approval because of modifications, and that the amount of alcohol consumed was insufficient to produce readings over the legal limit. They sought witness summonses against the manufacturer of the breath analysis devices used, pursuant to s 97(1), Magistrates' Courts Act 1980 as amended by s 169(2), Serious Organised Crime and Police Act 2005. The prosecution did not object in either case, and witness summonses were issued. They required the production of "unedited F11 settings"; engineers' reports and calibration/service sheets; and engineers' standard operating procedures.

The claimant appealed by way of judicial review, seeking the quashing of the witness summonses.

HELD: "9. [The claimant submits] that the test to be applied [under s 97(1)] … is whether (1) the person is likely to be able to give 'material evidence' or the document is likely to be 'material evidence' and in either case, (2) it is in the interests of justice to issue the summons. I agree with that submission and would stress the importance of both limbs being satisfied before any summons is issued. …

"27. … the disclosure test under section 8 of the [Criminal Procedure and Investigations Act 1996] is broader than the specific admissibility of evidence test under section 97 of the 1980 Act … if the documents in question do not fall to be disclosed as a matter of law under section 8 of the 1996 Act they do not satisfy the admissibility provisions of section 97 of the 1980 Act.

"21. … [In *Hastings*], once the deputy district judge was informed that the material was 'necessary to the defence and needed by the experts', and after hearing that the application was, in effect, unopposed, the witness summons was then issued without any further inquiry as to why the evidence was relevant or as to its materiality.

"22. … the deputy district judge failed to give full and proper consideration to the terms of section 97(1) of the 1980 Act. Had she done so, she would have concluded that the documents sought did not satisfy the materiality test required by section 97(1)(a).

"23. … it is for the party seeking production of the documents to 'satisfy the justices … that the documents are likely to be material'; … in the *Hastings* case there is nothing in [the] defence statement which demonstrates the materiality of the documents to any purported defence … Furthermore, … the documents requested were not material evidence because they were inadmissible without interpretation by expert witnesses and were thus not admissible evidence *per se*. …"

In the *Hastings* case, the witness summons was quashed. In the *West London* case the motorist pleaded guilty and the claim was not pursued. In the *Ealing* case, the witness summons was quashed for the same reasons as in *Hastings*.

Rothon v DPP

[2006] EWHC 3330 (Admin), 27 November 2006, QBD (Admin)

In the circumstances of this case (prosecution adducing expert evidence based on certain documents relating to the breath analysis device), the defendant's application for disclosure of those documents should have been allowed.

A motorist had been charged with driving with excess alcohol, contrary to s 5(1)(a), Road Traffic Act 1988. Intending to take expert advice on the reliability of the breath analysis device used in the case, he had sought disclosure of documents, in the possession of the prosecution, concerning the device. That application had been refused.

At the trial, the motorist called an expert witness (Dr Makin) who dealt generally with the workings of breath analysis devices, but said that he would need to see certain records in order to advise on the reliability of the device in question. It was again argued for the motorist that documents relating to the device, in the possession of the prosecution, should be disclosed to the defence, pursuant to s 8, Criminal Procedure and Investigations Act 1996 and art 6, European Convention on Human Rights. The prosecutor called an expert (Dr Rudram), who said that he had seen documents relating to the machine, and that there was nothing in them to suggest the machine in question was outside its type approval or unreliable; and that it had a self-checking system.

The motorist was convicted, and appealed.

QUESTION(S) FOR THE COURT: Whether the magistrates were correct in refusing the application for disclosure, given their acceptance of the evidence of the prosecution's expert that the machine was working correctly and was approved, even though the records, the subject of the motorist's application, were in the possession of the prosecution and not a third party.

HELD: "16. … given the situation prior to the calling of Dr Rudram, there was no basis for disclosure and the justices would have been perfectly entitled to refuse the application for disclosure. But the implication of the [question for the court] is that they were not necessarily of that view until they had heard Dr Rudram, despite the indication elsewhere in the stated case that they were relying on the presumption [that the instrument was reliable]. If they were going to hear Dr Rudram, it suggests that, but for his evidence, they might not have been satisfied as to the proper working of the machine. … Logically they should have ruled on the application for disclosure one way or the other before hearing Dr Rudram. Once they had heard Dr Rudram, it seems to me that natural justice, Article 6 considerations and common sense indicate that they should have acceded to an application for disclosure of the material. …

"17. [It was submitted] that out of a sense of fairness the prosecution were going further than they needed to go. In one sense that is true. Nevertheless, what eventually happened was that on the application for disclosure the justices relied on expert evidence, without any opportunity for the defence to … cross-examine that expert. That seems to me on any view to be contrary to principle. If the prosecution had relied on the statutory assumption and had argued that there was no basis either for displacing it or for disclosing the records, they would in my view have been on solid ground. But once Dr Rudram was called, in that unusual situation the magistrates should have acceded to the application for the records to be disclosed. Indeed, in that situation, if the prosecution were going to call Dr Rudram, it is extremely difficult to see why those records were not disclosed. They had them and they could have disclosed them."

The answer to the question was "no". Appeal allowed.

12. LATE EVIDENCE

Writtle v DPP

[2009] EWHC 236 (Admin), [2009] RTR 28, 20 January 2009, QBD (DC)

Justices were right to refuse to admit expert evidence served after the close of the prosecution case, that evidence not being relevant to the issues in the case and raising wholly new issues.

A motorist had been charged with failing without reasonable excuse to provide two specimens of breath for analysis, contrary to s 7(6), Road Traffic Act 1988. At the police station, she failed to provide specimens of breath, and a forensic medical examiner found no medical reason why not. At the case management conference, the court had before it a letter from the defendant's solicitors indicating that no novel or complex issues arose; the defence would be factual and the intention was to put the prosecution to proof of its case.

At the trial, the court heard the prosecution witnesses, and watched a CCTV recording of the procedure. The prosecution closed its case and the hearing was adjourned for lack of time to hear the defence.

Some 6 weeks later, the defence served an additional report from a Dr Trafford; he had seen the CCTV recording and was critical of the handling of the investigation, and suggested the machine user log should be examined and the service history requested.

At the resumed hearing, the justices decided not to admit Dr Trafford's report on the basis that it was not relevant to the issues in the case and sought to introduce wholly new issues. The defendant appealed.

QUESTION(S) FOR THE COURT: Whether the justices were wrong in law to refuse to admit Dr Trafford's evidence.

HELD: "11. … Rule 24(1) of the Criminal Procedure Rules sets out the requirement to disclose expert evidence as soon as is practicable and rule 24(3) states that the party that seeks to adduce expert evidence and fails to comply with rule 24(1) may not adduce the evidence without the leave of the court. …

"14. … either the defence knew the nature of the defence which was later set out in Dr Trafford's opinion and failed to raise it appropriately; or it did not, and contrived the defence after the prosecution case had closed. … in either case the approach is to be deplored. … the Justices were right in saying that the evidence was inadmissible since it did not relate to an issue which had been raised at the appropriate stage. The appropriate stage would have been a reasonable time before the cross-examination of [the police sergeant who conducted the procedure] so that he and the prosecution had an opportunity to consider it. Equally, it was … open to the Justices to refuse the application as a matter of discretion. The evidence on which Dr Trafford commented, the CCTV recording, had been disclosed at a very early stage. If the late application to adduce further expert evidence had been allowed, delay would undoubtedly have occurred. The prosecution would have needed to consider whether to call its own expert evidence in answer and whether to recall [the sergeant]. Doctor Trafford's opinion also raised possible doubts about the reliability of the equipment used, all of this after the prosecution had closed its case some months before. …

"15. … the present regime of case management should in general ensure that the issues in the case are identified well before a hearing. There will, of course, be cases where something occurs in the course of a trial which may properly give rise to a new issue, but this was not such a case. The days when the defence can assume that they will be able successfully to ambush the prosecution are over."

The answer to the question was "no". Appeal dismissed.

Chapter 8

Definitions

1. ATTEMPTING TO DRIVE

R v Farrance

(1978) 67 Cr App R 136, 19 December 1977, CA

A person sitting in the driving seat, attempting to start the car or to put it into gear, or accelerating the engine so as to try to make the car go forward, is attempting to drive it, even though some intervening factor (here a burnt out clutch) prevents fulfilment of the attempt.

A person had been charged with attempting to drive with excess alcohol, contrary to s 6(1), Road Traffic Act 1972. The clutch of the car he was driving had, unknown to him, burnt out and the car stopped on a bend. The driver thought this was a dangerous place to leave the vehicle, and he allowed it to run downhill, backwards, and across the road until the wheels rested on the kerb, the car then occupying almost half the road. He suffered from angina and could not push the car. He accelerated the engine, hoping to be able to drive a short distance but the car would not move. Police officers arrived and found the driver still in the driving seat with the engine running. They suspected he had been drinking. A blood specimen showed excess alcohol. He was convicted and appealed.

QUESTION(S) FOR THE COURT: Whether the appellant could be found guilty of attempting to drive a car which the prosecution conceded was incapable of being propelled by its engine and which, at the time of his arrest, was in a position from which he could not move it unaided.

HELD: "… [This] case can be looked at in one of two ways; the first is that the appellant was truly attempting to drive this car and that his attempt would have been successful but for the intervention of a burnt out clutch. It is quite different from the case of a man who attempts to steal from a pocket which is in fact empty or from those who attempt to handle goods which are no longer stolen goods. Those cases are fundamentally impossible. This is a clear case where all the steps constituting an attempt are taken but frustrated by the intervention of a burnt out clutch. …

"In this case, shortly afterwards, the police officer, having given the car a push, was able to drive it down the hill although the motive power was no longer driving the car. It is true that that particular method of driving the car was not possible for the appellant because of his heart condition but there was no impossibility about driving the car in principle. He was prevented from driving it in the way which he wanted to drive it because the clutch was burnt out, that alone prevented him from doing so.

"... if somebody is sitting at the driving seat of a car either attempting to start it or attempting to put it in gear or accelerating the engine so as to try to make the car go forward, he is attempting to drive it and the fact that there is some intervening factor which in the end will prevent him from fulfilling his attempt does not prevent it from being an attempt to drive. It is quite different from the case where the commission of the full offence is impossible from the very beginning. In a case such as this there is simply an impediment similar to the smallness of the tool which the burglar has, or the inadequacy of the quantity of poison which the poisoner has, which prevents the driving from taking place."

Appeal dismissed.

Kelly v Hogan

[1982] RTR 352, 11 March 1982, QBD

Sitting in the driving seat, inserting keys into the ignition, none of which fitted, amounted to attempting to drive.

A person had been convicted of attempting to drive when unfit through drink, contrary to s 5(1), Road Traffic Act 1972. Police officers came upon him sitting in the driver's seat of a vehicle, holding some keys. Unaware of the presence of the officers, he inserted a key on two separate occasions but was unable to turn it and start the engine. It was not known whether any of the keys fitted the vehicle. One of the officers noticed that the man's speech was slurred and his eyes glazed, and that he was drunk. He appealed.

QUESTION(S) FOR THE COURT: Whether, on the facts found by the justices, they could deduce that the defendant was attempting to drive.

HELD: "[It is submitted] that this is one of those cases where there could not be a conviction for an attempt because the commission of the full offence was impossible. [Referring to the judgment in *R v Smith (Roger)* [1975] AC 476, quoting *R v Donnelly* [1970] NZLR 980, setting out] various categories of cases which fell to be considered. The fourth and fifth categories were:

'Fourth, he may ... fail to complete the commission of the crime through ineptitude, inefficiency or insufficient means. The jemmy which he has brought with him may not be strong enough to force the window open. Fifth, he may find that what he is proposing to do is after all impossible – not because of insufficiency of means, but because it is for some reason physically not possible, whatever means be adopted'.

"That case is authority for the proposition that where facts fall within the fourth category, the offence can be committed. For my part, I am quite unable to see what is the difference, in principle, between a jemmy carried by a burglar, who is found not to be strong enough to open a window and an ignition key, carried by a drunken gentleman, who has it in mind to drive but who finds that whilst the key is strong enough, it is the wrong shape.

"[Referring to *R v Farrance*, above] For my part, I think that this case is stronger than … *Farrance* as it falls more clearly within the fourth category."

Appeal dismissed.

Mason v DPP

[2009] EWHC 2198 (Admin), [2010] RTR 11, 15 July 2009, QBD (Admin)

The act of opening the car door was merely preparatory to driving and did not amount to attempting to drive.

A person had been convicted of attempting to drive with excess alcohol in blood, contrary to s 5(1)(a), Road Traffic Act 1988. Knowing he could be over the limit, he opened the car door to get in and drive home, but was approached by a man with a knife who demanded the keys from him and drove off in the vehicle. The motorist appealed against conviction.

QUESTION(S) FOR THE COURT: Where a person with excess alcohol expresses an intention to drive and opens the door of the vehicle, whether opening the door is more than merely preparatory to the act of driving to justify a conviction of attempting to drive.

HELD: "12. … s 3 of the [Criminal Attempts Act 1981 – a person is guilty of an attempt … if, with intent to commit the relevant full offence, he does an act which is more than merely preparatory to the commission of that offence] applies to the offence of attempting to drive a motor vehicle under section 5(1)(a) of the 1988 Act. The [question] was therefore … whether the facts as found were more than merely preparatory to the commission of the full offence of driving with excess alcohol.

"20. The line is fine, … the appellant admitted his intention to drive the car, but *mens rea* absent sufficient *actus reus* is not enough to constitute guilt …

"21. … the acts of the appellant … were not capable of being characterised as more than merely preparatory. The appellant could not properly be convicted of an offence under section 5(1)(a)."

Appeal allowed.

Moore v DPP

[2010] EWHC 1822 (Admin), [2010] RTR 36, 2 March 2010, QBD (Admin)

A defendant who was over the limit and drove about 90 metres on a private car park, and would have driven onto the public road if he had not been stopped by a police officer, was guilty of attempting to drive with excess alcohol.

A motorist had been charged with attempting to drive with excess alcohol, contrary to s 5(1), Road Traffic Act 1988. He had been collecting his car from the recreational facility in the Atomic Weapons Establishment at Aldermaston, an area closed to the public. He asked a police officer manning the gate for permission to do so. The officer drove the defendant to the place where his car was, but smelt alcohol on the defendant's breath as he got out. The officer stopped the defendant as he was driving towards the open gate, but before he reached the public road. The defendant said he needed to drive someone home. He was arrested and breath analysis revealed excess alcohol. He was convicted and appealed.

QUESTION(S) FOR THE COURT: Whether the offence of attempting to drive a motor vehicle on a road after consuming alcohol in excess of the prescribed limit could be committed when the vehicle was not on a road.

HELD: "8. … there is no reason in law or logic why [the motorist] could not have been attempting to drive on a road simply by virtue of his having been driving …

"13. … I … am not persuaded that the critical distinction between driving and attempting to drive is the achievement of motion, and I therefore reject the argument … that, because the appellant was in fact driving … he could not have been attempting to drive. …

"14. … the appellant's intention [to drive his friend home] was plainly relevant …

"22. The appellant … drove a distance of approximately 90m from the car park to the open gate on to the A340. Had the police officer at the gate not intervened, the appellant would have driven onto the public road … the fact that there was an intervening factor which in the end prevented the appellant from fulfilling his attempt does not prevent it from being an attempt to drive on a public road.

"23. Under the Criminal Attempts Act 1981, acts that are 'merely preparatory' are excluded from the ambit of an attempt to commit an offence. But all acts short of those necessary for the commission of the intended substantive offence are in some sense preparatory. The introduction of the qualifying adverb 'merely' in the Criminal Attempts Act must have been intended by Parliament to distinguish acts which, although preparatory, are sufficiently close to the final act or acts to be properly regarded as part of the execution of the defendant's criminal course of conduct, from those which are not. All will turn on the facts of the case. On the uncontested facts of this case the deputy district judge was … entitled to conclude that the appellant's actions went beyond acts merely preparatory to the commission of the offence."

The answer to the question was "yes". Appeal dismissed.

2. BREATH

See also McNeil v DPP, page 60 – the fact that a breath specimen might have been affected by eructation did not give reasonable cause to believe that the device had not produced a reliable indication; DPP v Darwen, page 197 and Rweikiza v DPP, page 198, both on the sufficiency of a breath specimen; and Ng v DPP, page 571 – elevated mouth alcohol caused by eructation is capable of amounting to a special reason for not disqualifying.

Zafar v DPP

[2004] EWHC 2468 (Admin), [2005] RTR 220, 1 November 2004, QBD (DC)

The word "breath" has its ordinary meaning; the statutory provision refers to "breath" not "deep lung air".

A motorist had been charged with driving with excess alcohol, contrary to s 5(1)(a), Road Traffic Act 1988. He had been arrested and breath analysis showed excess alcohol.

He was convicted by magistrates and appealed to the Crown Court, where he said he suffered heartburn causing occasional reflux of the stomach contents to the mouth and had felt discomfort in the stomach during the evening in question. He adduced expert evidence to the effect that the breath analysis device is designed to detect alcohol in deep lung air, rather than mouth alcohol; if it detects mouth alcohol it should print out "mouth alcohol – unsatisfactory specimen". The expert said that machines of the type in question were generally inadequate for the purpose; he had tested many, including the one used in the case in question, which he found "very poor". The appellant contended that the prosecution had to show that the breath analysis reading related solely to deep lung alcohol, not to mouth alcohol.

The Crown Court accepted the prosecution's argument that although the breath analysis device was designed to make the distinction between "deep lung breath" and "mouth alcohol", such a distinction was not required by s 5, Road Traffic Act 1988 and that the word "breath" in that provision does not distinguish between the two meanings. It dismissed the appeal. The motorist appealed further.

QUESTION(S) FOR THE COURT: Whether the meaning of the word "breath" in s 5, Road Traffic Act 1988 and s 15(2), Road Traffic Offenders Act 1988 is to be confined to deep lung air, or whether it includes "all of that which is exhaled".

HELD: "10. … The basic submission … for the appellant is that the word 'breath' in section 5 … does not include all of what is exhaled, but that it is limited to 'deep lung air' and therefore it excludes 'mouth alcohol'. [Counsel for the Crown] disagrees as he contends that the word 'breath' includes mouth alcohol as it includes any exhaled air.

"11. … the *New Shorter Oxford English Dictionary*'s main definition of the word 'breath' is 'air exhaled from any thing'. This definition confirms my view of how the word 'breath' is used and understood in normal parlance … Thus, neither the dictionary definition nor the normal use of the word 'breath' limits its meaning to 'deep lung air' … unless there is any contrary intention expressed in the statutory provision, that definition of the word 'breath' should be adopted …

"22. … there is nothing in the RTA or in the RTOA, which suggests that the word 'breath' should have a special meaning or that the dictionary definition of 'breath' should not apply. … the statutory provision refers to 'breath' and not to 'deep lung air'. What [the appellant] is seeking to persuade us to do is to rewrite the statutory provision and that is not correct."

The answer to the question was "no". Appeal dismissed.

Woolfe v DPP

[2006] EWHC 1497 (Admin), [2007] RTR 16, 23 June 2006, QBD (DC)

The definition of breath is not confined to "deep lung air"; "consume" does not include the regurgitation of stomach contents; the fact that a defence was precluded does not preclude a finding of special reasons.

A motorist had been charged with driving with excess alcohol, contrary to s 5(1)(a), Road Traffic Act 1988. Breath analysis readings were 69 μg and 65 μg alcohol in 100 ml breath. The magistrates found that he suffered a medical condition of regurgitation of stomach content into the oesophagus with inadequate clearance by the oesophagus; and that he had drunk one pint of Castlemaine, two soft drinks and a Budweiser. Experts for each side agreed that such a quantity of alcohol would produce a reading of 10 μg alcohol in 100 ml breath. The magistrates accepted the defence expert's evidence that repeated reflux could account for the readings. They followed the finding in *Zafar v DPP* (above) that there is no difference between deep lung air and breath contaminated by alcoholic mouth contents (such as regurgitated alcohol from the stomach); a high reading could result from both. They convicted the defendant.

They made no finding on the meaning of the word "consume" but did not accept that regurgitation and absorption had to be implied from their having convicted the defendant.

The defendant appealed.

QUESTION(S) FOR THE COURT: (1) Whether the meaning of the word "breath" in s 5, Road Traffic Act 1988 and s 15, Road Traffic Offenders Act 1988 includes breath expelled that has been infused with alcohol contents of the stomach by way of oesophageal reflux, then giving a reading that does not reflect the blood alcohol level; (2) whether the word "consume" in s 15(3), Road Traffic Offenders Act 1988 includes the regurgitating of the contents of the stomach into the mouth or upper oesophagus and reabsorbing them; (3) (added in the course of judgment) whether the magistrates were wrong to conclude that the appellant's medical condition could not amount to a special reason not to disqualify under s 34(1), Road Traffic Offenders Act 1988 merely because the condition (if established and if relevant to the specimens provided) did not amount to a defence.

HELD: "[On (1), quoting from *Zafar v DPP*] 4. … 'there is nothing in [either Act] which suggests that the word "breath" should have a special meaning or that the dictionary definition of "breath" should not apply. It is noteworthy that the statutory provision refers to "breath" and not to "deep lung air".' … that analysis and conclusion are undoubtedly correct.

"6. … It is common ground that the second question [which would be in issue only on a secondary argument that, if the answer were yes, there may have been a further act of consumption after cessation of driving, raising the 'hip flask' defence] must be answered in the negative.

"7. … although at first sight *Zafar* may appear harsh, this has to be seen in context. … For regurgitation or reflux to prejudice a defendant, it must have occurred twice (once before each specimen) and with substantially similar results. In addition, the present prescribed procedure requires the suspect to be asked twice (once before and once after the evidential breath test procedure) whether he has brought up anything from his stomach. The scope for real injustice is extremely slight and, where it arises, there remains the further possibility of mitigating the penalty.

"[On (3)] 8. … the Justices were invited not to disqualify the Appellant because of 'special reasons' relating to his medical condition. His tendency to regurgitation/reflux was well documented, although his evidence was that he had no recollection of its occurrence at the material times. The Justices … found that there was 'not a special reason not to disqualify because this would undermine *Zafar* and the defence submission was closely linked with defence argument at trial'.

"9. … it is common ground that the approach of the Justices was legally flawed.

"10. … the error … was to exclude special reasons at least partly on the basis that, as *Zafar* precluded a defence, so it precluded a finding of special reasons. It is plain from … *Wickins* [*R v Wickins*, page 560] that this is incorrect."

The answer to question (1) was "yes"; the answer to question (2) was "no"; the answer to question (3) was "yes". Appeal allowed in part accordingly.

3. CONSUMING

See also Woolfe v DPP, above – "consume" does not include the regurgitation of stomach contents.

DPP v Johnson (David)

[1995] 1 WLR 728, [1995] 4 All ER 53, [1995] RTR 9, [1994] Crim LR 601, 7 March 1994, QBD (DC)

The court below was wrong to confine the word "consume" to the act of drinking and to exclude the introduction of alcohol by injection.

A motorist had been convicted of driving with excess alcohol, contrary to s 5(1), Road Traffic Act 1988. At the hearing, medical evidence was adduced that 5 weeks earlier the motorist had been injected with a slow-release pain-killing drug which, unknown to him, contained alcohol. The magistrate found there was a reasonable possibility that the injection had affected the Intoximeter reading, and that there was no evidence on which the magistrate could conclude that the consumption of alcohol by drinking wine, which the defendant admitted, had caused him to be over the limit. He found that the injection of the drug did not amount to "consumption" within the meaning and spirit of the Road Traffic Act 1988, and found the motorist not guilty. The prosecutor appealed.

QUESTION(S) FOR THE COURT: Whether the court was entitled to restrict the meaning of "consuming" to the act of drinking and to no other mode of introduction or injection of alcohol.

HELD: "… the word 'consume' is capable of a whole variety of meanings depending on the context … In the present context it is clear that section 5 was enacted in the context of a Parliamentary endeavour to diminish the number of those who drive whilst there is alcohol in their bodies. I would accept that it is probable that Parliament did not specifically consider the possible modes of entry of alcohol into the body …

"… it is possible, without doing violence to the chameleon-like qualities of this word, to construe it widely enough to embrace ingestion in any form. Should the magistrate have so construed it?

"… the sidenote against … section 5 reads as follows: 'Driving or being in charge of a motor vehicle with alcohol concentration above prescribed limit'. Approaching section 5 with the sidenote in mind, … the answer to the question posed by the magistrate is in the negative."

Appeal allowed.

4. CONVICTION

DPP v Haddigan

Unreported, CO-121-94, 27 May 1994, QBD (DC)

A guilty plea amounted to a conviction for the purposes of determining the minimum period of disqualification for driving with excess alcohol, even though the offender had not been sentenced.

Police stopped a motorist on 9 February 1992 and found he had been driving with excess alcohol. He was arrested and bailed to appear before magistrates the next day. He failed to appear and a warrant for his arrest was issued, resulting in his appearing before the court on 1 April 1992. On 15 April 1992 he pleaded not guilty to driving with excess alcohol; the case came for trial on 5 June 1992, when he changed his plea to guilty. The court adjourned the case for a pre-sentence report. The defendant was bailed to 29 June 1992, but failed to appear on that date. A warrant was again issued.

On 23 September 1993 the defendant was involved in a road accident and police again found that he was over the limit. He was arrested and the next day pleaded guilty to, *inter alia*, the second offence of driving with excess alcohol. On 22 October 1993 he came before the magistrates for sentencing for both excess alcohol offences. The question was whether, for the purposes of s 34, Road Traffic Offenders Act 1988 (periods of obligatory disqualification), the defendant had, in the period of 10 years before 23 September 1993, been convicted of an offence of driving with excess alcohol, i.e. was the offence to which he had pleaded guilty on 5 June 1992 but for which, by 22 October 1993, he had not been sentenced, an offence of which he had been convicted. If so, he had to be disqualified for not less than 12 months for the first offence and not less than 3 years for the second offence. But if he had not been convicted for the 1992 offence, he was liable to obligatory disqualification of only 12 months for the second offence.

The magistrates were advised that, as they had power to allow the defendant to withdraw his guilty plea at any time before sentence, he had not been convicted until he was sentenced; and that the word "conviction" included the imposition of sentence. They accordingly decided that the minimum obligatory period of disqualification for the second offence was 12 months; in fact they disqualified him for 18 months for the offence committed in 1992, and for 14 months, concurrent, for the offence committed in 1993. The prosecutor appealed.

QUESTION(S) FOR THE COURT: Whether the entering of a guilty plea without sentence to a relevant offence is a conviction for the purposes of s 34(3), Road Traffic Offenders Act 1988.

HELD: "… The words 'where a person is convicted of an offence' appear frequently throughout Part II [of the Road Traffic Offenders Act 1988], and they are conditions precedent to the requirements of the sections in which they appear … it is clear that the words 'where a person is convicted of an offence' against a provision of the Traffic Acts, must apply to a stage of the proceedings at which the maximum punishment or penalty has not yet been considered and the actual punishment or penalty has not been imposed. So in this context it is clear that the word 'convicted' has the meaning of 'found guilty of an offence', and does not include the sentencing component of the judicial determination of the case, or in a more succinct phrase, it has the narrower meaning. A conviction for the offence is clearly a condition precedent to the penalty which may be imposed, and in my judgment is similarly a condition precedent to consideration of the obligatory disqualifications contained in section 34(1).

"… therefore … the word 'convicted' means 'found guilty of the offence' … [but is] the court bound to give the word the wider meaning [as in] the case of *R v Brentwood JJ ex p Richardson* [(1992) 95 Cr App R 187, [1993] RTR 374] … where the word 'conviction' … had to be construed in the sense of including the process of sentencing. But merely because in [s 29] the word is given the wider meaning, that does not mean to say that where it appears elsewhere in Part II of the Act, it has to have the same meaning.

"… in section 34 the word 'convicted' has the narrower meaning and … when it fell to the magistrates to deal with the respondent for the offence which had been committed by him on 23 September 1993, it was obligatory for them to impose the period of three years disqualification."

Appeal allowed.

5. DRIVING

See also the cases in Chapter 12 under the heading "Proof of Driving", page 627; Jones v Pratt [1983] RTR 54, DC, where a passenger who deliberately took hold of the steering wheel for a moment to avoid an animal was not, on the facts, driving; and Planton v DPP, page 471, where a person who was in the driving seat, with the engine running and the lights on, waiting for the tide to recede from a causeway, was driving.

R v MacDonagh

[1974] QB 448, [1974] 2 WLR 529, [1974] 2 All ER 257, [1974] RTR 372, 1 February 1974, CA

"Driving" means the use of the driver's controls to direct the movement of a vehicle, but the word must also be given its ordinary meaning. Pushing a vehicle did not amount to driving it.

The defendant had been convicted of driving while disqualified, contrary to s 99, Road Traffic Act 1972. He maintained he had pushed the car, standing with his feet on the road, his shoulder against the door pillar and one hand inside the car on the steering wheel. The court found that he was driving and convicted him. He appealed.

QUESTION(S) FOR THE COURT: On the facts as stated by the defendant, whether or not he was driving.

HELD: "… The Act does not define … 'drive' and in its simplest meaning … it refers to a person using the driver's controls for the purpose of directing the movement of the vehicle. It matters not that the vehicle is not moving under its own power, or driven by the force of gravity, or even that it is being pushed by other well-wishers. The essence of driving is the use of the driver's controls in order to direct the movement, however that movement is produced.

"There are an infinite number of ways in which a person may control the movement of a motor vehicle, apart from the orthodox one of sitting in the driving seat and using the engine for propulsion. …

"He may be coasting down a hill with the gears in neutral and the engine switched off; … as in the present case, he may be standing in the road and himself pushing the car with or without using the steering wheel to direct it. Although the word 'drive' must be given a wide meaning, the courts must be alert to see that the net is not thrown so widely that it includes activities which cannot be said to be driving a motor vehicle in any ordinary use of that word in the English language. …

"… there must be a distinction between driving a car and pushing it. The dividing line will not always be easy to draw, and the distinction will often turn on the extent and degree to which the defendant was relying on the use of the driver's controls. Where, however, the defendant was walking beside a vehicle which was being pushed or moving under gravity, we do not think that the mere fact that he had his hand on the steering wheel is enough to say that he was driving in any ordinary sense of that word.

"… in the present case we do not think that any ordinary meaning of the word 'drive' could extend to a man who is not in the motor car, who has both feet on the road, and who is making no use of the controls apart from an occasional adjustment of the steering wheel.

"Cases such as these are near the borderline, and a different conclusion might well be open to the tribunal of fact if the accused had one foot in the car in order to make more effective use of the controls."

Appeal allowed.

Rowan v Chief Constable of the Merseyside Police

The Times 19 December 1985, 3 December 1985, QBD (DC)

The court below was not wrong to find that a person had been driving when he released the handbrake of a coach, then lost control so that it travelled onto a road.

The defendant had been charged, *inter alia*, with driving with excess alcohol, contrary to s 6(1), Road Traffic Act 1972 as substituted by s 25 and Sch 8, Transport Act 1981. He had been convicted by magistrates and appealed to the Crown Court. He had, with friends, boarded a coach, which was unlocked, and parked, on an obvious slope, on land belonging to the company which owned the coach. For a joke, he released the handbrake, but was then unable to control the coach and bring it to a stop. It travelled onto the public road, at which point the defendant abandoned his attempts to re-apply the handbrake; he and his friends alighted from the back of the coach; it then crashed into a wall. The Crown Court concluded that he had been driving for the purposes of s 6(1) and upheld his conviction. He appealed further.

QUESTION(S) FOR THE COURT: (1) If a person inside a motor vehicle which is parked on an obvious slope kneels on the driving seat and releases the handbrake and thereafter attempts to re-apply the handbrake, do his actions amount to "driving" the vehicle for the purposes of an offence under s 6(1), Road Traffic Act 1988? (2) If a person sets a vehicle in motion on private land by actions that amount to "driving" but abandons all control of the vehicle as it travels on to a road or other public place, can he properly be said to be "driving" that vehicle on a road or other public place if the vehicle subsequently travels from the private land on to a road?

HELD: "… [After reviewing the authorities] With some hesitation, I have reached the conclusion that it would be wrong to disturb the judgment of the circuit judge here and the justices … They were guided by the assistance provided in the cases … I see no justification whatsoever for coming to the conclusion that the learned judge did otherwise than apply the principles which emerged from those cases accurately … .

"It is in the end a question of fact and degree. I do not feel it right to say that the court has to be satisfied that a defendant used more than one control of a motor vehicle in order for it to be found that he was driving. Certain it is that it has to be shown that he was responsible for bringing about the movement of the vehicle and thereafter in some way to control or to endeavour to control that movement. Beyond that I am not prepared to acknowledge that it is necessary to go. But in every case it really depends upon the circumstances and how sensible people look at it … ."

Appeal dismissed.

McKoen v Ellis

[1987] RTR 26, [1987] Crim LR 54, 26 June 1986, QBD (DC)

The court below was not wrong to find that a defendant had been controlling the movement and direction of his motor cycle, and therefore driving it, given that the ignition was on, the lights were on, he was astride it and was wearing motor cyclist's clothing and a crash helmet.

The defendant had been convicted of driving with excess alcohol, contrary to s 6(1)(a), Road Traffic Act 1972 as substituted by s 25 and Sch 8, Transport Act 1981. He had propelled a motor cycle by pushing it an unspecified distance, deliberately setting it in motion; he pushed it, steered it and the lights were on; he used the brakes; the ignition had been turned on sufficiently to warm the exhaust pipe. When the police came upon him, he had his legs astride the machine and was wearing a crash helmet and other motor cycling gear.

At the hearing, he had argued he had not been "driving"; the justices rejected that submission and convicted him. He appealed.

QUESTION(S) FOR THE COURT: Whether it was open to the justices, as a question of fact and degree, to conclude that the defendant was driving his motor cycle.

HELD: "… The first question … is whether or not the defendant is making use of the driver's controls in order to direct the movement of the vehicle however that movement is produced … was the defendant in a substantial sense controlling the movement and direction of the vehicle? Assuming that he was, it is … then necessary [to] look at the matter in the round and ask … whether the activity in question falls within the ordinary meaning of the word 'drive'. If both of those tests are satisfied, then it is open to the court, entirely as a matter of fact and degree for their determination, to conclude that the defendant was the driver.

"… It seems to me perfectly proper here for the justices to have regard to the circumstances surrounding the defendant's conduct in controlling the movement and direction of his motor cycle on the night in question, namely, to the facts that the ignition was on, the lights were on, he was found standing astride the motor cycle and he was wearing motor cyclist's clothing and a crash helmet.

"… although this case might well be thought to come close to the borderline, it nevertheless falls within the bracket within which it is a question of fact and degree for the justices to determine, directing themselves properly in accordance with *R v MacDonagh* [page 444], whether the defendant could properly be said to be driving within the ordinary use of that words."

Appeal dismissed.

Gunnell v DPP

[1994] RTR 151, 4 March 1993, QBD (DC)

There was ample material to find that a defendant had been driving a moped when he was astride it and set it in motion by propelling it with his feet for 60 or 70 yards along a road.

The defendant had been charged with driving with excess alcohol, contrary to s 5(1)(a), Road Traffic Act 1988. He had been astride a moped which he was attempting to kick start, not wearing a crash helmet. The engine would not start. The defendant, still astride the moped, set it in motion by propelling it with his feet, proceeding some 60 or 70 yards along a road and back. The lights were not on; no keys were needed to start the engine; there was a fault with the spark plugs. Breath analysis later revealed that he was over the limit.

The motorist submitted that he had not been "driving" for the purposes of the Road Traffic Act 1988. The justices applied the test in *R v MacDonagh* (page 444) that "The essence of driving is the use of the driver's controls in order to direct the movement, however that movement is produced", and concluded that the defendant had had total control over the direction and movement of the moped; the fact that the vehicle had not been moving under its own power was irrelevant. Applying the further test that "drive" should not include "activities which cannot be said to be driving … in any ordinary use of that word", they found that the manner of use of the moped would unequivocally be seen and interpreted by any passer-by as "driving". They distinguished the facts in the present case from those is *R v MacDonagh.* They found that the defendant had been driving and convicted him. He appealed.

QUESTION(S) FOR THE COURT: Whether the defendant was driving within the meaning of the Road Traffic Act 1988.

HELD: "[After reviewing the cases and the justices' findings] … there was ample material to justify the conclusion reached by the justices … On the facts found by the justices, this defendant was … driving."

Appeal dismissed.

DPP v Alderton

[2003] EWHC 2917 (Admin), [2004] RTR 367, 25 November 2003, QBD (Admin)

"Wheel spinning" amounted to "driving".

A motorist had been charged with driving with excess alcohol, contrary to s 5(1)(a), Road Traffic Act 1988. Following an argument with his wife, he had been sitting in the driving seat of his car, which was on a grass verge outside his house. The verge formed part of the road. He was "wheel spinning", which "involved the engine running and the use of the accelerator, clutch and steering wheel, with the vehicle in gear and the handbrake on". Breath analysis showed that he was over the limit.

The justices found that the respondent had no intention of moving the vehicle from the grass verge and that "wheel spinning" did not involve moving the position of the vehicle either forwards or backwards. They acquitted the defendant. The prosecutor appealed.

QUESTION(S) FOR THE COURT: Whether the wheel spinning constituted driving.

HELD: "[Referring to *MacDonagh*, page 444] 11. Both parties agree that [the case sets out] the two relevant tests, namely whether the defendant was in a substantial sense controlling the movement and direction of the car and, secondly, whether the activity in question can fall within the ordinary meaning of the word 'driving'.

"[On the first test] 23. … It seems to me that the whole purpose of having the handbrake on was to prevent the car moving whilst the wheels were moving. … He was, in effect, using all the controls of the car – the clutch, the accelerator and the steering wheel – and the wheels were turning. The whole vehicle was in motion, save only for the handbrake preventing movement of the car backwards or forwards. The fact that there was no movement of the car due to the handbrake does not, in my judgment, prevent it being said that the respondent was driving the car. …

"25. … the first test … was satisfied in that there was a sufficient degree of control over the movement and direction of the vehicle being exercised by the respondent.…

"[On the second test] 27. In my judgment, a person wheel spinning is driving a vehicle in such a way as to seek to ensure that it does not go forward whilst its wheels are turning.

"28. … the justices erred in law in concluding that there had to be some movement of the vehicle before the respondent could be said to be driving it. Each case will depend on its own facts. But … on the facts of this case, the respondent was driving the vehicle … ."

Appeal allowed.

6. DRUG

See also the Drug Driving (Specified Limits) (England and Wales) Regulations 2014 (SI 2014/2868) and the Drug Driving (Specified Limits) (England and Wales) (Amendment) Regulations 2015 (SI 2015/911), designating certain drugs as specified controlled drugs.

Bradford v Wilson

(1984) 78 Cr App R 77, [1984] RTR 116, 29 March 1983, QBD (DC)

A substance taken into the body which is neither drink nor food but which affects the control of the body may be regarded as a drug for the purposes of s 5, Road Traffic Act 1988. Glue (Evo-Stik, containing toluene) was such a drug.

A motorist had been convicted of being in charge of a motor vehicle when unfit to drive through drink or drugs, contrary to s 5(2), Road Traffic Act 1972. Police had found him slumped over the steering wheel of his car, which was stationary and unlit at the side of a road. He was holding a plastic bag over his nose and face. He admitted he had been "glue sniffing". The bag and the glue (Evo-Stik) found in the car contained organic solvents; the principal solvent was toluene which, when inhaled, causes giddiness, light headedness, slurred speech and staggering – effects similar to those of alcohol.

The motorist appealed against conviction.

QUESTION(S) FOR THE COURT: Whether the justices were correct in finding that the constituent chemicals of Evo-Stik, in particular toluene, were a drug for the purposes of s 5, Road Traffic Act 1972 when deliberately inhaled by a person in charge of a motor vehicle thus rendering him unfit to drive.

HELD: "… Substances which are taken as medicines may be drugs, but equally, substances which are not taken as medicines may also be drugs.

"Plainly the mischief against which [s 5] is directed is preventing persons being in charge of vehicles when they have taken substances which could affect the control of their bodies in that particular activity.

"… without attempting to give a definition …, as a general rule, a substance which is taken into the human body by whatever means – for example by inhalation, or by injections, or by mouth – which does not fall within the description 'drink' (because that is specifically mentioned in the subsection) and which is not taken as a food, but which does affect the control of the human body, may be regarded as a drug for the purposes of the section. A particular example of such a substance is one which has a narcotic effect …

"… a person who sniffs glue and who thereby inhales toluene which … [has] effects, in short, similar to those of alcohol … is a person who has taken a drug. If it has such an effect upon him that he does not have proper control of a vehicle, then he is not fit to drive through a drug."

The answer to the question was "yes". Appeal dismissed.

R v Ealing Magistrates' Court ex p Woodman

[1994] RTR 189, [1994] Crim LR 372, 4 October 1993, QBD (DC)

A hypoglycaemic attack which is a direct result of an injection of insulin may amount to unfitness to drive, but on the facts of this case, there was no expert evidence that an injection of insulin many hours earlier was the real effective cause of unfitness.

A motorist had been charged with driving while unfit through drugs, contrary to s 4(1), Road Traffic Act 1988. He was a diabetic and had self-injected his usual dose of insulin 12 hours before he drove, suffered a hypoglycaemic attack, and crashed. At the time of the accident, his blood-sugar level was very low.

At the hearing, he adduced unchallenged medical evidence that the low blood sugar could have been caused by having taken either too much insulin or too little food; that it is difficult to maintain the appropriate blood-sugar balance; and that even a careful diabetic can suffer attacks.

The magistrate found that the motorist had unreasonably failed to follow medical advice to inject himself twice daily rather than once, as he had done; and that he had unreasonably failed to check his blood-sugar level on the day in question. The magistrate concluded that the motorist's unfitness to drive was caused by the drug insulin and convicted him. He was conditionally discharged and disqualified from driving.

The motorist wished to appeal against sentence, but the magistrate refused to state a case on the ground that the application was frivolous. The motorist therefore sought judicial review, initially for an order of *mandamus* directing the magistrate to state a case, but later also for substantive relief.

GROUND(S) FOR THE APPLICATION: That the court was wrong in law: (1) to find that insulin was a drug for the purpose of s 4(1); or (2) to reject the submission that a hypoglycaemic attack suffered by a diabetic was not a state of affairs that could be said in law to be caused through drink or drugs; or (3) to take into consideration the degree to which a particular diabetic followed the advice of his doctors or in other ways monitored and administered his own treatment.

HELD: "… section 4(1) is indeed apt to found the prosecution of a diabetic, if it can clearly be shown that his unfitness to drive as a result of a hypoglycaemic attack was the direct result of an injection of insulin, either because injected in too great a quantity, or because still clearly operative at the moment of the subsequent attack [but] that is as far as it goes … in … the present case … no one suggested that the injection of insulin, which the applicant administered on the afternoon before this accident was itself excessive or other than perfectly proper and appropriate.

"There was simply no evidence … whether or not that insulin, or part of it, still remained in his body at the time of this accident … so as to have produced the blood-sugar imbalance and the consequent hypoglycaemic attack … Nor … was there evidence … that either of the applicant's identified failures was itself productive of the attack. As to his injecting himself only once daily rather than twice as recommended, one should note the apparently undisputed evidence of the defence expert … [that] '… he doubted whether two insulins a day would have stopped such a reaction'.

"Nor does it seem … that, even had the applicant carried out the blood-sugar check, as he should have done, that would necessarily have averted the onset of this hypoglycaemic attack, or, even if it would have done, that that of itself could properly be said to make the presence of insulin in the blood 'the real effective cause of the [attack]'.

"… there simply was not before the magistrate such expert evidence as entitled him to be sure beyond reasonable doubt that the injection many hours earlier was 'the real effective cause' of the unfitness … On that narrow basis, I would accordingly allow the application … ."

R v Norman

[2022] EWCA Crim 1738, 3 November 2022, CA (Crim)

Different bases for the limits in alcohol and in drugs; the sentencing judge erred in equating the excess of cannabis over the specified limit with the excess of alcohol over the prescribed limit. See also R v Norman [2023] EWCA Crim 112, 1 September 2023, CA (Crim), where the same driver's appeal against conviction was dismissed.

A driver was convicted of causing death by careless driving when over the limit for a controlled drug, contrary to s 3A(1)(ba), Road Traffic Act 1988. He was sentenced to 9 years' imprisonment and disqualified for a total of 6½ years and until he passed an extended test. He had driven at 70 mph on a dual carriageway; he lost control; his van drifted to the left across both lanes and into a lay-by, colliding with a lorry and killing his passenger. He was almost three times over the limit for cannabis; he was a long-term daily user of cannabis. The sentencing judge found that the standard of driving fell not far short of dangerous. In assessing seriousness, the judge took the starting point at its highest, on the basis that in an alcohol case, being twice over the alcohol limit would take the case into that category. The driver appealed against sentence.

GROUNDS OF APPEAL: The sentencing judge erred in equating the level of drug in the blood with the amount of drug consumed and giving it an equivalence with alcohol levels; the judge placed the offending too high within the definitive sentencing guideline.

HELD: "20. [The sentencing] judge did fall into error in making a comparison between the extent to which the reading from the appellant exceeded the legal limit for cannabis and the Definitive Guideline's use of a figure double the legal limit for alcohol in assessing what should be treated as a 'high quantity' of drugs and hence in category 1 [high]. …

"22. [Referring to Parliament's zero-tolerance approach to the drug-drive offences, and to the Sentencing Council's guidance to the effect that it would be wrong to rely on the guideline for driving with excess alcohol when sentencing for an excess drugs offence], … it is inappropriate to make a comparison between lawful drug limits with the figures given in the Guideline for alcohol, in order to define whether the quantity of drugs involved in 'high', moderate' or 'medium'…

"25. [The appellant's argument that the case should be placed in the minimum category was rejected.] The approach taken by Parliament in the legislation requires the court to focus on the level of drug present compared to the legal limit. On any view, the level here was approaching three times the legal limit and that had to fall within the moderate category at the very least… .

"27. The judge was entitled to treat the appellant as having been substantially impaired … We will proceed on the basis that the concentration was 'moderate' rather than 'high'. [Given the aggravating and mitigating factors] Whilst … the sentence … was severe, … it was not manifestly excessive."

Appeal dismissed.

7. IN CHARGE

DPP v Webb

[1988] RTR 374, 12 October 1987, QBD (DC)

It was correct to acquit a defendant of being in charge where the allegation referred to the place at which the defendant was found, not the place where the motor vehicle was, but that did not justify acquitting on a charge of failing to provide breath specimens.

The defendant had been charged, *inter alia*, with, at Park Avenue, Gillingham, being in charge with excess alcohol, contrary to s 5(2), Road Traffic Act 1972 as substituted by s 25 and Sch 8, Transport Act 1981; and, in the course of an investigation into an offence under s 5, with failing without reasonable excuse to provide a specimen of breath for analysis, contrary to s 8(7), Road Traffic Act 1972 as likewise substituted. He was seen in Park Avenue tampering with two parked cars belonging to neighbours, both of whom saw him, considered he was drunk, saw he was smoking two cigarettes at the same time and fumbling with keys, and thought he was oblivious to his surroundings. He said he thought one of the cars was his own. Police officers arrived and found the defendant in possession of the keys to his own car, which was in fact parked in Seaton Road, some one fifth of a mile away. He was arrested for being drunk in charge. At the police station he refused to provide breath specimens for analysis, saying "On the basis that I didn't have a motor vehicle in that area, no".

The justices convicted the defendant, who appealed to the Crown Court. At the Crown Court the prosecution conceded that the "in charge" matter related to the defendant's car in Seaton Road, although the charge recited Park Avenue. On failure to provide, the Crown Court found that the confusion as to "which car at what venue" persisted. It was not clear to the defendant whether the offence giving rise to the demand for the specimen was made in respect of his own car or his neighbour's and that it was wrong to make a requirement on an "either/or" basis.

The Crown Court found no case to answer on both charges. The prosecutor appealed.

QUESTION(S) FOR THE COURT: (1) Whether there was *prima facie* evidence that the defendant was in charge of a motor vehicle within the meaning of s 5, Road Traffic Act 1972 as substituted, in view of the prosecution's case being directed at Seaton Road; (2) whether there was a *prima facie* case of failing to provide two specimens of breath for analysis since the police were investigating whether the defendant had committed any offence under s 5; (3) whether, if there was a *prima facie* case in respect of either of the two charges as originally laid, the Crown Court was wrong in law to dismiss the charges.

HELD: "[On being in charge] Section 5(2) of the Act of 1972 makes the geographic place critically the place where the motor vehicle is and not where the defendant is. The motor vehicle in the instant case was not in Park Avenue. It was in another street. Accordingly … the geographic location being flawed, the Crown Court were … correct in the conclusion which they reached …

"So far as the section 8(7) offence is concerned, the Crown Court ranked the destiny of that offence with the offence under section 5 … there is no such linkage. All that is required in relation to the section 8 offence is that there should be an investigation into whether an offence under section 5 has been committed. There was such an investigation here. Whether the arrest was lawful or not is immaterial … There is no question of reasonable excuse … ."

Appeal in respect of the s 5(2) offence dismissed. Appeal in respect of the s 8(7) offence allowed.

DPP v Watkins

[1989] QB 821, [1989] 2 WLR 966, [1989] 1 All ER 1126, [1989] RTR 324, 1 March 1989, QBD (DC)

Where a person is not the owner, lawful possessor or recent driver of a vehicle, he is in charge if he is voluntarily in de facto control of it or may imminently be expected to assume control. On the facts of this case, the defendant was in charge. To establish that a person is in charge there must be a close connection between that person and the control of the vehicle, but it is not necessary to prove likelihood of driving.

A person had been charged with, *inter alia*, being in charge while unfit, contrary to s 5(2), Road Traffic Act 1972 as substituted by s 25 and Sch 8, Transport Act 1981. He had been found seated in a car which was not his, was drunk, and had a key which fitted the ignition. The police did not know whether the owner of the vehicle had given the defendant permission to be in the car or for what purpose he was there; nor had they tested whether the key in the defendant's possession would turn on the engine.

The defendant asserted, *inter alia*, that although the key fitted the ignition, it would not start the engine and that there was no likelihood of his driving; and that there was therefore no case to answer.

The justices dismissed both matters. The prosecutor appealed.

QUESTION(S) FOR THE COURT: (1) Whether the justices were correct in finding no case to answer on the ground that there was insufficient evidence that the defendant was in charge of a motor vehicle; (2) whether in so finding they were right to take into account evidence that the car did not belong to the defendant, and doubts as to whether the car key found in his possession could in fact start the car; (3) whether the meaning of the phrase "in charge" necessitates a close connection between a defendant and the control of or likelihood of driving a motor vehicle.

HELD: "… the facts of this case … raise in acute form the question: what must the prosecution prove to establish that a defendant is 'in charge of a motor vehicle'.

"[Reviewing certain authorities and statutory provisions] Broadly, there are two distinct classes of case. (1) If the defendant is the owner or lawful possessor of the vehicle or has recently driven it, he will have been in charge of it, …

"(2) If the defendant is not the owner, the lawful possessor or recent driver but is sitting in the vehicle or is otherwise involved with it, the question for the court is, as here, whether he has assumed being in charge of it … [he] will be in charge if, whilst unfit, he is voluntarily in *de facto* control of the vehicle or if, in the circumstances, including his position, his intentions and his actions, he may be expected imminently to assume control. Usually this will involve his having gained entry to the car and evinced an intention to take control of it …

"The circumstances to be taken into account will vary infinitely but the following will usually be relevant: (i) whether and where he is in the vehicle or how far he is from it; (ii) what he is doing at the relevant time; (iii) whether he is in possession of a key that fits the ignition; (iv) whether there is evidence of an intention to take or assert control of the car by driving or otherwise; (v) whether any other person is in, at or near the vehicle …

"In the present case the defendant was not only in the driving seat; he was holding one of a bunch of keys between his thumb and forefinger. Those facts support an inference that he intended to take control of the car by starting it. There was no evidence of any other person at or near the car … there was sufficient to show either he was voluntarily in *de facto* control of the car or that he could be expected imminently to take such control. In those circumstances it was open … to conclude that he was in charge …

"But there was no burden of proof on the prosecution in regard to the likelihood of the defendant driving. The burden was upon him to establish that defence once a *prima facie* case of being in charge was made out … So the justices' approach to the uncertainty regarding the efficacy of the key put the burden of proof on the wrong party and their conclusion was premature."

The answers to the questions were: (1) "no"; (2) "… the justices were right to take into account evidence that the car did not belong to the defendant. They would have been right to take into account the presence of the key in the defendant's hand as that would go to his intention. However they were wrong to take into account doubts as to whether the car keys found in his possession could in fact start the car, i.e., the absence of proof of the likelihood of his driving." (3) "The meaning of 'in charge' does necessitate a close connection between the defendant and the control of a motor vehicle … It does not necessitate proof of a likelihood of the defendant driving the vehicle."

Appeal allowed.

DPP v Janman

[2004] EWHC 101 (Admin), [2004] RTR 522, [2004] Crim LR 478, 22 January 2004, QBD (DC)

A person supervising a learner driver is in charge of the vehicle, regardless of whether or not he is professionally qualified as a driving instructor. The competence of the learner is insufficient to establish the defence of no likelihood of driving.

A person had been charged with being in charge of a motor vehicle with excess alcohol, contrary to s 5(1)(b), Road Traffic Act 1988. He had been in the car with a learner driver (his partner); the police took the view that he was supervising his partner and therefore in charge of the vehicle. A roadside breath test was positive and they arrested him; breath analysis showed excess alcohol.

The justices found nothing to prove that the defendant had been anything other than a passenger, and not therefore in charge of the vehicle. They also found that the defendant had said, in interview with the police, that he did not need to supervise his partner as she was able to drive. The Crown gave no evidence on this and so did not rebut the defence in s 5(2), Road Traffic Act 1988 (no likelihood of driving while over the limit). The justices dismissed the charge. The prosecutor appealed.

QUESTION(S) FOR THE COURT: (1) Whether the fact that a person assumes the role of supervisor of a learner driver is a sufficient basis for finding that person to be a supervisor, or whether there should be evidence that the person is a qualified driver in accordance with reg 17, Motor Vehicles (Driving Licences) Regulations 1999 (SI 1999/2864); (2) if the justices should have found the respondent to have been supervising his partner, whether they should have concluded that he was 'in charge' of the car by virtue solely of his supervisory role; (3) alternatively, whether the justices should have found the respondent to be in charge of his partner's motor vehicle even if he was not supervising her driving; (4) if the answer to (2) or (3) is "yes", whether the justices were correct to find that the respondent had, during his police interview, satisfied the evidential burden to raise the defence in s 5(2), Road Traffic Act 1988.

HELD: "12. … A person supervising a learner driver may or may not be qualified to do so … If … as a matter of fact the driver of a car is the holder of a provisional licence requiring him or her to be supervised, and if a person is as a matter of fact performing the function of supervising that learner driver, then they are indeed the supervisor …

"13. … the prosecution does not have to establish positively that the person supervising was statutorily qualified to do so.

"15. … in any normal circumstances, if the holder of a provisional driving licence is in fact driving a motor vehicle on a road or other public place, the person supervising that driver will be in charge of the motor vehicle. That seems to me to be an obvious normal consequence of the requirement that such a person should be supervised …

"17. … the main burden of the present appeal turns on the question whether the prosecution had sufficiently rebutted the defence under section 5(2) …

"18. The case advanced on behalf of the respondent … was that … [the driver] was a good competent driver who did not need detailed supervision. In those circumstances there was no likelihood of his driving the vehicle.

"19. [The Crown] submits that the very statutory purpose of [requiring] somebody … to supervise the holder of a provisional driving licence when they are driving necessarily raises the … possibility that it may be necessary for the supervisor to assume control of the vehicle … in one or more of the following ways; by himself taking sole charge of the driving …; by himself operating one or more of the controls …; or by instructing his partner to control the vehicle's movement in a particular manner … He submits that any one of those would for the purpose of section 5(2) constitute his driving the vehicle. …

"21. Accordingly, it is submitted, and in my judgment correctly submitted, that the likelihood of driving the vehicle under section 5(2) of the 1988 Act extends to the kind of operations which the supervisor of a learner driver might be expected to have to undertake if that learner driver got into difficulties. …

"31. … The very statutory purpose of having a person supervising the holder of a provisional driving licence is because they are a provisional driver and by statute not yet regarded as competent to drive on their own. Apart from extraordinary facts which could conceivably arise but do not, in my judgment, arise in this case, it will normally be the case that any submission based on the learner driver's driving competence will be insufficient to establish that there was no likelihood of the supervisor driving the vehicle. …

"32. In my judgment, the facts advanced in the present case, although they raised the defence so that the prosecution had to deal with it, did not go so far as contributing to any finding that there was no likelihood of this respondent driving the vehicle. …"

Appeal allowed.

CPS v Bate

[2004] EWHC 2811(Admin), 22 November 2004, QBD (DC)

Being in charge is not synonymous with an intention to drive. On the facts of this case (defendant seen approaching his car, keys in hand, stumbling, sitting in driver's seat), the defendant was in charge.

A motorist had been charged with being in charge of a motor vehicle with excess alcohol, contrary to s 5(1)(b), Road Traffic Act 1988. He had been seen by a police officer approaching his car with the keys in his hand; he stumbled as he opened the driver's door. By the time the officer reached him, he was sitting in the driver's seat; the engine had not been started. A roadside breath test was positive; he was arrested; breath analysis revealed excess alcohol.

The magistrates found that the defendant had had no intention of taking or asserting control of the vehicle and therefore no intention of driving it. They dismissed the charge; the prosecutor appealed.

QUESTION(S) FOR THE COURT: In finding insufficient proof to establish that the defendant intended to take or assert control of the vehicle, whether the justices correctly applied the test in *DPP v Watkins* (see page 453); whether their decision was one which a reasonable bench of magistrates, properly directed, could have reached.

HELD: "16. [After reviewing *DPP v Watkins*] … It is not necessary for the prosecution to establish to the criminal standard an intention to drive in order to prove an offence under section 5(1)(b) if the evidence otherwise establishes that the defendant is in charge of the vehicle. Being in charge is not synonymous with an intention to drive, but an intention to drive may prove that charge of the vehicle has not been relinquished.

"18. … the Justices erred in their approach …

"19. … the respondent manifestly was in charge of the vehicle. Far from relinquishing his charge he had, by entering and sitting in the vehicle, reasserted his charge. … whether the respondent had an intention to drive would only have become material upon an examination of the statutory defence under section 5(2) … ."

The answers to both questions were "no". Appeal allowed.

8. INTERVIEW

See also DPP v Billington, page 216 – the procedure for taking specimens for analysis is not an interview; Brown (Kevin Mark) v DPP, page 351, where the circumstances did not amount to an interview; and Prouse v DPP, page 354, Ortega v DPP, page 355 and Charles v DPP, page 371, where interviews took place.

CPS v O'Shea

Unreported, CO/3689/97, 11 May 1998, QBD (DC)

On the facts of this case, an officer's question whether the suspect was driving his car at the time of an accident was an interview and the caution should have been administered. Compare Whelehan v DPP, page 15, where questioning did not amount to an interview.

A motorist had been charged with driving with excess alcohol, contrary to s 5(1)(a), Road Traffic Act 1988. A road traffic accident had occurred; there were no witnesses, but nearby residents heard a loud bang and came out of their houses. The defendant was seen near his Volvo and appeared to witnesses to be drunk. Police were called. An officer said to the defendant "An accident has just happened that is alleged was your fault. Were you driving your Volvo H569 WTV at the time of the accident?" He replied "yes". The breath test procedure was then administered and breath analysis later revealed 79 µg alcohol in 100 ml breath.

It was argued before the justices that the officer's question to the defendant constituted an interview as defined in PACE Code C, paragraph 11.1A of the Codes of Practice under s 66, Police and Criminal Evidence Act 1984; he should therefore have been cautioned but was not; and that the admission should be excluded under s 78, Police and Criminal Evidence Act 1984 (discretion to exclude evidence which would have such an adverse effect on the fairness of the proceedings that the court ought not to admit it). The justices found for the defendant, excluded the evidence and dismissed the case. The prosecutor appealed.

QUESTION(S) FOR THE COURT: (1) Whether the justices erred in law in finding that PACE Code C applied to the questioning of the respondent immediately prior to the administration of the roadside breath test. (2) Whether the justices were wrong in law to regard a failure to administer a caution as a breach of PACE Code C. (3) Whether the justices' decision to exclude the reply to the officer's questioning was one that a reasonable bench of magistrates properly directed could have made in exercising their discretion under s 78, Police and Criminal Evidence Act 1984.

HELD: "… under the current Code C: (1) there is an interview for the purposes of the Code if a question or questions is/are put to a person whom there are grounds to suspect of an offence, regarding involvement or suspected involvement in that offence, if his answers or his silence may be given in evidence to a court in a prosecution. (2) There is not an interview for the purposes of the Code if a question or questions is/are put for other purposes, for example: (i) solely to establish identity or ownership of any vehicle; (ii) to obtain information in accordance with any relevant statutory requirement; (iii) in furtherance of the proper and effective conduct of a search …; (iv) to seek verification of a written record in accordance with paragraph 11.13; and (v) where procedures are undertaken under section 7 of the Road Traffic Act 1988 (provision of specimens for analysis).

"In the present case the police officer said to the respondent: 'An accident has just happened that is alleged was your fault. Were you driving your Volvo H569 WTV at the time of the accident?' It is clear that the police officer knew the respondent's identity and knew that the respondent owned the Volvo: see the reference to 'your Volvo'. Thus the question was not solely 'to establish identity or ownership of any vehicle'. It is also clear from the words 'an accident has just happened that is alleged was your fault', and the facts found by the justices that, at the time of the question … the respondent was a person whom there were grounds to suspect of an offence … The thrust of the question was to seek an admission that the respondent was driving the Volvo at the relevant time. It was plain that the answer might be given in evidence to a court in a prosecution. It follows … that the justices were correct in ruling that the question posed was an interview …

"Section 78 afforded a wide discretion to the justices. This is not a case where this court should interfere with the exercise of that discretion … ."

Appeal dismissed.

DPP v Rous and Davis

[1991] Crim LR 911, [1992] RTR 246, 28 June 1991, QBD (DC)

The procedure under s 8, Road Traffic Act 1972 does not constitute an interview for the purposes of the Police and Criminal Evidence Act 1984.

In both cases, motorists had been charged with driving with excess alcohol, contrary to s 5(1), Road Traffic Act 1988.

In *Rous*, breath analysis had produced a lower reading of 48 µg alcohol in 100 ml breath, and the procedure under s 8(2), Road Traffic Act 1988 (lower breath reading no more than 50 µg alcohol in 100 ml breath – now repealed; see page v) was followed. The motorist contended that the parts of the Book 116 (the police contemporaneous record) containing questions and answers relating to the statutory option constituted an "interview" for the purposes of PACE Code C, paragraph 12 of the Codes of Practice under s 66, Police and Criminal Evidence Act 1984; that paragraph had not been complied with and the justices should therefore exercise their discretion under s 78, Police and Criminal Evidence Act 1984 (to exclude evidence which would have such an adverse effect on the fairness of the proceedings that the court ought not to admit it) to exclude evidence of compliance with the procedure as contained in the Book 116. The justices accepted that submission and dismissed the information.

In *Davis*, the defendant was a juvenile; breath analysis had proved positive. Before the justices he argued that the breath analysis printout should not be admitted in evidence because there had been a breach of PACE Code C, paragraph 13.1, which provides, *inter alia*, that a juvenile must not be "interviewed" in the absence of an appropriate adult. The justices accepted that the questions and answers leading to the taking of breath specimens constituted an "interview" and excluded the evidence. The charge was dismissed.

In both cases the prosecutor appealed.

QUESTION(S) FOR THE COURT: In *Rous*, whether the Book 116, containing a contemporaneous record of the statutory procedure, constituted an interview so that the procedures in PACE Code C had to be complied with.

In *Davis*, whether requesting breath specimens for analysis from a juvenile amounts to an interview covered by PACE Code C, paragraph 13 and so requires the presence of an appropriate adult.

HELD: "… in the notes for guidance C:6C it is provided 'Procedures undertaken under section 8 of the Road Traffic Act 1972 do not constitute interviewing for the purposes of this code' … Applying *DPP v Billington* [see page 216] neither the … procedure which was involved in *Davis* nor the … procedure which was involved in *Rous* constituted an interview within the passages in the code which were relied upon. Accordingly, there is no situation in which the justices could exercise their discretion under section 78 of the Act."

Appeals allowed.

R (Ridehalgh) v DPP

[2005] EWHC 1100 (Admin), [2005] RTR 353, 23 May 2005, QBD (Admin)

In the circumstances of this case (smell of alcohol on breath; no indication of how much alcohol had been consumed or whether the person had driven), asking if the person had been drinking was not an interview for the purposes of the Police and Criminal Evidence Act 1984.

A motorist had been charged with driving with excess alcohol, contrary to s 5(1)(a), Road Traffic Act 1988. He was a serving officer of the British Transport Police and on the date in question he went to a police station on police business. A sergeant smelled alcohol on him, and consulted an inspector; they asked the accused if he had been drinking; he said he had the night before, and that he had driven to the police station that morning. The inspector required a breath test, which was positive. The accused was arrested and cautioned. He then repeated the admissions.

At the trial, it was argued that the initial conversation was an interview and that the defendant should have been cautioned before it took place pursuant to PACE Code C, paragraphs 10.1 and 11.1A of the Codes of Practice under s 66, Police and Criminal Evidence Act 1984. The justices rejected that argument and convicted the defendant; he appealed.

HELD: "17. … Where police officers question people, in any circumstances in the course of possible investigations relating to the commission of a criminal offence, there inevitably comes a time when it begins to occur to them that an offence might have been committed. They need to make further enquiries to establish whether there are grounds for suspecting the particular person, the potential defendant, of committing the offence. If the stage comes when there are such grounds, then the duty to caution arises.

"19. … all that the officers had prior to the questioning of the appellant was a smell of alcohol on his breath; no indication as to when and how much alcohol had been taken; and no indication as to whether or not he had been driving. Under those circumstances, the magistrates were, in my judgment, fully justified in concluding that the conversation on those matters amounted simply to a conversation and not to an interview within the definition of the Code of Practice …

"20. Further, if I am wrong in that conclusion, it does seem to me inevitable that the justices would have reached precisely the same decision about the appellant's guilt in any event. It is difficult if not impossible to see how any unfairness could have arisen by the admission of that conversation. The appellant was himself a police officer, and once he was cautioned he not only freely admitted precisely the same matters as he had done in the previous conversation, he elaborated upon them. There could have been no unfairness. Under all those circumstances, this appeal is dismissed."

Sneyd v DPP

[2006] EWHC 560 (Admin), (2006) 170 JP 545, 24 February 2006, QBD (DC)

Where officers asked a person whom they had seen driving out of a pub car park if he had been drinking, and he said he had had 3 pints, that was not an interview for the purposes of the Police and Criminal Evidence Act 1984. Unchallenged oral evidence was sufficient to establish the breath alcohol level, and the calibration and reliability of the breath analysis device.

A motorist had been charged with driving with excess alcohol, contrary to s 5(1)(a), Road Traffic Act 1988. A police officer had seen him driving out of the car park of a public house; he stopped the driver and asked if he had been drinking; he said he had had 3 pints. A roadside breath test was positive and the driver was arrested. At the police station, the breath analysis device was checked and no problems were found. Breath analysis revealed a lower reading of 52μg alcohol in 100 ml breath.

It was argued that there had been a breach of PACE Code C of the Codes of Practice under s 66, Police and Criminal Evidence Act 1984 in that the driver had not been cautioned before being asked if he had been drinking; and that since the printout had not been produced there was no admissible evidence of the reading or that the machine had self-calibrated and was functioning correctly.

The magistrates rejected those arguments and convicted the defendant. He appealed.

QUESTION(S) FOR THE COURT (INTER ALIA): Whether the magistrates: (a) were right in law to hold that there had been no breach of PACE Code C; (b) were right in law to determine that there was admissible evidence on which they could conclude that the proportion of alcohol in the appellant's breath was 52 μg in 100 ml; (c) erred in law in rejecting the contention that they were not entitled to convict because there was no evidence of calibration of the Intoximeter machine.

HELD: "[On (a)] 14. … the requirement to caution exists under para 10.1 [of PACE Code C] when there are 'grounds to suspect of an offence' …

"17. … [the officer] said that when he stopped the appellant, he suspected that the appellant had been drinking; but to drink is not in itself a criminal offence and the officer did not say that he suspected that the appellant had committed or was committing an offence, nor … did he have grounds to suspect the appellant of an offence. The mere fact that the appellant was driving out of a public house car park at a late hour was not sufficient for that purpose. Accordingly, at the point when the officer asked the appellant if he had been drinking, paragraphs 10 and 11 of Code C were not engaged.

"18. Nor indeed were they engaged by the appellant's response that he had drunk 3 pints. The significance of that response was that it gave the officer reasonable cause to suspect that the appellant had alcohol in his body, which was sufficient to entitle him under section 6(1) of the Road Traffic Act 1988 to require the appellant to provide a specimen of breath. It was only once the breath test showed a positive result that the officer had grounds to suspect the appellant of an offence, so as to require the caution to be administered under paragraph 10.1 of Code C before any further questioning. It was at that point that a caution was duly given. …

"19. … There was no breach of Code C.

"[On (b) and (c)] 32. … it is well established that evidence both as to the results of the analysis and as to the reliability of the machine can be given either in the form of a written print-out or orally by the officer who carried out the procedure. …

"38. … oral evidence was given by the officer who carried out the procedure, evidence which was supported by the other officer who was present throughout. There was no challenge to that evidence in cross-examination. No objection was taken to its admissibility at the time and no challenge, indeed, to its correctness. … the oral evidence that was given covered in clear terms the results produced by the machine … [On the argument that the officer had given evidence of what he had seen on the printout, not on the screen] … I see no problem of oral evidence of the results shown on the print-out and no difference in principle between that and oral evidence of the results on the screen of the machine. These are just two different ways by which the machine displays its results. The same thing appears on both. In neither case … is oral evidence inadmissible hearsay.

"39. The evidence before the justices also covered in sufficiently clear terms the reliability of the machine, amply supporting the justices' finding that the machine was working correctly and was calibrated properly. … it was unnecessary for the officer to deal expressly with the calibration figures. If the machine was working correctly it follows that it was calibrated properly. It was for the defence to raise an issue concerning the calibrations by way of cross-examination of the officer if they had anything to raise.

"41. … the justices were … entitled to conclude that the machine was working correctly and had been calibrated properly."

The answer to questions (a) and (b) was "yes"; the answer to question (c) was "no". Appeal dismissed.

9. MOTOR VEHICLE

Croitoru v CPS

[2016] EWHC 1645 (Admin), 11 February 2016, QBD (DC)

On the facts, the appellant failed to bring his scooter within the statutory provisions which take an invalid carriage outside the definition of "motor vehicle"; the provisions on drink-driving therefore applied.

The appellant had been convicted of using a Motability scooter on a road with excess alcohol, contrary to s 5, Road Traffic Act 1988. He said he had bought the scooter for his elderly father, fitted it with a battery, and was testing it to see how far it would go. He argued that the case fell within s 20, Chronically Sick and Disabled Persons Act 1970, which disapplies (among other provisions) s 5, Road Traffic Act 1988 to a scooter if prescribed requirements and conditions of use are met. He claimed the scooter was being used in accordance with the conditions set out in reg 4, Use of Invalid Carriages on Highways Regulations 1988 (SI 1988/2268). He invoked para (b)(ii), claiming that the scooter was being used "by some other person for the purposes only of taking the invalid carriage to or bringing it away from any place where work of maintenance or repair is to be or has been carried out to" it. The Crown Court dismissed his appeal against conviction, finding that s 5, Road Traffic Act 1988 applied to the scooter.

The appellant appealed further.

QUESTION(S) FOR THE COURT: Whether, if a person is driving on a road an invalid carriage, which is also a mechanically propelled vehicle intended or adapted for use on a road, and has alcohol in his breath, blood or urine which exceeds the prescribed limit, he is guilty of an offence under s 5, Road Traffic Act 1998, if he is using it in accordance with s 20, Chronically Sick and Disabled Persons Act 1970 and reg 4(a)(ii), Use of Invalid Carriages on Highway Regulations 1988.

HELD "18. … section 20(1)(b) [of the Chronically Sick and Disabled Persons Act 1970] should be interpreted as meaning that a mechanically propelled invalid carriage – provided, of course, that it complies with the prescribed requirements and is being used in accordance with the prescribed conditions – is excluded from the definition of 'motor vehicle' for all the purposes of the Road Traffic Act 1988 save for the sole and specific exception of section 22A, and is also excluded from the ambit of the nine specified sections of the 1988 Act which apply to mechanically propelled vehicles.

19. … the Crown Court was wrong to interpret section 20 of the 1970 Act as it did, and that the answer to the certified question is No.

20. … [however] … The answer to the certified question is only in the negative if the invalid carriage is being used in accordance with the conditions specified in regulation 4 of the 1998 Regulations. In [this] case, the evidence on that issue was all one way. [The appellant] did not himself give and did not call any evidence at the hearing of the appeal. There was no evidence to contradict his assertion to the

police that he had fitted a new battery and taken the scooter out to see how far it would go. But the use of the scooter in such circumstances, in my view, cannot possibly be regarded as taking it to or bringing it away from a place where maintenance or repair had been or was to be carried out. Thus, far from raising any issue of using the scooter in accordance with the regulations, [the appellant] expressly excluded himself from such use.

21. In those circumstances there was no burden on the prosecution to prove that the 1970 Act did not apply … The effect of section 20 of the 1970 Act … is to create an exception in favour of the person accused of driving with excess alcohol, and there was therefore, at the very least, an evidential burden on [the appellant] to show that he was capable of coming within that exception. In my view, he did not begin to do so."

Appeal dismissed.

10. PUBLIC PLACE

See also Pugh v Knipe [1972] RTR 286 (QBD) – for private land to be a public place, it must be shown that the public has access to the place; Filmer v DPP, page 581, where the defence was not entitled to an adjournment to seek further evidence concerning whether a place was a public place; Hallett v DPP, page 478, on the need for evidence of public use; and Havell v DPP [1993] Crim LR 621, where it was held that a car park which was available only to members of a club or their guests was not a public place.

Bowman v DPP
[1991] RTR 263, [1990] Crim LR 600, 17 January 1990, QBD (DC)

On the facts of this case, there were no grounds for interfering with the justices' decision that a car park, which they knew to be left open at certain times, was a public place.

A motorist had been charged with driving on a public place with excess alcohol, contrary to s 6, Road Traffic Act 1972 as substituted by s 25 and Sch 8, Transport Act 1981. The place of the alleged offence was a National Car Parks car park; at the time the barrier at the entrance was raised and the car park was accessible from the street; other cars were parked there; the barrier was put across the entrance only during shopping hours.

At the hearing, it was argued on behalf of the motorist that the car park was not a public place. The justices rejected that, using their own knowledge of the car park that the barrier was left up at night and anyone could use it. They convicted the motorist. He appealed.

QUESTION(S) FOR THE COURT: (1) Whether there was any evidence upon which a reasonable tribunal might find that the car park was a "public place" within the meaning of s 6, Road Traffic Act 1972 as substituted; (2) upon such evidence, if any, whether the justices were correct in law in holding that the defendant had been driving in a public place.

HELD: "There is no doubt that justices are entitled, when weighing up the evidence …, to use their own local knowledge … That is not knowledge which is called judicial knowledge or the taking of judicial notice … It is actual local knowledge gained by justices as ordinary citizens of the place in which they live and in which they from time to time dispense justice …

"[Counsel for the appellant] has to persuade us that no reasonable bench of justices, armed with the local knowledge that these justices had, equipped with the oral evidence which they had heard, including that of the defendant himself, could properly have come to the conclusion that this car park was at the relevant time a public place … that is asking far too much of this court."

Appeal dismissed.

DPP v Vivier

[1991] 4 All ER 18, [1991] RTR 205, [1991] Crim LR 637, 11 March 1991, QBD (DC)

In the circumstances of this case, a privately owned campsite was a public place.

A motorist had been charged with driving on a road or other public place with excess alcohol, contrary to s 5(1)(a), Road Traffic Act 1988. He argued that the place where he had been driving was not a road as defined in s 192(1), Road Traffic Act 1988, i.e. it was not a "highway or other road to which the public has access".

The alleged offence had taken place at a privately owned campsite called Unity Farm, of about 80 acres with 3–4 miles of road; it opened from Spring to Autumn and accommodated up to 3,500 people. It was surrounded by a ditch and had one main gate; visitors entering were required to register and to have a car pass; fees were charged; security services were employed.

The justices found that the site was open only to a special class of members of the public; although that class was large, that did not make the site a public place. They dismissed the charge. The prosecutor appealed.

QUESTION(S) FOR THE COURT: Whether the justices were correct in finding that the holiday centre when open for business between 24 March and 26 October was not a public place for the purposes of the Road Traffic Acts.

HELD: "… are the caravanners, campers and guests to be regarded … as members of the public [in which case the site would be a public place] or are they instead … a special class of members of the public [in which case the site would not be a public place].

"… those seeking entry are … screened in the sense of having to satisfy certain conditions for admission. Does the screening process … endow those passing through with some special characteristic whereby they lose their identity as members of the general public and become instead a special class?

"… there was … no sufficient segregation or selection of the caravanners and campers passing through the control system … to cause them to cease to be members of the general public and to become instead a special class. They passed through the gate, not for any reason or characteristic personal to themselves, not because they were in any way selected, but rather because they wished to enter and were prepared to satisfy the modest conditions imposed upon them … Up to the boundary of this caravan site those seeking entry were unarguably members of the general public pure and simple … it is quite unreal to suggest that at the gate some transformation occurs whereby they alter their legal character, shed their identity as members of the general public and take on instead a different status as caravanners and campers."

The answer to the question was "no". Appeal allowed.

DPP v Coulman

[1993] RTR 230, 20 October 1992, QBD (DC)

Freight lanes at Dover Docks are a public place.

A lorry driver had been charged with driving on a road or other public place with excess alcohol, contrary to s 5(1)(a), Road Traffic Act 1988. He had disembarked from a cross-Channel ferry at Dover and was in the Inward Freight Immigration Lanes, Eastern Docks, Dover, when he was suspected of having consumed alcohol. He was later arrested and breath analysis revealed a lower reading of 85 μg alcohol in 100 ml breath.

He was convicted by magistrates and appealed to the Crown Court. On a preliminary issue, the Crown Court found that the lanes were not a public place. The prosecutor appealed.

QUESTION(S) FOR THE COURT: Whether it was wrong in law to find as a matter of fact that the Inward Freight Immigration Lanes, Dover Eastern Docks, were a public place within the meaning of the Road Traffic Act 1988.

HELD: "… The question is whether [the lanes] are roads to which the public have access.

That question may be refined to inquiring whether those who use the Lanes are doing so as members of the public … whether those who are permitted to use the Lanes … are so permitted because of some special characteristic or reason personal to themselves which is not possessed by the public at large …

"… those who enter … from the landward side are permitted to enter because of some special characteristics or reason which is relevant to entry and which they possess. That is to say, they were in the relationship of employee to the occupier or held a pass issued by him …

"However, what of those entering from seaward? … The only condition for being upon the Lanes is disembarkation. The necessity for being on the Lanes is the desire to achieve access to the shore … is so common a reason capable of removing those who enter the Lanes from seaward from their ordinary position as being ordinary members of the public? … no."

The answers to the questions were "yes, they were wrong in law". Appeal allowed.

Edwards v DPP

Unreported, Case 1782/93, 10 March 1994, QBD (DC)

On the facts of this case, a privately-owned car park in use by the public was a public place.

A motorist had been charged with driving in a public place with excess alcohol, contrary to s 5(1)(a), Road Traffic Act 1988. The place in question was a car park. It belonged to a limited company, which had not used it for about 2 years; the company had given a taxi company and a school permission to use it; they had also given an adjacent nightclub permission to use it between 6.30 pm and 8.00 am during the week and at all hours at weekends. The justices found that it was in fact used by the local community at large; at the time of the alleged offence (2.05 am), it was three quarters full; members of the public were standing on the car park and taxis were arriving; there were no signs, notices or effective barriers prohibiting any person from using the car park. The general public had been using the car park completely unhindered for the preceding 12 months. The owners, and the owners of the nightclub, were aware of that. There were no defined times during which the public were allowed to use it.

The justices found that the car park was a public place, and convicted the motorist. He appealed.

QUESTION(S) FOR THE COURT: Whether, on the facts as found, the justices were justified in finding that the car park was a public place within the meaning of s 5(1)(a), Road Traffic Act 1988 at the material time.

HELD: "… It is not essential, for the purposes of a car park being a public place for the purposes of the Road Traffic Act, that members of the public should have rights (enforceable at law if need be) to go to that place. The question is whether, as a matter of fact, they did use it with sufficient regularity, so that it had become *de facto* a public place, even though, if the owners of the land had sought to enforce their rights, they could have stopped its use in that manner. The issue is: how was the land being used at the date in question? The Justices' findings of fact make it clear that it was being used as a public place, both in the day time and after dark.

"I refer … to the specific finding relating to the day of the incident in question, when, … at five past two in the morning, members of the public were standing in the car park and taxis were arriving … it is not suggested that there was no evidence which entitled the Justices to reach that conclusion.

"This clearly was a matter when the Justices had ample evidence to make the finding that they did."

Appeal dismissed.

R v Colchester JJ ex p Wood

Unreported, CO 286 93, 11 March 1994, QBD (DC)

On the facts, there was no evidence entitling the magistrates to find that the defendant's car had been on a public place.

The defendant had been charged, *inter alia*, with being "in charge of a motor vehicle in a public place called field adjacent to Bakers Lane having consumed alcohol in such quantity that the proportion thereof in his breath exceeded the prescribed limit", contrary to s 5(1)(b), Road Traffic Act 1988. Bakers Lane was a public place; the field was a private place.

At the hearing, the prosecution applied for leave to amend the charge by removing the words "field adjacent to", which was refused.

No oral evidence was given, but there was a statement by a police officer that he had noticed a car "parked just off the road [Bakers Lane] to our nearside"; the engine was running and the defendant was asleep in the driver's seat. Another officer's statement said that he too had noticed the car "parked just off the road to my nearside". Photographs taken by a police photographer 2 months after the incident, showing the venue and a parked police car, and a statement from the owner of the field, were also in evidence.

The justices found that the defendant had been seated in his car at the side of the carriageway of Bakers Lane directly in front of the entrance to a field. They found that to be a public place and convicted. The defendant wished to appeal, but the justices refused to state a case on the ground that the application was frivolous. The defendant sought an order of *certiorari* requiring them to state a case.

HELD: "… the evidence consisted of the written statement together with [the] photographs. But … there was no evidence which linked … the position of the car as shown in the photographs to the position at which the defendant's car was alleged to have been at the time of the offence, even though the obvious inference was that that was what was intended …

"… the photographs are by no means clear as to whether the car was within the area of what might be called the road-side verges, which would be part of the highway and part of the public place, or sufficiently within the field, which, on the face of it, was a private place. There was no evidence which would have entitled the Justices to find that that private place was used by the public so as to make it a public place.

"… it would be pointless to require [the Justices] to state a case. It would simply be better the quash the conviction …

"I repeat, the only evidence as to where the applicant's car was at the time of the offence is that of the two police officers, that it was parked just off the road, that is Bakers Lane, 'to our near side'.

"Bearing in mind that the [charge] as laid referred to the car being 'on a public place called field adjacent to Bakers Lane', and quite clearly it is possible to say that a car in the field could be described as just off the road, in my judgment there was no evidence which entitled the Magistrates to come to the conclusion which they did."

Application granted.

Robinson v DPP

Unreported, CO 53/95, 10 March 1995, QBD (DC)

On the facts of this case, a lane to which the public had access was a public place.

A defendant was charged with driving with excess alcohol and with failing to provide a specimen for a breath test. It was accepted that he had driven on a "road"; the case turned on whether the public had access to that road and, therefore, whether it was a "public place" for the purposes of s 5(1)(a), Road Traffic Act 1988. The road in question was a lane; it was not made up, and had no road markings, pavements or tarmac. It was a cul-de-sac with nine houses, the last of which was the defendant's. It was approximately 70 yards long and unlit. The lane had no signs saying it was private or in any way indicating restricted access; there was no physical obstruction preventing access by the public; a public footpath led off it. Photographs of the lane, and copies of the definitive footpath map and statement accompanying it, prepared by the local county council, were admitted in evidence.

The justices concluded that the lane was in the nature of a road; even if it was not a road, it was a public place to which the general public had access. They based their findings on police evidence of a man walking his dog in the lane; the photographs produced in evidence; the fact that the lane was not fenced against the public so that they generally could enter it; the defendant's admission that members of the public have access to it and that visitors use it to visit his and other property; the fact that the lane led directly off a High Street so that any member of the public could walk or drive directly from one to the other; and the presence of the public footpath leading off the lane. While not convinced that access had to be by tolerance of the owner, the justices found clear evidence of tolerance by reason of the lack of fencing or preventative notices, or any means to prevent access. They convicted the defendant, who appealed.

QUESTION(S) FOR THE COURT: (i) Whether the justices were entitled in law to find on the facts that the lane was a road and/or a public place.

HELD: "... there is in my judgment sufficient evidence ... to justify [the magistrates] in reaching the conclusion that they did. The test to be applied does not mean that a very extensive use has to be established. It does not require that any particular number of people who, as members of the public, must be shown to have used [the lane] ... ."

Appeal dismissed.

Taussik v DPP

[2001] ACD 10, 7 June 2000, QBD (DC)

A cul-de-sac marked "Private Residents Only" was not a public place.

A motorist had been charged with being in charge of a motor vehicle with excess alcohol contrary to s 5(1)(b), Road Traffic Act 1988. The issue was whether the place at which she had been found in charge was a "public place" for the purposes of the Act. She had gone to visit her estranged husband in a block of flats on a council estate. She parked her car at the top of an access road leading to the block where her estranged husband lived. The access road was a cul-de-sac, which led off the highway. At the entrance to the cul-de-sac there was a large sign, "Private Residents Only". Two police officers gave evidence that other people parked in the cul-de-sac; they did not say how many or how often, and this evidence appeared to be based partly upon what they had been told by other people.

Two officials of the council were called, one on each side. Their evidence was similar – that the cul-de-sac was maintained by the Housing Department, not the Highways Department; and that the words on the sign meant exactly what they said – the cul-de-sac was private and for the use of residents only.

The motorist was convicted by magistrates. Her appeal to the Crown Court was dismissed. She appealed further.

QUESTION(S) FOR THE COURT: Whether the *locus in quo* was a public place.

HELD: "[After reviewing the authorities] … was there any evidence … that the *locus in quo* was a public place? … there was some evidence from the police officers, but [it was] of a very thin and unsatisfactory nature. It is not clear whether the Officers themselves had observed members of the public at large, as opposed to the residents themselves, parking their cars in that area. It is equally uncertain whether that evidence was based on what they had been told by other persons … That seems … to be a very unsatisfactory basis upon which to approach this difficult case …

"… the cul-de-sac was, by its very nature, not a thoroughfare. Therefore, the public were not likely to pass or repass along the cul-de-sac for the purposes of access to anywhere else other than the block of flats. Consequently … it is very difficult to say that the people who used the cul-de-sac at any time were merely residents or members of the public, as a general body, which is envisaged by the authorities. In other words, they may well have fallen into the specialist class of user, as it is put, mainly those who were residents of the block of flats …

"… the notice … meant what it said, and the Crown Court found that that was the position. It was a private area for residents only. The public at large were excluded by the terms of the notice … the Crown did not get anywhere near establishing that there was a tolerance of user to the public at large … ."

The answer to the question was "no". Appeal allowed.

Planton v DPP

[2001] EWHC Admin 450, [2002] RTR 107, 6 June 2001, QBD (DC)

A private causeway linking an island to the mainland was not a public place. Justices were entitled to find that a person was driving when he was in the driving seat, with the engine running and the lights on, waiting for the tide to recede from the causeway.

The defendant had been charged with driving with excess alcohol, contrary to s 5(1)(a), Road Traffic Act 1988. He had been found in the driver's seat of his car, which was not moving, on a man-made causeway linking an island in the Blackwater River in Essex to the mainland. The engine was running; his head was against the window. At the hearing, the defendant argued that the causeway was not a "public place" for the purposes of s 5(1)(a); nor had he been "driving".

The justices found that the causeway is sometimes passable and sometimes submerged by tidal water; a Royal Mail van uses it to deliver mail; from time to time persons have been rescued from it; access to the causeway from the mainland is not prevented by any physical obstruction; there is a barrier at the entrance to the approach road some distance from the causeway but it would extend across part only of the approach. Signs by the entrance to the approach road indicate that it is a private road, saying "Private Road Residents and Authorised Vehicles only"; "Private Road No Parking"; and "Danger Tidal Causeway Authorised vehicles only". They further found that the defendant was waiting for the tide to recede sufficiently for him to proceed.

The justices concluded that the causeway was a public place and that the defendant had been driving. They convicted him; he appealed.

QUESTION(S) FOR THE COURT: Whether the justices were entitled to be satisfied that: (a) Mr Planton was driving; and (b) that the causeway is a public place.

HELD: "19. [After reviewing the authorities] the evidence in this case is wholly insufficient to entitle a court to conclude that the Causeway was a public place within the meaning of section 5(1)(a). The use found to exist is compatible with access to the residences on the island and for purposes connected with those residences on the basis analysed by Lord MacDermott in *Montgomery v Loney* [1959] NI 171 …

"25. … the engine of the vehicle was running; the lights were on; the claimant was in the driving seat. Plainly he was waiting, as they found, for the tide to recede sufficiently for him to get across the Causeway. In waiting he may have dozed or was otherwise distracted so that he was awoken by the approach of the police officers. In my judgment, in circumstances such as these, the justices were entitled to hold that the claimant was driving the vehicle."

The answer to question (a) was "yes"; the answer to question (b) was "no", Conviction quashed.

DPP v Lloyd (David Michael)

[2002] EWHC 2977 (Admin), 13 December 2002, QBD (DC)

It was a necessary inference that a defendant had been driving on a public road when his van was found stuck in a ditch on private land, the only access to which was via a public road, and there was nothing to suggest he had taken an unorthodox route or that anyone else had driven.

A motorist had been charged with driving with excess alcohol, contrary to s 5(1)(a), Road Traffic Act 1988. His van had become stuck in a ditch on a private road, the only access to which was via a public road. He went to his former girlfriend's house, where her parents called the police. When they arrived at the scene, they took the view that the defendant had been driving the vehicle and suspected that he had been drinking. A breath test was positive; he was arrested; at the police station, breath analysis revealed excess alcohol.

The magistrates found that the evidence called by the prosecution concerned helping the defendant pull his vehicle from a ditch and that there had been no evidence that he had been driving on a public road. They dismissed the charge. The prosecutor appealed.

QUESTION(S) FOR THE COURT: (1) Whether any bench of justices, properly directed upon the facts and the law, could have acquitted the respondent; (2) Whether the court's decision was perverse.

HELD: "8. … There being no dispute but that the respondent was the driver when the vehicle got stuck in the ditch, there being no dispute that he was manifesting signs of intoxication at the time, the task of the magistrates must have involved asking whether it was a necessary inference that he had driven the vehicle from a public road into the private road and ultimately into the ditch. As there was not a single scrap of evidence suggesting that he had not or that any unorthodox route had been taken, or that anybody else had been involved in the driving of the car, in my judgment, it was indeed perverse of the magistrates to reach any conclusion other than the necessary conclusion that by inference, the respondent had been driving the car on the public road prior to its entrance into the private lane and ultimately its arrival in the ditch."

The answers to both questions were "no". Appeal allowed.

R (Lewis) v DPP

[2004] EWHC 3081 (Admin), 10 December 2004, QBD (Admin)

It was proper to infer that a car park attached to a public house was a public place; evidence of use was not necessary.

A motorist had been charged with driving on a road or other public place with excess alcohol, contrary to s 5(1)(a), Road Traffic Act 1988. He had driven on the car park of a public house; breath analysis showed that he was over the limit. The magistrates convicted him; he appealed.

QUESTION(S) FOR THE COURT: Whether the car park was a public place.

HELD: "[On the argument that there should have been, but was not, positive evidence that the car park in question was a public place] 17. … it simply was not necessary for the prosecution to adduce actual evidence of the users of this car park. This was a car park attached to a public house to which members of the public would be invited by the publican. That, in my view, clearly shows that it was a public place.

"18. [On the observation in *Pugh v Knipe* [1972] RTR 286 that] 'there must be evidence that the public utilises the access' – and it is in any case to be borne in mind that [that case did not concern] a public house – … that can just as well and appropriately be taken as meaning there must be evidence from which it may *properly be inferred* that the public utilises the access. It is absolutely plain that such an inference can properly be drawn in this case, having regard to the primary evidence that this was a public house car park. There was also primary evidence that [the appellant] was in his car during licensing hours. … not only were the magistrates entitled to reach the ultimate conclusion that they reached: they were positively bound to do so."

Appeal dismissed.

Cowan v DPP

[2013] EWHC 192 (Admin), 18 January 2013, QBD (Admin)

Evidence of public use must be before the court to establish that a place is a "road or other public place". See also Hallett v DPP, page 478, to the same effect in relation to a "road".

A motorist had been charged with driving with excess alcohol, contrary to s 5(1), Road Traffic Act 1988. He had been driving on an internal roadway in a university campus. A police officer gave evidence that the campus was accessed by an ordinary road; there was a barrier which opened using a pressure pad; no identification was needed to enter; anyone could go in; there were no "private" signs, although there were signs about parking prohibitions; the grounds were accessible to students and visitors; the roads were of normal layout and had normal signs; the entrance was one-way and there was no barrier at the exit.

The magistrates found that the place in question was used by members of the public at any time of day or night without restriction; access was not limited to a special class of members of the public. It was a public place. They convicted. The motorist appealed.

QUESTION(S) FOR THE COURT: (A) Whether there was sufficient evidence upon which a reasonable tribunal might find that the campus was a public place within the meaning of the Road Traffic Act 1988. (B) Upon such evidence, if any, whether the magistrates were correct in law in holding that the defendant had been driving on a public place.

HELD: "22. The unhelpful answer which I give to the first question is that I cannot tell from the case stated whether there was sufficient evidence upon which the Justices could properly find that the campus was a public place within the meaning of the Road Traffic Act 1998 at the time that the defendant was driving. If all that there was was evidence that students, their visitors and those with business employed at the University used the roadway and the campus, then the answer which I give to the stated question, is no. If there was in fact evidence of use by members of the public for not counting within those categories, the answer would be yes. I simply cannot tell from the case whether or not that was so. …

"[After lengthy discussion on the possible disposals] 85. … The evidence set out in the case does not support the conclusion [that the place on which the alleged offence occurred was a public place]. I am bound by the evidence in the case unless I choose to remit the case to the Justices for amendment under section 28(a). It is simply too late to do that. … I have concluded that the evidence does not support the findings."

The answers to the questions were "no". Appeal allowed.

Scott Richardson v DPP

[2019] EWHC 428 (Admin), [2019] 4 WLR 46, 28 February 2019, QBD (Admin)

On the facts – no evidence as to exactly where in a car park serving several businesses the appellant had parked; no evidence of use by the public; even if the public did use the car park, there was no evidence that they had permission to do so – the car park in question was not a public place.

The appellant had been convicted of being in charge of a motor vehicle on a road or other public place while unfit through drink, contrary to s 4(2), Road Traffic Act 1988. He had parked on a car park which served several businesses, including a pub where the appellant worked, although he was not working on the day in question. He argued that the car park was not a public place for the purposes of the offence. The justices found that the car park had no physical restrictions on access; there were a number of different signs for different parking spaces; and the appellant had parked as a member of the public as he was not working at the time. They convicted him and he appealed.

QUESTION(S) FOR THE COURT: Whether the prosecution had brought sufficient evidence for a reasonable tribunal properly directed to conclude that the relevant location was a public place.

HELD: "29. … The photographs [in evidence] show that the car park serves a number of businesses. There are a number of different forms of sign in different areas of the car park, all strongly indicating that parking by the public is not permitted. In some areas (and by one of the entrances) there are signs saying 'Private Property Strictly No Unauthorised Parking'. By other parking spaces there are signs saying 'Staff Parking', and by other spaces signs saying 'Private Car Park'. Strikingly, on a wall above two other spaces is a sign saying:

> Private Car Park
> These 2 spaces are private car park spaces
> Only for the use of our employees.
> If you park here you run the risk of being fined for trespass and/or blocked in.
> So, please do not park here at any time.

"30. … [The car park] … appears to comprise several different car parking areas, for use by different groups of persons, at least some of which were unquestionably and explicitly private. There was no finding by the justices as to exactly where the Appellant parked. If he had parked under the sign I have set out above, then there could be little question but that he had parked in a private area. The sign could be hardly more explicit. This deficiency alone means the conviction cannot stand. The Appellant had to be 'in charge' of his vehicle in a public place and given that … that question depended on exactly where in the car park he had parked, the absence of any evidence or finding about where he parked is fatal to the conviction.

"31. A second problem for the prosecution was the absence of evidence of any use by the public, as opposed to members of the public who happened to have business at the premises served by the car park …

"33. The third problem faced by the prosecution is the absence of any evidence that even if, contrary to the evidence and the signs in the photographs, the public did in fact use the car park, they had lawful permission to do so either explicitly, implicitly or as the result of tolerance by the owners of the land in question. Again, this absence of evidence and factual finding is fatal to the conviction.

"34. … The fact that there are no physical barriers is not of itself sufficient to establish that a car park is a public place … Also, true it is that the Appellant parked as a member of the public (in the sense that he was not at work at the pub at the time). But as I have said, there was no evidence that he was entitled to do so lawfully because there was no evidence of general tolerated use by the public. The mere fact that the photographs showed cars parked in the car park was not sufficient because they could have belonged to the staff of the businesses served by the car park, who were entitled to park there. And … the presence of signs … weighed against the prosecution. That is because, with the exception of [one particular] sign inviting patients to park, all of the other signs made clear in different ways that public parking was not allowed and that the car park was private."

Appeal allowed.

11. ROAD

See s 192(1), Road Traffic Act 1988: in relation to England and Wales, "road" means any highway and any other road to which the public has access, and includes bridges over which a road passes. See also Barrett v DPP [2009] EWHC 423 (Admin), [2010] RTR 2.

Lang v Hindhaugh

[1986] RTR 271, 17 March 1986, QBD (DC)

A footpath falling within the definition of "highway" was a road for the purposes of the Road Traffic Act 1972.

A motor cyclist had been convicted of, *inter alia*, driving a motor vehicle on a road with excess alcohol, contrary to s 6(1)(a), Road Traffic Act 1972 as substituted by s 25 and Sch 8, Transport Act 1981. He had been riding on a public footpath listed for that purpose under the National Parks and Access to the Countryside Act 1949; it was 4–5 feet wide; had formerly been surfaced but had deteriorated; there were potholes in it and bushes growing between the fences on either side; it was not designed for motor vehicles, not passable by a car, had no street lamps or bollards; there was no indication that motor cyclists were forbidden from using it and no barrier to prevent access.

The motor cyclist contended that the path was not a "road" for the purposes of s 196(1), Road Traffic Act 1972. The justices rejected that argument. The motor cyclist's appeal to the Crown Court failed, that court finding that although the path was not a road within the ordinary meaning of that word, it was a highway, and "road" in s 196(1), Road Traffic Act 1972 was to be construed as including any road to which the public had access and any highway.

QUESTION(S) FOR THE COURT: Whether: (i) for the purposes of the Road Traffic Act 1972 a highway which was not a road within the ordinary meaning of that word was a "road" within the meaning of s 196(1), Road Traffic Act 1972; (ii) whether the Crown Court was right to reject the defendant's submissions and dismiss the appeal.

HELD: "… [the path] was a highway because it was a public footpath and had been for quite a long time. It is conceded by [counsel for the appellant] that the finding that it was a highway cannot be challenged.

"… section 196(1) … is the general interpretation section of the Act. Highway is not defined … Road is defined. The definition is '… "road" means any highway and any other road to which public has access, and includes bridges over which a road passes …'.

"… Highways are anywhere that the public had a right to pass and re-pass, either on foot or with animals or in vehicles, as the case may be. If they are only fit for travelling on foot, they are footpaths, but they will still be highways if the public had the right to use them for that purpose. This clearly was a footpath. It also was that kind of a footpath which was a highway.

"… once it is established that this was a highway, this footpath fell within the definition of road in section 196 and accordingly the Crown Court were entirely correct in dismissing the appeal … whether a road is a road within the ordinary meaning of the word is irrelevant."

Appeal dismissed.

Brewer v DPP

[2004] EWHC 355 (Admin), [2005] RTR 5, 11 February 2004, QBD (DC)

A station car park, through which station staff drove to gain access to a staff car park, was not a road.

A motorist had been charged, *inter alia*, with driving with excess alcohol on a road, contrary to s 5(1)(a), Road Traffic Act 1988. He had been seen driving slowly but erratically on a railway station car park. He was arrested and blood analysis proved positive. The car park was bordered partly by a fence. Access was via a button-operated barrier. Pedestrians had access through the car park to one of the station platforms; staff drove through it to the staff car park. The motorist contended that the car park was not a road for the purposes of s 5(1)(a).

The magistrates found that the prime function of the car park was the parking of cars, but that both pedestrians and motorists also used it as a through route; they concluded that it was a road and convicted the motorist. He appealed.

QUESTION(S) FOR THE COURT: Whether, on the facts found, the justices were correct in law to find that the appellant was driving on a road as defined by the Road Traffic Act 1988.

HELD: "6. … It is to be noted that the prosecution … did not seek to amend the charge … so that it alleged driving on a road 'or other [public] place'.

"7. … having regard to [*Cutter v Eagle Star Insurance* [1998] 4 All ER 417] the characteristics of a road are that it is defined or definable as a way, that it has ascertained or ascertainable edges, that it leads from one point to another and that it has the function of serving as a means of access. …

"20. … the only feature of the present case, on the findings of the justices, which is capable of rendering this car park a road … is that staff drove cars through this car park on their way to the staff car park. In my judgment that is insufficient, having regard to the other considerations to which Lord Clyde [in *Cutter v Eagle Star*] draws attention, to render this car park capable of being a road. It follows that there are no findings made by the justices which are … capable of sustaining the conclusion that this car park was a road."

Appeal allowed.

R (Dunmill) v DPP

[2004] EWHC 1700 (Admin), 5 July 2005, QBD (Admin)

In this case, there was no evidence that a camp site was a road.

A motorist had been charged with driving with excess alcohol on a road, contrary to s 5(1)(a), Road Traffic Act 1988. His vehicle had collided with a caravan on a grass area of a camp site. He was arrested and breath analysis revealed excess alcohol. At the trial, the issue was whether the place where he had been driving was a road for the purposes of the Road Traffic Act 1988. The justices found that it was, and convicted the motorist. He appealed.

QUESTION(S) FOR THE COURT: Whether on the evidence the justices were entitled to find that: (1) the grass area on the camp site was a road for the purposes of the Act; (2) the motorist had driven on a road with excess alcohol.

HELD: "10. … the charge … was a charge of driving on a road within the meaning of the Act. The charge did not include the … words 'or other public place', which is the form in which such charges are normally preferred. There was no application … to amend the charge … notwithstanding … that one of the issues would be whether the relevant driving had occurred on what was properly to be termed 'a road' within the meaning of the Act.

"15. … it seems to me that … the justices did not adequately consider … whether the area on which [the appellant] had been driving was 'a road' … What [the justices] seem to have done … is to decide simply that a road was a place to which the public had access. That is not the only question to be resolved in deciding what is a road. The rest of their findings … are all related to the question of public access, without consideration as to whether this was a road at all. …

"16. Looking at the evidence … the only material that we find is that the collision … occurred on a grass area, and there was the evidence of … skid marks, not necessarily near the collision site, but apparently near the tent where the appellant had been staying, which strayed onto a roadway. It does not seem to me … that that slender evidence was sufficient to take the site in this case out of what one might generically have thought a caravan site to be, namely not 'a road' as such. Moreover, it seems to me that those two features of evidence were not sufficient in any event to establish this as being a road within the meaning of the charge."

The answers to both questions were "no". Appeal allowed.

Hallett v DPP

[2011] EWHC 488 (Admin), 8 March 2011, QBD (Admin)

Evidence of public use must be before the court to establish that the place where an offence is said to have been committed is a "road or other public place". See also Cowan v DPP, page 473, to the same effect in relation to a "public place".

A motorist had been charged with driving with excess alcohol, contrary to s 5(1), Road Traffic Act 1988. He had been driving on a service road running parallel to a main road; twenty houses led off the service road; forty or more people had access to the houses; the service road was open at both ends; there were "give way" markings at each end; it was not a cul-de-sac; the residents were responsible, by covenant, to maintain the road, but did not in fact maintain it; there was no signage indicating the road was private or that access was prohibited; pedestrians had access to the road to reach a footpath and to cross the road to continue along the footpath.

The motorist was convicted and appealed.

QUESTION(S) FOR THE COURT: Whether there was any evidence upon which a reasonable tribunal might find that the service road was a road or other public place with the meaning of the Road Traffic Act 1988.

HELD: "10. … The key question is whether there were before the Bench evidence of public use of the unmade 'service road'.

"14. … Photographs show that two swathes of green run parallel to each other and to the [main road]. Separating the swathes is a footpath, accepted as a public road. The public can walk along the footpath and continue its pedestrian progress without crossing the mouth of the 'service road'. There was nothing before the Bench to establish that individuals other than householders and those in a special class used the latter. In short, the Respondent led no evidence of public use.

"15. … There was no or no adequate evidence before the Bench of the use by the public of the "service road" such as to bring it within the definition of a public road set out in the authorities."

The answer to the question was "no". Case remitted to the magistrates' court with a direction to acquit.

Avery v DPP

[2011] EWHC 2388 (Admin), [2012] RTR 8, 28 July 2011, QBD (DC)

Where part only of a vehicle encroached onto a public place, even though the wheels remained on private property, the driver was nevertheless "on a road" for the purposes of the legislation.

A motorist had been charged with driving with excess alcohol, contrary to s 5(1), Road Traffic Act 1988. He had parked his car on his brother's drive. He had driven in, across the pavement, and parked the car so that the rear end faced the road. Later, he found that a neighbour's Ford Focus was also parked outside the same house, with the offside on the pavement and the onside on the road, but so that pedestrians could still pass along the pavement. He decided to adjust the position of his car, which he did by moving it backwards and forwards. During the course of these manoeuvres, the rear end of the defendant's car hit the Ford Focus. The wheels of the defendant's car did not leave his brother's property. The defendant was found to have excess alcohol. It was agreed that the pavement was part of the road. The magistrates convicted him and he appealed.

QUESTION(S) FOR THE COURT: Whether, if a vehicle encroaches onto an area which would constitute a road, but the tyres do not leave private land, the driver could be found to have driven "on a road".

HELD: "16. … it is not necessary that there should be any contact between vehicle and road surface. … the only issue is whether there has been sufficient occupation of road space for the protective purposes of the statute to be engaged. This is demonstrably the case where, as here, the encroachment on the road is sufficiently substantial to cause damage and to show a potential for causing injury to pedestrian and vehicular user alike, although the happening of an accident or a near miss is, I accept, not essential to show the necessary occupation of road space. …

"18. Any material encroachment on the air space vertically above the road is, in my view, sufficient to justify a conclusion that the vehicle concerned was on the road.

"19. Since the rear overhang of the car in the present case hit the Ford Focus, it can simply be asked …: was the boot of the car on the driveway when it hit the parked car? … the legislation seeks to protect the public from the effects of drunken driving in a place where they might be expected to pass and re-pass in safety. … If the answer is that the boot is not on the driveway, as the answer must be here, then where was it? … on the road. The extent to which the rest of the vehicle was still on private property does not matter, provided only that the intrusion into the road could not properly be described as minimal. That could not be the case here."

Appeal dismissed.

Chapter 9

Defences

1. AUTREFOIS ACQUIT

Broadbent v High
[1985] RTR 359, 25 October 1984, QBD (DC)

Where the prosecution elected to proceed on the basis of one of two informations, the doctrines of autrefois acquit and res judicata did not arise.

A motor cyclist had been convicted, under s 6(1), Road Traffic Act 1972 as substituted by s 25 and Sch 8, Transport Act 1981, of driving with excess alcohol. Breath analysis produced a reading of 40 µg alcohol in 100 ml breath; the motor cyclist elected, under s 8(6), Road Traffic Act 1972 (lower breath reading no more than 50 µg alcohol in 100 ml breath – since re-enacted as s 8(2), Road Traffic Act 1988 and now repealed; see page v), to provide a specimen of blood instead, which was found to contain not less than 83 mg alcohol in 100 ml blood. The information was originally in error in alleging that he had driven having consumed so much alcohol that the "proportion in his blood exceeded the prescribed limit, as ascertained by a specimen of breath …". Rather than amend the information, the prosecution had issued a new information, which correctly referred to blood. Before the trial began, the defendant put the prosecution to an election as to which information should be proceeded on; the prosecutor elected the second, and the justices dismissed the first. The motor cyclist appealed against conviction.

QUESTION(S) FOR THE COURT: Whether, in the circumstances, the second information should properly have been considered as *res judicata* and whether the justices were correct in allowing the prosecutor to proceed on the second information when no evidence had been offered on the original information.

HELD: "[In respect of the motorist's argument of *autrefois acquit*] Where, as here, there has been the kind of error, … by the prosecution and which has led to the justices quite properly – especially at the invitation of the defence – to put the prosecution to election as to which of two informations it would proceed on, the doctrine of *autrefois acquit* has in my judgment no place …

"The doctrine of *res judicata* has no application to these circumstances as there had been no trial on the merits … The justices were certainly correct … in allowing the prosecutor to proceed at his election on the second information having decided not to proceed on the first."

Appeal dismissed.

DPP v Porthouse

[1989] RTR 177, [1989] Crim LR 224, 20 October 1988, QBD (DC)

Where an information was so faulty in form and content that the defendant could never have been in jeopardy on it, its dismissal could not give rise to a defence of autrefois acquit on a second, corrected, information.

An information against the defendant alleged that he was "… in charge of a motor vehicle … in a public place … and was unfit to drive having consumed so much alcohol that the proportion in his breath exceeded the prescribed limit, contrary to section 5 of the Road Traffic Act 1972". When the matter came before the justices, the prosecutor substituted for the defective information an information that the defendant was "in charge of a motor vehicle … after consuming so much alcohol that the proportion of it in his breath exceeded the prescribed limit, contrary to section 6(1) of the Road Traffic Act 1972". The defendant had already pleaded not guilty to the first information, and pleaded not guilty to the second. The prosecutor elected to proceed on the second information and offered no evidence on the first, which the justices dismissed. It was submitted on behalf of the defendant that the second information should be dismissed on the principle of *autrefois acquit*, and the justices did so. The prosecutor appealed.

QUESTION(S) FOR THE COURT: (1) Whether the justices were entitled to find that the principle of *autrefois acquit* was applicable to the second information; (2) whether they were right to dismiss the second information before evidence had been heard in relation to either information.

HELD: "As an actual plea of *autrefois acquit* or *autrefois convict* can only be raised at a trial on indictment, it cannot be entered in a magistrates' court, but the same principles apply. More usually the issue in such cases is whether the offence charged on the second occasion 'is the same or is in effect or is substantially the same as' the offence charged on the first occasion … [Here], however, the real issue is whether the defendant was on risk in relation to the first information and whether there was a sufficient adjudication upon it by the justices to bring the principle into operation.

"The first information … was clearly defective. It referred to section 5 of the Road Traffic Act 1972 but the particulars combined sections 5 and 6 … [it] was clearly objectionable. If a conviction had been recorded upon it, that conviction would have been quashed.

"… the first information was so faulty in form and content that the defendant could never have been in jeopardy upon it and thus its dismissal could not give rise to any defence of *autrefois acquit* on the second information."

The answers to the questions were "no". Appeal allowed.

R v Truro & South Powder JJ ex p McCullagh

[1991] RTR 374, 18 June 1990, QBD (DC)

Where the defendant established the defence of no likelihood of driving and was acquitted of being in charge with excess alcohol, but was later charged with driving with excess alcohol at an earlier time, the acquittal on the first matter did not necessarily lead to acquittal on the second, and the defence of autrefois acquit was not available.

A motorist had been acquitted of being in charge with excess alcohol, contrary to s 6(1)(a), Road Traffic Act 1972 as substituted by s 25 and Sch 8, Transport Act 1981; he had established the statutory defence under s 6(2), Road Traffic Act 1972 as likewise substituted, that there was no likelihood of his driving while over the limit. The police then found witnesses who could testify that the motorist had been driving on the occasion in question, and charged him with driving with excess alcohol, contrary to s 6(1)(a), Road Traffic Act 1972 as likewise substituted. The motorist pleaded *autrefois acquit*, which was rejected by the justices.

The motorist sought, by way of judicial review, an order prohibiting the justices from proceeding with hearing the summons.

GROUND(S) FOR THE APPLICATION: (a) The essential ingredients of the charge of driving with excess alcohol would have been sufficient to have convicted on the first charge of being in charge with excess alcohol; the justices, therefore, should have exercised their general and inherent power to prevent the abuse of their process, the principle underlying the plea of *autrefois acquit* being available to the applicant; (b) the second information was laid 2 days before the expiration of the 6 months' limitation period; that delay was unconscionable and the justices should have exercised their discretion to stay the second summons; (c) the second summons was founded on the same facts as the first, and the justices should have exercised their discretion to stay it.

HELD: "The plea of *autrefois acquit* or the analogous defence available in the magistrates' court has been well known to the common law for many years … The test … is whether the acquittal on the first charge, that is of being in charge of a motor vehicle, necessarily involved an acquittal on the second charge, that is of driving a motor vehicle with excess alcohol in the body. It is quite plain that of course it did not … first, because the applicant was acquitted on the first charge on the ground, not that the justices were not satisfied that he was in charge of the motor vehicle, but by reference to the statutory defence; and, secondly, because the evidence in relation to the first charge related to a later time than the period during which it is alleged that the applicant was driving … the defence of *autrefois acquit* was not available … ."

Application dismissed.

Williams (Alan Davies) v DPP

[1991] RTR 214, 20 March 1991, QBD (DC)

On the facts of this case (error in the information; amended information issued), the defendant was never in jeopardy on the first information and the defence of autrefois acquit did not therefore arise. In the requirement to serve the certificate of blood analysis not later than 7 days before the hearing, "hearing" means the hearing at which the evidence is to be given, not a preliminary hearing.

A motorist had been charged with driving with excess alcohol, contrary to s 6(1)(a), Road Traffic Act 1972 as substituted by s 25 and Sch 8, Transport Act 1981. At the police station, breath analysis revealed less than 50 μg alcohol in 100 ml breath and the motorist elected to provide a blood specimen instead under s 8(6), Road Traffic Act 1972 as likewise substituted (lower breath reading no more than 50 μg alcohol in 100 ml breath – since re-enacted as s 8(2), Road Traffic Act 1988 and now repealed; see page v). The prosecutor later served a certificate of the positive blood analysis, but the summons referred to excess alcohol in breath. At the hearing, before a plea was taken, the motorist took as a preliminary point that the breath analysis could not be used since a blood specimen had been provided instead. That was accepted by the prosecutor, who applied for an adjournment so that the summons could be amended. The adjournment was refused and the magistrates dismissed the charge.

The prosecution later laid a fresh information alleging excess blood alcohol; the summons and a certificate of the blood analysis were served on the motorist 3 days before he was required to appear before the court. At that hearing, he pleaded not guilty and the matter was adjourned for trial for some 6 weeks. At the trial, the motorist submitted that the certificate had not been properly served, s 10(3), Road Traffic Act 1972 requiring that the certificate be served not later than 7 days before the hearing; and pleaded *autrefois acquit* on the basis that the original summons had been dismissed.

The magistrates rejected these submissions and convicted the motorist. He appealed.

QUESTION(S) FOR THE COURT: Whether the words "not later than seven days before the hearing" in s 10(5), Road Traffic Act 1972 referred to a preliminary hearing, as was the case when the plea was entered but no evidence called, or to a hearing where evidence was heard; (b) whether the defendant was acquitted of the charge when he first appeared before the court, no plea was entered and the original charge dismissed; and (c) whether the prosecution were entitled to proceed against the defendant in respect of the second information founded on the same facts, having regard to the dismissal of the first information.

HELD: "[On the argument of *autrefois acquit*] … we have to consider two possible situations in which a defendant may or may not be in jeopardy. The first is … whether the proceedings had reached such a stage that [the defendant] was in peril of conviction. The second is … whether the imperfection … of the proceedings which led to the original decision in the defendant's favour was of such a kind that he would never have been in danger of conviction …

"… the … time at which the defendant becomes in peril had to be some formal stage at or after the start of the proceedings …

"… in proceedings before justices [when the plea is taken] is the logical moment whereat a defendant begins to be in peril of a conviction. Although it could be said that when a preliminary point is taken before plea, battle has been joined, as it were, yet all that is due to happen at that stage is that the point is decided for or against the defendant; he is not in peril of conviction of the charge …

"… Realistically, the reason … the defendant escaped conviction on the first hearing was because the prosecution had framed the charge incorrectly … the defendant could never have been convicted. It follows … that he was never in jeopardy within the meaning of the phrase as applicable to the doctrine of autrefois acquit."

"[On the service of the certificate] … the sensible interpretation is that the hearing should refer to the hearing at which the purported evidence will be given."

Appeal dismissed.

2. CONSUMING ALCOHOL AFTER CEASING TO DRIVE

For the defence under s 15(3), Road Traffic Offenders Act 1988 (consumption of alcohol after ceasing to drive which took the driver over the limit), see page 314 et seq.

3. DURESS/NECESSITY

DPP v Jones (Jeremy)

[1990] RTR 33, 11 October 1989, QBD (DC)

Where a defendant drove to escape danger, the defence of necessity did not avail him except for the initial part of the journey.

A motorist had been charged with driving with excess alcohol, contrary to s 6(1)(a), Road Traffic Act 1972 as substituted by s 25 and Sch 8, Transport Act 1981. He had been drinking at a public house; a friend drove his car to the public house to pick him up; an altercation broke out in the car park; the motorist was confronted by another person who hit him on the head; the motorist tried to evade him; he got into the car and locked himself in. Finally, he decided his only means of escape was to drive away; he did drive away, but on the journey did not check whether he was being followed. When the police later arrived at his house, they suspected he had been drinking and breath analysis showed excess alcohol.

The magistrates accepted the motorist's argument that he had a defence of necessity, akin to the defence of duress, finding that the course adopted by him was reasonable in the circumstances; they acquitted him. The prosecutor appealed.

QUESTION(S) FOR THE COURT: (a) Whether the justices were correct in law to find that the defence of duress/necessity was available to the defendant on the evidence before them; (b) whether the justices were entitled to find that the defence of duress/necessity extended to excuse the whole period of the defendant's driving on the evidence before them.

HELD: "… I can quite follow how the defence of necessity was available for the defendant for a part of the journey to his house. Before the justices it was submitted on behalf of the prosecutor that there was no necessity for him to drive all the way home. The justices found as a fact that the defendant did not even bother to check whether he was being pursued …

"In these circumstances, … the defence of necessity did not avail the defendant other than for the initial part of the journey … He could easily … have pulled into a side road or into some other convenient place and proceeded for the rest of his journey home on foot."

The answers to both questions were "no". Appeal allowed.

DPP v Bell (Derek)

[1992] RTR 335, [1992] Crim LR 176, 1 November 1991, QBD (DC)

Where a defendant drove away in fear of personal injury, and there was no evidence that he drove for longer than was necessary, the defence of duress was upheld.

A motorist had been charged with driving with excess alcohol, contrary to s 6(1), Road Traffic Act 1972 as substituted by s 25 and Sch 8, Transport Act 1981. He had been drinking at various places with three friends; the defendant was driving them in his own car; at the end of the evening, the three friends got into the car, which was parked in a car park, and waited for the defendant to come and drive them home; he was talking to someone on a coach which was also in the car park; trouble broke out which caused the defendant to hurry back to his car, being pursued by others. His friends came to his aid, but were outnumbered. He drove off with one of his party, in terror of serious personal injury.

Before the justices, he contended that he had been driving under duress. The defence failed before the justices, but succeeded on appeal to the Crown Court, which quashed the conviction. The prosecutor appealed.

QUESTION(S) FOR THE COURT: Whether, in view of the finding of fact that, at the time the trouble arose in the car park, the defendant's intention was to continue to drive that evening and that there was no plan, as alleged by the defendant and his witness, for anyone other than the defendant to drive, the Crown Court was right to accept that the defence of duress of circumstances applied to the defendant's driving with excess alcohol away from the car park on account of the supervening threat of serious violence to the defendant's person at the hands of others in the car park.

HELD: "… the situation in duress by circumstances is one where the defendant gives way to the circumstances and acts in accordance with them. On the finding of fact here, the defendant did give way to the circumstance of threatened serious personal injury and acted in accordance with that circumstance for he drove off, as it was found, in terror … There is no finding that the defendant, whilst driving, … had ceased to act in accordance with the circumstances of terror …

"The prosecutor never sought to demonstrate that the defendant drove for a longer period than was necessary to respond to the circumstance of terror.

"… it being accepted the onus is on the prosecutor to negative the defence of duress once it is raised, it must … follow that the conclusion of the Crown Court was correct".

Appeal dismissed.

DPP v Davis; DPP v Pittaway

[1994] Crim LR 600, 19 November 1993, QBD (DC)

Duress is to be assessed objectively. On the facts, neither an unwelcome homosexual advance nor a jealous companion amounted to duress.

In both cases, a motorist had been charged with driving with excess alcohol, contrary to s 5(1)(a), Road Traffic Act 1988.

In *Davis*, the defendant had been off work suffering from anxiety and stress. On the day in question he accepted an invitation to go for a meal with a male acquaintance; he drove to that man's flat. From there they took a taxi; they drank wine, before returning by taxi to the other man's flat. The other man made an unwelcome homosexual advance to Mr Davis; he resisted and indicated that he wished to leave. The justices found that the advance had made the defendant afraid and in fear for his life. He ran downstairs and got into his car; the other man chased him and was violent and abusive and tried to pull Mr Davis from his car. He broke free and drove away. He had driven about 2 miles before the police stopped him; breath analysis was positive. At the time of arrest, he was neither asked for, nor gave, any explanation of why he was driving.

The justices found that the defence of duress was available where fear engendered by threats caused a person to lose complete control of his will; it was for the prosecution to negative the defence; and it was more likely than not that the defendant had lost complete control of his will; they applied a subjective test; they found that it was reasonable for the defendant to continue to drive for 2 miles because it would have been difficult to find a convenient place to stop. They acquitted; the prosecutor appealed.

In *Pittaway*, the defendant had been recently divorced and had been subjected to violence by her former husband, to the extent that a personal protection order, with a power of arrest, had been made in her favour. On the day in question she had been to a party with a Mr Perrins; they were drinking. He became jealous when she spoke to another man, and swung his arms at her; he left and she followed. Her car was parked outside her own home which was about 200 yards from the house where the party was being held. She followed Mr Perrins up the road, angry words were exchanged and Mr Perrins made unspecified threats.

The justices found that she believed she would suffer immediate violence from Mr Perrins. She hid in her car and some 4 or 5 minutes later, drove off. She drove some 200 or 300 yards before the police stopped her. Mr Perrins was not pursuing her, nor was he then in the vicinity. The justices found that the defendant was afraid of men and feared immediate violence from Mr Perrins. They applied the same tests as in *Davis* and found the defence of duress established. They acquitted. The prosecutor appealed.

QUESTION(S) FOR THE COURT: *Davis*: Whether it was open to the justices to find that an unwelcome homosexual advance accompanied by unspecified threats, taking account of the respondent's state of mental health, could amount to circumstances sufficient to support a defence of duress to a charge of driving with alcohol over the prescribed limit.

Pittaway: (a) whether the justices were correct in applying a subjective test based on the state of mind of the respondent, or should they have considered whether the respondent was impelled to act as she did as a result of what she reasonably believed to be the situation, thereafter going on to consider the effect upon a sober person of reasonable firmness, sharing the characteristics of the respondent; (b) whether the justices were entitled to find that the defence of duress was available to the respondent on the basis of threats made when the evidence was that the threats did not amount to threats of death or serious physical injury and where no history of violence had existed between the threatener and the respondent; whether they were also entitled to find the defence of duress extended to cover the act of driving given the time which had elapsed before driving commenced and the other possible courses of action open to the respondent.

HELD: *Davis*: "[Quoting from *R v Howe* [1987] 1 AC 417, [1987] 2 WLR 568, [1987] 1 All ER 771, (1987) 85 Cr App R 32] 'the definition of duress … [contains] an objective element … and this must involve a threat of such a degree of violence that "a person of reasonable firmness" with the characteristics and in the situation of the defendant could not have been expected to resist.'…

"… In the present case there is no [finding that the defendant was in terror of being caused serious injury], nor is there any finding that as he continued to drive he continued to be in such terror. On the contrary, the Justices' only reference to the defendant fearing for his life is when he was still in the flat following the unwelcome homosexual advance …

"… the Justices wrongly … applied a subjective test and never considered whether the defendant had good cause of this fear …

"The Justices also … adopted the wrong approach in relation to the two-mile journey. They concluded … that it was not unreasonable for the defendant to drive that distance … Had they considered, as … they should, whether it was necessary for him to continue driving, their conclusion might well have been different."

The answer to the question was "no". Appeal allowed.

Pittaway: "… [the magistrates' findings] do not … address the nub of this case, in three respects: first the objective considerations which Lord Lane emphasised

… secondly, the fact that the Justices expressly applied a subjective test; and, thirdly, the Justices comment in their questions that the threats did not amount to threats of death or serious physical injury …

"… the Justices … were wrong to apply subjective tests. They were wrong to approach the distance driven on the basis of whether it was unreasonable, rather than whether it was necessary. They failed adequately to consider the significance of the defendant sitting in her car for four or five minutes unpursued by Mr Perrins, or her state of mind during the following drive.

"… the Justices … should have considered whether there was good cause for Mrs Pittaway to fear when she drove. Had they done so it is, in my view, the inescapable conclusion that good cause did not arise …

"… they were not entitled to find duress was raised, nor was there any evidence that it had applied at the time of driving."

Appeal allowed.

DPP v Rogers

[1998] Crim LR 202, 15 October 1997, QBD (DC)

Where the justices failed to apply an objective test and ask whether the perceived danger was such that the defendant could not reasonably have been expected to act otherwise than he did, the defence of duress was not made out.

A motorist had been charged with driving with excess alcohol, contrary to s 5(1)(a), Road Traffic Act 1988. Police officers had responded to a report of an incident of domestic violence at the defendant's home, one of a pair of cottages on isolated farmland. Shortly after arriving there, they saw a van being driven away. They followed it along a track, at a distance of 70–80 yards; the officers were in a marked police vehicle but did not activate the siren or flashing lights. They were not sure whether they were using their headlights on main beam or dipped. There was no other lighting. Shortly before reaching the A505, the van stopped, as did the police car. The driver, the defendant, got out, walked towards the rear of the van, and looked towards the police vehicle for 20–30 seconds, before returning to the van, switching on the lights, and driving onto the road. The police vehicle followed the van onto the road where the officers activated their blue flashing lights and flashing headlights. The defendant accelerated away, but, after travelling about one mile on the road, pulled over. He cooperated with the breathalyser procedure; he appeared calm and not agitated; he did not seek to explain that the reason for his flight was that he feared violence from another person. Breath analysis showed 51 μg alcohol in 100 ml breath.

At the trial, the defendant submitted that the defence of duress of circumstances applied. He said that when he drove away from his home he was immediately aware of a vehicle following him. He thought it was driven by his neighbour, that his wife had told the neighbour about the dispute, and that the neighbour would inflict serious physical harm on him. The neighbour was said to be about 6 feet tall and of muscular build; he had a temper, shouted a lot when angry and was a disciplinarian.

The justices found that the respondent had formed a genuine fear of violence; that no direct threats had been made to him; that this fear had arisen from his activities that night; and that the defence of duress of circumstances was available to him and should be applied. They acquitted him. The prosecutor appealed.

QUESTION(S) FOR THE COURT: Whether the defence of duress can apply where there had been no threat of violence towards the accused person.

HELD: "[The justices] focus only on the respondent's belief, the subjective test. At no stage do they apply the second, objective test, as to whether it was reasonable for him to act as he did in driving the car under the influence of drink on to the main highway in that belief … They did not ask themselves, given the respondent's belief, however mistaken it may have been, that the car behind was being driven by this neighbour, who had the characteristics mentioned in their findings, whether it was reasonable for the respondent to drive his car, knowing as he did that he had been drinking that night, on to the main road, rather than taking some other form of evasive action, such as leaving the car and going by way of escape over the fields. In other words, the justices did not apply at all the second part of the test which required them to consider whether the danger which the respondent believed to exist might have been such that in all the circumstances he could not reasonably have been expected to act other than he did … ."

Appeal allowed.

DPP v Tomkinson

[2001] EWHC Admin 182, [2001] RTR 583, 16 February 2001, QBD (DC)

A sober woman of reasonable firmness would not, in the circumstances of this case (being assaulted and threatened by her husband) have responded by driving 72 miles; the defence of duress was not therefore available.

A motorist had been charged with driving with excess alcohol, contrary to s 5(1)(a), Road Traffic Act 1988. She had drunk one bottle of lager at about 4–5 pm on New Year's Eve and a large glass of red wine at about midnight. At about 2–3 am, at home in Harrogate, her husband, who was drunk, accused her of flirting and violently assaulted her, causing injuries. He threatened her and put her in fear. He also injured himself. He said he had called the police; he smashed the house telephone and the defendant's mobile telephone, and took all the money and credit cards from her purse. He then went to hospital by taxi, saying "you had better be gone when I get back".

The defendant waited until 5 or 6 am; the police had not arrived and she had no telephone to contact them. She decided to leave. She had only recently moved to Harrogate and was not familiar with the area; she had no money with her; she did not know her neighbours; she believed she was not over the limit to drive; she believed the only safe place was in Sale where her children would be. She drove

72 miles from Harrogate to Sale, where she was stopped by police. Breath analysis showed 52 µg alcohol in 100 ml breath.

The justices accepted the motorist's argument that she had a defence of duress and acquitted her. The prosecutor appealed.

QUESTION(S) FOR THE COURT: (1) Whether the justices were correct in concluding that a defence of duress was available when the defendant had driven after the person who had assaulted her had left the premises, thereby removing any immediate threat of death or really serious injury to her. (2) If so, whether the justices were correct in concluding that a defence of duress was available, having regard to the fact that the defendant drove with excess alcohol for a distance of 72 miles from Harrogate to Sale.

HELD: "[After reviewing the authorities] 31. … applying the principles of law … to the facts as found by the Justices, I am wholly unable to accept that when the Respondent left the immediate area of her home in her car and commenced the long journey from Harrogate to Sale, she was then subjected to any effective threat of violence at the hands of her husband. In any event, I am satisfied that there was no basis for the Justices' conclusion that a sober woman of reasonable firmness would or may have responded to the situation as the Respondent did and drive 72 miles over the Pennines … ."

The answers to the questions were "no". Appeal allowed.

DPP v Hicks

[2002] EWHC 1638 (Admin), 19 July 2002, QBD (Admin)

The defence of necessity was not, on the facts of this case, available to the defendant, who drove to a pharmacy to buy medication for his child.

A motorist had been charged with driving with excess alcohol, contrary to s 5(1)(a), Road Traffic Act 1988. He had been arrested and breath analysis revealed 49 µg and 50 µg alcohol in 100 ml breath. A blood specimen was taken, which also revealed excess alcohol. At the police station the motorist gave a false name.

At the hearing he gave evidence that he had been at his brother's house with his girlfriend and baby daughter. The child had become ill; she had a high temperature and was sick. He considered telephoning a doctor, but feared a doctor would not see the child immediately; in any event, there was no telephone in the house; he did not have enough money for a taxi; no one else could have driven him; he decided to drive his brother's car to a chemist to buy medication. While on this journey, he was stopped by the police. He did not mention the baby to the police or to the doctor who took the blood specimen.

The magistrates accepted a defence of necessity and acquitted. The prosecutor appealed.

QUESTION(S) FOR THE COURT: Whether the justices were correct: (1) in concluding that it was necessary for the purpose of avoiding death or serious harm to another for the defendant to drive (or for the defendant reasonably to believe it necessary to drive) to collect medication for his daughter; (2) in concluding that driving a motor vehicle with excess alcohol, viewed objectively, was reasonable and proportionate having regard to the circumstances relating to the defendant's daughter's health; (3) in acquitting the defendant.

HELD: "10. … [The defence of necessity] is available to a charge of driving with excess alcohol, but only in very closely prescribed circumstances. Once raised … the onus is on the prosecution to prove beyond reasonable doubt that the driver did not drive from necessity.

"11. Turning to the facts of this case, it seems to me that the defence was only available, firstly, if the driving was done to avoid consequences that could not otherwise have been avoided. Secondly, that those consequences were inevitable and involved serious harm either to the respondent or to some other person that he was bound to protect, in this instance his daughter. Thirdly, he did no more than was reasonably necessary to avoid the harm and, fourthly, the danger of driving a motor vehicle with excess alcohol in his system was not disproportionate to the harm that he sought to avoid.

"12. It is not disputed that he gave the wrong name to the police, although no mention is made of that fact in the justices' findings. Nor is it disputed that he told neither the police officers who stopped him, nor the police surgeon who took the blood sample, of the child's condition …

"13. In my judgment, there was no basis on which the defence of necessity could be found established on the facts that the justices heard and on the basis of their findings of fact."

The answers to all three questions were "no". Appeal allowed.

DPP v Mullally

[2006] EWHC 3448 (Admin), 9 November 2006, QBD (DC)

On the facts of this case (genuine fear for safety, but response not reasonable, police having attended), the defence of duress was not made out.

A motorist had been charged with driving with excess alcohol, contrary to s 5(1)(a), Road Traffic Act 1988. In the past she had suffered serious domestic violence. On the day in question she feared for her sister's safety at the hands of her sister's partner, and so drove to their home, with her daughter. There, she was assaulted and threatened by the sister's partner; she called the police, then left with her daughter. The police arrived just as they got to their car. The motorist nevertheless drove away; when she was stopped half a mile further on, a breath test was positive and breath analysis later showed 77 μg alcohol in 100 ml breath.

The defendant pleaded the defence of duress and was acquitted. The prosecutor appealed.

QUESTION(S) FOR THE COURT: Whether: (i) the respondent was impelled to act as she did as a result of holding a reasonable belief of an imminent threat of serious physical harm; (ii) from an objective viewpoint, the threat ceased to exist prior to the respondent being required to stop by the police.

HELD: "7. … The defence, once raised, involves the court determining two questions (the burden, in those circumstances, resting on the Crown): first, was the accused … driven to act as they did because they genuinely (even if mistakenly) believed that if they did not do so death or serious injury would result to themselves or someone [for] whose safety they would reasonably regard themselves as responsible? Second, if so, [would] a sober person of reasonable firmness, sharing the characteristics of the accused, have been driven in that situation into acting as he or she acted? If the answer to both those questions is yes, then the court must acquit … so long as the threat was effective at the time when the crime was committed and there was no available escape route or other means of dealing with the situation that a reasonable person in the defendant's situation would have taken …

"12. The justices found that the respondent's fear was genuine and at an appropriately high level, namely she feared imminent serious violence. Accordingly … [the] first (subjective) part of the ingredients of duress/necessity was not disproved by the prosecution. However … the court below fell into error as regards the second question, namely whether, from an objective standpoint, the respondent's response to the threat was reasonable. … from the moment she was aware that the police had attended at the premises, it ceased being necessary for her to continue to drive whilst over the limit in order to avoid a serious assault. Once a reasonable person knew that the police were at [the sister's] home … the only sustainable and reasonable reaction was to conclude that they would be given appropriate protection by the police.

"13. … there was no suggestion that [the sister's partner] was armed or that police officers would not be able to handle the situation. Accordingly … the only proper conclusion was that the threat of immediate and serious violence had been removed. Therefore, the half mile or so drive to the respondent's home fell demonstrably outside the response of a reasonable person. The only sustainable finding, in my view, was that the prosecution had disproved this (objective) element of the defence."

Appeal allowed.

CPS v Brown (Christopher)

[2007] EWHC 3274 (Admin), 20 December 2007, QBD (DC)

Where the driver drove for longer than was necessary to escape a threat, the defence of duress was not available.

A motorist had been charged with driving with excess alcohol, contrary to s 5(1)(a), Road Traffic Act 1988. He had invited three men to his home, where he lived with his parents; his parents were away. He had just met the men. One of them began to flirt with the motorist's girlfriend and he asked them all to leave. They did, but later the motorist received a threatening telephone call. He was afraid and decided to drive to his grandmother's home. As he left his house, he saw the three men but believed they did not see him; they did not follow him. He was stopped by police having covered about 3 miles, and was found to have 89 µg alcohol in 100 ml breath.

He pleaded the defence of duress. The magistrates accepted that it was reasonable for him to have driven away rather than call the police. They found the defence made out and dismissed the charge. The prosecutor appealed.

QUESTION(S) FOR THE COURT: Whether, in the light of the findings of fact, the magistrates were right to acquit.

HELD: "[After referring to the decision in *DPP v Jones (Jeremy)* (page 485) that the defence of necessity is not available to a defendant who drove for a longer period than was necessary] 13. I do not think that we need to consider whether the magistrates were right to conclude on the facts they found that the defence of duress was available in respect of the situation when the respondent first got into his car … [but] it is quite plain that the defence ceased to be available … long before he was stopped by the police. He was not being pursued and he had no grounds to think that he was being pursued, nor did he think that. … Despite the efforts of [counsel] to persuade us that the magistrates were justified in finding that the respondent was still acting under duress with regards to his driving when he was stopped, it is plain that that was not the case."

Case remitted to the magistrates' court with a direction to convict.

Stevens v DPP

[2017] EWHC 2839 (Admin), 10 November 2017, QBD (DC)

On the facts in this case (events of the night in question, history of relationship), the defence of duress did not apply.

A motorist admitted five driving offences, including driving with excess alcohol contrary to s 5, Road Traffic Act 1988. Police saw her car being driven erratically, mounting the kerb and veering from side to side. The officer activated the siren and the vehicle drove off at excessive speed and dangerously. The driver was stopped and taken to the police station, where she was found to be uninsured, disqualified from driving and over the prescribed limit of alcohol.

A statement served on her behalf set out a history of assaults against her by her partner, who had been a passenger in her car at the time of the offences. His conduct included threats to kill her children. She stated that on the night in question he had been drinking and taking cocaine; he had dragged her from her home partially dressed because he had wanted them to have sex in public; forced her to drive to McDonald's and when the police car came into view he threatened to kill her if she did not drive on; he was screaming at her throughout, punching her in the ribs and trying to grab the steering wheel. She gave evidence that she believed he would kill them both if she did not comply with his demands. Her partner was arrested for assault on the appellant on dates both before and after the driving offences.

The justices ruled that a reasonable and sober person would have stopped the vehicle and told the police that she was acting under duress; in fact, the issue was not raised until after her first court appearance, and her own description of the incident was that it was "not as bad as the others". The justices found that the defence of duress did not apply.

QUESTION(S) FOR THE COURT (INTER ALIA, AND AS AMENDED IN THE JUDGMENT): Whether the justices erred to the detriment of the appellant in the application of the test of duress in *R v Bowen* [1996] 2 Cr App R 157.

HELD: "24. The test in *R v Bowen* is well established. The test must be strictly applied …

"26. [The justices] found that [the appellant] had behaved in the way in question because of the threats and actual violence used. That was open to them on an application of the subjective elements of the test to the facts as they found them to be. They included in their considerations the events of the night in question and the history of the relationship.

"27. They were then required to apply the objective element of the test as set out in *R v Bowen* at 166 D *et seq*: [quoting from the judgment in *Bowen*] …

"28. A strict application of the principles in *R v Bowen* would have meant that [the justices] only considered the Appellant's age and sex. In fact, they adopted a test more favourable to the Appellant and also considered her personal history of domestic abuse. Even taking that background into account, they found that a reasonable person having experienced violence and threats which, on occasion, had not always been carried out, would not have acted as the Appellant did. A modified form of the test was applied adding a subjective element to the objective test. If there was an incorrect application of the law it was in the Appellant's favour.

"29. A proper application of the test in *Bowen* should have caused the Justices to ask themselves … 1. Did the Appellant behave in the way she did on the night because she believed her partner would seriously assault or kill her because he had behaved in that way in the past? 2. Would a reasonable woman of her age have responded to those threats in that way?

"30. Accordingly, in so far as the Justices misdirected themselves it was in the Appellant's favour. The Justices' second question should be amended to be: Did we err to the detriment of the Appellant in the application of the test of duress in *R v Bowen* [1996] 2 Cr App R 157?; the answer to which is 'No'."

Appeal dismissed.

4. INSANITY

R v Birmingham JJ ex p Jacobs

Unreported, CO/540/89, 11 October 1989, QBD (DC)

Where a defendant's mental state was such as to provide a reasonable excuse for failing to provide specimens, that did not necessarily mean that his mental state also afforded him a defence to an allegation of being in charge.

A motorist had been acquitted of failing without reasonable excuse to provide a specimen for a breath test, contrary to s 7(4), Road Traffic Act 1972 as substituted by s 25 and Sch 8, Transport Act 1981; but convicted of being in charge with excess alcohol, contrary to s 6(2), Road Traffic Act 1972 as likewise substituted. The case was adjourned for sentence. On sentencing, the stipendiary magistrate, after reading a psychiatric report on the defendant, queried how the defendant could have been convicted, and gave him an unconditional discharge. The psychiatric report said, *inter alia*, that the defendant was distraught and confused, preoccupied with religious thoughts, and wished to contact other born-again Christians; on the occasion in question, he had driven from London to Birmingham to find a particular person; he did not have a map, but thought God would guide him; he got lost; stopped his car and drank a bottle of wine intended for the person he was seeking out. He planned to sleep in the car.

The defendant's application for a case to be stated had been refused. He sought, by way of judicial review, an order of *mandamus* directing the magistrates to state a case.

GROUND(S) FOR THE APPLICATION: (a) In the light of the report, on what basis and in fact was it possible to come to any conclusion that the applicant had the necessary intention to drive; (b) in the light of the report, why did the stipendiary magistrate reject the defences of: (i) insanity; ... (c) given that the stipendiary magistrate dismissed an allegation of failing to provide a specimen of breath at the roadside for medical reasons, can he explain why those same medical reasons did not provide a defence to the allegation of being in charge?

HELD: "[On (c), and the argument that conviction of being in charge was wholly inconsistent with the acquittal for failing to provide a breath test] The two offences are quite different. In the one case the question was a question of reasonable excuse and it was perfectly open to the magistrate to come to the conclusion that ... the applicant was not capable of appreciating ... what was being asked of him.

"[On (b)] The defence of insanity is based wholly on the medical report. But the medical report makes it perfectly clear that this applicant, although he undoubtedly had delusions ... was capable of forming the intention ... of driving his car ... and in every other way leading a perfectly normal life with a full understanding of what he was doing ... There is no demonstration of insanity in any relevant sense and ... no connection whatever between the disease of his mind ... and this offence.

"[On (a)] Once it is accepted that this applicant was in charge of the car, as it is and has to be, the burden then falls upon the applicant to establish that there was no likelihood of him driving the car whilst he still had an excess of alcohol in his blood. There is no evidence whatever that there was no such likelihood."

Application dismissed.

DPP v Harper

[1997] 1 WLR 1406, [1998] RTR 200, 15 April 1997, QBD (DC)

Insanity is not a defence to driving with excess alcohol because no mens rea is required. Magistrates should not have acquitted where there was no evidence that the defendant was, at the material time, suffering from a disease of the mind such that he did not know the quality or nature of his act or that what he was doing was wrong.

A motorist had been charged with driving with excess alcohol, contrary to s 5(1)(a), Road Traffic Act 1988. He had a history of mental illness, including hypomanic mood disorder, for which he had been being treated for some 6 months before the incident in question. His doctor gave evidence, but did not say unequivocally that his patient had been in a condition of hypomanic mood disorder on the day of the alleged offence, as he had not seen him for about 6 weeks before the incident and for more than 2 weeks after. The magistrates nevertheless found, on the basis of other evidence, including the defendant's bizarre behaviour at the time, that on the day in question he was suffering a hypomanic mood disorder. They dismissed the charge. The prosecutor appealed.

HELD: "… insanity can be a defence in the Magistrates' Court, but only if the offence charged is one in which *mens rea* is an element. Every man is assumed to be sane at the time of an alleged office, and accordingly the burden is on the accused to establish insanity at the time of the commission of the offence on the balance of probabilities. The defence is based on the absence of *mens rea*, but none is required for the offence of driving with an excess of alcohol. Hence the defence of insanity has no relevance to such a charge as it is an offence of strict liability …

"… Disease of the mind is a matter of medical opinion. [The respondent's doctor] did not say in evidence that on the occasion that he was found to be driving with excess alcohol he was suffering from a disease of the mind which put him in a state where he did not know the quality or nature of his act or that what he was doing was wrong. Such evidence should have come from the doctor, if it was going to come at all. It could not be put together by bits of evidence from other people, and in particular from the fact that the appellant was behaving on the evening in question in a bizarre manner … ."

Appeal allowed.

R v Norman

[2023] EWCA Crim 1112, 1 September 2023, CA (Crim)

In a case of causing death by careless driving when over the limit for a controlled drug where experts in different medical disciplines had been instructed, it was correct not to put to the jury the experts' views on the cause of the collision. See also R v Norman [2022] EWCA Crim 1738, page 451, on the dismissal of the same driver's appeal against sentence.

A driver had been convicted of causing death by careless driving when over the specified limit for a controlled drug, contrary to s 3A(1)(ba), Road Traffic Act 1988. There had been a collision in which the driver's passenger was killed. The driver failed a roadside drug screening test. Analysis of a blood specimen taken some 4½ hours after the collision showed 5.5 µg of cannabis per litre of blood against the limit of 2 µg. After the accident, the driver was diagnosed with epilepsy, and argued that the accident had been brought about by an epileptic fit. The evidence was consistent with the accident having been caused either by drowsiness as a result of smoking cannabis, or by an epileptic fit. If an epileptic fit were the cause, the defence of insanity could be argued. Both sides instructed experts (on the effects of cannabis on driving, on epilepsy), but at the trial, both counsel agreed not to ask any of the experts which explanation was to be preferred; to do so would be outside the experts' respective areas of expertise and would usurp the function of the jury (to decide on questions of fact). The trial judge approved counsel's approach. The driver appealed against conviction.

GROUNDS FOR APPEAL: Whether the experts ought to have been allowed to give their opinions on whether, at the time of the accident, the appellant was suffering from the effects of cannabis use or had suffered an epileptic fit.

HELD: "11. Causing death by careless driving having taken drugs exceeding the specified limit is an offence of strict liability in the sense that it is not necessary for the prosecution to show that it was the effect of the drugs which caused an offender to drive carelessly so as to cause death. However, it was the prosecution's case that the cannabis … had in fact caused [the appellant] to be drowsy and to lose consciousness for a short while, thus causing the collision… .

"12. The appellant's defence was that at the time of the accident he suffered an epileptic fit which had caused him to lose control of his vehicle. As a matter of law this defence comes within the definition of insanity …

"13.… if the collision was caused by … an epileptic fit, the correct verdict would be not guilty by reason of insanity… for this defence to succeed, the burden was on the appellant on … the balance of probabilities. …

"20. Both parties instructed experts. The prosecution called … an expert on the effects of cannabis on driving, and … an expert on epilepsy. The defence instructed … a psychiatrist who was an expert in epilepsy, but in the event decided not to call him as there was no dispute that the appellant suffered from epilepsy and that the collision was consistent with being caused by an epileptic seizure. …

"33. … the view taken by counsel that the 'ultimate issue' [whether the appellant was suffering the effects of cannabis, or an epileptic episode] should not be explored with the experts was reasonable and appropriate in the circumstances … there were two very different expert disciplines in play … an expert on the effects of cannabis would not necessarily be able to comment usefully on the relative likelihood of cannabis on the one hand and epilepsy on the other being the cause of the collision.

"43. … there is no basis on which to conclude that the jury would have been assisted by the experts expressing a view about the more likely cause of the collision. It would have been speculation on the experts' part, straying outside their proper area of expertise, which is not permitted."

Appeal dismissed.

5. NO LIKELIHOOD OF DRIVING

See s 4(3), Road Traffic Act 1988 (person to be deemed not to have been in charge if there was no likelihood of driving while remaining unfit), s 5(2) (defence to charge of being in charge with excess alcohol – no likelihood of driving while over the limit) and s 5A(6) (defence to charge of being in charge with an excess of a specified controlled drug – no likelihood of driving). See also DPP v Janman, page 455 – the competence of a learner driver is insufficient to establish no likelihood of driving by the supervisor; CPS v Bate, page 457 – being in charge is not synonymous with an intention to drive; DPP v O'Connor and Other Cases, page 534 – expert evidence is usually needed to establish no likelihood of driving.

DPP v Frost

[1989] RTR 11, [1989] Crim LR 154, 21 June 1988, QBD (DC)

It was open to justices, without expert evidence, to find that a person accused of being in charge while unfit would no longer be unfit by the time he planned next to drive; but not to find that his breath alcohol would have been below the limit by that time.

The defendant had been charged with being in charge while unfit through drink or drugs, contrary to s 5(1), Road Traffic Act 1972 as substituted by s 25 and Sch 8, Transport Act 1981; and with being in charge with excess alcohol, contrary to s 6(1), Road Traffic Act 1972 as likewise substituted. He had driven to a party with his girlfriend; they intended to stay there the night. At about 3 am, he went outside for a breath of air, went for a short walk, and decided to sit in the car for a while rather than return to the party. He adjusted the driver's seat, where he then fell asleep and where police officers found him. The keys were in the ignition; he was difficult to rouse, befuddled and unsteady on his feet. Breath analysis revealed 97 μg alcohol in 100 mg breath; a doctor examined him and concluded he was unfit to drive. He was released from the police station after charge, and went back to the party venue, where he spent the night. At the hearing, he adduced no expert evidence.

The justices accepted that it was unlikely he would have driven before about 9 am the following morning, and dismissed both charges. The prosecutor appealed.

QUESTION(S) FOR THE COURT: Whether, on either of the matters before the justices, there was evidence upon which, properly directing themselves, they could properly conclude that the defendant, on whom the onus lay, had established the defences which the statute makes available to him.

HELD: The relevant statutory provisions were s 5(3), Road Traffic Act 1972 as likewise substituted (person not be deemed to have been in charge if … there was no likelihood of his driving so long as he remained unfit) and s 6(2) (defence of proving that there was no likelihood of driving while proportion of breath … remained likely to exceed the limit).

"There is a distinction between sections 5 and 6 … but essentially the enquiry centres around the effect of the lapse of … time … on the condition of the defendant, his unfitness to drive: section 5; or his blood/breath-alcohol level: section 6 …

"So far as section 5 is concerned … [t]he inquiry is as to a matter about which laymen can be expected to hold views and to be able, without always having expert assistance, to express opinions – namely, fitness or unfitness to drive … On the facts of the present case, [there was] evidence on which the justices could conclude that the defendant had discharged the onus … A considerable time was to elapse before 9 a.m. or thereabouts, when he planned next to drive, and … it was open to the justices, without expert assistance, on those facts, to reach the conclusion that he had proved that by 9 a.m. or thereabouts the likelihood was that he would no longer be unfit to drive.

"[Turning to s 6] the position is … quite different. There the justices were addressing a question which was not in any sense within the ordinary experience of laymen, namely the rate of decline over a given period of the blood- or breath-alcohol level. What evidence was there before the justices on which they could form an opinion as to whether the defendant had discharged the onus that lay upon him? … none … The time interval, though not insignificant, was relatively short. The alcohol level found on analysis was nearly three times the limit. There was … no material on which the justices could properly reach a conclusion as to what would have been the position at 9 a.m. or thereabouts the following morning … ."

Appeal in respect of the s 5 offence dismissed. Appeal in respect of the s 6 offence allowed.

Drake v DPP

[1994] RTR 411, [1994] Crim LR 855, 21 March 1994, QBD (DC)

There was no likelihood of driving a vehicle which had been wheel-clamped, and the presence of the wheel clamp did not constitute damage for the purposes of s 5(3), Road Traffic Act 1988.

A person had been accused of being in charge of a motor vehicle with excess alcohol, contrary to s 5(1)(b), Road Traffic Act 1988. He had left his vehicle in a car park where it had been wheel-clamped because the parking fee had not been paid. On his return, he refused to pay the release fee; he was angry and shouting; he tried to remove the clamp with a hammer. He was arrested and at the police station breath analysis revealed excess alcohol. He was convicted by magistrates and appealed to the Crown Court.

The defendant argued that he had a defence under s 5(2), Road Traffic Act 1988 (no likelihood of driving while over the limit). The prosecutor contended that the attempt to remove the wheel clamp gave rise to a sufficient likelihood of driving for the purposes of s 5(2); and that the application of the wheel clamp could be "damage to the vehicle", which, under s 5(3), the court was entitled to ignore when considering the likelihood of driving.

The Crown Court found that the vehicle was still clamped at the time of arrest; that there was no evidence to suggest it could be removed except by paying the unclamping fee; and that the defendant was in charge of the vehicle and would have driven it away had he been able to unclamp it. It upheld the conviction. The defendant appealed further.

QUESTION(S) FOR THE COURT: (a) Whether there was, at the time of the alleged offence, a likelihood of the defendant's driving while over the limit, given that the vehicle was wheel-clamped and that there was no evidence to suggest that it was possible to remove the clamp other than by paying a fee to the appropriate authority; (b) whether evidence that a vehicle was wheel-clamped was a factor which a court might regard as "any damage to the vehicle" pursuant to s 5(3), Road Traffic Act 1988 in determining whether there was such a likelihood.

HELD: "… the court was plainly entitled to hold that the defendant was in charge of the vehicle within section 5(1)(b) …

"… on any sensible view of these facts, there was no likelihood whatever of the car being driven at the relevant time.

"… a reasonable court must have concluded, on the uncontested evidence, that the section 5(2) defence succeeded unless the last point about 'damage' is right. The question then is, can the application of a wheel clamp to a vehicle constitute damage to that vehicle within section 5(3)? … there must be something which as a matter of ordinary language is capable of being described as 'damage' … there must be some intrusion into … the 'integrity of the object in question'. There was no such intrusion here. There was nothing which … could sensibly be regarded as damage to the car."

The answers to the questions were "no". Appeal allowed.

Sheldrake v DPP; Attorney General's Reference (No 4 of 2002)

[2004] UKHL 43, [2005] 1 AC 264, [2004] 3 WLR 976, [2005] 1 All ER 237, [2005] RTR 13, 14 October 2004, HL

The reverse burden of proof in s 5(2) does not infringe human rights. It imposes a legal burden of proof (that is, on the balance of probabilities) rather than an evidential burden (that is, to raise a reasonable doubt which the prosecution must then negative).

A motorist had been charged with being in charge of a motor vehicle with excess alcohol, contrary to s 5(1)(b), Road Traffic Act 1988. It was argued on his behalf that s 5(2), Road Traffic Act 1988 (defence to prove there was no likelihood of driving while remaining over the limit) infringed the presumption of innocence guaranteed by art 6(2), European Convention on Human Rights if it were interpreted so as to impose a legal burden on him. He argued that once the prosecutor had proved that he was in charge of a motor car in a public place while over the prescribed limit, it was presumed that he would have driven the car while over the limit unless he proved otherwise. If he failed to discharge that legal burden he would be convicted on the basis that he would have driven the car whilst over the limit. The risk of driving was an essential element of the offence, and the prosecution should be required to prove the presence of that risk beyond reasonable doubt; s 5(2) should therefore be interpreted as imposing an evidential burden only.

The justices found that he had not proved, on a balance of probabilities, that there was no likelihood of his driving whilst over the prescribed limit, and that s 5(2) did not interfere with the presumption of innocence, but that, if it did, it pursued a legitimate aim and was proportionate.

The motorist appealed; the High Court allowed the appeal; the prosecutor appealed further.

HELD: "41. It may not be very profitable to debate whether section 5(2) infringes the presumption of innocence. It may be assumed that it does. Plainly the provision is directed to a legitimate object: the prevention of death, injury and damage caused by unfit drivers. Does the provision meet the tests of acceptability identified in the Strasbourg jurisprudence? In my view, it plainly does. I do not regard the burden placed on the defendant as beyond reasonable limits or in any way arbitrary. It is not objectionable to criminalise a defendant's conduct in these circumstances without requiring a prosecutor to prove criminal intent. The defendant has a full opportunity to show that there was no likelihood of his driving, a matter so closely conditioned by his own knowledge and state of mind at the material time as to make it much more appropriate for him to prove on the balance of probabilities that he would not have been likely to drive than for the prosecutor to prove, beyond reasonable doubt, that he would. I do not think that imposition of a legal burden went beyond what was necessary. If a driver tries and fails to establish a defence under section 5(2), I would not regard the resulting conviction as unfair … I find no reason to conclude that the conviction of Mr Sheldrake was tainted by any hint of unfairness.

"44. I would allow the Director's appeal, reinstate the justices' decision and answer the certified question by saying that the burden of proof provision in section 5(2) of the Road Traffic Act 1988 imposes a legal burden on an accused who is charged with an offence contrary to section 5(1)(b) of that Act."

CPS v Thompson

[2007] EWHC 1841 (Admin), [2008] RTR 5, 12 July 2007, QBD (DC)

The fact that the defendant did not intend to drive until he was below the limit was not, of itself, sufficient to establish the defence in s 5(2) in the circumstances of this case.

A motorist had been charged with being in charge of a motor vehicle whilst unfit through drink, contrary to s 5(1)(b), Road Traffic Act 1988. Police had found him asleep across the front seats of his van; the reversing lights were illuminated but the engine was not running; the keys were in the ignition; the heater fan was on; the gear stick was in the reverse position; an opened bottle of wine was on the front passenger seat. Breath analysis later revealed 106 μg alcohol in 100 ml breath.

The magistrates accepted the defendant's argument that he had had no intention of driving when he got into the vehicle, or when he was woken by the police officers; they dismissed the charge. The prosecutor appealed.

QUESTION(S) FOR THE COURT: (1) Whether the justices were correct in dismissing the case. (2) Whether the intention of a driver at the time of getting into his vehicle would ever be enough to establish the defence under s 5(2), Road Traffic Act 1988.

HELD: "9. … Section 5(2) is not primarily concerned with the person's intentions. They may be a factor to be considered, but the questions to be addressed are: whether a defendant has shown that there is no likelihood of his driving the vehicle whilst the alcohol in his body remains likely to be above the prescribed limit.

"10. The Justices have simply not asked those essential questions. They have stopped short. They have merely found what Mr Thompson's intentions were at particular times. A defendant's subjective intention cannot be decisive in circumstances such as these where he is: (1) affected by drink; (2) well above the prescribed level; (3) intends to drive when he feels 'alright'; (4) would have no way of knowing when his blood/alcohol level would fall below the prescribed limit; and (5) has put forward no scientific evidence to indicate when that point might be reached.

"11. I would answer the first question posed in the negative. I would answer the second question posed by holding that there might be circumstances in which the evidence of the driver's intention could satisfy the statutory defence. I would envisage them as most likely to arise where that evidence is accompanied by other compelling circumstantial evidence, or by expert scientific evidence. However, I can envisage circumstances where the evidence of the defendant alone might suffice if it showed that he would not drive until he was in fact below the prescribed level. That would be a matter for a court to consider in the individual circumstances of any given case, and no general answer to the question that has been proposed by the Justices can be given."

Appeal allowed.

Chapter 10

Special Reasons

See s 34, Road Traffic Offenders Act 1988 – disqualification for a minimum period for certain offences unless the court for special reasons thinks fit to disqualify for a shorter period or not at all.

1. THE MEANING OF "SPECIAL"

Whittall v Kirby

[1947] KB 194, [1946] 2 All ER 552, November 1946, KBD (DC)

The four criteria for finding special reasons.

The defendant had pleaded guilty to driving while under the influence of drink, contrary to s 15, Road Traffic Act 1930. He argued that there were special reasons for not disqualifying, under s 15(2), Road Traffic Act 1930. The magistrates had no knowledge of any previous motoring convictions against the defendant; they found that retention of his licence was essential to his livelihood; in setting the fine they took account of that fact that they did not intend to disqualify him. They did not disqualify. The prosecutor appealed.

HELD: "… none of the facts found by the justices can amount to a special reason …

"… The limited discretion [not to disqualify] must be exercised judicially. The reasons inducing the court to exercise it must be special, and special is the antithesis of general. The facts that a man is a first offender or that he has committed no motoring offence for many years are reasons of the most general character … There is no indication in the Act that Parliament meant to draw any distinction between drivers who earn their living by driving or who drive for purposes connected with their business and any other users of motor cars …

"What then can be said to be a special reason beyond saying that it must be one that is not of a general character? … the reasons must be special to the offence, and not to the offender … [Quoting from the judgment in the Northern Ireland case of *R v Crossan* [1939] 1 NI 106] 'A "special reason" within the exception is one which is special to the facts of the particular case, that is, special to the facts which constitute the offence. It is, in other words, [1] a mitigating or extenuating circumstance, [2] not amounting in law to a defence to the charge, yet [3] directly connected with the commission of the offence, and [4] one which the court ought properly to take into consideration when imposing punishment.

A circumstance peculiar to the offender as distinguished from the offence is not a "special reason" within the exception.' I respectfully and entirely agree with and adopt this passage … ."

Appeal allowed.

Chatters v Burke

[1986] 1 WLR 1321, [1986] 3 All ER 168, [1986] RTR 396, 17 June 1986, QBD (DC)

Seven-point checklist for assessing whether special reasons exist. See also the cases under the heading "The Distance Driven and the Degree of Danger", page 540 et seq, where the checklist was applied.

The defendant had pleaded guilty to, *inter alia*, driving with excess alcohol, contrary to s 6(1)(a), Road Traffic Act 1972 as substituted by s 25 and Sch 8, Transport Act 1981. He had been to a party. On leaving, he thought he had had too much drink and asked someone else to drive. The driver lost control; the car left the road and stopped in a field. The defendant then drove the car off the field and back onto the road; he immediately stopped the car, which now had a flat tyre, got out, and waited for the police. Breath analysis later revealed 51 µg alcohol in 100 ml breath.

The justices accepted the defendant's submission that there were special reasons for not disqualifying under s 93(1), Road Traffic Act 1972, on the ground of the very short distance driven. They did not disqualify him from driving. The prosecutor appealed.

QUESTION(S) FOR THE COURT: Whether on the facts the justices came to a correct determination and decision in point of law.

HELD: "… seven matters … ought to be taken into account by justices [on] a submission … that special reasons exist … First of all they should consider how far the vehicle was in fact driven; secondly, in what manner it was driven; thirdly, … the state of the vehicle; fourthly, whether it was the intention of the driver to drive any further; fifthly, the prevailing conditions with regard to the road and the traffic upon it; sixthly, whether there was any possibility of danger by contact with other road users; and finally, what was the reason for the vehicle being driven at all.

"Of those seven matters … item six [is] the most important, but clearly the distance which is driven is of itself not a sufficient determinant as to whether special reasons should be found or not.

"[Looking at] the matters which the justices took into account, … The distance actually driven … was very short and that which he drove upon the highway was minimal. The manner of his driving is not commented upon as having caused any difficulty. The state of the car, apart from its flat tyre, was without any particular unusual feature …

"... [The defendant] was not intending to drive the vehicle further ... The conditions of the road are not spelt out in the case ... As to the possible risk of danger, the justices clearly had in mind the shortness of the travel upon the highway; and as to the reason for moving the vehicle, the defendant said that he had thought that it was the right thing to do ...

"Reviewing the decision of the justices against the seven criteria to which I have made reference, it seems to me that there was more than one factor taken into account here and that the evidence was sufficient to justify the view which the justices took."

Appeal dismissed.

2. EMERGENCIES

Taylor v Rajan; Fraser v Barton

[1974] QB 424, [1974] 2 WLR 385, [1974] 1 All ER 1087, [1974] RTR 304, [1974] Crim LR 188, 21 January 1974, QBD (DC)

Where the facts disclose a special reason, that does not mean that the driver automatically escapes disqualification. When exercising the discretion whether or not to disqualify on the grounds of emergency, the court must consider, objectively, all the circumstances, and distinguish the outward and return journeys. On the facts of these cases, the drivers should have been disqualified.

In both cases a motorist had pleaded guilty to driving with excess alcohol, contrary to s 6(1), Road Traffic Act 1972, but argued that there were special reasons for not disqualifying under s 93(1), Road Traffic Act 1972.

In *Taylor v Rajan*, the defendant was suffering from influenza and had arranged for someone else to take his place at one of the restaurants he managed; he was at home and intended to remain there; he had been drinking brandy. He received a telephone call saying his deputy was himself ill and unable to be at work; there was no responsible person at the restaurant to secure the premises and remove the cash. The defendant therefore drove to the restaurant. He could have asked his father, who owned the restaurant, to go, but he preferred not to trouble his father. The defendant stayed at the restaurant for 1½ hours, and did not drink while there. He was stopped for speeding while driving home, and blood analysis later revealed 102 mg alcohol in 100 ml blood.

In *Fraser v Barton*, the defendant returned home at 11.30 pm, having consumed a large amount of alcohol. At 1.30 am he received a telephone call from a friend who said she was having serious domestic trouble and asked him to go and see her at once; he telephoned for a taxi but could not get one; he called the only minicab number he had, but there was no answer. He then drove to his friend's home; he was stopped while driving on his return journey, and blood analysis later revealed 230 mg alcohol in 100 ml blood.

In both cases the justices found special reasons and did not disqualify. The prosecutor appealed.

QUESTION(S) FOR THE COURT: (Both cases): (1) Whether the circumstances in which the respondent decided to drive were such that the justices were entitled to find a special reason in respect of that journey; (2) if so, whether the special reason could continue so as to cover the journey home.

HELD: *Taylor v Rajan*: "… If a man, in the well-founded belief that he will not drive again, puts his car into the garage, goes into his house, and has a certain amount to drink in the belief that he is not going to drive again, and if thereafter there is an emergency which requires him … to take his car out … then that … can in law amount to a special reason for not disqualifying …

"… The mere fact that the facts disclosed a special reason does not mean that the driver is to escape disqualification as a matter of course …

"One of the most important matters which justices have to consider in the exercise of this discretion is whether the emergency … was sufficiently acute to justify the driver taking his car out …

"The court … must consider the whole of the circumstances … the nature and degree of the crisis or emergency; … whether there were alternative means of transport, or methods of dealing with the crisis … They should have regard to the manner in which the defendant drove … and … to whether the defendant acted responsibly or otherwise.

"… the test is not a subjective one … The matter must be considered objectively and the quality and gravity of the crisis must be assessed in that way.

"Last … if the alcohol content in the defendant's body is very high, that is a very powerful reason for saying that the discretion should not be exercised in his favour. Indeed if the alcoholic content exceeds 100 milligrammes per 100 millilitres of blood, the justices should rarely, if ever, exercise this discretion in favour of the driver.

"… there will often be a distinct difference in the situation presented to the driver on his outward journey when he goes to deal with the emergency, and on his homeward journey when the emergency has been dealt with. It will generally be much more difficult for the driver to justify using his car to go home, the emergency having been dealt with …

"[In *Taylor v Rajan*, if the justices] had really considered the nature of the emergency and seriously weighed it up in an objective way, I think it extremely unlikely they would have regarded it as an emergency at all. It was convenient for this man to drive his own car … he made no attempt to find alternative transport having got to the restaurant and having dealt with whatever crisis existed there. He drove himself home … without apparently making any attempt to find alternative transport.

"To make matters worse, on his journey home he was … exceeding the speed limit."

Appeal allowed.

Fraser v Barton: "… the degree of emergency described in the justices' case is … wholly insufficient to amount to a special reason … if all that happened was [the respondent] had been rung up by a woman friend at 1.30 a.m. and asked to advise her on a matrimonial problem, the use of a motor car to drive in those circumstances cannot be justified at all … even if one assumes there was an emergency … it is quite impossible … for any responsible bench to come to the conclusion that a man would be justified in driving to the succour of his friend with 230 milligrammes of alcohol in 100 millilitres of blood … it is out of the question that anyone should suggest that a man in that condition should drive on the road and his driving should be in any way excused at all.

"Accordingly in this case it is really sufficient … to say that the justices erred on that point alone, but if that had not been sufficient I … would have been interested to discover what steps the respondent took before embarking on his return journey … when the crisis was over. We are told by counsel he again tried to telephone for a taxi … [but] if he could not get a taxi or alternative transport, what is to stop him sleeping in the car … ."

Appeal allowed.

Thompson v Diamond

[1985] RTR 316, 29 October 1984, QBD (DC)

The facts of this case (emergency admission of his mother to hospital, defendant driving to see her without first inquiring the nature of her illness or whether it was necessary to visit immediately) did not amount to an emergency.

A motorist had pleaded guilty to driving with excess alcohol, contrary to s 6(1), Road Traffic Act 1972. He submitted that there were special reasons for not disqualifying under s 93(1), Road Traffic Act 1972. He had been giving a family lunch party at home and had consumed alcohol; his sister telephoned to say their mother had been admitted to hospital as an emergency patient. Without inquiring the nature of his mother's indisposition, he immediately set off in his car to drive from the Wirral to collect his sister and go on to the hospital in Torbay. Public transport was not available. He did not inquire about hiring a taxi or seek private assistance. He was stopped on the way by police, and blood analysis later revealed 125 µg alcohol in 100 ml blood.

The justices found special reasons, and did not disqualify. The prosecutor appealed.

QUESTION(S) FOR THE COURT: Whether the justices were correct in finding that there was an emergency; that the defendant had shown there was no alternative but for him to drive; that he had explored every reasonable alternative; and that there were therefore special reasons under s 93(1) for not disqualifying him.

HELD: "Viewing the facts here objectively … was there any emergency of any kind? The defendant had not taken the trouble … to inquire of the hospital as to whether there was any need for him to proceed to the hospital at Torbay that day or … if it was necessary to go that day, he could have left the making of the journey until some time later in the day when he could, with safety, have driven

… The sister did not give him any indication of what his mother had been admitted for. He did not ask her … precisely why his mother had been taken in.

"… If [the justices] had, as they should have, asked themselves firstly whether there was an emergency of any kind, they would, in my judgment, have been bound to say that there was not … ."

Appeal allowed.

Williams v Tierney

[1988] RTR 118, 24 February 1987, QBD (DC)

On the facts and findings in this case, the justices' conclusion that there were special reasons was not open to challenge.

A motorist had been convicted of driving with excess alcohol, contrary to s 6(1)(a), Road Traffic Act 1972 as substituted by s 25 and Sch 8, Transport Act 1981. He submitted that there were special reasons for not disqualifying under s 93(1), Road Traffic Act 1972. He had been at a public house with his wife, intending to stay the night with his wife's sister who lived nearby. As they emerged from the public house at the end of the evening, the ex-husband of the defendant's wife, who had a history of violence against his former wife, ran towards them. The defendant and his wife were afraid for their safety; the wife was hysterical; they got into their car; the defendant accidentally collided with another parked car; the defendant drove home; another car, which they believed contained the ex-husband and others, followed them. The defendant drove about 4¼ miles and pulled into a driveway, so shaking off the car which had been following. He then drove a further three-quarters of a mile home, stopping briefly at his mother-in-law's house to telephone the police and report the accident at the car park.

The justices found that the defendant and his wife had been extremely frightened and in fear for their safety; the only means of immediate transport was the car; the defendant initially drove in an emergency; the emergency continued until the time the defendant and his wife were no longer being followed; at that point the defendant was still distressed; the vehicle was then driven a very short distance without danger to others; the defendant intended to drive no further than to his home; a reasonable person would not have considered other means of transport at the time of night and in the circumstances. They found special reasons and did not disqualify. The prosecutor appealed.

QUESTION(S) FOR THE COURT: Whether the justices were entitled in law to find special reasons not to disqualify.

HELD: "… one could only properly challenge the conclusions of the justices about what a reasonable man would objectively have done and that the special reasons extended for the two minutes' journey from the mother-in-law's home to the defendant's home, if they were conclusions of fact to which no reasonable bench of justices, properly directing themselves in accordance with the law … could have come. When one looks at the case in that way, it immediately becomes apparent that the findings by the justices in this case are not properly open to challenge."

The answer to the question was "yes". Appeal dismissed.

DPP v Waller

[1989] RTR 112, 11 February 1988, QBD (DC)

On the facts of this case (driving to the rescue of a person who was in fear, then driving her away), there was an emergency on the outward journey but not on the return journey.

A motorist had pleaded guilty to driving with excess alcohol, contrary to s 6(1)(a), Road Traffic Act 1972 as substituted by s 25 and Sch 8, Transport Act 1981. He argued special reasons for not disqualifying; he had not planned to drive on the day in question, but, at her request, went to the rescue of his fiancée, who was at a restaurant. Her estranged husband, against whom she had been granted a decree *nisi* of divorce on the grounds of unreasonable behaviour, had telephoned and threatened to go to the restaurant. There was no time for the motorist to call a taxi. While driving his fiancée away from the restaurant, he lost control of the car and caused extensive damage. He was arrested and breath analysis revealed 78 µg alcohol in 100 ml breath.

The justices accepted the submission and did not disqualify. The prosecutor appealed.

QUESTION(S) FOR THE COURT: Whether the justices were correct in finding a special reason for not ordering disqualification.

HELD: "[The prosecution conceded that an emergency existed when the defendant drove to the restaurant, but in relation to the journey from the restaurant] The defendant had a duty to consider whether there was any means of concealing his fiancée from the expected husband other than taking her away in his car, and he chose, nonetheless, and with the knowledge of his alcohol consumption, to take the course which he did.

"… the justices erred in finding, albeit that the emergency continued after his arrival at the restaurant, that it continued after the defendant had collected his fiancée from the restaurant."

Appeal allowed.

DPP v Sendell

Unreported, CO/1592/87, 18 April 1988, QBD (DC)

On the facts of this case (driving to see an infirm mother-in-law who was in difficulty, then driving home), there was an emergency on the outward journey but not on the return journey.

A motorist had pleaded guilty to driving with excess alcohol, contrary to s 6(1), Road Traffic Act 1972 as substituted by s 25 and Sch 8, Transport Act 1981. He said there had been an emergency; his mother-in-law, who was 86 years old and infirm, had telephoned and said she could not see anything; the defendant, who had been at home and had been drinking, drove to his mother-in-law's home; there was no other way of dealing with the emergency. When he arrived, he found that a fuse had blown. On his way home, a collision occurred, giving rise to the breath testing procedure.

The justices found that the emergency would have continued until the motorist arrived back at his own house, and that there was a special reason for not disqualifying under s 93(1), Road Traffic Act 1972. The prosecutor appealed.

QUESTION(S) FOR THE COURT: Whether any reasonable tribunal was entitled to find that there was an emergency justifying the court's decision that the respondent's driving in the circumstances constituted special reasons not to order disqualification.

HELD: "To suggest that the matters relied upon, even the … additional matters [the respondent had telephoned his wife from his mother-in-law's house to ask her to come and collect him, but she was not at home; he knew that when his wife got home and found him not there she would assume her mother was ill; medication had to be taken to the mother-in-law from the respondent's home; the respondent had left the oven on with something in it] could possibly constitute a continuing emergency is … entirely fallacious. The idea that somebody with food in the oven, in a large city such as Cardiff, would be justified in driving when he recognises that he has had more to drink than he should have done is … an impossible contention; likewise the suggestion about the worry about what his wife might feel or the necessity to get the pills. There were all sorts of other ways in which adequately and sensibly those problems could and should have been dealt with …

"… failing, as they did, to appreciate the distinction to be drawn between the outward and the return journey, the justices … fell into error."

The answer to the question was "no". Appeal allowed.

DPP v Feeney

(1989) 89 Cr App R 173, *The Times* 13 December 1988, 30 November 1988, QBD (DC)

Driving a friend with a defective colostomy bag to her home was an emergency, but driving home afterwards was not.

A motorist had pleaded guilty to driving with excess alcohol, contrary to s 6(1)(a), Road Traffic Act 1972 as substituted by s 25 and Sch 8, Transport Act 1981. He submitted there were special reasons for not disqualifying under s 93(1), Road Traffic Act 1972. He had been drinking at a party with another person, "Miss L"; her colostomy bag had become detached and was leaking; he had thought of calling a taxi to take her home, but decided that that would be embarrassing in the circumstances; he had driven her home himself, and, 45 minutes later, drove to his own home, some 1,000 yards away. He was stopped by police during this latter journey, and found to be driving with excess alcohol.

The justices accepted that there had been an emergency, which lasted until the motorist arrived at his own home, and did not disqualify him. The prosecutor appealed.

QUESTION(S) FOR THE COURT: (1) Whether the justices were wrong in law in finding that the facts amounted to an emergency justifying the respondent driving; (2) whether they were wrong in law in finding that the emergency continued even after dropping Miss L.

HELD: "… we would not wish to fault the justices in their conclusion that, in taking Miss L home, after the accident with the colostomy bag, the respondent was attending upon an emergency …

"However, the second journey, that is the journey from Miss L's house to the respondent's house … is in a different position. The emergency … had been disposed of and was ended."

Appeal allowed.

DPP v Knight

[1994] RTR 374, 19 December 1988, QBD (DC)

Driving home because the baby-sitter had received a number of threatening telephone calls, given the efforts made to avoid driving, amounted to special reasons.

A motorist had been charged with driving with excess alcohol, contrary to s 6(1)(a), Road Traffic Act 1972 as substituted by s 25 and Sch 8, Transport Act 1981. She had been out and had been drinking, leaving her small child at home in the care of a 14-year girl. At 11 pm, she telephoned the baby-sitter and learned there had been a number of threatening telephone calls; the baby-sitter pleaded with her to return home. The motorist made various attempts to find other ways of getting home, but without success, and in the end she drove herself. She was stopped on the way by police, and found to be driving with excess alcohol.

The justices found that she would not have driven but for the emergency, and that the facts amounted to a special reason not to disqualify. The prosecutor appealed.

QUESTION(S) FOR THE COURT: Whether the reasons put forward in this case by the respondent amount to special reasons.

HELD: "[After quoting the principles set out in *Taylor v Rajan* (see page 507)] "the attempts that the respondent made to avoid driving herself [were] sufficient in the circumstances to discharge the obligation upon her to avoid driving herself if she could …

"There is … no point of principle involved in this case. The case was, on the facts found by the magistrates, as clear and compelling an example as could be contemplated of a crisis or emergency which moved the respondent to use her car."

Appeal dismissed.

DPP v Doyle

[1993] RTR 369, 7 December 1992, QBD (DC)

A special reason could not be made out where the defendant drank knowing that she would drive afterwards.

A motorist had been convicted of driving with excess alcohol, contrary to s 5(1)(a), Road Traffic Act 1988 and submitted there were special reasons for not disqualifying under s 34(1), Road Traffic Offenders Act 1988. She had successfully sought injunctions against her former boyfriend by reason of his behaviour towards her, both violent and otherwise. Two and a half weeks before the incident in question, he had taken her car without permission. On the day in question, she went to his address to retrieve the car; she intended also to retrieve certain goods he had taken. While there, he assaulted her and damaged the car. The motorist then drove to a friend's home, where she called the police and arranged to meet them at the former boyfriend's address. While waiting for a telephone call to say the police had arrived, she consumed brandy sufficient to take her over the limit, which the police in due course detected.

The magistrates found special reasons, being of the opinion that an emergency had arisen; the motorist had had a genuine fear for her personal safety and for the safety of her property. They were satisfied she had considered alternative methods of transport and that her unwillingness to abandon her car was reasonable. The prosecutor appealed.

QUESTION(S) FOR THE COURT: Whether on the facts as found the justices were correct in finding special reasons, namely, that an emergency existed which could be dealt with in no way other than by the defendant driving a motor vehicle whilst the proportion of alcohol in her breath exceeded the prescribed limit.

HELD: "… where a driver has deliberately taken a decision to drink knowing that he will or probably will drive, it is not open to justices to find that a special reason exists …

"… The reality of this case is that the defendant, having rescued her motor car from the clutches of her former boyfriend and having driven some distance to her friend's house, clearly contemplated that she would continue driving … It was then that she drank brandy. Had the justices considered the matter, it seems to me to be inevitable that they must have concluded that when she drank the brandy she did indeed intend to drive … it follows that it was not open to the justices to find special reasons."

The answer to the question was "no". Appeal allowed.

DPP v Upchurch

[1994] RTR 366, 15 December 1993, QBD (DC)

Where a 17-year-old drove his injured friends to hospital, having been told no ambulances were available and having tried unsuccessfully to get a taxi, the justices' finding of special reasons and their decision not to disqualify could not be faulted.

The defendant had pleaded guilty to driving with excess alcohol, contrary to s 5(1)(a), Road Traffic Act 1988. He submitted that there were special reasons for not disqualifying under s 34(1), Road Traffic Offenders Act 1988. He was 17 years old; he went to a restaurant with three friends; they went on foot because they expected to be drinking. A serious disturbance took place in the town that evening; 200 people and police officers from two forces were involved. The defendant and his friends became innocently caught up in it. The friends were all injured on the head; the defendant asked a police officer to call an ambulance, but none was available. They walked back to their accommodation; the friends were seriously unwell. The defendant telephoned for a taxi, but the taxi company would not send a car, in view of the disturbance in the town. The defendant then drove his friends 3 miles to a hospital. He drove at 62 mph when the limit was 30 mph, but otherwise drove perfectly properly. He was stopped by police. Breath analysis showed 45 µg alcohol in 100 ml breath. In the event, the friends were found not to be seriously hurt; they were examined in the casualty department and discharged after about 10 minutes. They left by taxi.

The justices found that there had been an emergency which amounted to a special reason, and did not disqualify the defendant. The prosecutor appealed.

QUESTION(S) FOR THE COURT: (1) Whether, on the basis of the evidence given, the justices were correct in finding that the defendant had proved that a special reason existed; (2) if so, whether the justices were correct, in all the circumstances, in exercising their discretion in favour of not disqualifying.

HELD: "It is well established law that driving in an emergency can amount to special reasons … The first question … was whether the justices were entitled to come to the conclusion that this was an emergency … head injuries are notoriously difficult to assess. The justices were entitled to consider that factor. They also were entitled to consider the defendant was a young man of 17 and that he took the decision to drive to hospital in good faith. He had been told by a policeman that there were no ambulances available. He had telephoned for a taxi and been told the taxi could not come out … He accepted in evidence that now he did realise there were other taxi firms and he should have tried other taxis, but … it was not unreasonable of him to form the view that … he would be unlikely to get a taxi if he rang other taxi firms … it was … open to the justices to come to the conclusion that the circumstances of this case did indeed amount to a genuine emergency.

"… the justices next had to consider whether in their discretion they should in fact refuse to disqualify. There were clearly factors there which entitled them [to do so] and … their decision not to disqualify cannot be faulted."

Appeal dismissed.

DPP v Bird

Unreported, CO 1606/93, 24 February 1994, QBD (DC)

On the facts of this case (driving to see a suicidal friend, drinking while there, then driving home, taking away pills) there was no special reason for not disqualifying.

A motorist who had driven with excess alcohol, contrary to s 5(1)(a), Road Traffic Act 1988, argued that there were special reasons for not disqualifying him under s 34(1), Road Traffic Offenders Act 1988. He received a telephone call from a close friend; she was in distress and said she did not want to live any more; she had in the past attempted suicide; he went to her home, as he had done in similar situations before. The friend gave him gin. Normally, he would have stayed the night at her home, but she became angry, threatened to take an overdose of tablets, and told him to leave. She would not let him use the telephone to call a taxi. There was no telephone box in the immediate vicinity. The defendant decided to take the tablets away with him. He drove home, and was stopped by police on the way.

The magistrates found that the defendant had considered walking home, but it was dark, and a country area; the distance was 6 miles along unlit roads; and that was not a viable option. They found that "there was no alternative means of transport available. The necessity to drive was brought about by the serious risk of suicide to the defendant's friend and the need to remove the means". They found special reasons not to disqualify. The prosecutor appealed.

QUESTION(S) FOR THE COURT: Whether the justices were wrong in law to find special reasons.

HELD: "… for there to be a finding of a special reason … there has to be an emergency acute enough to impel the defendant to drive. No doubt in this case there was an emergency for him to get rid of the pills. But what I cannot accept is that there was an emergency to drive them away … he could have hidden the pills. Mr Bird [said he did not think of that] … He conceded that he only needed to walk about a mile and a half and he would have come to the houses of friends and indeed to a public telephone box … his intentions were of the best, but we have to apply the law.

"… the Justices were really finding that a special reason existed in the need for the Respondent to drive home, because he was six miles from home and had no other means of transport … that was not capable of amounting to a special reason."

Appeal allowed.

DPP v Enston

[1996] RTR 324, 9 February 1995, QBD (DC)

On the facts of this case (woman crying rape and demanding money, driving with her to a cash machine), the justices' finding of special reasons was not perverse.

A motorist had pleaded guilty to driving with excess alcohol, contrary to s 5(1)(a), Road Traffic Act 1988. He submitted that there were special reasons for not disqualifying under s 34(1), Road Traffic Offenders Act 1988. On the evening in question he had met a woman whom he knew; she had been drinking; he agreed to drive with her to a public house, where she drank more alcohol; the defendant drank only Coca-Cola. On leaving the public house, they went to the defendant's flat; the defendant thought he would not be driving again that night, the woman having said she would stay at his flat. He drank 2½ cans of strong lager. The woman then became aggressive, demanding £25 and saying she would accuse him of rape if he did not drive her home. The defendant was frightened; he suggested ordering a taxi; she refused and threatened to scream if he did not do as she asked; he drove with her to a cash machine where he withdrew £30 and gave £25 to the woman. On the return journey he was stopped by police; he did not tell them of the threats because the woman was still in the car and he was afraid of her.

The justices found that the facts amounted to mitigating or extenuating circumstances, did not amount to a defence, and were directly connected with the commission of the offence. Applying an objective test, they found there had been an emergency and that the defendant was subject to duress as a result of a potential false accusation of rape which was such as to make any reasonable man act as the defendant had done; the duress did not end when the money was handed over; he had had no alternative but to drive. They found special reasons and did not disqualify. The prosecutor appealed.

QUESTION(S) FOR THE COURT: (i) Whether on the evidence supplied to the justices there was an emergency; (ii) if there was, whether there was no alternative but to drive and every reasonable alternative had been explored before driving.

HELD: "... This bench ... went through the various stages in an impeccable fashion ... they made the necessary findings of fact before approaching their conclusion. Basic to their task was to decide whether the story told them by the defendant was true.

"... justices should be on the alert not to be taken in by hard luck stories, not least in the field of special reasons ... but they saw the defendant give his evidence. It was for them to believe him or not. They appear to have been totally convinced that he was telling the truth. Once they were over that hurdle, was there any reason in law why they should not proceed to exercise their discretion not to disqualify him?

"... I do not feel able to say that a situation in which a woman blackmails a man by a threat to cry rape cannot amount to an emergency ... it is argued that the defendant had alternatives to driving ... [he] could have immediately telephoned the police, or ejected the woman from his premises, or insisted that they walk to the nearest cash point. By the way the woman was behaving … any such action or insistence on his part would certainly have caused her to cry rape … any decision by him to dump her at the cash point and not drive her home could well have had the very consequences that [the defendant] feared.

"I certainly cannot say that the justices' conclusion on the facts was perverse."

Appeal dismissed.

DPP v Whittle

[1996] RTR 154, 27 April 1995, QBD (DC)

On the facts, the justices were wrong to find that there had been a medical emergency justifying the defendant in driving, and wrong to find special reasons.

A motorist had pleaded guilty to driving with excess alcohol, contrary to s 5(1)(a), Road Traffic Act 1988. He submitted that there were special reasons for not disqualifying under s 34(1), Road Traffic Offenders Act 1988. He had been out drinking with friends; his wife was driving but complained of dizziness and blurred vision; the defendant decided to take over driving. He drove in a suburban area of Manchester; there was a telephone in the car. Breath analysis revealed 61 µg alcohol in 100 ml breath.

At the hearing, the motorist argued that there had been a medical emergency; he adduced medical evidence that his wife suffered from a condition characterised by attacks of intermittent pain in the neck and limitation of neck movement; the evidence did not refer specifically to the evening in question.

The justices found there had been a medical emergency and that the defendant had explored every reasonable possible alternative; they found special reasons and did not disqualify. The prosecutor appealed.

QUESTION(S) FOR THE COURT: (1) Whether there was evidence upon which the justices were entitled to conclude that special reasons existed; and (2) whether the facts found by the justices were capable of amounting in law to special reasons.

HELD: "… there was no suggestion before the justices that … the defendant thought his wife was in need of urgent medical attention … the justices proceeded to find that the defendant thought it was a medical emergency and could see no alternative but to drive himself … there was no evidence on which any reasonable person could genuinely be in either of such states of mind … there was no special reason arising in the first place and, therefore, no discretion in the justices could have possibly arisen. The decision not to disqualify was perverse."

Appeal allowed.

DPP v Cox

[1996] RTR 123, 22 May 1995, QBD (DC)

On the facts (the steward of a golf club driving 300 yards to the club house, which had been burgled before, etc), the justices were entitled to find there had been an emergency.

A motorist had pleaded guilty to driving with excess alcohol, contrary to s 5(1)(a), Road Traffic Act 1988. He submitted that there were special reasons for not disqualifying under s 34(1), Road Traffic Offenders Act 1988. He was the steward of a golf club and a key holder; the club premises were about 300 yards from his home; about half of that distance was on a public road. The premises had been burgled a number of times. On the day in question, he had finished work, locked up and went home, where he drank four or five cans of lager, having previously drunk two half pints while at work. He did not intend to drive. The alarm company telephoned to say the burglar alarm at the premises had been activated. Without thinking of the amount he had drunk, alternative methods of transport, or contacting other key holders, he drove to the club premises. No other traffic was on the road other than police vehicles en route to the club premises.

The justices found there had been an emergency which amounted to a special reason; they did not disqualify. The prosecutor appealed.

QUESTION(S) FOR THE COURT: Whether the justices were entitled to find special reasons, and, if so, whether they were correct in exercising their discretion in the defendant's favour.

HELD: "... For [the prosecutor] to succeed on [the argument that if there was an emergency the justices exercised their discretion wrongly in not disqualifying] it would be necessary ... to establish that no reasonable bench of justices could have found as this bench did. I certainly would not hold so ... the action was very understandable.

"[On whether there was an emergency, the prosecutor] argues that there were other reasonable methods of meeting this emergency ... the strongest is that [the defendant] should have walked ... the test is an objective one ...

"[Counsel for the respondent] has pointed out ... that had the defendant walked, he would not have arrived there as quickly ... the situation was not a static one; it was a developing one. The situation at the clubhouse could have been getting worse by the minute. [The defendant] could not be sure how soon the police would get there and the intruder or intruders in the meantime might be vandals smashing the place ...

"Having regard to all those points and after some hesitation ... the justices were entitled to take the view they did. They were entitled to conclude that this was an emergency ... ."

Appeal dismissed.

DPP v Bristow

[1998] RTR 100, 17 October 1996, QBD (DC)

Where a sober, reasonable and responsible friend would advise against driving, and there were other solutions to the problem which had arisen (fear for the safety of children), there were no special reasons.

A motorist had pleaded guilty to driving with excess alcohol, contrary to s 5(1)(a), Road Traffic Act 1988. He submitted that there were special reasons for not disqualifying under s 34(1), Road Traffic Offenders Act 1988. He had been at home, drinking. His daughter and his niece were with friends at the local park, about 200 yards away. One of the daughters returned home; she told her father that her sister and cousin had been assaulted and were being held in a house against their will. The motorist did not think of calling the police; the niece's mother was at the house and could have driven; the motorist did not ask anyone else in the house to drive; he did not tell others present what his daughter had told him; he drove the 400–500 yards to the place where he understood the children to be. Police arrived; they arrested the driver; breath analysis revealed 73 µg alcohol in 100 ml breath.

The justices found, *inter alia*, that an acute emergency had arisen; it was reasonable for the driver to act immediately; he panicked; it would have been unreasonable to expect him to enquire into all the alternative methods of dealing with the situation; his actions were not dangerous to other road users or pedestrians. They found special reasons and did not disqualify. The prosecutor appealed.

QUESTION(S) FOR THE COURT: Whether the justices were entitled to find that special reasons existed for not disqualifying the defendant, having regard to: (a) the level of alcohol; (b) the circumstances which led to the defendant driving his motor vehicle; and (c) both factors taken together.

HELD: "… the key question … is this: what would a sober, reasonable and responsible friend of the Defendant present at the time, but himself a non-driver and thus unable to help, have advised in the circumstances: drive or do not drive? The Justices could only properly find special reasons and exercise their discretion not to disqualify if they thought it a real possibility rather than merely an off chance that such a person would have advised the Defendant to drive. Amongst the most critical circumstances influencing that advice would, of course, be these: (1) How much has the Defendant had to drink? (2) Having regard to that, what threat would he pose to others when driving in that condition, given the distance he was proposing to drive, the likely state of the roads and the condition of his vehicle? (3) How acute a problem is there? (4) What, if any, alternatives are open to the defendant to solve that problem?

"… with regard to the facts of the present case …: (1) The Respondent had drunk a good deal … (2) The Respondent was only proposing to drive some four or five hundred yards … in a well maintained van on quiet and pedestrian free roads … (3) The problem was undoubtedly both acute and urgent … (4) Several alternatives were clearly open to the Respondent here.

"… The only sober advice that could possibly have been given to him was that he had had far too much to drink and that there were other solutions to the problem readily available. Had the Justices approached the matter in the way I have suggested, I believe that they too must inevitably have come to that view … ."

The answer to the question was "no". Appeal allowed.

DPP v Tucker

Unreported, CO/1572/96, 6 November 1996, QBD (DC)

On the facts of this case (defendant driving to business premises following activation of burglar alarm, justices properly considering all relevant matters), the finding of special reasons was not susceptible to challenge.

A motorist had been charged with driving with excess alcohol, contrary to s 5(1)(a), Road Traffic Act 1988. Breath analysis showed 89 µg alcohol in 100 ml breath. He was convicted and submitted that there were special reasons for not disqualifying under s 34(1), Road Traffic Offenders Act 1988.

He had been at home and had been drinking. At about 1.30 am, he received a telephone call from a burglar alarm company to the effect that the alarm at the premises of his jewellery business had been activated; the first key holder was not available, and the police would attend. Items of substantial value were kept at the business premises; his insurance company expected him to attend within 20–30 minutes of activation of the alarm. There had been burglaries and a robbery at the premises on 14 occasions in the previous year. The motorist had considered alternative courses for someone to attend the business premises.

The justices found that an emergency had arisen and that the respondent had a genuine fear for the safety of his business; they were satisfied that he had been justified in responding to the emergency himself, and that he had rejected alternative methods of transport on reasonable grounds. They found special reasons for not disqualifying. The prosecutor appealed.

QUESTION(S) FOR THE COURT: (1) Whether the justices were entitled on the basis of the evidence given to find that the respondent had proved that a special reason existed for not disqualifying him; and (2) if such a special reason existed, whether the justices were entitled, in all the circumstances referred to by the evidence given, to exercise their discretion in favour of not disqualifying the respondent.

HELD: "… no point of principle arises in this case. The first question is … whether there was material justifying the Justices in reaching a conclusion that there were special reasons. The answer to that, in the light of the findings which the Justices made, seems to me to be plainly 'yes'.

"The next question is whether there was an exercise of discretion by the Justices. I accept … that the word 'discretion' is not expressly incorporated in the Justices' case. However, when one considers the terms of the opinion which they express, it seems to me to be impossible to contend that they did not exercise their discretion having regard to the factors to which they refer.

"The final question is whether there was material before the Justices, properly considered by them, entitling them to exercise the discretion in the way in which they did. No factor is suggested to which they improperly had regard. No factor is identified to which they should have had regard, but to which they did not have regard … it follows that the decision of the Justices … is not susceptible to challenge in the way [counsel for the appellant] suggests."

The answers to both questions were "yes". Appeal dismissed.

DPP v Goddard

[1998] RTR 463, 19 January 1998, QBD (DC)

On the facts of this case (escaping assailants by driving to sister's house, then driving away from there), the emergency was over by the time the defendant was found driving with excess alcohol; there were therefore no special reasons.

The defendant had been drinking in one public house, then went on to another, "The Castle". On the way, he was assaulted by a number of persons; he arrived at The Castle, where an ambulance was called; he left his car in the car park of The Castle. The next day, Saturday, he went back to The Castle at lunch time for a drink. Then he decided to go to his car to collect his coat, intending to walk to his sister's house, but two of the assailants from the evening before approached him; one hit him in the face, breaking his nose which began to bleed profusely. The defendant ran to his car, got in, locked the driver's door, then drove to his sister's house. He next realised that one of the men lived close to his sister, and might have known he usually went to this sister's house on Saturday afternoons. He therefore decided to drive the 8½ miles to his own home. He was found to be driving with excess alcohol in blood.

The magistrates found that the motorist had been placed in an emergency situation where the only means of readily escaping was to drive and he would not have done so otherwise; they considered the emergency would continue until he arrived at a place of security; he had tried to make a shorter journey; they found special reasons and did not disqualify. The prosecutor appealed.

QUESTION(S) FOR THE COURT: Whether the evidence entitled the justices to find that there had arisen an emergency which acted on the respondent's mind and subsisted throughout his 8½-mile journey and that there were special reasons for not ordering disqualification.

HELD: "[Counsel for the prosecution] accepts that in relation to the first journey from the public house to his sister's place, there was indeed, arguably, an emergency, and the Magistrates were entitled so to find. She submits that at that time Mr Goddard was in a safe house, albeit with a bleeding nose, but with a number of options which were open to him, and driving eight-and-a-half-miles whilst over the limit with a bleeding nose was not one which was a reasonable option for him to take when he was snugged in his sister's house to which he obviously had access.

"... I am satisfied that she is right. This was not a case where, by the time Mr Goddard arrived at his sister's house, he effectively had no sensible option save to go and drive these eight-and-a-half-miles to his own house. There were a number of options which must have been available to him, including calling the police ... ."

The answer to the question was "no". Appeal allowed.

DPP v Ellis

Unreported, CO/3358/98, 2 November 1998, QBD (DC)

The facts of this case (spouse in pain, alternatives to driving home not explored) did not amount to an emergency and there was therefore no special reason.

A motorist pleaded guilty to driving with excess alcohol, but submitted that there were special reasons for not disqualifying. The defendant's wife had been injured in a hunting accident on the day in question; she was taken home, then to hospital where she was given strong pain killers and allowed home. The defendant had consumed two whiskies, one at about 11 am and one at about noon, but had not eaten during the day. He and his wife attended a dinner that evening; the defendant had arranged to drive to the dinner but to be driven home by a friend afterwards. At the dinner, the defendant drank a whisky and water, but no other alcohol. After the dinner, his wife was in pain and wished to return home, although she was not in such pain as to need a doctor. The person who was to have taken them home was not prepared to leave early; no one else was asked if they could drive; the defendant did not telephone for a taxi because, when he had done so a few weeks earlier, no taxi had been available. The defendant drove home and was stopped by police. Breath analysis revealed 67 µg alcohol in 100 ml breath.

The justices found that the defendant had not intended to drive, and that an emergency had arisen. They found special reasons and exercised their discretion not to disqualify. The prosecutor appealed.

QUESTION(S) FOR THE COURT: (i) Whether there was evidence upon which the justices were entitled to conclude that special reasons existed; and (ii) whether evidence put forward to the court amounted in law to special reasons having regard to: (a) the level of alcohol in the respondent's breath; (b) the circumstances which led to his driving his motor vehicle; (c) both factors taken together.

HELD: "... there are a number of question marks. The first and most obvious one is that the defendant was found to have almost double the legal limit of alcohol in his breath ...

"Furthermore, we do not know how far it was that he had to drive home. Nor do we know the precise circumstances which led [the friend] to decline to honour the agreement [to drive the defendant and his wife home]. We do not know whether any other guests lived near enough to offer a lift ... [the defendant] had not telephoned for a taxi ... That apparently was what [the justices] relied on to justify their conclusion that Mr Ellis was acting wholly reasonably in not seeking to find out whether a taxi might be available.

"… The test is an objective one. It is not what appeared to the defendant at the time. Looking at it and considering all the facts, was it a reasonable thing for the defendant to have done at the time? …

"… I find it impossible to say that there was here an emergency … The respondent took no steps to find out even whether a taxi might be available or whether there was any alternative to driving his car in the circumstances … The pain suffered by [his wife] cannot have been that intense … she did not require any doctor to be called, nor when she returned home did she seek any medical assistance. One can well understand her discomfort, but in my judgment it falls far short of giving a reason for driving when the alcohol content in the breath was as high as it was.

"… there was no evidence which entitled [the justices] to conclude that special reasons existed … ."

Appeal allowed.

DPP v Ubhi

[2003] EWHC 619 (Admin), 11 February 2003, QBD (Admin)

In this case, the justices did not apply the objective test of what a reasonable person would have done in the circumstances (perceived medical emergency), and there was no special reason.

A motorist had pleaded guilty to driving with excess alcohol, contrary to s 5(1)(a), Road Traffic Act 1988. He had been drinking with his girlfriend, his sister and her boyfriend, in a student hall of residence. Around midnight he was awoken by his sister screaming, having fallen in the bathroom. Her boyfriend tried to call an ambulance, then a taxi, but without success. The brother decided to drive her to hospital. He was stopped on the way; the police called an ambulance for the sister.

The magistrates found, *inter alia*, that the defendant believed there was a genuine medical emergency, and had, via his friend who made the telephone calls, explored other ways of getting help. They found special reasons for not disqualifying under s 34(1), Road Traffic Offenders Act 1988. The prosecutor appealed.

QUESTION(S) FOR THE COURT: Whether the justices were correct: (b) in finding that a genuine medical emergency had arisen given that the sister was released from hospital within an hour of arrival; (c) to find special reasons when the defendant himself made no inquiry to establish alternatives to driving; (d) to find special reasons when not all available alternatives to driving had been explored by the defendant, or others on his behalf; (f) to find that the defendant himself did not need to make any inquiry as to the alternatives to him driving but was entitled to rely on what someone else had told him.

HELD: "6. … The justices failed to consider what a reasonable person would have done, faced with the screaming which roused them from the sister falling in the bathroom. The only finding was that the respondent believed there was a genuine medical emergency …. But there is no finding as to whether a reasonable person would have acted that way.

"7. Secondly, the justices record that they found that the respondent believed that the other ways of getting help had been explored. Again, that is not the correct test. … It was important that they found whether a reasonable person would have reacted … in the way that the respondent acted. There is no such finding. …

"9. Having regard to those failures in the findings of the justices to look at the objective evidence of what a reasonable person faced with those circumstances would have done, it is plain that this decision cannot stand. …

"[On (b)] 10. … the correct question is whether a reasonable person faced with those facts would have treated it as a genuine medical emergency. …

"[On (c)] … the justices were not correct in law to find special reasons without examining and making findings as to whether a reasonable person would have made further enquiries to establish alternatives.

"[On (d)] It is not clear … from [the] question what other alternatives they are referring to, but it does seem to me that it is vital that any justices look at … whether a reasonable person would have made enquiries as to alternatives, and as to whether that reasonable person would have discovered that there were alternatives available. Should there, in fact, have been alternatives available, it will be rare indeed that special reasons could be found because the driver had not himself established the availability of those other alternatives. …

"[On (f)] … there may be circumstances in which a driver need not make an inquiry himself. It will all depend upon what the reasonable person would have done, faced with the situation that he was presented with, and what inquiries he would have made of the person to whom he had delegated the task of seeking help.

"11. … the many questions asked do not go to the root of the defect of the findings of the justices. That defect was in failing to consider the objective evidence, both as to the emergency and as to the steps that were taken to deal with that emergency."

Appeal allowed.

R (Khan) v DPP

[2004] EWHC 2505 (Admin), 12 October 2004, QBD (DC)

On the facts (perceived emergency, defendant could have woken his wife and asked her to drive), the justices correctly applied the objective test and were right not to find special reasons.

A motorist had been charged with driving with excess alcohol, contrary to s 5(1)(a), Road Traffic Act 1988. He and his wife had been out; he had been drinking but his wife had not and she drove home. Later that night, having heard that there had been a road traffic accident about a mile from his home, and fearing his sons might be involved, he had tried to rouse his wife to take him there, but she did not wake and he drove himself to the scene of the accident. He had had a previous experience of a serious road traffic accident involving a young person whom he regarded as family, and which had left him traumatised. At the scene of the accident, he was arrested and blood analysis later revealed excess alcohol. He was convicted. The justices rejected his argument that there were special reasons for not disqualifying under s 34(1), Road Traffic Offenders Act 1988. He appealed.

QUESTION(S) FOR THE COURT: Whether the justices: (1) accepting the facts of the case, could reasonably have come to their decision; (2) made an error of law in considering the case on a purely objective basis when reaching their decision as to the advice of a sober, reasonable and responsible friend.

HELD: "14. … the Magistrates approached this matter carefully and thoroughly, and faithfully applying the test as set down in *Taylor v Rajan* [page 507] and other such cases. True it is that, on the evidence, the appellant was presented with what he perceived, understandably, to be an emergency involving potentially a serious accident relating to his two sons, in circumstances where he had had a dreadful experience of that in the past. But … he was at that time at the very least two and a half times over the limit. Moreover … [the appellant's wife] was, herself, perfectly capable of driving. …

"15. … the conclusion of the Justices, to the effect that they were very strongly of the opinion that Mr Khan could have made more effort to wake up his wife who was asleep in bed, was justified. … I find it unsurprising that, looking at the position objectively, the Justices concluded that the appellant would have been advised by a sober, reasonable and responsible friend not to drive himself but rather to wake his wife who then, and in very short order no doubt, would have got dressed and driven the car herself."

The answer to question (1) was "yes"; the answer to question (2) was "no". Appeal dismissed.

DPP v Heathcote

[2011] EWHC 2536 (Admin), 5 July 2011, QBD (Admin)

On the facts of this case (driving in pursuit of a stolen vehicle; high breath alcohol reading; obvious danger; no imminent fear or threat to life and limb; no consideration of alternative courses of action), there was no special reason for not disqualifying.

A motorist had pleaded guilty to driving with excess alcohol contrary to s 5(1)(a), Road Traffic Act 1988. He had got into his van and was pursuing someone who had stolen his quad bike. He drove for about 10 minutes, covering a distance of about 1½ miles. He then saw police officers and attempted to report the theft. They smelt alcohol on him and asked if he had been drinking. Breath analysis revealed 57 μg alcohol in 100 ml breath.

The justices found there had been an emergency in that a crime was in progress and there was a realistic prospect of recovering the quad bike and a possibility of apprehending the perpetrator(s); the defendant acted instinctively; there was little other traffic and few pedestrians; the defendant had not planned to drive that night; they concluded that there was a special reason for not disqualifying under s 34(1), Road Traffic Offenders Act 1988, and did not disqualify. The prosecutor appealed.

QUESTION(S) FOR THE COURT: Whether there was evidence upon which the justices were entitled to conclude that special reasons existed, and whether the facts found were capable of amounting to special reasons.

HELD: "[After reviewing the authorities] 28. I cannot see that any sober, reasonable or responsible friend of this respondent, being unable to drive themselves, would have advised this respondent to drive. … the respondent had a considerable amount to drink, reflected by the blood alcohol content of nearly twice the permitted intake. Secondly, the danger to road users must have been obvious: it is clear that the police immediately suspected alcohol consumption. The distance to be driven was uncertain: there could be no idea how long it might be before the thieves were caught or lost in the chase. A chase in itself imports more risk than normal driving. The respondent drove for one and a half miles for some ten minutes. Thirdly, the problem was theft of valuable property but not imminent fear or threat to life and limb. A normal friend advising the respondent might well have considered that property of this nature was likely to be insured and the matter should be left to the police. Fourthly, no consideration seems to have been given to the alternatives and the facts as found suggest that there were other qualified drivers present in the vicinity who could have taken Mr Heathcote's place. …"

The answers to the questions were "no". Appeal allowed.

Key v CPS

[2013] EWHC 245 (Admin), 24 January 2013, QBD (Admin)

Where the district judge gave a reason why the motorist had not considered the alternatives to driving, she nevertheless, on the facts, applied the correct objective test.

The defendant had been convicted of driving with excess alcohol. He had been to a party, 5 minutes' walk from his home. He drove there, intending to walk back. There was a fight at the party; he was attacked by six young men. When he left the party he saw two of them outside. He got into his car. The two men came up to him and screamed and shouted as he drove off. He argued that his fear of being attacked amounted to an emergency and that there was therefore a special reason for not disqualifying under s 34(1), Road Traffic Offenders Act 1988.

The district judge found that his fear was that his car would be damaged, not that he would be assaulted, and that he drove it to avoid its being damaged. Even if he was in fear for his own safety, alternatives were open to him; he could have gone back into the party, or to any of the nearby houses, to ask for help; he had a phone but did not use it. The district judge said he did not consider these because he was impaired by drink, and rejected the special reasons argument. The motorist appealed.

QUESTION(S) FOR THE COURT: Whether the district judge erred in applying an objective test to how the defendant dealt with the emergency by finding that, because of intoxication, he had not explored other avenues as to what to do, rather than consider what he did in the circumstances he faced.

HELD: "4. …The test is indeed an objective one. …

"5. … it is quite clear that [the district judge] was entitled to decide that the emergency faced, so far as the appellant was concerned, was concern that his car would be damaged, not initially that he would be assaulted, and he got into the car in order to remove the car from, as he thought, the danger zone; but there were alternatives that were available to him, and he made no use of any such reasonable alternatives. That would be quite sufficient to justify the decision reached that this was not a case where it was appropriate to find special reasons.

"6. However, the District Judge then went on to say that the alternatives were not considered because of his impairment by drink. …

"7. … the District Judge was entirely correct. She did apply the objective test, she knew that that was the appropriate test, and the reference to the reason why, in the circumstances, he might not have considered the alternatives … certainly does not indicate that she was applying a wrong test overall."

Appeal dismissed.

3. LACED DRINKS

On eligibility for legal aid for a laced drinks argument, see R v Gravesham Magistrates' Court ex p Baker, page 634.

Pugsley v Hunter

[1973] 1 WLR 578, [1973] 2 All ER 10, [1973] RTR 284, [1973] Crim LR 247, 20 February 1973, QBD (DC)

To establish that his drinks were "laced", the defendant must show, on a balance of probabilities, that the excess alcohol is attributable to the additional drink unknowingly consumed; medical evidence is usually necessary.

A motorist had pleaded guilty to driving with excess alcohol, contrary to s 1(1), Road Safety Act 1967; he argued there were special reasons for not disqualifying, under s 5(1), Road Traffic Act 1962. He had been at a public house where he consumed two light ales and a shandy. Unknown to him, two double vodkas were added to his drinks. He was later seen driving in the centre of the road; he was speeding; he failed to accord precedence to pedestrians on two pedestrian crossings; and failed to give traffic signals. A breath test was positive, and blood analysis later revealed 161 mg alcohol in 100 ml blood. No expert evidence was adduced as to whether the added drink accounted for the excess alcohol.

The magistrate found special reasons and did not disqualify; the prosecutor appealed.

QUESTION(S) FOR THE COURT: Whether the magistrate came to a correct decision in law and whether the procedure followed was correct.

HELD: "… the onus of proof of the relevant and material facts rests on the defendant … it is for the defendant to show that the quantity of alcohol in his blood in excess of the statutory authorised maximum is attributable to the additional drink which was put into his glass unknown to him …

"… the standard of proof required is proof on a balance of probabilities that the offence was caused by the added drink, and nothing else.

"… [The onus] must be discharged … by the calling of admissible and relevant evidence … there are some cases where it can be said to be obvious to a layman that the added drink, once its nature and quality have been discovered, was the cause of the commission of the offence. An example is where the alcoholic content in the blood is only marginally above the statutory limit, and the added drink taken to the satisfaction of the court without the knowledge of the defendant is substantial … But there may be occasions in which such a conclusion is not obvious … but … unless the case really is an obvious one, unless the case is one where a layman can reliably and confidently say that the added liquor must explain the excess of alcohol, then the only way in which a defendant can discharge the onus is by calling medical evidence …

"[In the present case] … whether the magistrate took that view [that the question was whether it was obvious to a layman that the vodka was responsible for the excess] or would take that view is difficult to say, because … he did not really decide the case on that consideration … [he] should be given an opportunity to reconsider this question … ."

Appeal allowed.

Pridige v Gant

[1985] RTR 196, 27 June 1984, QBD (DC)

Where the magistrate had not allowed the prosecutor to put to the defendant that he should have realised he was not fit to drive, a finding of special reasons could not be upheld.

A motorist had pleaded guilty to driving with excess alcohol in blood, contrary to s 6(1), Road Traffic Act 1972. Blood analysis had revealed 180 mg alcohol in 100 ml blood. He submitted that there were special reasons for not disqualifying under s 93(1), Road Traffic Act 1972; he had not drunk alcohol for some years because he had a duodenal ulcer; he drank only non-alcoholic lager; on the occasion in question he had been to a party and believed he had been drinking only non-alcoholic lager; unknown to him, it had been laced with vodka; he ascribed his state of fatigue at the time of the offence to the long and arduous day he had experienced.

The magistrate did not allow the prosecutor to put to the motorist that, with 180 mg alcohol in 100 ml blood, he should have realised he was not in a fit state to drive a motor vehicle.

The magistrate found special reasons and exercised his discretion not to disqualify. The prosecutor appealed.

QUESTION(S) FOR THE COURT: Whether there were sufficient grounds in law to support a finding of "special reasons" and, if so, whether on the facts of the case, the magistrate was correct in law in exercising his discretion not to order disqualification of the defendant and not to order endorsement of his driving licence.

HELD: "… the proper way of approaching the plea raised in this case is in two stages. The first stage is to decide whether or not 'special reasons' existed … [the prosecutor] concedes that the fact that the defendant's drinks were laced without his knowledge and that he, at that time, had no reason to think he was taking in any alcohol, provides a special reason …

"The most serious matter is … the disallowance of the question as to whether the defendant should have realised, with this quantity of alcohol in his body, that he was not in a fit state to drive. The importance of that is not so much that the answer was not received by the court as the fact that the disallowance of the question suggests that the magistrate, in my view quite wrongly, then excluded the second stage from his mind – the consideration that even if at the time of the party the defendant had no reason to suspect that he was taking in any alcohol, as was found as a fact, he should nevertheless have realised before he got into his car that his drinks might have been laced and that he was not in a fit state to drive, due to his having taken in alcohol."

Appeal allowed.

Smith v Geraghty

[1986] RTR 222, 24 October 1985, QBD (DC)

When considering a "laced drinks" argument, justices were right not to take into account the prosecution's back-calculations of the blood alcohol level at the time of the offence.

A motorist had been charged, *inter alia*, with driving with excess alcohol, contrary to s 6(1), Road Traffic Act 1972 as substituted by s 25 and Sch 8, Transport Act 1981. He had opted to provide a blood specimen under s 8(6), Road Traffic Act 1972 as likewise substituted (lower breath reading no more than 50 µg alcohol in 100 ml breath – now repealed; see page v). The blood analysis revealed 92 mg alcohol in 100 ml blood. He pleaded guilty but argued special reasons for not disqualifying, under s 93(1), Road Traffic Act 1972, on the basis that, unknown to him, his drink had been "laced".

The defendant adduced expert evidence with a view to showing that at the time of driving his blood alcohol had been lower than the prescribed limit, and that it was the "laced" drink which had taken him over the limit; the prosecutor made counter-submissions on "back-calculating" the level of alcohol to the time of driving. The justices decided it would be unjust to attempt a back-calculation, but that the alcohol unknowingly consumed had accounted for the excess over the limit and this was a "special reason"; they did not disqualify the motorist. The prosecutor appealed against sentence.

QUESTION(S) FOR THE COURT: (b) When considering special reasons for not disqualifying the defendant by reason of a "'laced drink" mitigation … was the prosecutor entitled to show that, at the time of the offence, the defendant's blood alcohol concentration was higher than that shown in his certified analysis tendered to the court for the purpose of proving the offence? (c) If the prosecutor is entitled to back-calculate, whether, in the circumstances of this case, the justices were correct in deciding that there existed a special reason.

HELD: "… when … the question of whether there are or are not special reasons arises, the onus of proving that is on the defendant … on the balance of probabilities …

"… what a court is concerned to ascertain, if it is possible to ascertain it when special reasons are in contemplation, is what was the level of alcohol in the blood at the time when the offence was committed, that is to say, at the time when the defendant was driving, and what difference would have been made if the 'suspect' drink or drinks had not been consumed … once one leaves the reasonable certainty of an analysis of a blood sample … and one ventures on to calculation, one inevitably enters into a sphere in which there are a number of uncertainties … it is most undesirable that justices should be drawn into or allow themselves to be drawn into considering detailed calculations … even if those calculations are put before them by way of expert evidence … Going back to the level of alcohol in the blood at the time of driving is clearly permissible but only practicable … provided there is reasonably clear, straightforward and relatively simple evidence to show it … had the defendant pleaded not guilty, the prosecution would not have been entitled to seek to put the printout from the Lion Intoximeter 3000 in evidence, … does this apply equally to consideration of special reasons? … I conclude that it [does]."

The answer to question (b) was "yes"; the answer to question (c) was: "In the circumstances of this case the justices were entitled to find special reasons". Appeal dismissed.

James v Morgan

[1988] RTR 85, 27 January 1987, QBD (DC)

Where the evidence of laced drinks consisted solely of what the defendant's friends had told him, the magistrates were wrong to find special reasons.

A motorist had been convicted of driving with excess alcohol, contrary to s 6(1)(a), Road Traffic Act 1972 as substituted by s 25 and Sch 8, Transport Act 1981. The justices had accepted the motorist's uncorroborated evidence that his drinks had been laced and found that that amounted to a special reason, under s 93(1), Road Traffic Act 1972, for not disqualifying. The prosecutor appealed.

QUESTION(S) FOR THE COURT: Whether the justices were correct in finding special reasons and exercising discretion in not disqualifying the defendant on his uncorroborated evidence that his drinks had been laced.

HELD: "… First, [the defendant] had to satisfy the justices that the drink had been laced; and, secondly, he had to satisfy them that the quantity of alcohol in excess of the prescribed limit was attributable to the alcohol added to his drink …

"… the defendant's evidence that he had had his drinks laced depended solely upon what he must have been told by one or more of his mates. In those circumstances the argument is that there was no relevant and admissible evidence before the justices … upon which they could rely in accepting the defendant's argument … [that argument] is correct … the justices allowed pure hearsay evidence to be given. That evidence was not admissible and should not have been accepted … the defendant fails at the first hurdle."

Appeal allowed.

DPP v Younas

[1990] RTR 22 (note), 22 May 1989, QBD (DC)

It was not possible to say that the justices' decision – that it was obvious that the amount consumed would not have put the defendant over the limit – was perverse.

A motorist had been convicted of driving with excess alcohol, contrary to s 6(1), Road Traffic Act 1972 as substituted by s 25 and Sch 8, Transport Act 1981. He advanced special reasons for not disqualifying under s 93(1), Road Traffic Act 1972, in that, unbeknown to him, his drink had been laced.

The magistrates heard evidence from the motorist, and from a person who had laced one pint of lager with a double measure of spirits, and witnessed the like lacing of another; no medical or other expert evidence was adduced. They found that the motorist would not have been over the limit but for the "lacing", and that it was obvious to them that the amount he had drunk excluding the added spirits – 1¾ pints of lager – would not have put him over the limit. There was therefore a special reason and they did not disqualify. The prosecutor appealed.

QUESTION(S) FOR THE COURT: (a) Whether the justices were right to find special reasons in the absence of medical and/or expert evidence; and (b) whether on the facts found the justices were right to find special reasons.

HELD: "… each case depends on its own facts and … it is quite impossible … to say that the justices were perverse here in reaching the conclusion to which they came. It was open to them, if they took the view that it was obvious that the amount consumed by the defendant was such that it could not have put him over the limit, to say so … it is impossible to say that that conclusion was perverse."

Appeal dismissed.

Smith (Ian Philip) v DPP

[1990] RTR 17, 20 June 1989, QBD (DC)

There was no basis for saying that the court's decision (that it was not obvious that the additional alcohol took the defendant over the limit) was perverse.

A motorist pleaded guilty to driving with excess alcohol in blood, contrary to s 6(1), Road Traffic Act 1972 as substituted by s 25 and Sch 8, Transport Act 1981. He said he had drunk 1½ pints of lager, then asked for a fruit drink, to which, unknown to him, a single measure of vodka had been added. His submission that this was a special reason for not disqualifying under s 93(1), Road Traffic Act 1972, failed.

The Crown Court rejected his appeal, on the ground that, in the absence of medical evidence, he had not established that it was the vodka which had taken him over the limit. He further appealed.

QUESTION(S) FOR THE COURT: Whether the Crown Court was justified in concluding that they did not have sufficient evidence before them to satisfy them that the defendant had established special reasons.

HELD: "… the Crown Court decided that it could not say or was not prepared to say that it was obvious to that court that it was the vodka which had taken this defendant above the limit … that was a conclusion of fact to which the court, on the evidence, was entitled to come … in the absence of … medical or scientific evidence, … I am not prepared to say that the decision of the Crown Court was perverse."

Appeal dismissed.

R v Cambridge Magistrates' Court ex p Wong

[1992] RTR 382, 19 March 1991, QBD (DC)

The fact that a motorist had taken cough linctus which, unknown to him, contained alcohol, was capable of amounting to a special reason, but a finding of special reasons would not necessarily mean that the defendant would escape disqualification.

A motorist had pleaded guilty to a charge of driving with excess alcohol. The breath analysis reading was 40 μg alcohol in 100 ml breath. He had been drinking alcohol and had also taken cough linctus, which, unknown to him, contained alcohol. He pleaded special reasons for not being disqualified from driving, citing the general practice, set out in Home Office Circular 46/83, of not prosecuting where the reading is less than 40 μg, and adducing evidence that, but for the cough linctus, the reading would have been below 40 μg.

The justices found that, as a matter of law, the facts were not capable of amounting to special reasons. The motorist applied for judicial review of that decision.

GROUND(S) FOR THE APPLICATION: (1) The justices were wrong in law in finding that the facts put were not capable of amounting to special reasons; (2)

even if it was possible so to find, natural justice required the justices to invite argument thereon, particularly as the prosecution had conceded that the facts were indeed capable of amounting to special reasons; and (3) the circumstances were capable of amounting to special reasons and the justices should have gone on to consider whether the applicant should have realised that he was not fit to drive by reason of the alcohol in his body.

HELD: "… the appellant was unaware that the [cough linctus] contained alcohol … [he] was only just at the figure justifying prosecution. There was no bad driving … the Crown has properly conceded that the case was one where the justices could regard the facts as being capable in law of amounting to special reasons …

"Since the justices … indicated that they had found against the applicant as a matter of law, it is clear that they fell into error.

"[The appellant] submits that the circumstances were such that the justices, once accepting that the facts were capable of amounting to special reasons, could have come to no other conclusion than that they did so … He submits that this court should … substitute its view for that of the justices as to whether special reasons should apply to oust … the imposition of a disqualification.

"However, … there are two stages … whether to find special reasons and whether those reasons should excuse disqualification … Although, therefore, the circumstances may be thought here to be strongly in the applicant's favour on the second question, it would not … be appropriate for this court to impose its view or to pre-empt the view of the justices."

Certiorari granted to quash the justices' decision; *mandamus* granted ordering the justices to continue the hearing.

DPP v O'Connor and Other Cases

(1992) 95 Cr App R 135, [1992] RTR 66, 2 July 1991, QBD (DC)

The court should first determine whether special reasons exist (the onus being on the defendant, on the balance of probabilities), and then whether or not to exercise its discretion. The defendant must show that his drink was laced, without his knowledge, and that, but for the laced drink, he would not have been over the limit. Expert evidence is usually highly relevant. Even when special reasons are found, disqualification may nevertheless follow. Expert evidence is usually also needed to establish the defence of no likelihood of driving.

The cases concerned offences connected with the consumption of alcohol under s 5(1), Road Traffic Act 1988 and the evidence required to establish special reasons to avoid disqualification under s 34(1), Road Traffic Offenders Act 1988. One of the cases, *Allen*, concerned the defence of no likelihood of driving in relation to an allegation of being in charge while over the limit. They all featured drivers whose drinks had been laced.

QUESTION(S) FOR THE COURT: The questions concerned whether special reasons had been established; and whether or not medical evidence was necessary.

HELD: "The cases … indicate that some justices require guidance as to how they should evaluate evidence … in 'special reasons' cases …where a defendant seeks to rely upon special reasons the court is required to go through a two-stage process. First, it should determine whether there are special reasons, and then it should ask itself whether it is a case where, in its discretion, having regard to the special reasons, it should not disqualify … or disqualify for a shorter period than the normal … 12 months.

"… the onus of establishing special reasons is on the defendant but of course the standard of proof is the lesser one of balance of probabilities.

"… the matters which the defendant has to establish on the balance of probabilities … are three-fold. By admissible and relevant evidence, the driver is required to show, first of all, that his drink has been laced; secondly, that he did not know or suspect his drink had been laced; and, thirdly, if he had not taken the laced drink, the level of alcohol in his body would not have exceeded the prescribed limit …

"… expert evidence is usually highly relevant for two reasons. The first reason is because the expert evidence will indicate whether or not the amount of drink which the driver admits that he knowingly consumed was an amount which would result, in any event, in his alcohol level being above the prescribed limit. The evidence is also important because it will indicate whether or not the account which is being put forward … is credible …

"Turning to the issue of discretion, … because special reasons are established it does not follow that automatically the normal consequences of a finding of guilt of an offence of this sort should not follow … where there is erratic driving, or … a substantial amount of alcohol above the prescribed limit, … justices will want to consider carefully whether, even if special reasons are established, this is a case where the defendant should have appreciated that he was not in a condition in which he should have driven. If he should there would be no ground for mitigating the normal consequences of the conviction.

"In cases [like *Allen*] where a defendant is relying on the statutory defence provided by section 5(2) he is under the onus of proving that defence on the balance of probabilities … [Quoting from *DPP v Frost*, see page 499], 'the defendant must ordinarily call evidence appropriate to that which it is sought to be established. If [he was] only marginally above the limit and persuades the court that he would not have driven for a long period thereafter, then the court may properly find it to be obvious that the defence has been made out; but if a defendant [was] well over the limit and the court is satisfied that he would probably have driven in the space of a few hours, then it will not be at all obvious that the defence has been made out. In such a case the court cannot rely on general knowledge or common sense or personal experience but will require clear, cogent and reliable evidence as to the relative rate at which the particular defendant would have been likely to lose the alcohol …'."

Appeals disposed of applying the above principles.

Woodward (Mark de Maine) v DPP

Unreported, CO 2641/94, 23 February 1995, QBD (DC)

Magistrates were in error not to take into account an expert's back-calculations and forward calculations to show that the defendant's breath alcohol level would have been below the limit but for the lacing of his drink.

A motorist had pleaded guilty to driving with excess alcohol, contrary to s 5(1)(b), Road Traffic Act 1988. He argued that there were special reasons for not disqualifying under s 34(1), Road Traffic Offenders Act 1988 in that his drinks had been laced. He adduced evidence from a forensic scientist to the effect that "The forward calculation result indicates that Mr Woodward's breath alcohol level would have been below 35 μg …; the back calculation indicates that [his] breath alcohol level … would have been approximately 39 μg. This is … marginally below the level at which a prosecution will normally follow … Based on Mr Woodward's stated known consumption of alcohol, his breath alcohol level would have been below the permitted limit for driving at the time of the incident."

The justices found that special reasons did not exist. The motorist appealed.

QUESTION(S) FOR THE COURT: (1) Since the justices accept the appellant's evidence of the amount of drink he had consumed, were they entitled to rely on the figure produced by the forensic scientist's back-calculation approach (a breath alcohol reading of 39 μg) rather than on the forward calculation method (a reading of 28 μg)? Was the justices' finding that the appellant's evidence about the amount of alcohol he had consumed earlier in the day so unreasonable as to amount to an error in law? (2) Having found that the appellant's breath alcohol level was below that at which a prosecution is normally brought, were the justices entitled as a matter of law not to consider exercising their discretion to find special reasons? (3) Given that the justices found that the appellant's breath alcohol level would have been 39 μg but for the "lacing" of his drinks, should the justices have communicated this finding to the parties in open court and invited representation on the consequences of such a finding?

HELD: "… to succeed in establishing special reasons, a defendant must prove, on a balance of probability that (a) his drink was laced, (b) he did not know or suspect that his drink was laced and (c) if his drink had not been laced the alcohol level in his breath, blood or urine would not have exceeded the prescribed limit …

"As far as (c) is concerned, the plea of special reasons is available where a defendant has provided a specimen of breath, if, had his drink not been laced, his breath alcohol level would have been less than 40 microgrammes in 100 millilitres of breath. That is because of the policy of all police forces of not prosecuting … where the analysis is between 35 and 39 microgrammes. That the justices would have learned had they been referred … to the case of *R v Cambridge Magistrates' Court ex p Wong* [see page 533].

"Then finally, [w]here … a special reason is made out, the Magistrates must then go on to consider whether or not to exercise their discretion in favour of the defendant …

"It is apparent ... that the Justices did go wrong here ... there was a statement from a Forensic Scientist ... before the court ... It follows from [the relevant parts of that statement] that whether one does the back calculation or the forward calculation, either way it was established in this case that special reasons could apply."

Appeal allowed.

DPP v Vincent

Unreported, CO/1825/96, 16 July 1996, QBD (DC)

Where there was nothing to suggest that the magistrates had not considered the appropriate matters, their decision to find special reasons, while surprising, was not perverse.

A motorist had pleaded guilty to driving with excess alcohol, contrary to s 5, Road Traffic Act 1988. He submitted there were special reasons for not disqualifying under s 34(1), Road Traffic Offenders Act 1988. The defendant and his wife had been to a club, although the wife was unwell. She became increasingly ill during the evening. The defendant decided to drink an amount of alcohol which he believed would allow him to be able to drive home without exceeding the limit; he drank Coca-Cola between 3 pints of beer. He was stopped by police while driving home; he was speeding; breath analysis revealed a lower reading of 71 µg alcohol in 100 ml breath.

At the hearing, a friend of the defendant, who had been at the club with him, gave evidence that he had seen the defendant drink 2½ pints of beer, and that others had been pouring drinks from tumblers into pint glasses. There was expert evidence that if the defendant had drunk only 3 pints, that would have produced a breath alcohol reading of 20 µg. The justices concluded that the defendant's drinks had been laced; they found special reasons and did not disqualify. The prosecutor appealed.

QUESTION(S) FOR THE COURT: (1) Whether the justices were entitled to find, on the evidence given, that someone or some persons deliberately or misguidedly laced the respondent's drinks. (2) Whether the justices were entitled to find that the respondent had no reason to suspect or believe that he had consumed more than he intended and that on the balance of probabilities the evidence adduced by the defendant amounted to special reasons. (3) Assuming that the justices were entitled to find that special reasons were established, whether they correctly exercised their discretion not to disqualify.

HELD: "... From the authorities the following principles can be established. Firstly, it is for the defendant on the balance of probability to establish that his drink has been laced unknown to him. Secondly, it is very rarely that a court will be justified in drawing such an inference without direct evidence of it. Thirdly, the court should decide whether the accused would not have exceeded the legal limit if his drinks had not been laced. Fourthly, he did not know or suspect that his drinks had been tampered with in that way. The authorities also show that it is seldom that what I have called point 3 can be established without medical or scientific evidence, but they do not say that it is impossible for the justices to reach that conclusion without there being scientific evidence … [W]hilst it may be somewhat surprising that [the justices] reached the conclusion they did, I am not prepared to say that that conclusion was perverse or that it could not be justified on the evidence …

"[On (3)] … there are some circumstances which would justify magistrates not disqualifying, despite the fact that the amount of alcohol … is appreciably in excess of that permitted … They were entitled to look at the manner of the driving … they specifically found that the reason for the respondent driving at the speed at which he did was because of his anxiety to get his sick wife home. They clearly found … that he did not feel as though he was under the influence of alcohol, but it is clear that despite that, they should then have asked, … should he have appreciated that he was over the limit? … they were clearly referred to the case of *Barker* [*DPP v Barker*, see page 574]. It is, in our judgment, inconceivable that they were not aware of the duty to ask themselves that question. Reading the case as a whole, we are not prepared to say that their decision not to disqualify was perverse."

The answer to questions (1) and (2) was "yes"; the answer to question (3) was "yes, subject to this caveat, that the question should be understood as asking: did they ask themselves the right question and were they entitled to come to the conclusion to which they did come?". Appeal dismissed.

DPP v Winfield-Grant

Unreported, CO/3243/1999, 8 June 2000, QBD (DC)

The facts of this case revealed no error on the part of the magistrates.

A motorist had been convicted of driving with excess alcohol and of another road traffic offence. She argued that there were special reasons for not disqualifying. She believed she had drunk only two glasses of wine, and adduced expert evidence that the consumption of such an amount between the times in question would leave her below the statutory limit. The prosecutor argued that she had knowingly drunk vodka as well as the two glasses of wine. The justices accepted the defendant's argument that she did not know or believe that she had consumed any alcoholic drink other than the two glasses of wine, and that the lacing of her drinks was the deciding factor as to the excess alcohol. They found special reasons not to disqualify. The prosecutor appealed.

QUESTION(S) FOR THE COURT: Not recited in the judgment.

HELD: "… the justices here applied the correct standard and burden of proof. They found as a fact that this lady had knowingly only consumed two glasses of wine and that therefore the alcohol shown to be in her body as a result of the breath test must have been there as a result of her drinks having been laced by someone unknown to her. In those circumstances, I can find no reason to hold that the justices were in error in exercising their discretion in the way they did.

Once having found that there were special reasons, they were entitled to decline to disqualify."

Appeal dismissed.

Robinson v DPP

[2003] EWHC 2718 (Admin), (2004) 168 JP 522, 3 November 2003, QBD (DC)

Where a defendant was not aware that he had drunk alcohol, but had made no inquiries about what he was drinking, a special reason for not disqualifying could not be made out.

A motorist pleaded guilty to driving with excess alcohol, contrary to s 5(1)(a), Road Traffic Act 1988. He argued that there were special reasons for not disqualifying under section 34(1), Road Traffic Offenders Act 1988, in that he had not been aware he had drunk alcohol. He had been a Rastafarian for 7 years and it was contrary to his belief to take alcohol, although he had drunk alcohol in the past and knew its taste. He was at a funeral where refreshments were being served. He drank what he thought was fruit juice but which was in fact alcoholic punch. The magistrates found that he had made no enquiries about the contents of the drink he took and rejected his argument. He appealed against disqualification.

QUESTION(S) FOR THE COURT: (a) Whether there was a positive duty on the appellant to make enquiries about the contents of the drink; (b) if so, whether failure to make such enquiries entitled the magistrates to find that special reasons had not been established.

HELD: "16. … A driver who, at a party where alcohol is being served, assumes without enquiry that a cup available for consumption is alcohol-free is taking a risk, and if he turns out to be mistaken he must pay the price. … if there is to be any mitigation of penalty, the driver must show that he or she has done all that could reasonably be expected of him to avoid the risk of committing the offence."

The answers to both questions were "yes". Appeal dismissed.

DPP v Sharma

[2005] EWHC 879 (Admin), [2005] RTR 361, 27 April 2004, QBD (Admin)

Where the magistrates had considered the appropriate matters, their decision to find special reasons, while surprising, was not perverse.

A motorist had been convicted of driving with excess alcohol, contrary to s 5(1)(a), Road Traffic Act 1988. A friend had bought her two 250 ml bottles of "Smirnoff Ice", which contained vodka. To each, he had added 100 ml of vodka. The defendant was unaware that the vodka had been added; she did not experience any effects of intoxication or display any signs of impairment and the police who stopped her noticed nothing unusual. Expert evidence was adduced to the effect that if she had drunk only the two Smirnoff Ice drinks, she would not have been over the limit. The magistrates found that there were special reasons for not disqualifying under s 34(1), Road Traffic Offenders Act 1988. The prosecutor appealed.

HELD: "9. [On the magistrates' finding that the respondent was unaware of the additional alcohol and that her ability to drive was unimpaired] … it is not possible for me to say that the Justices' finding, surprising though it may seem to an outside observer, was one to which they were not entitled to come on the evidence that they heard – in other words, that their findings on the facts were legally perverse. I am not satisfied that they were.

"13. … They found all the necessary facts, they reached a conclusion which not every bench of Justices might have done on those facts, and they reached a conclusion which was not perverse or wrong in law, and reached it by a process which was not wrong in law or influenced by errors of law. For those reasons, surprising though the outcome may seem, this is not a case in which it is for … a reviewing judge, to interfere."

Appeal dismissed.

4. THE DISTANCE DRIVEN AND THE DEGREE OF DANGER

See also Chatters v Burke, page 506 – the seven-point checklist for assessing whether special reasons exist.

Redmond v Parry

[1986] RTR 146, 22 April 1985, QBD (DC)

Driving a very short distance may amount to a special reason not to disqualify.

A motorist pleaded guilty to driving while unfit through drink or drugs, contrary to s 5(1), Road Traffic Act 1972 as substituted by s 25 and Sch 8, Transport Act 1981, and to failing without reasonable excuse to provide a specimen for a breath test, contrary to s 7(4), Road Traffic Act 1972 as likewise substituted. He had been at a dinner with his wife; they had arranged that his wife would drive home; at the end of the evening, his wife did not want to reverse the car out of the position in which it was parked; the defendant did so, but collided with another parked car.

He submitted that there were special reasons for not disqualifying under s 93(1), Road Traffic Act 1972, in that he had driven only a short distance, intended to drive the car no further, and had not realised he was committing an offence. The justices rejected that submission. The motorist appealed against disqualification.

QUESTION(S) FOR THE COURT: Whether, on the facts as found, the justices were right to conclude that there were no special reasons not to disqualify.

HELD: "… a special reason must be a mitigating or extenuating circumstance, not amounting in law to a defence to the charge, directly connected with the commission of the offence and one which the court ought properly to take into consideration when imposing sentence …

"… [The justices' conclusion] was not a correct conclusion in law. It is clear from [*Coombs v Kehoe* [1972] 1 WLR 797, [1972] 2 All ER 55, [1972] RTR 224, [1972] Crim LR 560 (DC) and *James v Hall* [1968] Crim LR 507, [1972] 2 All ER 59 (note), [1972] RTR 228 (note) (DC)] that the fact that the defendant drove for a very short distance, in the circumstances … was something which was capable of amounting to a special reason for not disqualifying him. Whether or not it was appropriate for the justices in the circumstances to find that it was a special reason, is a matter which … we should leave to them."

Appeal allowed.

DPP v Thomas (Graham Derek)

Unreported, CO/664/89, 20 June 1989, QBD (DC)

Driving away from home after a row, albeit for less than half a mile, did not amount to an emergency or to a special reason.

A motorist pleaded guilty to driving with excess alcohol, contrary to s 6(1), Road Traffic Act 1972 as substituted by s 25 and Sch 8, Transport Act 1981. He submitted there were special reasons for not disqualifying under s 93(1), Road Traffic Act 1972. He had been out with his wife and had drunk a considerable amount; they went home by taxi; they quarrelled during the journey and after arriving home; he left the house in a temper, taking his small son with him; he got into his car and drove it for less than half a mile, when he stopped at a telephone kiosk and telephoned a relative asking to be collected.

The magistrates accepted there were special reasons and did not disqualify – the motorist had found himself in a situation which justified his use of a motor vehicle; he drove for no longer than was necessary; the distance driven was short; and no danger was likely to be caused to other road users or pedestrians. The prosecutor appealed against the finding of special reasons.

QUESTION(S) FOR THE COURT: (a) Whether the justices were correct in law to find special reasons not to disqualify, on the evidence before them; (b) whether the justices were entitled to find that the distance travelled by the respondent brought him within the ambit of the principles laid down in *Chatters v Burke* (see page 506) on the evidence before them.

HELD: "… the respondent was found to have driven on a road late at night for nearly half a mile through a residential area when in a very bad mood and having consumed a considerable amount of alcohol. The only reason for doing so was that he had had an argument with his wife and decided to leave home taking his small son with him … I find myself quite unable to understand how the justices could have come to the conclusion that this was a situation which justified the use of a motor vehicle. Cases show that it is only where clear and compelling circumstances arise, amounting to an acute emergency, that the situation could be capable of amounting to special reasons … the situation in the present case falls far short of being described as an emergency, let alone an acute emergency."

The answers to both questions were "no". Appeal allowed.

DPP v Corcoran (Joseph Patrick)

[1991] RTR 329, 28 January 1991, QBD (DC)

On the facts of this case, the short distance driven and absence of danger justified a finding of special reasons.

A motorist pleaded guilty, *inter alia*, to driving with excess alcohol, contrary to s 5(1)(a), Road Traffic Act 1988. He had been going to the theatre, intending to leave his company car in a car park overnight; he had arranged for it to be collected from there by a colleague the next morning. But he was late, and so parked on the street. At the end of the performance he drank alcohol while still in the theatre, then drove his car to the car park. On the way, he was stopped by police and found to be driving with excess alcohol.

The justices found the motorist had driven only about 40 yards; no other vehicles were visible and there was no danger to other road users, and that there were therefore special reasons not to disqualify or endorse the licence. The prosecutor appealed.

QUESTION(S) FOR THE COURT: Whether a reasonable bench, having heard the evidence in this case and applying their minds to the proper considerations, could have found special reasons in law under s 34, Road Traffic Offenders Act 1988 for not ordering disqualification and endorsement taking into account the criteria laid down in *Chatters v Burke* (see page 506).

HELD: "[After reviewing the factors to be taken into account, as set out in *Chatters v Burke*] Having regard to the facts found by the justices, and in particular the absence of any danger to the public and the relative shortness of the distance travelled, this was a case where the justices were entitled to find special reasons".

The answer to the question was "yes". Appeal dismissed.

DPP v Williams (Shane)

Unreported, CO 3632/93, 22 June 1994, QBD (DC)

The shortness of the distance driven cannot be directly connected with the commission of the offence of failing to supply specimens, and so did not amount to a special reason.

A motorist had pleaded guilty to failing without reasonable excuse to provide two specimens of breath for analysis, contrary to s 7(6), Road Traffic Act 1988. He submitted that there were special reasons for not disqualifying under s 34(1), Road Traffic Offenders Act 1988. He had been suffering from depression and phobia; his medical condition had deteriorated because of marital and domestic problems; on the evening in question he had been out drinking, but intended to stay the night with a friend and not drive after drinking; while waiting for the friend, he reversed his car about 10 yards to a safer parking place; the lights were not on. The police approached him; he refused to provide a specimen for a roadside breath test, saying "Come on, you are not going to do me for 10 yards, are you?" At the police station, he refused to provide breath specimens for analysis.

The magistrates found that the respondent had reasonably refused to supply a specimen because of the circumstances leading up to the request including the short distance driven and the factors on his mind at the time; and that the respondent felt "cornered" and anxious while at the police station. They found special reasons and did not disqualify. The prosecutor appealed.

QUESTION(S) FOR THE COURT: Not recited in the judgment.

HELD: "… There [are] four minimum criteria for special reasons. We are only concerned here with the third of them: the matter relied on must be directly connected with the commission of the offence. It is essential to bear in mind … what the offence was, namely, refusing to supply a specimen of breath.

"There is authority that the short distance that a car has been driven can be the subject of a special reason, but that is in a case where the man is charged with driving with excess alcohol. The special reason must be directly connected with the commission of the offence. I find it impossible to understand how it could be thought here that it was connected with the commission of the offence. [The respondent] had done the driving, short as it was, and he was now being asked to supply the specimen. How then could the driving of the short distance, which had already occurred, be related to that offence? … there was no justification here for … finding special reasons."

Appeal allowed.

Costello v DPP

Unreported, CO 3504/94, 8 March 1995, QBD (DC)

On the facts found in this case, there was a possibility of danger, and the distance driven was not short enough to give rise to a special reason.

The defendant had pleaded guilty to driving with excess alcohol, but argued that there were special reasons for not disqualifying under s 34(1), Road Traffic Offenders Act 1988.

He had come upon a van belonging to his companion's father; it was being reversed into the road. The driver then decamped, leaving the van in the middle of the road. The ignition lock had been tampered with by someone attempting to steal the van. The defendant drove the van to another car parking space at least 80 yards away.

The defendant said he had driven the van to the further place because the van was insecure and in a dark place. There was nothing improper in his manner of driving; the roads on which he drove were part of a housing development giving access to a substantial number of houses; numerous cars were parked in and adjacent to these roads. There was no other traffic on the roads at the time.

The magistrates dismissed his submission of special reasons. His appeal to the Crown Court was also dismissed, that court finding that he could have simply driven forward into the space the van had just come from, and that there was a possibility of danger having regard to the nature of the area.

The motorist appealed further.

QUESTION(S) FOR THE COURT: Whether on the facts as the court found them: (b) as a matter of law special reasons existed; (c) their opinion that there was a possibility of danger was one which no properly directed tribunal could have come to.

HELD: "[The Crown Court] specifically concluded that there was a possibility of danger … [T]here was … evidence for such a finding in the present case. Certainly I am not prepared to say that no reasonable tribunal could have arrived at such a finding, properly directed.

"Secondly, it is argued that the Crown Court was wrong in law to have taken into account the fact that the defendant need not have driven as far as he did … It seems to me that [this] is highly relevant to the decision which the trial Court had to make. If this factor had to be put into one of the categories spelt out in *Chatters v Burke* [see page 506], it would seem to fall into the final one; that is to say, the reason for the vehicle being driven at all … The defendant was in essence driving the vehicle in order to put it into a parking space which was better lit … That was the reason for the van being driven on that particular stretch of road where it was stopped by the police, rather than the emergency (if that is what it was) created by the van blocking the road. That latter problem could have been dealt with by driving the vehicle back into the position that it originally occupied …

"Lastly, [counsel for the appellant] has taken us through the various factors in *Chatters v Burke* and argued that almost all of them were in favour of a finding of special reasons … But … the assessment of the various factors is a matter for the trial court … This is not a matter where one can simply add up the number of factors on one side and the number of factors on the other and say that one is more numerous than the other … The Court is entitled to attach great weight to a factor such as the possibility of danger … ."

Appeal dismissed.

DPP v Craddock

Unreported, CO 3836/95, 2 April 1996, QBD (DC)

The emergency in this case (violence from spouse) did not justify driving 12–15 miles and so was not a special reason.

A motorist had pleaded guilty to driving with excess alcohol, contrary to s 5(1)(a), Road Traffic Act 1988. He submitted there were special reasons for not disqualifying under s 34(1), Road Traffic Offenders Act 1988. His wife was suffering post-natal depression and sometimes used violence towards her husband. On the day in question, the defendant and his wife were staying at her father's home. At about midnight, the wife attacked the defendant, beating him, stubbing out a cigarette on his body and demanding that he leave her father's house. He went out and sat in his car. His wife followed, threatening to break the window unless he left. The defendant drove some 12–15 miles; he was not followed. He did not consume alcohol after leaving his father-in-law's house. He fell asleep in his car. Police officers arrived and breath analysis later showed 52 µg alcohol in 100 ml breath.

The magistrates found that the circumstances of violence constituted an emergency; that the defendant was genuine in considering he had no alternative but to drive off; and that, in hindsight, he would not have done so. They found special reasons and did not disqualify. The prosecutor appealed.

QUESTION(S) FOR THE COURT: (i) Whether the facts found by the Justices could, in the circumstances, amount to special reasons; (ii) if the facts found could amount to special reasons for commencing to drive, whether they could continue throughout the duration of the driving to be special reasons.

HELD: "… the Justices have not, in my view, applied themselves to the question of what other steps Mr Craddock could have taken to deal with the emergency which presented itself, viewed objectively. In other words, what other steps would a reasonable person have taken at that time of night in that situation … Mr Craddock himself said that '… in hindsight he would not have done the same thing. He would have walked off somewhere and tried to find an hotel'.

"… it is quite impossible to see why Mr Craddock was justified in driving 12 to 15 miles. If the emergency did justify him removing his car from outside his father-in-law's house … he could have driven a short distance and found some suitable place in which to park for the night …

"He did not take either course and for that reason alone I cannot find that the second of Lord Widgery's criteria [in *Taylor v Rajan*, see page 507 – alternative means of transport or method of dealing with the crisis] was met.

"… This is a man who had taken so much drink that four hours later he had the equivalent of 120 milligrammes of alcohol per 100 millilitres of blood in his body … Clearly this was a very high reading. If the Magistrates had taken it properly into account on that ground alone it is difficult to see … how they could have concluded that there were special reasons."

The answers to both questions were "no". Appeal allowed.

DPP v Elsender

[1999] EWHC Admin 529, 9 June 1999, QBD (DC)

Where there was no good reason for driving in the first place, the shortness of the distance driven and absence of danger were irrelevant; there was no special reason for not disqualifying.

Police answered a call regarding a disturbance. They found the defendant outside the address of her ex-boyfriend; she was in a distressed state with cuts to her wrist, blood on her legs and crying. The police constable smelt alcohol on her breath. She admitted that she had driven to the house. She failed the roadside breath test procedure and was arrested and taken to the police station. Breath analysis revealed 73 µg alcohol in 100 ml breath.

She was convicted of driving with excess alcohol, but asked the justices to find special reasons for not disqualifying. On hearing further evidence, the justices found that the respondent had driven a relatively short distance – approximately half a mile; the journey was undertaken when there was little traffic on the road; there was no evidence to suggest the vehicle was not well maintained; and, having regard to the facts of the case, the respondent intended to drive no further than her declared destination. They found no evidence of any possibility of danger to other road users. These amounted to special reasons not to disqualify.

The prosecutor appealed.

QUESTION(S) FOR THE COURT: (1) Whether, as a matter of law, the distance driven was short enough to justify consideration of special reasons. (2) If so, whether the justices should have concluded that the respondent's vehicle was unlikely to be brought into contact with other road users or danger was likely to arise.

HELD: "… The answer to [question (1)] is quite clearly … no. The driving of a vehicle for half a mile could not in itself amount to a special reason. If there were good reason, such as some emergency, for driving that sort of distance, in all the circumstances then special reasons might possibly be found. But the justices here do not say that there was any particular emergency or any good reason why the respondent should have driven her vehicle at all. It seems from the material that we have that she had decided to go over to her ex boyfriend's house in an emotional state and no doubt drink played a part in that decision, and she then created a disturbance outside the premises.

"The answer to [question (2)] is that they should not have reached that conclusion." Appeal allowed.

CPS v Humphries

[2000] 2 Cr App R (S) 1, [2000] RTR 52, 1 November 1999, QBD (DC)

Where the defendant intended to drive some distance but succeeded in moving the vehicle only a few feet, the shortness of the distance driven did not amount to a special reason for not disqualifying for attempting to drive with excess alcohol.

A witness saw the headlights of a parked car flashing. He saw the defendant sitting in the driver's seat with someone else in the passenger seat. He then saw the passenger get out of the car and start to push it towards the main road. The vehicle moved forward about one or two car lengths before falling back to its original position. He then saw the defendant switch off the lights of the car and get out of it. The witness called the police. The police arrived 5 minutes later and found the defendant sitting half in and half out of the car fiddling with a knife with the wires underneath the steering column. He was arrested. Breath analysis revealed 66 µg of alcohol in 100 ml breath. The defendant admitted to the police that he had been extremely drunk when he was arrested because he had been drinking all day; he said he had to get home that evening; he had no intention of walking, so he decided to steal the car. Either he or his friend were attempting to "hot wire" it to enable him to do so.

He was convicted of, *inter alia*, attempting to drive the car with excess alcohol. His solicitor argued that there were special reasons for not disqualifying because of the short distance which the vehicle had travelled and because the defendant would never have been able to drive the vehicle anyway.

The justices found, *inter alia*, that there was an intention to drive, but the engine was never started; the defendant attempted to drive the vehicle but was too intoxicated to get it started and, in any event, he was interrupted by the arrival of the witness and the police. They concluded that the shortness of distance driven amounted to a special reason for not imposing a mandatory disqualification. The prosecutor appealed.

QUESTION(S) FOR THE COURT: Whether any bench of justices, properly directed, could have found the respondent had established special reasons, particularly in light of their finding that the respondent had intended to drive the vehicle home had he not been so intoxicated and would have done so but for the arrival of the police.

HELD: "… Where one is looking at a conviction for attempt, the Court must look not only at what the attemptor actually achieved (which, because he was so drunk was very little in this case) but what he had intended. I think that if the Justices in this case had looked at what was intended, which was to take this stolen car in a very drunken state out on to the public road and drive it some considerable distance, they could only have reached one conclusion and that is there were no special reasons to justify non-disqualification of the respondent.

"… it was not the fact that the car was only driven for six feet which mattered, it was the fact that the driver, the Appellant, intended to drive it out into the public highway in order to get home with all the attendant danger which that entailed given that on his own admission he was completely unfit to drive."

The answer to the question was "no". Appeal allowed.

DPP v Conroy

[2003] EWHC 1674 (Admin), [2004] 1 Cr App R (S) 37, (2003) 167 JP 418, 23 June 2003, QBD (DC)

The facts of this case – speeding through a town centre, erratically, with pedestrians in the vicinity, while twice over the limit – did not justify a finding of special reasons.

A motorist had been convicted of driving with excess alcohol, contrary to s 5(1)(a), Road Traffic Act 1988. He had driven, at speed and erratically, for no more than one mile, including half a mile through the centre of Congleton at 3 am; he intended to drive a further 200 yards beyond the place at which he was stopped by police; the car was in good condition; traffic was light and there were only a few pedestrians in the area; he had with him his girlfriend who suffered from a condition rendering it difficult for her to walk, although it was not contended that her condition gave rise to a medical emergency. On the basis of the shortness of the distance driven, the justices found special reasons for not disqualifying under s 34(1), Road Traffic Offenders Act 1988.

The prosecutor appealed.

QUESTION(S) FOR THE COURT: Not recited in the judgment.

HELD: "18. … The fact that this car was driven for a mile and would have been driven for a further 200 yards; the fact that it was driven in excess of the speed limit in a built-up area; the fact that it was driven about half a mile through Congleton; the fact that it was driven in an erratic manner; the fact that, being driven where it was, despite the time at which it was being driven, meant that there were likely to be some pedestrians about with which there might well be contact, because of the excessive speed and erratic driving – all those circumstances, in my judgment, rendered the only conclusion open to the Justices, in a proper exercise of their discretion, to be that there were no special reasons for refusing to disqualify … it was wrong in law … to find special reasons, having found that the vehicle had been driven, because of the condition of his passenger, 'for no more than a mile through a town centre in an erratic manner in light traffic with several pedestrians in the vicinity whilst being twice over the prescribed limit'."

Appeal allowed.

DPP v Oram

[2005] EWHC 964 (Admin), 5 May 2005, QBD (Admin)

Shortness of distance driven alone is insufficient to establish special reasons.

A motorist had been convicted of driving with excess alcohol (91 mg in 100 ml blood), contrary to s 5(1)(a), Road Traffic Act 1988. He had been in a public house; he drank a pint of beer; he was with friends and they persuaded him to have another pint. He then remembered he had valuable tools in his van and decided to drive the van home rather than leave it in the pub car park. He drove some 350 yards home. The van had a defective rear lamp.

On the basis of the shortness of the distance driven, the justices found special reasons for not disqualifying under s 34(1), Road Traffic Offenders Act 1988. The prosecutor appealed

QUESTION(S) FOR THE COURT: Whether the decision to find a special reason was one that no reasonable bench could have reached on the facts found.

HELD: "[After reviewing the authorities] 11. … The fact that any act of driving is only over a short distance cannot … alone justify the exercise of a discretion not to disqualify … In each and every case it is necessary to look at all the circumstances. Not surprisingly, those cases most likely to attract the exercise of discretion will be those which arise when the driver does not expect to drive and has done so in some sort of emergency or unforeseeable circumstances. ... I do not describe a definitive test but merely point to the circumstances.

"12. In this case there is no question of any emergency. ... the respondent's difficulties were entirely of his own making. Further, although the Justices concluded that the road was likely to be free of other traffic, such that the danger was extremely low, the test is whether there is a possibility of danger by contact with other road users. This has to be considered against the background that although he was driving down a cul de sac, at least one of his lights was in fact defective.

"13. I return to the question posed [in *DPP v Bristow*, page 520]: What would a sober, reasonable and responsible friend of the defendant, present at the time but himself a non-driver and thus unable to help, have advised in the circumstances: Drive or do not drive? ... the only possible answer ... was that a friend would advise not to drive in those circumstances."

The answer to the question was "yes". Appeal allowed.

DPP v Harrison

[2007] EWHC 556 (Admin), 1 March 2007, QBD (DC)

On the facts of this case (defendant who had been subjected to harassment drove 446 yards, giving rise to a real prospect of danger to others), there were no grounds to find special reasons.

A motorist had pleaded guilty to driving with excess alcohol, contrary to s 5(1)(a), Road Traffic Act 1988. He submitted there were special reasons for not disqualifying under s 34(1), Road Traffic Offenders Act 1988. He had suffered harassment from a gang of youths which took the form of verbal abuse, damage to his vehicle and bottles being thrown into his property. On the evening in question, he had been drinking at home and was in bed. At about 12.30 am, he was awakened by the sound of breaking glass and verbal abuse. He saw youths attacking a neighbour's property. He telephoned the police who told him to stay at home. The youths then went to the defendant's property, broke the back gate and threw a brick through his patio doors. The police had not arrived. The defendant got dressed, took a baseball bat, and went outside. The youths were going away. The defendant got into his car and drove after the youths; he stopped and got out, seeking to identify the youth who had smashed his patio doors. He was hit in the face, and went back to his vehicle for the baseball bat. A passing police car approached, and the youths scattered. The defendant was arrested on suspicion of driving with excess alcohol and breath analysis later showed 54 μg alcohol in 100 ml of the defendant's breath.

The magistrates accepted the special reasons argument and did not disqualify. The prosecutor appealed.

QUESTION(S) FOR THE COURT: Whether a reasonable bench, having heard the evidence and applying the proper considerations, could have found special reasons in law under s 34 for not ordering disqualification.

HELD: "17. In my judgment … the Justices did reach a conclusion that was not properly open to them. First, there is the very length which the respondent actually drove; some 446 yards … this is a significantly greater distance than could in itself justify a finding of special reasons. Moreover … the driving took place on the A666 road, a major arterial road between Bolton and Manchester. … there inevitably would have been a real prospect of danger to other users of that road predictably out even at that late hour of night …

"18. Further, … the Justices found that this particular respondent exceeded the breath limit by quite a significant amount, [but] made no mention of the general principle that exceeding the breath limit by the amount in question here of itself would disincline Justices to exercise discretion.…

"19. In addition, there were in fact alternatives open to this respondent … He could have asked … one of the neighbours to drive him; but he did not do so. He could have perhaps chased after the youths by foot, but again decided not to do so. It cannot be said that the only option available to him was simply to pursue them driving in his car. Moreover … this respondent had been advised by the police to stay in his house. That was advice he elected … to ignore.

"20. … having regard to the facts as found and whether one takes those facts individually or cumulatively, the Justices could not properly find that special reasons existed in this case."

The answer to the question was "no". Appeal allowed.

DPP v Cove

[2008] EWHC 441 (Admin), 14 February 2008, QBD (DC)

On the facts of this case (motorist drove 250 metres to avoid paying an excess parking charge), the magistrates should not have found special reasons.

A motorist had pleaded guilty to driving with excess alcohol, contrary to s 5(1)(a), Road Traffic Act 1988. The reading was 60 μg alcohol in 100 ml breath. She had driven 250 metres, from a car park, to avoid incurring an excess parking charge. She submitted there were special reasons for not disqualifying under s 34(1), Road Traffic Offenders Act 1988. The magistrates found that 250 metres was not an excessive distance; the vehicle was unlit; the state of the car was not an issue; there was no intention to drive further; the road was not busy; the weather was dry; there were other road users in the vicinity but they were few; and that the vehicle was driven to avoid paying an excess parking charge. They found special reasons not to disqualify. The prosecutor appealed.

QUESTION(S) FOR THE COURT: Whether the magistrates correctly applied the case law concerning shortness of distance driven, bearing in mind the totality of the evidence; in particular, whether the magistrates gave appropriate weight not only to how far the vehicle was driven and whether the defendant intended to drive further, but also to the manner in which the vehicle was driven, the reason for the vehicle being driven and whether there was a possibility of danger by coming into contact with other road users and pedestrians.

HELD: "15. The events occurred at about 3 o'clock in the morning … But given the location, the prospective presence of other road users, including pedestrians, was still a real one. The respondent drove, and was seen to drive, for some 250 metres. That included driving around a roundabout, and it was a journey taken throughout without lights. The respondent had drunk a significant amount of alcohol.

"17. … it is apparent that the magistrates focused, not on what prospectively the usage of the road would have been … but on what the usage actually was on the evidence. That seems to me to indicate a departure from the approach required by *Chatters v Burke* [see page 506] and the other authorities, recalling that the sixth of the matters referred to … was 'whether there was any possibility of danger by contact with other road users'.

"18. To that extent, it seems to me that the magistrates misdirected themselves. However, that is not the only concern. In acceding to the points made on behalf of the respondent in relation to the distance driven, the lack of lights and the reason for driving, namely in order to avoid the possibility of a car park surcharge, it seems to me that the magistrates reached a decision which no reasonable bench of magistrates could have reached on that evidence. This was not a case of emergency."

The answers to the questions were "no". Case remitted to the magistrates' court for the imposition of disqualification.

5. UNAWARE OF BEING OVER THE LIMIT

DPP v O'Meara

[1989] RTR 24, 4 February 1988, QBD (DC)

A defendant who had been drinking the night before and thought he would be below the limit when he drove 12 hours later did not have a special reason for not disqualifying.

A motorist pleaded guilty to driving with excess alcohol, contrary to s 6(1), Road Traffic Act 1972 as substituted by s 25 and Sch 8, Transport Act 1981. He had been drinking the evening before, and some 12 hours had elapsed between his last drink and the offence. The magistrates accepted his submission there were special reasons for not disqualifying under s 93(1), Road Traffic Act 1972. The prosecutor appealed.

QUESTION(S) FOR THE COURT: Whether the ignorance of the long-term effect of alcohol can constitute a special reason for not disqualifying.

HELD: "[Applying the four tests in *Whittall v Kirby* (see page 505)] … The argument really centres round the third test. Is the fact that the defendant, having consumed a quantity of alcohol on the previous night, did not think or believe that the following morning the amount in his blood would still be above the legal limit, directly connected with the commission of the offence?

"Put shortly, in my view it is not … it is a matter connected with … the offender … if a man either has convinced himself that the amount in his blood will, by the time he drives, have subsided to something less than the legal limit but is mistaken, or … does not think about it at all but assumes that by the following morning he is below the legal limit, those are matters relating to him and not to the offence … the facts of this case did not provide a special reason."

The answer to the question was "no", but in the circumstances, there was no order to remit to the justices.

DPP v White

[1988] RTR 267, 8 February 1988, QBD (DC)

The fact that a roadside screening test was negative, and a later roadside screening test was positive, the defendant having drunk nothing in between, was not a special reason.

A motorist pleaded guilty to driving with excess alcohol, contrary to s 6(1)(a), Road Traffic Act 1972 as substituted by s 25 and Sch 8, Transport Act 1981. He had stopped at a railway station to drop off passengers, where police had asked him to take a roadside screening test, which was negative. He continued his journey and was stopped by different police officers some time later. On this occasion a screening test was positive. The motorist was arrested and taken to the police station, where breath analysis proved positive.

The justices accepted that he had not drunk between the two screening tests, and that when he resumed driving after the first screening test he honestly and reasonably believed he was within the legal limit. They therefore found special reasons for not disqualifying under s 93(1), Road Traffic Act 1972. The prosecutor appealed.

QUESTION(S) FOR THE COURT: Whether there were sufficient grounds in law to support a finding of special reasons and if so, whether, on the facts of the case, the justices were correct in law in exercising their discretion not to order disqualification.

HELD: "[The defendant] must inevitably have consumed alcohol to such an extent that it put him at risk of driving with alcohol in his bloodstream above the permitted limit. It is inescapable, as any citizen must know, that where one consumes alcohol the alcohol is not immediately released into the bloodstream. It is released into the bloodstream gradually on an ascending … curve. It is clear that having consumed alcohol … the defendant, when he drove to [the station], was at risk that the concentration of alcohol in his blood would be above the permitted limit. It is inescapable that when he drove from [the station] he was running the like risk.

"… the decision to drive was not a decision that he made by reason of the clear breath test at [the railway station]. The only effect upon him was that it was not present to his mind that he was taking any risk at all.

"… the justices had no proper ground on which to find that there were special reasons."

Appeal allowed.

Bryant v DPP

Unreported, CO/132/88, 9 June 1988, QBD (DC)

The defendant's belief that he would not be over the limit was not a matter to be taken into account in relation to penalty, and it was peculiar to the offender rather than the offence; it was not therefore a special reason.

A motorist had pleaded guilty to driving with excess alcohol, contrary to s 6(1), Road Traffic Act 1972 as substituted by s 25 and Sch 8, Transport Act 1981, and submitted there were special reasons for not disqualifying under s 93(1), Road Traffic Act 1972.

The justices found that on the day in question, he had not fully recovered from a stomach upset; he had nevertheless consumed alcohol; he had had very little to eat that day and for the preceding 2 days; he believed that the alcohol would have cleared from his system when he began driving. The justices concluded there was no special reason and disqualified. The motorist appealed.

QUESTION(S) FOR THE COURT: Whether the justices were right in finding that the evidence disclosed no special reasons.

HELD: "… the high point of the justices' finding … is that the defendant believed the alcohol he consumed would have cleared from his system when he commenced driving. There is no finding that had the appellant not been suffering from the gastric condition … the alcohol which he drank would not have resulted in his being above the prescribed limit … what he certainly did know was that such alcohol as he took, he took while he was suffering from a gastric disorder at a time when he had had virtually nothing to eat for a very long period. It is … well-known … that to drink alcohol on an empty stomach is likely to have more dramatic effects than to drink the same quantity of alcohol in the course of a normal day when one is eating normal meals …

"… the magistrates were amply justified in concluding … that this was not a case in which the facts … could constitute special reasons. They chose to justify their conclusion by specific reference to the fourth of the requirements [in *Whittall v Kirby*, page 505], namely that this was not a matter which should properly be taken into account in relation to the penalty … I would also … hold that the facts … could not amount to a special reason, being peculiar to the offender and not the offence."

Appeal dismissed.

DPP v Jowle

The Times, 13 December 1997, (1999) 163 JP 85, 30 October 1997, QBD (DC)

A person who had taken a large amount of mouthwash which, unknown to him, contained alcohol, should have realised he was not fit to drive; there was no special reason for not disqualifying.

A motorist had been charged with driving with excess alcohol, contrary to s 5(1)(a), Road Traffic Act 1988. He had been stopped by police after consuming 800 ml of Listerine mouthwash; his vehicle had swerved, failed to take a bend correctly and crossed to the wrong side of the road. Breath analysis later revealed 94 μg alcohol in 100 ml breath. Listerine mouthwash contained 26.9% by volume of alcohol, although the presence of alcohol was not indicated on the bottle. The respondent was a member of Alcoholics Anonymous and had not knowingly drunk alcohol for 21 years.

The justices found that the motorist had become addicted to Listerine and, although familiar with the effects of alcohol, did not associate the "lift" he obtained from drinking the mouthwash with the effects of alcohol consumption. He submitted that there were special reasons for not disqualifying under s 34(1), Road Traffic Offenders Act 1988. The justices were of the opinion that special reasons could be found where the offender showed that he did not know or suspect that he had been drinking a liquid containing alcohol, and that that applied here; they could not say that he should have realised that he was not in a fit state to drive. They did not disqualify him. The prosecutor appealed.

QUESTION(S) FOR THE COURT: Whether the justices were entitled to find that the facts put forward by the respondent amounted to special reasons.

HELD: "… The simple fact here is that, over a period of a considerable amount of time, this offender knew that if he took Listerine mouthwash it gave him a lift. On the day on which he was stopped he had taken a considerable amount of that substance from which it follows he had a lift. He drove in a way which was plainly erratic. In those circumstances, I … find it impossible to conclude, as did the Justices, that they were entitled to say that he should not have realised that he was not in a fit state to drive. It seems to me plain on the evidence that anyone in his position should have realised that he was not in a fit state to drive.

"Accordingly I would set aside that finding as perverse … there is no room for a finding of special reasons."

Appeal allowed.

DPP v Anderson (Marilyn)
[1998] COD 363, 29 June 1998, QBD (DC)

On the facts of this case (wine stronger than usual) the defendant did not discharge the burden of proving that she would have been below the limit but for the alcohol she unknowingly consumed. She did not have a special reason.

A motorist had pleaded guilty to driving with excess alcohol in blood contrary to s 5(1)(a), Road Traffic Act 1988, but argued that there were special reasons for not disqualifying under section 34(1), Road Traffic Offenders Act 1988. She had consumed two 175 ml glasses of red wine at a public house before driving on the occasion in question; she did not believe the wine would take her above the limit; she did not inquire about the strength of the wine. The landlord of the public house gave evidence that he ordinarily served wine which was 11.5% proof but on the day in question, and since the preceding Christmas, had been selling a wine which was 13.5% proof. Expert evidence was called on behalf of the defendant to the effect, *inter alia*, that there was a 50 to 1 chance against the wine consumed giving rise to a reading of 80 mg when the blood specimen was taken, and an even lower probability that the reading would have been the 100 mg it was; if the defendant had consumed 11.5% strength wine instead of 13.5% strength, her blood alcohol would have been between 83 mg and 88 mg per 100 ml; i.e. she could still have been above the limit.

The justices found the expert evidence confusing and inconclusive, but that the defendant had consumed only two glasses of wine and that she was misled about the quality in that it was considerably stronger than she was expecting; but for that, she would have been below the limit when tested; they found special reasons for not disqualifying and for not endorsing. The prosecutor appealed.

QUESTION(S) FOR THE COURT: Whether any bench of justices properly directed could have found the respondent had established special reasons.

HELD: "… [The justices found] that [the respondent] had only consumed two glasses of wine. That is a question of fact. The justices were perfectly entitled to make it … [They] go on to say that [the respondent] was clearly misled by the quality of wine supplied that evening, which was considerably stronger than she was expecting. It is indeed true on the facts as found that the wine … turned out to be stronger than she had thought. There was, however, no active misleading and no finding that she had ever asked for, or been given, any indication as to the strength of the wine … The inference must therefore be … that if [the respondent] had been told that the wine was unusually strong she would or might have drunk less of it. The fact is, however, that she never at any stage was given any indication of any kind one way or the other as to the strength of the wine … The justices then go on … to find that taking account of the expert evidence the justices believed that [the respondent] would have been below the limit when the blood sample was taken if the wine had been of its usual strength. This finding appears to be based on expert evidence which the justices had already described as 'confusing and inconclusive'. As I understand their summary of that evidence, it appears to have been that she might have very well been above the limit even if the wine had been of the lower strength … The evidence given … could not be relied on to support [the justices'] conclusion, given that the burden of proving special reasons lay squarely on [the respondent]. It seems as plain as could be that the evidence she adduced did not discharge that burden.

"This was … a very plain case of a person who both drank and drove. She thought that what she drank would not take her over the limit, but she took no adequate steps to satisfy herself that such would be the case, and in the event she was proved wrong … ."

Appeal allowed.

DPP v Wynne

[2001] EWCA Admin 21, 15 January 2001, QBD (DC)

A defendant who said she had drunk two half pints of lager and eaten three slices of cake to which whiskey had been added, failed to establish a special reason.

A motorist had been charged with driving with excess alcohol, contrary to s 5(1)(a), Road Traffic Act 1988. She argued that there were special reasons for not disqualifying under s 34(1), Road Traffic Offenders Act 1988. She said she had drunk two half pints of lager which would not have taken her over the limit, but she had also eaten three large slices of Christmas cake which, unknown to her, had been liberally soaked in whiskey during preparation. It was said that up to one half of a 70 cl bottle of whiskey had been added; the defendant had eaten about a quarter of the cake. She called an expert witness who said that the pint of lager would have an alcohol concentration of about 57 mg, but that if she had a normal rate of elimination of 15 mg per hour, by the time the blood sample was taken, the lager would have represented less than 9 mg of the 86 found in her blood. He could not say how much whiskey was in the cake after allowing for evaporation, which he had not tested, but that if she had drunk an eighth of a bottle of whiskey in the time in question, the blood alcohol reading would have been over the limit.

The magistrates accepted the argument and did not disqualify. The prosecutor appealed.

HELD: "9. … it seems to me most improbable that the respondent could have drunk an eighth of a bottle of whiskey through eating the cake, without realising it. If she had consumed that amount, she would probably have been over the limit and must therefore have been aware of its effect. Second, the notion that a cake could contain within it a half a bottle of whiskey without becoming mushy so that it was eaten rather than drunk, seems to me to be unlikely.

"10. Third, the evidence of the expert was speculative as he had not tested the alcoholic potential of the cake … The magistrates' approach to the expert evidence shows an error in law … What they said was that [in the absence of any contrary evidence and on the basis that his evidence was not discredited by cross-examination, they accepted the opinion he formed].

"11. … What they should have done was to ask themselves whether there was any evidential value to the opinion expressed by the expert rather than concentrating on whether there was other expert evidence to contradict what he had said.

"12. Fourth, the evidence about the cake and its contents was admitted by a written statement when there was no evidence that its maker could not have been called so she could be cross-examined. The evidence of that person was not just the formulation of a recipe, but also … as to … how much alcohol she put into a cake …

"13. Fifth, the back calculations which can be made in this case show that if the totality of the Respondent's consumption of the cake and lager was true, then she would not have been below the prescribed minimum for the amount of alcohol in the blood at [the time the specimen was taken].

"14. In my view one has only to stand back from the facts of this case in order to appreciate that the suggestion that two halves of lager and three slices of cake, consumed over a five hour period, could have accounted for the reading taken two hours later must have been flawed."

Appeal allowed.

6. PERSONAL CIRCUMSTANCES

Bullen v Keay

[1974] RTR 559, [1974] Crim LR 371, 4 April 1974, QBD

An apparent suicide attempt was peculiar to the offender, not the offence, and did not constitute a special reason.

A motorist had driven to a lay-by where he took a quantity of barbiturates, intending to commit suicide. He expected to go into a coma; he became unconscious, but then drove erratically and there was an accident. He pleaded guilty to driving while unfit through drugs, contrary to s 5(1), Road Traffic Act 1972, but argued that there were special reasons for not disqualifying under s 93(1), Road Traffic Act 1972.

The magistrates found that he had not intended to drive after taking the drug and that when he did drive he was not in control of his actions. They found that the four criteria in *R v Wickins* (see page 560) were fulfilled and that there were therefore special reasons. They did not disqualify. The prosecutor appealed.

QUESTION(S) FOR THE COURT: Whether the facts found amounted to special reasons for not disqualifying.

HELD: "… [On the finding that] it had not been the defendant's intention to drive after taking the tablets … What he had in mind when he took the tablets does not … have any effect on the succeeding history of the matter, which is that he did drive and did drive at a time when he was very heavily under the influence of drugs. Even if there is some substance in the first reason, … it is a reason peculiar to the offender and not to the offence, and accordingly … should not be treated as a special reason. …

"… this is a case in which … it was as clear an example as one could possibly have in which the mandatory disqualification, and perhaps something more, should have followed. The argument that, because the defendant was heavily under the influence of drugs it would in some way be an excuse for his conduct produces the perverse consequence that, if a man drinks so much that he cannot understand what he is doing, he can then go on the road and not be at the risk of having his licence taken away … ."

Appeal allowed.

DPP v Hyland

Unreported, CO/575/87, 6 July 1987, QBD (DC)

A driver who was suicidal and took to drink, then drove, did not have a special reason.

A motorist was convicted of driving with excess alcohol, contrary to s 6(1)(a), Road Traffic Act 1972 as substituted by s 25 and Sch 8, Transport Act 1981. The justices accepted her difficult personal circumstances as special reasons, under s 93(1), Road Traffic Act 1972, for not disqualifying. The prosecutor appealed against the non-disqualification.

HELD: "… [The defendant] had become extremely depressed … she was … driven to despair. She was beside herself and she was suicidal. She decided to leave home in that state and take to drink … [After quoting the criteria in *Whittall v Kirby*, see page 505] I should have thought that the justices, having been told of those criteria – as indeed they were – could have come instantly to no other conclusion than that none of the four criteria applied in this case."

Appeal allowed.

DPP v Crawford

Unreported, CO 725/93, 22 June 1994, QBD (DC)

On the facts of this case, the justices erred in finding special reasons; the circumstances (domestic problems, anxiety about absent spouse) related to the offender, not the offence.

A motorist had been charged with reckless driving; failing without reasonable excuse to provide a specimen for a breath test, contrary to s 6(4), Road Traffic Act 1988; failing without reasonable excuse to provide two specimens of breath for analysis, contrary to s 7(6), Road Traffic Act 1988; and wilfully obstructing a police officer in the execution of his duty. All the charges arose out of the same incident. He pleaded guilty to three and was found guilty of the fourth.

A witness had seen him at midnight driving erratically; other witnesses later observed the car, heard loud squealing of brakes and shouting, and saw the car mount the kerb on more than one occasion and swerve across the road. Police went to his home. The defendant poured a full glass of brandy and drank it in one gulp. The officer warned him not to drink any more but he drank another full glass of brandy, despite physical restraint by the officer. He was restrained from taking any further alcohol. He was arrested after a struggle. At the police station, he was aggressive and belligerent.

At the hearing, the evidence about the manner of driving was unchallenged. The defendant submitted that there were special reasons for not disqualifying under s 34(1), Road Traffic Offenders Act 1988. The magistrates found that he was emotionally upset because he had had domestic problems with his wife over the preceding 12 months; she had been absent from home since midday on the day of the offence and had not returned by 9.30 pm. They found the defendant had consumed two cans of lager at a friend's home at some time after 9.30 pm (there was no evidence as to the time at which he had left the friend's home); at the police station he was "physically, mentally and emotionally beside himself with the trauma of not knowing where his wife was and with the violence of the arrest". They believed he was suffering "an unusual trauma when the request to take a breath test was made by the circumstances of his arrest and a deep concern for his wife. This acted on his mind in such a way as to prevent him making a rational decision whether to provide a breath sample for analysis, grossly affecting his judgment … In addition, on the balance of probabilities, [they] were of the opinion that the Respondent, when he ceased driving, was not over the prescribed limit … ."

They found special reasons and did not disqualify. The prosecutor appealed.

HELD: "… The conclusion [that the respondent was not over the limit when he ceased driving] was entirely regardless of the unchallenged evidence [of the witnesses who had seen him driving]. The driving that they described only makes sense in all the circumstances if the Respondent had at the time of driving already consumed far too much …

"I … therefore find this conclusion one that no reasonable bench of Justices … could possibly have arrived at. In any event, it seems to me to have nothing to do with special reasons …

"… to amount to a special reason a matter must (a) be a mitigating or extenuating circumstance; (b) not amount in law to a defence …; (c) be directly connected with the commission of the offence and (d) be one which the court ought properly to take into consideration when imposing sentence. In this matter we are concerned with (c) … this is not a case where there was some intervening medical condition. This was a man who was very upset by reason of his wife being absent that evening, having had far too much to drink, being aggressive when police attempted to arrest him, and being taken off to the police station. There is no doubt at all he was, for all those reasons together, in a distressed state, where he may well have been acting out of his usual sensible character. However … this is about as far removed from any question of a special reason as one can imagine. It has something to do with the offender. It seems to me to have nothing whatsoever to do with the commission of the offence."

Appeal allowed.

DPP v Phillips (Richard Charles)

Unreported, CO 1055/94, 22 June 1994, QBD (DC)

The illness of the defendant's spouse and his anxiety about it were connected to the offender not the offence; they did not therefore amount to a special reason not to disqualify.

A motorist had pleaded guilty to driving with excess alcohol, contrary to s 5(1)(a), Road Traffic Act 1988. He submitted that there were special reasons for not disqualifying under s 34(1), Road Traffic Offenders Act 1988. His wife suffered a rare form of bone cancer and was being treated at hospital; she was rarely allowed home. On the day in question, he had been told she could come home; he drove to the hospital but when he arrived was told that, after all, she was not well enough. The defendant drove home in a distressed state. Later, he went to a public house, drank alcohol, and was stopped by police on the way home. Breath analysis revealed 69 µg alcohol in 100 ml breath.

The magistrates found that the illness of the motorist's wife and her having to stay in hospital had been operating on his mind at the time in question and was directly connected to the commission of the offence. They found special reasons and did not disqualify him. The prosecutor appealed.

HELD: "The essence of this case is that this man was driving with greatly excessive alcohol, because he was, with very good cause, extremely unhappy … unhappiness, however justified, causing one to drink to excess, cannot be a special reason leading to non-disqualification.

"… the Respondent simply could not bring himself within the third test [in *R v Wickins*; see below]; in other words, … [the matter relied on] was not directly connected with the commission of the offence. It was all to do with the unhappy circumstances of the offender. That will not do at law."

Appeal allowed.

7. MEDICAL CONDITION

See also Kinsella v DPP, page 95 – abnormal alcohol metabolism is not a special reason.

R v Wickins

(1958) 42 Cr App R 236, [1958] Crim LR 619, 14 July 1958, CCA

A defendant who did not know he suffered diabetes had a special reason – he would not have been driving under the influence of drink if he had not had diabetes.

A motorist had pleaded guilty to driving when under the influence of drink. He argued that there were special reasons, under s 15(2), Road Traffic Act 1930, why he should not be disqualified. He suffered diabetes but had not been aware of that at the time of driving. Had he not been diabetic, the small amount he had drunk would not have affected his ability to drive. The argument was rejected by the

Recorder, who imposed a nominal fine and 12 months' disqualification. The motorist appealed to the Court of Criminal Appeal against disqualification.

HELD: "… if one takes the essence of [the definition of 'special reason' in *Whittall v Kirby*; see page 505], there are four conditions there laid down which have to be satisfied. The first is that it must be a mitigating or an extenuating circumstance. There is no doubt about that here. The next is that it must not amount in law to a defence to the charge. Equally, that is the case here. The third is that it must be directly connected with the commission of the offence. In our judgment, the circumstances here are directly connected with the commission of the offence. If it had not been for the fact that the appellant was suffering from diabetes, the offence would not have been committed at all, because he had not taken sufficient drink to affect the mind of an ordinary man who was not suffering from that disease. The fourth is that the matter is one which the court ought properly to take into consideration when imposing punishment. That fourth condition is clearly satisfied here … ."

Appeal allowed.

R v Jackson; R v Hart

[1970] 1 QB 647, [1969] 2 WLR 1339, [1969] 2 All ER 453, [1970] RTR 165, 11 March 1969, CA

The general state of health or a bodily defect of an offender is peculiar to the offender and not to the offence; it makes no difference whether or not that state of health or its effect are known to the offender. The circumstances in these two cases were peculiar to the offenders and so did not amount to special reasons.

In *Jackson*, a motorist had pleaded guilty to driving with excess alcohol, contrary to s 1(1), Road Safety Act 1967. He had been stopped at 12.50 am by police because of his erratic driving, and blood analysis was positive. He said he had had no food during the day, had been engaged on business all day, and had driven considerable distances. At 7 pm, he drank 2 pints of brown ale, had dinner, with which he drank one third of a glass of wine, followed by four brandies. At 10.40 pm he began driving. He also said he was unaware that he had a defective liver. A doctor gave evidence that the defendant suffered from high blood pressure, a lamentable diet and a lamentable way of life; he spoke of a malfunctioning liver; these factors had the effect that alcohol would be retained in the blood for longer than would be expected; the build-up of alcohol in the blood was below normal and excretion slow.

In *Hart*, a motorist had pleaded guilty to failing without reasonable excuse to provide a specimen for a laboratory test, contrary to s 3(3), Road Safety Act 1967. He was a polio victim and his right lower arm had been amputated; he drove an invalid car. He was stopped by police and asked to provide a specimen for a breath test; he refused, saying he had "had a few drinks". At the police station he again refused to provide specimens. At the hearing, he said he had refused as a matter of personal principle.

Both argued, unsuccessfully, that there were special reasons for not disqualifying, under s 5(1), Road Traffic Act 1962. They appealed.

HELD: "[After reviewing the authorities, and applying *Whittall v Kirby*, page 505] … this court is prepared to make the following assumptions: first, – albeit with considerable hesitation, – that in neither case was there evidence that drink consumed by the driver had impaired his capacity to drive … Secondly, that in the case of *Hart*, he was a cripple unable to get home … without his invalid car, unless he hired a taxi or had transport assistance from a friend. Thirdly, that in the case of *Jackson* the evidence established an idiosyncratic state of his liver which, when combined with his blood pressure, caused the duration of retention of alcohol in the blood to be longer than usual to some unspecified extent and degree, and that he did not know of that idiosyncrasy.

"None of these facts thus assumed can constitute a special reason as regards an offence created by section 1 or by section 3 of the Act of 1967.

"… this court finds itself quite unable to comprehend how any tribunal could find that the fact the driver was a cripple who required transport was a special reason in relation to the offence of unreasonably refusing to give a specimen. The refusal in the instant case was stated to be 'on principle'. Indeed, this court finds difficulty in conceiving what could be a special reason in relation to an unreasonable refusal.

"… any general state of health of an offender or bodily defect … can only be peculiar to the offender and not to the offence: at any rate as regards offences under sections 1 and 3 of the Act of 1967. It makes no difference whether or not that state of health or its effect are known to him."

Appeals dismissed.

DPP v Williams (Rhys Aubrey)

Unreported, CO 512/94, 22 June 1994, QBD (DC)

The facts of this case revealed no evidence of any medical condition which would justify finding a special reason.

A motorist had pleaded guilty to driving with excess alcohol, contrary to s 5(1)(a), Road Traffic Act 1988. He submitted that there were special reasons for not disqualifying under s 34(1), Road Traffic Offenders Act 1988. He had drunk one pint of beer with his father; he was profoundly deaf; he had undergone treatment to reconstruct his mouth as a result of which he had to take an alcohol-based mouthwash four times a day; he had periodic gastric problems. Agreed medical evidence was to the effect that, *inter alia*, his disabilities were "rather indeterminate" and that the records did not mention any liver or kidney dysfunction.

The magistrates found that the motorist had consumed only one pint of beer; and that due to his ongoing and indeterminate medical problems he would not have been aware that he would be over the limit. They found special reasons and did not disqualify. The prosecutor appealed.

HELD: "Looking first at [the point on] unawareness that he would be over the limit, that can shortly be disposed of having regard to the case of *DPP v O'Meara* [see page 551] … The fact that he was not aware that he would be over the limit is neither here nor there.

"… the Justices speak of 'due to his ongoing and indeterminate medical problem …'. What these medical problems were, other than deafness, I have no idea … Specifically, the doctor says that there is no mention in the records whatsoever of any liver or kidney dysfunction. If there had been any such evidence, that might have been an explanation of the fact that, although he said he had only consumed one pint of beer, the proportion of alcohol in his breath was found to be 84 [μg] in 100 millilitres of breath …

"… the evidence … simply did not establish any medical condition of relevance … he obviously had the medical condition of profound deafness, but that had nothing whatsoever to do with the case … there was no justification whatsoever for the Justices' finding of special reasons."

Appeal allowed.

8. OTHER ARGUMENTS

See also Bobin v DPP, page 55 – officer saying that failure to provide would not mean "definite disqualification" may amount to a special reason; Grix v Chief Constable of Kent, page 91 – offering a urine specimen in response to a requirement for blood was not a special reason; Kinsella v DPP, page 95 – abnormal alcohol metabolism was not a special reason; Dickinson v DPP, page 249 – being unable to raise the defence of post-driving consumption was not a special reason; Beauchamp-Thompson v DPP, page 309 – where the motorist made no inquiry about what wine he was drinking, but later claimed he was drinking stronger wine than usual, he did not have a special reason; Griffiths (Richard Stephen) v DPP, page 313 – hoping to complete the journey before the breath alcohol reached the limit was not a special reason; Daniels v DPP, page 350, where failure to tell a motor cyclist that he was no longer suspected of stealing the motor cycle could amount to a special reason; Woolfe v DPP, page 440 – something which is precluded as a defence may nevertheless be a special reason; and Stewart v DPP, unreported, CO/4440/98 (DC), 14 December 1998, where the fact that the defendant had had a leg amputated did not amount to a special reason. See also R (Gatenby) v Newton Ayecliffe Magistrates' Court, page 593, where the court's refusal to allow a short adjournment denied the defendant the opportunity to argue special reasons.

Lodwick v Brow

[1984] RTR 394, (1984) 6 Cr App R (S) 38, 27 January 1984, QBD (DC)

The fact that the defendant had lost his portion of the blood specimen did not amount to a special reason not to disqualify.

A motorist pleaded guilty to driving with excess alcohol in blood, contrary to s 6(1), Road Traffic Act 1972. There had been an accident and the motorist had been taken to hospital; the doctor in charge gave permission for specimens to be taken. Blood was taken and the motorist retained part of the specimen. Later, he could not remember having given a blood specimen, and his part of it could not be found. Analysis on behalf of the prosecutor revealed 82 μg alcohol in 100 ml blood.

The motorist submitted that there were special reasons for not disqualifying under s 93(1), Road Traffic Act 1972. Following *Whittall v Kirby* (see page 505), that a special reason had to be a reason special to the facts which constituted the offence, the justices found that the alcohol-testing procedures were directly connected with the commission of the offence and could not be separated therefrom. They therefore found special reasons and exercised their discretion not to disqualify. The prosecutor appealed.

QUESTION(S) FOR THE COURT: Whether the facts were capable in law of amounting to special reasons.

HELD: "… the decision in *Doyle v Leroux* [[1981] RTR 438, [1981] Crim LR 631 (DC)] was *per in curiam* and should not hereafter be looked upon as an authority for the proposition that the loss of a specimen, occurring as it must after the offence, can be treated as a special reason … to allow such an argument based on post traumatic amnesia would open the door to anyone to allege that they lost their part of the specimen … and that they therefore should not be liable to be disqualified.

"… Quite clearly the blood-alcohol test took place after the offence had been completed and the loss thereafter of the specimen could not be a special reason which related to the commission of the offence."

Appeal allowed.

Vaughan v Dunn

[1984] RTR 376, 20 February 1984, QBD (DC)

A police officer on a special assignment which involved visiting public houses did not have a special reason for not being disqualified.

A motorist pleaded guilty to driving with excess alcohol, contrary to s 6(1)(a), Road Traffic Act 1972 as substituted by s 25 and Sch 8, Transport Act 1981. He had collided with a lamp post. Breath analysis revealed 100 μg alcohol in 100 ml breath.

He submitted that there were special reasons for not disqualifying under s 93(1), Road Traffic Act 1972. He was a police officer on a special assignment with other officers; they were visiting public houses, ingratiating themselves with people they met there with a view to gathering information. The defendant was being paid a special allowance to buy alcoholic drinks; he worked extremely long hours; on the occasion in question he had visited several licensed premises; he would have brought suspicion on himself had he consumed only soft drinks.

The justices accepted that this was an exceptional case and that the defendant was at risk of consuming alcohol beyond the legal limit; they found special reasons and exercised their discretion not to disqualify. The prosecutor appealed.

QUESTION(S) FOR THE COURT: Whether it was correct in law that the circumstances of the case could amount to a special reason for not disqualifying.

HELD: "… the … discretion [not to disqualify] should only be exercised in clear and compelling circumstances. I do not think that the present case could possibly be described as one where there were clear and compelling circumstances.

"The next matter is the manner in which the defendant drove … the man was so drunk that he simply drove his car straight into a lamp post, without any other vehicle being involved.

"Then … it will be a very powerful reason against exercising the discretion in favour of the defendant if the relevant alcohol content is very high. In the present case, the alcohol content in the defendant's breath exceeded the permitted limit by nearly 200 per cent.

"… even in cases of emergency … it is much more difficult for a driver to justify using a car to go home, the obvious reason being that he can, if necessary, take steps to obtain alternative transport. He can get a lift, hire a taxi or, if it is available, use public transport.

"… none of these matters could have been taken into account by the justices … The present case … is not one of emergency. It is one where the defendant went round public houses. He went out with the obvious intention of drinking in those public houses, and he went out with the intention of driving after he had drunk in those public houses; and he carried out that intention.

"… I cannot conceive of a case which includes those facts where it could be said that it was a proper case for exercising the discretion under the section not to disqualify."

The answer to the question was "no". Appeal allowed.

Bolliston v Gibbons

(1984) 6 Cr App R (S) 134, [1985] RTR 176, 29 March 1984, QBD (DC)

Where a defendant had had special reasons for not disqualifying for an earlier offence, that did not mean that he escaped the minimum 3-year disqualification on a second offence.

A motorist had pleaded guilty, on 16 March 1983, to a charge of driving with excess alcohol, contrary to s 6(1), Road Traffic Act 1972. His driving licence revealed that he had been convicted on 30 April 1973 of an identical offence, committed on 9 November 1971; on that occasion the court had found special reasons for not disqualifying from driving – the motorist had been taking a tonic which, unknown to him, contained alcohol.

The motorist submitted that the special reasons for not disqualifying for the earlier offence equally amounted to special reasons in respect of the later offence; and that an offender who had knowingly committed the offence once only should not be punished in the same way as a person who had knowingly committed the same offence twice.

The magistrate rejected that argument, finding that she could have regard only to special reasons relating to the offence with which she was dealing, namely the later offence. The motorist was, *inter alia*, disqualified from driving for 3 years. He appealed.

QUESTION(S) FOR THE COURT: Whether on a true construction of s 93(1) (obligatory disqualification for not less than 12 months unless there are special reasons) and (4) (substituting a minimum period of disqualification of 3 years for a person convicted twice within 10 years) of the Road Traffic Act 1972, a court when deciding whether there were special reasons for not disqualifying the second-time offender for a period less than the statutory minimum of 3 years, was entitled to, and should, take into account the circumstances of both offences; or whether the magistrate was bound to disqualify the defendant for a minimum period of 3 years.

HELD: "… [the magistrate] was entirely right in her construction of these two provisions and … she was bound to disqualify the defendant for a period of three years, since there were no special reasons relating to the offence with which she was concerned … ."

Appeal dismissed.

McCormick v Hitchins

[1988] RTR 182, 3 December 1985, QBD (DC)

Having no intention to drive was a special reason for not disqualifying or endorsing for failing to provide.

A motorist had pleaded guilty to failing without reasonable excuse to provide a specimen of breath for analysis while in charge of a motor vehicle, contrary to s 8(7), Road Traffic Act 1972 as substituted by s 25 and Sch 8, Transport Act

1981. He had left his car in the car park of a public house a few days before the incident giving rise to the charge, and had not driven it since. On the evening in question, he was in the public house and, on being told there had been an accident involving his car, went out and found it had been moved by a number of youths and had collided with another car. The police were called; the motorist had the car keys in his pocket; he refused to provide a sample for a roadside breath test; at the police station, he refused to provide a specimen of breath for analysis.

The magistrates found special reasons not to disqualify in that there had been no likelihood of driving; but found no special reasons not to endorse under s 19(1) and Sch 7, Pt II, Transport Act 1981. They endorsed his licence with 10 penalty points. He appealed against the decision to endorse.

QUESTION(S) FOR THE COURT: Whether, having exercised their discretion not to disqualify on the grounds that there was no likelihood of his driving whilst the proportion of alcohol in his breath remained likely to exceed the prescribed limit, the justices were entitled to find that there were no special reasons for not ordering his licence to be endorsed with 10 penalty points.

HELD: "… If one takes the essence of [the definition of] 'special reason' in *R v Wickins* [see page 560], there are four conditions … which have to be satisfied. The first is that it must be a mitigating or an extenuating circumstance. There is no doubt about that here. The next is that it must not amount in law to a defence to the charge. Equally, that is the case here. The third is that it must be directly connected with the commission of the offence … in the circumstances here relied upon the whole of them related not to the defendant personally but to the offence which he freely confessed to having committed … His reasons for not providing [the] sample were simply that he had no intention of driving. He was believed about that, and so could not have constituted any kind of danger or menace upon the road … here was a special reason. No reasonable bench of justices properly directed on the law could … have avoided such a conclusion."

Appeal allowed.

Jane v DPP

Unreported, CO/1081/87, 26 October 1987, QBD (DC)

Being only marginally over the limit is not a special reason.

A motorist had pleaded guilty to driving with excess alcohol in breath, contrary to s 6(1)(a), Road Traffic Act 1972 as substituted by s 25 and Sch 8, Transport Act 1981. He advanced special reasons for not disqualifying under s 93(1), Road Traffic Act 1972, saying the publican had, by mistake, given him different lager from the one he had ordered. He adduced expert evidence that if he had been drinking the type of lager he had asked for, in the quantities which he had undoubtedly consumed, his alcohol level would have been between 36 µg and 39 µg alcohol in 100 ml breath. Although this was over the prescribed limit, local policy was not to prosecute where the reading was below 40 µg.

The justices ordered disqualification. The motorist appealed.

HELD: "… the question arises as to whether or not [the defendant] is entitled to pray in aid that practice [of not prosecuting when the reading was under 40 μg] when urging that there are special reasons for not disqualifying …

"The simple fact is that on any view of the matter this Appellant was and always would have been over the prescribed limit …

"There is … ample authority … for the proposition that it cannot be a special reason to be only marginally above the prescribed limit. If it cannot be a special reason to be only marginally over the prescribed limit, it would be strange indeed if police practice could be prayed in aid to say that such a finding would not normally lead to a prosecution …

"There was nothing in the evidence … which could have enabled [the magistrates] to come to the conclusion that there were special reasons for not disqualifying … ."

Appeal dismissed.

DPP v Kinnersley

[1993] RTR 105, 10 December 1992, QBD (DC)

On the facts of this case, a fear of contracting AIDS was capable of amounting to a special reason.

A motorist had been charged with failing without reasonable excuse to provide a specimen for a breath test, contrary to s 6(4), Road Traffic Act 1988; and with failing without reasonable excuse to provide two specimens of breath for analysis, contrary to s 7(6), Road Traffic Act 1988. He had refused to provide a roadside specimen, and at the police station, refused to provide specimens for analysis. He gave no reason.

At the hearing, he submitted that he believed the provision of a specimen would entail a substantial risk to his health in that he feared contracting the HIV virus and that this amounted to a reasonable excuse. The justices convicted him on both charges, and the motorist then submitted, on the same grounds, that he had special reasons for not disqualifying under s 34(1), Road Traffic Offenders Act 1988.

The justices were of the opinion that his exceptional fear of contracting HIV was justified, particularly as he had knowledge of the condition and how it may be contracted, and the sealed mouthpieces of the testing devices had not been shown or explained to him. They found special reasons and did not disqualify. The prosecutor appealed.

QUESTION(S) FOR THE COURT: (1) Whether the justices were right to say that the test of reasonable excuse was objective; (2) whether, having convicted the defendant, the justices were then entitled to consider the circumstances in which the defendant refused to provide the breath specimens and the arguments put forward as to the reasonableness of his excuse for refusing as constituting special reasons; (3) whether, on the evidence heard and facts found, the justices were entitled to find that the defendant had established special reasons.

HELD: "… the justices in this case were on the evidence entitled to find that there were special reasons … The driver's failure to give an explanation at the time of the refusal does not exclude as a matter of law the possibility of a finding that special reasons existed, though it will usually be an important factor in the court's deliberations upon the evidence before conclusions are reached … Failure to give an early explanation may reflect on the *bona fides* of the defendant …

"All the relevant circumstances must be considered by the court, including the fact that the defendant has been arrested and cautioned and the fact that the constable is not under a legal duty to explain to a driver that mouthpieces are sterile …

"… [The justices] were entitled to conclude … that to a man with the defendant's knowledge there were mitigating circumstances not amounting to a defence, yet directly connected with the commission of the offence and properly taken into consideration when imposing punishment …

"I am very far from saying that where a person who fears AIDS is required to provide a specimen of breath the circumstances of a refusal will often permit a finding of special reasons."

The answers to the questions were "yes". Appeal dismissed.

DPP v Daley (No 2)

[1994] RTR 107, 4 October 1993, QBD (DC)

Facts which do not amount to a reasonable excuse may amount to a special reason, but the facts must be made out.

A motorist had been charged with failing without reasonable excuse to provide a specimen for a breath test, contrary to s 6(4), Road Traffic Act 1988; and with failing without reasonable excuse to provide two specimens of breath for analysis, contrary to s 7(6), Road Traffic Act 1988.

The justices found that he had done his best, but had been physically unable to provide specimens and dismissed the charge. The prosecutor appealed to the Divisional Court which found that there had been no evidence of medical inability, allowed the appeal, and remitted the case to the justices with a direction to convict (see *DPP v Daley*, page 224).

Following conviction and disqualification, the motorist appealed against sentence to the Crown Court, which accepted the same facts as amounting to special reasons for not disqualifying under s 34(1), Road Traffic Offenders Act 1988. The prosecutor appealed against the finding of special reasons.

QUESTION(S) FOR THE COURT: (1) Whether a finding that the defendant had "done his best" to provide specimens could, without more, entitle a court to find special reasons; (2) whether it was necessary for the defendant to establish such facts and circumstances to explain his failure to provide as would entitle the court to find that those facts and circumstances amounted to a sufficient mitigating or extenuating circumstance, directly connected to the commission of the offence, as should be properly taken into consideration when imposing punishment; (3) whether a court, in relation to a defendant who had been convicted of failing without reasonable excuse to provide breath specimens, was entitled to consider the same facts and circumstances, put forward as to the reasonableness of the excuse for that failure, as constituting special reasons; (4) whether the court was entitled to find that the defendant had established special reasons.

HELD: "… it is clear … that it is possible for circumstances which do not amount to a reasonable excuse to afford the foundation for a finding that there were special reasons. It is an unusual situation, but such a situation can from time to time arise. But … if such a situation is to arise, the court must be in a position where it accepts the factual basis … In the present case, the factual basis which was relied on by the defendant when submitting that there was a reasonable excuse … was effectively demolished by the judgment of this court … The Divisional Court [on an earlier appeal in the same case] … came to the clear conclusion that the factual basis could not be sustained … it must necessarily follow that the special reasons were not and could not have been established."

Appeal allowed.

DPP v Murray (David John)

[2001] EWHC Admin 848, 25 October 2001, QBD (DC)

Not knowing that a motorised foot scooter is a motor vehicle did not amount to a special reason for not disqualifying.

The defendant pleaded guilty to, *inter alia*, driving a "Go-ped" motorised scooter with excess alcohol, contrary to s 5(1)(a), Road Traffic Act 1988. He argued that there were special reasons for not disqualifying under s 34(1), Road Traffic Offenders Act 1988, in that, at the time of the offences, the law relating to foot scooters as motor vehicles was unclear. Some 5 months after the offences, the High Court decided that the type of scooter in question is a motor vehicle and that a driving licence and insurance are necessary before using it. There was no evidence of any instructions to inform the purchaser of such a scooter that it is classed as a motor vehicle.

The magistrates found that the defendant had, before buying the scooter, searched the internet for information about whether or not it was a motor vehicle, and that he had used it as though it were a bicycle. They recognised that although it is an offence to use a bicycle when over the limit, conviction does not result in disqualification from driving. The magistrates found special reasons and did not disqualify. The prosecutor appealed.

QUESTION(S) FOR THE COURT: (1) Whether ignorance of the nature of a motorised foot scooter can, as a matter of law, amount to a special reason; (2) whether the justices' decision that special reasons existed was the correct one on the facts of this case.

HELD: "14. … In *Chief Constable of North Yorkshire Police v Saddington* [[2001] RTR 15, [2001] Crim LR 41], … it was held that a Go-ped was a motor vehicle as defined by section 185 of the Road Traffic Act 1988. A Go-ped is a mechanically propelled vehicle intended for use on roads. A driving licence and third-party insurance are required.

"[After reviewing other authorities, including *R v Wickins* (see page 560) and *DPP v Powell* [1993] RTR 236] 23. In the present case, as to driving having consumed alcohol in excess of the prescribed limit, there was no mitigating or extenuating circumstance directly connected with the commission of the offence … Any ignorance of the law on the part of [the appellant] was peculiar to him, and not to the facts of the offence of driving having consumed excess alcohol … the respondent used the motorised scooter as an alternative to his other motor vehicles to drive home after drinking alcohol in a public house.

"[On (1)] 25. Ignorance as to the nature of a motorised foot scooter cannot, as a matter of law, amount to a special reason. …

"26. [The answer to (2) was] No. The Justices' decision that special reasons existed was not correct on the facts of the particular case. There were no mitigating or extenuating circumstances directly connected with the commission of the offences of driving a motor vehicle after consuming alcohol in excess of the prescribed limit and without insurance."

Appeal allowed.

Ng v DPP

[2007] EWHC 36 (Admin), [2007] RTR 35, 26 January 2007, QBD (Admin)

Elevated mouth alcohol caused by eructation (belching) is capable of amounting to a special reason for not disqualifying.

A motorist had been charged with driving with excess alcohol, contrary to s 5(1)(a), Road Traffic Act 1988. He argued that the breath analysis was affected by eructation (belching) and that if the reading had thereby been artificially inflated, that would amount to a special reason for not disqualifying under s 34(1), Road Traffic Offenders Act 1988. The district judge found that the presence of elevated mouth alcohol could not amount to a special reason because it was connected to the offender and not the offence. She convicted the motorist; he appealed.

QUESTION(S) FOR THE COURT: (1) Whether it was right to conclude that the elevated mouth alcohol was a circumstance special to the offender and not the commission of the offence and thus not capable of amounting to a special reason. (2) Following *Zafar v DPP* (page 439), whether the district judge was bound to conclude that evidence of mouth alcohol could not amount to a special reason in any event as no distinction could be made between deep lung breath and any other breath or air exhaled for the purpose of the specimen.

HELD: "[On (2), following *Woolfe v DPP*, page 440] 5. … the question should be answered in the negative. …

"[On (1) and the argument that an increased concentration of alcohol in the appellant's breath as a consequence of eructation could not amount to a special reason because it was a circumstance peculiar to the offender rather than the offence] 10. I do not agree. The evidence upon which the appellant sought to rely went directly to the commission of the offence. If accepted it could provide an explanation as to why the level of alcohol in the appellant's breath exceeded the prescribed level, notwithstanding that on his case the alcohol that he had consumed would not have had that effect. The case is analogous to the line of authority arising out of cases in which … 'the drinks consumed immediately before the offence had, without the knowledge of the offender, been laced or combined with some extraneous substance (drugs or chemicals), or affected by some extraneous incident without the offender being aware of the potential effects', see *R v Jackson* [page 561]."

The answers to both questions were "no". Appeal allowed. Case remitted to the magistrates' court for consideration of special reasons.

9. EXERCISING THE DISCRETION NOT TO DISQUALIFY/ENDORSE

See also Taylor v Rajan, page 507 – when the facts disclose a special reason, that does not mean that the defendant automatically escapes disqualification.

R v Ashford and Tenterden Magistrates' Court ex p Wood

[1988] RTR 178, 5 May 1987, QBD (DC)

Where the defendant would have driven had he not been prevented from doing so, and the justices found special reasons, they were entitled to exercise their discretion to order endorsement.

A person been charged, *inter alia*, with failing without reasonable excuse to provide a specimen of breath for analysis, contrary to s 8(7), Road Traffic Act 1972 as substituted by s 25 and Sch 8, Transport Act 1981. There had been a road accident; the defendant had not been driving at the time; he had intended to, but someone else had intervened and taken over the wheel, the defendant taking the passenger seat.

The justices dismissed other charges, but convicted the defendant of the s 8(7) offence, endorsing his licence with 10 penalty points under s 19(1), Transport Act 1981. The defendant contended he had a special reason for not endorsing; the justices agreed there was a special reason, but, because the defendant would have been driving but for the intervention of another person, they exercised their discretion to order the endorsement.

The justices refused to state a case for the opinion of the Divisional Court. The defendant sought an order of *mandamus* directing the justices to do so.

GROUNDS FOR THE APPLICATION: The case sought to be stated was, where a defendant is found guilty of an offence under s 8(7), Road Traffic Act 1972 and it is also found that at the material time he was not the driver of the motor vehicle but merely a passenger therein, whether it should be held that there are special reasons for not endorsing his licence or disqualifying him, having regard in particular to the dictum of Watkins LJ in *Bunyard v Hayes* [1985] RTR 348 (DC).

HELD: "… the justices … might have concluded that no special reason existed. They did not do that, but chose to deal with the matter in this way: that the fact that the applicant intended to and would have driven his car but for the [other person's] intervention was a reason for declining to exercise their discretion not to endorse … the justices directed themselves correctly as to the law and exercised their discretion in a way in which they were entitled to do on the facts … ."

Application dismissed..

Mayhew v DPP

Unreported, CO/313/87, 13 October 1987, QBD (DC)

Where special reasons were found but the breath alcohol level was very high, the Crown Court's decision to disqualify was not irrational.

A motorist pleaded guilty to a charge of driving while unfit through drink, contrary to s 5(1), Road Traffic Act 1972 as substituted by s 25 and Sch 8, Transport Act 1981. The lower of two breath analyses was 119 µg alcohol in 100 ml breath. The magistrates dismissed a submission of special reasons for not disqualifying under s 93(1), Road Traffic Act 1972.

The motorist appealed to the Crown Court against the disqualification imposed. The Crown Court found special reasons; that that gave it a discretion not to disqualify; but that they would not exercise that discretion in favour of the motorist. The motorist appealed further.

QUESTION(S) FOR THE COURT: Whether or not the Crown Court was correct in directing themselves that they had a discretion, and were they correct in exercising the discretion as they did, or were they bound, having found special reasons, to give effect to that finding by allowing the appeal and ordering disqualification for less than 3 years or ordering no disqualification?

HELD: "[Quoting from *Taylor v Rajan*, see page 507], 'The mere fact that the facts disclose a special reason does not mean that the driver is to escape disqualification as a matter of course … if the alcohol content in the defendant's body is very high, that is a very powerful reason for saying that the discretion should not be exercised in his favour …'.

"[Quoting from *Vaughan v Dunn*, see page 564] 'The discretion should only be exercised in clear and compelling circumstances' … There is … abundant authority that there is a discretion … That being so, the exercise of the discretion could only be flawed on the basis that it was irrational … I do not think for one moment that this decision was in measurable distance of irrationality … ."

Appeal dismissed.

DPP v Barker

[1990] RTR 1, 6 November 1989, QBD (DC)

On the facts of this case (total loss of knowledge following laced drink), the magistrates, having found a special reason, were correct not to disqualify.

A motorist had pleaded guilty to a charge of driving with excess alcohol, contrary to s 6(1), Road Traffic Act 1972 as substituted by s 25 and Sch 8, Transport Act 1981. She had submitted there were special reasons for not disqualifying under s 93(1), Road Traffic Act 1972. She was required to drive in the course of her employment; she was unused to alcohol; at the time, she was distressed, depressed and emotionally weak; she had drunk wine at a restaurant and had later been given orange juice to which, unknown to her, vodka had been added; she did not detect the alcohol; she had no reason to drive on the evening in question; she remembered nothing after the first laced drink; she had woken the following morning unaware that she had driven, been arrested, given breath specimens and brought home by the police.

Expert evidence on the effects of the amount of alcohol taken was called by both prosecutor and defendant, on the basis of which the justices concluded, *inter alia*, that the alcohol consumed by the motorist would have had an immediate effect.

The motorist contended that she had unknowingly consumed alcohol, but for which she would not have been over the limit, and that the justices should exercise their discretion not to disqualify. The justices accepted her argument and did not disqualify. The prosecutor appealed.

QUESTION(S) FOR THE COURT: Whether the justices were correct in law, on the facts found: (1) to find that special reasons existed; (2) to exercise their discretion not to disqualify.

HELD: "[The prosecution] does not challenge the finding [of] special reasons, but … submits that the justices erred in law because, when considering whether to exercise their discretion, they did not ask themselves … whether the defendant should have realised that she was not fit to drive due to the presence of alcohol in her body … The findings are … that the defendant could not detect the presence of alcohol in the orange juice and that the effect of it upon her was sudden … [she] remembered nothing after the first drink and was indeed even unaware of the fact that she had driven her motor car, had been arrested and been taken to a police station. The important finding of fact is … that 'the defendant suffered a total loss of knowledge of her actions and was not aware that her condition was influenced by the consumption of alcohol.' … With such total loss of knowledge it seems to me inevitably to follow that the defendant could not have appreciated that she was unfit to drive through drink."

The answers to both questions were "yes". Appeal dismissed.

Donahue v DPP

[1993] RTR 156, 3 March 1992, QBD (DC)

Where the justices found special reasons, but also found that the motorist must have realised he was not fit to drive and so disqualified him, there was nothing to suggest that the justices had misdirected themselves.

A motorist had pleaded guilty to driving with excess alcohol, contrary to s 6(1)(a), Road Traffic Act 1972 as substituted by s 25 and Sch 8, Transport Act 1981. He was a sales representative and had been entertaining customers in a hospitality tent. He had asked to be served only alcohol-free wine, but that request had not been observed. He drove away, and was involved in an accident. Breath analysis revealed 99 µg alcohol in 100 ml breath. He did not mention to the police that he believed he had been drinking alcohol-free wine only.

At the hearing, he submitted there were special reasons for not disqualifying under s 93(1), Road Traffic Act 1972. He adduced medical evidence to the effect that his excess of alcohol on the day in question could mimic the effect of excessive tiredness following broken sleep the night before.

The justices found that there were special reasons, but that the motorist must have realised he was not fit to drive; his conduct and answers to the police supported that, as did the high reading. They did not therefore exercise their discretion to refrain from disqualifying him from driving. The motorist appealed.

QUESTION(S) FOR THE COURT: Whether the justices were justified in their decision, having decided that there were special reasons for not disqualifying the defendant, nevertheless in determining that he merited disqualification in the circumstances.

HELD: "… the justices found as a fact that the defendant, who was not an inexperienced or young man, must have realised that he was not fit to drive through alcohol. They had taken into account the evidence of the doctor that the effects of alcohol might be confused with those of excessive tiredness. I can find in the stated case no circumstance which would justify the conclusion that in exercising their discretion the justices misdirected themselves, failed to take into account evidence which was relevant to the issues which they had to decide or approached the exercise of their discretion on any wrong principle."

Appeal dismissed.

Lane v DPP

Unreported, CO 11/95, 10 March 1995, QBD (DC)

Having found special reasons, a court should not then invite further evidence before exercising the discretion whether or not to disqualify; it should take into account only the factors within R v Wickins, page 560.

A motorist had pleaded guilty to driving with excess alcohol, contrary to s 5(1)(a), Road Traffic Act 1988. She submitted that there were special reasons, under s 34(1), Road Traffic Offenders Act 1988, for not disqualifying, or for disqualifying for a period shorter than the minimum. She thought she had had no alcohol on the evening in question; unknown to her, her drinks had been laced; had they not been, she would not have been over the limit.

The justices found special reasons did exist, but before deciding whether or not to exercise their discretion in her favour, they asked the defence advocate if he wished to address the court on this point. In response, the motorist's representative attempted to introduce new evidence about his client's personal circumstances. The justices found that personal circumstances were not relevant. They disqualified the motorist for 14 days. She appealed.

QUESTION(S) FOR THE COURT: Whether, after finding special reasons which give rise to a discretion not to disqualify or to disqualify for a period other than the statutory minimum, the magistrates are limited to taking into account only matters connected with the commission of the offence, or are they entitled to take account of matters of personal mitigation?

HELD: "[Counsel for the appellant] accepts that special reasons must relate to the offence. He submits, however, that there is a further stage at which the Court is entitled, before reaching its decision, to consider the personal circumstances of the defendant. [He] seeks to rely upon the decision of this Court in *DPP v O'Connor* [see page 534] …

… [In *DPP v O'Connor*] Woolf LJ did not have in mind that, at the final stage, considerations other than those covered by the expression 'special reasons' as defined in the authorities should be considered. He was not intending to depart from the approach of the Court in *Wickins* [*R v Wickins*, page 560] … Neither … did Woolf LJ have in mind that Magistrates should first announce that they had found special reasons and then invite further evidence and submissions on whether to disqualify."

Appeal dismissed.

Dixon-Watmough v Preston Justices

Unreported, CO/2474/96, 22 November 1996, QBD (DC)

In exercising the discretion, justices should not have taken into account the fact that the defendant was unable to call as a witness the person who had laced her drink.

A motorist had pleaded guilty to driving with excess alcohol, but submitted that there were special reasons for not disqualifying under s 34(1), Road Traffic Offenders Act 1988. With friends, she visited two public houses and drank 2 pints of shandy. A person whom she had not met before offered to buy her a drink and she asked for Coke. He twice gave her a drink; on neither occasion did she see the drink poured. She was stopped by police while driving home, and breath analysis revealed 46 μg alcohol in 100 ml breath.

At the hearing she called expert evidence to show that the 2 pints of shandy would not have accounted for the amount of alcohol in her breath, and argued that therefore the two glasses of Coke must have been contaminated with alcohol. The motorist suffered from multiple sclerosis as a result of which she was unable to detect the taste of alcohol.

The justices found there were special reasons in that the motorist's drinks had been laced without her knowledge, but did not exercise their discretion not to disqualify.

QUESTION(S) FOR THE COURT: Whether the justices were correct in law on the facts found in not exercising their discretion not to disqualify.

HELD: "… it is the law than even where special reasons are found, the Justices still have a discretion to exercise as to whether they will disqualify or not …

"… [in exercising their discretion the justices] rightly took into account that the driver should be responsible for what she drinks, that Miss Dixon-Watmough had accepted drinks from a stranger of short acquaintance, and that as she was unable to taste alcohol because of her multiple sclerosis she ought to take care as to what drinks of any kind she has and who they come from. They rightly concluded that she took a great risk in accepting drinks from a stranger in the public house.

"Thus far, the Justices' reasoning is beyond criticism. [But,] dealing with discretion, they say she was not present at the bar when the drinks were purchased and because the identity of the customer was unknown she was unable to adduce evidence to support her contention that her drinks had been tampered with. The latter part of that last sentence was wholly irrelevant to the question whether they should exercise their discretion to disqualify her or not once they found special reasons. Having found special reasons without the benefit of evidence from the unknown customer …, they had no need to consider what evidence he might have given, nor were they entitled to attribute any importance to the fact that he had not given evidence. It might have made sense if they had taken the absence of that man as a witness into account in deciding whether to accept that there had been special reasons, but they did not. It would appear that they regarded it as relevant to their discretion whether or not to order disqualification once special reasons had been established.

"This … is a very borderline case. But I do not think we can be confident that the Justices approached this question of discretionary disqualification in the right way. It seems distinctly possible that they took quite an irrelevant factor into account … ."

Appeal allowed.

R v St Albans Crown Court ex p O'Donovan

[2000] 1 Cr App R (S) 344, 9 July 1999, QBD (DC)

On the facts of this case (finding of special reasons, absence of danger) disqualification for 20 months was excessive.

A police officer observed a motorist manoeuvring his vehicle in the car park of a public house and colliding with another vehicle. Breath analysis later revealed 103 µg of alcohol per 100 ml breath.

At the hearing, it was accepted that the defendant lived close by; he was not going to drive out of the car park, but was simply attempting to move his car a few yards to clear an access. The magistrates convicted him. They found special reasons for not disqualifying under s 34(1), Road Traffic Offenders Act 1988, but nonetheless disqualified him for 20 months (one third less than the period recommended in the Magistrates' Association Sentencing Guidelines, but 8 months longer than the mandatory minimum), subject to a reduction of 5 months if he successfully completed a rehabilitation course. They also fined him and ordered him to pay costs.

His appeal to the Crown Court was dismissed. He appealed further.

HELD: "… The applicant's essential argument is that, in the light of the special reasons …, no reasonable tribunal could have imposed so long a disqualification as twenty months … [I]t would be insufficient for his purpose to establish merely that the sentence is: '… severe, perhaps even unduly severe or surprisingly severe.' Rather [it must be shown] that it is: '… so far outside the normal discretionary limits as to enable this court to say that its imposition must involve an error of law …'.

"Neither counsel has been able to find any previous case in which justices (or a Crown Court on appeal), despite finding the existence of special reasons, have then gone on to impose a period of disqualification in excess of the mandatory twelve months. I certainly do not go so far as to say that there could never be a case where such an approach would be appropriate … But I do say that where, as here, special reasons are found to exist and where no-one has sought to suggest that the actual driving undertaken or contemplated could have posed any appreciable risk of danger to anyone at all, it would be hard to justify a period of disqualification in excess of the mandatory twelve months.

"… I think that the overall period of disqualification imposed here … was wholly disproportionate to the gravity of this particular offence … ."

Disqualification reduced from 20 to 12 months, to be further reduced by 3 months on completion of a drink driving course.

Chapter 11

Other Issues

1. ADJOURNMENTS

Walden v Highbury Corner Magistrates' Court; Stern v Highbury Corner Magistrates' Court

[2003] EWHC 708 (Admin), [2003] All ER(D) 285 (Mar), 19 March 2003, QBD (Admin)

Where adjournments were granted without rigorous scrutiny of the applications, and in the absence of representations from the prosecutor or the justices on the appeal, the orders granting the adjournments were quashed.

In *Walden*, a motorist had been charged with being in charge of a motor vehicle with excess alcohol on 10 November 2001, contrary to s 5(1)(b), Road Traffic Act 1988. In *Stern*, a motorist had been charged with driving with excess alcohol on 22 April 2001, contrary to s 5(1)(a), Road Traffic Act 1988. Both had pleaded not guilty and their cases had been adjourned to await the decision in *DPP v Brown; DPP v Teixeira* (see page 297). Trial dates were then fixed for 3 September 2002 and 26 September 2002, respectively. On both trial dates, no prosecution witnesses were present, having not been warned. The prosecution sought adjournments. The justices asked for an outline of the facts of the allegations; they did not ask why the witnesses had not been warned. In *Stern*, the defendant had become seriously ill. The magistrates granted the adjournments, in *Walden*, citing the seriousness of the charge, and in *Stern* without giving reasons. The defendants appealed.

HELD: "9. The position today is this: in a word, no one is any the wiser. No evidence has been filed on behalf of the defendant court. An acknowledgment of service was lodged by the defendant court in each case, but no submissions were made. There has been no response either from the Crown Prosecution Service, who again had been served in each case as an interested party … Neither the justices, nor the Crown Prosecution Service, are represented at today's hearing. …

"[After reviewing the authorities] 16. … The justices have an obligation formally to examine the circumstances leading to an application, the reasons for it, and the consequences, both to the prosecution and to the defence. As Bingham LJ observed [in *R v Hereford Magistrates' Court ex p Rowlands* [1998] QB 110], 'applications for adjournments must be subjected to rigorous scrutiny', and that observation applies regardless of which side is making the application.

"17. The single inquiry made in each of these cases was for an outline of the prosecution's case. The prosecution was not, for example, sent away to investigate the … non-attendance of witnesses. Finally, the court gave no reasons in the case of Mr Stern for its conclusion; and in the case of Mr Walden, gave limited reasons which did not reveal that any regard had been had for any other considerations save for the two identified. Furthermore, these reasons were given in the absence of any 'rigorous scrutiny' …

"18. With some hesitation … I have come to the conclusion, in the absence of any representations made on behalf either of the justices or the Crown Prosecution Service, that it is in each of these cases appropriate for the court to interfere. In my judgment, each of these applications for an adjournment should have been refused, with the inevitable consequence that each case would have been dismissed. The order granting the adjournment will accordingly be quashed, as will the decision to refuse to dismiss each of these cases."

Appeals allowed.

Essen v DPP

[2005] EWHC 1077 (Admin), 12 May 2005, QBD (DC)

Where magistrates allowed the prosecution's application to adjourn, and the case stated gave no reasons for that decision, it was overturned.

A motorist had been charged with, *inter alia*, driving, on 4 July 2001, while unfit through drink or drugs, contrary to s 4(1), Road Traffic Act 1988. There had been a number of pre-trial hearings and a trial date of 30 December 2002 was set. The defence then sought to vacate that date on the grounds that it was inconvenient for defence witnesses; the magistrates refused the application. On 30 December, the prosecution sought an adjournment because no prosecution witnesses had attended. The defendant opposed the application, but the magistrates granted it; the case stated gave no reasons for this decision. There were then various applications concerning the admissibility of evidence. The trial eventually opened on 17 April 2003 but did not conclude until 7 April 2004, when the defendant was convicted. She appealed.

QUESTION(S) FOR THE COURT: Whether, having refused the defence application to adjourn the original trial date of 30 December 2002, it was *Wednesbury* unreasonable to have on the day then granted the same application when made by the prosecution and opposed by the defence.

HELD: "28. … the court has the benefit of the case stated, but … this does not give the reasons for granting the prosecution's application for an adjournment on that day.

"30. … we have no information before us upon which we can be satisfied that the Justices did take into account relevant considerations and exclude irrelevant considerations. It is possible that what weighed them was the factor referred to by

Bingham LJ in [*R v Aberdare Justices ex p DPP* (1990) 155 JP 324]. That is the interest of the prosecution that a serious charge properly preferred by the defendant should be the subject of proper adjudication and that the result of refusing an adjournment would … be the collapse of the prosecution. If this was the case and if they had articulated this, … it is very unlikely that this court would interfere with their decision.

"31. … it is not possible to say anything other than that this was a decision which could have gone either way. In those circumstances, since no reasons were given, given that applications for adjournments must be subjected to rigorous scrutiny [Lord Bingham CJ in *R v Hereford Magistrates' Court ex p Rowlands* [1998] QB 110] … with some reluctance, I am constrained to the conclusion that this court is unable to uphold the decision. I would set aside the decision of the Justices granting the adjournment and allow the appeal."

Filmer v DPP

[2006] EWHC 3450 (Admin), [2007] RTR 28, 1 November 2006, QBD (DC)

On the facts of this case, the defence had been given sufficient notice of the issues to be tried and was not entitled to an adjournment to seek further evidence.

A motorist had been charged with driving, on the parking area of commercial premises, with excess alcohol, contrary to s 5(1)(a), Road Traffic Act 1988. He at first pleaded guilty, but was then allowed to vacate his plea to enable him to argue that the parking area was not a public place.

The magistrates heard evidence from a police officer that the car park had an entrance and exit without barriers, and was, outside normal trading hours, used as a pedestrian shortcut, a turning circle, and for parking. At the close of the prosecution case, the defendant submitted there was no case to answer. When that submission was rejected, he sought an adjournment to gather more evidence about the parking area, claiming "prosecution by ambush". In fact, the advance disclosure had included a statement from the witness that, "the forecourt itself is an open area of tarmac which is accessible to vehicles at two points but which has a brick wall partially across the front". The magistrates refused the application to adjourn and convicted the motorist. He appealed.

QUESTION(S) FOR THE COURT: Whether: (a) refusing the adjournment was a proper exercise of discretion; (b) it was *Wednesbury* unreasonable to accept the police evidence that the area in question was a public place.

HELD: "19. … [The appellant cited] two generally accepted propositions which relate to the fundamental preconditions of a fair trial. First, the requirement that criminal proceedings should not proceed by way of ambush … and second, the concomitant requirement that the prosecution must normally serve written versions of the evidence they propose to adduce in sufficient time before the hearing to enable the defendant fairly to deal with it …

"25. … [The Crown] argues that the appellant had clear prior knowledge of the issues in the case such as to enable him to prepare his case fully for trial, and that the evidence called by the Crown was sufficient to justify a conviction …

"28. The central complaint as regards disclosure is that the appellant had received no sufficient notification of the details of the respondent's case that the car park was a public place so as to enable him to anticipate it and to gather evidence in rebuttal. I am unable to accept that argument. The appellant's guilty plea was vacated in order for this very issue to be resolved, and the appellant knew full well that it was the prosecution's submission that this was a public place for the purposes of this legislation.

"29. Additionally, [the] statement which was served in advance of trial, had revealed the essential elements of their case. …

"31. The additional evidence given [at the trial] was no more than … examples of how the public, to [the witness's] knowledge, had utilised this car park. The appellant was fully aware that he had the option of calling witnesses if any could be found who were in a position to rebut the prosecution assertion that this was private land to which the public had access at the time in question."

The answer to question (a) was "yes"; the answer to question (b) was "no". Appeal dismissed.

Williams v DPP

[2009] EWHC 2354 (Admin), 24 July 2009, QBD (DC)

Amending the charge, out of time, from failing to provide breath to failing to provide urine, was permissible in that both offences arose from the same facts, but, in the absence of any compelling reason, an adjournment following the amendment was not, on the facts, in the interests of justice.

A motorist had provided insufficient breath for analysis, saying he suffered from bronchitis. He was then asked if there was any medical reason why a specimen of blood could not be taken, and he said he was afraid of needles. When asked to provide a urine specimen, he failed to do so. He was charged with failing to provide specimens of breath, contrary to section 7(6), Road Traffic Act 1988. Following a case management hearing at which the question of the charge was not raised, and some 7 months after the date of the offence, the Crown Prosecution Service wrote to the defendant indicating that it would, on the date set for trial, seek to amend the charge from failing to provide a specimen of breath to failing to provide a specimen of urine. On the date set for the trial, the justices allowed the amendment and adjourned the trial for a further 3½ months.

QUESTION(S) FOR THE COURT: Not recited in the judgment.

HELD: "16. [Citing *R v Scunthorpe Justices ex p Kerry McPhee and ex p Gallagher* (1998) 162 JP 635, an information can be amended out of time if] the different offence or offences allege the 'same misdoing' as the original offence, and the amendment can be made in the interests of justice. … The phrase 'same misdoing' [is understood] to mean that the new offence should arise out of the same (or substantially the same) facts as gave rise to the original offence. …

"20. … The offence created under s.7(6) is one that covers in one sub-paragraph the failure to provide a specimen of breath, and in the second sub-paragraph, the failure to provide a specimen of urine.

"21. … the offences do arise out of the same, or substantially the same, facts. …

"28. Modern case management, set out in the Criminal Procedure Rules, requires a proper attention to case management duties. There was no excuse whatsoever … for the failure to raise the application to make the amendment at the case management hearing on 3 July 2007, given that was over 5 months after the charge and the case was a simple one. Even if that could be excused, there is no excuse for the failure to apply to the court for a short hearing to determine the question of the amendment once the point was appreciated on 7 August 2007. …

"30. … the condition for allowing the amendment … was not met in relation to the interests of justice condition. The interests of justice under our modern procedural code required the amendment to have been refused, if (as we must assume to be the case) there would have been an adjournment [from 19 October 2007] to February 2008. In fact, it transpired that the adjournment was for an even longer period, until 19 March 2008. Why that happened is … not clear, but there can have been no way in which the case should have been allowed to proceed in the circumstances set out, given the assumption on which we must proceed, that an adjournment was required."

Case remitted to the justices with a direction to refuse leave to amend the charge.

Visvaratnam v Brent Magistrates' Court

[2009] EWHC 3017 (Admin), 28 October 2009, QBD (DC)

Where the prosecution failed to warn its principal witness or to serve that witness's evidence, and failed to respond to another witness's notice that he could not attend the trial, the prosecution was not entitled to an adjournment.

A motorist had been charged with driving while unfit through drugs, contrary to s 4(2), Road Traffic Act 1988. A doctor was to give critical evidence of the unfitness, but was not warned to attend the trial, nor was his evidence disclosed to the defendant. The analyst of the defendant's blood specimen, who was to have given evidence of his findings, had given ample warning that he would not be available on the date set for trial. On the trial date, the defendant attended with counsel, but no witnesses for the prosecution attended, and the prosecution sought an adjournment, on the grounds that the allegation was serious and justice required that the case be heard. The adjournment was granted but detailed reasons were not given. The defendant appealed against the decision to adjourn.

HELD: "[After reviewing the authorities] 17. The magistrates here had to balance the public interest in the … trial … against the gravity of a series of very serious errors made by the prosecution, which were unexplained and indeed inexplicable. There was no indication of when it would be possible to refix the trial, but we all know that very frequently trial dates are set in the Magistrates' Courts very many months in the future. … this would have caused further anxiety and costs to the claimant. It is true that this was the first date that the case was set for trial and there was no history of other ineffective hearings. It is also true that this was not a case which depended upon recollection.

"18. The prosecution must not think that they are always allowed at least one application to adjourn the case. If that idea were to gain currency, no trial would ever start on the first date set for trial.

"19. … there is a high public interest in trials taking place on the date set for trial, and … trials should not be adjourned unless there is a good and compelling reason to do so. The sooner the prosecution understand … that they cannot rely on their own serious failures properly to warn witnesses the sooner the efficiency in the Magistrates' Court system improves. An improvement in timeliness and the achievement of a more effective and efficient system of criminal justice in the Magistrates' Court will bring about great benefits to victims and to witnesses and huge savings in time and money."

The decision to adjourn was quashed and the defendant acquitted.

Balogun v DPP

[2010] EWHC 799 (Admin), [2010] 1 WLR 1915, 12 March 2010, QBD (DC)

The prosecution failed to identify and bring to court a crucial witness, and the district judge allowed the prosecution's application for an adjournment. On appeal, it was held that the district judge had not subjected the application to adjourn to appropriate rigorous scrutiny.

A motorist had been charged with driving with excess alcohol, contrary to s 5(1)(a), Road Traffic Act 1988. The defence gave notice that it would put the prosecution to strict proof of every element of the alleged offence, and that there was an issue concerning the taking of a blood specimen and its analysis.

On the trial date, the district judge adjourned the case, giving as his reasons that: (1) the prosecution admitted having failed to identify a particular police officer as a relevant witness and warn her to attend; although other prosecution witnesses could have given evidence and the case could then have been adjourned part heard, the parties urged against doing so; these witnesses were police or other professional people and questions or loss of memory of relevant events were therefore unlikely; (2) this was the first listing for trial and neither party had sought further directions concerning the service of evidence since the case management hearing; (3) it was proper to decide whether or not to grant an adjournment before identifying a new trial date; (4) once the defendant had a reasonable expectation that his case would be concluded on the trial date, it was open to him to apply for costs if he was acquitted, or for wasted costs of the day originally set for trial; (5) there was a legitimate public interest that the charge would be adjudicated on.

The defendant was convicted at the adjourned hearing and appealed.

QUESTION(S) FOR THE COURT: Whether the district judge erred in granting an adjournment.

HELD: "[After reviewing the authorities to the effect that a decision to adjourn is discretionary, that the higher court will interfere only reluctantly, and that applications should be subject to rigorous scrutiny, and after referring to the Criminal Procedure Rules 2005 (SI 2005/384), and after reciting the appellant's challenges to each of the reasons given for the adjournment – which included delays in obtaining and serving a witness statement from the missing witness, failure to take into account the position of defence witnesses who attended on the first trial date, that the next available trial date should have been identified and taken into account] 27. … there are sufficient and legitimate and proper criticisms of the approach of the deputy district judge to justify the challenge advanced … that he did not submit the application to adjourn to appropriate rigorous scrutiny. Each of the reasons which the judge provides, if not flawed, is open to challenge."

The court did not quash the conviction, but allowed the applicant to apply out of time for judicial review of the decision of the magistrates to conduct the hearing which eventually took place.

Cherpion v DPP

[2013] EWHC 615 (Admin), 5 February 2013, QBD (DC)

On the facts in this case (including its long history and the attendance of witnesses), the magistrates were right to refuse an adjournment. On the facts, the doctor who saw the driver at hospital and agreed that a blood specimen could be taken was the medical practitioner in charge of the case.

A motorist had been involved in an accident and was taken to hospital. A blood specimen was taken which, when analysed, revealed excess alcohol. There was a long history of hearings and adjournments. On 12 July 2012 (the adjourned date of trial), the prosecution first sought an adjournment because its three witnesses, although correctly warned, had not appeared. The defence asked the court to proceed, but it then became clear that the witnesses were in fact on their way; they had been told to go to the wrong court. The defence then sought an adjournment on the basis that Dr Kropelnicki, a hospital doctor who saw the defendant, was not present; she had not been asked to attend, even though the prosecution had indicated, at an earlier hearing, that she would be called.

The magistrates refused the adjournment on the basis of the already lengthy history of the case; that the other witnesses were present and ready to give evidence; that the defence had at first itself cited delay as a reason not to adjourn; that the prosecution had agreed not to rely on certain matters said to be hearsay; that the attendance of Dr Kropelnicki had not been identified as necessary until late in the case and in any event the defence could have called her; and that no defence statement had been served.

On an argument that Dr Kropelnicki was not the "doctor in charge" for the purposes of s 9(1), Road Traffic Act 1988 (hospital patient not to be required to provide a specimen unless the medical practitioner in immediate charge of the case has been notified and does not object), the magistrates found that a PC Shaw had been with the appellant from the time he attended the scene of the accident and handed him over to Dr Kropelnicki, whom he described as "the doctor in charge of Mr Cherpion's welfare". Dr Kropelnicki agreed to a blood test to be taken by a police forensic examiner. PC Shaw handed over the motorist to PS Suddick, identifying Dr Kropelnicki as the person responsible for the motorist's welfare. PS Suddick conducted the procedure and, on the *pro forma*, noted that Dr Kropelnicki was the doctor in charge. The forensic medical examiner took the specimen, confirming that the police had obtained consent although she could not remember from which doctor. The motorist agreed that Dr Kropelnicki took care of his leg and sent him for an X-ray. The magistrates found that Dr Kropelnicki was the doctor in immediate charge of the appellant.

The appellant appealed against conviction (the offence charged is not recited in the judgment).

QUESTION(S) FOR THE COURT: (a) Whether the magistrates were wrong to refuse the adjournment on 12 July 2012; (b), whether, on the evidence before the magistrates, they were correct to convict.

HELD: "28. Having said they would do so, the prosecution were plainly at fault in not requesting Dr Kropelnicki to attend. That said, the magistrates had to deal with the position as it was before them. I have no doubt they were entitled to refuse to adjourn. The case had already taken far too long. Although not spelled out as such in their reasons, the magistrates plainly thought that this delayed request for the doctor to attend was no more than a speculative attempt to see whether the appellant might avoid the consequences of his admitted driving with excess alcohol. No reliance was to be placed on the suggested hearsay evidence.

"29. … It was entirely a matter for the discretion of the magistrates. They reached a conclusion which they were entitled to reach. …

"[On the finding that Dr Kropelnicki was in charge] 30. The magistrates … were entitled to look at the evidence … as a whole and draw common sense conclusions from it.

"31. The police officer, PC Shaw, delivered the appellant to Dr Kropelnicki. He described her as the doctor in charge of Mr Cherpion's welfare. The appellant appears to bear that out. She it was who, according to him, examined his leg. She it was who sent him for x-ray. She it was who permitted the blood test to take place.

"32. On that evidence the magistrates were entitled to conclude she was the doctor in charge."

The answers to both questions were "yes". Appeal dismissed.

DPP v Petrie

[2015] EWHC 48 (Admin), 21 January 2015, QBD (DC)

On the facts (viewable CCTV not available at trial, prosecution application for adjournment refused), magistrates were in error to grant a stay of proceedings. *See also DPP v Spalluto, page 670.*

A motorist had been charged with driving with excess alcohol, contrary to s 5(1), Road Traffic Act 1988. It was agreed that CCTV footage of the custody area at the police station would be required at the trial, but, on the day of the trial, the prosecution supplied it in a format such that it could not be viewed. The prosecutor applied for an adjournment to make enquiries about the possibility of obtaining the original footage that day. The defendant applied for a stay of the proceedings on the ground of abuse of process. The magistrates refused the adjournment and granted the stay. The prosecutor appealed.

QUESTION(S) FOR THE COURT: Whether the court was correct in law: (1) in refusing the Crown Prosecution Service's request to adjourn the trial; (2) in acceding to the defendant's request to stay the case as an abuse of process.

HELD: "[On refusing the adjournment] 20. … It is essential that parties to proceedings in the magistrates' court should proceed on the basis of a need to get matters right first time; any suggestion of a culture readily permitting an opportunity to correct failures of preparation should be firmly dispelled. …

"22. … the [CCTV] footage supplied had not been formatted and could not be played on any equipment at the court. As to resolving that conundrum, the prosecution application for an adjournment did not go beyond making enquiries about '… possibly obtaining that day the original footage from [the] Police Station …'. To put it no higher, the magistrates were thus faced with the likelihood that the trial could not go ahead on that day should the adjournment have been granted. The magistrates were aware that the prosecution were otherwise ready to proceed, albeit that counsel for the Respondent had already indicated that he would raise an argument of abuse of process, if the adjournment was refused.

"23. The refusal of the adjournment may well have been a robust case management decision by the justices; if so, it was none the worse for that. On any view, I am wholly unable to conclude that the decision was one to which the Bench was not entitled to come.

"[On granting the stay, after reviewing *R (Ebrahim) v Feltham Magistrates' Court* [2001] EWHC Admin 130, [2001] 2 Cr App R 23, on the two categories of case in which the power to stay proceedings for abuse of process may be invoked] 33. … the justices were plainly wrong or erred in law or principle … However regrettable the prosecution failure to furnish the CCTV footage in a playable format, it fell well short of justifying a stay. …

"34. First, the decision was wholly speculative. The facts in the case do not disclose that anyone had ever watched the CCTV footage. It is not known, for instance, whether the recording covered the relevant part of the procedure or, if it did, whether it captured the precise details of what was said. Accordingly, the magistrates had no basis for concluding that the CCTV footage … would have assisted the Respondent. It follows that the foundation for the justices' conclusion and the exercise of the exceptional jurisdiction to stay proceedings – that the Respondent could not have a fair trial without the CCTV footage – simply disappears.

"35. Secondly, the trial could and should have proceeded on the basis of the available evidence. The prosecution would have called the police officer (who was present at Court) and the defence could, if they so chose, have called the Respondent. The burden of proof was on the Crown to prove the case to the requisite criminal standard of proof, against the background that if there was or might have been any relevant failure of procedure … the Respondent would have been entitled to an acquittal …

"36. Thirdly and assuming that at the conclusion of the live evidence … the justices were driven to the view that the interests of justice did require the viewing of the CCTV footage, they could *at that stage* have revisited the question of an adjournment. They would still, it is fair to say, have needed to grapple with the difficulty that the assistance to be obtained from the footage remained speculative. That said, consideration of an adjournment at this later stage would have arisen with knowledge of the other available evidence and as a matter of last resort."

The answer to question (1) was "yes"; the answer to question (2) was "no". Appeal allowed; case remitted to a differently constituted bench for further consideration.

R (Jenkins) v Hammersmith Magistrates' Court

[2015] EWHC 3961 (Admin), 3 December 2015

Where the prosecution had done nothing to prepare for trial, its application for an adjournment, made on the trial date, should not have been allowed.

A motorist had been charged with driving with excess alcohol in blood contrary to s 5, Road Traffic Act 1988. He raised a number of issues in his defence, including that he had not consented to the taking of the blood specimen. Directions given at a case management hearing (4 May 2015) included that the Crown serve a statement of the health care professional who had taken the specimen. The defence then requested disclosure of further items. On the date set for trial, the prosecution applied for an adjournment, which was granted by the deputy district judge. The motorist sought judicial review of that decision.

GROUND(S) FOR THE APPLICATION: That the deputy district judge erred in law when she granted the prosecution application for an adjournment; her decision was unreasonable, unfair and/or irrational.

HELD: "27. … there were failures on a number of different fronts. No statement from [the health care professional] had been served. [The health care professional] was not present in court on the date fixed for the trial. There was no statement from [the] custody officer … There was no CCTV footage of the blood specimen breath test procedure. Indeed it seems that there had been no disclosure made at all. The CPS were in breach of an order of the court to serve a statement by [the health care professional]. …

"28. … the legal adviser's note [of the adjournment hearing] does not disclose any close examination of what had gone wrong with the conduct of this case by the Crown Prosecution Service or indeed why it had gone wrong. It seems to me that there was a failure here on the part of the judge to demand an explanation as to what had happened. Moreover, it appears from the legal adviser's note that there had been no explanation offered by the CPS at all. The note by the legal adviser has the Deputy District Judge asking whether anyone had looked at the file since the case management hearing but there is nothing in the response as summarised to indicate that the CPS were pressed at all on what had gone wrong. …

"32. The case is put by the applicant on the basis of an error of law or unreasonableness. I consider that the judge did not exercise her discretion in accordance with authority. Indeed, there was to my mind simply no basis on which the judge could reasonably grant an adjournment in this case. It is necessary to have regard to the public interest that those charged with driving under the influence of alcohol should be brought to trial and the charge adjudicated upon, but it also necessary to have regard to the further public interest that this should be done promptly, fairly and efficiently. In particular it is not appropriate in my view to put upon the defence the burden of remedying the situation brought by such inertia on the part of the Crown Prosecution Service.

"33. … the grant of an adjournment did result in the circumstances of this case in substantial unfairness to the applicant. It was common ground that had an adjournment been refused, the Crown could not have proceeded and the applicant would have been acquitted."

The order for an adjournment was quashed and acquittal directed.

DPP v Woods

[2017] EWHC 1070 (Admin), 24 February 2017, QBD (DC)

Where a prosecution application to vacate a trial date was misleading in suggesting the defence was at fault, whereas in fact the prosecution had failed to warn its own principal witness, and the application was first granted, then reversed, the reversal was upheld.

A motorist had been charged with driving while unfit through drink contrary to s 4(2), Road Traffic Act 1988 and, in the alternative, with driving with excess alcohol, contrary to s 5(2), Road Traffic Act 1988. On the day before the date fixed for trial, a legal team manager, acting under delegated authority, granted the prosecution's written application to vacate the trial date. The next day (the trial date), however, a district judge reversed that decision, on the basis that the prosecutor's application for adjournment had been misleading in suggesting the defence was not ready, whereas in fact the prosecution, having earlier failed to comply with orders to serve its evidence, had not warned its principal witness, whose attendance had been required from the start.

The prosecution appealed.

QUESTION FOR THE COURT: Where the court has been misled or given incorrect information about the basis for an application to vacate a trial (namely, whether or not a witness was required to attend) and granted the application, is it permissible for the same court to revisit that decision (and hear renewed submissions) when the correct information is provided?

HELD: "15. [After setting out a chronology of the case spanning some 7 months and four case management hearings, the prosecution's written application to vacate] stated that [the prosecution's expert] 'was not required when the trial date was fixed'. It then went on, against the background of alleged failures by the defence to comply with their duties in relation to disclosure issues, to assert that the defence had failed to trigger the preparation of an SFR2 [Streamlined Forensic Report 2 under the Streamlined Forensic Report Protocol], in accordance with the staged reporting of forensic expert evidence …

"… whether expressly or impliedly, this clearly placed the blame for the last-minute nature of the application to vacate on the defence.

"The reality … was significantly different. It had been made clear since the [first] Case Management Hearing … , that [the prosecution expert] was required to give evidence; the SFR1 [Streamlined Forensic Report 1] … had not been served by the prosecution until some six months after it should have been; and the court had twice ordered the prosecution to serve its evidence by certain dates and the prosecution had failed to do so. In contrast, and albeit without serving a Defence Statement, the defence had set out the issues in broad terms (both to the prosecution and the court) from the outset; had sent numerous letters trying to progress the consideration of expert issues; and had served their own expert report … two months in advance of the date ordered by the court and five months in advance of the eventual trial date.

"… the mischaracterisation of these events by the prosecution was the substantial cause of [the team leader's] decision …

"… the prosecution's application was misleading. Had the true position been appropriately crystallised to [the legal team leader] it is inconceivable that he would have granted the application to vacate what was the third date of trial. Equally he was wrong to reject the defence assertion that … they were ready for trial. Although they were not in an ideal position, we accept that they were ready."

The answer to the question was "yes". Appeal dismissed.

Decani v City of London Magistrates' Court and CPS

[2017] EWHC 3422 (Admin), 25 October 2017, QBD (Admin)

Justices were wrong to allow an adjournment where the Crown Prosecution Service had simply failed to warn the vital witness and get him to court, despite having known for some time that his attendance was necessary.

A motorist had been charged with driving with excess alcohol, contrary to s 5(1), Road Traffic Act 1988. He disputed the charge on several grounds, and required the attendance at trial of the police sergeant who had operated the breath analysis device. On the trial date, the officer did not appear; the Crown Prosecution Service had not warned him that he was required. The justices granted a prosecution application for an adjournment. The motorist sought judicial review of that decision.

HELD: "21. … It seems that the factors which were taken into account as influencing the exercise of [the justices'] discretion were the failings of the CPS … to get the required witness to court, the short period between the alleged offence and the trial date which was slightly more than eight weeks, and therefore, the fact that the case would not involve significant delay in coming to trial… .

"23. … all of the lawyers in court before the justices were satisfied that the police sergeant's attendance was vital. … This claimant was not raising every conceivable point in order to frustrate the administration of justice. The points which were raised … were within a relatively narrow compass and in relation to [the police sergeant] arose from the claimant raising his statutory right under s.16(4) of the [Road Traffic Offenders Act 1988 – inadmissibility of certificate if the accused has served notice requiring the attendance of the signatory] to have a certificate proved… . there was no suggestion on any side before the justices that this was a claimant who was playing games. He was pursuing a legitimate defence, supported by evidence. He was making a positive case, not needlessly putting the prosecution to proof …

"25. … [there appears to be] a legitimate concern that the adjournment application in this case was not, as the authorities specifically direct, subjected to the necessary rigorous scrutiny before the decision was taken … . there is in truth little evidence … that [the principles in *CPS v Picton* [2006] EWHC 1108 (Admin)] were carefully and thoroughly examined in weighing up the factors at play in the decision to be made."

The decision to adjourn was quashed and the matter remitted to the magistrates with an order to acquit the claimant.

Bourne v Scarborough Magistrates' Court

[2017] EWHC 2828 (Admin), [2018] 4 WLR 29, 10 November 2017, QBD (DC)

A legal adviser authorised to manage a case should not have made decisions on a contested application for adjournment without full information.

The applicant had pleaded not guilty to a charge of driving with excess alcohol contrary to s 5(1)(a), Road Traffic Act 1988. His defence was that he had not consumed sufficient alcohol to take him over the limit; he questioned the reliability of the breath specimen, the functionality of the breath analysis device and the procedure at the police station. Eight days before the trial date, a court legal adviser, nominated to manage the case pursuant to r 3.5, Criminal Procedure Rules 2015 (SI 2015/1490), granted a prosecution application to vacate the trial date. The applicant sought to have that decision reviewed at an oral hearing, which was at first allowed, but the next day, the legal adviser reversed that decision. The appellant sought judicial review of the decisions.

THE ISSUES: (a) Whether the legal adviser had power to rule on a contested application for an adjournment; (b) if so, whether his decision to do so was unreasonable, irrational, outwith his discretion or wrong in law; (c) whether, having received written representations and granted the adjournment, he had power to refuse to list the applicant's application for an oral hearing before the magistrates; (d) whether his refusal to allow the appellant to apply to vary the direction to adjourn was unreasonable, irrational, outwith his discretion or wrong in law.

HELD: "46. … The plain terms of [CPR] rule 3.5(2)(f) empower a nominated case manager to 'adjourn a hearing' … 'hearing' in this context must include a trial …

"47. … the legal adviser did have power by virtue of rule 3.5(2)(f) to adjourn the trial on the prosecution's application.

"48. … however, he fell into error in making his decision to vacate the fixed trial date and there are at least three reasons why [that] decision cannot stand.

"49. First, … he did not have sufficient information to enable him properly to grant an adjournment without at least requiring further details from CPS. It might be doubted whether any application for an adjournment was actually being made to him: [correspondence from the Crown Prosecution Service] … said that the Crown 'will be seeking an adjournment', but those words arguably fall short of making an application.

"50. Secondly, … the legal adviser granted the adjournment with no knowledge of its duration … .

"51. Thirdly, … the [appellant's] solicitors … had specifically asked, if the court were minded to accede to the prosecution's application, for a hearing at which 'our full submissions can be made', … I do not think it was right for the legal adviser to treat [those emails] as written representations, on the basis of which a decision would be made.

"52. For those reasons [the legal adviser] made a decision which … was not properly open to him. Put shortly, he did not have sufficient information to enable him to make a properly-informed decision in accordance with the principles set out in *Picton* [*CPS v Picton* [2006] EWHC 1108 (Admin)]. He should either have permitted the parties to make their submissions at an oral hearing, or should have invited them to submit further written representations on the explicit basis that he would then make a decision on the papers and without a hearing …

"[Concerning the refusal to allow an oral hearing] 55. … In the circumstances of this case it was not open to the legal adviser to refuse to grant the application to vary as he did: he should either have directed a hearing, or at the very least have given both parties an explicit opportunity to make full written submissions."

Both decisions were quashed and the case remitted to the magistrates' court with a direction that it be listed for trial as soon as possible and in any event within 10 weeks from the date on which this judgment was handed down.

R (Gatenby) v Newton Ayecliffe (sic) Magistrates' Court

[2017] EWHC 3772 (Admin), 1 December 2017, Admin

Where the court declined a request for a short adjournment to obtain a copy of a relevant law report with the result that the defendant was denied the opportunity to make a special reasons argument, that amounted to procedural unfairness and vitiated the proceedings thereafter.

The applicant had been charged with failing without reasonable excuse to provide a specimen of breath for analysis, contrary to s 7(6), Road Traffic Act 1988. He pleaded guilty on the basis that he had not been driving or in charge at the relevant time, so that disqualification would be discretionary rather than obligatory (Sch 2, Road Traffic Offenders Act 1988), allowing him to argue special reasons for not endorsing his licence (s 44(2), Road Traffic Offenders Act 1988). At the hearing, neither the prosecutor nor the court's legal adviser accepted that if the accused had not been driving or attempting to drive at the material time, that could amount to a special reason. The court declined a request for a short adjournment to obtain a copy of the report of *McCormick v Hitchins* ([1988] RTR 182, (1986) 83 Cr App R 11, DC, see page 566). The applicant was fined, his licence was endorsed with 10 penalty points and he was ordered to pay costs and a victim surcharge. He sought judicial review of the decision to endorse his licence.

GROUND(S) FOR THE APPLICATION: Procedural unfairness, in that the applicant was not given a fair opportunity to lay before the court case law which would have had a material effect on the issue of special reasons for not endorsing.

HELD: "[On the question whether judicial review is the appropriate route of challenge] 5. … judicial review does lie in this case … the exhaustion of alternative remedies of appeal is not, as a matter of principle, necessary when seeking to challenge a magistrate's decision. This is particularly so … when, as in this case, procedural unfairness is relied on.

"6. … The key to any successful challenge on procedural unfairness is that the complaint is one which does go to vitiate the proceedings … .

"30. I have no doubt that there was procedural unfairness in this case. It beggars belief … that the prosecution, and the Legal Adviser, and … the court, the magistrates, were not aware of their responsibility to ensure that the law governing special reasons was properly before the court … .

"42. … the procedural unfairness in this case was so unfair that this court would not be giving proper recognition to that unfairness if it dismissed this claim or refused the remedy sought. The effect of dismissing the claim and/or refusing the remedy is that the claimant will be prevented from having a first opportunity on the issue going to special reasons by giving evidence in the Magistrates Court and obtaining a determination on the issue from the magistrates before deciding whether he needs to utilise his right of appeal to the Crown Court. His only opportunity to give evidence and to obtain that determination will be in the Crown Court on appeal and this will be for the first and only time. This on the face of things is unfair.

"43. … the failure of the Magistrates Court to allow the claimant a short adjournment, likely to have been a very short one, to obtain the reported legal authority and the failure of the Legal Adviser to advise the magistrates that it was essential, if it be an issue, that the applicable legal principles relating to special reasons be laid before the court in proper form, if a proper decision was on special reasons was to be made, did vitiate the proceedings thereafter … .

"45. … the whole proceedings thereafter were vitiated, and … the claimant has, in effect, been denied a fair hearing on the issue of special reasons."

The sentence was quashed and the matter remitted to the magistrates for a fresh sentencing hearing.

R (DPP) v Sunderland Magistrates' Court and Hanson; R (Kharaghan) v City of London Magistrates and CPS

[2018] EWHC 229 (Admin), 14 February 2018, QBD (DC)

Material mistake of fact resulting in unfairness may be a ground of challenge by way of judicial review in criminal proceedings. In the specific circumstances of the City of London case, as they were believed to be at the time, the justices were entitled to grant an adjournment.

In both cases, the magistrates' court had acted on a material mistake of fact when determining, on the day fixed for trial, a contested application to adjourn.

The *Sunderland* case concerned a charge of criminal damage. The DPP sought judicial review of the magistrates' decision to refuse an adjournment and dismiss the charge. The Divisional Court held that material mistake of fact resulting in unfairness may be a ground of challenge by way of judicial review not only in civil proceedings (as in *E v Secretary of State of the Home Department* [2004] EWCA Civ 49, [2004] QB 1044), but also in criminal proceedings, providing the five preconditions set out in *E v SSHD* are met. On the facts, all five conditions were met. There had been a material mistake of fact resulting in unfairness. The decision of the court below to refuse an adjournment applied for on the day set for trial was quashed and the case remitted to the magistrates' court for rehearing.

In the *City of London* case, a motor cyclist had been charged with riding a motor cycle with excess alcohol contrary to s 5, Road Traffic Act 1988. At the first hearing, he pleaded not guilty and the court made an order for the prosecution to serve its evidence and initial disclosure by a given date. The prosecution did not comply by the deadline. Although the motor cyclist's solicitor contacted the prosecution about disclosure following the expiry of the deadline for service, he did not point out that the order as to service had not been met. Nor did he provide a secure email address, so the prosecution had to send its documents by post. The documents were eventually served over a month late and only some 12 days before the trial date; they were not received by the claimant's solicitor until the day before the trial. CCTV and the custody record were not served. The defendant's solicitor did not tell the court that the disclosure requirements had not been met and that the defence was not ready for trial. On the trial date, counsel for the prosecutor and the justices mistakenly understood that the prosecution had done nothing at all to comply with the order for disclosure. The prosecution applied for an adjournment to enable it to serve its case, which was granted. The motor cyclist challenged that decision by way of judicial review.

HELD: [The judgment contains a review of the cases on material mistake of fact resulting in unfairness as a ground for challenge in claims for judicial review in criminal proceedings; the relevant provisions of the Criminal Procedure Rules 2015 (SI 2015/1490) and Criminal Practice Direction; and the case law on applications to adjourn in magistrates' court and the ability to challenge decisions made on such applications by judicial review.]

"103. These claims are concerned with the judicial review of discretionary decisions made on applications to adjourn trial hearings in the Magistrates' Court – which, as was made clear in *Balogun v DPP* [see page 584], should only be mounted in exceptional circumstances and, if brought, must be pursued as a matter of great urgency. …

"111. The first question in the *City of London* case is whether, on the facts as they were mistakenly believed to be at the time, the Justices' decision to adjourn was within the legitimate exercise of their discretion.

"112. Although it appeared at the time that the Prosecution had not complied at all with the order to serve and disclose by [date], the Claimant and his advisers had clearly failed to comply with their duties to bring that to the attention of the court at an early stage, and thereafter to warn the court about their consequent lack of readiness for trial.

"113. … for the reasons advanced on behalf of [the prosecution – the justices had given the application the appropriate degree of scrutiny, considered the relevant authorities, the conduct of the parties and the real issues; the public interest in criminal charges being adjudicated upon; the lack of prejudice to the claimant if the trial was adjourned; the public interest in prosecuting those charged with driving while intoxicated; the documents which the prosecution should have served (except the CCTV footage and the custody record) could all have been served on the trial day; the witnesses were present)] … in the specific circumstances … as they were believed to be at the time, the Justices were entitled, in the exercise of their discretion, to grant the adjournment.

"114. In those circumstances, it is not necessary to consider whether the five conditions in relation to the ground of mistake of fact leading to unfairness are met in the *City of London* case."

Claim dismissed.

R (Parashar) v Sunderland Magistrates' Court and CPS

[2019] EWHC 514 (Admin), 6 March 2019, QBD (DC)

Where the trial had been set for a date on which the prosecution expert (who had been instructed late) could attend, but the defence expert (whose report had been served in good time) could not, it was wrong to refuse the defence application to vacate the trial date; this was an exceptional case in which judicial review was appropriate.

A motorist had been charged with driving with excess alcohol, contrary to s 5, Road Traffic Act 1988. He pleaded not guilty. The defence served its expert's statement, to which the Crown Prosecution Service did not respond. The prosecution failed to serve all its evidence as directed. The defence sought a hearing, on the basis that it would be an abuse of process to allow the prosecution to continue; dates for that hearing, and for the trial, were set. The abuse of process hearing did not go ahead. At this point, there was no suggestion that the prosecution would instruct an expert. A legal arguments hearing would take place on the date set for trial, and a new trial date was set. The date for the legal arguments hearing was vacated by email from the court. The prosecution then served its own expert report challenging the defence expert; the defence did not agree it. The defence expert was not available to attend court on the date set for trial. The defendant's advance application to vacate that date was refused. He sought judicial review of that refusal.

HELD: "28. … If the trial had proceeded [on the date set] the court would have had to decide between the evidence of two experts, one of whom was present and one of whom was not. It is not clear to me how the court could have determined the issues between the experts. It would have been particularly unfair to have adhered to the date since it was one which (apparently) suited [the prosecution], whose report had been served on 11 October 2018, but not [the defence], whose report had been served on 30 May 2018.

"29. The issue of the late service of [the prosecution expert's] report and the consequence that the prosecution required permission to adduce it was simply ignored …

"[On whether or not judicial review was an appropriate method of challenge, after reviewing the authorities] 42. In *Bourne* v *Scarborough Magistrates' Court* [2017] EWHC 2828 (Admin) [see page 591] … it was 'common ground' that an application for judicial review may in principle be an appropriate means by which to challenge a decision of a magistrates' court as to an adjournment, though only in exceptional circumstances. We asked [counsel for the prosecution in the present case] to suggest what those circumstances might be. His answer, with which [counsel for the defence] agreed, was as follows:

(1) Where it is properly arguable that the ability of the defendant to present his defence is so seriously compromised by the decision under challenge that an unfair trial is inevitable.

(2) Where an important point of principle is raised, likely to affect other cases.

(3) Where the case has some other exceptional feature which justifies the intervention of the High Court.

"43. I agree with this formulation, with the proviso that it will only be in rare cases that this court will consider an interlocutory challenge once the trial is under way … But this is not such a case: indeed the decision under scrutiny is accurately described not as a refusal to grant an adjournment, but as a refusal to vacate a trial date in advance. The threshold of exceptionality is less high in such a case. …

"45. … Unlike many reported cases concerning driving with excess alcohol where the defence have played games with the system, here the defence were not at fault at all. The prosecution had caused the difficulty by instructing an expert very late in the day and after having raised no objection to the defence expert's report being admitted under s 9 Criminal Justice Act 1967. They could and in my view should either have supported the defence application for the trial to be on a date on which both experts could attend, or indicated that they would not pursue the application to adduce the evidence of [their expert].

"46. … the decision to fix a date for a trial at which the prosecution expert could attend and the defence expert (whose report had been served in good time) could not was clearly wrong. If the trial had proceeded on that basis the defendant's ability to present his defence would have been seriously compromised and the trial would inevitably have been unfair. This is therefore an exceptional case in which this court should intervene at the pre-trial stage.

"47. I would grant judicial review accordingly. This case should now proceed to trial … ."

Saunders v Bristol Magistrates' Court and CPS

[2022] EWHC 2544 (Admin), 12 October 2022, KBD (Admin)

On the facts, the justices' grant of an application to adjourn a trial date was vitiated by their failure to give adequate reasons and apparent bias.

A driver was charged with failing to provide a specimen of blood for analysis, contrary to s 7, Road Traffic Act 1988. The custody doctor had been unable to take a specimen. The circumstances were contentious, the defendant arguing that she had been willing, but had suffered a panic attack. The driver pleaded not guilty. The prosecution planned to call as witnesses two police officers and the custody doctor. The defence required the doctor (and there was initially confusion about the doctor's identity) to attend, but the doctor was not warned, nor was a statement by the doctor served as had been directed. Three days before the trial date, the prosecution applied to the court to change the trial date, saying the witness had not been called because there had been confusion about the witness's identity. Lay justices granted the adjournment, saying it was in the interests of justice to do so, but without giving further reasons other than saying, when asked to expand, "the failure on the admin side should not affect the interests of justice". It later transpired that one of the justices had told the legal adviser, in the retiring room, that the defendant "can't get away with it because there has been an admin error"; the justices maintained their position despite being asked by the legal adviser to check their thinking. Such was the legal adviser's concern about their approach, that she spoke to the defendant's representative about it.

The driver sought judicial review of the decision to grant the adjournment.

GROUND FOR THE APPLICATION: The decision to adjourn demonstrated bias, failed to give adequate reasons and took into account an irrelevant consideration.

HELD: "46. … the presiding justice … expressed a conclusion: that an adjournment was justified in the interests of justice … but did not explain why it was in the interests of justice to adjourn the trial. Describing the prosecution's failure to serve [the doctor's] statement or warn him to attend the trial as an 'admin error' did not help. Overall, what the presiding justice said did not demonstrate that he had taken account of the factors identified as relevant in the Practice Direction [Criminal Practice Directions 2015, PD 24C – Trial adjournment in magistrates' courts] and authorities. The 'reasons' were therefore inadequate …

"47. … this case involves a combination of features: the lack of adequate reasons for the adjournment decision; [the justice's] comment while the justices were deliberating in private; and the reaction of the very experienced Legal Advisor. Taking these three features into account, a fair-minded and informed observer not present when the comment was made would in my view place considerable weight on the reaction of someone who was, particularly someone with [the legal adviser's] training and experience. She regarded it as sufficiently concerning to raise it with [the defence representative]. That fact tips this case over the line so that the test for apparent bias is met.

"48. It follows that … the decision to adjourn was vitiated by two public law errors: failure to give adequate reasons and apparent bias."

The decision to adjourn was quashed and the case remitted to the justices with a direction to acquit.

2. THE CASE STATED

See also Roberts v DPP, page 668 – the magistrates should not have dismissed as frivolous a request to state a case on whether the place in question was a "road or other public place"; R (Clarke) v Ipswich Crown Court, page 603, and R (Usman) v Reading Magistrates' Court, page 607, where appeal by way of case stated, rather than by applying for judicial review, was the correct course.

R v City of London JJ ex p Ocansey

Unreported, CO/2021/94, 17 February 1995, QBD (DC)

On the facts of this case, the applicant had no arguable case, and so had no grounds for requiring that a case be stated.

A motorist had been convicted of failing without reasonable excuse to provide two specimens of breath for analysis, contrary to s 7(6), Road Traffic Act 1988. He sought to appeal by way of case stated but the justices refused to state a case on the ground that the application was frivolous. The motorist sought judicial review of that refusal.

QUESTION(S) FOR THE COURT: The questions which the applicant sought to raise by way of case stated were: "(i) In the absence of any evidence that [the sergeant who administered the breath analysis procedure] was entitled to ask for a specimen of breath were we right to convict the defendant of failing to provide a specimen; … (iii) Were we entitled to hold that [the sergeant] was an officer trained and experienced in the use of the Intoximeter in view of the fact that: (a) he did not know how long a subject was given … to blow into it before it treated him as having failed to give a sample; (b) he said that 5 stars appeared on the screen which … had to be eliminated before the machine could carry out an analysis, whereas the unchallenged evidence of the Defence expert witness was that … as the subject blows into the machine bars appear on the screen in increasing numbers to a possible maximum of 5; and (c) he thought that in order to provide a sample of breath a subject was legally entitled to only one attempt at blowing into the machine whereas the unchallenged evidence of the Defence expert witness was that a subject could blow as many times as he was able in 3 minutes until he successfully provided a sample; (iv) Were we right to hold that [the expert] had the necessary qualifications to give expert evidence about the functioning of the Intoximeter 3000."

HELD: "[On (i)] … The question … was whether the prosecution laid a *prima facie* case that the Applicant had committed one of the offences specified by either s 3A, s 4 or s 5 … the Applicant … admitted that he had been driving immediately prior to his arrest. The officer … gave evidence and described how he required the Applicant to provide samples of breath in accordance with the provisions of s 7. [He] was not challenged when he gave this evidence. It was not suggested … that the sergeant was not then investigating whether the Applicant had committed an offence under one of the sections … or that he was not entitled to ask for a specimen. There was in fact no issue before the Justices as to the lawfulness or otherwise of the sergeant's conduct … There is no arguable case open to the Applicant in relation to this point …

"[On (iii)] … I am wholly unable to accept that any point of law is raised … The point is unarguable.

"[On (iv)] … The Doctor gave evidence as a medical expert, not as an expert on the functioning of the Intoximeter … this question has no merit at all. At best, it raises a question of fact."

Application dismissed.

R v Warrington JJ ex p Worsley; R v Cheshire JJ ex p Henshaw

[1996] COD 346, 12 March 1996, QBD (DC)

A recognisance to prosecute an appeal by way of case stated may be required before a draft case is sent to an applicant.

Two motorists had been convicted of driving with excess alcohol and sought to appeal by way of case stated. The clerk to the justices declined to send draft cases to the applicants unless and until they entered into recognisances. They sought judicial review of the decision of the clerk to the justices.

HELD: "… It seems to me that requiring a person to enter into a recognisance does not constitute a refusal to state a case … The question is whether the recognisance can be required before the draft case is sent or not until the case is formally stated. That depends on whether the sending of the draft case is part of the process of stating the case.

"The purpose of the power to require a recognisance is to ensure that the Applicant is in earnest, and also to safeguard the court against costs incurred. Although it may indeed be helpful to an Applicant to know [from a draft case stated] what facts the Justices have found and what their reasoning was before proceeding with a request for a case to be stated, that is not how the legislation is structured. … an application has to be made to state a case. Once that occurs the Applicant can be required to enter into a recognisance. The provision of a draft case is seen to be part of the process of stating a case …

"… If when an Applicant receives the draft case he at once decides to abandon his appeal, and so informs the Justices, they may well decide not to forfeit all or any of the recognisance."

Applications dismissed.

R v Fylde and Wyre JJ ex p Gornall

[1996] COD 434, 13 May 1996, QBD (DC)

Lodging an appeal to the Crown Court does not debar an appeal by way of case stated.

A motorist had been convicted of driving with excess alcohol. He immediately served notice of appeal to the Crown Court against conviction. Thirteen days later an application to state a case was received by the magistrates' court, who took the view that since the appeal to the Crown Court had not been abandoned in accordance with r 11, Crown Court Rules 1982 (SI 1982/1109), the application to state a case was defective. The motorist sought judicial review of that decision.

HELD: "… [counsel for the applicant argues] that by making the application … for stating of the case there was an automatic consequence in the form of any right of appeal disappearing and that therefore the Magistrates' Court Clerk was wrong to seek to reject that application on the grounds that the appeal had not been abandoned in accordance with the Crown Court Rules. I agree with that submission … It seems to me quite clear that … by making an application, which at that stage was in perfectly good order for a case to be stated, the right of appeal of the applicant, that is to say, the right to go to the Crown Court, was lost.

"… although an application for stating a case debars any appeal, there is no corresponding provision that an appeal debars any right to seek a case."

Application granted.

R (DPP) v Chorley Magistrates' Court

[2006] EWHC 1795 (Admin), 8 June 2006, QBD (DC)

On the facts, justices should not have declined to state a case. (Obiter): the Criminal Procedure Rules 2005 (SI 2005/384) effected a sea change.

A motorist had been charged with driving with excess alcohol in blood, contrary to s 5(1)(a), Road Traffic Act 1988. A number of hearings took place at which the defendant was not represented and at which he did not indicate a defence. He was, however, represented at the trial. The prosecution sought to adduce the evidence of the certificate of analysis of the blood. The defence objected on the basis that service could not be proved. The justices accepted that the certificate had been sent, and the defendant said he had received the package in which the certificate was said to have been included. But they acceded to a submission of no case to answer and later refused the prosecution's request to state a case.

The prosecutor appealed against the refusal to state a case.

HELD: "19. … [After referring to s 16(3), Road Traffic Act Offenders 1988 (certificate admissible only if a copy has been served)], the Justices accepted that the certificate had actually been sent. It is clear … from the evidence of [the motorist] that [he] accepted having received the package. Unfortunately, there is no finding by the Justices as to whether the package … contained the certificate.

"21. In the circumstances … we have no doubt at all that the justices must be directed to state a case.…

"24. In April 2005 the Criminal Procedure Rules came into effect. … They have effected a sea change in the way in which cases should be conducted … The rules make clear that the overriding objective is that criminal cases be dealt with justly; that includes acquitting the innocent and convicting the guilty, dealing with the prosecution and the defence fairly, respecting the interests of witnesses, dealing with the case efficiently and expeditiously, and also, of great importance, dealing with the case in a way that takes into account the gravity of the offence, the complexity of what is in issue, the severity of the consequences to the defendant and others affected and the needs of other cases. …

"25. Rule 3.2 imposes upon the court a duty to further that overriding objective by actively managing the case.

"26. The pertinent part relevant … in this case is the early identification of the real issues. … what should have happened is that at the first hearing … the defendant should have been asked first what was in issue. … he should then have been asked what witnesses did he need. … [He] should, thirdly, have been asked what issues were taken by the defence. … The days of ambushing and taking last-minute technical points are gone. They are not consistent with the overriding objective of deciding cases justly, acquitting the innocent and convicting the guilty."

DPP v Vince; Kang v DPP

[2016] EWHC 3014 (Admin), 25 November 2016, QBD (Admin)

Importance of properly drafting a case stated.

In *Vince*, the facts concerning the breath analysis procedure were largely the same as in *Kang* (page 63 – ambient fail; breath analysis procedure recommenced). At the conclusion of the prosecution evidence, the defendant submitted that there was no case to answer. The magistrates accepted that submission and the prosecution appealed.

QUESTIONS FOR THE COURT: (1) Whether the court was right to exclude the evidence of the Intoxilyser reading in light of the inconsistencies and contradictions in the evidence of the two officers concerned. (2) Whether the court was correct to conclude that the prosecution had failed to prove an essential element of the case, namely the level of alcohol in the defendant's breath, and therefore that there was no case to answer.

HELD: "39. Unfortunately the poor drafting of the case stated makes it difficult to give a clear answer to the questions posed. …

"40. As to the first question, the inconsistencies and contradictions to which the magistrates refer are nowhere identified in the case stated. This was a serious error by the magistrates. As a result it is impossible to tell whether there were such inconsistencies and contradictions or, if there were, how significant they were. In any event the evaluation of inconsistent and contradictory evidence is a part of the fact-finding process which does not give rise to any question of law suitable for decision by way of case stated. …

"41. As to the second question, the case stated does not explain in what respects the procedure adopted was not in accordance with what was required by section 7 of the 1988 Act. …

"43. At all events, it does appear that the magistrates concluded that the test reading obtained was not reliable. … although their reasoning is obscure, it is not possible to say from the case stated that they were wrong in law.

"44. … despite the unsatisfactory drafting of the case stated and the uncertainty about the magistrates' reasoning, I would dismiss this appeal. The alternatives –

either to send the case stated back for re-drafting when no representations were made on behalf of the prosecution as to the contents of the case stated or to start again before a differently constituted panel – would be even less satisfactory."
Both appeals dismissed.

3. JUDICIAL REVIEW

On the availability of judicial review, see also Balogun v DPP, page 584; Bourne v Scarborough Magistrates' Court, page 591; R (Gatenby) v Newton Ayecliffe (sic) Magistrates' Court, page 593; R (Olajide) v Stratford Magistrates' Court, page 343; R (DPP) v Sunderland Magistrates' Court and Hanson; R (Kharaghan) v City of London Magistrates and CPS, page 594; R (Parashar) v Sunderland Magistrates' Court and CPS, page 596; Hoar-Stevens v Richmond Magistrates' Court, page 661; Miller v DPP, page 375.

R (Clarke) v Ipswich Crown Court

[2013] EWHC 1129 (Admin), 24 January 2013, QBD (Admin)

Where a claim for judicial review was effectively an appeal against the decision made by the court below on the evidence, judicial review was not appropriate; the correct procedure would have been an appeal by way of case stated.

The claimant had been convicted of driving with excess alcohol, contrary to s 5, Road Traffic Act 1988 and appealed to the Crown Court. He argued that it was alcohol consumed after driving which caused him to be over the limit and adduced expert evidence to that effect. That evidence was, however, based on what the claimant himself said he had drunk and when, which was uncorroborated and was not accepted by the court. The Crown Court decided to disregard the expert evidence and dismissed his appeal. The claimant sought judicial review of that decision.

GROUNDS FOR THE APPLICATION: That the Crown Court had acted irrationally and unreasonably, and in a manner which no properly directed tribunal or circuit judge could act, in wrongly rejecting the claimant's expert evidence on the basis that that evidence could be disregarded because of the unreliability of the claimant's evidence.

HELD: "[On whether judicial review was an appropriate remedy] 17. … it was wholly inappropriate in this case to bring what was effectively an appeal against the court's conclusions in relation to the evidence, by way of judicial review proceedings. The … only appropriate way to challenge the Crown Court's decision… was to have adopted the normal and statutory prescribed method of appeal, namely by way of case stated. That is the appropriate procedure when, as here, there is an out-and-out challenge to the conclusion reached by the court on the evidence before it, as opposed to a situation where the challenge is based, for example, on an allegation of unfairness, bias or procedural irregularity, when judicial review may be an appropriate procedure. …

"21. … Irrespective of the procedural point, however, it is clear … that this claim is wholly without merit.

"22. The court … was clearly entitled to conclude that the claimant had not proved that the statutory assumption in section 15(2) of the Road Traffic Offenders Act [assumption that the proportion of alcohol in the breath, blood or urine at the time of an alleged offence not less than in the specimen] should be displaced."

Claim dismissed.

R (Hi) v Willesden Magistrates' Court and CPS

[2016] EWHC 1760 (Admin), [2018] 4 WLR 3, 14 July 2016, QBD (Admin)

Where an application for judicial review had been refused as totally without merit, that decision could not be reconsidered at an oral hearing; on the facts, the claim was totally without merit.

The claimant had been charged with driving with excess alcohol contrary to s 5, Road Traffic Act 1988. At trial, the district judge refused her application for an adjournment for the production of CCTV footage of the custody suite, and proceeded to trial. The claimant was convicted and her application for judicial review was dismissed on the basis that it was totally without merit. The claimant sought to have that decision reconsidered at an oral hearing.

GROUNDS FOR THE CLAIM: (i) Whether the court has jurisdiction to permit its decision to be reconsidered at an oral hearing, notwithstanding r 54.12(7), Civil Procedure Rules 1998 (SI 1998/3132) (where permission for judicial review has been refused as being totally without merit, the claimant may not request the decision be reconsidered at an oral hearing); (ii) whether or not the claim was totally without merit.

HELD: "4. As a general rule, when permission to apply for judicial review has been refused and recorded as totally without merit, that decision is not the end of the road for the claimant. That is because CPR 52.15(1A) entitles the claimant to apply to the Court of Appeal for permission to appeal (with that application to be determined on the papers without an oral hearing). However, there is no such right where the decision of which judicial review is sought was made in criminal proceedings because section 18(1)(a) of the Senior Courts Act 1981 provides that (subject to an exception not relevant here) no appeal shall lie to the Court of Appeal from any judgment of the High Court in any criminal cause or matter… .

"7. … If the intention had been that CPR 54.12(7) should not apply to claims for judicial review in any criminal cause or matter, the rule would have been bound to say so. The unequivocal and unqualified language used is simply not capable, in my view, of being interpreted as impliedly excluding from its scope criminal cases (or any other category of claims for judicial review)… .

"10. … I do not think it arguable that the court has jurisdiction in this case to reconsider its decision at an oral hearing.

"[On whether the claim was totally without merit] 11. The reason … for recording the claim as being totally without merit was that there was clearly an adequate alternative remedy … in the form of an appeal to the Crown Court … this reason was inadequate and … should have addressed the substance of the claim. …

"12. … it is clear from the material which was before the court when the order was made that the claim was … bound to fail.

"16. … the decisions of the district judge to refuse an adjournment and to refuse to order disclosure of the custody suite CCTV were unassailable. It cannot be said that the district judge ought to have granted an adjournment for a reason – namely, the fact that the CCTV was identified as disclosable in the schedule of unused material – which was not relied on by the defence as a reason for seeking an adjournment at the time. Furthermore, the district judge was not merely entitled but plainly right to regard the suggestion that the CCTV footage might undermine the prosecution case or assist the case for the defence as wholly speculative."

Application dismissed.

DPP (Blakeley) v Manchester and Salford Magistrates' Court;
DPP (Whyte) v Manchester and Salford Magistrates' Court
[2017] EWHC 3719 (Admin), 7 July 2017, QBD (DC)

Jurisdiction to hear application for judicial review; on the facts, there was no evidential basis for concluding that materials sought to be disclosed were reasonably capable of undermining the prosecution or of assisting the defence.

In both cases, a motorist had been charged with driving with excess alcohol, contrary to s 5(1), Road Traffic Act 1988. The same solicitors acted for both defendants. The defendants claimed to have drunk insufficient alcohol to give rise to positive readings and challenged the reliability of the Lion Intoxilyser used. They applied under s 8, Criminal Procedure and Investigations Act 1996 (application by accused for disclosure) for disclosure of documentation concerning the device. Disclosure of certain items was ordered in both cases. The Director of Public Prosecutions challenged the disclosure orders by way of judicial review.

HELD: "[On whether or not the court had jurisdiction to hear the applications for judicial review, after reviewing the authorities] 14. … a challenge to an interlocutory order or decision should not lightly be made but may, exceptionally, be justified where the challenge raises issues likely to have general or wider application and is not dependent on the ultimate result and there is no other means by which the order or decision can be challenged. …

"[After referring to a witness statement by a Crown Prosecution Service prosecutor, describing a pattern of disclosure requests of this sort being made routinely in excess alcohol cases in Greater Manchester, and the consequent costs, delay and calls on resources] 17. The lawfulness of the disclosure orders could not sensibly be challenged by the CPS in the event of a conviction. Where there was an acquittal, the disclosed material may have played no part in the acquittal; it might not even have been admitted in evidence. The CPS is bound to comply with court orders, even if it intends to challenge them later if possible; it should not wait until it faces the consequences of non-compliance, for example in the refusal to admit the printout in evidence, and then seek to remedy the consequences of non-compliance by challenge to the order it failed to comply with. A costs order if made, and paid, will not establish any general principle in relation to the making of a disclosure order; and will not cover the disruptive effect of delays on the trial process …

"19. In the circumstances, we reject the challenge to our jurisdiction."

"[On the question whether the district judge could rationally conclude on the evidence that (the materials sought) were reasonably capable of undermining the prosecution or advancing the defence cases] 54. … the answer to that is no, and disclosure should not have been ordered …

'55. … there must be a proper evidential basis for concluding that the material sought is reasonably capable of undermining the prosecution or of assisting the defence, or that it represents a reasonable line of enquiry to pursue. … there is no evidential basis upon which the disclosure should have been ordered.

'56. … it is not enough … to say that the defence case is that the amount drunk would not put the defendant over the limit or anywhere near it, and therefore the machine must be unreliable. What the evidence needed to do, in order to provide a basis for such a disclosure order was to address two critical features.

'57. The first requirement is the basis for contending how the device might produce a printout which, on its face, demonstrated that it was operating in proper fashion, but which could generate a very significantly false positive reading, where, on the defence case, the true reading would have been well below the prosecution limit. The second requirement is to identify how the material which was sought could assist to demonstrate how that might have happened. Those are the two issues which arise and which the expert evidence in support of disclosure should address. Unless that evidence is provided, the disclosure is irrelevant.

"58. But [the defence] simply ignored the printout, and the way in which the device is designed and operates. They provide no explanation as to how the device could have malfunctioned in the way they say it must have done and still have produced a positive reading so far from the true reading which they say it would have produced. … Their generalised assertions that the machine could be unreliable and that its reliability needed to be verified was accompanied by no evidence that the disclosure sought could cast any light on its reliability in that way.

"59. … this is not to say that the machine must be taken to be infallible. ... However, unless the disclosure application addresses the two questions which we have identified, this extensive disclosure would have to be given in every case in which a defendant alleged that his alcohol consumption had been too low to sustain a positive reading, and in effect proof of reliability would always be required and the presumption of accuracy would be displaced."

The disclosure order in *Blakeley* was quashed. In *Whyte*, disclosure had taken place; it would be for the trial judge to decide on its admissibility and the weight to be attached to it.

See also *R (DPP, Davies) v Caernarfon Crown Court* [2019] EWHC 767 (Admin), where the principles in *DPP v Manchester and Salford* were applied in the context of a speeding offence and a speed measurement device.

R (Usman) v Reading Magistrates' Court

[2017] EWHC 2153 (Admin), 13 July 2017, QBD (Admin)

Judicial review was not available where an alternative remedy (here, an appeal to the Crown Court) was available.

The applicant disputed a charge of driving with excess alcohol. On the trial date, there was insufficient time for his solicitor to take instructions on additional evidence from the prosecution received about 15 minutes before the trial was listed to start. There was a conflict of evidence between the applicant and his solicitor about the time the applicant arrived at court. The solicitor asked the magistrates for a half-hour adjournment to read and take instructions. They refused the application and the solicitor withdrew from the case. The case proceeded, and the defendant, now unrepresented, was convicted. He appealed against conviction to the Crown Court and later also sought judicial review of the refusal to adjourn, on the ground that it was wrong to insist on proceeding when he had expected to be represented by a specialist solicitor. His application was refused and he renewed it.

HELD: "11. … the applicant has at least an arguable case on the merits ….

"12. [But] … there is here an important question about whether it is a proper case for the grant of what could be a discretionary remedy of judicial review. The pending appeal to the Crown Court carried with it the considerable benefit of a suspension of the disqualification from driving which followed the magistrates' decision. That suspension has already benefitted the applicant for some eight or nine months …

"13. Secondly, it is important to identify precisely what it is that the applicant seeks by these proceedings. His appeal to the Crown Court provides him with a re-hearing at which the … issues … can properly be considered by a court of competent jurisdiction.

"14. … in considering the grant of judicial review as a discretionary remedy, it is … very important … to bear in mind that a refusal of judicial review would not leave the applicant without remedy. It would leave him with the opportunity to pursue his issues at a full hearing before the Crown Court. I also have regard to the timetable here [the appeal to the Crown Court had been served promptly, while the application for judicial review was not issued until the relevant time limit had almost expired]. …

"15. … those are circumstances in which the granting of judicial review is not an appropriate remedy. Should it ever be necessary to explore the circumstances in which the adjournment was requested and refused by the magistrates, the very fact that there is a conflict of evidence between applicant and his solicitor adds to my feeling that judicial review is not the appropriate course … ."

Renewed application dismissed.

R v Wilson, Walmsley, York & Senior

[2019] EWCA Crim 2410, 3 December 2019, CA (Crim)

On the jurisdiction of the Court of Appeal Criminal Division in relation to convictions for summary offences sent to the Crown Court pursuant to s 51, Crime and Disorder Act 1988.

Three of the appellants had been convicted of a number of offences, including drug-driving contrary to s 5A(1)(a) and (2), Road Traffic Act 1988. All the drug-drive cases were based on blood analyses carried out by Randox (see *R v Bravender*, page 151). The summary drug-drive offences had been committed to the Crown Court, along with other charges, under s 51, Crime and Disorder Act 1988 (sending cases to the Crown Court). The defendants had pleaded guilty to the drug-drive charges following convictions for other offences dealt with on indictment. Senior's appeal against conviction had been allowed (*R v Senior*, page 153) without reference to the issues now raised.

GROUNDS FOR THE APPLICATION: (a) Whether the Court of Appeal Criminal Division has jurisdiction under s 9, Criminal Appeal Act 1968 to hear an appeal for a summary offence which was committed to the Crown Court under s 51, Crime and Disorder Act 1988 when a guilty plea was entered following conviction for an offence or offences on indictment. (b) If not, whether the High Court has jurisdiction to consider the conviction. (c) The approach to be followed if either the Court of Appeal or the High Court has jurisdiction to consider the conviction.

HELD: "24. An appeal by way of case stated would not … be an appropriate route by which to challenge a conviction on the ground that fresh evidence renders the convictions unsafe. This is because it could not be said that the conviction was wrong in law or in excess of jurisdiction (see s 28(1), Senior Courts Act 1981).

"25. The question then arises as to whether the High Court is able to intervene if the decision did not involve an error of law, there was no unfairness on the part of the tribunal and malpractice on the part of the prosecution is not alleged. …

"32. … We have no doubt that the four cases before the court meet the particular requirements established in *Scally* [*R v Bolton Justices ex p Scally*, page 145]. The prosecution concedes that the three Randox cases (*Wilson*, *Walmsley* and *Senior*) were analogous to fraud in that the evidence, as now known, would not make out the offence with which each man was charged. The fault lay entirely with the prosecution. The accused were denied a proper opportunity to decide whether to plead guilty or not guilty. Indeed, they were wrongly denied a complete defence to the charge. There was no real dispute as to the facts and there was a certainty of acquittal.

"[Settling the matter of jurisdiction by reconstituting itself as a Divisional Court] 34. In the cases of [*Wilson* and *Walmsley*], sitting as a Divisional Court, we grant permission to apply for judicial review, we dispense with the issue and service of the judicial review claim form, we abridge all times as necessary and, as set out, we have considered the merits of the claims for judicial review. We grant the applications and the individual summary convictions in the cases of [*Wilson* and *Walmsley*] are quashed.

"35. [In *Senior*] it is clear that the decision on his appeal was flawed on jurisdictional grounds but the decision and the order quashing the conviction remain valid unless and until set aside."

DPP (Bhusal) v Walsall Magistrates' Court; DPP (Thaiss) v Lincoln Magistrates' Court

[2019] EWHC 3317 (Admin), 5 December 2019, QBD (DC)

On the facts (issues of wide application, not dependent on the final result, no other way effectively to challenge the decisions in question), intervention by way of judicial review was justified. The requirements for disclosure as set out in the authorities were not met on the facts in these cases; quality of defence evidence.

In both cases, a motorist had been charged with driving with excess alcohol, contrary to s 5(1), Road Traffic Act 1988. The DPP sought judicial review of disclosure orders made pursuant to s 8, Criminal Procedure and Investigations Act 1996 (application by accused for disclosure). In *Bhusal*, disclosure of logs and historical test data relating to the Intoxilyser used was ordered on the basis that the gas calibration certificate for the Intoxilyser had expired some 2 months before the date of the breath analysis in question. In *Thaiss*, disclosure of logs, memory downloads, calibration certificates and pre-release breath tests was ordered on the basis that the alcohol reading was close to the limit and the prosecution had not properly responded to the application for disclosure. The same expert had prepared reports on behalf of both defendants.

The DPP argued that in both cases the material sought was not relevant because it could not reasonably be considered capable of undermining the prosecution case or assisting the defence case (under s 7A, Criminal Procedure and Investigations Act 1996). The DPP also argued that in the *Thaiss* case, the defence had delayed seeking to have its application for disclosure heard such that it was unreasonable to grant it.

HELD "30. The issue central to both cases … was whether it had been open to the District Judge to decide that the material was such as might be considered capable of undermining the case for the prosecution or of assisting the case for the defence …

"[On the availability of judicial review] 46. Challenges to [interlocutory orders made in the court below] are sparingly entertained in this court. However, in cases like the two before us the court's intervention is justified: the issues raised are of wide application, they are not dependent on the final result and there is no other way by which the orders for disclosure may be effectively challenged. ..."

The requirements to be met when seeking disclosure, as set out *Cracknell v Willis* (page 270) and *DPP v Manchester and Salford Magistrates' Court* (page 605), were reviewed.

"[In *Bhusal*] 51. In the absence of any supporting evidence ..., the District Judge's first instinct, namely to refuse the application, was right. The District Judge was persuaded that the expiry of the gas calibration certificate overcame that difficulty. We respectfully disagree. He was right to adjourn the trial to enable the attendance of experts to speak to the relevance, if any, of that fact to the accuracy of the Intoxilyser readings; but that circumstance alone could not justify ordering the wider disclosure in the absence of any evidence establishing its relevance. ...

"[In *Thaiss*, the expert's report] 52. ... purported to give some evidence in support of the application for disclosure, but it was in our view inadequate, falling far short of the necessary relevance ... [it contained] a series of generalised and, for the most part, unexplained assertions. ...

"53. ... courts faced with evidence purporting to call into question the reliability of a type-approved device should scrutinise such evidence very carefully for its actual meaning and its relevance to the particular test results under examination. ...

"57. ... The delay in pursuing the application for disclosure was a further reason for refusing it."

The applications were allowed and both disclosure orders were quashed.

The court went on to draw attention to Part 19, Criminal Procedure Rules, on expert evidence, and in particular r 19.4 on the contents of an expert report, and criticised the expert reports in the present cases for failures to comply.

"69. ... Given that the printout is the key evidence in relation to the breath-alcohol test results which [the defence expert] considers and the reliability of which he apparently seeks to question, it is an omission that his reports do not examine and discuss the entries on the printout, in particular the results of the device's self-calibration checks. ...

"72. [His] failure to deal in his reports with contrary views previously expressed by [the prosecution's expert witness] in other cases is a further factor undermining the reliability of his evidence.

"73. ... It is the responsibility of defence representatives to ensure that experts like [the expert in the present cases] understand the requirements of the Criminal Practice Rules and Directions, and that the expert reports which they serve on behalf of their clients are reliable and admissible; further that if such reports are to be relied upon for the purposes of seeking further disclosure in relation to a type-approved machine, they address all the matters identified ... in the *Manchester Justices* case."

4. CHARGES

See also Worsley v DPP, page 352, where a charge of failing without reasonable excuse to provide a specimen was not duplicitous.

Thomson v Knights

[1947] KB 336, [1947] 1 All ER 112, 17 December 1946, KBD

The words "drink or drugs" create a single offence.

A motorist had been convicted of being unlawfully in charge of a motor vehicle whilst under the influence of drink or a drug to such an extent as to be incapable of having proper control of the vehicle, contrary to s 15, Road Traffic Act 1930. He appealed against conviction on the ground that it was bad for uncertainty; he had been convicted of two offences in the alternative – being in charge while under the influence of drink, and being in charge while under the influence of a drug.

HELD: "... The offence is driving, or attempting to drive, or being in charge of a vehicle, when ... incapable of having proper control of the vehicle, and that incapacity is caused by drink or a drug. I do not think Parliament here meant to create one offence of being incapable by reason of a drug and another offence of being incapable by reason of drink. What Parliament intended to provide was that a man driving or attempting to drive, or being in charge of a motor car in a self-induced state of incapacity, whether that incapacity was due to drink or drugs, ... commits an offence in each of those cases. In my opinion the conviction is not for an alternative offence nor can it be said to be in respect of two offences. The offence was being in charge of the car when in this particular state of incapacity."

Appeal dismissed.

Jones v Thomas (John Barrie)

[1987] RTR 111, [1987] Crim LR 133, 21 October 1986, QBD (DC)

A reference in the information to s 6(1), Road Traffic Act 1972 "as amended" when the section had in fact been substituted did not render the information defective.

A motorist had been charged with being in charge of a motor vehicle with excess alcohol, contrary to s 6(1), Road Traffic Act 1972 as substituted by s 25 and Sch 8, Transport Act 1981. The justices dismissed the information on the ground that it referred to "section 6(1) of the Road Traffic Act 1972 as amended", but that s 6, Road Traffic Act 1972 had in fact been substituted by the Transport Act 1981; the charge was therefore defective. The prosecutor appealed.

QUESTION(S) FOR THE COURT: Whether the justices were correct to regard the information as defective.

HELD: "... The words 'as amended' were plainly a reference to the fact that, if the defendant wanted to read the statutory provision under which he was charged, he should not get out the Act of 1972 as originally enacted, but that Act in its currently amended form.

"The form of the charge, in my judgment, satisfied the requirements of rule 100 of the Magistrates' Courts Rules 1981 [information sufficient if … it contains a reference to the section of the Act … creating the offence] and, further, was incapable of misleading either layman or lawyer. The information was not defective … ."

Appeal allowed.

DPP v Gane

[1991] Crim LR 711, 11 March 1991, QBD (DC)

Where a person was charged both with driving with excess alcohol and with being in charge with excess alcohol, both arising out of the same facts, and was convicted on the former, the magistrates should not have dismissed the second allegation without consulting the prosecutor.

A person had been charged, *inter alia*, with being in charge of a motor vehicle with excess alcohol, contrary to s 5(1)(b), Road Traffic Act 1988, and of driving with excess alcohol, contrary to s 5(1)(a), Road Traffic Act 1988. The charges arose out of the same facts.

The justices found that the defendant had in fact been driving. They convicted him of driving with excess alcohol, but dismissed the allegation of being in charge, on the grounds that it would have been oppressive not to do so, the charges appeared to be alternatives, and both arose from the same facts. The prosecutor appealed against the dismissal of the charge.

QUESTION(S) FOR THE COURT: Whether the justices were correct in concluding that the proper course was to dismiss the "in charge" allegation: (a) when they had not been invited to do so by the prosecutor's offering no evidence; or (b) because they were satisfied that course was proper on the merits of the evidence.

HELD: The prosecution argument was that the justices could either have convicted and imposed no penalty, or made no adjudication on the "in charge" matter; having dismissed it, if the motorist successfully appealed against the conviction for driving with excess alcohol, he would in effect have gone scot-free.

"The answer … depends upon what approach the prosecution chose to take … Once [the justices] convicted of the offence of driving with excess alcohol, the Crown should have been invited and should have indicated whether they wished to pursue the alternative charge of being in charge … If the Crown had taken the view that they did not wish to pursue that charge they could have withdrawn it … If, however, the prosecution had … wished to keep its position open, pending any possible appeal, certain alternatives were available …

"… The justices could … have adjourned the alternative charge *sine die*, which would have left it open for them to pursue it to conviction had the matter been referred back after a successful appeal on [the charge of driving with excess alcohol]. Alternatively, they could have convicted of it and imposed a concurrent disqualification on that charge but no further penalty … The result of that would have been that if a successful appeal had been mounted in regard to the driving charge there would still have remained a conviction on the alternative offence … with an appropriate disqualification, although of course no fine.

"The course which the justices did adopt was … inappropriate."

Appeal allowed.

R v Chichester Magistrates' Court ex p DPP

[1994] RTR 175, 15 March 1993, QBD (DC)

Charges of failing to provide a specimen of breath for analysis and failing to provide a specimen for a laboratory test are not inconsistent with each other; when both were charged arising out of the same facts, they should have been tried together.

A motorist had been charged with failing without reasonable excuse to provide a specimen of breath for analysis, and with failing without reasonable excuse to provide a specimen of blood or urine for a laboratory test, both contrary to s 7(6), Road Traffic Act 1988.

At the police station, the motorist said he could not provide breath specimens unless he had with him a "puffer", because he suffered a heart complaint. The officer administering the procedure decided to request a blood or urine specimen, in case it transpired that there was a medical reason why the motorist could not provide breath specimens. He failed to do so.

The justices refused to try the two charges together on the grounds that they were inconsistent with each other and ordered they be tried separately by differently constituted benches.

The prosecutor applied for an order of *mandamus* directing the justices to try the two charges together, and for an order of *certiorari* to quash their decision not to do so.

GROUND(S) FOR APPEAL: Whether: (1) the justices erred in law in determining that the charges were inconsistent with each other; (2) charges arising out of one and the same incident should be tried together even if inconsistent; (3) relevant authorities had not been cited in argument or taken into account by the justices, who failed to take account of the advantages of trying the charges together; (4) there was no rational reason for refusing to try the charges together …

HELD: "… *White & Gaskell v Proudlock* [see page 26] … makes it clear … that these two charges can both be made against one defendant in respect of the same facts and factual situation and indeed those charges are not inconsistent one with the other …

"… the facts and circumstances relating to the two charges are so inter-related that in fact no justice in the true sense of the word could be done as between the prosecution and [the motorist] without those two charges being heard together.

"… there are no good reasons whatever for the trial of these separate charges by separate benches which would give rise to the consequent risk of inconsistent decisions … there was no rational basis on which the justices could take the decision to direct that the two charges should be tried separately by differently constituted benches … ."

Application granted.

Butterworth v DPP

[1995] 1 AC 381, [1994] 3 WLR 538, [1994] 3 All ER 289, [1994] RTR 330, [1995] Crim LR 71, 21 July 1994, HL

A charge under s 7(6), Road Traffic Act 1988 (failing to provide breath specimens for analysis) need not specify the offence being investigated; that question is relevant only after conviction and goes to the appropriate penalty.

A person had been charged, *inter alia*, with failing without reasonable excuse to provide two specimens of breath for analysis, contrary to s 7(6), Road Traffic Act 1988.

He was convicted by magistrates, and, on appeal to the Divisional Court, argued that the charge was bad for duplicity (s 7 providing that, "In the course of an investigation into whether a person has committed an offence under section 4 or 5 …"). The Divisional Court held that it was not. The motorist appealed further.

CERTIFIED QUESTION(S): (1) Does s 7(6), Road Traffic Act create more than one offence? (2) Does an information which merely alleges that the accused failed to provide a breath sample for analysis comply with r 12(1), Magistrates' Courts Rules 1981 (SI 1981/552) (magistrates' court not to proceed to try an information that charges more than one offence)? (3) In order to comply with rr 12(1) and 100 (information sufficient if it describes the specific offence in ordinary language … and gives such particulars as may be necessary for giving reasonable information of the nature of the charge; information to refer to the section of any Act creating the offence), Magistrates' Courts Rules 1981, must an information alleging an offence under r 12(1) give sufficient information so that it is manifest what is the maximum penalty for the offence?

HELD: "The central test for the purpose of an offence under section 7(6) is whether the constable is carrying out an investigation into whether a person has committed an offence under section 4 or 5 of the Act … this … plainly means an investigation into whether the person has committed any offence under section 4 or 5. It does not have to be shown that the constable had in his mind a specific offence under one of those sections and that he was investigating that specific offence. It is not therefore necessary to specify in the charge which, if any, specific offence was being investigated by the constable. The substance of the offence is the refusal in the course of a general investigation for the purposes of section 4 and 5. If the test is positive, then it may be necessary to decide which, if any of the substantive offences under section 4 or 5 have been committed …

"Is this reading of section 7(6) vitiated by the fact that separate penalties are provided for driving or attempting to drive on the one hand, and being in charge on the other? … it is clearly not so vitiated. The question whether the person was driving or in charge of the motor vehicle is not part of the enquiry into whether there has been a refusal for the purposes of section 7(6). That question only becomes relevant after conviction and goes to the appropriate penalty. For the purposes of the enquiry into the appropriate penalty the defendant will need to be told precisely what is alleged (e.g. driving or being in charge) though evidence as to this is likely to have been gone into during the investigation of his guilt of the section 7(6) offence but it is not an essential part of the offence. There has, thus, to be a separate and distinct inquiry and a distinct decision by the justices after conviction …

"… The charge here was accordingly not bad for duplicity and there was no failure to comply with rule 12(1) or rule 100 of the Magistrates' Courts Rules 1981."

The answer to question (1) was "no"; the answer to question (2) was "yes"; the answer to question (3) was "no". Appeal dismissed.

DPP v Corcoran (Terence) [1993] 1 All ER 912, [1992] RTR 289, (1993) 97 Cr App R 13 (DC) overruled.

R v Bolton JJ ex p Khan (Zafer Alli)

[1998] EWHC QB 1040, 4 November 1998, QBD (DC)

Section 5(1)(a), Road Traffic Act 1988 establishes six offences; if the appropriate alternative is not specified in the charge, it is duplicitous.

A motorist had been convicted of driving with excess alcohol, contrary to s 5(1)(a), Road Traffic Act 1988. He had been stopped by police and a roadside breath test was positive. He sought, and was granted, leave to apply for judicial review on the ground that the police had followed the wrong procedure under s 8(2), Road Traffic Act (lower breath reading no more than 50 µg alcohol in 100 ml breath giving rise to the "driver's option" – now repealed; see page v). It was also later said that the charge of driving after consuming so much alcohol that the proportion of it in his "breath/blood/urine" exceeded the prescribed limit was duplicitous.

HELD: "[It is submitted that s 5(1)(a)] contains within it six different offences, namely driving or attempting to drive with excess alcohol in (1) breath, (2) blood or (3) urine. The appropriate charge will depend on whether the defendant had been driving or attempting to drive and whether he has supplied a specimen of breath, of blood or of urine.

"… In order to establish the offence, it must be shown that the excess of alcohol is in breath, blood or urine as the case may be. The exact wording of each statutory provision must be considered. In our judgment, this provision contains, as [counsel for the appellant] submitted, six different offences. The prosecution will always know whether breath, blood or urine is appropriate and if an error is made in failing to delete from the *pro forma* charge the otiose words, an amendment can be made without any prejudice to the defendant. That should have happened in this case.

"Our conclusion on the question of duplicity makes it unnecessary to consider whether the plea of guilty should prevent the grant of relief despite the failure to tell the applicant that the breath specimen provided a reading not exceeding 50 microgrammes. But, since the point has been argued, we will state our conclusions briefly. …

"Here there can be no question that the prosecutor's actions came anywhere near being analogous to fraud. This was not a case of a failure to disclose vital information which only the prosecutor knew. … The failure of the prosecutor to appreciate its significance was matched by the failure of the applicant and his advisers. Furthermore, the applicant was not at all prejudiced by the failure. He gave a specimen of blood willingly having been correctly told that he had the option to do so. If he had not, he would have been prosecuted for the offence of excess alcohol in his breath … Accordingly, we would in any event have refused relief in the exercise of our discretion."

Order of *certiorari* to quash the conviction.

DPP (R) v Short

[2001] EWHC Admin 885, 26 October 2001, QBD (Admin)

On the facts, the magistrates should have allowed an error in the information to be corrected.

A motorist had been charged with using (rather than driving or attempting to drive) a motor vehicle on a road with excess alcohol, contrary to s 5(1)(a), Road Traffic Act 1988. At the close of the evidence the prosecution applied to amend the information by substituting the word "drove" for "used", to bring it within the terms of s 5. The magistrates refused the application, finding that the error was so fundamental that it could not be amended. The prosecutor appealed.

QUESTION(S) FOR THE COURT: Whether the ruling that the prosecution should not be allowed to amend the information in all the circumstances was reasonable.

HELD: "[After reviewing s 123, Magistrates' Courts Act 1990 and the case law] 21. … The information must be looked at as a whole. The reference to the statutory provision cannot be ignored. If account is taken of the reference to Section 5 of the Road Traffic Act, it cannot be said that the information does not disclose an offence known to law. … the justices erred in holding that the defect in the information fell into the category of errors that are so fundamental that they cannot be cured by amendment.

"22. … the effect of Section 123 of the Magistrates' Court Act is to give a wide discretion to the court to amend an information; … the discretion will ordinarily be exercised in favour of an amendment unless that would result in injustice to the defendant. In this case no injustice will flow from the proposed amendment. The defendant has been fully aware at all times of the case made against him. … the magistrates should have exercised their discretion to permit the amendment of the information."

Appeal allowed; case remitted to the justices with a direction to convict.

R v Phipps

[2005] EWCA Crim 33, 14 January 2005, CA (Crim)

Where a motorist had pleaded guilty to drink driving, it was an abuse of process, in the absence of special or exceptional circumstances, later to charge him with dangerous driving arising out of the same incident.

A motorist had been charged with driving with excess alcohol, contrary to s 5(1)(a), Road Traffic Act 1988. He had been driving in the wrong direction on a dual carriageway and collided head-on with another vehicle, causing injury. He was arrested and found to have excess alcohol. He pleaded guilty and was convicted.

Some weeks later, apparently in response to press reports of the case, he was summonsed for dangerous driving in relation to the same incident. At the trial, it was submitted that it was an abuse of process for the Crown to proceed with a charge of dangerous driving arising out of the same or substantially the same facts as those in respect of which the defendant had been convicted for driving with excess alcohol. The court rejected this argument and, on his guilty plea, convicted the defendant for dangerous driving. He appealed.

HELD: "11. [On the appellant's argument that no one should be punished twice for an offence arising out of the same or substantially the same set of facts unless there are special or exceptional circumstances, these propositions] are correct. They are soundly based on the authorities …

"12. The only scope for possible debate is whether the principle applies not only where the facts are the same but also where they are substantially the same and precisely what that means.

"21. The authorities do not consider in detail what is meant by the same or substantially the same facts but … they essentially mean that the Crown should not be permitted, save in special or exceptional circumstances, to bring a second set of proceedings arising out of the same incident as the first set of proceedings after the first set of proceedings has been concluded. The principle … is that the Crown should decide at the outset, or at the latest before the conclusion of the first set of proceedings, what charges it wishes to bring arising out of the same incident. Any other approach is unfairly oppressive to a defendant. …

"23. … the burden of establishing special or exceptional circumstances is on the Crown and the question is not whether a fair trial is possible.

"29. … both these prosecutions and the allegations in them arose out of the same or substantially the same facts, namely driving the appellant's car on the A3 at Malden. They both arose out of the same incident …

"31. [The prosecutor] correctly concedes that, if that is so, there are no special circumstances in this case which would entitle the Crown to bring the second set of proceedings. It follows that … the judge should have stayed the second proceedings as an abuse of process and that this appeal against conviction must be allowed."

Crann v CPS

[2013] EWHC 552 (Admin), 27 February 2013, QBD (Admin)

On the facts, the magistrates' decision to allow the late amendment of the charge was (somewhat reluctantly) upheld, on the basis that the magistrates addressed the interests of justice and must also have taken into account the need to ensure that justices is dispensed with promptitude.

A motorist had been arrested on suspicion of driving with excess alcohol, contrary to s 5(1), Road Traffic Act 1988. When asked to provide breath specimens he said he was "not right in the head", and was apparently threatening to self-harm. He did not provide breath specimens. The officer accepted this as a valid reason for not providing breath and went on to request a specimen of blood. The motorist refused, saying he was terrified of needles. The motorist was charged with failing without reasonable excuse to provide a specimen of breath for analysis, contrary to s 7(6), Road Traffic Act 1988.

At the first hearing, the motorist's advisers pointed out that the charge should refer to blood, not breath. After a number of hearings and adjournments, the charge was eventually amended on the grounds that the amended charge arose out of the same, or substantially the same, facts as the original charge; and on the ground that the accused would not face a more serious charge than had already been charged; he would not therefore be prejudiced by the amendment. The motorist pleaded guilty to the amended charge, but then appealed by way of case stated against the decision to adjourn on the ground that it was contrary to the interests of justice.

QUESTION(S) FOR THE COURT: Not recited in the judgment.

HELD: "20. [It is accepted] that the failure to ensure that the appropriate charge was brought represented a 'particularly lamentable failure' on the part of the CPS. …

"23. Every case depends upon its own facts, the essential question being whether the principles appropriate to the question of whether the discretionary exercise involved in deciding whether to grant the amendment to the charge were observed.

"24. The stated case shows that the magistrates took into account the fact that there would be no prejudice to the appellant if the amendment was to be allowed.

"25. That, as it seems to me, was a judgment the magistrates were entitled to make and it would be one with which I would find it impossible to interfere.

"26. The question is did they address the issue of the need to ensure that justice was dispensed with promptitude in the way in which Thomas LJ suggested [in *Williams v DPP* [2009] EWHC 2354 (Admin); see page 582] should be the case? They did not say expressly that they took into account the need for the delivery of justice with promptitude. …

"29. Undoubtedly, the whole of the case of *Williams* was drawn to the attention of the magistrates … and it would be difficult to believe that considerations of the kind that I have mentioned (namely, the requirement for justice to be dispensed expeditiously) were not well and truly in the minds of the justices who had to make the decision. It must have become commonplace to consider these issues in the climate that is referred to in the case of *Williams*.

"30. I am not entirely convinced that every bench of magistrates would have granted the amendment at the late stage that it was granted in this case, but my task is simply to decide whether the decision was outside the band of reasonable responses to the issues that fell to the magistrates to consider.

"31. On balance, I do not think that I can characterise their decision in that way and for those reasons the appeal is dismissed."

5. COSTS

Ho-Shing v CPS

[2022] EWHC 3137 (Admin), 3 November 2022, KBD (Admin)

Where the nature of the defence was not made clear until the first hearing, and the case was then discontinued, costs incurred before the first hearing were not recoverable.

The appellant had been charged with failing without reasonable excuse to provide a specimen for analysis, contrary to s 7(6), Road Traffic Act 1988. Before appearing at court, she agreed to pay her solicitors a total of £1,600 plus VAT to represent her up to and including her first appearance at court. At the first hearing she made clear her defence would be that, at the time she was asked for specimens, she was asleep in a police cell. The police had CCTV footage of the cell showing that she was indeed asleep, but did not provide it to the Crown Prosecution Service until after a number of requests and a case management meeting. The Crown Prosecution Service then discontinued the case. The appellant applied for her costs.

The district judge hearing the application proceeded on the basis of the Costs in Criminal Cases (General) Regulations 1986 (SI 1986/1335) and the case law arising from them. He applied the test of whether there had been an unnecessary or improper act or omission, as a result of which costs were incurred by another party such that the court would have a discretion to order the party responsible to meet those costs. Quoting *Evans v Serious Fraud Office*

[2015] EWHC 263 (QB), such awards are "generally restricted to those exceptional cases where the prosecution has acted in bad faith or made a clear and stark error". Here, the Crown Prosecution Service should have reviewed the CCTV footage before the first appearance, so that the case could have been discontinued much earlier, but the failure did not meet the test in *Evans*, since it was only at the first appearance that the nature of the defence was made clear. By that time, the appellant's costs had been incurred. The appellant appealed.

QUESTION(S) FOR THE COURT: Whether the judge erred in law or approach or reached a decision that was not open to him on the evidence.

HELD: "14. … . the judge accepted that an error had been made prior to the first appearance – the question before him was what sort of error. Was it a clear and stark error or something less than that? That was a highly fact-sensitive question of evaluation for him.

"15. … the reasons he gave were intelligible, coherent and sufficient to explain why he considered that the line between an error *simpliciter* and a clear and stark error of the kind needed to justify an award of costs had been crossed … after the first appearance and not before that.

"16. … the judge was well-placed to identify the point at which that line was crossed … . The judge had a close understanding of the context of the case, as demonstrated by his detailed ruling … The judge considered the significance of the evidence deployed by the prosecution. The regulations … conferred a discretion on him. It was for him … to exercise that discretion. In my judgment, there was no error of law or approach. The conclusion he reached was properly open to him."

Appeal dismissed.

6. DISQUALIFICATION FROM DRIVING

See Sch 2, Road Traffic Offenders Act 1988 for the lists of offences in relation to which disqualification from driving is obligatory and those in relation to which disqualification is at the discretion of the court. See also Cawley (Stephen) v DPP, page 84 – where the defendant claimed he had not been driving and the prosecution did not call evidence on the point, disqualification from driving was discretionary not mandatory; DPP v Haddigan, page 442 – a guilty plea amounted to a conviction for the purposes of determining the minimum period of disqualification; Butterworth v DPP, page 614 – a charge of failing to provide breath specimens need not specify the offence being investigated; that question is relevant only after conviction and goes to the appropriate penalty.

George v DPP

[1989] RTR 217, 6 October 1988, QBD (DC)

Where a motorist failed to provide specimens, having been found in charge of his vehicle, disqualification was discretionary rather than mandatory.

A motorist had pleaded guilty to failing without reasonable excuse to provide a specimen of breath for analysis, contrary to s 8(7), Road Traffic Act 1972 as substituted by s 25 and Sch 8, Transport Act 1981. He had been found asleep in his car on the hard shoulder of a motorway; he was arrested and taken to the police station; the allegation against him was not that he had been driving, but that he had been in charge with excess alcohol. He refused to supply specimens of breath.

At the hearing the motorist contended that no evidence of the reason for requiring the specimens had been adduced; if they had been required in connection with an offence of driving with excess alcohol, the case would fall within the category of case for which disqualification is mandatory; but if in connection with any other offence, it would fall within the category of case for which disqualification is discretionary. The prosecution argued that, since the motorist had admitted he had been driving, the specimens had been required in connection with an offence attracting obligatory disqualification.

The justices found that the case fell within Sch 4, Part I, column 4 (a), Road Traffic Act 1972 as likewise substituted (specimen required to ascertain proportion of alcohol when driving – obligatory disqualification). They disqualified the motorist for 3 years; he appealed.

QUESTION(S) FOR THE COURT: Whether there was any or sufficient evidence upon which the court could find that the specimen was required to ascertain liability to drive or proportion of alcohol at the time the offender was driving or attempting to drive.

HELD: "… although … there was just enough evidence on which the justices were entitled to find that this was a driving case rather than an 'in charge' case, … that seems to me to be wholly contrary to the justice of this prosecution, being run, as it was, on an 'in charge' basis. The justices ought … to have found that that was the only basis upon which they could sentence, that the evidence only went to that particular basis … accordingly they were wrong to reach the conclusion that this was an obligatory disqualification case rather than a discretionary disqualification case."

The answer to the question was "no". Appeal allowed.

R v Loughborough JJ ex p Smith (Steven)

[1992] COD 299, 11 February 1992, QBD (DC)

Where a motorist failed to provide specimens, but had not been driving or attempting to drive or in charge, and the magistrates endorsed his licence, a case should be stated to elucidate the principles upon which special reasons apply in such circumstances.

A motorist had pleaded guilty to failing without reasonable excuse to provide a specimen of breath for analysis, contrary to s 7, Road Traffic Act 1988. He submitted that there were special reasons for not disqualifying under s 34(1), Road Traffic Offenders Act 1988: he had not driven or attempted to drive, or been about to drive, nor had he been in charge of a motor vehicle. The justices granted an absolute discharge but endorsed the motorist's licence with 10 penalty points.

The magistrates declined to state a case for the opinion of the Divisional Court on the ground that the application was frivolous. The motorist sought an order of *mandamus* directing them to state a case.

HELD: "… I do not agree that the application was frivolous … the justices speak of the fact that, even though there was no driving or attempting to drive, none the less an endorsement was obligatory … having regard to the … second schedule to the Road Traffic Offenders Act 1988.

"… the justices may have failed to appreciate that the question of special reasons only arises [where] an endorsement would otherwise be obligatory or, where there is a disqualification, in those cases in which a disqualification would otherwise be obligatory. Moreover this case is unusual in the sense that a person may commit an offence under section 7 of the Road Traffic Act 1988, albeit he has not driven or attempted to drive, is not about to drive and has not been in charge of a motor vehicle. It may be that the application to such a case of the principles upon which special reasons can be found would be usefully elucidated by this court."

Application granted.

Shaw v DPP and Other Cases

[1993] RTR 45, 12 November 1992, QBD (DC)

The circumstances of, and penalty for, an offence of failing to provide specimens are for independent ascertainment if they do not emerge during a trial.

Motorists had been convicted of failing without reasonable excuse to provide specimens for analysis, contrary to s 7(6), Road Traffic Act 1988. They appealed.

QUESTION(S) FOR THE COURT: (i) Whether s 7(6), Road Traffic Act 1988 created two offences; (ii) whether a charge alleging an offence under s 7(6) should state on its face whether the defendant was being investigated for an offence under either s 4(1) or (2), or 5(1)(a) or (b), Road Traffic Act 1988; (iii) whether a failure on its face of a charge under s 7(6) to specifically identify which other sections of the Road Traffic Act 1988 were said to apply, so that the defendant could not determine the penalty for the offence for which he was charged, meant that the charge was defective (*Shaw*). The remaining appeals were brought on, essentially, the same basis.

HELD: "The maximum punishment for failing to provide a specimen pursuant to section 7(6) is higher 'where the specimen was required to ascertain ability to drive or proportion of alcohol at the time the offender was driving or attempting to drive' than it is in any other case; see Schedule 2 to the Road Traffic Offenders Act 1988 … It was held by the Divisional Court in *DPP v Corcoran* [[1993] 1 All ER 912, [1992] RTR 289, (1993) 97 Cr App R 13, since overruled by *Butterworth v DPP*, see page 614] … that (a) by reason of that difference in maximum punishment section 7(6) creates two offences, and (b) an information in terms of section 7(6) alone is therefore bad for duplicity …

"It is, of course, understandable that a defendant should wish to be aware as precisely as possible of the likely consequences in terms of punishment of his admitted conduct or that found by the court to have been committed. But that cannot affect the construction of a plain straightforward provision creating an uncomplicated offence as section 7(6) undoubtedly does. It stands in isolation from other circumstances prior to and succeeding its commission. The matter of penalty and other circumstances which may affect it are for independent ascertainment … if they have not emerged during a trial … Whether it would be more just that the prosecution at some early stage inform a defendant of relevant circumstances sought to be relied upon is a matter which goes to procedural fairness and is, we think, easily resolved by a suitable procedure."

Appeal dismissed; applications refused.

Crampsie v DPP

[1993] RTR 383, 21 December 1992, QBD (DC)

On a charge of failing to provide, the question whether the defendant was driving or attempting to drive goes to sentence alone, and must be proved beyond reasonable doubt.

The defendant had been charged with, having been driving or attempting to drive a motor vehicle on a road, failing without reasonable excuse to provide two specimens of breath for analysis, contrary to s 7(6), Road Traffic Act 1988. The police found his car dangerously parked and unattended, seemingly having collided with another vehicle. At the police station, he provided a specimen of breath for analysis which showed 92 µg alcohol in 100 ml breath. He failed to provide a second specimen, saying he suffered from asthma.

At the hearing, the motorist said he had parked his car outside a public house; it was not double parked and he had not collided with any other vehicle. He went to the public house and drank 6 or 7 pints of beer. Then he went to a nearby take-away, which was only about 10 minutes walk from his home; on emerging, he saw police officers near his car and approached them. He said he had not been driving or attempting to drive, but only in charge. The motorist submitted there was no case to answer.

The justices found a case to answer, since the issue whether the specimen was required in connection with driving or with being in charge was not relevant. They convicted the defendant and disqualified him from driving on the basis that it was mandatory to do so under s 34(3), Road Traffic Offenders Act 1988. The defendant appealed.

QUESTION(S) FOR THE COURT: (a) Where an accused is convicted of an offence under s 7(6), Road Traffic Act 1988 which alleges that the specimen was required to ascertain the proportion of alcohol at the time he was driving or attempting to drive and the court finds as a fact that he was in charge of the vehicle, and may well have been driving or attempting to drive, is the court bound by the wording of the charge to impose a mandatory disqualification despite that finding of fact, or should that finding of fact lead to the conclusion that any disqualification will be discretionary? (b) Did the court err in law in omitting formally to determine whether the appellant was driving or attempting to drive, or was in charge of the vehicle, prior to the making of the requirement for a specimen for analysis, before proceeding to consider its powers of sentence?

HELD: "… there was no necessity on the issue of whether the specimen was required to ascertain the defendant's alcohol content to establish whether he was driving or attempting to drive or merely in charge of a motor vehicle. This was not relevant to the question of innocence and guilt but was only material in relation to the court's powers of sentence following conviction.

"Thus the justices cannot be faulted in convicting on the evidence that he had refused to supply a specimen and that there was no reasonable excuse for his refusal … However, whether or not to impose the mandatory disqualification depended upon a finding of fact whether at the material time he had been driving or attempting to drive. As this was a criminal matter it called for the prosecution to discharge the burden of proof and the standard of proof required was that of being satisfied beyond reasonable doubt.

"The justices [stated in the case that] 'whilst the evidence supported the submission that the defendant was in charge of his vehicle, it did not go so far as to establish that he was not driving or attempting to drive at the time the specimen was required.' This passage on its face appears to suggest that they were applying the wrong burden of proof … a much fairer reading of it is that they were not satisfied beyond reasonable doubt … that the appellant had been driving or attempting to drive … This being so it was not open to the justices … to disqualify the appellant mandatorily. They were, however, sure that he had been in charge and thus the discretionary sanction as appropriate."

The answer to question (a) was "no"; the answer to question (b) was "yes". Appeal allowed in part.

R (Cawley) v Warrington Crown Court
[2001] EWHC Admin 494, 22 June 2001, QBD (DC)

Where refusal to provide specimens was on the basis that the defendant had been in charge, there being no proof of driving or attempting to drive, a 3-year disqualification, taking account of an earlier conviction, was unreasonable.

A motorist had pleaded guilty to failing without reasonable excuse to provide a specimen for a roadside breath test, contrary to s 6(4), Road Traffic Act 1988, and was convicted by magistrates on 26 April 1999 of a further offence of failing to provide a specimen of blood, contrary to s 7(6), Road Traffic Act 1988. The offences were committed on 12 July 1998. The magistrates disqualified the applicant from driving for 3 years.

The applicant appealed to the Crown Court against conviction for failing to provide a specimen of blood, and against sentence. The appeal against conviction was dismissed and the 3-year disqualification upheld. The recorder at the Crown Court believed that such a disqualification was mandatory since the applicant had been convicted of drink driving in March 1990; disqualification would have been mandatory if it had been proved that the applicant had been driving on 12 July 1998.

The applicant's appeal by way of case stated came before the Divisional Court on 24 January 2001. The Divisional Court held that the recorder had been wrong to impose what he believed was a mandatory disqualification of 3 years because there was no sufficient evidence that the applicant had been driving. At the Crown Court the police officers involved in the case had not given evidence that the applicant was driving; they had first seen him on foot. The applicant gave evidence that someone else, not he, had been driving. The recorder and justices rejected that evidence and concluded, wrongly as the Divisional Court found, that the applicant had been driving. The Divisional Court remitted the case to the Crown Court with an indication that a discretionary, rather than a mandatory, disqualification might be appropriate.

On 9 March 2001 the matter came before the same recorder sitting with justices; the recorder appeared to maintain that the applicant had been driving, despite the conclusion of the Divisional Court that there was no sufficient evidence of that. Although disqualification was discretionary, rather than mandatory, 3 years disqualification was still imposed.

The appellant sought judicial review and permission was granted by a single judge on 11 April.

HELD: "8. As a matter of history … the applicant has served approximately six months by way of disqualification … the imposition of the same period of disqualification, when disqualification was known to be discretionary, as that which had been thought to be appropriate when that period of disqualification was mandatory, raises a question mark as to the propriety of the decision.

"9. … submissions … on behalf of the applicant, draw attention to a number of ways in which [it is submitted] the recorder misdirected himself and those sitting with him in reaching the conclusion which he did. He referred to the court having reminded itself of the facts of the offence, but he did not identify which particular facts of the offence were those on which the court relied. Nor was any explanation given as to why three years was thought to be appropriate, save by reference to the previous conviction. The recorder also referred to the court being obliged to take into account the previous offence. As there was no question of mandatory disqualification that is a misapprehension of the position if by the word 'obliged' the recorder was seeking to indicate some legal or statutory obligation. Undoubtedly, the fact that there was a previous conviction was a matter to be taken into account but the court was not 'obliged' to take it into account in the way in which it would have been had disqualification been mandatory.

"10. … Taking [the] history into account, however, and taking into account that the refusal to provide specimens in this case can only have been on the basis that the applicant was in charge of the motorcar, there being no proof that he was driving or attempting to drive, it seems to me that the three-year disqualification … was manifestly unreasonable … I would quash the three-year disqualification."

7. EQUIVOCAL PLEA

Ankrah v DPP

[1998] RTR 169, 20 February 1995, QBD (DC)

On the facts of this case, the defendant's guilty plea was not equivocal and there was nothing to suggest that it was entered under a mistake of law.

A motorist had been charged with driving with excess alcohol, contrary to s 5(1)(a), Road Traffic Act 1988, and with failing without reasonable excuse to provide a specimen of blood for analysis, contrary to s 7(6), Road Traffic Act 1988. He pleaded guilty to the second charge and was sentenced. He pleaded not guilty to driving with excess alcohol; no evidence was offered and the charge was dismissed.

He then appealed to the Crown Court on the grounds that his guilty plea had been equivocal, or had been based on an error of law; and that the charge to which he had pleaded guilty had been duplicitous. The appeal was dismissed and the motorist appealed further.

QUESTION(S) FOR THE COURT: (ii) Was the appellant's plea in the lower court unequivocal? (iii) Was the Crown Court right to dismiss the appeal?

HELD: "[On the appellant's argument that the procedure followed by the police did not fully comply with the requirements laid down in *DPP v Warren* (see page 75) and that the court had before it facts which made his plea equivocal] [t]he only facts put before the court after the plea was entered are those contained in the Statement of Facts … Nothing was said as to the detail of the procedure which was in fact followed and therefore the court was not either expressly or inferentially alerted to the fact that the procedure which was followed was in any way unlawful … Nothing said by or on behalf of the Appellant raised any doubt as to the certainty of his plea. It was not in any sense, therefore, equivocal.

"The related point is … that [the] plea of guilty was entered under a mistake of law …

"There is considerable doubt as to whether a mistake of law in the Appellant's mind at the time when he enters a plea can form the basis of such a recantation … Assuming for present purposes however that it is open for an Appellant to say that his plea is equivocal because he entered it under a mistake as to the law, there was absolutely no material in the instant case upon which the Crown Court could have concluded that the plea was entered upon any such basis … There is … nothing to support the submission that the plea was entered under a mistake of law.

"The third point … is a simple plea for justice, based on the premise that this Appellant, in fact, committed no offence and … the Crown Court ought to have had jurisdiction to hear his appeal …

"The answer to this submission is to be found in the provisions of section 108, which proscribe the right of appeal against conviction … if someone pleads guilty he has no right of appeal to the Crown Court against conviction. The only exception is if the plea is equivocal … ."

The answers to the questions were: (ii) "yes"; (iii) "yes". Appeal dismissed.

8. PROOF OF DRIVING

See also Whelehan v DPP, page 15 – admission of driving and grounds for inference of having driven; Tobi v Nicholas, page 45, where hearsay evidence of the identity of the driver was disallowed; Porceddu v DPP, page 357, Davis (Karl) v DPP, page 360 and R (Marsh (Ian)) v DPP, page 370, all on the admissibility of identification evidence; and Watson v DPP, page 392, where the driver's admission of driving was admissible.

Patterson v Charlton

[1986] RTR 18, 18 February 1985, QBD (DC)

The defendant's unchallenged admission that he had been driving needed no corroboration.

A charge under s 6(1) and Sch 4, Road Traffic Act 1972 as substituted by s 25(3) and Sch 8, Transport Act 1981, of driving with excess alcohol, had been dismissed. A police officer arrested two men whom he suspected had stolen a car. The defendant said he was the owner of the car and that he had driven it. The police sergeant then suspected him of having taken alcohol; a breath test was positive. The police officer had not seen the defendant drive the car.

The justices found that, in the absence of independent evidence that the vehicle had been driven by the defendant, admissions by him were not sufficient to merit the case proceeding further. The prosecutor appealed.

QUESTION(S) FOR THE COURT: Whether or not the unchallenged admission made by the defendant that he had driven the vehicle on the road was an admission sufficient to establish a *prima facie* case that he was the driver of the vehicle; and whether the justices were right in dismissing the matter.

HELD: "… any suggestion that an admission from a defendant that he has been the driver of the vehicle needs some sort of corroboration or reinforcement from other witnesses is untenable … Once the defendant had admitted driving the vehicle … and once the sample showed that he had an excess of alcohol … section 10 [presumption that alcohol level at the time of the offence not less than in the specimen, etc] operated to transfer the burden to the defendant to displace the assumption made under that section that he was over the limit … ."

Appeal allowed.

DPP v Williams (Charles Anthony)

Unreported, CO/744/89, 25 July 1990, QBD (DC)

Justices should not have dismissed a charge of driving with excess alcohol where the defendant called no evidence but submitted there was no case to answer because, at the time of the arrest, the officer did not have reasonable cause to suspect he had been driving or that he still had alcohol in his body.

A motorist had been charged with driving with excess alcohol, contrary to s 6(1)(a), Road Traffic Act 1972 as substituted by s 25 and Sch 8, Transport Act 1981. Police officers located a car they had been looking for; without examining the car, they then found the driver in a nearby home. He admitted he had driven the car; the police detected alcohol on him; he said he had last had a drink some 5 hours earlier. He was taken to the police station, where breath analysis showed excess alcohol.

At the close of the prosecution case, the motorist submitted there was no case to answer on the grounds that the only evidence of his having driven the car was his own admission to the police; and that the prosecution had failed to prove that the motorist had been over the prescribed limit at the time of driving. The magistrates accepted the submission and dismissed the charge.

The prosecutor appealed successfully, the Divisional Court finding that the effect of s 10(2), Road Traffic Act 1972 as likewise substituted is to require a court to assume, unless an accused on a balance of probabilities proves the contrary, that he had had at least as much alcohol in his body when he was last driving as shown in the specimen taken from him.

The case had been sent back to the justices. The motorist called no evidence but again argued that there was no case to answer because, on the undisputed facts, the police officer at the time of the arrest did not have reasonable cause to suspect that the motorist had been driving or attempting to drive or in charge with excess alcohol and that he still had alcohol in his body as prescribed by s 7(1)(b). Again, the justices accepted the submission and dismissed the charge. The prosecutor appealed.

QUESTION(S) FOR THE COURT: Whether, on the undisputed facts found and the defence not having given any evidence or called any witnesses, the justices were wrong in law to dismiss the allegation.

HELD: "... The requirements are that it should be proved that a person had been driving ... with alcohol in his body and that the person still has alcohol in his body. [The undisputed evidence] involved the assertion by the officer that he had spoken to the defendant and asked him if he had been driving. He was told that he had and at the time he had smelt alcohol on his breath. Plainly there was, as it were, subsequent corroboration of that latter piece of evidence in the light of the finding on the analysis of breath.

"... there was incontrovertible evidence that the requirements of section 7(1)(b) had been satisfied. It was not open ... to the justices on the second occasion to accede to the submission that was made ... the case was abundantly proved by undisputed evidence. The only way in which the defendant could have secured an acquittal following the determination of the first appeal was by himself calling evidence in order to satisfy the burden of proof imposed upon him by section 10(2)."

Appeal allowed.

Brown v Stott (Procurator Fiscal, Dunfermline) and Another

[2003] 1 AC 681, [2001] 2 WLR 817, [2001] 2 All ER 97, DRA No 3 of 2000, 5 December 2000, Privy Council

A requirement under s 172, Road Traffic Act 1988, that the registered keeper of a vehicle disclose the name of the driver, does not infringe art 6, European Convention on Human Rights.

The defendant had been charged with theft and with driving with excess alcohol contrary to s 5(1)(a), Road Traffic Act 1988. She had been arrested for theft at a supermarket; she appeared to have been drinking; she pointed out a car in the car park, saying it was hers. At the police station, the police, pursuant to s 172(2)(a), Road Traffic Act 1988, required her to say who had been driving; she admitted it had been her. She was required to provide a specimen of breath; she did so and it revealed excess alcohol. At the trial, she argued that it would be incompatible with her rights under art 6, European Convention on Human Rights (the right to a fair trial), for the prosecutor to be allowed to rely on her admission. The High Court accepted that argument. The prosecutor appealed further.

HELD: "... while the overall fairness of a criminal trial cannot be compromised, the constituent rights comprised, whether expressly or implicitly, within article 6 are not themselves absolute. Limited qualification of these rights is acceptable if reasonably directed by national authorities towards a clear and proper public objective and if representing no greater qualification than the situation calls for

… There being a clear public interest in enforcement of road traffic legislation, the crucial question … is whether section 172 represents a disproportionate response, or one that undermines a defendant's right to a fair trial, if an admission of being the driver is relied on at trial.

"I do not … consider that section 172 … does represent a disproportionate response to this serious problem, nor do I think that reliance on the respondent's admission … would undermine her right to a fair trial. I reach that conclusion for a number of reasons.

"… Section 172 provides for the putting of a single, simple question. The answer cannot of itself incriminate the suspect, since it is not without more an offence to drive a car. … it is not easy to see why a requirement to answer a question is objectionable and a requirement to undergo a breath test is not. Yet no criticism is made of the requirement that the respondent undergo a breath test. … All who own or drive motor cars know that by doing so they subject themselves to a regulatory regime which does not apply to members of the public who do neither. Section 172 forms part of that regulatory regime. If … one asks whether section 172 represents a disproportionate legislative response to the problem of maintaining road safety, whether the balance between the interests of the community at large and the interests of the individual is struck in a manner unduly prejudicial to the individual, whether (in short) the leading of evidence would infringe a basic human right of the respondent, I would feel bound to give negative answers."

Appeal allowed.

Huntley v DPP

[2004] EWHC 870 (Admin), 2 April 2004, QBD (Admin)

The fact that a person was arrested on suspicion of driving with excess alcohol was insufficient to prove that he was in fact driving.

A motorist had been charged with driving with excess alcohol, contrary to s 5(1)(a), Road Traffic Act 1988. At the start of the trial, his representative indicated that he took no issue with the prosecution evidence concerning events up to the motorist's arrival at the police station. Following the prosecution evidence of the breath testing procedure at the police station, the defendant's representative submitted there was no case to answer since the prosecution had adduced no evidence that the defendant had been driving.

The magistrates referred to the agreed statement of an officer present when the defendant was arrested, that he had been arrested on suspicion of driving while having had too much to drink, and not simply on suspicion of having had too much to drink. They convicted him; he appealed.

QUESTION(S) FOR THE COURT: Whether the fact of the arrest on suspicion of driving proved to the requisite standard that the appellant had been driving.

HELD: "4. … The question is … whether the fact of the arrest on suspicion of driving proved to the requisite standard that [the appellant] had been driving. That question has to be answered in the negative given the specific finding by the justices that the arrest was on suspicion of driving. Suspicion that the appellant was driving does not amount to evidence proving that he was. There was no other evidence to the effect that he was driving.

"5. It is also to be noted that the evidence of [the officer who witnessed the arrest] with regard to the critical matters was in fact hearsay. But be that as it may, there was simply no basis upon which the justices could properly have come to the conclusion that the case had been proved against the appellant."

Appeal allowed.

Jones (Vivian Mary) v DPP

[2004] EWHC 3165 (Admin), [2005] RTR 184, 22 October 2004, QBD (DC)

Where police statements referred to the identity of the defendant, the defence should, if it wished to challenge identification, have called the witnesses and cross-examined them. Where a specimen is taken at hospital, there is no requirement to explain why a breath specimen cannot be taken. Putting a blood sample into the defendant's handbag which was with her personal belongings on a hospital trolley constituted supply.

A motorist had been charged with driving with excess alcohol, contrary to s 5(1)(a), Road Traffic Act 1988. Police saw her being helped from her driver's seat by ambulance staff, following a road traffic accident. At hospital, a specimen of blood was taken.

At trial, the evidence of the police officers at the scene was by way of statements under s 9, Criminal Justice Act 1967. The defendant was convicted and appealed.

QUESTION(S) FOR THE COURT: (1) Whether, upon a submission of no case to answer, a reasonable bench properly directing itself, could have found evidence that the appellant had driven a motor vehicle; (2) whether the police followed the correct procedure in that they did not tell the appellant why she could not supply a specimen of breath; (3) whether the magistrates were right to find that the appellant had been supplied with a sample of her own blood.

HELD: "[On (1)] 4. [two police officers] were … at the scene at the same time. The burden of [the statement of one of them] was that the driver was identified as the appellant at the time. [The other officer] saw a woman being helped from the driver's seat. The magistrates found that the statement of [the first officer] could be interpreted as indicating that he had identified the appellant himself. Neither [officer] was cross-examined.

"5. … if identity were an issue the defence should have called for the relevant witnesses to be cross-examined and objection should have been taken to the admission of the relevant extract from [the] statement. …

"[On (2)] 9. … the procedure for taking specimens for analysis was carried out from first to last while the appellant was in hospital. Section 7(2) of the Road Traffic Act 1988 provides: 'A requirement under this section to provide specimens of breath can only be made at a police station.' There was accordingly no power to take a specimen of breath from the appellant at the hospital. … there is no conceivable good reason in a section 7(2) case to require the police to explain to the suspect why a breath test cannot be taken. Her response to such information cannot affect what is to be done. Parliament has said that there shall be no breath specimen taken in such circumstances, and that is an end of it. …

"[On (3), quoting from the case] 15. '[the officer] told the court that the doctor took the blood sample, which was then divided into two canisters and placed in a sealed plastic container. He offered one of the samples to the defendant and put it into an envelope sealed and signed by him. The item was then placed into the defendant's handbag, which was with her personal belongings on the hospital trolley.'

"17. The [appellant's] argument is that she was not supplied with the sample merely by its having been put into her handbag. She claims that she never found it there and the policeman did not tell her he had put it there. She said she was moved to another ward and the sample was lost.

"19. … the justices were entitled to find, as they did, that this defendant had indeed been supplied with the sample … ."

The answers to all three questions were "yes". Appeal dismissed.

Premananthan v CPS

[2013] EWHC 3419 (Admin), 11 October 2013, QBD (Admin)

In all the circumstances of this case, the magistrates were entitled to infer that the defendant had been driving.

The defendant had been charged with driving with excess alcohol, contrary to s 5(1)(a), Road Traffic Act 1988. The sole prosecution witness gave evidence that he had heard a crash, looked out of his window, and saw the defendant leaning against the bonnet of a car; no one else was in the vicinity. The defendant offered the witness £2,000 but did not say what it was for. The accused was over the limit. The justices rejected a submission of no case to answer, drew an adverse inference from the accused's silence at trial, and, looking at the combination of circumstances, convicted the accused. He appealed.

QUESTION(S) FOR THE COURT: (1) Whether the justices were correct to reject the submission of no case to answer. (2) Whether there was sufficient evidence to entitle the justices to convict.

HELD: "[On the argument that there had been no case to answer since there was no evidence that the car had been recently driven, no finding concerning the whereabouts of the keys, no evidence that the car had been involved in the crash the witness heard, and no evidence about the length of time the car had been in the position in which it was found, and there were various explanations for the offer of £2,000] 15. Questions of credibility and reliability and of the weight to be attached to evidence are fundamentally questions for the court of trial to determine having regard to the whole of the evidence …

"16. … circumstantial evidence … can be powerful evidence. It is the whole picture that is important, the combination of all the different strands of the evidence that is accepted, and upon which the ultimate question is whether the facts as they are found to be lead the court to the sure and inescapable conclusion that a defendant is guilty.

"21. … the justices found that [the witness], who was the sole live witness at trial, gave clear and credible evidence. They therefore accepted his account that … he had heard a crash or bang outside his home; that he had almost immediately, within a matter of seconds, looked outside his window and had seen the appellant leaning on the bonnet of his car on the driver's side; that there was no one else in the vehicle, in the immediate vicinity of the vehicle or in the general area; that he had gone outside and found the appellant to be in a drunken state; that no one else was present at the scene; and that the appellant said he would give him £2,000 without any explanation as to why he was offering him that sum of money.

"22. The evidence as to the appellant being over the prescribed alcohol limit was undisputed.

"23. While each one of these facts on its own would be unlikely to be considered sufficient to found a case to answer, it is the combination of all these facts and circumstances which, in my judgment, entitled the court to reject the submission of no case to answer.

"24. … While … there could be other, innocent explanations for the offer of £2,000, the circumstances in which that offer was made, together with all the other facts found, entitled these justices to reject the submission of no case and, ultimately, to infer that the appellant had been driving the vehicle and that he was offering the witness money in order to dissuade him from calling the police."

The answers to both questions were "yes". Appeal dismissed.

9. LEGAL AID

R v Richmond Magistrates' Court ex p Gawel

Unreported, CO-317-94, 22 November 1994, QBD (DC)

On the facts of this case (charges of driving with excess alcohol and when unfit; risk of custodial sentence; risk of loss of job), it was in the interests of justice to grant legal aid.

A motorist had been charged with driving with excess alcohol, contrary to s 5(1), Road Traffic Act 1988, and with driving when unfit, contrary to s 4(1), Road Traffic Act 1988. He applied for legal aid to defend the charges, saying he was in real danger of a custodial sentence and of losing his job, and that a substantial question of law was involved. Legal aid was refused on the ground that it was not desirable in the interests of justice to grant it.

He renewed his application, saying that additional/new information was relevant, in that he had taken some medication ("Buttercup Syrup") before driving; the medication contained menthol; but for that, he might have passed the breath test; he therefore may have had a defence to both charges and that expert evidence would be needed. The renewed application was refused, the magistrates saying there was no real danger of a custodial sentence because the reading was not high and there were no previous convictions; on the risk of his losing his job, that disqualification was compulsory on conviction unless a defence or special reasons were made out; and they found no substantial question of law. The applicant applied for judicial review of the refusal.

HELD: "[On the magistrates' decision that there was no real danger of a custodial sentence] … That may of course be relevant to the charge under Section 5, but the question of the possibility of a custodial sentence under Section 4(1) seems to me dependent very much on the nature of the offence as it turned out to be proved.

"[On the magistrates' decision on the risk of the applicant's losing his job], it does not seem to take into account in any way the length of the possible disqualification.

"[On the magistrates' decision that no substantial point of law was involved], I agree.

"[Counsel for the appellant] is able to produce two matters which suggest that the magistrates did not give proper consideration to this request for legal aid. The first is that there was not merely an offence charged under Section 5 [driving with excess alcohol], but there was a separate charge under Section 4 of being unfit to drive … For that offence it might well have been appropriate for the Applicant to have had legal aid because the facts as proved on that charge might have been very relevant to the seriousness of the offence which could, at the very least, have clearly affected the possibility of a custodial sentence on that charge and also as to the length of disqualification.

"Similarly, the factual grounds established as to the degree of the danger of the Applicant's driving in this case could also have been relevant to the length of disqualification imposed under the Section 5 charge.

"For those reasons it seems to me that this was a case where the interests of justice did really require that the Applicant should be granted legal aid."

Application granted.

R v Gravesham Magistrates' Court ex p Baker

[1998] RTR 451, 16 April 1997, QBD

Legal aid should have been granted for a "special reasons" argument based on laced drinks.

A motorist had been charged with driving with excess alcohol, contrary to s 5(1)(a), Road Traffic Act 1988. She did not wish to defend the allegation but wished to argue that her drinks had been spiked and there was therefore a special reason under s 34, Road Traffic Offenders Act 1988 (disqualification for a minimum period for certain offences unless the court for special reasons thinks fit to disqualify for a shorter period or not at all; see Chapter 10). The justices refused her application for legal aid on the grounds that, at the end of the case, the motorist could apply for the costs of her expert witness from central funds, and that there was no substantial point of law in issue. The motorist sought judicial review of the refusal of legal aid.

HELD: "[After referring to the matters which must be proved to establish special reasons, set out in *DPP v Vincent* (page 537) and *DPP v O'Connor* (page 534)] In the present case it seems to me a scientific expert is required for two reasons. First, to examine the analysis and give evidence whether the defendant's explanation is consistent with the scientific facts. Secondly, to say whether the amount of alcohol the defendant admits having drunk on the occasion in question would have resulted in any event in the defendant being over the prescribed limit.

"Furthermore, that scientific report is likely to be needed by the defendant to cross-examine, if necessary, any expert called by the prosecutor. A scientific expert needs to be found to assist the defendant with the cross-examination of any expert to another effect.

"Legal aid is also needed because witnesses have to be found, witnesses of the facts, a proper proof taken and the story has to be extracted in the witness-box from those witnesses and indeed from the defendant herself. In my judgment, this is plainly a case where it would not only be to the benefit of the defendant but to the benefit of the court itself if legal aid is granted.

"In my judgment, the order refusing legal aid should be quashed and the justices should be directed to grant the defendant legal aid."

Application allowed.

R v Slough Magistrates' Court ex p Noble

Unreported, CO/2423/97, 3 December 1997, QBD (DC)

On the facts of this case (a combination of difficult legal points and the need for expert cross-examination, including cross-examination of the defendant's ex-partner), the refusal of legal aid could not be justified.

The defendant had been charged with being in charge of a motor vehicle when unfit through drink or drugs, contrary to s 4(2), Road Traffic Act 1988; and with failing without reasonable excuse to provide two specimens of breath for analysis, contrary to s 7(6), Road Traffic Act 1988. She had herself called the police. They found her in a parked car. She intended to defend the charges on the grounds that she feared an attack from her ex-partner and was sheltering in her car until the police arrived; and that she had drunk only some three bottles of cider during the day. She applied for legal aid, but was refused on the ground that it was not in the interests of justice. She sought judicial review of that refusal.

HELD: "... [Counsel for the applicant] essentially relies upon three of [the] considerations [set out in s 22(2), Legal Aid Act 1988] ...

"… First of all, she says that there is a potential for a conviction in this case to damage [the applicant's] reputation as a foster parent. That …, taken alone would not be a strong ground for the grant of legal aid. More weightily, [counsel] submits that there are a number of difficult legal points arising in this case. Firstly, the car was … parked in a parking place, and a point arises whether or not that was a public place or a place to which the public had access. I can see that there may be a point of law here. Secondly, [counsel] submits that a clear point arises of some legal difficulty whether [the applicant] was (if her account is accepted) in charge of this vehicle, her case being that she was only in it as a means of avoiding her ex-partner … that is a point of legal substance and may be of some difficulty. The third point, it may be of law, arises from the evidence … of [a] manager of [a] public house. That goes to the question of the extent to which the applicant had been drinking during the day … the admissibility of this evidence … is … something which would require very careful handling …

"The next submission … is that it may be necessary for there to be expert evidence to deal with [the appellant's] state of intoxication. I am not impressed by that submission … There is more force, perhaps, in the submission that expert cross-examination of police officers may well be necessary in defence of the second charge of refusing to provide a specimen.

"The final … submission … is that … there will [be] a need to cross-examine [the applicant's] ex-partner and his son, and that it would really be asking too much for an unrepresented lady defendant to have to ask what could be embarrassing questions of a partner or ex-partner with whom she appears to have fallen out. That last point … by itself would not carry this application. However, the burden, in summary, of the submission that we have heard is that there is a combination of difficulties and complications in this case, such that the refusal of legal aid cannot be justified."

Application granted.

R v Cheshire JJ ex p Rolt

Unreported, CO/2565/97, 24 February 1998, QBD (DC)

On the facts of this case (lorry driver said to be four times over the limit – risk of imprisonment and of losing livelihood; evidence needed to challenge breath analysis; spouse an invalid), it was in the interests of justice to grant legal aid.

A motorist, a heavy goods vehicle driver, had been charged with driving with excess alcohol contrary to s 5(1)(a), Road Traffic Act 1988. Breath analysis had produced a lower reading of 130 µg alcohol in 100 ml breath. The motorist wished to argue that he had not consumed sufficient alcohol to explain the breath analysis readings and that the breath analysis device must have been functioning incorrectly. He sought legal aid to defend the case, which was refused, first by the clerk to the justices, then by a magistrate, in both instances on the ground that the grant of legal aid did not appear to be in the interests of justice. He sought an order of *mandamus* directing the magistrates to grant legal aid.

HELD: "… The grant of legal aid in these circumstances is governed by section 21 of the Legal Aid Act 1988 [the 'interests of justice' test] …

The decision whether to grant legal aid accordingly depends on the judgment of the magistrates' court of what appears to it to be desirable in the interests of justice … a form of words which accords a generous, but not unfettered, discretion to the justices …

"In applying the statutory test, section 22 of the Act [factors to be taken into account in determining the interests of justice test] … gives guidance …

"The applicant points out that the reading in his case shows that he was nearly four times over the limit. He accordingly submits that, if convicted he is at grave risk of imprisonment … if convicted and disqualified, he would lose his livelihood. That is almost certainly so.

"The applicant also places reliance on the nature of his defence. From the brief description given of it, it is not an easy defence to mount. It seems safe to assume that the applicant himself would be called to testify to the approximate quantity of alcohol he had consumed before the tests were performed. To stand any reasonable prospect of acceptance the applicant's evidence would need to be corroborated or supported by other factual witnesses, who would need to be traced and interviewed in order to obtain apparently reliable written statements. Such factual evidence on its own however, would scarcely be enough to throw doubt on the Intoximeter reading … in the absence of expert evidence adduced by the defence to challenge that reading. It would be necessary for the defence to suggest an inconsistency between the amount of alcohol consumed and the Intoximeter reading obtained …

"Lastly, the applicant points out that his wife is an invalid … whose freedom to leave her house is dependent on his ability to drive her …

"If … we ask … whether there is a real risk that the denial of legal aid may cause significant injury to this applicant, it seems to me that the clear answer must be 'yes' … ."

Application granted.

R (Matara) v Brent Magistrates' Court

[2005] EWHC 1829 (Admin), (2005) 169 JP 576, 20 July 2005, QBD (DC)

On the facts of this case (defendant with poor English charged with failing to provide specimens of breath; defence of not having understood the requirement), it was in the interests of justice to grant legal aid.

A motorist had been charged with failing to provide two specimens of breath for analysis, contrary to s 7(6), Road Traffic Act 1988. When asked whether there were any medical reasons for not providing breath specimens, the claimant had replied "I don't understand you". The police officer did not offer an interpreter, finding that although English was not the motorist's first language, his command of English was "sufficient and competent to provide all the details".

The defendant's case was that although he could speak some English, he had not understood what was required of him and therefore had a reasonable excuse for not providing the specimens. He twice applied for legal aid, which was refused. Written advice from counsel was obtained; it was to the effect that legal representation was necessary in the interests of justice as, *inter alia*, he was likely to receive a short custodial sentence if convicted, and that his English was sufficiently poor to raise a serious issue. The application was renewed on the basis of this advice, but was again refused on the grounds that there was no risk of serious damage to the claimant's reputation; there was no substantial or complex issue of law; and that an interpreter was to be provided; these were substantially the same grounds as for the earlier refusals.

The defendant sought judicial review of the decision to refuse legal aid.

HELD: "[After referring to the 'interests of justice' test in Sch 3, para 5, Access to Justice Act 1999, and the factors to be taken into account when applying the test] 15. [Counsel for the claimant] submits … that the case meets at least three relevant criteria: first, whether the claimant is likely to lose his liberty or livelihood; secondly, whether the determination of any matter arising in the proceedings may involve consideration of a substantial question of law; and thirdly, whether the individual may be unable to understand the proceedings or state his own case.

"16. … [She further submits that] the only way the claimant could seek to be acquitted was by demonstrating to the court that he was wholly unable to understand any of the relevant procedures … [and] that the grant of an interpreter does not negate the need for legal representation …

"18. … at least one of the criteria is met, which makes the refusal of legal aid unreasonable to a degree which entitles this court to intervene. It is important not to lose sight of the fact that the test is a test of 'the interests of justice'. Whatever the basis of the application for legal aid before [counsel's] advice was tendered, the contents of that advice raised a compelling and unanswered argument that it was in the interest of justice that the claimant should be granted legal aid. The availability of an interpreter does not meet the point that it is the claimant's case that he was unable to understand what was being said at the time of his arrest. This is a point which lies at the heart of his defence. It goes to his ability to state his own case and the overall fairness of the trial."

Refusal of legal aid quashed.

R v Dean Thomas

[2020] EWCA Crim 117, 29 January 2020, CA (Crim)

On the facts, the trial court was correct to find the defendant fit to plead and to refuse to appoint an intermediary.

A driver had been convicted of causing death by careless driving when over the limit for drugs, contrary to s 3A(1)(ba) Road Traffic Act 1988. He collided with a cyclist on a roundabout and the cyclist died from his injuries. Analysis of the driver's blood had shown 289 μg benzoylecgonine (BZE) per litre.

The defendant suffered from a number of vulnerabilities, including inability to concentrate or focus for any length of time and difficulty retaining information, exacerbated by medication for pain. At the pre-trial review he applied to the court for the appointment of an intermediary to assist him throughout the trial. The application was based on expert reports from an intermediary and a psychologist.

The judge ruled against the application, indicating that the facts were largely agreed and the issues were not complex. The appellant would have an appropriate opportunity to discuss all relevant issues with his legal team. Regular breaks would be granted and the appellant could stand in the dock and stretch if this became necessary. The difficulties experienced by the accused were not such that a fair trial required the appointment of an intermediary.

On the first day of the trial, the accused argued that he was not fit to stand trial. The judge ruled that he could have the assistance of an intermediary if he chose to give evidence and if an intermediary was available, but if no intermediary could be secured, the requirements for a fair trial could still be met. Funding to instruct an intermediary was not available and the court again ruled against the court's appointing one. The argument that he was not fit to stand trial was rejected.

The driver was convicted and appealed.

GROUNDS OF APPEAL: The judge erred in: (1) refusing to grant the application for the appointment of an intermediary; (2) finding the appellant fit to plead; and (3) deciding it was not appropriate to use the court's inherent powers to instruct an intermediary.

HELD: The Court of Appeal reviewed paras 3F.12, 13, 16 and 17 of the Criminal Practice Directions 2015 (see now Criminal Practice Directions 2023, ch 6) on intermediaries for defendants.

"… the appointment of an intermediary for the defendant's evidence will be a rare occurrence and … it will be exceptionally rare for a whole trial order to be made. …

"Intermediaries should not be appointed as a matter of routine trial management, but instead because there are compelling reasons for taking this step, it being clear that all other adaptations to the trial process will not sufficiently meet the defendant's needs to ensure he or she can effectively participate in the trial.

"… although we readily appreciate the appellant had a range of significant difficulties, the issues he needed to address were notably straightforward and were relatively few in number … he needed to testify as to whether he was tired or under the influence of drugs whilst driving, whether the sun was in his eyes, whether his view was obstructed by the structure of the car, whether he had looked properly for other road users as he approached the roundabout and whether he saw the cyclist. … With clear, precise questioning and with appropriate breaks, these subjects could have been addressed successfully without the assistance of an intermediary, albeit the latter would no doubt have assisted in the process if retained. It follows that we do not fault the judge for not using the court's inherent power to appoint an intermediary."

Appeal against conviction dismissed.

10. THE MAGISTRATES

See also Jarvis v DPP, page 51 – magistrates may not use personal knowledge that only one breath analysis device is available at a particular police station.

Owen v Jones

[1988] RTR 102, 26 January 1987, QBD (DC)

Where the justices knew that a defendant would lose his job and his home if he was disqualified, they were not wrong to rely on their own knowledge, without evidence being called, to find exceptional hardship and refrain from disqualifying for accumulating 12 penalty points.

A motorist, a serving CID officer, had been convicted of being in charge with excess alcohol, contrary to s 6(1), Road Traffic Act 1972 as substituted by s 25 and Sch 8, Transport Act 1981. The justices ordered his licence be endorsed with 10 penalty points; he already had 3 points and so was liable for disqualification under s 19, Transport Act 1981 (12 or more points). The justices were told by the motorist's solicitor that police policy was to the effect that the motorist would lose his job and his home if disqualified; already aware of this policy themselves, they declined to hear mitigating evidence on the point; they found exceptional hardship under s 19(6)(b), Transport Act 1981, and so did not order disqualification. The prosecutor appealed.

QUESTION(S) FOR THE COURT: (1) Whether, having found the defendant guilty and imposed 10 points, the defendant already having 3 points which made him liable for disqualification, it was necessary to hear evidence of mitigating circumstances before deciding not to disqualify. (2) Whether it is correct in law that the possibility of the defendant's losing his job, and with it his house which belonged to his employer, as a result of disqualification, can alone amount to exceptional hardship under s 19(6)(b), Transport Act 1981.

HELD: "I can see no reason … why justices should not be entitled to rely upon that which they believe to be true providing their belief is founded upon knowledge of what has happened in previous similar cases, especially those which have arisen in their locality …

"… I see no reason at all why, if justices are in such a position, they should not be allowed to say to a defendant that they are fully apprised of the fact sought to be asserted … and … do not require evidence of it.

"… Justices should not easily come to the conclusion that their belief is sufficient for the purpose, unless they are confident that it is well founded on fact positively known to them from a past event … In the vast majority of cases justices will need evidence to satisfy them of exceptional hardship. But … there are cases – and I find this to be one – where they can rely on their knowledge, gathered from past events and experience, so as to be able to say they can dispense with evidence whether it is tendered to them or not and so be satisfied that exceptional hardship is established."

The answer to question (2) was "yes". Appeal dismissed.

R v Downham Market Magistrates' Court ex p Nudd

[1989] RTR 169, [1989] Crim LR 147, 13 April 1988, QBD (DC)

Charges of failing to provide specimens should not have been heard by a bench whose chairman had, not long before, participated in sentencing the defendant for other offences, read a social inquiry report on him and seen his criminal record; the public might have perceived the chairman to be biased.

A motorist had been convicted of failing without reasonable excuse to provide a specimen for a breath test, contrary to s 7(4), Road Traffic Act 1972 as substituted by s 25 and Sch 8, Transport Act 1981; and of failing without reasonable excuse to provide a specimen of breath for analysis, contrary to s 8(7), Road Traffic Act 1972 as likewise substituted.

The local bench comprised only eleven justices, and the defendant's solicitor sought to have the hearing listed before a different chairman. The clerk to the justices decided not to seek to list the case in another petty sessional division because the magistrates who were to deal with it were not precluded from so doing by s 42, Magistrates' Court Act 1980 (justice precluded from trying an issue if in the course of the same proceedings he has been informed, for bail purposes, of previous convictions); and on the ground there is no rule of law that a magistrate is disqualified from hearing a case by reason of having been concerned with the same defendant in other proceedings.

The defendant sought an order of *certiorari* to quash both convictions.

GROUND(S) FOR THE APPLICATION: There was ostensible bias in that, *inter alia*: (a) the chairman of the bench which convicted him had, a month before, with other justices, imposed a suspended prison sentence on him for threats to kill; the chairman had read a social inquiry report on him and had seen his criminal record, including a previous conviction for driving while unfit; (b) the same chairman had recently, with other justices, sentenced him for failing to leave licensed premises when required to do so and for using abusive language.

HELD: "… the clerk was aware that the chairman had crucial knowledge of the criminal record of the applicant which … included an offence of driving whilst unfit through drink … If the clerk had asked himself … whether it would be right in the interests of justice for the chairman to sit on this occasion, then he would … have been asking himself the right question …

"[Quoting from an article in *Justice of the Peace*] 'mere knowledge of the defendant's previous convictions does not necessarily preclude the court from trying the case. It would only be wrong for the magistrates to proceed where the previous convictions are disclosed to the court in a way which might lead to bias or a suggestion of bias in the minds of the public'… in applying that test one has to conclude that it was wrong for the chairman to sit in his customary position on this occasion. The public could not, in my judgment, have come to any other conclusion than, try as he might, experienced though he was, he might not have been able to put out of his mind what he knew about this applicant … ."

Order of *certiorari* granted.

DPP v Quinn

The Times 13 October 1988, 7 October 1988, QBD (DC)

Justices should not have found no case to answer without having heard submissions.

A motorist had been charged with failing without reasonable excuse to provide a specimen of breath for analysis, contrary to s 8(7), Road Traffic Act 1972 as substituted by s 25 and Sch 8, Transport Act 1981. He had been arrested on suspicion of having stolen the car he was driving; at the police station he was asked to provide breath specimens, which he refused to do, in forceful language.

At the hearing, having heard police evidence of those facts, the justices retired without hearing submissions from either prosecution or defendant. They concluded that the defendant had been confused when he made his reply to the request for breath specimens, decided there was no case to answer, and dismissed it. The prosecutor appealed.

HELD: "[The justices] had no evidence whatsoever to come to the conclusion that the respondent was confused when confronted with a perfectly lawful request for the provision of a specimen of breath. If they were to come to a contrary conclusion, they should have heard from the respondent himself as to what it was he thought he was being asked for. There undoubtedly was a case to answer."

Appeal allowed.

R v Highbury Corner Magistrates' Court ex p Tann

[1994] RTR 5, 26 November 1992, QBD (DC)

On the facts of this case (sentence, defendant indicating he wished to come back and advance further mitigation, then changing his mind), the purported rescission, over a year later, of the original sentence was unlawful.

On 27 November 1990 a motorist pleaded guilty to driving with excess alcohol, contrary to s 5(1)(a), Road Traffic Act 1988. He was fined £100 and disqualified from driving for 12 months, and his driving licence was endorsed. Later the same day he came back before the magistrate and asked for an adjournment to enable him to advance further mitigation. The magistrate granted an adjournment of one week.

The motorist then changed his mind and decided to accept the original sentence; on the adjournment date, he handed in to the court a letter to that effect, but he did not stay until the case came before the magistrate. When it did come before the magistrate, the magistrate took the view that the motorist had yet to be sentenced and issued a warrant for his arrest. The motorist had taken the view that the original fine and disqualification would stand; he refrained from driving for the period of disqualification and the warrant was not executed during that time. He wrote to the court about paying the fine, but received no reply.

About a year later, the motorist applied to the Driver and Vehicle Licensing Centre for the return of his licence; the police then executed the warrant. On 6 February 1992, he was brought back before the court and the magistrate imposed a fine of £100 and disqualification for 12 months, to run from 6 February 1992.

HELD: "… The first question is whether the purported decision of the magistrate was an exercise of his powers under section 142(1) [Magistrates' Courts Act 1980 – power to vary or rescind sentence, exercisable only within 28 days] …

"Secondly, … the applicant maintains that, if the magistrate did … effectively exercise his power … to rescind the sentence imposed earlier that day … he had no power to revisit it in any way outside the statutory 28 day period …

"… on the facts before the magistrate on 27 November 1990, there does not appear to have been any suggestion from the applicant or otherwise that he would seek to advance on the adjourned hearing any special reasons why he should not be disqualified for the minimum period, nor do the papers disclose any particular concern expressed by him then or now about the modest fine imposed … The applicant's concern … was that the minimum disqualification would bear hardly on him. However, there was nothing that the magistrate could do about that, either on originally sentencing him or, as it must have appeared to him, at any adjourned hearing. It was not therefore a case of a type which would justify the exercise by the magistrate of his statutory power to rescind the sentence that he had just imposed … the magistrate's purported exercise of his power of rescission was not only inappropriate in the circumstances as a route to possible future variation but, on the particular facts before him, was *Wednesbury* unreasonable. It was unlawful. It follows from that that the original sentence of 27 November 1990 … stands, and that the purported sentence of 6 February 1992 should be quashed."

Application granted.

Huchard v DPP

[1994] COD 459, 17 June 1994, QBD (DC)

Knowledge of a previous conviction for driving with excess alcohol did not give rise to a serious danger of bias by a bench hearing a special reasons argument.

A motor cyclist pleaded guilty to driving with excess alcohol, contrary to s 5(1), Road Traffic Act 1988. He argued that there were special reasons – the shortness of the distance driven – for not disqualifying, under s 34(1), Road Traffic

Offenders Act 1988. The stipendiary magistrate rejected that argument and disqualified the motor cyclist from driving.

The motor cyclist appealed to the Crown Court against disqualification. The documents provided for the Crown Court revealed that the motor cyclist had been disqualified for 3 years, indicating that he had a previous conviction for driving with excess alcohol. It was submitted before the Crown Court that such knowledge would prejudice the bench and that they ought to disqualify themselves. The bench rejected that argument, considering itself able to determine the appeal on the evidence alone. The Crown Court dismissed the appeal. The motor cyclist appealed further.

HELD: "… knowledge of previous convictions … does not necessarily render a verdict even of a jury unsafe … there is no absolute rule that Justices … with knowledge of previous convictions should not sit … the test now … for all tribunals where there was concern about any sort of bias, except financial interest, which does not arise in this case, is to be found in *R v Gough* [1993] AC 646, [1993] 2 WLR 883, [1993] 2 All ER 724] …

"There are two points of some importance to be noted. The first is that the conviction of which the recorder and his colleagues gained knowledge was indeed a conviction for the same offence as that which the Appellant had been convicted of in the case before them. However, … all that conviction told those Justices was that on a previous occasion this gentleman had driven with excess alcohol, and that issue was not an issue in the present case, because he had pleaded guilty to that matter. Therefore, it is difficult to see how, in any event, knowledge of that conviction would seriously bias the Justices when they were considering the matter before them; that is to say, whether there were special reasons why the accused should not be disqualified.

"Secondly, … the Recorder and Justices did consciously consider the problem that their knowledge presented to them in the context of this case … They directed their minds to the problem, said that they did not find the matter to be prejudicial, and that they had considered the appeal on evidence before them and on that evidence alone.

"In the light of that conscious and careful consideration by a professional Judge, a Recorder of the Crown Court, and two experienced Magistrates sitting in the Crown Court, I am certainly not prepared to say that … there was a real danger of bias … ."

Appeal dismissed.

R v Newcastle upon Tyne Magistrates' Court ex p Currie

Unreported, CO 2476/94, 20 February 1995, QBD (DC)

Magistrates who believed that the defendant had been convicted of, and disqualified for, an earlier offence should not have adjudicated on a charge of driving with excess alcohol.

The defendant had been charged with driving while disqualified and with driving with excess alcohol; both offences were said to have been committed on the same day. There was an issue of identity in respect of both charges. At the hearing before the magistrates, no evidence that the defendant had been disqualified from driving was called. The defendant therefore contended that there was no case to answer. The prosecutor replied that there was no need to call evidence of the disqualification because the case had been opened on that basis and the justices could take judicial notice of the fact that the defendant had been disqualified, as he had been disqualified by the court in which the present case was proceeding. The justices ruled there was a case to answer; the defence called no evidence; the justices convicted on both charges.

The solicitor for the defendant then wrote to the magistrates' court, which accepted that a mistake had been made, and the matter came before them again. The magistrates' attention was drawn to s 142(2), Magistrates' Courts Act 1980 (power to direct rehearing by different justices), but they did not order that the charge of driving while disqualified be reheard by different magistrates; instead, apparently, they rescinded that conviction although it appeared they had no power to do that. The prosecutor apparently offered no evidence. The magistrates further decided that the conviction for driving with excess alcohol was to stand. The defendant sought an order of *certiorari* to quash that conviction.

HELD: "… there was one issue in the case, we are told, and that was whether this man was rightly identified as the driver of the car … once the Justices had proved to them, as they obviously believed they had, that he was a man who had been guilty of a previous offence (a convicted man) but also had been disqualified, his credibility would inevitably have nose-dived. [Counsel for the Crown Prosecution Service] invited us to say that the Justices would have been capable of putting that out of their heads. I think that is simply expecting too much of human nature. They believed that this man had been proved to have been convicted and disqualified on a previous conviction. No such thing had, in fact, been proved. There was no evidence of it. They should not have known of it, and … it is too much to expect that that knowledge which they should not have had, did not colour their decision in respect of driving with excess alcohol.

"It follows that I am of the view that the Justices should have decided that this too was a conviction which could not stand … ."

Application granted.

R v Chelmsford Magistrates' Court ex p Hammond

Unreported, CO 521/94, 7 March 1995, QBD (DC)

The prosecutor's application to cross-examine the defendant by referring to previous convictions prejudiced the bench and they should not have continued to hear the case. It is undesirable for a legal adviser to retire with the justices when the only issue to be determined is one of fact.

A motorist had been charged with failing without reasonable excuse to provide a specimen for a breath test, contrary to s 6(4), Road Traffic Act 1988, and with failing without reasonable excuse to provide two specimens of breath for analysis, contrary to s 7(6), Road Traffic Act 1988. He pleaded not guilty.

At the hearing the police officer concerned gave evidence, saying that at no time did the defendant put forward any medical reason for not complying with the request and that there appeared to be nothing wrong with him. The defendant said he had given a medical reason why he could not provide breath, and disputed what the police officer had said. The prosecutor, having earlier told defence counsel of her intention so to do, then sought leave to cross-examine the defendant pursuant to s 1(f)(ii), Criminal Evidence Act 1898, by referring to previous convictions. The request was made in the presence of the magistrates, and the prosecutor emphasised that her intention was to discredit the defendant. The magistrates refused the application.

Defence counsel then submitted that the justices should disqualify themselves because they would be prejudiced by their knowledge that the defendant had previous convictions. They declined to do so, heard the case, retired with their clerk to consider their verdicts, and convicted the defendant of both charges. He sought judicial review to quash both convictions.

HELD: "… I am surprised that the prosecuting solicitor made the application. There was a serious dispute of fact between a prosecution witness and the defendant … The Justices found that it was the nature of the prosecuting solicitor's questioning which had led the defendant to assert his case as firmly as he did, and I am surprised that the application was made in the particular circumstances …

"The point for decision in this case, however, is as to what should happen once the application had been heard and rejected. It is common ground that there is no strict rule that there must be a fresh trial …

"… in this particular case the convictions must be quashed …

"The application was made with the result that the Justices knew the defendant had previous convictions, and the reason why those were sought to be put to him was emphasised by the prosecutor … Try as the Justices might … to try the case fairly upon the evidence, there was in my judgment a real danger that in the circumstances disfavour would be shown to the defendant on the issue of credibility as between him and the police sergeant.

"… I need consider only briefly the other complaint of the Applicant, namely that the Clerk retired with the Justices when the question of fact came to be considered by them … I propose to do no more than repeat the undesirability of Clerks retiring with the Justices … when it appears plain that the only issue to be determined is one of fact."

Application granted.

11. RE-OPENING THE CASE

See also Leeson v Haringey JJ and DPP, page 339, R v Pydar JJ ex p Foster, page 346 and Greenaway v DPP, page 407, on the court's discretion to admit the printout after the close of the prosecution case.

MacDonald v Skelt

[1985] RTR 321, 16 January 1985, QBD (DC)

Where the magistrates had not reached a conclusion on the issues before them, they were not functus officio. On the facts of this case (submission that the evidence did not show the blood analysed was that taken from the defendant), the magistrates' decision to allow the prosecutor to re-open the case was neither perverse nor wrong in principle.

A motorist had been charged with driving with excess alcohol in blood, contrary to s 6(1), Road Traffic Act 1972. At the police station, a blood specimen was taken. It was divided into two parts and one was given to the motorist. The police officer administering the procedure completed a label on the part retained, showing the doctor's name, the officer's name, the police force, the date, the time, and the name of the police station. At the hearing, the prosecutor adduced evidence of an analyst that the blood contained in "Securitainer no 42329" had been analysed and showed 84 mg alcohol in 100 ml blood; and that the Securitainer had been labelled with the doctor's name, the officer's name, the police force, the date, the time, and the name of the police station. At the close of the prosecution case, the motorist submitted there was no case to answer on the grounds that the evidence did not show that the specimen of blood which had been taken was one and the same as that tested by the analyst.

The justices accepted this argument, but invited counsel for both parties to consider whether the omission in the evidential chain was of a technical nature which would enable the justices to consider allowing the prosecutor to re-open the case to call the necessary linking evidence. There was then argument on whether the justices were by then *functus officio*; or, if not, whether they should allow the prosecutor to re-open the case. The justices adjourned the case pending the outcome of the motorist's appeal by way of case stated.

QUESTION(S) FOR THE COURT: (1) Did the rulings made, after the defence submissions of no case to answer, amount to a finding of no case to answer and in the circumstances were the justices *functus officio* and thereby prevented from considering the prosecutor's application to re-open his case and call further evidence? (2) Were the justices right to rule that the prosecutor should be allowed to re-open his case and introduce further evidence?

HELD: "[On (1)] … For there to be a state of *functus officio*, the justices would have to indicate clearly that they had reached a conclusion on the issues which were being argued and, further, that in consequence of their conclusion they were giving a decision on the outcome of the case … in saying that they ruled in favour of the defendant, all they were really doing was indicating that on the state of the evidence at that stage there was not sufficient proof of the sample that was analysed being the sample taken from the defendant. The fact that immediately they had said that, their clerk invited counsel to consider whether this was a situation in which further evidence should be allowed for the prosecution, clearly shows that what they were doing was not coming to a final decision … this was not a case in which the justices were *functus officio* …

"[On (2)] … the decision here of the justices to allow the prosecutor to re-open his case was neither perverse nor wrong in principle and their exercise of discretion cannot be faulted … no point had been taken on behalf of the defendant during the evidence given on behalf of the prosecutor as to the sample being the right sample, or any possible mistake in that regard. In the circumstances, justice required that the justices should give serious consideration to the application made on behalf of the prosecutor."

Appeal dismissed.

R v Aylesbury Crown Court ex p Lait

Unreported, CO/2348/97, 13 March 1998, QBD (DC)

On the facts of this case, the Crown Court was outside the reasonable bounds of its discretion in allowing the prosecution to re-open its case to call further evidence from a forensic analyst, and then adjourn it for rehearing because the analyst was no longer available that day.

A motorist had been convicted of driving with excess alcohol and appealed to the Crown Court. At the Crown Court, a forensic analyst gave evidence seeking to prove that the motorist's blood alcohol level was over the prescribed limit and produced a computer printout for that purpose; the analyst did not give evidence to establish that the computer was operating correctly (Police and Criminal Evidence Act 1984, s 69(1), now repealed). After the prosecution had closed its case, and after the defence had begun its case, the Crown Court allowed the prosecution to re-open its case, to recall the analyst to give further evidence; and adjourned the case for rehearing because the analyst was no longer available and it was late in the day.

The motorist sought judicial review of the order allowing the case to be re-opened.

HELD: "… Each case will depend on its own circumstances. In my judgment, in this case, … the Crown Court did step outside the reasonable bounds of its discretion in giving leave to the prosecution to call further evidence and then in adjourning the case for rehearing because of non-availability of [the analyst] and the time of day.

"I cannot accept [the prosecutor's] submission as generally correct that, if the prosecution have no idea that a point will be taken, then that is ground for allowing them to call further evidence. It is for the Prosecution to prepare their case, to identify the points upon which evidence is to be given, and to call evidence on those points and each of them. There is no doubt that one of the points on which evidence had to be given in this case was to establish that the machine was operating properly. I cannot, in the circumstances of this case, find an obligation in defence counsel to raise the point, if he was going to raise it at all, while the prosecution witness was giving evidence …

"… The further relevant aspect of this case is the need, if the prosecution are correct, for a complete rehearing. That was going to involve substantial delay and there is an interest in finality in this litigation. I regard this as a relevant factor which distinguishes this case from one where the evidence sought to be given could be given on the same day and as a part of the same trial …

"The general practice is that prosecution evidence must be called at the appropriate time. When the prosecution close their case ordinarily they will not be permitted to reopen it … ."

Appeal allowed.

Jolly (Christopher) v DPP

[2000] Crim LR 471, 31 March 2000, QBD (DC)

In the circumstances of this case, the magistrates were not wrong to allow the prosecutor to call further evidence after the close of its case; they should consider the interests of justice and any risk of prejudicing the defendant.

A motorist had been required to provide a specimen of blood for analysis. The result was positive and the defendant was charged with driving with excess alcohol contrary to s 5(1)(a), Road Traffic Act 1988. A forensic scientist gave evidence that the blood specimen had been analysed by gas chromatography. The raw data from the chromatographs went directly into a computer which calculated and printed out the results of the analyses.

In the final submission on behalf of the defendant, an argument was raised that the court could not rely on the results of the analyses because there was no evidence to show that the computer used to obtained those results had been working correctly at all times, as required by s 69, Police and Criminal Evidence Act 1984 (now repealed). The magistrate allowed the prosecutor to recall the forensic scientist, who gave further evidence about the calibration of the machines and that she was satisfied that they had been working correctly. The magistrate accepted her evidence. The defendant appealed.

QUESTION(S) FOR THE COURT: Whether the magistrate was wrong to exercise discretion by allowing the respondent to call evidence of the correct working of the computer after the close of the case.

HELD: "[After reviewing the authorities] 4. … any trial court must recognise that it is the duty of the prosecution to call its evidence before closing its case. But it is now beyond argument that there is a general discretion to permit the calling of evidence at a later stage, which extends in a Magistrates Court up to the time when the Bench retires. Before exercising that discretion, the Court will look carefully at: (1) the interests of justice overall, and in particular – (2) the risk of any prejudice whatsoever to the defendant.

"The result will be that the discretion will be sparingly exercised, but I venture to doubt whether it assists any longer to speak in terms of 'exceptional circumstances' … ."

The answer to the question was "no". Appeal dismissed.

R v Cook ex p DPP

[2001] Crim LR 321, 19 December 2000, QBD (DC)

A prosecution application to re-open its case and recall a witness to deal with evidence previously omitted by oversight may properly be granted; there must be no absence of good faith on the part of the prosecutor and no possible material prejudice to the defendant.

A motorist had been charged with driving with excess alcohol, contrary to s 5(1)(a), Road Traffic Act 1988. He had been convicted by magistrates and appealed to the Crown Court. At the Crown Court, the officer who had conducted the breath testing procedure gave evidence; he did not specifically say that he had warned the motorist of the consequences of refusing to provide specimens, or that he had completed a declaration pursuant to s 69, Police and Criminal Evidence Act 1984 (admissibility of a statement in a document produced by a computer – now repealed). He merely said that he had complied with the procedure and completed the *pro forma*. The motorist gave evidence of the amount he had drunk that night; he was supported by a witness. An expert's report was to the effect that the quantity of alcohol referred to by the motorist would not have produced a reading above the prescribed limit on the timescale in question. The motorist also said he had driven the car only because he had been invited to do so by a police officer.

It was argued, first, that if the magistrates accepted that the appellant was told to drive the car, the court should apply s 78, Police and Criminal Evidence Act 1984 (discretion to exclude evidence which would have such an adverse effect on the fairness of the proceedings that the court ought not to admit it) in the exercise of their discretion. Secondly, the amount the motorist had drunk could not have given rise to a suspicion of his being unfit; there was no evidence that he had been warned by the station sergeant of the consequences of failing to supply a sample and no evidence that the computer in the breath analysis device was working correctly.

The prosecutor then applied to re-open his case. The Crown Court judge decided that that application was a matter of law for him to decide, without consulting the other members of the court. He allowed the sergeant to be recalled. The sergeant then gave evidence which complied with s 69 and the motorist was invited to call further evidence if he wished. The court decided the factual matters in favour of the prosecutor and dismissed the appeal. The motorist appealed further.

QUESTION(S) FOR THE COURT: (1) Was the question of allowing the prosecutor to re-open the case one of law, or should the judge have consulted his lay justices? (2) In any event, was the judge right on the facts of this particular case to allow the respondent's application?

HELD: "30. ... each of the questions ... is to be answered affirmatively. The decision to re-open the case by recalling the sergeant was essentially a question of admissibility and therefore one to be taken by him alone ... It is perfectly right that each case will turn on its own peculiar facts, but ... the effect of Kennedy LJ's decision and review of the authorities in *Jolly* [above] ... is further to limit the opportunities for the ambush defence once so popular in drink driving litigation. In a proper case, applications to recall a witness may properly be granted, provided ... that there has been no absence of good faith on the part of the prosecution and, even more significantly, where no possible material prejudice can redound to a defendant, who will be given every possible opportunity, as the appellant was here, to deal with the evidence heard by way of recall. In such circumstances an application to recall a witness to deal with evidence previously admitted [*sic*] by mere oversight may properly be granted."

Appeal dismissed.

Steward v DPP

[2003] EWHC 2251 (Admin), [2004] 1 WLR 592, [2004] 4 All ER 1005, [2004] RTR 16, 30 July 2003, QBD (Admin)

Where magistrates found no case to answer, having confused evidence of the taking of a blood specimen with the analyst's certificate, and the defendant's solicitor agreed there had been an error, the magistrates were in order to re-open the case and receive evidence of the taking of the specimen.

A motorist had been charged with driving with excess alcohol, contrary to s 5(1)(a), Road Traffic Act 1988. The lower breath analysis reading was 41 µg alcohol in 100 ml breath. He was therefore offered the option to provide a blood or urine specimen, under s 8(2), Road Traffic Act 1988 (lower of two breath readings not more than 50 µg alcohol in 100 ml breath – now repealed; see page v). He accepted the option and provided a blood specimen, which, in due course, revealed excess alcohol.

At the trial, the prosecution's analyst gave evidence (by way of witness statement), producing his certificate of the proportion of alcohol in the specimen. At the end of the prosecution case, the defence argued there was no case to answer in that there had been no oral evidence or a certificate from the doctor who took the specimen. The magistrates found no case to answer, but it then became clear they had confused the analyst's certificate with the doctor's certificate; all parties agreed this, and the magistrates reversed their decision. They went on to accept the police officer's evidence that the specimen had been taken with the defendant's consent by a medical practitioner. They convicted the defendant; he appealed.

QUESTION(S) FOR THE COURT: (1) Whether the justices were entitled to re-open the case after finding that there was no case to answer.

HELD: "[On (1)] 10. ... This is not a case like [*R v Essex Justices ex p Final* [1963] 2 QB 816] where a Bench was persuaded to re-open the case and, in effect, hear further submissions as to the evidence. It is a case of an error having been identified, having been agreed by the defendant's solicitor and having been admitted to by the magistrates. I do not consider that that comes within the principles set out in the *Essex Justices* case, or in the case of [*S v Recorder of Manchester* [1971] AC 481, [1970] 2 WLR 21, [1969] 3 All ER 1230] in which Lord MacDermott referred ... to the point where: '... the process of adjudication ... had been completed and was effective in point of law,' as the cut off point."

Appeal dismissed.

Khatibi v DPP

[2004] EWHC 83 (Admin), (2004) 168 JP 361, 28 January 2004, QBD (DC)

On the facts of this case, justices were entitled to allow the prosecution to re-open its case to bring further evidence on the blood specimen and to adjourn the case for that purpose. On the evidence, the magistrates were entitled to find that the blood analysed was that of the appellant.

A motorist had been charged with driving with excess alcohol, contrary to s 5(1)(a), Road Traffic Act 1988. Breath analysis showed 42 and 41 μg alcohol in 100 ml breath; she was therefore offered the option to provide a blood or urine specimen, under s 8(2), Road Traffic Act 1988 (lower of two breath readings not more than 50 μg alcohol in 100 ml breath – now repealed; see page v). She accepted the option and gave a blood specimen which was duly taken and divided. A sample marked with the names of the doctor who had taken the blood, the police officer who had conducted the procedure, the name of the police station, the date and time of taking the specimen, and the name of the defendant, was analysed by a forensic scientist with the help of an assistant. It revealed excess alcohol.

At the trial, the defendant submitted, *inter alia*, that the forensic scientist's evidence was inadmissible since it depended in part on the evidence of his assistant; and that there was no evidence of how the specimen had been labelled and therefore no inference could be drawn that the blood analysed was the defendant's. The bench retired to decide the second point; they were satisfied that the blood analysed was that of the defendant. The prosecutor then applied to re-open its case and adjourn to allow the forensic scientist's assistant to be called. The justices agreed and adjourned the case for some 5 months.

When the trial resumed, the defence argued that the case should be dismissed as the memories of the magistrates would have faded over the 5-month delay. The bench rejected this submission. The assistant to the forensic analyst gave evidence that she had analysed the specimen under the supervision of the forensic analyst; she was not cross-examined.

The defendant appealed against conviction.

QUESTION(S) FOR THE COURT: (i) Whether the justices were right to adjourn the case for the purpose of hearing further evidence and then doing so; (ii) whether they were right to continue with the trial after adjourning it for 5 months; (iii) whether there was evidence upon which a reasonable bench, properly directing itself, could have found that the blood analysed was that of the appellant.

HELD: "[On (i)] 17. There is a general discretion to admit evidence after the close of the prosecution case which is not confined to the two well established exceptions of rebuttal and mere formality. The discretion must be exercised with great caution …

"18. Lord Justice Kennedy in [*Jolly (Christopher) v DPP*; page 649] reviewed the authorities before concluding that there was a general discretion to permit the calling of evidence at a stage later than the closing of the prosecution case but prior to the moment the justices retire and said that before exercising that discretion the court will look carefully at the interests of justice overall and in particular the risk of any prejudice whatsoever to the Defendant. …

"29. I am satisfied that after retiring to consider their decision on the continuity submission the Justices were right to hear further argument … on the admissibility of the forensic science evidence, and in view of the submissions being made on behalf of the Appellant were right to adjourn the case for the purpose of hearing further evidence and then doing so.

"[On (ii)] 34. … The only evidence to be called was that of [the assistant analyst] whose evidence was already known and indeed not in the event challenged … the bench were right to continue with the trial after adjourning it for five months …

"[On (iii)] 39. … the prosecution accepted that there was a gap in the prosecution case in that there was no evidence as to who had written the details on the label but submitted that the contents on the label were sufficient for the magistrates to infer that the blood in the container analysed was the Appellant's. The contents of the label were admissible under sections 24 [business, etc documents] and 26 [statements in documents that appear to have been prepared for purposes of criminal proceedings or investigations] of the Criminal Justice Act 1988 and could therefore have been ruled admissible by the bench had the question of admissibility been raised by the Appellant. …

"40. … the label gives details of the exact time at which the sample was taken, namely 0015 hrs on 13 November 2001, which is entirely consistent with the evidence of [the doctor] that he took the sample between 1210 and 1220 a.m. on that date. In addition the name of the arresting officer … is also correctly stated as is the name of the doctor who took the sample … and where he took it … [The assistant analyst's] evidence confirmed that that sample so labelled had been received at the laboratory on 15 November 2001. 'Document' and 'statement' under the 1988 Act are widely defined in schedule 2 paragraph 5. 'Document' means anything in which information of any description is recorded and 'statement' means any representation of fact however made.

"42. It is, [the prosecutor] submits, an irresistible inference on the facts that the label was created by a police officer in the course of his work and that therefore the information contained in the label was supplied by a person who had personal knowledge of the matters dealt with. Any other inference would be unreasonable. Hence section 24(1)(i) and (ii) are satisfied. …

"43. As to section 26, the prosecution submit that it was in the interests of justice to admit the statement which resulted in no unfairness to the accused other than establishing the true facts.

"45. … the Justices were entitled to conclude … that there was evidence upon which, properly directing itself, the bench could have found that the blood analysed … was that of the Appellant."

The answers to all three questions were "yes". Appeal dismissed.

Malcolm v DPP

[2007] EWHC 363 (QB), [2007] 1 WLR 1230, [2007] 2 Cr App R 1, [2007] RTR 27, 27 February 2007, QBD (DC)

On the facts of this case (defence raising, in its closing speech, whether the warning under s 7(7) had been given), magistrates were right to exercise their discretion to allow the prosecution to recall a witness to give evidence of the procedure, even though they had started to consider their verdict.

A motorist had been charged with driving with excess alcohol, contrary to s 5(1)(a), Road Traffic Act 1988.

At the hearing, the officer who conducted the breath analysis procedure gave evidence but was not cross-examined. The defendant argued the defence of duress. In her closing speech, counsel for the defendant submitted that the warning required by s 7(7), Road Traffic Act 1988 (of the consequences of failing to provide) had not been given and that there was therefore no admissible evidence of the breath analysis or that the correct procedure had been followed. The magistrates retired to consider the submissions. They returned to court and announced that they accepted there had been no evidence that the s 7(7) warning had been given. They had made no decision on the defence of duress, assuming the case would be dismissed on the ground that there was no admissible evidence of excess alcohol.

The prosecutor then asked to recall the police officer to give further evidence of the procedure, arguing that there would be no prejudice since the officer had not been cross-examined. The magistrates allowed the witness to be recalled and heard further evidence from him. They went on to find that the motorist had been properly warned and that the evidence of excess alcohol was therefore admissible; and that the defence of duress was not made out. They convicted the motorist but found special reasons for not disqualifying her. She appealed against conviction.

QUESTION(S) FOR THE COURT: Whether the magistrates were right to exercise their discretion to admit further evidence after they had started to consider their verdict and had returned to court and started to announce their decision on the point of law concerning s 7(7).

HELD: "22. … magistrates have a discretion to receive further evidence after they have retired to consider their verdict, but special circumstances are required if the discretion is to be exercised …

"31. … It is the duty of the defence to make its defence and the issues it raises clear to the prosecution and to the court at an early stage …

"32. That was not done in this case. At no time before her final speech did [defence counsel] raise any issue as to the police's compliance with section 7(7). [The officer] was not cross-examined on the point … If there was an issue as to whether the warning required by section 7(7) had been given, and she contended that as a result the officer's evidence of the proportion of alcohol in the appellant's breath was inadmissible [counsel] should have objected to the admission of the officer's evidence as to the proportion of alcohol in the appellant's breath. [Counsel] did neither of these things … in these circumstances she should not have been permitted to raise the issue under section 7(7) in her final speech unless the prosecution was given the opportunity to call evidence to deal with the point.

"33. To take the section 7(7) point in the final speech was a classic and improper defence ambush of the prosecution …

"37. … the matters [referred to above] were special circumstances justifying the recall of [the police officer] notwithstanding the fact that the justices had retired and had partially announced their decision … The appellant was available to be recalled to dispute the officer's evidence, if it was disputed. In fact it was not. There was no injustice … the magistrates were fully entitled to exercise their undoubted discretion as they did."

The answer to the question was "yes". Appeal dismissed.

12. RECKLESS DRIVING

Hand v DPP

[1991] RTR 225, [1991] Crim LR 473, 20 February 1991, QBD (DC)

The fact that a person is guilty of driving with excess alcohol does not of itself prove that he was driving recklessly.

A motorist had been charged, *inter alia,* with reckless driving, contrary to s 2, Road Traffic Act 1988, and with driving with excess alcohol, contrary to s 5(1)(a), Road Traffic Act 1988. He had been drinking; some 5 hours later he drove his car and there was a fatal accident; the motorist was found to be over the limit.

He pleaded guilty to the excess alcohol charge. The justices convicted him of reckless driving, considering that any reasonable person assessing his ability to drive a motor vehicle would have appreciated an obvious and serious risk of causing injury should he proceed to take the risk and drive. The motorist appealed against the conviction for reckless driving.

QUESTION(S) FOR THE COURT: Whether to drive a motor vehicle having consumed such a quantity of alcohol that the proportion of it in one's breath obviously exceeded the prescribed limit could without more be reckless.

HELD: "… the first part of the *Lawrence* [*R v Lawrence (Stephen)* [1982] AC 510, [1981] 2 WLR 524, [1981] 1 All ER 974, [1981] RTR 217, [1981] Crim LR 409 (HL)] test requires proof by the prosecution that the manner of driving was such as to create an obvious and serious risk.

"The only finding … is … that [the defendant] was involved in a road traffic accident … There is no finding as to the circumstances in which the accident occurred, … as to the state of the road, or the visibility, or the condition of either vehicle …

"… unless one can tell from other evidence what the cause of the accident was and how it can be related in some way to the driving of the defendant, the mere fact that the defendant is over the legal limit of alcohol cannot by itself satisfy the first limb of the *Lawrence* test …

"… the *Griffiths* decision [*R v Griffiths (Gordon Rupert)* [1984] Crim LR 628, [1990] RTR 244 (CA)] does not constitute authority for the proposition that the consumption of alcohol in excess of the limit alone can support a charge that the defendant, while driving a car with the amount of alcohol in his body, has driven recklessly …

"… driving with excess alcohol is not the same thing as reckless driving. There was no evidence that this defendant drove in a reckless manner and therefore he should not have been convicted of reckless driving."

The answer to the question was "no". Appeal allowed.

13. STAY OF PROCEEDINGS AND ABUSE OF PROCESS

See also DPP v Petrie, page 587, where magistrates were in error to grant a stay.

R v Bishop's Stortford JJ ex p DPP

Unreported, CO 3169/96, 17 April 1997, QBD (DC)

Where delay, to which the defendant had contributed, did not prejudice the defendant, proceedings should not have been stayed.

A motorist had been stopped, arrested and charged with driving with excess alcohol on 14 August 1993. He was bailed to appear before magistrates on 9 September 1993. A warrant for his arrest in connection with another matter was outstanding and, also on 14 August, the police arrested him on that warrant and bailed him to another magistrates' court to appear on 25 August. On 9 September he failed to appear on the drink-drive matter and the justices issued a warrant for his arrest.

On 24 March 1994, the defendant's then solicitor telephoned the Crown Prosecution Service, saying the defendant would surrender to custody on 6 April 1994, pursuant to the warrant. He failed to do so and the warrant remained unexecuted until either 29 February or 1 March 1996. The defendant had been before a magistrates' court on 21 September 1994 and thought the drink-drive offence in question had been dealt with then; in fact it had not. The present case was listed for trial on 22 July 1996.

On 22 July 1996, counsel for the defence applied for a stay of the proceedings on the basis that to continue would be an abuse of process, in view of the length of time since the date of the alleged offence; it was said that the defendant had been prejudiced by the delay in that it prevented him from providing adequate instructions to his lawyers, and that his own failure to surrender to custody was partly explained by the fact that in September 1994 when he had been at a court on other matters, he had been told by a police officer that there were no outstanding warrants against him.

The magistrates ordered the prosecution be stayed and the defendant acquitted. The prosecutor appealed.

HELD: "... Having regard to the history of the matter and to the charges which this accused faced, it seems to me that had the Justices asked themselves the question whether the delay in this case had been contributed to by the actions of the Defendant himself ... there could only be one answer and that is that it had. In those circumstances it should not be the foundation for a stay ... the decision of the Magistrates to stay the proceedings ... was wrong. The chances of prejudice were remote, the degree of potential prejudice was very small, the risk of any unfairness in the conduct of a trial being produced as a result of delay was infinitesimal and in any event, the case was in no way so exceptional as to justify the ruling which the magistrates made. If they had asked themselves the question whether the delay had prejudiced the Defendant so that he was unable to obtain a fair trial as a result of it, the answer must have been 'No'."

Application granted.

DPP v Edgar

Unreported, CO 21/2/2000, 21 February 2000, QBD

On the facts (agreement to plead guilty to two charges and for a third charge to be withdrawn), the third charge should not have been reinstated when it was realised that the withdrawal was based on an error as to the law.

A defendant pleaded guilty to offences of failing to stop and give her name after an accident and of failing to report an accident as soon as reasonably possible; a charge of driving with excess alcohol, contrary to s 5, Road Traffic Act 1988, was withdrawn. The prosecutor, having first thought there was an error in the drink-drive procedure, and then having realised there was not, sought to reinstate the excess alcohol charge. The charge was reinstated. The defence argued that there had been an agreement that the prosecution would withdraw the charge, and the reinstatement was an abuse of process. The magistrates accepted this argument and did not proceed with the allegation of driving with excess alcohol. The prosecutor appealed.

QUESTION(S) FOR THE COURT: Whether the justices were correct in law to conclude that the reinstatement of the charge of driving with excess alcohol was capable of being, and amounted to, an abuse of process.

HELD: "11. … a careful reading of the case does lead to the conclusion that the Magistrates considered that a deal had been done. …

"14. There is no indication in the case that the prosecution ever argued that there had not been an earlier agreement to this effect. …

"15. … For my part, I think we are justified in proceeding on the basis that there was such an agreement.

"16. However, that is not automatically the end of the case because the magistrates had to make a decision whether, given there had been such an agreement, they would allow the prosecution, who had entered into it under a mistake of law, to put matters right …

"17. … I do see some difficulty in finding that the defendant has been prejudiced personally … by what went on. I do not know whether the magistrates, in finding the defendant had been prejudiced, were actually doing more than saying that it was wrong to try to go back on a bargain that has been made in good faith by both sides. Perhaps they were, although it is not entirely clear …

"20. … compromises of this kind between prosecution and defence, where the defence agrees to plead to some charges in return for the prosecution dropping others, are a commonplace of our criminal proceedings and they occur in magistrates courts and crown courts. It is important in principle that such compromises should generally be stuck to and the integrity of the criminal process requires that they should be.

"21. … on the facts of the case, it was well within the magistrates' discretion to decide that to go back on that agreement was something which would amount to an abuse of process. They so decided. I do not think it would be right for this Court to interfere in these circumstances … ."

The answer to the question was "yes". Appeal dismissed.

DPP v Garrety

Unreported, CO3546/00, 11 December 2000, QBD (DC)

In the circumstances of this case (video evidence not disclosed because there was no such evidence, the officer having made an error in his report book), the justices were wrong to stay proceedings as an abuse of process.

A motorist had been charged with driving while unfit through drugs, contrary to s 4(1), Road Traffic Act 1988. She had been in a road traffic accident. An officer who attended marked his accident report book to the effect that there was video evidence. On the trial date, the Crown had not served any primary disclosure material under s 3(1)(a), Criminal Procedure and Investigations Act 1996 or stated that no such material existed, but the prosecutor stated that there was in fact no video, and that the reference to a video had been an error; he further said that all material that did exist had been served. The justices concluded that the absence of the video and the Crown's non-compliance with its disclosure obligations had severely prejudiced the defendant, to the extent that a fair trial was not possible. They stayed the proceedings as an abuse of process. The prosecutor appealed.

QUESTION(S) FOR THE COURT: Whether the justices were right: (1) to determine that the non-retention and non-disclosure of the police video was an abuse of process given the nature of the charge and the lack of relevance that any video would have had in law to its determination by the court; and (2) to refuse the prosecution further time to seek more information for the court before it made its decision above.

HELD: "27. … [The] matter could have been resolved by [the officer's] attendance at court that morning … it was the Respondent … who objected to such a proposed solution …

"31. … the Justices declined, contrary to the principles established by the authorities, to consider properly an alternative solution short of staying the proceedings as an abuse of process. …

"37. … It was entirely speculative as to how any video evidence, assuming such existed, was or might have been relevant to any issue in the case. The Defence provided no detail of what possible relevance any such video would have or to what issue it might go. Their approach was to argue that there must have been a video because of the single ringed entry in one officer's notebook that had been disclosed by the Prosecution, and that the Respondent was thereby, in some unspecified manner, disadvantaged and therefore, the proceedings ought to be stayed as an abuse of process.

"38. … on the material before them and the submissions made, the Justices exceeded any reasonable exercise of their discretion in … staying the proceedings as an abuse."

The answers to both questions were "no". Appeal allowed.

R (Bozkurt) v Thames Magistrates' Court

[2001] EWHC Admin 400, [2002] RTR 15, 14 May 2001, QBD (DC)

On the facts, there was no unfairness where the same interpreter acted at the drink-drive procedure and at the trial, even though the interpreter might have been called as a prosecution witness.

A person was found asleep across the front seat of his car and showed signs of being drunk. He was arrested and taken to the police station. He spoke little English and an interpreter was called to interpret the drink-drive procedure. A doctor attended. The suspect was charged with being in charge of the vehicle while unfit and of being in charge with excess alcohol, contrary to s 4, Road Traffic Act 1988. He appeared at the magistrates' courts 2 days later. The same interpreter was in attendance. Although the interpreter might have been called as a witness for the prosecution, she did not tell the duty solicitor that she had been the interpreter at the police station, and interpreted a conversation between the unrepresented defendant and the duty solicitor, including advice to plead not guilty.

The deputy district judge rejected argument that it was an abuse of process or unfair for the prosecution to rely on the evidence of the interpreter concerning the procedure at the police station. He found that it was doubtful that the interpreter's evidence would do more than describe the interpretation of the drink-drive procedure; if there were any issues of unfairness they could be explored at trial. There was no suggestion that the interpreter had acted improperly. She was bound by strict rules of confidentiality, and there was no suggestion of a breach.

The applicant sought judicial review of the deputy district judge's decision.

GROUND(S) FOR THE APPLICATION: Whether the proceedings, as a whole, including the way the evidence was taken, were fair.

HELD: "[After reviewing the authorities] 27. … if an interpreter is required to be present during an interview between a solicitor and his client, the interpreter is subject to exactly the same duties in relation to confidentiality as the solicitor who is giving the advice. If there had been no question of the interpreter giving evidence, as was intended in this case, obviously there could be no objection to an interpreter being present. Does the fact that the interpreter was to be a witness make a difference? The deputy district judge was right … in coming to the conclusion that it made no difference which could not be properly dealt with at a trial. …

"[On the argument that the very fact that the interpreter was to be a witness meant that, automatically, the proceedings were flawed, where, as here, the interpreter's evidence was necessary] 28. The interpreter's evidence which was necessary was evidence at a different time from that of the interview between the solicitor and the applicant. The interpreter's evidence is formal evidence as to what happened at the police station prior to the charge. At this stage it cannot be anticipated that there is going to be any issue in relation to that evidence which could possibly be affected by what took place between the solicitor and the applicant. If any issue of that sort arose at the hearing, that would be a matter which the trial judge would have to deal with and apply section 78 of the Police and Criminal Evidence Act 1984 [discretion to exclude evidence which would have such an adverse effect on the fairness of the proceedings that the court ought not to admit it] to what occurred at the trial. … although it is unfortunate that the interpreter did not obtain the consent of the solicitor and the applicant to her acting as interpreter at the interview, there is no reason to think that any prejudice could have or could appear to have occurred by reason of her presence at the interview. … she is bound by a firm duty of confidence not to disclose anything which occurred at the interview. … The events which occurred in this case are undesirable because … they arguably create a perception of unfairness. However, on examination of the facts, I am satisfied that that perception is dispelled."

Application refused.

R v Boyd

[2002] EWCA Crim 2836, [2004] RTR 2, 18 November 2002, CA (Crim)

Where the defendant's part of a blood specimen was not properly stored before being supplied to her, so that she could have it analysed, the proceedings should have been stayed as an abuse for process.

A motorist had been charged with causing death by careless driving while unfit through drink or drugs, contrary to s 3A(1), Road Traffic Act 1988. Following a fatal accident, a blood specimen was taken from the motorist. Analysis for the prosecution gave a positive screening for free morphine and opiate drugs. The defendant disputed the finding but could not conduct a comparative analysis because, in error, the specimen had not been refrigerated and had become unfit for testing. At the trial, a chartered biologist for the defence gave evidence in a *voir dire* that a second test might have yielded results favourable to the defendant. The judge decided to exclude the evidence of the blood analysis, but rejected the defence submission that the case be stayed as an abuse of process. The motorist was convicted and appealed.

HELD: "19. … The evidence of [the chartered biologist] demonstrated that, in the first place, the conclusion reached on behalf of the prosecution in interpreting the sample tested by them was open to challenge … what was revealed by the test was no more than a borderline positive and, therefore, should be regarded as negative from the appellant's point of view. Furthermore, had another sample been examined by the defence, it may have established … that there was no heroin materially affecting the appellant at the time she drove. That being so … the defence was deprived by the prosecution of the opportunity of establishing a defence which might have been open to them. …

"20. … the judge, having excluded the blood sample, ought … to have taken the further step of ordering that the proceedings should be stayed. The fairness of the trial required that this be done."

Appeal allowed; conviction quashed.

Hoar-Stevens v Richmond Magistrates' Court; Christopher Boucher, Interested Party

[2003] EWHC 2660 (Admin), 23 October 2003, QBD (DC)

Proceedings in the magistrates' court should not be stayed for guidance from a higher court; the correct procedure is to proceed to the end of the trial and to test a matter by way of case stated.

A motorist had been charged with driving with excess alcohol, contrary to s 5(1)(a), Road Traffic Act 1988. He had been arrested and breath analysis was positive. The defence wished to explore the reliability of the breath analysis device used and sought certain records. Various documents were disclosed and directions made.

At the trial the district judge found that the prosecution had not fully complied with its duty of disclosure under the Criminal Procedure and Investigations Act 1996 and the Attorney General's Guidelines, in that it had not enquired of the Home Office as to the existence of relevant material and had not sought from the manufacturers of the device copies of the engineers' reports. She refused a defence application to stay the proceedings on the basis that the prosecution had not made adequate disclosure. She was then asked to consider excluding material under s 78, Police and Criminal Evidence Act 1984 (discretion to exclude evidence which would have such an adverse effect on the fairness of the proceedings that the court ought not to admit it). She decided it was not appropriate to consider the question until after the defence's closing submission. She invited the parties to test her decision by judicial review because the issue of disclosure had arisen in several cases and there was no guidance from a higher court. The defence obtained leave to do so, and the proceedings in the magistrates' court were stayed.

HELD: "18. … there are powerful reasons for accepting the guidance offered by [*R v Rochford Justices ex p Buck* (1978) 68 Cr App R 114]. It is of the utmost importance that the course of a criminal trial in the Magistrates' Court should not be punctuated by applications for an adjournment to test a ruling in this court, especially when in reality if the case proceeds the ruling may turn out to be of little or no importance. In the present case the district judge has yet to rule in relation to s. 78. If her ruling were to favour the claimant the prosecution would fail. That may or may not be a realistic possibility, but I am satisfied that even when, as here, there is an important substantive point which arises during a trial this court should not and indeed cannot intervene. The proper course is to proceed to the end of the trial in the lower court and then to test the matter, almost certainly by way of case stated."

Appeal dismissed; stay discharged.

DPP v Meakin

[2006] EWHC 1067 (Admin), 4 May 2006, QBD (DC)

Proceedings should not be stayed unless the defendant will suffer such prejudice that a fair trial is not possible. Where the prosecution erred in failing to disclose the name of a witness, the magistrates were wrong to order a stay.

A motorist had been charged with driving with excess alcohol, contrary to s 5(1)(a), Road Traffic Act 1988. A woman had telephoned the police reporting that a car had been driven into a garden wall. A police officer went to the scene where he found two men standing by the car. One of the men admitted he had been driving; a roadside breath test was positive; he was arrested and breath analysis later revealed excess alcohol.

The prosecution did not disclose to the defence the identity of the woman who had made the telephone call and the defence did not ask for it. At the trial, the defence put the prosecution to strict proof, including proof that the defendant had been driving. The defence complained about the non-disclosure of the woman's identity, but did not apply for disclosure. The court found that the defendant could not have a fair trial and that there had been an abuse of process, and stayed the proceedings. The prosecutor appealed.

QUESTION(S) FOR THE COURT (INTER ALIA): Whether in the circumstances the magistrates were wrong to have: (a) found that the defendant could not have a fair trial; (b) found an abuse of process; (c) stayed the proceedings as an abuse of process.

HELD: "… If [the person who made the telephone call – 'the caller'] was a witness to what passed, her evidence might be capable of undermining the prosecution or assisting the defence, and, if so, then the identity of that witness should have been disclosed … the prosecution are now right to concede that … [her] name should have been disclosed. …

"The real issue was whether the caller could give any material evidence. The point was unclear at the time, and … remains unclear even now, although the high likelihood is that the caller could not give material evidence and certainly not any material evidence which could assist [the appellant]. Since the caller is not and never has been a witness on whom the prosecution intended to rely, there is no question of the prosecution being under any duty to secure the attendance of the caller to tender her for cross-examination. …

"The question now … is whether the defence intended to call her. If they do, then a witness summons should have been issued by the defence and served by them after they had made proper enquiries as to her name and particulars. The failure to do so is as much their fault in failing to ask for her details as it is of the prosecution in failing to supply those details. …

"[On abuse of process and stay of proceedings] the principles are clear. The imposition of a stay is now wholly exceptional. A stay should not be imposed unless the defendant shows that he will suffer such prejudice that a fair trial is not possible. The defence did not and do not here allege bad faith or serious misconduct. There was no affront to justice in the case proceeding. The highest it can be put is that the prosecution erred in failing to disclose the name of the witness. To my mind, that was at least matched by the defence failure to ask for those particulars."

The answers to the questions were "yes". Appeal allowed.

Ivic v DPP

[2006] EWHC 1570 (Admin), 9 June 2006, QBD (Admin)

The circumstances of this case (delay between arrest and trial; CCTV tape lost) were not such that a stay of proceedings on the ground of abuse of process was appropriate. The fact that a police radio was on in the breath analysis room did not render the breath analysis inadmissible. An award of costs of £4,000 against the motorist was upheld.

A motorist had been charged with driving with excess alcohol, contrary to s 5(1)(a), Road Traffic Act 1988. He had been arrested and breath analysis revealed excess alcohol.

The date of the alleged offence was 3 November 2001; there were various applications and adjournments and the trial did not take place until March 2005. The district judge declined to stay the proceedings as an abuse of process because of the delays. Nor would she order a stay on the ground that a CCTV video of the procedure had not been provided to the defendant, or exclude evidence of the breath analysis because a police officer had had his radio on while the testing was being conducted. The defendant was convicted and fined £500 and ordered to pay £4,000 costs. He appealed.

QUESTION(S) FOR THE COURT: Whether the district judge was right to reject the application to stay the proceedings as an abuse of process because of delay or because a CCTV video had not been produced; whether the district judge was right to reject the application to exclude the evidence of the breath test when a police constable had his police radio on in the room while the analysis was being carried out; whether it was *Wednesbury* unreasonable for the district judge to order a fine of £500 and costs of £4,000 without an exact breakdown of the costs.

HELD: "[On delay, the appellant] 4. … submits now that the district judge should have stayed proceedings on [the] basis that evidence [of what the appellant had drunk and that he had suffered a reflux before breathing into the breath analysis device] would have been more credible if given close in time to the date of arrest …

"5. … It is appropriate to stay proceedings for delay if a fair trial is not possible or if it would be unfair to try the defendant … On the submissions made to her … the district judge was undoubtedly right to reject the application. The case would turn on expert evidence about the intoximeter device which would not be affected by the passage of time. A fair trial was possible and it would not have been unfair to try the defendant. …

"6. … [The CCTV tape] had gone missing … [the appellant argues] that it might have shown that the appellant burped and whether the police officer who administered the tests had followed the manufacturer's recommended procedure. …

"7. The district judge rejected the submission, holding… that there was no suggestion of bad faith and that it was unclear whether the CCTV footage would have recorded relevant events. In any event, two police officers were available to be cross-examined about these matters and one of them completed a form contemporaneously recording the administration and results of the test. The district judge's conclusion is clearly right. The suggestion that the CCTV footage might have assisted the defence was, to put it politely, speculative or more bluntly far-fetched. …

"[On the presence of the police radio] 10. … The *pro forma* completed by the administering police officer contained the printed notation: 'As a precaution radio sets and mobile phones should be switched off in the immediate vicinity of substantive breath testing devices'. It was accepted that a police officer had left his police radio on throughout the procedure in the room in which it was performed. [Counsel for the appellant] submitted that the district judge should therefore have excluded the evidence of the test under Section 78 of the Police and Criminal Evidence Act 1984 [discretion to exclude evidence which would have such an adverse effect on the fairness of the proceedings that the court ought not to admit it]. The district judge directed herself in accordance with [*DPP v Carey*, page 72]. … In addition, she had [expert evidence] that the police radio being switched on would not affect the accuracy or reliability of the machine. She rejected the submissions. … the district judge was right to [reject the application].

"[On costs] 14. … At first sight the order for costs appears not to be proportionate to the fine, thus offending the normal rule that costs should not, in the ordinary way, be grossly disproportionate to the fine. … However the normal rule does not provide a licence to defendants or their advisers to cause very substantial costs to be incurred, far beyond those required to prosecute and defend the case in the normal way, at no financial risk. It should be clearly understood that defendants who instruct, or are unwise enough to accept advice from, their lawyers to pursue hopeless technical defences to breathalyser prosecutions which inflate the costs of the case will pay those costs if their defence fails. The normal rule in such circumstances should, in my view, be that those who cause the costs to be incurred should pay them.

"15. … No schedule of costs was provided to [the district judge] before she made her order. It should have been. Recognising that, she gave the defendant an opportunity of deferring the assessment of costs but warned him that he would be at risk of incurring further costs if he did so. … he gave the answer no. The appellant thereby elected … to accept an assessment by the district judge without a schedule. She did not exceed the margin of the discretion conferred upon her in assessing the costs by making the order that she did."

Appeal dismissed.

Murphy (Gerard) v DPP

[2006] EWHC 1753 (Admin), 20 June 2006, QBD (DC)

In the circumstances of this case, the district judge had been right to refuse to stay proceedings because of delay. A defendant does not lose the right to secondary disclosure because of a short delay in serving the defence statement. Where there was no evidence to the contrary, the breath analysis device was assumed to be type approved and to have installed the approved software and gas delivery system; the district judge was not required to consider the latter. The approval order does not constitute expert evidence. Where the roadside breath testing device generates and stores analysis figures, the prosecutor is not required to adduce those figures.

A motorist had been charged with driving with excess alcohol, contrary to s 5(1)(a), Road Traffic Act 1988. He had been stopped and a roadside breath test was positive. He was arrested and at the police station breath analysis by means of an Intoximeter EC/IR revealed excess alcohol.

There had been 44 appearances before magistrates before the matter eventually came to trial, and an interval of a little over 4 years between the date of the offence and the trial. The adjournments were, *inter alia*, for experts to examine the Intoximeter; for service of reports; for the attendance of experts; to await decisions of the High Court in similar cases; for the filing of submissions; for the service of a defence case statement; for secondary disclosure; for service of details of modifications to the Intoximeter; and for disclosure of documents.

Eventually, the defendant was convicted, and appealed.

QUESTION(S) FOR THE COURT: (1) Whether the district judge erred in law in holding that a defendant is entitled to secondary disclosure of unused material only if a defence statement had been served on the prosecution within 14 days of the service on him of primary disclosure; … (3) whether the district judge was entitled to find that the breath analysis device used was of a type approved by the Secretary of State within s 7, Road Traffic Act 1988; (4) whether there was any evidence on which to hold that the device used had the approved software and approved gas delivery system, and whether the district judge was required to consider this issue in the absence of any evidence called by either party on the subject; (5) whether the Breath Analysis Devices (No 2) Approval Order 1988 constitutes expert evidence for the purpose of the Magistrates' Court (Advance Notice of Expert Evidence) Rules 1997 (SI 1997/705); … (7) whether the district judge erred in law in holding that s 15(2), Road Traffic Offenders Act 1988 (assumption that the proportion of alcohol at the time of an alleged offence not less than in the specimen) did not compel the respondent to adduce the result in figures of the breath analysis carried out at the roadside by a Lion Alcometer device; (8) whether the district judge erred in law in refusing the defence application to stay the proceedings for delay, when the case came on for trial.

HELD: "[After summarising, and deploring, the history of the case, on (8)] 22. The district judge was unquestionably right … to refuse to stay the proceedings. The issues raised in the amended defence case statement did not turn to any extent on the reliability of the memory of any witness including the appellant, but on his truthfulness and upon technical evidence, to the extent that it was led, as to type approval and perhaps the functioning of the intoximeter EC/IR device. There was no challenge to any of the police evidence as to the administering of the three breath tests, or any other aspect of the procedure. If there was a defence, it was not affected by the passage of time.

"[On (1), following *DPP v Wood; DPP v McGillicuddy*, page 428] 26. … It cannot have been Parliament's intention that a defendant should lose the right to disclosure of material, or to apply to the court for disclosure of material in the possession of the prosecution which might reasonably assist his case, by delay, even for a short period, in serving his defence statement. My answer to question (1) is, therefore, yes. …

"30. The answer to question (3) is yes. … there was no evidence to the contrary. The district judge's finding was the only one open to him.

"31. Question (4) raises two questions: (1) was the district judge entitled to conclude that the device had the approved software and delivery system? (2) was he required to consider the issue in the absence of evidence called by either side on the point? The answer to the first part of question (4) is yes, and to the second part, no. The district judge was entitled to assume that the device had installed within it the software and gas delivery system of the type it contained when it was approved by the Secretary of State: see the court's acceptance of the respondent's submission to that effect in *Skinner v DPP* [page 265].

"[On (5)] 32. It is common ground that the order is not expert evidence: it is a public document, proved under section 2 of the Documentary Evidence Act 1868, without the need for proof of the Minister of State's signature: see s 1, Evidence Act 1845. The answer to question (5) is, therefore, no.

"[On (7)] 36. both sides made … admissions [that the Alcolmeter stores the analytical results of breath tests; police can download pass/warn/fail records, but only the manufacturers can download the actual digital results].

"37. [Counsel for the appellant] submitted that section 15(2) of the Road Traffic Offenders Act 1988 required the prosecution to obtain and produce in evidence the analysis which had been stored in the memory of the Lion Alcolmeter by which the roadside test had been administered. …

"38. Free of authority, I would hold that evidence of the proportion of alcohol in a specimen [in s 15(2)] meant … no more than evidence actually placed before the court by either party. If no evidence was adduced of the proportion of alcohol in a specimen, there is no requirement for a court to take it into account. Thus, though evidence of the proportion of alcohol in a specimen of breath provided in a roadside breath test still in the memory of the Lion Alcometer device is admissible in evidence if it is retrieved, if it is not there is no evidence to take into account.

"40. … nothing in [*Badkin v DPP*, page 46] leads to the conclusion that in every case the prosecution must obtain from the manufacturers an analysis of the proportion of alcohol in the specimen provided in the roadside breath test and put that result in evidence. Accordingly, I answer the seventh question no."

Appeal dismissed.

Roberts v DPP

[2008] EWHC 643 (Admin), 19 March 2008, QBD (DC)

On the facts of this case, the prosecution's failure to produce a video recording of the custody area was not an abuse of process, but the magistrates should not have dismissed as frivolous a request to state a case on whether the place where the alleged offence occurred was a "road or other public place".

A motorist had been charged with failing without reasonable excuse to provide two specimens of breath for analysis, contrary to s 7(6), Road Traffic Act 1988. Disputing that the MG DD/A form had been completed in his presence or that he had been warned under s 7(7) (of the consequences of failing to provide), he sought disclosure of a video recording of the custody area. By the time the prosecutor became aware of the request for the video, the recording had been overwritten. The justices found that there was no abuse of process and declined to stay the proceedings.

The officer who had conducted the procedure gave evidence that he had completed the form in the presence of the defendant, and the justices took note of a number of initialled responses; in particular, the defendant's response to the warning under s 7(7) had been initialled. They accepted the police evidence and convicted the defendant.

He appealed against the refusal of the justices to stay the prosecution as an abuse of process. He also applied to extend the case to require the justices to deal with the question whether there was any evidence on which a reasonable bench, properly directing themselves, could have held that the road the subject of the proceedings was a "road or other public place" for the purposes of the Road Traffic Act 1988. The justices declined to do so on the ground that the application was frivolous.

QUESTION(S) FOR THE COURT: Whether it was *Wednesbury* unreasonable to hold that there was no abuse of process when a video recording of the breathalyser procedure had, deliberately and contrary to the codes of practice and a defence request, been re-used by the police, and which recording would have conclusively proved whether or not the correct procedures had been followed at the police station.

HELD: "9. … It was open to the Justices, having heard the sergeant, to accept that he performed his responsibilities accurately. Equally, it was open to the Justices to accept the evidence of the appellant that this task had not been done in the way the sergeant did it. Although the officer asserted that this procedure had been conducted in the custody area, if that material was not on the tape it would not have established that the procedure was not conducted properly, merely that it was not conducted in the place where it was believed to have been conducted.

"10. … it was entirely open to the Justices to conclude that this prosecution was not an abuse of process … We do not accept that such a recording would necessarily conclusively have proved whether or not the correct procedure had been followed at the police station.

"[On the question of the road] 15. … in the light of *Deacon v AT* [1976] RTR 244, it seems to me that it is quite wrong to conclude that the request to state [a case on whether or not the place in question was a road] was frivolous."

The answer to the question was "no". Case remitted to the magistrates' court to state a case.

Morris v DPP

[2008] EWHC 2788 (Admin), 14 November 2008, QBD (Admin)

The prosecution is not automatically required to retain CCTV evidence which might record the giving of the warning under s 7(7), Road Traffic Act 1988; on the facts (issue of giving of warning not raised in advance, doubt that CCTV would have picked up conversation, video tape not requested and not disclosed), it was not Wednesbury unreasonable to have found no abuse of process.

A motorist had been convicted by magistrates of driving with excess alcohol in blood, contrary to s 5(1)(a), Road Traffic Act 1988. He appealed to the Crown Court. At a pre-trial review he said the issue at trial would be a challenge to the statutory procedure and to the reliability of the blood analysis; no further details were given. At trial, he argued that the statutory warning under s 7(7), Road Traffic Act 1988 (of the consequences of failing to provide) had not been given and that the blood analysis was therefore inadmissible. The investigating officer, who had completed the Form MG DD/B, on which was recorded the s 7(7) warning, mentioned in cross-examination that there was CCTV in the custody suite. In accordance with usual procedure, the video tape had been kept for 3 months, then, in the absence of anyone wanting to look at it, it had been destroyed; nobody had thought it relevant or significant. The Crown Court thought it highly unlikely that the precise detail of what had been said would be apparent from the tape, finding that a fair trial was possible and there was no abuse of process. It concluded that the procedure had been correctly followed and dismissed the appeal. The motorist appealed further.

QUESTION(S) FOR THE COURT: (1) Whether the prosecution is automatically required to retain CCTV evidence in every case where it might record the administering of the statutory warning under s 7(7), regardless of whether or not the defence raises the giving of the warning as an issue before trial; (2) whether it was *Wednesbury* unreasonable to have refused to allow the appeal on the grounds of abuse of process.

HELD: "[On (1), after reviewing the Attorney General's Guidelines on Disclosure and the Code of Practice pursuant to section 23, Criminal Procedure and

Investigations Act 1996] 27. [the appellant's] agreement that in certain cases there is no requirement on the prosecution to retain CCTV evidence where it might record the administering of the statutory warning … necessarily leads to his acceptance that the answer to the first question … is 'No' and I so find. …

"[On (2), after reviewing the authorities] 42. [the appellant] did not indicate before trial whether he accepted or contested that the … warning … had been given …. The case therefore falls within the middle ground as to which there are competing contentions by the parties as to the circumstances in which there is an obligation to retain and disclose material. …

"47. … it was not apparent nor were the prosecution put on notice that the giving of the … warning was to be challenged. … there was considerable doubt as to whether any CCTV recording in the custody area would have picked up conversation between the officer and [the appellant].

"48. The Crown Court gave proper consideration to the appropriate question 'can the Appellant have a fair trial in these particular circumstances?' … It considered whether there was a requirement to preserve the CCTV evidence pending the outcome of the case. On the evidence before it the Crown Court observed 'nobody, apparently, thought this video tape was relevant or significant at all.' The Court was entitled to take into account the fact that the defendant's legal advisors had been involved in a substantial number of such cases and that with all 'of that experience and knowledge nobody thought this was a significant feature of the case until the cross-examination of the officer at trial.'"

The answers to both questions were "no". Appeal dismissed.

DPP v Spalluto

[2015] EWHC 2211 (Admin), 23 June 2015, QBD (Admin)

The prosecution's failure to serve CCTV footage with audio was not a proper basis for accepting a defence argument that the defendant could not have a fair trial without it.

A motorist had been charged with failing without reasonable excuse to provide a specimen of breath for analysis, contrary to s 7(6), Road Traffic Act 1988. Numerous points were raised by the defence, including whether the officer had warned the respondent about the consequences of failing to provide (he could not remember having been warned), and, if so, whether the respondent had understood the warning, his first language not being English. There were numerous hearings and trial dates vacated. The prosecution served a CCTV recording, which had no sound. At a case management hearing, the court set a deadline for serving the CCTV with audio, or confirming that such a recording did not exist. That order was not complied with. The justices found that the defendant was prejudiced by the absence of CCTV with audio and could not have a fair trial. They stayed the proceedings as an abuse of process. The prosecution appealed.

QUESTION(S) FOR THE COURT: Whether the justices were justified in staying the proceedings as an abuse of process in so far as they found that the respondent could not have a fair trial.

HELD: 20. … in [*DPP v Petrie* [2015] EWHC 48 (Admin), page 587] … there was a straightforward issue as to the validity of the statutory process but the court made the point … that even without CCTV, which might of course help the prosecution rather than the defence, in a given case fairness to the prosecution is as important as fairness to the defence in considering whether there is an abuse of process in that the defendant could not have a fair trial. The issue would be dealt with through evidence given by the police officers who administered the procedure and it is a matter which the defence would rely on that there was a failure to produce CCTV and this might have shown that he was correct. It is also to be noted that he was not raising a positive defence that it was not properly administered, merely that he could not recall that it had been and that might have something to do, no doubt, with his difficulty with the English language. Again, that is a matter that could be gone into, no doubt would be gone into with the police officers who administered the necessary process.

"22. … we should follow the approach in *Petrie* and apply the way in which the court dealt with this, in particular in paragraph 35 of the judgment, where this was said:

> 'Secondly, the trial should and could have proceeded on the basis of the available evidence. The prosecution would have called the police officer who was present at court and the defence could, if they so chose, have called the respondent. The burden of proof was on the Crown to prove the case to the requisite criminal standard of proof and against the background that if there was or might have been any relevant failure of procedure the respondent would have been entitled to an acquittal.
>
> 'Furthermore, the respondent could have properly made play of the fact that the CCTV footage which he had requested was not available through no fault of his own. In this way the trial process could safely and fairly have dealt with the hole in the case arising from the prosecution failure.
>
> 'Having weighed all these matters in accordance with the burden and standard of proof, the magistrates could fairly have concluded the trial, and depending on the view they took, either acquitted or convicted the respondent. Underlying this approach was the recognition and emphasis that is saved for an exceptional remedy of last resort.'

"23. Those observations apply, in my judgment, perhaps with added force, to the circumstances of this case."

The answer to the question was "no". Appeal allowed.

14. VERDICTS

Macphail v DPP

Unreported, CO/80/96, 1 July 1996, QBD (DC)

A Crown Court is bound by an acquittal in a magistrates' court.

Magistrates had dismissed an allegation against a motorist of driving with excess alcohol, contrary to s 5(1)(a), Road Traffic Act 1988, but convicted him of driving whilst unfit, contrary to s 4(1), Road Traffic Act 1988. Both alleged offences had arisen out of the same episode. The motorist had been to a wine bar on his way home; he said he had drunk three glasses of wine before continuing his journey home. He was seen driving erratically and collided with a lamp post. A neighbour arrived at the scene and took him home, where, he said, he consumed more alcohol. The police arrived; the motorist was taken to hospital; blood analysis revealed 265 mg alcohol in 100 ml blood.

The justices found he had drunk three large glasses of wine; he had been weaving and drifting from side to side while driving, resulting in the collision; alcohol had been smelt on his breath; he had been drinking before he drove, which impaired his ability to drive. They found him guilty of driving whilst unfit.

He appealed to the Crown Court, which "accepted the evidence of the Appellant's expert witnesses that if the Appellant had drunk only three glasses of wine … prior to driving (as he said he did in the witness box) … he would have been perfectly fit to drive. We did not find that evidence of any assistance to us because the Appellant had consumed far more alcohol than he had stated as we did not accept that the Appellant had consumed the amount of alcohol he claimed after he had ceased to drive. Blood alcohol concentration of about 3–4 time[s] the legal limit was clearly evidence that the Appellant was unfit to drive. Although we accepted that the Appellant had drunk some alcohol after the accident, he had failed to prove on a balance of probabilities that it was solely the post-driving consumption of alcohol which had made him unfit to drive …".

The Crown Court dismissed the appeal. The motorist appealed further.

QUESTION(S) FOR THE COURT: (1) Whether the court was right to hold that as a matter of law it could not be told the reasons why the appellant was acquitted of the s 5(1)(a) offence; (2) whether the court was bound by the appellant's acquittal and whether it was bound to accept that the appellant had not committed the offence of which he had been acquitted.

HELD: "… [Counsel for the appellant] submits that his client had been acquitted by a court of competent jurisdiction of the charge of driving with excess alcohol, and that acquittal was binding upon the Crown Court. It was not open to the Crown Court to regard itself as not bound by that acquittal nor could the Crown Court in its own trial process make any finding which ran counter to the acquittal or undermined it … The Justices in terms had found that when the appellant was driving he had consumed only three glasses of wine and, consequently, was not over the limit. Hence their dismissal of the first charge.

"By making the finding that the Appellant must have had more than three glasses of wine prior to driving the Crown Court effectively found that the Appellant was over the limit in direct contradiction of the acquittal by the Magistrates. That submitted [counsel for the Appellant] was a flawed … process in the Crown Court.

"… The Crown Court … fell into error … It is an irresistible inference from the fact that the Justices dismissed the blood/alcohol charge and that they were not satisfied that the analysis reading represented the level at the time of driving or anything like it. The finding [of the Crown Court that the Appellant had failed to rebut the presumption that the amount of alcohol in his blood specimen was the same as the amount of alcohol in his blood at the time of driving] ran counter to the acquittal and was not open to the Crown Court …".

The answer to question (a) was "no"; the answer to question (2) was "yes". Appeal allowed.

DPP v Chajed

[2013] EWHC 188 (Admin), [2013] 2 Cr App R 6, [2013] Crim LR 603, 17 January 2013, QBD (DC)

Magistrates may not revise a verdict on the basis of submissions made after they announce their verdict.

A motorist had been charged with failing without reasonable excuse to provide specimens of breath for analysis, contrary to s 7(6), Road Traffic Act 1988. At the trial, it was accepted that the officer conducting the procedure did not, as advised in the *pro forma* MG DD/A, ask whether the suspect had brought up anything from his stomach within the preceding 20 minutes.

The magistrates found the motorist guilty. Immediately after the verdict was announced, defence counsel rose, arguing that there had not been a lawful requirement to provide a specimen since the question had not been put. Without giving the prosecutor any opportunity to make submissions on this point, and without saying they were going to reconsider their verdict, the bench retired. They returned soon after and substituted a verdict of not guilty. The prosecutor appealed.

QUESTION(S) FOR THE COURT: (1) Whether the magistrates were wrong to reconsider their verdict once they had announced their original verdict. (2) Whether, if they were not wrong in law to reconsider their verdict, they were wrong in law to find the defendant not guilty, given their finding that there was no lawful requirement to provide a specimen because of procedural irregularity.

HELD: "20. … This case concerns, not an infraction of the statutory provisions, but a failure to follow the step-by-step approach of Form MG DD/A. Whilst no doubt the form provides a helpful guide to the statutory procedures, it does not have any statutory force itself … In any event, a failure to follow the guidance can only possibly affect the reliability of any specimen in fact provided: it does not have any possible relevance where, as in this case, the charge involves a failure to provide a specimen at all. …

"23. … the only power under which the magistrates could reconsider their decision was s.142 [Magistrates' Courts Act 1980 – powers of magistrates' court to re-open cases to rectify mistakes, etc]. However, the purpose and scope of the provisions in that section are very limited. …

"26. … where there has been a simple mistake (or something akin to such), s.142 enables a magistrates' court to rectify it … However, … once a guilty verdict has been pronounced … it does not enable a convicted defendant to make further submissions with a view to persuading the bench to change its mind and substitute a not guilty verdict … nor does it empower the court to hear such submissions with a view to their mind being turned. … it is … antagonistic to the principle of finality in justice for a defendant in the face of a pronounced guilty verdict to seek to re-argue a point in that way. If the magistrates have got a decision wrong on the merits of the submissions made to them, then the appropriate course for the offended party is to appeal to the Crown Court or by way of case stated to this court.

"27. In this particular case, the magistrates' reconsideration of their verdict on its merits was compounded by their procedural failure – serious, in my view – to give the prosecution an opportunity to respond to the submissions made on behalf of the defendant. Had that opportunity been given and the prosecution made submissions, then, upon their reconsideration, perhaps the magistrates would not have proceeded to find the defendant not guilty.

The answers to both questions were "yes". Appeal allowed.

R v Roberts (Samantha Ann)

[2016] EWCA Crim 502, 4 February 2016, CA (Crim)

On the facts, the jury had not been pressurised to return a majority verdict.

A motorist had been charged with causing death by careless driving when under the influence of alcohol, contrary to s 3A(1)(b), Road Traffic Act 1988. Evidence had been given over a Wednesday and Thursday. On the Friday, the jury retired at 13.09. After 2 hours 20 minutes, the judge raised with counsel the question of a majority direction. Six minutes later, the jury returned and was given a majority direction, together with a direction that they were not under pressure to reach a verdict that afternoon. Some 8 minutes later they returned a verdict of guilty by a majority of 10 to 2. The motorist appealed.

GROUND OF APPEAL: The majority direction was not in proper form and put improper pressure on the jury by reason of its timing.

HELD: "14. The real complaint here is that in giving the jury the majority direction just before 4 o'clock on a Friday afternoon the judge put unnecessary pressure on them and therefore the resulting conviction is arguably unsafe. …

"15. It is said that the speed with which the jury returned their verdict demonstrates that they felt under pressure. We disagree; it simply demonstrates that the jury had, at that stage, reached a verdict upon which at least 10 of them had already agreed. In the light of the issues they had to determine this was not surprising. … the case was sensitive and emotionally difficult but it was not complex. Furthermore, the judge had made it crystal clear that there was no pressure on the jury to reach a verdict that afternoon. He said in terms: '… it is Friday afternoon, I appreciate ... but the fact that I am giving you this direction should not be taken by you to put any pressure on you at all to reach a verdict in the time that is allowed today'.

"16. He then went on to explain to them they would sit until the normal time of 4.15 or 4.30 and they would not, in the manner of old practice, be expected to stay in retirement over the weekend. …

"17. It is … not arguable that that direction put the jury under pressure; on the contrary it did the opposite and in those circumstances we find there is no arguable ground to appeal in relation to the conviction."

Appeal dismissed.

15. PERVERTING THE COURSE OF JUSTICE BY AVOIDING DETECTION

R v Clark (Mark)

[2003] EWCA Crim 991, [2003] 2 Cr App R 23, 4 April 2003, CA (Crim)

Driving away after a road accident so as to avoid detection of excess alcohol did not amount to an act tending and intended to pervert the course of public justice.

A driver who was under the influence of alcohol knocked over and killed a cyclist. There were no witnesses, and the driver drove away. He reported the accident the next morning, when he was no longer under the influence of alcohol. He said he thought he had hit a badger, and admitted he had drunk 7 or 8 pints the night before. He was charged with doing an act tending and intended to pervert the course of public justice, and appealed against conviction.

GROUNDS OF APPEAL: The facts alleged by the Crown could not constitute the offence alleged.

HELD: "10. Perverting the course of justice is a common law offence which covers a wide variety of situations …. There is no closed list of acts which may give rise to the offence and it would be wrong to confine it to the specific instances or categories which have so far appeared in the reported cases. The offence undoubtedly covers fabricating, concealing or destroying evidence with intent to influence the outcome of criminal proceedings, which include criminal investigations. Fabrication and destruction of evidence are likely to involve positive acts which will obviously fall within the ambit of the offence. Concealment is more difficult. It may involve a positive act such as hiding a body or a weapon … There is authority however that some positive act is required. That is implicit in the definition of the offence with its reference to doing an act or embarking on a course of conduct …

"12. There is little doubt that the offence has not so far been extended to cover facts such as those in this case. …

"16. … the appellant's actions after the accident provided ample evidence of intent to commit the offence. However it is important not to allow this to obscure the need to identify and examine the act or course of conduct relied on as tending to pervert the course of justice (i.e. the *actus reus*). …

"18. The essence of the Crown's argument is that the appellant concealed evidence that he had excess alcohol in his blood. We do not accept that the logic of this argument is that every driver who is over the limit must hand himself in to avoid prosecution for perverting the course of justice … because no-one is required to incriminate himself in this way. … Charging a man who has simply gone home in this way with this serious criminal offence cannot be justified. Without more he has not perverted the course of justice.

Appeal allowed.

Appendices

ROAD TRAFFIC ACT 1988, SECTIONS 3A TO 11

[1]3A.— Causing death by careless driving when under influence of drink or drugs

(1) If a person causes the death of another person by driving a mechanically propelled vehicle on a road or other public place without due care and attention, or without reasonable consideration for other persons using the road or place, and—

(a) he is, at the time when he is driving, unfit to drive through drink or drugs, or

(b) he has consumed so much alcohol that the proportion of it in his breath, blood or urine at that time exceeds the prescribed limit, or

[2](ba) he has in his body a specified controlled drug and the proportion of it in his blood or urine at that time exceeds the specified limit for that drug, or

(c) he is, within 18 hours after that time, required to provide a specimen in pursuance of section 7 of this Act, but without reasonable excuse fails to provide it, [or

(d) he is required by a constable to give his permission for a laboratory test of a specimen of blood taken from him under section 7A of this Act, but without reasonable excuse fails to do so,[3]]

he is guilty of an offence.

(2) For the purposes of this section a person shall be taken to be unfit to drive at any time when his ability to drive properly is impaired.

(3) Subsection (1)(b) [,(ba)[4]] [, (c) and (d)[5]] above shall not apply in relation to a person driving a mechanically propelled vehicle other than a motor vehicle.

4.— Driving, or being in charge, when under influence of drink or drugs

(1) A person who, when driving or attempting to drive a [mechanically propelled vehicle[6]] on a road or other public place, is unfit to drive through drink or drugs is guilty of an offence.

(2) Without prejudice to subsection (1) above, a person who, when in charge of a [mechanically propelled vehicle[7]] which is on a road or other public place, is unfit to drive through drink or drugs is guilty of an offence.

(3) For the purposes of subsection (2) above, a person shall be deemed not to have been in charge of a [mechanically propelled vehicle[8]] if he proves that at the material time the

---

1 Section 3A inserted by Road Traffic Act 1991, s 3, in force 1 July 1992.

2 Paragraph (ba) inserted by Crime and Courts Act 2013, Sch 22, para 2(2), in force in England and Wales 2 March 2015.

3 Words in square brackets inserted by Road Safety Act 2006, s 31(2), in force 24 September 2007.

4 Paragraph number in square brackets inserted by Crime and Courts Act 2013, Sch 22, para 2(3), in force in England and Wales 2 March 2015.

5 Words in square brackets substituted by Road Safety Act 2006, s 31(3), in force 24 September 2007.

6 Words in square brackets substituted by Road Traffic Act 1991, s 4, in force 1 July 1992.

7 *Ibid.*

8 *Ibid.*

circumstances were such that there was no likelihood of his driving it so long as he remained unfit to drive through drink or drugs.
(4) The court may, in determining whether there was such a likelihood as is mentioned in subsection (3) above, disregard any injury to him and any damage to the vehicle.
(5) For the purposes of this section, a person shall be taken to be unfit to drive if his ability to drive properly is for the time being impaired.
[9]

5.— Driving or being in charge of a motor vehicle with alcohol concentration above prescribed limit

(1) If a person—

(a) drives or attempts to drive a motor vehicle on a road or other public place, or
(b) is in charge of a motor vehicle on a road or other public place,

after consuming so much alcohol that the proportion of it in his breath, blood or urine exceeds the prescribed limit he is guilty of an offence.
(2) It is a defence for a person charged with an offence under subsection (1)(b) above to prove that at the time he is alleged to have committed the offence the circumstances were such that there was no likelihood of his driving the vehicle whilst the proportion of alcohol in his breath, blood or urine remained likely to exceed the prescribed limit.
(3) The court may, in determining whether there was such a likelihood as is mentioned in subsection (2) above, disregard any injury to him and any damage to the vehicle.

[10]5A.— Driving or being in charge of a motor vehicle with concentration of specified controlled drug above specified limit

(1) This section applies where a person ("D")—

(a) drives or attempts to drive a motor vehicle on a road or other public place, or
(b) is in charge of a motor vehicle on a road or other public place,

and there is in D's body a specified controlled drug.
(2) D is guilty of an offence if the proportion of the drug in D's blood or urine exceeds the specified limit for that drug.
(3) It is a defence for a person ("D") charged with an offence under this section to show that—

(a) the specified controlled drug had been prescribed or supplied to D for medical or dental purposes,
(b) D took the drug in accordance with any directions given by the person by whom the drug was prescribed or supplied, and with any accompanying instructions (so far as consistent with any such directions) given by the manufacturer or distributor of the drug, and
(c) D's possession of the drug immediately before taking it was not unlawful under section 5(1) of the Misuse of Drugs Act 1971 (restriction of possession of controlled drugs) because of an exemption in regulations made under section 7 of that Act (authorisation of activities otherwise unlawful under foregoing provisions).

(4) The defence in subsection (3) is not available if D's actions were—

---

[9] Subsections (6)–(8), and an earlier version of s 4 applying to Scotland only, repealed by Serious Organised Crime and Police Act 2005, Sch 7(1), para 27(2), in force 1 January 2006.

[10] Section 5A inserted by Crime and Courts Act 2013, s 56, in force in England and Wales 2 March 2015.

(a) contrary to any advice, given by the person by whom the drug was prescribed or supplied, about the amount of time that should elapse between taking the drug and driving a motor vehicle, or
(b) contrary to any accompanying instructions about that matter (so far as consistent with any such advice) given by the manufacturer or distributor of the drug.

(5) If evidence is adduced that is sufficient to raise an issue with respect to the defence in subsection (3), the court must assume that the defence is satisfied unless the prosecution proves beyond reasonable doubt that it is not.

(6) It is a defence for a person ("D") charged with an offence by virtue of subsection (1)(b) to prove that at the time D is alleged to have committed the offence the circumstances were such that there was no likelihood of D driving the vehicle whilst the proportion of the specified controlled drug in D's blood or urine remained likely to exceed the specified limit for that drug.

(7) The court may, in determining whether there was such a likelihood, disregard any injury to D and any damage to the vehicle.

(8) In this section, and in sections 3A, 6C(1), 6D and 10, "specified" means specified in regulations made—
(a) by the Secretary of State, in relation to driving or attempting to drive, or being in charge of a vehicle, in England and Wales;
(b) by the Scottish Ministers, in relation to driving or attempting to drive, or being in charge of a vehicle, in Scotland.

(9) A limit specified under subsection (2) may be zero.

[11]6.— Power to administer preliminary tests

(1) If any of subsections (2) to (5) applies a constable may require a person to co-operate with any one or more preliminary tests administered to the person by that constable or another constable.

(2) This subsection applies if a constable reasonably suspects that the person—
(a) is driving, is attempting to drive or is in charge of a motor vehicle on a road or other public place, and
(b) has alcohol or a drug in his body or is under the influence of a drug.

(3) This subsection applies if a constable reasonably suspects that the person—
(a) has been driving, attempting to drive or in charge of a motor vehicle on a road or other public place while having alcohol or a drug in his body or while unfit to drive because of a drug, and
(b) still has alcohol or a drug in his body or is still under the influence of a drug.

(4) This subsection applies if a constable reasonably suspects that the person—
(a) is or has been driving, attempting to drive or in charge of a motor vehicle on a road or other public place, and
(b) has committed a traffic offence while the vehicle was in motion.

(5) This subsection applies if—
(a) an accident occurs owing to the presence of a motor vehicle on a road or other public place, and
(b) a constable reasonably believes that the person was driving, attempting to drive or in charge of the vehicle at the time of the accident.

(6) A person commits an offence if without reasonable excuse he fails to co-operate with a preliminary test in pursuance of a requirement imposed under this section.

---

[11] Sections 6–6E substituted by Railways and Transport Safety Act 2003, Sch 7, para 1, in force in part 29 March 2004, the remainder, 30 March 2004.

(7) A constable may administer a preliminary test by virtue of any of subsections (2) to (4) only if he is in uniform.

(8) In this section—

- (a) a reference to a preliminary test is to any of the tests described in sections 6A to 6C, and
- (b) "traffic offence" means an offence under—
  - (i) a provision of Part II of the Public Passenger Vehicles Act 1981 (c. 14),
  - (ii) a provision of the Road Traffic Regulation Act 1984 (c. 27),
  - (iii) a provision of the Road Traffic Offenders Act 1988 (c. 53) other than a provision of Part III, or
  - (iv) a provision of this Act other than a provision of Part V.

6A.— Preliminary breath test

(1) A preliminary breath test is a procedure whereby the person to whom the test is administered provides a specimen of breath to be used for the purpose of obtaining, by means of a device of a type approved by the Secretary of State, an indication whether the proportion of alcohol in the person's breath or blood is likely to exceed the prescribed limit.

[12](2) A preliminary breath test administered in reliance on section 6(2) to (4) may be administered only at or near the place where the requirement to co-operate with the test is imposed.

(3) A preliminary breath test administered in reliance on section 6(5) may be administered—

- (a) at or near the place where the requirement to co-operate with the test is imposed, or
- (b) if the constable who imposes the requirement thinks it expedient, at a police station specified by him.

6B.— Preliminary impairment test

(1) A preliminary impairment test is a procedure whereby the constable administering the test—

- (a) observes the person to whom the test is administered in his performance of tasks specified by the constable, and
- (b) makes such other observations of the person's physical state as the constable thinks expedient.

(2) The Secretary of State shall issue (and may from time to time revise) a code of practice about—

- (a) the kind of task that may be specified for the purpose of a preliminary impairment test,
- (b) the kind of observation of physical state that may be made in the course of a preliminary impairment test,
- (c) the manner in which a preliminary impairment test should be administered, and
- (d) the inferences that may be drawn from observations made in the course of a preliminary impairment test.

(3) In issuing or revising the code of practice the Secretary of State shall aim to ensure that a preliminary impairment test is designed to indicate—

- (a) whether a person is unfit to drive, and
- (b) if he is, whether or not his unfitness is likely to be due to drink or drugs.

---

[12] Subsections (2) and (3) added by Railways and Transport Safety Act 2003, Sch 7, para 1, in force in part 29 March 2004, the remainder, 30 March 2004.

(4) A preliminary impairment test may be administered—

(a) at or near the place where the requirement to co-operate with the test is imposed, or

(b) if the constable who imposes the requirement thinks it expedient, at a police station specified by him.

(5) A constable administering a preliminary impairment test shall have regard to the code of practice under this section.

(6) A constable may administer a preliminary impairment test only if he is approved for that purpose by the chief officer of the police force to which he belongs.

(7) A code of practice under this section may include provision about—

(a) the giving of approval under subsection (6), and

(b) in particular, the kind of training that a constable should have undergone, or the kind of qualification that a constable should possess, before being approved under that subsection.

6C.— Preliminary drug test

(1) A preliminary drug test is a procedure by which a specimen of sweat or saliva is—

(a) obtained, and

(b) used for the purpose of obtaining, by means of a device of a type approved by the Secretary of State, an indication whether the person to whom the test is administered has a drug [in his body and if so—

(i) whether it is a specified controlled drug;

(ii) if it is, whether the proportion of it in the person's blood or urine is likely to exceed the specified limit for that drug.[13]]

(2) A preliminary drug test may be administered—

(a) at or near the place where the requirement to co-operate with the test is imposed, or

(b) if the constable who imposes the requirement thinks it expedient, at a police station specified by him.

[14](3) Up to three preliminary drug tests may be administered.

6D.— Arrest

(1) A constable may arrest a person without warrant if as a result of a preliminary breath test [or preliminary drug test the constable reasonably suspects that—

(a) the proportion of alcohol in the person's breath or blood exceeds the prescribed limit, or

(b) the person has a specified controlled drug in his body and the proportion of it in the person's blood or urine exceeds the specified limit for that drug.[15]]

[16](1A) The fact that specimens of breath have been provided under section 7 of this Act by the person concerned does not prevent subsection (1) above having effect if the constable who imposed on him the requirement to provide the specimens has reasonable cause to

---

[13] Words in square brackets inserted by Crime and Courts Act 2013, Sch 22, para 3(2), in force in England and Wales 2 March 2015.

[14] Subsection (3) inserted by Crime and Courts Act 2013, Sch 22, para 3(3), in force in England and Wales 2 March 2015.

[15] Words in square brackets substituted by Crime and Courts Act 2013, Sch 22, para 4, in force in England and Wales 2 March 2015.

[16] Subsection 1A inserted by Serious Organised Crime and Police Act 2005, s 154(2), in force 1 July 2005.

believe that the device used to analyse the specimens has not produced a reliable indication of the proportion of alcohol in the breath of the person.

(2) A constable may arrest a person without warrant if—

(a) the person fails to co-operate with a preliminary test in pursuance of a requirement imposed under section 6, and

(b) the constable reasonably suspects that the person has alcohol or a drug in his body or is under the influence of a drug.

[17](2A) A person arrested under this section may, instead of being taken to a police station, be detained at or near the place where the preliminary test was, or would have been, administered, with a view to imposing on him there a requirement under section 7 of this Act.

(3) A person may not be arrested under this section while at a hospital as a patient.

6E.— Power of entry

(1) A constable may enter any place (using reasonable force if necessary) for the purpose of—

(a) imposing a requirement by virtue of section 6(5) following an accident in a case where the constable reasonably suspects that the accident involved injury of any person, or

(b) arresting a person under section 6D following an accident in a case where the constable reasonably suspects that the accident involved injury of any person.

(2) This section—

(a) does not extend to Scotland, and

(b) is without prejudice to any rule of law or enactment about the right of a constable in Scotland to enter any place.

7.— Provision of specimens for analysis

(1) In the course of an investigation into whether a person has committed an offence under [section 3A, 4 or[18]] 5 of this Act a constable may, subject to the following provisions of this section and section 9 of this Act, require him—

(a) to provide two specimens of breath for analysis by means of a device of a type approved by the Secretary of State, or

(b) to provide a specimen of blood or urine for a laboratory test.

[19](1A) In the course of an investigation into whether a person has committed an offence under section 5A of this Act a constable may, subject to subsections (3) to (7) of this section and section 9 of this Act, require the person to provide a specimen of blood or urine for a laboratory test.

[20](2) A constable may make a requirement under this section to provide specimens of breath only if—

(a) the requirement is made at a police station or a hospital,

---

[17] Subsection 2A inserted by Serious Organised Crime and Police Act 2005, s 154(3), in force 1 July 2005. For the wording applying in Scotland, see Criminal Justice (Scotland) Act 2016, Sch 2, para 36, in force 25 January 2018.

[18] Words in square brackets substituted by Road Traffic Act 1991, Sch 4, para 42(a), in force 1 July 1992.

[19] Subsection (1A) inserted by Crime and Courts Act 2013, Sch 22, para 5(2), in force in England and Wales 2 March 2015.

[20] Subsections (2)–(2D) substituted for subs (2) by Serious Organised Crime and Police Act 2005, s 154(5), in force 1 July 2005. Subsection (2) further substituted by Deregulation Act 2015, Sch 11, pt 1, para 3(2), in force 10 April 2015.

(b) the requirement is imposed in circumstances where section 6(5) of this Act applies, or

(c) the constable is in uniform.

21

(2C) Where a constable has imposed a requirement on the person concerned to co-operate with a relevant breath test at any place, he is entitled to remain at or near that place in order to impose on him there a requirement under this section.

[22](2CA) For the purposes of subsection (2C) "a relevant breath test" is a procedure involving the provision by the person concerned of a specimen of breath to be used for the purpose of obtaining an indication whether the proportion of alcohol in his breath or blood is likely to exceed the prescribed limit.

(2D) If a requirement under subsection (1)(a) above has been made at a place other than at a police station, such a requirement may subsequently be made at a police station if (but only if)—

(a) a device or a reliable device of the type mentioned in subsection (1)(a) above was not available at that place or it was for any other reason not practicable to use such a device there, or

(b) the constable who made the previous requirement has reasonable cause to believe that the device used there has not produced a reliable indication of the proportion of alcohol in the breath of the person concerned.

(3) A requirement under this section to provide a specimen of blood or urine can only be made at a police station or at a hospital; and it cannot be made at a police station unless—

(a) the constable making the requirement has reasonable cause to believe that for medical reasons a specimen of breath cannot be provided or should not be required, or

(b) [specimens of breath have not been provided elsewhere and[23]] at the time the requirement is made a device or a reliable device of the type mentioned in subsection (1)(a) above is not available at the police station or it is then for any other reason not practicable to use such a device there, or

[24](bb) a device of the type mentioned in subsection (1)(a) above has been used [(at the police station or elsewhere)[25]] but the constable who required the specimens of breath has reasonable cause to believe that the device has not produced a reliable indication of the proportion of alcohol in the breath of the person concerned, or

[26](bc) as a result of the administration of a preliminary drug test, the constable making the requirement has reasonable cause to believe that the person required to provide a specimen of blood or urine has a drug in his body, or

---

21 Subsections (2A) and (2B) omitted by Deregulation Act 2015, Sch 11, pt 1, para 3(3), in force 10 April 2015.

22 Subsection (2CA) inserted by Deregulation Act 2015, Sch 11, pt 2, para 3(4), in force 10 April 2015.

23 Words in square brackets inserted by Serious Organised Crime and Police Act 2005, s 154(6)(a), in force 1 July 2005.

24 Paragraph (bb) inserted by Criminal Procedure and Investigations Act 1996, s 63(1), in force 1 April 1997.

25 Words in square brackets substituted by Serious Organised Crime and Police Act 2005, s 154(6)(b), in force 1 July 2005.

26 Paragraph (bc) inserted by Railways and Transport Safety Act 2003, Sch 7, para 2, in force 30 March 2004.

(c) the suspected offence is one under section 3A [, 4 or 5A[27]]of this Act and the constable making the requirement has been advised by a medical practitioner [or a registered health care professional[28]] that the condition of the person required to provide the specimen might be due to some drug;

but may then be made notwithstanding that the person required to provide the specimen has already provided or been required to provide two specimens of breath.

(4) If the provision of a specimen other than a specimen of breath may be required in pursuance of this section the question whether it is to be a specimen of blood or a specimen of urine [and, in the case of a specimen of blood, the question who is to be asked to take it shall be decided (subject to subsection (4A)) by the constable making the requirement[29]].

[30](4A) Where a constable decides for the purposes of subsection (4) to require the provision of a specimen of blood, there shall be no requirement to provide such a specimen if—

(a) the medical practitioner who is asked to take the specimen is of the opinion that, for medical reasons, it cannot or should not be taken; or

(b) the registered health care professional who is asked to take it is of that opinion and there is no contrary opinion from a medical practitioner;

and, where by virtue of this subsection there can be no requirement to provide a specimen of blood, the constable may require a specimen of urine instead.

(5) A specimen of urine shall be provided within one hour of the requirement for its provision being made and after the provision of a previous specimen of urine.

[31][(5A) A constable may arrest a person without warrant if—

(a) the person fails to provide a specimen of breath when required to do so in pursuance of this section, and

(b) the constable reasonably suspects that the person has alcohol in his body.]

(6) A person who, without reasonable excuse, fails to provide a specimen when required to do so in pursuance of this section is guilty of an offence.

(7) A constable must, on requiring any person to provide a specimen in pursuance of this section, warn him that a failure to provide it may render him liable to prosecution.

[32]7A.— Specimens of blood taken from persons incapable of consenting

(1) A constable may make a request to a [medical or health care practitioner[33]] for him to take a specimen of blood from a person ("the person concerned") irrespective of whether that person consents if—

(a) that person is a person from whom the constable would (in the absence of any incapacity of that person and of any objection under section 9) be entitled under section 7 to require the provision of a specimen of blood for a laboratory test;

(b) it appears to that constable that that person has been involved in an accident that constitutes or is comprised in the matter that is under investigation or the circumstances of that matter;

---

27 Section numbers in square brackets substituted by Crime and Courts Act 2013, Sch 22, para 5(3), in force in England and Wales 2 March 2015.

28 Words in square brackets inserted by Deregulation Act 2015, Sch 11, pt 1, para 5, in force 10 April 2015.

29 Words in square brackets substituted by Police Reform Act 2002, s 55(1), in force 1 April 2003.

30 Subsection (4A) inserted by Police Reform Act 2002 s 55(2), in force 1 April 2003.

31 Subsection (5A) inserted by Deregulation Act 2015, Sch 11, pt 1, para 3(5), in force 10 April 2015.

32 Section 7A inserted by Police Reform Act 2002, s 56(1), in force 1 October 2002.

33 Words in square brackets substituted by Deregulation Act 2015, Sch 11, pt 1, para 8(2), in force 10 April 2015.

(c) it appears to that constable that that person is or may be incapable (whether or not he has purported to do so) of giving a valid consent to the taking of a specimen of blood; and

(d) it appears to that constable that that person's incapacity is attributable to medical reasons.

(2) A request under this section—

(a) shall not be made to a [medical or health care practitioner[34]] who for the time being has any responsibility (apart from the request) for the clinical care of the person concerned; and

(b) shall not be made to [a practitioner other than a police medical or health care practitioner[35]] unless—

(i) it is not reasonably practicable for the request [to be made to a police medical or health care practitioner[36]]; or

(ii) it is not reasonably practicable for such a [[37]] practitioner (assuming him to be willing to do so) to take the specimen.

(3) It shall be lawful for [a medical or health care practitioner[38]] to whom a request is made under this section, if he thinks fit—

(a) to take a specimen of blood from the person concerned irrespective of whether that person consents; and

(b) to provide the sample to a constable.

(4) If a specimen is taken in pursuance of a request under this section, the specimen shall not be subjected to a laboratory test unless the person from whom it was taken—

(a) has been informed that it was taken; and

(b) has been required by a constable to give his permission for a laboratory test of the specimen; and

(c) has given his permission.

(5) A constable must, on requiring a person to give his permission for the purposes of this section for a laboratory test of a specimen, warn that person that a failure to give the permission may render him liable to prosecution.

(6) A person who, without reasonable excuse, fails to give his permission for a laboratory test of a specimen of blood taken from him under this section is guilty of an offence.

[39](7) In this section—

"medical or health care practitioner" means a medical practitioner or a registered health care professional;

"police medical or health care practitioner" means a medical practitioner, or a registered health care professional, who is engaged under any agreement to provide medical or health care services for purposes connected with the activities of a police force.

---

34 Words in square brackets substituted by Deregulation Act 2015, Sch 11, pt 1, para 8(2), in force 10 April 2015.

35 Words in square brackets substituted by Deregulation Act 2015, Sch 11, pt 1, para 8(3), in force 10 April 2015.

36 Words in square brackets substituted by Deregulation Act 2015, Sch 11, pt 1, para 8(4), in force 10 April 2015.

37 Word "medical" omitted by Deregulation Act 2015, Sch 11, pt 1, para 8(5), in force 10 April 2015.

38 Words in square brackets substituted by Deregulation Act 2015, Sch 11, pt 1, para 8(6), in force 10 April 2015.

39 Subsection (7) substituted by Deregulation Act 2015, Sch 11, pt 1, para 8(7), in force 10 April 2015.

8.— Breath specimen showing higher alcohol level to be disregarded[40]

(1) [ ][41] Of any two specimens of breath provided by any person in pursuance of section 7 of this Act that with the lower proportion of alcohol in the breath shall be used and the other shall be disregarded.

9.— Protection for hospital patients

(1) While a person is at a hospital as a patient he shall not be required [to co-operate with a preliminary test[42]] or to provide a specimen [under section 7 of this Act[43]] unless the medical practitioner in immediate charge of his case has been notified of the proposal to make the requirement; and—

(a) if the requirement is then made, [it shall be for co-operation with a test administered, or for the provision of a specimen, at the hospital[44]], but

(b) if the medical practitioner objects on the ground specified in subsection (2) below, the requirement shall not be made.

[45](1A) While a person is at a hospital as a patient, no specimen of blood shall be taken from him under section 7A of this Act and he shall not be required to give his permission for a laboratory test of a specimen taken under that section unless the medical practitioner in immediate charge of his case—

(a) has been notified of the proposal to take the specimen or to make the requirement; and

(b) has not objected on the ground specified in subsection (2).

(2) The ground on which the medical practitioner may object is—

(a) in a case falling within subsection (1), that the requirement or the provision of the specimen or (if one is required) the warning required by section 7(7) of this Act would be prejudicial to the proper care and treatment of the patient; and

(b) in a case falling within subsection (1A), that the taking of the specimen, the requirement or the warning required by section 7A(5) of this Act would be so prejudicial.

10.— Detention of persons affected by alcohol or a drug

(1) Subject to subsections (2) and (3) below, a person required [under section 7 or 7A[46]] to provide a specimen of breath, blood or urine may afterwards be detained at a police station [(or, if the specimen was provided otherwise than at a police station, arrested and taken to and detained at a police station) if a constable has reasonable grounds for believing[47]] that,

---

40 Subsections (2), (2A), (3) and (4) omitted, and s 8 re-titled by Deregulation Act 2015, Sch 11, pt 1, para 1(1) and (3), in force 10 April 2015.

41 Words omitted by Deregulation Act 2015, Sch 11, pt 1, para 1(3), in force 10 April 2015.

42 Words in square brackets substituted by Railways and Transport Safety Act 2003, Sch 7, para 3(a), in force 30 March 2004.

43 Words in square brackets substituted by Serious Organised Crime and Police Act 2005, s 154(8), in force 1 July 2005.

44 Words in square brackets substituted by Railways and Transport Safety Act 2003, Sch 7, para 3(b), in force 30 March 2004.

45 Subsections (1A)–(2) substituted for subs (2) by Police Reform Act 2002, s 56(2), in force 1 October 2002.

46 Words in square brackets inserted by Railways and Transport Safety Act 2003, Sch 7 para 4, in force 30 March 2004.

47 Words in square brackets substituted by Serious Organised Crime and Police Act 2005, s 154(10)(a), in force 1 July 2005.

were that person then driving or attempting to drive a [mechanically propelled vehicle[48]] on a road, he would [commit[49]] an offence under section 4 [, 5 or 5A[50]] of this Act.
(2) [Subsection (1) above does not apply to the person if it ought reasonably to appear to the[51]] constable that there is no likelihood of his driving or attempting to drive a [mechanically propelled vehicle[52]] [whilst—

(a) the person's ability to drive properly is impaired,
(b) the proportion of alcohol in the person's breath, blood or urine exceeds the prescribed limit, or
(c) the proportion of a specified controlled drug in the person's blood or urine exceeds the specified limit for that drug.[53]]

[54](2A) A person who is at a hospital as a patient shall not be arrested and taken from there to a police station in pursuance of this section if it would be prejudicial to his proper care and treatment as a patient.
(3) A constable must consult a medical practitioner on any question arising under this section whether a person's ability to drive properly is or might be impaired through drugs and must act on the medical practitioner's advice.

11.— Interpretation of sections 4 to 10
(1) The following provisions apply for the interpretation of [sections 3A to 10[55]] of this Act.
(2) In those sections—

[56]

[57]"controlled drug" has the meaning given by section 2 of the Misuse of Drugs Act 1971,
"drug" includes any intoxicant other than alcohol,
"fail" includes refuse,
"hospital" means an institution which provides medical or surgical treatment for in-patients or out-patients,
"the prescribed limit" means, as the case may require—

(a) 35 microgrammes of alcohol in 100 millilitres of breath,
(b) 80 milligrammes of alcohol in 100 millilitres of blood, or

---

48 Words in square brackets substituted by Road Traffic Act 1991, Sch 4 para 43, in force 1 July 1992.
49 Word in square brackets substituted by Serious Organised Crime and Police Act 2005, s 154(10)(b), in force 1 July 2005.
50 Section numbers in square brackets inserted by Crime and Courts Act 2013, Sch 22, para 6(2), in force in England and Wales 2 March 2015.
51 Words in square brackets substituted by Serious Organised Crime and Police Act 2005, s 154(11), in force 1 July 2005.
52 Words in square brackets substituted by Road Traffic Act 1991, Sch 4 para 43, in force 1 July 1992.
53 Words in square brackets substituted by Crime and Courts Act 2013, Sch 22, para 6(3), in force in England and Wales 2 March 2015.
54 Subsection (2A) inserted by Serious Organised Crime and Police Act 2005, s 154(12), in force 1 July 2005.
55 Numbers in square brackets substituted by Road Traffic Act 1991, Sch 4 para 44, in force 1 July 1992.
56 Definition of "breath test" repealed by Railways and Transport Safety Act 2003, Sch 8 para 1, in force 30 March 2004.
57 Definition inserted by Crime and Courts Act 2013, s 56(2)(a), in force in England and Wales 2 March 2015.

(c) 107 milligrammes of alcohol in 100 millilitres of urine,

or such other proportion as may be prescribed by regulations [...[58]].

[59]"registered health care professional" means a person (other than a medical practitioner) who is—

(a) a registered nurse; or

(b) a registered member of a health care profession which is designated for the purposes of this paragraph by an order made by the Secretary of State.

[60]"specified" in relation to a controlled drug, has the meaning given by s 5A(8).

[61](2ZA) Regulations under subsection (2) may be made—

(a) by the Secretary of State, in relation to driving or attempting to drive, or being in charge of a vehicle, in England and Wales;

(b) by the Scottish Ministers, in relation to driving or attempting to drive, or being in charge of a vehicle, in Scotland.

[62](2A) A health care profession is any profession mentioned in section 60(2) of the Health Act 1999 (c. 8) other than the profession of practising medicine and the profession of nursing.

(2B) An order under subsection (2) shall be made by statutory instrument; and any such statutory instrument shall be subject to annulment in pursuance of a resolution of either House of Parliament.

(3) [A person does not co-operate with a preliminary test or provide a specimen of breath for analysis unless his co-operation or the specimen[63]]—

(a) is sufficient to enable the test or the analysis to be carried out, and

(b) is provided in such a way as to enable the objective of the test or analysis to be satisfactorily achieved.

[64](4) A person provides a specimen of blood if and only if—

(a) he consents to the taking of such a specimen from him; and

(b) the specimen is taken from him [[65]] either by a medical practitioner or by a registered health care professional.

---

[58] Words repealed by Scotland Act 2012, s 20(6), in force 3 July 2012. For the limit in Scotland, see the Road Traffic Act 1988 (Prescribed Limit) (Scotland) Regulations 2014 (SI 2014/328): 22 µg of alcohol in 100 ml of breath; 50 mg alcohol in 100 ml of blood; and 67 mg alcohol in 100 ml of urine.

[59] Definition inserted by Police Reform Act 2002, s 55(3), in force 1 April 2003.

[60] Definition inserted by Crime and Courts Act 2013, s 56(2)(b), in force in England and Wales 2 March 2015.

[61] Subsection 2(ZA) inserted by Scotland Act 2012, s 20(7), in force 3 July 2012.

[62] Subsections (2A) and (2B) inserted by Police Reform Act 2002, s 55(4), in force 1 April 2003.

[63] Words in square brackets substituted by Railways and Transport Safety Act 2003, Sch 7, para 5(b), in force 30 March 2004.

[64] Subsection (4) substituted by Police Reform Act 2002, s 55(5), in force 1 April 2003.

[65] Words omitted by Deregulation Act 2015, Sch 11, pt 1, para 9, in force 10 April 2015.

ROAD TRAFFIC OFFENDERS ACT 1988, SECTIONS 15, 16, 34, 35

15.— Use of specimens in proceedings for an offence under [any of sections 3A to 5A[1]] of the Road Traffic Act

(1) This section and section 16 of this Act apply in respect of proceedings for an offence under [any of sections 3A to 5A[2]] of the Road Traffic Act 1988 (driving offences connected with drink or drugs)[3]]; and expressions used in this section and section 16 of this Act have the same meaning as in [sections 3A to 10[4]] of that Act.

(2) Evidence of the proportion of alcohol or any drug in a specimen of breath, blood or urine provided by [or taken from[5]] the accused shall, in all cases [(including cases where the specimen was not provided [or taken[6]] in connection with the alleged offence)[7]], be taken into account [and—

- (a) it is to be assumed, subject to subsection (3) below, that the proportion of alcohol in the accused's breath, blood or urine at the time of the alleged offence was not less than in the specimen;
- (b) it is to be assumed, subject to subsection (3A) below, that the proportion of a drug in the accused's blood or urine at the time of the alleged offence was not less than in the specimen.[8]]

[9](3) [The assumption in subsection (2)(a) above[10]] shall not be made if the accused proves—

- (a) that he consumed alcohol before he provided the specimen [or had it taken from him[11]] and—
  - (i) in relation to an offence under section 3A, after the time of the alleged offence, and
  - (ii) otherwise, after he had ceased to drive, attempt to drive or be in charge of a vehicle on a road or other public place, and
- (b) that had he not done so the proportion of alcohol in his breath, blood or urine would not have exceeded the prescribed limit and, if it is alleged that he was unfit to drive through drink, would not have been such as to impair his ability to drive properly.

---

1 Words in square brackets inserted by Crime and Courts Act 2013, Sch 22, para 10(2), in force in England and Wales 2 March 2015.

2 Words in square brackets inserted by Crime and Courts Act 2013, Sch 22, para 10(3), in force in England and Wales 2 March 2015.

3 Words in square brackets substituted by Road Traffic Act 1991, Sch 4, para 87(2), in force 1 July 1992.

4 *Ibid.*

5 Words in square brackets inserted by Police Reform Act 2002, s 57(1)(a), in force 1 October 2002.

6 Words in square brackets inserted by Police Reform Act 2002, s 57(1)(b), in force 1 October 2002.

7 Words in square brackets inserted by Road Traffic Act 1991, Sch 4, para 87(3), in force 1 July 1992.

8 Words in square brackets inserted by Crime and Courts Act 2013, Sch 22, para 10(4), in force in England and Wales 2 March 2015.

9 Subsection (3) substituted by Road Traffic Act 1991, Sch 4, para 87(4), in force 1 July 1992.

10 Words in square brackets substituted by Crime and Courts Act 2013, Sch 22, para 10(5), in force in England and Wales 2 March 2015.

11 Words in square brackets inserted by Police Reform Act 2002, s 57(2), in force 1 October 2002.

[12](3A) The assumption in subsection 2(b) above is not to be made if the accused proves—

(a) that he took the drug before he provided the specimen or had the specimen taken from him and—

(i) in relation to an offence under section 3A, after the time of the alleged offence, and

(ii) otherwise, after he had ceased to drive, attempt to drive or be in charge of a vehicle on a road or other public place, and

(b) that had he not done so the proportion of the drug in his blood or urine—

(i) in the case of a specified controlled drug, would not have exceeded the specified limit for that drug, and

(ii) if it is alleged that he was unfit to drive through drugs, would not have been such as to impair his ability to drive properly.

(4) A specimen of blood shall be disregarded [unless—

(a) it was taken from the accused with his consent [by a medical practitioner or a registered health care professional[13]]; or

(b) it was taken from the accused by a medical practitioner [or a registered health care professional[14]] under section 7A of the Road Traffic Act 1988 and the accused subsequently gave his permission for a laboratory test of the specimen.[15]]

(5) Where, at the time a specimen of blood or urine was provided by the accused, he asked to be provided with such a specimen, evidence of the proportion of alcohol or any drug found in the specimen is not admissible on behalf of the prosecution unless—

(a) the specimen in which the alcohol or drug was found is one of two parts into which the specimen provided by the accused was divided at the time it was provided, and

(b) the other part was supplied to the accused.

[16](5A) Where a specimen of blood was taken from the accused under section 7A of the Road Traffic Act 1988, evidence of the proportion of alcohol or any drug found in the specimen is not admissible on behalf of the prosecution unless—

(a) the specimen in which the alcohol or drug was found is one of two parts into which the specimen taken from the accused was divided at the time it was taken; and

(b) any request to be supplied with the other part which was made by the accused at the time when he gave his permission for a laboratory test of the specimen was complied with.

16.— Documentary evidence as to specimens in such proceedings

(1) Evidence of the proportion of alcohol or a drug in a specimen of breath, blood or urine may, subject to subsections (3) and (4) below and to section 15(5) [and (5A)[17]] of this Act, be given by the production of a document or documents purporting to be whichever of the following is appropriate, that is to say—

---

[12] Subsection (3A) inserted by Crime and Courts Act 2013, Sch 22, para 10(6), in force in England and Wales 2 March 2015.

[13] Words in square brackets substituted by Deregulation Act 2015, Sch 11, pt 1, para 10(a), in force 10 April 2015.

[14] Words in square brackets substituted by Deregulation Act 2015, Sch 11, pt 1, para 10(b), in force 10 April 2015.

[15] Words in square brackets substituted by Police Reform Act 2002, s 57(3), in force 1 April 2003.

[16] Subsection (5A) inserted by Police Reform Act 2002, s 57(4), in force 1 October 2002.

[17] Words in square brackets inserted by Police Reform Act 2002, s 57(5), in force 1 October 2002.

(a) a statement automatically produced by the device by which the proportion of alcohol in a specimen of breath was measured and a certificate signed by a constable (which may but need not be contained in the same document as the statement) that the statement relates to a specimen provided by the accused at the date and time shown in the statement, and

(b) a certificate signed by an authorised analyst as to the proportion of alcohol or any drug found in a specimen of blood or urine identified in the certificate.

(2) Subject to subsections (3) and (4) below, evidence that a specimen of blood was taken from the accused with his consent by a medical practitioner [or a registered health care professional[18]] may be given by the production of a document purporting to certify that fact and to be signed by a medical practitioner [or a registered health care professional[19]].

(3) Subject to subsection (4) below—

(a) a document purporting to be such a statement or such a certificate (or both such a statement and such a certificate) as is mentioned in subsection (1)(a) above is admissible in evidence on behalf of the prosecution in pursuance of this section only if a copy of it either has been handed to the accused when the document was produced or has been served on him not later than seven days before the hearing, and

(b) any other document is so admissible only if a copy of it has been served on the accused not later than seven days before the hearing.

(4) A document purporting to be a certificate (or so much of a document as purports to be a certificate) is not so admissible if the accused, not later than three days before the hearing or within such further time as the court may in special circumstances allow, has served notice on the prosecutor requiring the attendance at the hearing of the person by whom the document purports to be signed.

(5) In Scotland—

(a) a document produced in evidence on behalf of the prosecution in pursuance of subsection (1) or (2) above and, where the person by whom the document was signed is called as a witness, the evidence of that person, shall be sufficient evidence of the facts stated in the document, and

(b) a written execution purporting to be signed by the person who handed to or served on the accused or the prosecutor a copy of the document or of the notice in terms of subsection (3) or (4) above, together with, where appropriate, a post office receipt for the registered or recorded delivery letter shall be sufficient evidence of the handing or service of such a copy or notice.

(6) A copy of a certificate required by this section to be served on the accused or a notice required by this section to be served on the prosecutor may[—

(a) if the proceedings mentioned in section 15(1) take place in England and Wales, be served in accordance with Criminal Procedure Rules, or

(b) if the proceedings take place elsewhere,[20]] be served personally or sent by registered post or recorded delivery service.

---

[18] Words in square brackets inserted by Police Reform Act 2002, s 57(6), in force 1 April 2003.

[19] *Ibid.*

[20] Words in square brackets inserted by Judicial Review and Courts Act 2022, Sch 1, para 11(4), in force 28 June 2022.

[21][(6A) Where the proceedings mentioned in section 15(1) of this Act are proceedings before a magistrates' court inquiring into an offence as examining justices this section shall have effect with the omission of subsection (4).]

(7) In this section "authorised analyst" means—

(a) any person possessing the qualifications prescribed by regulations made under [section 27 of the Food Safety Act 1990[22]] as qualifying persons for appointment as public analysts under those Acts, and

(b) any other person authorised by the Secretary of State to make analyses for the purposes of this section.

34.— Disqualification for certain offences

(1) Where a person is convicted of an offence involving obligatory disqualification, the court must order him to be disqualified for such period not less than twelve months as the court thinks fit unless the court for special reasons thinks fit to order him to be disqualified for a shorter period or not to order him to be disqualified.

[23](1A) Where a person is convicted of an offence under section 12A of the Theft Act 1968 (aggravated vehicle-taking), the fact that he did not drive the vehicle in question at any particular time or at all shall not be regarded as a special reason for the purposes of subsection (1) above.

[24](2) Where a person is convicted of an offence involving discretionary disqualification, and either—

(a) the penalty points to be taken into account on that occasion number fewer than twelve, or

(b) the offence is not one involving obligatory endorsement,

the court may order him to be disqualified for such period as the court thinks fit.

(3) Where a person convicted of an offence under any of the following provisions of the Road Traffic Act 1988, that is—

[25](aa) section 3A (causing death by careless driving when under the influence of drink or drugs),

(a) section 4(1) (driving or attempting to drive while unfit),

(b) section 5(1)(a) (driving or attempting to drive with excess alcohol), [...[26]]

[27](ba) section 5A(1)(a) and (2) (driving or attempting to drive with concentration of specified controlled drug above specified limit)

(c) section 7(6) (failing to provide a specimen) where that is an offence involving obligatory disqualification,

[28](d) section 7A(6) (failing to allow a specimen to be subjected to laboratory test) where that is an offence involving obligatory disqualification;

---

21 Subsection (6A) inserted by Criminal Procedure and Investigations Act 1996, s 47, Sch 1, pts II and III, in force 8 March 1997, and repealed for specified purposes by Criminal Justice Act 2003, Sch 37, pt 4.

22 Words in square brackets inserted by Food Safety Act 1990, s 59(1), Sch 3, para 38, in force 1 February 1991.

23 Subsection (1A) inserted by Aggravated Vehicle-Taking Act 1992, s 3(2), in force 1 April 1992.

24 Subsection (2) substituted by Road Traffic Act 1991, s 29(2), in force 1 July 1992.

25 Paragraph (aa) inserted by Road Traffic Act 1991, s 29(3), in force 1 July 1992.

26 Words repealed by Police Reform Act 2002, s 56(3)(a), in force 1 October 2002.

27 Paragraph (ba) inserted by Crime and Courts Act 2013, Sch 22, para 12, in force in England and Wales 2 March 2015.

28 Paragraph (d) inserted by Police Reform Act 2002, s 56(3)(b), in force 1 October 2002.

has within the ten years immediately preceding the commission of the offence [("the new offence")[29]] been convicted of any such offence, subsection (1) above shall apply in relation to him as if the reference to twelve months were a reference to [the period specified in subsection (3A).[30]]

[31](3A) The period is—

(a) six years, where—

(i) an offence of which the person was convicted within the ten years mentioned in subsection (3) falls within paragraph (aa) of that subsection, and

(ii) the new offence also falls within that paragraph;

(b) in any other case (but subject to subsection (4ZA)), three years.

[32](4) Subject to subsection (3) above [and subsection (4ZA) below[33]], subsection (1) above shall apply as if the reference to twelve months were a reference to two years—

(a) in relation to a person convicted of—

(i) manslaughter, or in Scotland culpable homicide, or [34]

[35](iia) an offence under section 1A of [the Road Traffic Act 1988[36]] (causing serious injury by dangerous driving or),

[37](iib) an offence under section 3ZC of that Act (causing death by driving: disqualified drivers), or

(iic) an offence under section 3ZD of that Act (causing serious injury by driving: disqualified drivers),[38]]

(b) in relation to a person on whom more than one disqualification for a fixed period of 56 days or more has been imposed within the three years immediately preceding the commission of the offence.

[39](4ZA) Subsection (1) shall apply as if the reference to twelve months were a reference to five years in relation to a person convicted of—

(a) an offence under section 1 of the Road Traffic Act 1988 (causing death by dangerous driving), or

---

29 Words in square brackets inserted by Police, Crime, Sentencing and Courts Act 2022, ss 86(5)(a), in force 28 June 2022.

30 Words in square brackets substituted by Police, Crime, Sentencing and Courts Act 2022, s 86(5)(b), in force 28 June 2022.

31 Subsection (3A) inserted by Police, Crime, Sentencing and Courts Act 2022, s 86(6), in force 28 June 2022.

32 Subsections (4) and (4A) substituted for subs (4) by Road Traffic Act 1991, s 29(4), in force 1 July 1992.

33 Words in square brackets inserted by Police, Crime, Sentencing and Courts Act 2022, s 86(7)(a), in force 28 June 2022.

34 Subparagraph (ii) repealed by Police, Crime, Sentencing and Courts Act 2022, s 86(7)(b)(i), in force 28 June 2022.

35 Subparagraph (iia) inserted by Legal Aid, Sentencing and Punishment of Offenders Act 2012, Sch 27, para 5, in force 3 December 2012.

36 Words in square brackets substituted by Police, Crime, Sentencing and Courts Act 2022, s 86(7)(b)(ii), in force 28 June 2022.

37 Subparagraphs (iib) and (iic) inserted by Criminal Justice and Courts Act 2015, Sch 6, para 4, in force 13 April 2015.

38 Subparagraph (iii) and the word "or" repealed by Police, Crime, Sentencing and Courts Act 2022, ss 86(7)(b)(iii), in force 28 June 2022.

39 Subsection (4ZA) inserted by Police, Crime, Sentencing and Courts Act 2022, ss 86(8), in force 28 June 2022.

(b) an offence under section 3A of that Act (causing death by careless driving when under the influence of drink or drugs),

but this is subject to subsection (3) in cases within paragraph (a) of subsection (3A).

(4A) For the purposes of subsection (4)(b) above there shall be disregarded any disqualification imposed under section 26 of this Act or [section 147 of the Powers of Criminal Courts (Sentencing) Act 2000[40]] [or section 164 of the Sentencing Code[41]] or section 223A or 436A of the Criminal Procedure (Scotland) Act 1975 (offences committed by using vehicles) and any disqualification imposed in respect of an offence of stealing a motor vehicle, an offence under section 12 or 25 of the Theft Act 1968, an offence under section 178 of the Road Traffic Act 1988, or an attempt to commit such an offence.

[42](4AA) For the purposes of subsection (4)(b), a disqualification is to be disregarded if the period of disqualification would have been less than 56 days but for an extension period added pursuant to—

(a) section 35A or 35C,

(b) section 248D of the Criminal Procedure (Scotland) Act 1995, or

(c) section 147A of the Powers of Criminal Courts (Sentencing Act 2000 or section 166 of the Sentencing Code[43]].

[44](4B) Where a person convicted of an offence under section 40A of the Road Traffic Act 1988 (using vehicle in dangerous condition etc.) has within the three years immediately preceding the commission of the offence been convicted of any such offence, subsection (1) above shall apply in relation to him as if the reference to twelve months were a reference to six months.

(5) The preceding provisions of this section shall apply in relation to a conviction of an offence committed by aiding, abetting, counselling or procuring, or inciting to the commission of, an offence involving obligatory disqualification as if the offence were an offence involving discretionary disqualification.

[45](5A) In relation to Scotland, references in this section to the court include the [justice of the peace court[46]].

(6) This section is subject to section 48 of this Act.

35. Disqualification for repeated offences

(1) Where—

(a) a person is convicted of an offence [to which this subsection applies[47]], and

---

40 Words in square brackets substituted by Powers of Criminal Courts (Sentencing) Act 2000, Sch 9, para 121, in force 25 August 2000.

41 Words in square brackets inserted by Sentencing Act 2020, Sch 24, para 100(2), in force 1 December 2020.

42 Subsection (4AA) inserted by Coroners and Justice Act 2009, Sch 21, para 90(2), in force 16 July 2018.

43 Words in square brackets inserted by Sentencing Act 2000, Sch 24, para 100(3), in force 1 December 2020.

44 Subsections (4B) and (5) inserted by Road Safety Act 2006, s 25(2), in force 24 September 2007.

45 Subsection (5A) inserted by Criminal Proceedings etc. (Reform) (Scotland) Act 2007 (Powers of District and JP Courts) Order 2007 (SI 2007/3480), arts 1(1) and 2(1)(b), in force 10 December 2007.

46 Words in square brackets substituted by Criminal Proceedings etc. (Reform) (Scotland) Act 2007 Sch, para 7(d), in force from different dates for certain specified purposes.

47 Words in square brackets substituted by Road Traffic Act 1991, Sch 4, para 95(2), in force 1 July 1992.

(b) the penalty points to be taken into account on that occasion number twelve or more,

the court must order him to be disqualified for not less than the minimum period unless the court is satisfied, having regard to all the circumstances, that there are grounds for mitigating the normal consequences of the conviction and thinks fit to order him to be disqualified for a shorter period or not to order him to be disqualified.

[48](1A) Subsection (1) above applies to—

(a) an offence involving discretionary disqualification and obligatory endorsement, and

(b) an offence involving obligatory disqualification in respect of which no order is made under section 34 of this Act.]

(2) The minimum period referred to in subsection (1) above is—

(a) six months if no previous disqualification imposed on the offender is to be taken into account, and

(b) one year if one, and two years if more than one, such disqualification is to be taken into account;

and a previous disqualification imposed on an offender is [subject to subsection (2A),[49]] to be taken into account if it [was for a fixed period of 56 days or more and was imposed[50]] within the three years immediately preceding the commission of the latest offence in respect of which penalty points are taken into account under section 29 of this Act.

[51](2A) A previous disqualification imposed on an offender for a fixed period is not to be taken into account for the purposes of subsection (2) if that period would have been less than 56 days but for an extension period added pursuant to—

(a) section 35A or 35C,

(b) section 248D of the Criminal Procedure (Scotland) Act 1995, or

(c) section 147A of the Powers of Criminal Courts (Sentencing) Act 2000 [or section 166 of the Sentencing Code[52]].]

(3) Where an offender is convicted on the same occasion of more than one offence [to which subsection (1) above applies[53]]—

(a) not more than one disqualification shall be imposed on him under subsection (1) above,

(b) in determining the period of the disqualification the court must take into account all the offences, and

(c) for the purposes of any appeal any disqualification imposed under subsection (1) above shall be treated as an order made on the conviction of each of the offences.

(4) No account is to be taken under subsection (1) above of any of the following circumstances—

(a) any circumstances that are alleged to make the offence or any of the offences not a serious one,

---

48 Subsection (1A) inserted by Road Traffic Act 1991, Sch 4, para 95(3), in force 1 July 1992.

49 Words in square brackets inserted by Coroners and Justice Act 2009, Sch 21, para 90(6)(a), in force 16 July 2018.

50 Words in square brackets substituted by Road Traffic Act 1991, Sch 4, para 95(4), in force 1 July 1992.

51 Subsection 35(2A) inserted by Coroners and Justice Act 2009, Sch 21, para 90(6)(b), in force 16 July 2018.

52 Words in square brackets inserted by Sentencing Act 2020, Sch 24, para 101(2), in force 1 December 2020.

53 Words in square brackets substituted by Road Traffic Act 1991, Sch 4, para 95(5), in force 1 July 1992.

(b) hardship, other than exceptional hardship, or

(c) any circumstances which, within the three years immediately preceding the conviction, have been taken into account under that subsection in ordering the offender to be disqualified for a shorter period or not ordering him to be disqualified.

(5) References in this section to disqualification do not include a disqualification imposed under section 26 of this Act or [section 147 of the Powers of Criminal Courts (Sentencing) Act 2000[54]] [or section 164 of the Sentencing Code[55]] [or section 223A or 436A of the Criminal Procedure (Scotland) Act 1975 (offences committed by using vehicles) or a disqualification imposed in respect of an offence of stealing a motor vehicle, an offence under section 12 or 25 of the Theft Act 1968, an offence under section 178 of the Road Traffic Act 1988, or an attempt to commit such an offence[56]].

[57](5A) The preceding provisions of this section shall apply in relation to a conviction of an offence committed by aiding, abetting, counselling, procuring, or inciting to the commission of, an offence involving obligatory disqualification as if the offence were an offence involving discretionary disqualification.

(6) In relation to Scotland, references in this section to the court include the [justice of the peace court[58]].

(7) This section is subject to section 48 of this Act.

---

54 Words in square brackets inserted by Powers of Criminal Courts Act 2000, Sch 9, para 122, in force 25 August 2000.

55 Words in square brackets inserted by Sentencing Act 2000, Sch 24, para 101(3), in force 1 December 2020.

56 Words in square brackets substituted by Road Traffic Act 1991, Sch 4, para 95(6), in force 1 July 1992.

57 Subsection (5A) inserted by Road Traffic Act 1991, Sch 4, para 95(7), in force 1 July 1992.

58 Words in square brackets substituted by Criminal Proceedings etc (Reform) (Scotland) Act 2007, Sch, para 7(d), fully in force 22 February 2010.

Index

References are to page numbers.